| ITALY | 00 | 99 | 98 | 97 | 96 | 95 | 94 | 93 | 92 | 91 |
|---|---|---|---|---|---|---|---|---|---|---|
| Barolo, Barbaresco | 9◑ | 9◑ | 9◑ | 9◑ | 9◑ | 8● | 6● | 7● | 4● | 5● |
| Chianti Classico Ris. | 8◑ | 9◑ | 8◑ | 10◑ | 8● | 9● | 7● | 8● | 5● | 6● |
| Brunello | 8◑ | 9◑ | 9◑ | 10◑ | 6◑ | 9● | 8● | 8● | 5● | 7● |
| Amarone | 9◑ | 7◑ | 7◑ | 10◑ | 7◑ | 10● | 7● | 8● | 5● | 5● |
| **SPAIN** | | | | | | | | | | |
| Ribera del Duero | 7◑ | 8◑ | 7● | 6● | 9● | 8● | 9● | 4◑ | 6● | 8● |
| Rioja (R) | 7◑ | 6◑ | 6● | 7● | 8● | 8● | 9● | 5◑ | 6● | 7● |
| **PORTUGAL** | | | | | | | | | | |
| Alentejo | 8◑ | 8◑ | 6● | 8● | 6● | 8● | 7● | 5◑ | 6● | 7● |
| Dão | 8◑ | 7◑ | 6● | 8● | 8● | 7● | 7● | 4◑ | 7● | 7● |
| Port (vintage) | 9◑ | 7◑ | 6○ | 8◑ | 7○ | 8○ | 10◑ | 2○ | 9◑ | 8◑ |
| **USA** | | | | | | | | | | |
| California Cabernet | 8◑ | 8◑ | 8◑ | 9◑ | 7◑ | 8◑ | 9● | 7● | 8● | 9● |
| California Chardonnay | 8◑ | 8◑ | 7◑ | 7● | 6● | 8● | 8● | 7● | 7● | 9● |
| Oregon Pinot Noir | 9◑ | 9◑ | 8◑ | 5● | 7● | 5● | 9● | 7● | 9◑ | 8● |
| Wash. State Cabernet | 9◑ | 8◑ | 9◑ | 8◑ | 9◑ | 8◑ | 9● | 7● | 9● | 8● |
| **AUSTRALIA** | | | | | | | | | | |
| Coonawarra Cabernet | 8◑ | 8◑ | 9◑ | 7◑ | 8◑ | 5● | 8● | 7● | 7● | 9● |
| Hunter Semillon | 9◑ | 8◑ | 9◑ | 6● | 8● | 8● | 7● | 7● | 5● | 9● |
| Barossa Shiraz | 8◑ | 7◑ | 10◑ | 8◑ | 9● | 8● | 9● | 7● | 6● | 8● |
| Marg. River Cabernet | 8◑ | 8◑ | 6◑ | 9◑ | 9◑ | 8◑ | 8● | 9● | | ?◑ |
| **NEW ZEALAND** | | | | | | | | | | |
| M'lborough Sauvignon | | | | | | | | | | |
| Hawke's Bay Cabernet | | | | | | | | | | |
| **SOUTH AFRICA** | | | | | | | | | | |
| Stellenbosch Cabernet | 8◑ | | | | | | | 5◑ | 8● | 7◑ |

Numerals (1–10) represent ... overall rating for each year.  ◑ Not ready
● Just ready   ● At peak   ◑ Past best   ○ Not generally declared

# **Oz** Clarke's
## Pocket **Wine** Book
# **2002**

WEBSTERS

LITTLE, BROWN AND COMPANY
BOSTON   NEW YORK   LONDON

A LITTLE, BROWN/WEBSTERS BOOK

This edition first published in 2001 by
Little, Brown and Company (UK)
Brettenham House
Lancaster Place
LONDON WC2E 7EN

Created and designed by
Websters International Publishers Limited
Axe and Bottle Court
70 Newcomen Street
London SE1 1YT
*www.websters.co.uk*
*www.ozclarke.com*

10th edition. First published in 1992. Revised editions published annually.

A CIP catalogue for this book is available from the
British Library.

ISBN 0-316-85727-0

Printed and bound in Belgium

*CORPORATE SALES*

**Companies, institutions and other organizations wishing to make bulk pur-
chases of this or any other Oz Clarke title published by Little, Brown should
contact the Special Sales Department on +44(0)20-7911 8089.**

Thanks are due to the following people for their invaluable help with the
2002 edition and the generous spirit in which they have shared their
knowledge: Jim Budd, Bob Campbell MW, Elizabeth Eyre, Giles
Fallowfield, Anthony Gismondi, Tom Hyland, James Lawther MW,
Angela Lloyd, Dan McCarthy, Dave McIntyre, Sally Marden, David
Moore, Jasper Morris, Kim Parsons, Stuart Pigott, Victor de la Serna,
Phillip Williamson.

# CONTENTS

# HOW TO USE THE A–Z

The **A–Z** section starts on page 42 and includes over 1600 entries on wines, producers, grapes and wine regions from all over the world. It is followed on page 291 by a **Glossary** of some of the more common winemaking terms that are often seen on labels.

Detailed **Vintage Charts** with information on which of the world's top wines are ready for drinking in 2002 can be found on the inside front and back covers; the front chart features vintages back to 1991; the back chart covers a selection of older vintages for premium wines.

---

**Glass Symbols**　These indicate the wines produced.

♥ Red wine　　　　♥ Rosé wine　　　♀ White wine

The order of the glasses reflects the importance of the wines in terms of volume produced. For example:

♥♀ White followed by rosé wine

♥♀ Red followed by white wine

♥♥♀ Red followed by rosé, then white wine

---

**Grape Symbols**　These identify entries on grape varieties.
✿ Red grape　　　　✿ White grape

---

**Star Symbols**　These indicate wines and producers that are highly rated by the author.

★　　A particularly good wine or producer in its category
★★　　An excellent wine or producer in its category – one especially worth seeking out
★★★　　An exceptional, world-class wine or producer

---

**Best Years**　Recommended vintages are listed for many producer and appellation entries. Those listed in bold, e.g. **2000**, **99**, indicate wines that are ready for drinking now, although they may not necessarily be at their best; those appearing in brackets, e.g. (2000), (99), are preliminary assessments of wines that are not yet ready for drinking.

---

**Cross References**　To help you find your way round the A–Z, wine names, producers and regions that have their own entries elsewhere in the A–Z are indicated by SMALL CAPITALS. Grape varieties are not cross-referred in this way, but more than 70 varieties are included.

---

**Special Features**　The A–Z section includes special 2-page features on the world's most important wine styles, regions and grape varieties. These features include recommended vintages and producers, as well as lists of related entries elsewhere in the A–Z.

---

**Index**　The Index on page 298 will help you find over 3700 recommended producers, including all of those that don't have their own entry in the A–Z.

# INTRODUCTION

I was most offended this week. I was reading a report from the International Office of Vines and Wine, and it accused me of not drinking enough. Well, not just me. Every one of us wine lovers. I must admit I thought I'd been doing my share, and I'm sure most of you did too, but it's not enough. We must all try harder! Because it seems that there is a global surplus of between 6.7 billion and 8.7 billion bottles of wine. Yes, that's billion, not million. Which will take some shifting. After all, there are only 6 billion people – most of them not wine drinkers – on the whole planet. And by the time this guide is published, the surplus will be even bigger, because the surpluses seem to be rising by 30% a year – and that's the conservative estimate!

The thing is, all over Northern Europe wine drinking is booming. In North America it's booming. It's even begun a cautious increase in the traditional countries like Portugal and Spain and other European stalwarts whose vast thirst for wine had been in decline for about 30 years or more. But it's not enough. And for once it isn't just the European wine lake to blame. The biggest culprits in the increase in production are the New World producers who were planting like fury during the 1990s and who are still covering land with vines in this new century. It shows the amazing self-belief of these guys that they all think they won't have a surplus problem because everyone wants *their* wine at the expense of their competitors, especially their competitors in Europe. But they will have a problem. A big one, since their governments won't bail them out the way governments do in Europe. And when that happens – welcome to Wine Wars.

Until then – and it won't be in the too distant future – here's how I'm going to try to help out this year. I might as well start with the New World and its most aggressive performer, **Australia**. Well, there's no doubt I'll be drinking Australian – like just about everyone else. The world in general seems to have gone batty for Aussie Shiraz, which is lucky, really, as their plantings of Shiraz are projected to have risen sevenfold in the decade up to 2003. So I'll drink some of that – not always the beautiful brawny beasts of **Barossa** and **McLaren Vale**; the dark-hearted peppery and damson delights of the **Clare Valley**, **Coonawarra** and central **Victoria** (particularly the areas of **Bendigo**, **Grampians** and **Pyrenees**) will slake some of my thirst too. Talking of thirst, have you ever tried an Australian Riesling? An amazing number of wine enthusiasts haven't. Well, join me in enjoying the fabulous 1999s and 2000s from **Clare Valley**, **Eden Valley**, **Victoria** and **Tasmania**. Whenever the sun is high in the sky, these refreshing, lime-fruited lovelies are what I'll be reaching for.

Unless it's a **New Zealand** white. I was a bit worried that the Kiwis had lost the plot on whites, but the typically cool 2000 vintage showed that they can still make Sauvignon Blanc with gorgeous crunchy attack, as well as fragrant Gewürztraminer and Pinot Gris and lush Chardonnay. They're starting to say Pinot Noir is their best wine. Not yet it isn't, but I'll be merrily checking out progress during the year.

**South Africa**'s most individual wine is Pinotage – which doesn't usually taste one bit like Pinot Noir, even though it's related. But it's a true original and I'll have some of that, as well as trying their increasingly good Shiraz and surprisingly tangy Sauvignon Blanc.

I also thought I'd be drinking loads of new-wave wine from **Argentina**, but now I'm not so sure. The 1999 vintage was supposed to be a triumphant recovery from the uncharacteristically poor 1998 crop, but there seem to be a rather large number of dull wines. So I'll have to wait for the 2000s, which so far seem to be far more full of fruit and tango rhythms.

And I'll drink **Chilean** instead. Chile's had its hiccups too, trying to maintain the price–quality relationship that made it so irresistible a few years ago. I'm still not a fan of the overpriced 'mega-premium' wines, but there's lovely Carmenère, Merlot, Cabernet and Sauvignon Blanc around at fair prices.

There's lots of good juicy stuff to be had in **California**, too, and with vast vintages to soak up, prices are becoming less daunting – if you get away from the best-known areas like Napa Valley, and from overpopular varieties like Merlot and Cabernet. I'm getting particularly excited by the number of wines using Rhône Valley and Italian grape varieties. But stay away from the cheap branded wines, which seem to be getting sweeter and more dumbed down. Stick to the good guys, who are making some of California's best ever wines. Given the tremendous hype I've been hearing from the Pacific North West, I thought I'd be drinking lots of **Oregon** Pinot Noir from 1998, 99 and 2000, but I've been a little disappointed by them, as I have been by recent **Washington** efforts, too many of which seem rather flat and unfocused. Maybe the best stuff is being snapped up at the cellar door before I can get there. Ah well, I'll drown my sorrows in **Canadian** icewine, a lovely, high-class, individualistic, intensely sweet wine – which the EU has finally decided is no threat to the livelihood of European winegrowers. And Canada has more to offer than icewine. I'm getting increasingly keen on the delightful, cool, refreshing whites coming out of British Columbia's **Okanagan Valley**.

When it comes to Europe, I'll certainly be drinking **French**, but not uncritically. I do still occasionally pick out a bottle of mature red **Bordeaux** from my dwindling hoard, to remind me how lovely Bordeaux can be, but I rarely reach for wine from a recent vintage. I virtually stopped drinking **Champagne** last year in reaction to rising prices and a slump in quality post-Millennium. The rest of the world obviously agreed with me and Champagne sales abroad dropped by 22% in 2000. Which means stocks of older, softer Champagne will have risen, so perhaps this Christmas I'll cautiously give them another go. **Burgundy** I shall drink – there's lots of good stuff from a whole bunch of dynamic growers – and I enjoy the fresh, unoaky style of most **Loire** wines. There's really rather too much oak being used now in the South of France on wines whose ripe sunny character make extra oak-aging quite unnecessary, but there's so much good red and white in the **Rhône**, and so much good red in the **Languedoc** appellations – though, sadly, not in the Vin de Pays d'Oc – that this is where I'll do most of my French drinking.

Elsewhere in the Mediterranean, for the first time almost ever, I'll be making a beeline for **Tuscany**. All the efforts of the 1990s are now bearing fruit, with Tuscan reds and whites now better than ever before. **Piedmont**, too, is sharing in the quality surge, and not just with its top Nebbiolo reds; the lesser regions and grapes like Barbera and Dolcetto are making some beauties – and I'll be drinking them. As for **Sicily** and **southern Italy**, both reds and whites go from strength to strength and don't cost the earth. Count me in for some of them.

Yet I won't be drinking as many **Spanish** reds as usual. The last few years have seen price rise after price rise in famous areas like Rioja and Ribera del Duero, without any accompanying leap in quality. Fine – I'll drink elsewhere – **La Mancha**, **Valdepeñas**, and the resurgent wines of areas like **Calatayud** and **Campo de Borja** in Aragón and **Toro** in Castilla y León.

**Portugal** hasn't gone silly on price, and quality in the **Douro** and all over the south of the country has been thrilling since 1999. For big, juicy reds, that's where I'll be going.

And when I'm tired of all that heady ripeness, I'll head back north to the cool climes of the Mosel, the Rhine and the Danube. **Germany**, **Austria** and **Hungary** have been making fantastic white wines – and some pretty fair reds – during the past few years. Outside their own countries, relatively few people seem to drink them – but I shall, and I urge you to follow my lead. Phew. That should be a few more bottles off the global surplus.

# WINES OF THE YEAR

Now that the world of wine has flung its doors wide open, the swirling throng of wine names, grapes and places can sometimes obscure the real gems that are out there, just waiting to be discovered. So here is my guide to the hidden treasure. All the wines, regions and producers here are on an exciting roll in terms of quality – they're not definitive 'best wines', but they're all worth tracking down. You can find out more about them in the A–Z on pages 42 to 290: the cross-references in SMALL CAPITALS will guide you to the relevant entries.

## WORLD CLASS WINES THAT DON'T COST THE EARTH

- Tim ADAMS Shiraz, CLARE VALLEY, Australia
- Allandale Chardonnay, HUNTER VALLEY, Australia
- Briego, RIBERA DEL DUERO, Spain
- Quinta do CRASTO, DOURO, Portugal
- Forrest Estate Sauvignon Blanc, MARLBOROUGH, New Zealand
- Nieto Senetiner Malbec, MENDOZA, Argentina
- NYETIMBER Classic Cuvée, England
- SANTA RITA Triple C, MAIPO, Chile
- STEENBERG Merlot, CONSTANTIA, South Africa
- VALDESPINO Inocente Fino, Spain

## BEST LOOKALIKES TO THE CLASSICS

### Bordeaux-style red wines
- Larose, STONYRIDGE, WAIHEKE ISLAND, New Zealand
- Sorella, ANDREW WILL, WASHINGTON STATE, USA
- THELEMA Cabernet Sauvignon, STELLENBOSCH, South Africa

### Burgundy-style white wines
- Allandale Chardonnay, HUNTER VALLEY, Australia
- Cervaro della SALA, UMBRIA, Italy
- GROSSET, Piccadilly Chardonnay, Australia
- VELICH, Tiglat Chardonnay, Austria

### Champagne-style wines
- PIPERS BROOK Pirie, TASMANIA, Australia
- SCHRAMSBERG Reserve Brut, CALIFORNIA, USA
- SEAVIEW Edwards & Chaffey Pinot Noir-Chardonnay, Australia

## REGIONS TO WATCH

- ALENTEJO, Portugal
- CLARE VALLEY, Australia
- COTEAUX DU LANGUEDOC, France
- Luján de Cuyo, MENDOZA, Argentina
- MORELLINO DI SCANSANO, Italy
- OKANAGAN VALLEY, Canada
- Soprón, Hungary
- TORO, Spain
- Waipara, CANTERBURY, New Zealand
- Walla Walla, WASHINGTON STATE, USA

## PRODUCERS TO WATCH

- BRIGHT BROTHERS, RIBATEJO, Portugal
- CRAGGY RANGE, HAWKE'S BAY, New Zealand
- CUILLERON, CONDRIEU, France
- Hewitson, BAROSSA, Australia
- LA AGRICOLA, MENDOZA, Argentina
- NYETIMBER, England
- PLANETA, SICILY, Italy
- David Ramey, CARNEROS, USA
- Rijckaert, BURGUNDY WHITE WINES, France
- Telmo Rodriguez, RIBERA DEL DUERO and TORO, Spain

## THE 10 BEST-KEPT SECRETS

- Traditional, bone-dry amontillado SHERRY
- Argentinian Barbera, Bonarda and Sangiovese reds
- Australian Riesling
- Chilean Carmenère reds
- English sparkling wine
- Germany's MOSEL Riesling Kabinetts

- Hungarian whites
- PIC ST-LOUP reds from the LANGUEDOC
- South African Sauvignon Blanc
- Southern Italian PRIMITIVO DI MANDURIA and Negroamaro reds

*TOP VALUE WINES*
- Argentinian Torrontés
- Calatayud DO Garnacha, ARAGON, Spain
- CAVA fizz from Spain
- CONO SUR Pinot Noir, Chile
- FAIRVIEW Pinotage, South Africa
- Peter LEHMANN Grenache, Australia
- LINDEMANS Bin 65 Chardonnay, Australia
- Trincadeira, RIBATEJO, Portugal

- MONTANA Sauvignon Blanc, New Zealand
- Vin de Pays d'OC Viognier, France

*VINTAGES TO DRINK NOW*
(See also Vintage Charts)
- Bordeaux reds: 90 85 83 82
- Burgundy reds: 96 95 93 91
- Rhône: 95 91 90 89
- Loire: 97 96 95 90 89
- Tuscany: 97 96 95 94 93 90 88
- Piedmont: 95 93 90 89 88 85 82
- Rioja: 96 95 94 90 89
- Germany: 97 95 93 90 89 88 85
- California Cabernet: 95 93 92 91 90 87 86
- California Chardonnay: 96 95 94 93 92 91
- Barossa: 96 95 94 91 90 88

# SOME OF MY FAVOURITES

If you imagine it's an act of pure indulgence to sit down and select a few of my favourite wines, think again. I found it a real sweat to limit all these lists to just 10 entries, so if your favourite isn't here, perhaps it was number 11 on my list.

*AUSTRALIA*
- Tim ADAMS Aberfeldy Shiraz
- DE BORTOLI Noble One Botrytis Semillon
- Freycinet Pinot Noir, TASMANIA
- GROSSET Watervale Riesling
- HENSCHKE HILL OF GRACE Shiraz
- MORRIS Old Premium Liqueur Tokay
- PENFOLDS GRANGE
- PETALUMA Tiers Chardonnay
- WYNNS John Riddoch Cabernet Sauvignon
- YARRA YERING Dry Red No. 1

*BORDEAUX*
- Ch. ANGELUS (red)
- Dom. de CHEVALIER (white)
- Ch. GRAND-PUY-LACOSTE (red)
- Ch. LAFAURIE-PEYRAGUEY (sweet)
- Les Forts de LATOUR (red)
- Ch. LEOVILLE-BARTON (red)
- Ch LYNCH-BAGES (red)

- Ch. PICHON-LONGUEVILLE-LALANDE (red)
- Ch. RIEUSSEC (sweet)
- Ch. SMITH-HAUT-LAFITTE (white)

*BURGUNDY*
- CARILLON, Bienvenues-BATARD-MONTRACHET (white)
- R Chevillon, NUITS-ST-GEORGES les St-Georges (red)
- COCHE-DURY, CORTON-CHARLEMAGNE (white)
- Dugat-Py, Charmes-CHAMBERTIN (red)
- J-N GAGNARD, BATARD-MONTRACHET (white)
- Anne Gros, CLOS DE VOUGEOT (red)
- LAFON, VOLNAY Santenots (red)
- D Mortet, GEVREY-CHAMBERTIN Lavaux-St-Jacques (red)
- M Rollin, CORTON-CHARLEMAGNE (white)
- E Rouget, ECHEZEAUX (red)

## CALIFORNIA

- AU BON CLIMAT Chardonnay Le Bouge
- Chateau Potelle Zinfandel VGS, MOUNT VEEDER
- Harlan Estate Red, NAPA VALLEY
- LAUREL GLEN Cabernet Sauvignon
- NEWTON Unfiltered Chardonnay
- QUPE Bien Nacido Reserve Syrah
- David Ramey Chardonnay Hudson, CARNEROS
- RIDGE Santa Cruz Mountains Chardonnay
- SHAFER Hillside Select Cabernet Sauvignon
- STAG'S LEAP WINE CELLARS SLV Reserve Cabernet Sauvignon

## ITALIAN REDS

- ALLEGRINI La Poja
- BANFI Mandrielle
- Caggiano, TAURASI
- GAJA LANGHE
- ISOLE E OLENA Cepparello
- ORNELLAIA Masseto
- Castello della Paneretta Terrine (see SUPER-TUSCANS)
- POLIZIANO Le Stanze
- Le Pupille Saffredi, MORELLINO DI SCANSANO
- SELVAPIANA Riserva Bucerchiale

## RHÔNE AND SOUTHERN FRANCE

- Ch. de BEAUCASTEL Roussanne Vieilles Vignes (white)
- Dom. du Chêne, ST-JOSEPH
- CLOS DES PAPES, CHATEAUNEUF-DU-PAPE
- CUILLERON, CONDRIEU les Chaillets
- Dom. Gourt de Mautens, COTES DU RHONE-VILLAGES Rasteau
- GRAILLOT, CROZES-HERMITAGE la Guiraude
- JAMET, COTE-ROTIE
- Dom. de la Janasse, CHATEAUNEUF-DU-PAPE Vieilles Vignes
- Ch. de St-Cosme, CONDRIEU
- VERSET, CORNAS

## CABERNET SAUVIGNON

- GAJA Darmagi, PIEDMONT, Italy
- Ch. GRAND-PUY-LACOSTE, PAUILLAC, France
- Les Forts de LATOUR, PAUILLAC, France
- Ch. LEOVILLE-BARTON, ST-JULIEN, France
- RIDGE Monte Bello, CALIFORNIA, USA
- SANTA RITA Triple C, MAIPO, Chile
- SHAFER Hillside Select, CALIFORNIA, USA
- STAG'S LEAP WINE CELLARS SLV, CALIFORNIA, USA
- VINA CASABLANCA Santa Isabel Estate, Casablanca, Chile
- WYNNS John Riddoch, COONAWARRA, Australia

## CHARDONNAY

- CARILLON, Bienvenues-BATARD-MONTRACHET, France
- CHAPEL HILL Reserve, MCLAREN VALE, Australia
- COCHE-DURY, CORTON-CHARLEMAGNE, France
- CRAGGY RANGE, HAWKE'S BAY, New Zealand
- J-N GAGNARD, BATARD-MONTRACHET, France
- GROSSET Piccadilly, ADELAIDE HILLS, Australia
- KISTLER Kistler Vineyard, CALIFORNIA, USA
- NEWTON Unfiltered, CALIFORNIA, USA
- M Rollin, CORTON-CHARLEMAGNE, France
- KUMEU RIVER, AUCKLAND, New Zealand

## MERLOT

- ANDREW WILL, WASHINGTON, USA
- Ch. ANGELUS, ST-EMILION, France
- Ch. AUSONE, ST-EMILION, France
- Ch. CHEVAL-BLANC, ST-EMILION, France
- ERRAZURIZ, Aconcagua, Chile
- Esk Valley Merlot-Malbec-Cabernet Franc, HAWKE'S BAY, New Zealand (see VILLA MARIA)
- LEONETTI CELLAR, WASHINGTON, USA

- ORNELLAIA Masseto, TUSCANY, Italy
- NEWTON, CALIFORNIA, USA
- Ch. PETRUS, POMEROL, France

## PINOT NOIR

- ATA RANGI, MARTINBOROUGH, New Zealand
- AU BON CLIMAT Talley's Rosemary's Vineyard, CALIFORNIA, USA
- R Chevillon, NUITS-ST-GEORGES les St-Georges, France
- Dugat-Py, Charmes-CHAMBERTIN, France
- FELTON ROAD, CENTRAL OTAGO, New Zealand
- Freycinet, TASMANIA, Australia
- Anne Gros, CLOS DE VOUGEOT, France
- LAFON, VOLNAY Santenots, France
- Rex Hill Reserve, OREGON, USA
- E Rouget, ECHEZEAUX, France

## RIESLING

- Domaine Paul BLANCK, ALSACE Grand Cru Furstentum, France
- H DONNHOFF Niederhäuser Hermannshöhle, NAHE, Germany
- GROSSET Watervale, CLARE VALLEY, Australia
- GUNDERLOCH Nackenheimer Rothenberg, RHEINHESSEN, Germany
- Fritz HAAG Brauneberger Juffer Sonnenuhr, MOSEL, Germany
- Franz KUNSTLER Hochheimer Hölle, RHEINGAU, Germany
- Dr LOOSEN Erdener Prälat, MOSEL, Germany
- MAXIMIN GRUNHAUS, Ruwer, Germany
- Mount Horrocks, CLARE VALLEY, Australia

## SAUVIGNON BLANC

- Clifford Bay, MARLBOROUGH, New Zealand
- Lucien CROCHET, SANCERRE, France
- Didier DAGUENEAU, POUILLY-FUME, France
- Forrest Estate, MARLBOROUGH, New Zealand

- Nepenthe, ADELAIDE HILLS, Australia
- PALLISER ESTATE, Martinborough, New Zealand
- Ch. SMITH-HAUT-LAFITTE, PESSAC-LEOGNAN, France
- Springfield Estate, ROBERTSON, South Africa
- STEENBERG, CONSTANTIA, South Africa
- Ch. de Tracy, POUILLY-FUME, France

## SYRAH/SHIRAZ

- Tim ADAMS Aberfeldy, CLARE VALLEY, Australia
- BOWEN ESTATE, COONAWARRA, Australia
- BROKENWOOD Graveyard, HUNTER VALLEY, Australia
- CHAVE, HERMITAGE, France
- HENSCHKE HILL OF GRACE, Eden Valley, Australia
- JAMET, COTE-ROTIE, France
- MOUNTADAM Patriarch, Eden Valley, Australia
- PENFOLDS GRANGE, Australia
- QUPE Bien Nacido Reserve, CALIFORNIA, USA
- VERSET, CORNAS, France

## SPARKLING WINE

- BILLECART-SALMON Cuvée N-F Billecart CHAMPAGNE, France
- CLOUDY BAY Pelorus, MARLBOROUGH, New Zealand
- DEUTZ Blanc de Blancs CHAMPAGNE, France
- Alfred GRATIEN Vintage CHAMPAGNE, France
- Charles HEIDSIECK Mis en Caves CHAMPAGNE, France
- Charles MELTON Sparkling Shiraz, BAROSSA, Australia
- NYETIMBER, England
- PIPERS BROOK Pirie, TASMANIA, Australia
- POL ROGER Vintage CHAMPAGNE, France
- ROEDERER ESTATE L'Ermitage, CALIFORNIA, USA

# MODERN WINE STYLES _____

Not so long ago, if I were to outline the basic wine styles, the list would have been strongly biased towards the classics – Bordeaux, Burgundy, Sancerre, Mosel Riesling, Champagne. But the classics have, over time, become expensive and unreliable – thus opening the door to other, less established regions, and giving them the chance to offer us wines that may or may not owe anything to the originals. *These* are the flavours to which ambitious winemakers now aspire.

*WHITE WINES*

**Ripe, up-front, spicy Chardonnay** Fruit is the key here: round, ripe, apricot, peach, melon and pineapple, spiced up with the vanilla and butterscotch richness of some new oak – often American oak – to make a delicious, approachable, easy-to-drink fruit cocktail of taste. Australia created this style and still effortlessly leads the field.

**Green, tangy Sauvignon** New Zealand was the originator of this style – all zingy, grassy, nettles and asparagus and then green apples and peach – but has lost its way a little recently, and South Africa and Hungary are taking up the slack. Chile has the potential to produce something similar and there are hopeful signs in southern France. Bordeaux and the Loire are the original sources of dry Sauvignon wines, and at last we are seeing an expanding band of committed modern producers matching clean fruit with zippy green tang.

**Bone-dry, neutral whites** This doesn't sound very appetizing, but as long as it is well made it will be thirst-quenching and easy to drink. Many Italian whites fit this bill. Southern French wines, where no grape variety is specified, will be like this; so will many wines from Bordeaux, the South-West, Muscadet and Anjou. Modern young Spanish whites and Portuguese Vinho Verdes are good examples, as are Swiss Fendant and southern German Trocken (dry) wines. I don't like seeing too much neutrality in New World wines, but cheap South African and California whites are 'superneutral'.

**White Burgundy** By this I mean the nutty, oatmealy-ripe but dry, subtly oaked styles of villages like Meursault at their best. Few people do it well, even in Burgundy itself, and it's a difficult style to emulate. California makes the most effort. Washington, Oregon and New York State each have occasional successes, as do top Australian and New Zealand Chardonnays.

**Perfumy, off-dry whites** Gewurztraminer, Muscat and Pinot Gris from Alsace will give you this style and in southern Germany Gewurztraminer, Scheurebe, Kerner, Grauburgunder and occasionally Riesling may also do it. Riesling in Australia is often aromatic and mildly fruity. In New Zealand Riesling and Gewurztraminer can be excellent, as can Argentinian Torrontés and Hungarian Irsai Oliver.

**Mouthfuls of luscious gold** Good sweet wines are difficult to make. Sauternes is the most famous, but the Loire, and sometimes Alsace, can also come up with rich, intensely sweet wines that can live for decades. Germany and Austria's top sweeties are stunning, and exciting examples are appearing in Australia and New Zealand.

## RED WINES

**Spicy, warm-hearted reds** Australia is out in front at the moment through the ebullient resurgence of her Shiraz reds – ripe, almost sweet, sinfully easy to enjoy. France's Rhône Valley is also on the up and the traditional appellations in the far south of France are looking good. In Italy Piedmont is producing delicious beefy Barbera and juicy exotic Dolcetto. Spain's Ribera del Duero and Portugal's south also deliver the goods, as does Malbec in Argentina.

**Juicy, fruity reds** This used to be the Beaujolais spot, but there hasn't been much exciting Beaujolais recently. Grenache and Syrah vins de pays are better bets, as are grassy, sharp Loire reds. Modern Spanish reds from Navarra, Valdepeñas and La Mancha do the trick, while in Italy young Chianti and Teroldego hit home. Newcomer Argentina has some delicious examples.

**Blackcurranty Cabernet** Australia leads the field here, but New Zealand also strikes the blackcurrant bell in a much greener, sharper way. California only sometimes hits the sweet spot, and often with Merlot rather than Cabernet. Chilean Cabernets get there less often than they used to. Eastern Europe, in particular Hungary, is doing well, as is southern France. And what about Bordeaux? Only a few of the top wines reach the target; for the price, Tuscan Cabernet is often more exciting.

**Tough, tannic long-haul boys** Bordeaux does lead this field, and the best wines are really good after 10 years or so – but don't expect wines from minor properties to age in the same way. It's the same in Tuscany and Piedmont – only the top wines last well – especially Chianti Classico, Barolo and Barbaresco. In Portugal there's plenty of tannin and some increasingly good long-lasting Douro reds.

**Soft, strawberryish charmers** Good Burgundy definitely tops this group. Rioja in Spain can sometimes get there too, as can Navarra and Valdepeñas. Pinot Noir in California is frequently delicious, as it is in New Zealand, and occasionally Chile and Australia get it right. Germany hits the spot with Spätburgunder (Pinot Noir) now and then. Italy's Lago di Caldaro often smooches in; and over in Bordeaux, of all places, both St-Émilion and Pomerol can do the business.

## SPARKLING AND FORTIFIED WINES

**Fizz** This can be white or pink or red, dry or sweet, and I sometimes think it doesn't matter what it tastes like as long as it's cold enough and there's enough of it. Champagne can be best, but frequently isn't – and there are lots of new-wave winemakers making good-value lookalikes. Australia is tops for tasty bargains, followed by California and New Zealand. Spain pumps out oceans of good basic stuff.

**Fortified wines** For once in my life I find myself saying that the old ways are definitely the best. There's nothing to beat the top ports and sherries in the deep, rich, sticky stakes – though for the glimmerings of a new angle look to Australia and California – and don't forget the luscious Muscats made all round the Mediterranean.

# MATCHING FOOD AND WINE

Give me a rule, I'll break it – well, bend it anyway. So when I see the proliferation of publications laying down rules as to what wine to drink with what food, I get very uneasy and have to quell a burning desire to slosh back a Grand Cru Burgundy with my chilli con carne.

The pleasures of eating and drinking operate on so many levels that hard and fast rules make no sense. What about mood? If I'm in the mood for Champagne, Champagne it shall be, whatever I'm eating. What about place? If I'm sitting gazing out across the shimmering Mediterranean, hand me anything, just as long as it's local – it'll be perfect.

Even so, there are some things that simply don't go well with wine: artichokes, spinach, kippers and mackerel, chilli, salsas and vinegars, chocolate, all flatten the flavours of wines. The general rule here is avoid tannic red wines and go for juicy young reds, or whites with plenty of fruit and fresh acidity. And for chocolate, liqueur Muscats and Asti Spumante are just about the only things that work. Don't be afraid to experiment. Who would guess that salty Roquefort cheese and rich, sweet Sauternes would go together? But they do, and it's a match made in heaven. So, with these factors in mind, the following pairings are not rules – just my recommendations.

## FISH

**Grilled or baked white fish** White Burgundy or other fine Chardonnay, Pessac-Léognan or Graves, Viognier, Australian and New Zealand Riesling.

**Grilled or baked oily or 'meaty' fish** (e.g. salmon, trout, tuna, swordfish) Alsace Riesling, fruity New World Chardonnay or Semillon, Chinon or Bourgueil, New World Pinot Noir.

**Fried/battered fish** Simple, fresh whites, e.g. Soave, Mâcon-Villages, Pinot Gris, white Bordeaux, or a Spätlese from the Rheingau or Pfalz.

**Shellfish** Chablis or unoaked Chardonnay, Pinot Blanc; *clams and oysters* Aligoté, Vinho Verde, Seyval Blanc; *crab* Riesling Spätlese, Viognier; *lobster, scallops* white Burgundy or other fine Chardonnay, Champagne, Viognier; *mussels* Muscadet, Italian Pinot Grigio.

**Smoked fish** Ice-cold basic fizz, manzanilla or fino sherry, Alsace Gewurztraminer or Pinot Gris, lightly oaked Chardonnay, New World Riesling.

## MEAT

**Beef/steak** *Plain roasted or grilled* tannic reds, top Bordeaux, New World Cabernet Sauvignon, Ribera del Duero, Super-Tuscans, South African Pinotage.

**Lamb** *Plain roasted or grilled* top red Burgundy, top red Bordeaux, especially Pauillac or St-Éstephe, Rioja Reserva, fine New World Pinot Noir or Merlot.

**Pork** *Plain roasted or grilled* full, spicy dry whites, e.g. Alsace Pinot Gris, lightly oaked Chardonnay; smooth reds, e.g. Rioja, Alentejo; *ham and bacon* young, fruity reds, e.g. Beaujolais, Teroldego, unoaked Tempranillo, Mendoza Malbec, Lambrusco; *prepared pork products* rustic/young reds from Beaujolais, Provence, Puglia, and from Merlot, Zinfandel, Pinotage grapes.

**Veal** *Plain roasted or grilled* full-bodied whites, e.g. Alsace, German, Austrian Pinot Gris, Grüner Veltliner, Vouvray, Châteauneuf-du-Pape; soft reds, e.g. Dolcetto, Baden Pinot Noir, or mature Rioja, Burgundy or Margaux; *with cream-*

based sauce full, ripe whites, e.g. Alsace Pinot Blanc or Pinot Gris, Vouvray, oaked New World Chardonnay; with rich red-wine sauce (e.g. osso buco) young Italian reds, Zinfandel.

**Venison** *Plain roasted or grilled* Barolo, St-Estèphe, Pomerol, Côte de Nuits, Hermitage, big Zinfandel, Alsace or German Pinot Gris; *with red-wine sauce* Piedmont and Portuguese reds, Pomerol, St-Émilion, New World Syrah/Shiraz or Pinotage, Priorat.

**Chicken and turkey** *Plain roasted or grilled* fine red or white Burgundy, red Rioja Reserva, New World Chardonnay or Semillon.

**Duck** *Plain roasted* Pomerol, St-Émilion, Côte de Nuits, Rhône reds, New World Syrah/Shiraz (including sparkling) or Merlot; also full, soft whites such as Austrian Riesling; *with orange* German Riesling Auslese, or Barsac.

**Game birds** *Plain roasted or grilled* top reds from Burgundy, Rhône, Tuscany, Piedmont, Ribera del Duero, New World Cabernet; also full whites such as New World Semillon.

**Casseroles and stews** Match the dominant ingredient, e.g. red wine for *boeuf bourguignon* or *coq au vin*, dry whites for a fricassee. The weight of the wine should match the richness of the sauce. For strong tomato flavours see under Pasta.

## ETHNIC CUISINES

**Chinese** Riesling or Gewürztraminer, unoaked New World Chardonnay; mild German and Austrian reds.

**Indian/Tex-Mex** Spicy whites, e.g. Gewürztraminer, Mosel Kabinett or Spätlese, New World Sauvignon Blanc, Viognier; non-tannic reds, such as Rioja, Valpolicella, Merlot, Grenache,

Syrah/Shiraz.

**Thai** Riesling, Gewürztraminer, New World Sauvignon Blanc.

## EGGS

Champagne and traditional-method fizz; light, fresh reds such as Beaujolais or Chinon; full, dry unoaked whites; New World rosé.

## PASTA

*With tomato sauce* Barbera, Soave, Verdicchio, New World Sauvignon Blanc; *with meat-based sauce* north or central Italian reds, French or New World Syrah/Shiraz, Zinfandel; *with cream- or cheese-based sauce* soft, full, dry unoaked whites from northern Italy, light Austrian reds; *with seafood/fish sauce* dry, tangy whites, e.g. Verdicchio, Vermentino, Grüner Veltliner, Muscadet; *with pesto* New World Sauvignon Blanc, Dolcetto, Minervois.

## SALADS

Sharp-edged whites, e.g. New World Sauvignon Blanc, dry Riesling, Vinho Verde.

## CHEESES

**Hard** Full reds from Italy, France or Spain, New World Merlot or Zinfandel, dry oloroso sherry, tawny port.

**Soft** LBV port, rich, fruity Rhône reds, Shiraz, Zinfandel, Alsace Pinot Gris, Gewürztraminer.

**Blue** Botrytized sweet whites such as Sauternes, vintage port, old oloroso sherry, Malmsey Madeira.

**Goats'** Sancerre, Pouilly-Fumé, New World Sauvignon Blanc, Chinon, Saumur-Champigny.

## DESSERTS

**Chocolate** Australian Liqueur Muscat, Asti Spumante.

**Fruit-based** Sauternes, Eiswein, Moscatel de Valencia.

# MATCHING WINE AND FOOD ─────────

With very special bottles, when you have found an irresistible bargain or when you are casting around for culinary inspiration, it can be a good idea to let the wine dictate the choice of food.

Although I said earlier that rules in this area are made to be bent if not broken, there are certain points to remember when matching wine and food. Before you make specific choices, think about some basic characteristics and see how thinking in terms of grape varieties and wine styles can point you in the right direction.

In many cases, the local food and wine combinations that have evolved over the years simply cannot be bettered (think of ripe Burgundy with *coq au vin* or *boeuf bourguignon*; Chianti Riserva with *bistecca alla Fiorentina*; Muscadet and Breton oysters). Yet the world of food and wine is moving so fast that it would be madness to be restricted by the old tenets. Californian cuisine, fusion food, and the infiltration of innumerable ethnic influences coupled with the re-invigoration of traditional wines, continuous experiment with new methods and blends and the opening up of completely new wine areas mean that the search for perfect food and wine partners is, and will remain, very much an on-going process.

Here are some of the characteristics you need to consider, plus a summary of the main grape varieties and their best food matches.

**Body** As well as matching the taste of the wine to the flavour of the food you need to match the weight or body of the wine to the intensity of that flavour. A heavy alcoholic wine will not suit a delicate dish; and *vice versa*.

**Acidity** The acidity of a dish should balance the acidity of a wine. High-acid flavours, such as tomato, lemon or vinegar, need matching acidity in their accompanying wines. Use acidity in wine to cut through the richness of a dish but for this to work, make sure the wine is full in flavour.

**Sweetness** Sweet food makes dry wine taste unpleasantly lean and acidic. With desserts and puddings your task is very clear: find a wine that is at least as sweet as the food (sweeter than the food is fine). However, many savoury foods, such as carrots, onions and parsnips, taste slightly sweet and dishes in which they feature prominently will go best with wines that also have a touch of sweetness.

**Age/Maturity** Pay the wine the compliment of rewarding it for aging well. The bouquet of a wine is only acquired over time and should be savoured and appreciated: with age many red wines acquire complex flavours and perfumes and a similar degree of complexity in the flavour of the food is often a good idea.

**Wine in the food** If you want to use wine in cooking it is best to use the same style of wine as the one you are going to drink with the meal (it can be an inferior version though).

**Oak** Oak flavours in wine vary from the satisfyingly subtle to positively strident. This latter end of the scale can conflict with food, although it may be suitable for smoked fish (white wines only) or full-flavoured meat or game.

## RED GRAPES

**Barbera** Wines made to be drunk young have high acidity that can hold their own with sausages, salami, ham, and tomato sauces. Complex older wines from the top growers need to be matched with rich Piemontese food: beef casseroles and game dishes.

**Cabernet Franc** Best drunk with plain rather than sauced meat dishes, or, slightly chilled, with grilled or baked salmon or trout. Try it with Indian food.

**Cabernet Sauvignon** All over the world the Cabernet Sauvignon makes full-flavoured reliable red wine: the ideal food wine. Classic combinations include Cru Classé Pauillac with roast lamb; Super-Tuscan *vini da tavola* with *bistecca alla Fiorentina*; softer, riper New World Cabernet Sauvignons with roast turkey or goose. Cabernet Sauvignon seems to have a particular affinity for lamb but it partners all plain roast or grilled meats and game well and would be an excellent choice for many sauced meat dishes such as *boeuf bourguignon*, steak and kidney pie or rabbit stew and any substantial dishes made with mushrooms.

**Dolcetto** Dolcetto produces fruity purple wines that go beautifully with hearty local north Italian meat dishes such as calves' liver and onions or casseroled game with polenta.

**Gamay** The grape of red Beaujolais, Gamay, makes wine you can drink whenever, wherever, however and with whatever you want. It goes particularly well with charcuterie products such as pâtés and

sausages because its acidity provides a satisfying foil to their richness. It would be a good choice for many vegetarian dishes. If in doubt you are unlikely to go far wrong with Gamay.

**Grenache** Generally blended with other grapes, Grenache nonetheless dominates, with its high alcoholic strength and rich, spicy flavours. These are wines readily matched with food: casseroles, charcuterie and grills for concentrated older wines; almost anything – from light vegetarian dishes to *soupe de poissons* – for lighter reds and rosés.

**Merlot** The Bordeaux grape that has come into its own all over the world, Merlot makes soft, rounded, fruity wines that are some of the easiest red wines to enjoy without food, yet are also a good choice with many kinds of food. Spicier game dishes, herby terrines and pâtés, pheasant, pigeon, duck or goose all blend well with Merlot; substantial casseroles made with wine are excellent with top Pomerol châteaux; and the soft fruitiness of the wines is perfect for pork, liver, turkey, and savoury foods with a hint of sweetness such as honey-roast or Bayonne ham.

**Nebbiolo** Fruity, fragrant, early-drinking styles of Nebbiolo wine are best with local salami, pâtés, *bresaola* and lighter meat dishes. The best Barolos and Barbarescos need substantial food: *bollito misto*, rich hare or beef casseroles and *brasato al Barolo* (a large piece of beef marinated then braised slowly in Barolo) are just the job in Piedmont, or anywhere else for that matter.

**Pinot Noir** The great grape of Burgundy has taken its food-friendly complexity all over the wine world. However, nothing can beat the marriage of great wine with sublime local food that is Burgundy's heritage, and it is Burgundian dishes that spring to mind as perfect partners for the Pinot Noir: *coq au vin*, *boeuf bourguignon*, rabbit with mustard, braised ham, chicken with tarragon, steaks from prized Charolais cattle with a rich red-wine sauce ... the list is endless.

Pinot Noir's subtle flavours make it a natural choice for complex meat dishes but it is also excellent with plain grills and roasts and, in its lighter manifestations from, say, the Loire or Oregon, a good match for salmon or salmon trout.

In spite of the prevalence of superb cheese in Burgundy, the best Pinot Noir red wines are wasted on cheese.

**Sangiovese** Tuscany is where Sangiovese best expresses the qualities that can lead it, in the right circumstances, to be numbered among the great grapes of the world. And Tuscany is very much food with wine territory. Sangiovese wines such as Chianti, Rosso di Montalcino, Vino Nobile di Montepulciano, and the biggest of them all, Brunello, positively demand to be drunk with food. Drink them with *bisteca alla Fiorentina*, roast meats and game, calves' liver, casseroles, hearty pasta sauces, *porcini* mushrooms and Pecorino cheese.

**Syrah/Shiraz** Whether from France (in the Northern Rhône), Australia, California or South Africa, this grape always makes powerful, rich, full-bodied wines

that are superb with full-flavoured food. The classic barbecue wine, Shiraz/Syrah also goes with roasts, game, hearty casseroles and charcuterie. It can also be good with tangy cheeses.

**Tempranillo** Spain's best native red grape makes aromatic wines for drinking young, and matures well to a rich (usually) oaky flavour. Tempranillo is good with game, local cured hams and sausages, casseroles and meat grilled with herbs; it is particularly good with lamb. It can partner some Indian dishes and goes well with strong soft cheeses such as ripe Brie.

**Zinfandel** California's much-planted, most versatile grape is used for a bewildering variety of wine styles from bland, slightly sweet pinks to rich, elegant, fruity reds. And the good red Zinfandels themselves may vary greatly in style. If they aren't too oaky they are good with barbecued meats, venison and roast chicken. The hefty old-style wines are a great match with the spicy, mouthfilling San Francisco cuisine. The pale blush style of Zin goes well with tomato sauce.

*WHITE GRAPES*
**Aligoté** This Burgundian grape can, at its best, make very versatile food wine. It goes well with many fish and seafood dishes, smoked fish, salads and snails in garlic and butter.

**Chardonnay** More than almost any other grape Chardonnay responds to different climatic conditions and to the winemaker's art. This, plus the relative ease with which it can be grown, accounts for the marked gradation of flavours and styles: from steely, cool-climate austerity to almost tropical lusciousness. The relatively sharp end of the spectrum is one of the best choices for simple fish dishes; most Chardonnays are superb with roast chicken or other white meat; the really full, rich, New World blockbusters need rich fish and seafood dishes. Oaky Chardonnays are a good choice for smoked fish.

**Chenin Blanc** One of the most versatile of grapes, Chenin Blanc makes wines ranging from averagely quaffable dry whites to the great sweet whites of the Loire. The lighter wines can be good as apéritifs or with light fish dishes or salads. The sweet wines are good with most puddings and superb with those made with slightly tart fruit.

**Gewürztraminer** Spicy and perfumed, Gewürztraminer has the weight and flavour to go with such hard-to-match dishes as *choucroute* and smoked fish. It is also a good choice for Chinese or indeed any oriental food.

**Marsanne** These rich, fat wines are a bit short of acid so match them with simply prepared chicken, pork, fish or vegetables.

**Muscadet** The dry, light Muscadet grape (best wines are *sur lie*) is perfect with seafood.

**Muscat** Fragrant, grapy wines ranging from delicate to downright syrupy. The drier ones are more difficult to pair with food; the sweeties come into their own with most desserts. Sweet Moscato d'Asti, delicious by itself, goes well with rich Christmas pudding or mince pies.

**Pinot Blanc** Clean, bright and appley, Pinot Blanc is very food-friendly. Classic white wine dishes, modern vegetarian dishes, pasta and pizza all match up well.

**Pinot Gris** Rich, fat wines that need rich, fat food. Go (in Alsace) for *choucroute*, *confit de canard*, rich pork dishes. The Italian Pinot Gris (Grigio) wines are lighter and more suited to pizza or pasta.

**Riesling** Good dry Rieslings are really best appreciated without food. Luscious sweet ones on the other hand are very pudding-friendly. In between, those with a slight acid bite can counteract the richness of, say, goose or duck, and the fuller examples can be good with oriental food and otherwise hard-to-match salads.

**Sauvignon Blanc** This grape makes wines with enough bite and sharpness to accompany quite rich fish dishes as well as being an obvious choice for seafood. The characteristic acid intensity makes a brilliant match with dishes made with tomato, but the best match of all is Sancerre and local Loire goats' cheese.

**Sémillon/Semillon** Dry Bordeaux Blancs are excellent with fish and shellfish; fuller, riper New World Semillons are equal to spicy food and rich sauces, often going even better with meat than with fish; sweet Sémillons can partner many puddings, especially rich, creamy ones. Sémillon also goes well with many cheeses, and Sauternes with Roquefort is a classic combination.

**Viognier** A subtle and characterful grape, Viognier is at its best as an apéritif. It can also go well with spicy Indian dishes.

# MAKING THE MOST OF WINE

Most wine is pretty hardy stuff and can put up with a fair amount of rough handling. Young red wines can knock about in the back of a car for a day or two and be lugged from garage to kitchen to dinner table without coming to too much harm. Serving young white wines when well chilled can cover up all kinds of ill-treatment – a couple of hours in the fridge should do the trick. Even so, there are some conditions that are better than others for storing your wines, especially if they are on the mature side. And there are certain ways of serving wines which will emphasize any flavours or perfumes they have.

*STORING*

Most wines are sold ready for drinking, and it will be hard to ruin them if you store them for a few months before you pull the cork. Don't stand them next to the central heating or the cooker, though, or on a sunny windowsill.

Light and extremes of temperature are also the things to worry about if you are storing wine long-term. Some wines, Chardonnay for instance, are particularly sensitive to exposure to light over several months, and the damage will be worse if the bottle is made of pale-coloured glass. The warmer the wine, the quicker it will age, and really high temperatures can spoil wine quite quickly. Beware in the winter of garages and outhouses, too: a very cold snap – say –4°C (25°F) or below – will freeze your wine, push out the corks and crack the bottles. An underground cellar is ideal, with a fairly constant temperature of 10°–12°C (50°–53°F). And bottles really do need to lie on their sides, so that the cork stays damp and swollen, and keeps out the air.

*TEMPERATURE*

The person who thought up the rule that red wine should be served at room temperature certainly didn't live in a modern, centrally heated flat. It's no great sin to serve a big beefy red at the temperature of your central heating, but I prefer most reds just a touch cooler. Over-heated wine tastes flabby, and may lose some of its more volatile aromas. In general, the lighter the red, the cooler it can be. Really light, refreshing reds, such as Beaujolais, are nice lightly chilled. Ideally, I'd serve Burgundy and other Pinot Noir wines at larder temperature (about 15°C/59°F), Bordeaux and Rioja a bit warmer (18°C/64°F), Rhône wines and New World Cabernet at a comfortable room temperature, but no more than 20°C/68°F.

Chilling white wines makes them taste fresher, emphasizing their acidity. White wines with low acidity especially benefit from chilling, and it's vital for sparkling wines if you want to avoid exploding corks and a tableful of froth. Drastic chilling also subdues flavours, however – a useful ruse if you're serving basic wine, but a shame if the wine is very good. A good guide for whites is to give the cheapest and lightest a spell in the fridge, but serve bigger and better wines – Australian Chardonnays or top white Burgundies – perhaps half-way between fridge and central-heating temperature. If you're undecided, err on the cooler side, for whites or reds.

## OPENING THE BOTTLE

There's no corkscrew to beat the Screwpull, and the Spinhandle Screwpull is especially easy to use. Don't worry if bits of cork crumble into the wine – just fish them out of your glass. Tight corks that refuse to budge might be loosened if you run hot water over the bottle neck to expand the glass. If the cork is loose and falls in, push it right in and don't worry about it.

Opening sparkling wines is a serious business – point the cork away from people! Once you've started, never take your hand off the cork until it's safely out. Remove the foil, loosen the wire, hold the wire and cork firmly and twist the bottle. If the wine froths, hold the bottle at an angle of 45 degrees, and have a glass at hand.

## AIRING AND DECANTING

Scientists have proved that opening young to middle-aged red wines an hour before serving makes no difference whatsoever. The surface area of wine in contact with air in the bottle neck is too tiny to be significant. Decanting is a different matter, because sloshing the wine from bottle to jug or decanter mixes it up quite thoroughly with the air. The only wines that really need to be decanted are those that have a sediment which would cloud the wine if they were poured directly – mature red Bordeaux, Burgundy and vintage port are the commonest examples. Ideally, if you are able to plan that far in advance, you need to stand the bottle upright for a day or two to let the sediment settle in the bottom. Draw the cork extremely gently. As you tip the bottle, shine a bright light through from underneath as you pour in a single steady movement. Stop pouring when you see the sediment approaching the bottle neck.

Contrary to many wine buffs' practice, I would decant a mature wine only just before serving; elderly wines often fade rapidly once they meet with air, and an hour in the decanter could kill off what little fruit they had left. By contrast, a good-quality young white wine can benefit from decanting.

## KEEPING LEFTOVERS

Leftover white wine keeps better than red, since the tannin and colouring matter in red wine is easily attacked by the air. Any wine, red or white, keeps better in the fridge than in a warm kitchen. And most wines, if well made in the first place, will be perfectly acceptable, if not pristine, after 2 or 3 days re-corked in the fridge. But for better results it's best to use one of the gadgets sold for this purpose. The ones that work by blanketing the wine with heavier-than-air inert gas are much better than those that create a vacuum in the air space in the bottle.

# FRANCE

I've visited most of the wine-producing countries of the world by now, but the one I come back to again and again, with my enthusiasm undimmed by time, is France. The sheer range of its wine flavours, the number of wine styles produced, and indeed the quality differences, from very best to very nearly worst, continue to enthral me, and as each year's vintage nears, I find myself itching to leap into the car and head for the vineyards of Champagne, of Burgundy, of Bordeaux and the Loire.

*CLIMATE AND SOIL*

France lies between the 40th and 50th parallels north, and the climate runs from the distinctly chilly and almost too cool to ripen grapes in the far north near the English Channel, right through to the swelteringly hot and almost too torrid to avoid grapes overripening in the far south on the Mediterranean shores. In the north the most refined and delicate sparkling wine is made in Champagne. In the south, rich, luscious dessert Muscats and fortified wines dominate. In between is just about every sort of wine you could wish for.

The factors that influence a wine's flavour are the grape variety, the soil and climate, and the winemaker's techniques. Most of the great wine grapes, like the red Cabernet Sauvignon, Merlot, Pinot Noir and Syrah, and the white Chardonnay, Sauvignon Blanc, Sémillon and Viognier, find conditions in France where they can ripen slowly but reliably – and slow, even ripening always gives better flavours to a wine. Since grapes have been grown for over 2000 years in France, the most suitable varieties for the different soils and meso-climates have naturally evolved. And since winemaking was brought to France by the Romans, generation upon generation of winemakers have refined their techniques to produce the best possible results from their different grape types. The great wines of areas like Bordeaux and Burgundy are the results of centuries of experience and of trial and error, which winemakers from other countries of the world now use as role models in their attempts to create good wine.

*WINE REGIONS*

White grapes generally ripen more easily than red grapes and they dominate the northern regions. Even so, the chilly Champagne region barely manages to ripen its red or white grapes on its chalky soil. But the resultant acid wine is the ideal base for sparkling wine, and the acidity of the young still wine can, with good winemaking and a few years' maturing, transform into a golden honeyed sparkling wine of incomparable finesse.

Alsace, on the German border, is warmer and drier than Champagne but still produces mainly white wines. The German influence is evident in the fragrant but dry wine styles from grapes like Riesling, Pinot Gris and Gewurztraminer.

South-east of Paris, Chablis marks the northernmost tip of the Burgundy region, and the Chardonnay grape here produces very dry wines, usually with a streak of green acidity, but nowadays with a fuller softer texture to subdue any harshness.

It's a good 2 hours' drive further south to the heart of Burgundy – the Côte d'Or which runs between Dijon and Chagny. World-famous villages such as Gevrey-Chambertin and Vosne-Romanée (where the red Pinot Noir dominates) and Meursault and Puligny-Montrachet (where Chardonnay reigns) here produce the great Burgundies that have given the region renown over the centuries. Lesser Burgundies – but they're still good – are produced further south in the Côte Chalonnaise, while between Mâcon and Lyon are the white Mâconnais wine villages and the villages of Beaujolais, famous for bright, easy-going red wine from the Gamay grape.

South of Lyon in the Rhône Valley red wines begin to dominate. The Syrah grape makes great wine at Hermitage and Côte-Rôtie in the north, while in the south the Grenache and a host of supporting grapes make full, satisfying reds of which Châteauneuf-du-Pape is the most famous. The white Viognier makes lovely wine at Condrieu and Château-Grillet in the north.

The whole of the south of France is now changing and improving at a bewildering rate. Provence and the scorched Midi vineyards are learning how to produce exciting wines from unpromising land and many of France's tastiest and most affordable wines now come under a Vin de Pays label from the south. In the Languedoc the red wines can now be exceptional, and in the Roussillon the sweet Muscats and Grenache-based fortifieds are equally fine.

The South-West of France is dominated by the wines of Bordeaux, but has many other gems benefiting from the cooling influence of the Atlantic. Dry whites from Gascony and Bergerac can be exciting. Jurançon down in the Basque country produces some remarkable dry and sweet wines, while Madiran, Cahors and Bergerac produce good to excellent reds.

But Bordeaux is the king here. The Cabernet Sauvignon and Merlot are the chief grapes, the Cabernet dominating the production of deep reds from the Médoc peninsula and its famous villages of Margaux, St-Julien, Pauillac and St-Estèphe. Round the city of Bordeaux are Pessac-Léognan and Graves, where Cabernet and Merlot blend to produce fragrant refined reds. On the right bank of the Gironde estuary, the Merlot is most important in the plump rich reds of St-Émilion and Pomerol. Sweet whites from Sémillon and Sauvignon Blanc are made in Sauternes, with increasingly good dry whites produced in the Entre-Deux-Mers, and especially in Graves and Pessac-Léognan.

The Loire Valley is the most northerly of France's Atlantic wine regions but, since the river rises in the heart of France not far from the Rhône, styles vary widely. Sancerre and Pouilly in the east produce tangy Sauvignon whites, the centre of the river produces fizzy wine at Vouvray and Saumur, sweet wine at Vouvray and the Layon Valley, red wines at Chinon and Bourgueil, and dry whites virtually everywhere, while down at the mouth of the river, as it slips past Nantes into the Atlantic swell, the vineyards of Muscadet produce one of the world's most famous and often least memorable dry white wines.

## CLASSIFICATIONS

France has an intricate but eminently logical system for controlling the quality and authenticity of its wines. The system is divided into 4 broad classifications (in ascending order): Vin de Table, Vin de Pays, VDQS (Vin Délimité de Qualité Supérieure) and AC (Appellation Contrôlée). Within the laws there are numerous variations, with certain vineyards or producers singled out for special mention. The 1855 Classification in Bordeaux or the Grands Crus of Alsace or Burgundy are good examples. The intention is a system which rewards quality. Vin de Pays and VDQS wines can be promoted to AC, for example, after a few years' good behaviour. The AC system is now under increasing attack from critics, both inside and outside France, who feel that it is outmoded and ineffectual and that too many poor wines are passed as of Appellation Contrôlée standard.

*2000 VINTAGE REPORT*

Bordeaux has all the hallmarks of an exceptional vintage and comparisons are already being made with 1990 and 82. Despite gloomy weather at the beginning of the year a hot, dry August provided perfect ripening conditions, and the Indian summer that followed enabled producers to harvest at will at optimum levels of maturity. Reds have deep colour, good natural alcohol levels and a concentration of ripe tannins and fruit. Dry whites are balanced and flavoursome. The only blot on the landscape is in Sauternes, where the dry weather in September delayed the onset of botrytis and then heavy rain in October washed away any hopes of a quality harvest. A tiny quantity of quality wine has been produced at some top estates.

In Burgundy, a poor July left fragile Pinot Noir grapes which, in the Côte de Beaune, suffered from a violent September storm; the Côte de Nuits looks much better. The white grapes remained healthy and a bumper crop of high-quality wines has been made throughout the region. I don't think there will be too much millennium hype with prices either, except possibly for the grandest wines.

Following on from 1999, there was another fine vintage in both the northern and southern Rhône. Good, concentrated wines are likely, and there should be some ripe, forward whites. Châteauneuf-du-Pape saw a smaller than normal crop. Provence also looks like enjoying another fine vintage.

In the Languedoc-Roussillon a relatively cool July followed by hot, sunny weather in August and September has produced appealing wines with attractive fruit expression and finely honed tannins. The Mediterranean varieties of Carignan, Grenache and Mourvèdre all faired well and only the Syrah, in certain zones, suffered from the semi-drought conditions that prevailed around the harvest.

The Loire had a wet, very cold July, but the weather improved in August and September. The weather broke early in October and much of the autumn was wet. The two extremities – Muscadet and Sancerre/Pouilly – had the best time of it. Elsewhere 1999 is likely to prove better than 2000, although red wines will probably be enjoyable young. Rigorous selection allowed some producers to make small quantities of quite good sweet Coteaux du Layon wines.

A potentially promising year for Alsace: a successful flowering was followed by a generally fine and warm summer, although intermittent rain during the vintage will certainly produce uneven results. In spite of this, there could be many rich, balanced, ripe and structured wines.

In Champagne a cool, wet summer with July hailstorms was followed by a dry, warm period just before the harvest, which greatly improved its potential. Quality is likely to be variable.

---

See also ALSACE, BORDEAUX RED WINES, BORDEAUX WHITE WINES, BURGUNDY RED WINES, BURGUNDY WHITE WINES, CHAMPAGNE, CORSICA, JURA, LANGUEDOC-ROUSSILLON, LOIRE VALLEY, MIDI, PROVENCE, RHONE VALLEY, ROUSSILLON, SAVOIE, SOUTH-WEST FRANCE; and individual wines and producers.

# ITALY

The cultivation of the vine was introduced to Italy over 3000 years ago, by the Greeks (to Sicily and the south) and by the Etruscans (to the north-east and central zones). Despite their great tradition, Italian wines as we know them today are relatively young. New attitudes have resulted, in the last 25 years or so, in a great change in Italian wine. The whole industry has been modernized, and areas like Tuscany are now among the most dynamic of any in the world.

## GRAPE VARIETIES AND WINE REGIONS

Vines are grown all over Italy, from the Austrian border in the north to the island of Pantelleria in the far south, nearer to North Africa than to Sicily. The north-west, especially Piedmont, is the home of many of the best Italian red grapes, like Nebbiolo, Dolcetto and Barbera, while the north-east (Friuli-Venezia Giulia and Alto Adige) is more noted for the success of native white varieties like Garganega,

Tocai and Ribolla, as well as imports like Pinot Grigio, Chardonnay and Sauvignon. The central Po Valley is Lambrusco country. Moving south, Tuscany is best known for its red Chianti and Brunello wines from the native Sangiovese grape. South of Rome, where the Mediterranean climate holds sway, the traditional heavy whites and reds are gradually giving way here and there to some admirable wines.

## CLASSIFICATIONS

**Vino da Tavola**, or 'table wine', is used for a wine that is produced either outside the existing laws, or in an area where no delimited zone exists. Both cheap, basic wines and inspired innovative creations like Tignanello and other so-called Super-Tuscans used to fall into this anonymous category. Now the fancy wines have become either DOC (particularly in Piedmont with its Langhe DOC) or IGT (a lot of Super-Tuscans are now IGT). Remaining Vino da Tavola are labelled simply as *bianco*, *rosso* or *rosato* without vintages or geographical indications.

**IGT** (Indicazione Geografica Tipica) began taking effect with the 1995 vintage to identify wines from certain regions or areas as an equivalent of the French Vin de Pays. A great swathe of both ordinary and premium wines traded their Vino da Tavola status for a regional IGT.

**DOC** (Denominazione di Origine Controllata) is the main classification for wines from designated zones made following traditions that were historically valid but often outdated. Recently the laws have become more flexible, encouraging producers to lower yields and modernize techniques, while bringing quality wines under new appellations that allow for recognition of communes, estates and single vineyards.

**DOCG** (Denominazione di Origine Controllata e Garantita) was conceived as a 'super-league' for DOCs with a guarantee of authenticity that promised high class but didn't always provide it. Still, despite some dubious promotions to this élite category, wines must be made under stricter standards that have favoured improvements. The best guarantee of quality, however, remains the producer's name.

## 2000 VINTAGE REPORT

Like 1999, another early vintage for Italy. In Piedmont growers are anticipating the sixth very good vintage in a row despite slightly uneven ripening. In the North-East ripe healthy grapes were harvested, though Friuli experienced some problems with August rain. In Tuscany and the centre sugar levels and consequently alcohol levels are high but wines might not show the superb structure of 1999 or the extraordinary 1997 vintage. The south also looks very good; in places, the lack of rain combined with intense heat has stressed the vines, but expect top wines from the best producers.

See also ABRUZZO, ALTO ADIGE, CALABRIA, CAMPANIA, EMILIA-ROMAGNA, FRIULI-VENEZIA GIULIA, LAZIO, LIGURIA, LOMBARDY, MARCHE, PIEDMONT, PUGLIA, ROMAGNA, SARDINIA, SICILY, TRENTINO, TUSCANY, UMBRIA, VALLE D'AOSTA, VENETO; and individual wines and producers.

# GERMANY

Although exports of German wines are still dominated by semi-sweet Liebfraumilch-type wines, these are falling rapidly. This is focusing attention on the estates more and more, and here quality is significantly better than a decade ago.

*GRAPE VARIETIES*

The best wines come from Riesling, Scheurebe, Grauburgunder/Ruländer (Pinot Gris), Weissburgunder (Pinot Blanc), Gewürztraminer and Silvaner, although the widely planted Müller-Thurgau produces much of the simpler wine. Good reds can be made in the south of the country from Spätburgunder (Pinot Noir), Lemberger and Dornfelder or blends of these.

*WINE REGIONS*

Many of the most delectable Rieslings come from villages such as Bernkastel, Brauneberg, Ürzig and Wehlen on the Mosel, and Eltville, Johannisberg and Rüdesheim in the Rheingau. The Nahe also makes superb Rieslings in Schlossböckelheim and Niederhausen, and Traisen has the best vineyards in the entire region. Franken is the one place the Silvaner grape excels, often made in a powerful, dry, earthy style. Rheinhessen is unfortunately better known for its sugary Niersteiner Gutes Domtal than it is for the excellent racy Rieslings produced on steep slopes in the villages of Nackenheim, Nierstein and Oppenheim. The Pfalz is climatically similar to Alsace and has a similar potential for well-rounded, dry whites, plus rapidly improving reds. Baden produces wine styles which appeal to an international market increasingly reared on fuller, drier wines. In Württemberg most of the red wines are thin and dull, but there are a few producers who understand the need for weight and flavour in red winemaking. The other smaller wine regions make little wine and little is exported.

*CLASSIFICATIONS*

Germany's classification system is based on the ripeness of the grapes and therefore their potential alcohol level. In 2000, 2 new designations for dry wine have been introduced: Classic for 'good' typical varietal wines and Selection for 'top quality' varietal wines.

**Tafelwein** (table wine) is the most basic term used for any basic blended wine, accounting for only a tiny percentage of production.

**Landwein** (country wine) is a slightly more up-market version, linked to 17 regional areas. These must be Trocken (dry) or Halbtrocken (medium-dry).

**QbA** (Qualitätswein bestimmter Anbaugebiete) is 'quality' wine from one of 13 designated regions, but the grapes don't have to be very ripe, and sugar can be added to the juice to increase alcoholic content.

**QmP** (Qualitätswein mit Prädikat) or 'quality wine with distinction' is the top level. There are 6 levels of QmP (in ascending order of ripeness): Kabinett, Spätlese, Auslese, Beerenauslese, Eiswein and Trockenbeerenauslese. The addition of sugar is strictly forbidden.

*2000 VINTAGE REPORT*

German growers got used to rainy harvests in the 1990s, but this still did not prepare them for the torrential rains that swept over the country during late September and most of October; November was not much better. The majority of the wines will therefore be modest in quality due to dilution. Only those top producers who selected rigorously will have made wines that rise above the average.

See also AHR, BADEN, FRANKEN, HESSISCHE BERGSTRASSE, MITTELRHEIN, MOSEL-SAAR-RUWER, NAHE, PFALZ, RHEINGAU, RHEINHESSEN, SAALE-UNSTRUT, SACHSEN, WÜRTTEMBERG; and individual wine villages and producers.

# SPAIN

Spain has more land under vine than any other country in the world, yet because of its harsh climate, and outmoded viticultural methods in some regions, the average grape yield in Spain is still small. In some areas, however, increases since 1990 have been swift, even worrying.

## WINE REGIONS

Galicia in the green, hilly north-west grows Spain's most aromatic whites. The heartland of the great Spanish reds, Rioja, Ribera del Duero and Navarra, is situated between the central plateau and the northern coast. Cataluña is principally white wine country (much of it sparkling Cava), though there are some great reds in Priorat. The central plateau of La Mancha makes mainly cheap reds and whites, though non-DO producers are improving spectacularly. Valencia in the south-east can rival La Mancha for fresh, unmemorable but inexpensive reds and whites. Andalucía's specialities are the fortified wines, sherry, Montilla and Málaga.

## CLASSIFICATIONS

**Vino de Mesa**, the equivalent of France's Vin de Table, is the lowest level, but is also used for a growing number of non-DO 'Super-Spanish'.

**Vino de la Tierra** is Spain's equivalent of France's Vin de Pays.

**DO** (Denominación de Origen) is the equivalent of France's AC, regulating grape varieties and region of origin.

**DOC** (Denominación de Origen Calificada) is a super-category, but so far Rioja is the only region to have been promoted to DOC.

30

*2000 VINTAGE REPORT*
A carbon copy of 1999 and 98, with torrential September rains after a torrid, dry summer, making for an uneven vintage in Ribera del Duero and particularly in Rioja, where increasing yields emphasized dilution problems. Still, top producers are managing very good results through green harvesting and late picking. A small-quantity vintage in Galicia and a great, ripe one in central Spain.

# PORTUGAL

Investment and a new dynamic approach seem to be paying off in this varied and attractive country, with climates that vary from the mild, damp Minho region in the north-west to the subtropical island of Madeira. Innovative use of native grape varieties means that Portugal is now a rich source of inexpensive yet characterful wines.

*WINE REGIONS*
The lush Vinho Verde country in the north-west gives very different wine from the parched valleys of the neighbouring Douro, with its drier, more continental climate. In Beiras, which includes Bairrada and Dão, soils are more important in determining the character of the wines. Estremadura and Ribatejo supply generous quantities of wine from regions either influenced by the maritime climate, or softened by the river Tagus. South of Lisbon, the Terras do Sado and Alentejo produce some exciting table wines. And Madeira is unique, a volcanic island 400km (250 miles) out in the Atlantic Ocean.

*CLASSIFICATIONS*
**Vinho Regional** is equivalent to French Vin de Pays, with laws and permitted varieties much freer than for IPR and DOC.
**IPR** (Indicação de Proveniência Regulamentada) is the intermediate step for wine regions hoping to move up to DOC status. Many were promoted in 1999, leaving just 9 IPRs. Their wines are referred to as Vinhos de Qualidade Produzidos em Região Determinada (VQPRD).
**DOC** (Denominação de Origem Controlada) Equivalent to France's AC. There are now 38 DOC regions and sub-regions.

*2000 VINTAGE REPORT*
A promising vintage if early reports are anything to go by. A dry warm winter was followed by a poor spring, resulting in widespread mildew and poor fruit set. However, from the end of May temperatures rose and conditions remained mostly hot and dry, with some welcome showers in the Douro in late September.

---

See also (SPAIN) ANDALUCIA, ARAGON, CANARY ISLANDS, CASTILLA-LA MANCHA, CASTILLA Y LEON, CATALUNA, GALICIA; (PORTUGAL) ALENTEJO, ALGARVE, BEIRAS, ESTREMADURA, RIBATEJO, TERRAS DO SADO, TRAS-OS-MONTES; and individual wines and producers.

# USA

The United States has more varied growing conditions for grapes than any other country in the world, which isn't so surprising when you consider that the 50 states of the Union cover an area that is larger than Western Europe; and although Alaska doesn't grow grapes in the icy far north, Washington State does in the north-west, as does Texas in the south and New York State in the north-east, and even Hawaii, lost in the pounding surf of the Pacific Ocean, manages to grow grapes and make wine. Altogether there are over 40 states that make wine of some sort or another; it ranges from some pretty dire offerings which would have been far better distilled into brandy or used for marinating the sirloin, to some of the greatest and most original wine flavours to be found in the world today.

California is far and away the most important state for wine production. In its determination to match the best red Bordeaux and white Burgundy, California proved that it was possible to take the classic European role models and successfully re-interpret them in an area thousands of miles away from their home. However, there is more to California than this. The Central Valley produces the majority of the simple beverage wines that still dominate the American market. Napa and Sonoma counties north of San Francisco Bay do produce great Cabernet and Chardonnay, but grapes like Zinfandel and Merlot are making their mark and Carneros and Russian River Valley are highly successful for Pinot Noir, Chardonnay and sparkling wines. In the north, Mendocino and Lake Counties manage to produce good grapes, while south of San Francisco, in the cool, foggy valleys

Main vineyard areas

Seattle
WASHINGTON STATE
Portland

OREGON

MENDOCINO
NORTH COAST
LAKE
SONOMA
NAPA
San Francisco
CALIFORNIA
CENTRAL COAST
CENTRAL VALLEY
San Luis Obispo
Santa Barbara
Los Angeles
SOUTH COAST

0    150 km
0    100 miles

between Santa Cruz and Santa Barbara, exciting cool-climate flavours are appearing, especially from Pinot Noir and Chardonnay.

There are those that say that much of California is too hot for the best table wines – and many of the critics are based in Oregon and Washington, both keen to wrest the quality crown from California. Oregon, with a cooler but capricious climate, perseveres with Pinot Noir, Chardonnay, Pinot Gris, Pinot Blanc and Riesling with patchy success. Washington, so chilly and misty on the coast, becomes virtual desert east of the Cascade Mountains and it is here, in irrigated vineyards, that superb reds and whites are made with thrillingly focused fruit. New Yorkers are showing that Long Island has all the makings of a classic region: this warm, temperate claw of land to the east of New York City is well suited to Merlot, Cabernet Sauvignon, Cabernet Franc and Chardonnay. Finger Lakes and the Hudson Valley are increasingly turning from hybrid to vinifera grapes and have made a name with Riesling and Chardonnay, and improved vineyard management has led to advances with reds, especially Pinot Noir and Cabernet Franc.

Of the other states, Texas has the most widespread plantings of classic vinifera wine varieties, but producers of excellence also exist in Maryland, Virginia and Pennsylvania on the east coast, and Idaho and New Mexico in the west.

## CLASSIFICATIONS

A rudimentary appellation system was established during the 1970s. AVA (American Viticultural Area) merely defines a spread of land and decrees that at least 85% of the wine's volume must be derived from grapes grown within that AVA.

## 2000 VINTAGE REPORT

In Napa, Sonoma and Mendocino counties the growing season saw three heat spells that shattered some berries and threatened to bring a very early harvest. Cool temperatures in September brought things back to normal. The size of the crop was bigger than either 1999 or 98 but smaller than 97. Most varieties look fine, but with less acidity than in 1999; Cabernets look to be medium-term aging wines, while Chardonnays will be best in the short term. Warm, even weather throughout the growing season has produced good results in the Central Coast area. New plantings led to a record year in the Central Valley.

Warm weather during flowering and a long growing season followed by fine harvest conditions (cool in Washington, relatively warm in Oregon) suggest very positive results from both states.

See also CALIFORNIA, NEW YORK STATE, OREGON, WASHINGTON STATE; and individual wine areas and wineries.

# AUSTRALIA

Australian wine today enjoys a reputation well out of proportion to the quantity of wine produced (total output is about one-tenth of Italy's). The heavy, alcoholic wines of the past are long gone; sheer volume of fruit aroma and flavour is the hallmark of today's styles. Production of fortified wines has plunged while sparkling wines boom and fine white and red table wines are the bread and butter.

*GRAPE VARIETIES AND WINE REGIONS*

Most of Australia's wine regions are in the south-east, in South Australia, Victoria and New South Wales. Other important wine zones, including Margaret River and Great Southern, are in Western Australia. Semillon and Shiraz have long been key varietals and are over-taking Chardonnay and Cabernet Sauvignon as the most fashionable. The use of small oak barrels for aging is important in modern reds as well as Chardonnays. Pinot Noir is yielding much local success and is something of a new darling, and Riesling is very trendy again.

*CLASSIFICATIONS*

Formal appellation control is unknown except in the tiny regions of Mudgee and Tasmania, and there it is more a guarantee of authenticity than a guide to quality. In a country so keen on inter-regional blending, a system resembling France's AC could be problematic. The Label Integrity Program (LIP) guarantees all claims made on labels and the Geographical Indications (GI) committee is busy clarifying zones, regions and sub-regions – albeit with plenty of lively, at times acrimonious, debate.

*2001 VINTAGE REPORT*
Favourable winter weather followed by spring rains meant healthy vines that were able to withstand January heat stress in some areas, and ill-timed but relatively moderate rain in March elsewhere. Generally, however, harvest conditions were dry, and the heat meant that the vintage was a week or two earlier than usual. Western Australia appears to have escaped unfavourable weather and expects excellent reds and whites for the second consecutive year – but quality looks good throughout Australia. Conditions were slightly more favourable to red wines, but both reds and whites fared well. In terms of size it will be a record crop.

# NEW ZEALAND

New Zealand's wines are characterized by intense fruit flavours, zesty acidity and pungent aromas – the product of cool growing conditions and high-tech winemaking. Styles are diverse due to regional differences, vintage variation and winemaking philosophy.

*GRAPE VARIETIES AND WINE REGIONS*
Nearly 1600km (1000 miles) separate New Zealand's northernmost wine region from the country's (and the world's) most southerly wine region, Central Otago. In terms of wine styles it is useful to divide the country into two parts. Hawke's Bay and further north, including Gisborne, Auckland and Northland, produce the best Cabernet Sauvignon, Merlot, Cabernet Franc and Syrah. From Martinborough and further south, including Marlborough, Nelson, Canterbury and Central Otago, come the best Sauvignon Blanc, Riesling, Pinot Noir and fizz. Chardonnay and Pinot Gris perform well everywhere, with riper, fleshier styles in the north and finer, zestier styles to the south.

*2001 VINTAGE REPORT*
A vintage of adversity and diversity. Hawke's Bay suffered badly from frost, Marlborough had a fire; North Island vineyards, with the exception of Martinborough, had a wet vintage; other areas experienced drought. Expect very good Marlborough Sauvignon and Martinborough Pinot Noir. Hawke's Bay reds and Chardonnay will be variable.

---

See also (AUSTRALIA) NEW SOUTH WALES, SOUTH AUSTRALIA, TASMANIA, VICTORIA, WESTERN AUSTRALIA; (NEW ZEALAND) AUCKLAND, CANTERBURY, CENTRAL OTAGO, GISBORNE, HAWKE'S BAY, KUMEU/HUAPAI, MARLBOROUGH, MARTINBOROUGH, NELSON, WAIHEKE ISLAND; and individual wineries.

# SOUTH AMERICA

Several countries in this vast continent have vines, but in only a few places does the climate favour the production of fine wines.

## ARGENTINA

Such is foreign faith in this country that even Chileans are investing in MENDOZA vineyards. Yet quality has still to arrive consistently at the top end, although encouraging commercial blends are now appearing regularly on the shelves. Watch out for aromatic white Torrontés, and reds from Malbec, Tempranillo, Sangiovese, Barbera and Syrah. There's promising Chardonnay from Tupungato Valley, and the outlying regions of Salta (to the north) and Rio Negro (to the south) are becoming known for Torrontés and Sauvignon Blanc respectively.

## CHILE

Chile is making full use of rejuvenated vineyards and a new self-belief among the indigenous winemaking talent. New projects are sprouting everywhere, helped by a predictable climate, an asset that France and California have been quick to invest in. The search for a second cool region to equal CASABLANCA for whites continues, while the RAPEL region is generating most excitement. And, at last, greater risk-taking is delivering stunning results at the premium end of the market. However, Chile still stands first and foremost for good-value wines. While the big 4 grapes – Cabernet, Merlot, Chardonnay and Sauvignon Blanc – dominate, the new star is Carmenère, as an increasing amount of what was called Merlot is now being produced in exciting varietal examples. Good Malbec, Pinot Noir and Syrah are also on the increase. See also Valle Central, Colchagua, Curicó, Maipo, Maule.

## 2001 VINTAGE REPORTS

For Chile, 2001 promises to be a good vintage following a relatively dry if somewhat cool growing season. Yields are average but down around 20% on the bountiful 2000 harvest. Whites have good acidity and reds from good vineyards are ripe and concentrated. In Argentina too, most producers are more than satisfied with the outcome but here, even more so than in Chile, truly premium wines can only be expected to emerge from well-balanced vineyards. Too often nature's generous gift is wasted by a tendency to over-irrigate and over-crop.

## OTHER COUNTRIES

With its main wine region sitting on roughly the same latitude as the Barossa in Australia, Uruguay has greater climatic potential than Brazil for producing good wines. Clean, international styles can be made, with best results coming from the tough, black-berried Tannat, smoothed over with some Merlot.

In Brazil, where winemaking is confined to the southern corner, rot can be a problem due to the generally damp, subtropical climate. Vinicola Aurora and Palomas are the only serious export producers. See also Rio Grande do Sul.

# SOUTH AFRICA

Problems of oversupply at the bulk end of the market are not yet solved and there are fears that the many new red plantings coming on line will cause something of a glut themselves, but there is a better understanding that the right price will sell. At the pinnacle of the quality pyramid, where quantities remain strictly limited, the increase in breadth and depth of quality wines is more noticeable every year.

*GRAPE VARIETIES AND WINE REGIONS*

Due to much uprooting as well as extensive planting, South Africa's vineyards remain close to 100,000 ha (250,000 acres). The Cape's winelands, which run roughly 400km (250 miles) north and east of Cape Town, are divided into districts under the Wine of Origin (WO) system. The major grape varieties are planted over the entire Cape; Chenin Blanc still holds sway with nearly 24% of plantings. Between them, Chardonnay, Sauvignon Blanc, Cabernet Sauvignon, Merlot and Shiraz account for just over 24% of vineyard area. There is little typicity of origin, although some areas are historically associated with specific varieties or styles. STELLENBOSCH currently produces some of the best red wines; CONSTANTIA, with its sea-facing slopes, is acknowledged as ideal for Sauvignon Blanc; cooler areas also include Walker Bay in OVERBERG where the focus is Pinot Noir. The inland, warmer areas are noted for fortifieds, both Muscadets and port-styles.

*2001 VINTAGE REPORT*

A worrying shortage of water and a Chardonnay crop reduced by as much as 70% in some vineyards didn't augur well at the start of the season. However, the absence of prolonged heatwaves, combined with low night-time temperatures, saved the day – apart from a generally lower crop, except in Stellenbosch – and one of the warmest, driest winters on record preceded the 2001 harvest. This vintage promises exceptional, ageworthy wines from all major varieties.

# OTHER WINE COUNTRIES

**ALGERIA** The western coastal province of Oran produces three-quarters of Algeria's wine, including soft but muscular wines of the Coteaux de Tlemcen, and dark, beefy reds of the Coteaux de Mascara. A replanting programme is now under way.

**AUSTRIA** Much of Austria's viticulture falls either side of the Danube. The WACHAU produces great Riesling and excellent peppery-dry Grüner Veltliner. Next along the Danube are KAMPTAL and KREMSTAL, also fine dry white regions with a few good reds. Austria's best reds are from BURGENLAND, south of Vienna. Further south, in STEIERMARK, use of oak-aging for Chardonnay and Sauvignon is increasing. In Burgenland, around the Neusiedlersee, superb dessert wines in Germanic and Sauternes styles are made. See also Donauland, Thermenregion, Wien.

**BULGARIA** Eastern Europe's biggest success story of the 1980s fell into disarray in the early 1990s, but investment programmes, land reforms, and the use of American oak are improving quality once again. International varieties (Cabernet, Merlot, Pinot Noir, Chardonnay, Riesling, Sauvignon) abound and local red varieties, such as the plummy Mavrud, the meaty Gamza, the deep Melnik, Dimiat and Misket, can be good. Best wineries include Assenovgrad, DOMAINE BOYAR and SUHINDOL.

**CANADA** The strict VQA (Vintners Quality Alliance) maintains high standards in British Columbia and Ontario, and there has been enormous progress in the 2 most important regions – OKANAGAN VALLEY in British Columbia and the NIAGARA PENINSULA in Ontario – where the move from hybrid to vinifera varieties is rapid. Sweet icewine is still Canada's main trump card. Pinot Gris, Chardonnay, Riesling and Gewürztraminer lead the way in non-sweet whites; Merlot and Cabernet Franc show potential in reds.

**CHINA** The Chinese wine industry is changing: official policy is promoting wine, the area under vine (190,000ha/469,000 acres) and winery capacity are expanding rapidly. The leading wineries are a mix of Western and Chinese investment (HUADONG/Allied DOMECQ, Great Wall/TORRES, Dynasty/Rémy-Cointreau, Dragon Seal/Pernod Ricard). International grape varieties are being planted, notably Chardonnay, Riesling, Gamay, Cabernet Sauvignon and Merlot.

**CROATIA** Inland Croatia produces mainly bulk whites; the best vineyards are on the Dalmatian coast, turning out gusty, mouthfilling Postup, Peljesac and Faros reds. Best of all is full-bodied Plavac Mali from small private producers. GRGICH of California has a winery on the Peljesac peninsula.

**CYPRUS** The island has not had a high reputation for wine since the Crusades, when COMMANDARIA was reputedly a rich, succulent nectar worth risking your neck for. Cyprus is modernizing and, supported by the government, regional press houses and wineries are being built in or near the vineyards. Encouraging results are already being seen with both local and international grapes. Major producers Etko, Keo, Sodap and Loel are investing heavily.

**THE CZECH REPUBLIC** After the division of Czechoslovakia, the Czech Republic has the vineyards of Bohemia and Moravia. These mainly cool-climate vineyards are planted with white varieties – Pinot Blanc, Muscat, Grüner Veltliner and the indigenous Irsay Oliver – with pockets of red. Western investment and consultancy is helping, but the occasional sample suggests they still have a long way to go.

**ENGLAND** With less than 1000ha (2470 acres) of vineyards, England remains a statistically insignificant wine-producing nation. The most popular winemaking counties are Kent (Biddenden, CHAPEL DOWN) and Sussex (BREAKY BOTTOM, CARR TAYLOR, Hidden Spring, Nutbourne Manor, NYETIMBER), with other top producers in Berkshire (VALLEY VINEYARDS), Dorset (The Partridge), Gloucestershire (THREE CHOIRS), Oxfordshire (Chiltern Valley), Somerset (Pilton Manor, Wootton) and Surrey (DENBIES). Good wines are coming through every year as producers find that the most successful grape varieties – the hybrid Seyval Blanc and German-developed crosses like Schönburger, Huxelrebe, Bacchus, Kerner and Ortega – are those that can hold off disease while waiting for the last rays of October sunshine; that is, of course, if those rays ever come. Sparkling wines are proving England's best commercial card, as award-winning RIDGEVIEW and NYETIMBER show.

**GEORGIA** With its subtropical to moderate continental climate, frost-free winters and hugely diverse soils, Georgia produces a great diversity of wine styles; the most 'international' of these come from the central Kartli area. Saperavi, an excellent red grape, is a promising indigenous variety. GWS (Georgian Wines and Spirits Company), established in 1993 (Pernod Ricard owns 50%), is the main producer.

**GREECE** Production and sales of Greece's best-known wine, Retsina, are falling sharply, and large companies like Achaia-Clauss, Boutari, Kourtakis and Tsantalis are producing clean, modern wines. But the real interest comes from estates like ANTONOPOULOS, CHATEAU LAZARIDIS, Gerovassiliou and Skouras. Best results are powerful, concentrated reds, using both native Greek and international varieties. Leading winemakers are creating their own vineyards, especially in Nemea, home to top red variety Agiorgitiko. The sweet Muscat from SAMOS and Mavrodaphne from Patras remain affordable classics.

**HUNGARY** Hungary's great wine traditions did not prosper under the Communists, but inspired winemaking, initially by flying winemakers, now by top Hungarian winemakers such as Tibor Gal and Akos Kamocsay, has produced a tremendous range of high-quality wines, though it is still mainly a white wine country. Foreign investment in TOKAJI, commitment to quality and renewed interest in its native grape varieties are putting Hungary back on the international wine map as it moves towards membership of the European Union.

**INDIA** A large country with a tiny wine industry. Only 10% of the 50,000ha (123,500 acres) of vines is used for wine. Better vineyards are 300m (985ft) above sea level. Chateau Indage, southeast of Bombay, holds 70% of the market. International varieties such as Chardonnay and Pinot Noir are planted here and, using French expertise, produce a range of sparkling wines, in particular OMAR KHAYYAM.

**ISRAEL** Much of Israel's wine is sweet red, but there are excellent dry red and white wines from the GOLAN HEIGHTS WINERY and Carmel. Askalon, also called Segal, is making good Cabernet-based reds. There is a move towards Merlot and more plantings in Galilee.

**JAPAN** Some quality wines have been produced in Japan from home-grown grapes, as those of Chateau Lumière show, but much Japanese wine is produced from imported grapes, juice or wine. SUNTORY's large winery and vineyards at Yamanashi are producing good wines.

**LEBANON** CHATEAU MUSAR is Lebanon's talisman of courage and quality. Watch out also for Chateau Kefraya and Ksara.

**LUXEMBOURG** Luxembourg's wines are somewhat reminiscent of those of Alsace. Mainly white, from Elbling, Pinot Gris, Riesling and Rivaner, they're usually light, scented and very pleasant.

**MEXICO** In the far north-west of Mexico, in Baja California, some excellent reds are being made by L A CETTO. New investment from companies such as González Byass, Seagram and Suntory may be the spur for further improvements. High-altitude areas such as the Parras Valley and Zacatecas have the most potential for quality wines. Promising grape varieties include Nebbiolo, Petite Syrah and Barbera, with Viognier and Riesling also being planted.

**MOLDOVA** PENFOLDS, and winemakers Jacques Lurton and Hugh Ryman, have tried hard to overcome the lack of investment here. Bordeaux-like Rochu and Negru red wines from the Purkar winery are first-class. Cabernet from the Cricova winery can also be good. Hincesti is producing good premium wines.

**MONTENEGRO** The Vranac grape makes full-throated, burly reds in this red wine-dominated part of the former Yugoslavia.

**MOROCCO** Known for rich, sweet-fruited reds that found a ready blending market in France, Morocco still produces supple reds such as Tarik and Chante Bled, as well as refreshing but heady rosés. Massive investment by Castel Frères is resulting in good single and blended varietals.

**ROMANIA** An ancient wineland with great traditional vineyards on the Black Sea and the Moldovan border that can provide wonderful sweet wines. The Dealul Mare region can produce good Pinot Noir, Merlot and Cabernet, but quality has been erratic. Good results have been achieved with botrytized Chardonnay and Pinot Gris in the MURFATLAR region. Huge investment by Halewood International may improve quality and consistency; the new Prahova Valley range has been erratic so far.

**SLOVAKIA** The eastern part of the old Czechoslovakia, with cool-climate vineyards for white wines from Pinot Blanc, Rhine Riesling, Gewürztraminer and Irsay Oliver, plus some reds. Western investment, particularly at the Nitra winery, is rapidly improving quality.

**SLOVENIA** Many of the old Yugoslav Federation's best vineyards are found here, either on the Italian or the Austrian borders. Lutomer Laski Rizling comes from north-east Slovenia. Brda is an area with potential to watch.

**SWITZERLAND** Fendant (Chasselas) is the main grape for snappy, neutral whites from the VALAIS. Like the fruity DOLE reds, they are best drunk very young. German-speaking cantons produce light reds and rosés from Pinot Noir (Blauburgunder), and whites from Müller-Thurgau (Rivaner). Italian-speaking TICINO concentrates on Merlots, juicy at best but often lean and grassy. Serious wines use Cabernet, Chardonnay and traditional varieties like Arvine and Amigne. See also Neuchâtel, Vaud.

**TURKEY** The world's fifth-largest grape producer, but 97% ends up as raisins and the rest makes pretty poor red and white wines.

**UKRAINE** The Crimea is the most important region here. The greatest wines are the historical treasures of the Massandra winery – once destined for the Tsar's palace. Present-day winemaking lacks focus.

**ZIMBABWE** The first wines were produced in 1965 but the industry has only become fully modern in the last decade. There are just two companies: Mukuyu and Stapleford.

# A–Z

## OF WINES,
## PRODUCERS, GRAPES
## & WINE REGIONS

In the following pages there are over
1600 entries covering the world's top wines, as well as
leading producers, main wine regions and grape
varieties, followed on page 291 by a glossary of wine
terms and classifications.

*On page 4 you will find a full explanation of
How to Use the A–Z. On page 298 there is an index
of all wine producers in the book, to help you find the
world's best wines.*

**ABRUZZO** *Italy* East of Rome, this region stretches from the Adriatic coast to the mountainous Apennine interior. White Trebbiano d'Abruzzo DOC is usually dry and neutral; the MONTEPULCIANO D'ABRUZZO DOC is sometimes rosé called Cerasuolo, but generally a strapping, peppery red of real character. Overproduction is a problem, but there are a number of good producers.

**ACACIA** *Carneros AVA, California, USA* Leading producer of Chardonnay and Pinot Noir from the CARNEROS region for almost 2 decades. Reserve Chardonnay★★ is consistently exciting and the regular Carneros bottling restrained but attractive. Pinot Noirs include the stunning DeSoto★★★ as well as a Beckstoffer Vineyard★★ and a Carneros★ – the wines have moved to a riper, meatier style of late. Also a voluptuous Carneros Viognier★ and Brut fizz. Best years: (reds) 1999 98 97 96 95 94 93 92 91 90; (whites) 1999 98 97 96 95 94 93 92 91.

**TIM ADAMS** *Clare Valley, South Australia* Important maker of fine, old-fashioned wine from his own and bought-in local grapes. Classic dry Riesling★★, subtly wooded Semillon★★, and rich, opulent Shiraz★★ and Cabernet★★. The botrytis Semillon★ can be super, and minty, peppery Aberfeldy Shiraz★★★ is a remarkable, at times unnerving, mouthful of brilliance from 100-year-old vines growing near WENDOUREE. Best years: (Aberfeldy Shiraz) (1999) 98 97 96 95 94 93 92.

**ADELAIDE HILLS** *South Australia* Small and exciting region 30 minutes' drive from Adelaide. High altitude affords a cool, moist climate ideal for fine table wines and superb sparkling wine. Also Australia's finest, most consistently good Sauvignon Blanc. Best producers: Ashton Hills, Chain of Ponds, HENSCHKE★★★, LENSWOOD VINEYARDS★★, Nepenthe★★, PETALUMA★★, SHAW & SMITH★.

**ADELSHEIM VINEYARD** *Willamette Valley AVA, Oregon, USA* This vineyard first hit the headlines with wine labels depicting various local beauties, including the owner's daughter. Adelsheim has established a reputation for excellent, generally unfiltered, Pinot Noir – especially cherry-scented Elizabeth's Reserve★★ and Seven Springs Vineyard★★ – and rich Chardonnay Reserve★★. Also a bright, fresh Pinot Gris★. Best years: (Elizabeth's Reserve) 1999 98 97 96 94.

ADELSHEIM
POLK COUNTY
PINOT NOIR 1996
*Seven Springs Vineyard*

**AGE** *Rioja DOC, Rioja, Spain* A huge investment to build Rioja's largest vinification plant may yet improve the whole range. The Siglo Saco red Crianza is its best-known wine, perhaps because it comes wrapped in a hessian sack – but, luckily, this does not affect the taste. Best years: (reds) 1996 95 94 91 89.

**AGLIANICO DEL VULTURE DOC** *Basilicata, Italy* Red wine from the Aglianico grape grown on the steep slopes of Mt Vulture. Despite being one of Italy's most southerly DOCs the harvest is later than in BAROLO, 750km (470 miles) to the north-west, because the Aglianico grape ripens very late. The best wines are structured, complex and long-lived. Best producers: Consorzio Viticoltori Associati del Vulture (Carpe Diem★), D'Angelo★★, Armando Martino, Paternoster★★, Sasso. Best years: (1998) 97 96 95 94 93 90 88.

**AHR** *Germany* The Ahr Valley is a small, mainly red wine region south of Bonn. Chief grape varieties are the Spätburgunder (Pinot Noir) and (Blauer) Portugieser. Most Ahr reds used to be made sweet for the day-trippers from Bonn and Cologne, but this style is on the way out. Meyer-Näkel has achieved a certain international reputation by making serious dry reds.

**AIGLE** *Vaud, Switzerland* Village in the CHABLAIS sub-region of the VAUD, making white wines from the Dorin (as the locals call the Chasselas grape) and reds from the Pinot Noir. Best known are the whites, with their 'flinty' bouquet, light and refreshing from their slight prickle. Best producers: Henri Badoux, Landolt, Urs Saladin, J & P Testuz.

**AIRÉN** Spain's – and indeed the world's – most planted white grape can make fresh modern white wines, or thick, yellow, old-fashioned brews. Airén is grown all over the centre and south of Spain, especially in La MANCHA, VALDEPEÑAS and ANDALUCIA (where it's called Lairén). Any new plantings are now forbidden in the CASTILLA-LA MANCHA region.

**AJACCIO AC** *Corsica, France* Situated in the west of the island around the town of Ajaccio, this is one of the better Corsican ACs. The reds often need 2–3 years in bottle to show at their best. Best producers: Clos d'Alzeto★, Clos Capitoro, Comte Péraldi★.

**ALBANA DI ROMAGNA DOCG** *Romagna, Italy* In the hills south of Bologna and Ravenna, Italy's first white DOCG was a 'political' appointment that caused outrage among wine enthusiasts because of the totally forgettable flavours of most Albana wine. Though also made in dry and sparkling styles, the sweet *passito* version is the best. Best producers: (passito) Celli, Conti, Ferrucci, Giovanna Madonia (Chimera★), Paradiso, Riva, Tre Monti, Uccellina★, Zerbina (Scacco Matto★★).

**ALBARIÑO** Possibly Spain's most characteristic white grape. It grows in GALICIA in Spain's rainy north-west and, as Alvarinho, in Portugal's VINHO VERDE region. When well made, Albariño wines have fascinating flavours of apricot, peach, grapefruit and Muscat grapes, refreshingly high acidity, highish alcohol – and unrefreshingly high prices.

**ALCAMO DOC** *Sicily, Italy* One of SICILY's better-known DOCs. Made from the indigenous Catarratto grape of western Sicily, grown between MARSALA and Palermo, the few good examples are dry, nutty and rounded. Drink young. Best producers: Principe di Corleone, MID, Pellegrino (Duca di Castelmonte), Rapitalà Adelkam★, Spadafora.

**ALEATICO** Rarely seen, ancient, native Italian grape that produces sweet, high-alcohol after-dinner wines in central and southern Italy. Best producers: AVIGNONESI, Candido (delicious Aleatico di Puglia★).

**ALENQUER DOC** *Estremadura, Portugal* Maritime-influenced hills north of Lisbon, producing ESTREMADURA's best wines from, mostly, local grape varieties, but also Cabernet and Chardonnay. Many wines are simply labelled Estremadura. Best producers: Quinta da Abrigada★, D F J VINHOS★, Quinta de Pancas★, Casa SANTOS LIMA★. Best years: (2000) **99 98 97 96 95**.

43

**ALENTEJO** *Portugal* A large chunk of southern Portugal east of Lisbon and, along with the DOURO, one of Portugal's fastest improving red wine regions. Has had its own DOC since 1999, and there are also 8 DOCs for sub-regions. Potential is far from realized but already some of Portugal's finest reds come from here. Best producers: (reds) Caves ALIANÇA (Quinta da Terrugem★★), Fundação Eugénio de Almeida (Cartuxa★, Pera Manca★★), BORBA CO-OP, Quinta do CARMO★, Cortes de Cima★★, D F J VINHOS★★, ESPORAO (Reserva★★), José Maria da FONSECA★, J P VINHOS★★, Mouchão★, Quinta do Mouro★, João Portugal RAMOS★★, Redondo co-op, Roquevale, SOGRAPE. Best years: (reds) (2000) **99 97 95 94 91 90 89**. See also Borba, Reguengos.

**ALEXANDER VALLEY AVA** *California, USA* Important AVA centred on the Russian River, where the climate is fairly warm with only patchy summer fog. Cabernet Sauvignon is highly successful here, with lovely, juicy fruit not marred by an excess of tannin. Chardonnay may also be good but doesn't give such ripe, round flavours. Zinfandel and Merlot can be outstanding from hillside vineyards. Best producers: Alexander Valley Vineyards★, Chateau Souverain, CLOS DU BOIS★, GEYSER PEAK★, JORDAN★, Murphy-Goode★★, Seghesio★★, SILVER OAK★★, SIMI★. See also Russian River Valley AVA, Sonoma County.

**ALGARVE** *Portugal* Holiday region with feeble-flavoured, mostly red wines in 4 DOCs: Lagoa, Lagos, Portimão and Tavira. The broad Vinho Regional Algarve classification suffices for D F J VINHOS' ripe-fruited Cataplana★.

**ALIANÇA, CAVES** *Beira Litoral, Portugal* Based in BAIRRADA, Aliança makes crisp, fresh whites and soft, approachable red Bairradas. Also made, either from its own vineyards or bought-in grapes or wines, are reds from the DAO, DOURO and ALENTEJO (Quinta da Terrugem★★). Best, though, are the varietal Touriga Nacional★★ and Tinta Roriz★★ made for Quinta da Cortezia in ESTREMADURA.

**ALIGOTÉ** French grape, found mainly in Burgundy, whose basic characteristic is a lemony tartness. It can make extremely nice wine, especially from old vines, but is generally rather dull and lean. In ripe years it can resemble Chardonnay, especially if a little new oak is used. The best comes from Bouzeron in the COTE CHALONNAISE. Bouzeron is the only village in Burgundy with its own appellation for Aligoté. Occasionally also found in Moldova and Bulgaria. Drink young. Best producers: (Burgundy) Denis Bachelet, COCHE-DURY★, A Ente★, JAYER-GILLES★, Denis Mortet★★, RION★, TOLLOT-BEAUT, Villaine★.

**ALLEGRINI** *Valpolicella, Veneto, Italy* A medium-sized, high-profile producer in VALPOLICELLA Classico. Allegrini has concentrated increasingly on quality, and especially on the single-vineyard La Grola★★★ and Palazzo della Torre★★. These are now sold under the regional IGT – partly to further distance them from the continuing low regard in which much of Valpolicella is held. Barrique-aged La Poja★★, made solely with the Corvina grape, has shown the great potential that exists in Valpolicella. Outstanding AMARONE★★★ and RECIOTO (Giovanni Allegrini★★). Best years: (Amarone) 1997 **96 95 94 93 90 88 86 85**.

**ALL SAINTS** *Rutherglen, Victoria, Australia* Old winery recently revived with great flair and sold to Peter Brown of the BROWN BROTHERS family in 1998. Superb fortifieds Show Reserve Tokay★★★, Muscat★★, Tawny★★, Madeira★★ and Amontillado★ have rediscovered past glory. Classic Release★★ fortifieds are very good but younger, while table wines can surprise. Pink Aleatico is unusual, to say the least.

**ALMAVIVA**★★★ *Valle del Maipo, Chile* Joint venture between CONCHA Y TORO and Baron Philippe de Rothschild, and currently Chile's most expensive red – possibly its finest to date. Purposeful investment in the winery and a careful choice of vineyard sites mean it could be a great wine, but it is too early to know if it will achieve its potential. Can be drunk at 5 years but can age for 10. Best years: (1999) (98) 97 **96**.

**ALOXE-CORTON AC** *Côte de Beaune, Burgundy, France* An important village at the northern end of the COTE DE BEAUNE producing mostly red wines from Pinot Noir. Its reputation is based on the 2 Grands Crus, CORTON (red and very occasional white) and CORTON-CHARLEMAGNE (white only). Other vineyards in Aloxe-Corton used to be a source of tasty, good-value Burgundy, but nowadays the reds rarely exhibit their former characteristic blend of ripe fruit and appetizing savoury dryness. Almost all the white wine is sold as Grand Cru; straight Aloxe-Corton Blanc is very rare. Best producers: CHANDON DE BRIAILLES★★, M Chapuis★, Marius Delarche★, Dubreuil-Fontaine★, Follin-Arvelet★, Antonin Guyon★, JADOT★, Rapet★, Comte Senard★, TOLLOT-BEAUT★★, Michel Voarick★. Best years: (reds) 1999 98 **97** 96 **95** 93 90.

**ALSACE AC** *Alsace, France* Tucked away on France's eastern border with Germany, Alsace produces some of the most individual white wines of all, rich in aroma and full of ripe, distinctive flavours. Alsace is almost as far north as Champagne, but its climate is considerably warmer. Since 1975 the best vineyard sites in Alsace can call themselves Grands Crus. There are currently 50 of these, but the list is expanding. Riesling, Muscat, Gewurztraminer and Pinot Gris (sometimes labelled Tokay-Pinot Gris) are generally considered the finest varieties in Alsace and are the only ones permitted for Grand Cru wines. Sylvaner and Pinot Blanc can produce good wines, too, but Pinot Noir, the area's only red grape, is usually confined to less well-appointed vineyards and produces pale wines that are closer to a rosé than a red BURGUNDY. Alsace was one of the first regions to label its wines by grape variety. Apart from Edelzwicker, which is a blend, and CREMANT D'ALSACE, all Alsace wines are made from a single grape variety. Best producers: L Albrecht, Barmès-Buecher, J Becker, Léon Beyer, P BLANCK, Bott-Geyl, A Boxler, E Burn, DEISS, Dirler, HUGEL, Josmeyer, Kientzler, Kreydenweiss, KUENTZ-BAS, S Landmann, A MANN, Meyer-Fonné, Muré/Clos St-Landelin, Ostertag, Pfaffenheim co-op, Rolly Gassmann, M Schaetzel, C Schleret, SCHOFFIT, Bruno Sorg, M Tempé, TRIMBACH, TURCKHEIM co-op, WEINBACH, ZIND-HUMBRECHT. Best years: (2000) 99 98 97 96 **95 94 90** 89 88 85 83. See also Alsace Vendange Tardive.

**ALSACE VENDANGE TARDIVE** *Alsace, France* Vendange Tardive means 'late-harvest'. The grapes (Riesling, Muscat, Pinot Gris or Gewurztraminer) are picked late and almost overripe, giving higher sugar levels and potentially more intense flavours. The resulting wines are usually rich and mouthfilling and often need 5 years or more to show their personality. A further sub-category of Alsace wines is Sélection de Grains Nobles – late-harvest wines made exclusively from super-ripe grapes of the same 4 varieties. Invariably sweet and usually affected by noble rot, they are among Alsace's finest, but are very expensive to produce (and to buy). Best producers: (Vendange Tardive) Léon Beyer★★, P BLANCK★★★, Bott-Geyl★★★, E Burn★★, Rolly Gassmann★★, HUGEL★★★, Kientzler★★★, Kreydenweiss★★★, Muré★★, Ostertag★★★, SCHOFFIT★★, Tempé★★★, WEINBACH★★, ZIND-HUMBRECHT★★. Best years: 1998 97 96 95 94 **93 92 90 89 88 85 83 76**.

**ALTARE** *Barolo DOCG, Piedmont, Italy* Elio Altare crafts some of the most stunning of Alba's wines: excellent Dolcetto d'Alba★★ and BARBERA D'ALBA★ and even finer BAROLO Vigneto Arborina★★★ and new Barolo Brunate★★★. Though a professed modernist, his wines are intense, full and structured while young, but with clearly discernible fruit flavours, thanks largely to tiny yields. He also makes 3 barrique-aged wines under the LANGHE DOC: Arborina★★★ (Nebbiolo), Larigi★★★ (Barbera) and La Villa★★ (Nebbiolo-Barbera). Best years: (Barolo) (1998) 95 **94 93 90 89 88 86 85**.

**ALTO ADIGE** *Trentino-Alto Adige, Italy* A largely German-speaking province, originally called Südtirol. The region-wide DOC covers 25 types of wine. Reds are almost invariably varietal and range from light and perfumed when made from the Schiava grape, to fruity and more structured from the Cabernets or Merlot, to dark and velvety if Lagrein is used. Whites include Chardonnay, Pinot Bianco, Pinot Grigio, Riesling and Sauvignon, and are usually fresh and fragrant. There is also some good sparkling wine. Much of the wine comes from well-run co-ops. Subzones include the previously independent DOCs at SANTA MADDALENA and Terlano. Best producers: Abbazia di Novacella★, Caldaro co-op★, Casòn Hirschprunn★, Colterenzio co-op★★, Peter Dipoli★, Franz Gojer★, Giorgio Grai★★, Franz Haas★, Haderberg★, Hofstätter★, LAGEDER★, Laimburg★, J Niedermayr★, Ignaz Niedriest★, Heinrich Plattner★, Peter Pliger-Kuenhof★★, Prima & Nuova/Erste & Neue★, Hans Rottensteiner★, San Michele Appiano co-op★★, Schloss Salleg★, Schwanburg★, Tiefenbrunner★, Elena Walch★, Baron Widmann★. See also Trentino.

**ALVARINHO** See Albariño.

**AMA, CASTELLO DI** *Chianti Classico DOCG, Tuscany, Italy* Model estate of CHIANTI CLASSICO, with outstanding single-vineyard bottlings★★ (Bellavista and La Casuccia). L'Apparita★★★ is one of Italy's best Merlots; less impressive Il Chiuso is made from Pinot Nero. Also good VIN SANTO★. Best years: (Chianti Classico) (1999) (98) **97 96 95 94 93** 91 **90 88 85**.

**AMARONE DELLA VALPOLICELLA** *Valpolicella DOC, Veneto, Italy* A brilliantly individual, bitter-sweet style of VALPOLICELLA made from grapes shrivelled on mats for months after harvest. The wine, which can reach up to 16% of alcohol, differs from the sweet RECIOTO DELLA VALPOLICELLA in that it is fermented to dryness. Classico is generally the best, though an exception can be made for DAL FORNO. Best producers: Stefano Accordini★★, ALLEGRINI★★★, Bertani★★, Bolla★, Brigaldara★★, Brunelli★,

Tommaso Bussola★★, Michele Castellani-I Castei★★, DAL FORNO★★★, Guerrieri-Rizzardi★★, Lonardi★, MASI★, Mazzi★, QUINTARELLI★★★, Le Ragose★★, Le Salette★★, Serègo Alighieri★, Speri★★, Tedeschi★, Tommasi★, Villa Monteleone★★, Villa Spinosa★, Zenato★★, Fratelli Zeni★. Best years: 1999 (98) 97 **95 93 90 88 86 85 83 81**.

**AMIGNE** Swiss grape variety that is virtually limited to the region of Vétroz in the VALAIS. The wine has an earthy, nutty intensity and benefits from a few years' aging. Best producers: Germanier Bon Père, Granges Frères (Escalier de la Dame), Caves Imesch.

**AMITY VINEYARDS** *Willamette Valley AVA, Oregon, USA* Myron Redford was one of the pioneers in Oregon, opening his winery in 1976. The Gewürztraminer★★ is outstanding and Riesling★ is almost as good. The showpiece is the Pinot Noir, notably the Winemakers Reserve★. Pinot Blanc★ has replaced Chardonnay. Fruity, floral Gamay Noir remains fine value. Best years: (Pinot Noir) 1999 98 **97 96**.

**ANDALUCÍA** *Spain* Fortified wines, or wines naturally so strong in alcohol that they don't need fortifying, are the speciality of this southern stretch of Spain. Apart from sherry (JEREZ Y MANZANILLA DO), there are the lesser, sherry-like wines of Condado de Huelva DO and MONTILLA-MORILES DO, and the rich, sometimes treacly-sweet wines of MALAGA DO. These regions now also make some modern but bland dry whites; the best are from Condado de Huelva.

**ANDREW WILL WINERY** *Washington State, USA* Sourcing the best grapes and striving for elegance in his wines, winemaker Chris Camarda is making what many critics believe to be the finest Washington Merlots★★. The focus is on vineyard-designated wines, with particularly fine bottlings from Klipsun★★, Pepper Bridge★★ and Ciel du Cheval★★★. His Cabernets★★ are not far behind and Sorella★★★, a BORDEAUX blend, is outstanding. Best years: (reds) (2000) (99) 98 97 **96 95**.

**CH. ANGÉLUS★★★** *St-Émilion Grand Cru AC, 1er Grand Cru Classé, Bordeaux, France* One of the best-known ST-EMILION Grands Crus with an energetic owner and talented winemaker. Increasingly gorgeous wines throughout the 80s, recognized by promotion to Premier Grand Cru Classé in 1996. Best years: (2000) 99 98 97 96 95 94 **93 92** 90 **89 88 86 85**.

**MARQUIS D'ANGERVILLE** *Volnay AC, Côte de Beaune, Burgundy, France* With over half a century's experience and meticulous attention to detail, Marquis Jacques d'Angerville produces an exemplary range of elegant Premiers Crus from VOLNAY, the classiest of the COTE DE BEAUNE's red wine appellations. Clos des Ducs and Taillepieds are ★★★. All should be kept for at least 5 years. Best years: 1999 98 **97** 96 95 93 **91 90 89**.

**CH. D'ANGLUDET★** *Margaux AC, Cru Bourgeois, Haut-Médoc, Bordeaux, France* This English-owned château makes one of my favourite BORDEAUX. Always of Classed Growth standard, it has one of the best price–quality ratios in Bordeaux and ages superbly for a decade or more. Best years: (2000) 98 97 96 95 **94 90 89** 88 86 85 83 82.

**ANJOU BLANC AC** *Loire Valley, France* Ill-defined AC; ranges from bone dry to sweet, from excellent to dreadful; the best are dry. Up to 20% Chardonnay or Sauvignon can be added, but many of the leading

47

producers use 100% Chenin. Best producers: M Angeli★★, Bidet, Cady, Fesles★, Haute-Perche, V Lebreton, Ogereau★, Pierre-Bise★, J Pithon★★, RICHOU★, Soucherie★, Yves Soulez★, la Varière★. Best years: (2000) **99 98 97 96 95**.

**ANJOU ROUGE AC** *Loire Valley, France* Anjou is best known for ROSE D'ANJOU but reds (from Cabernets Sauvignon and Franc or Pineau d'Aunis) are increasingly successful. Usually fruity, easy-drinking wine, with less tannin than ANJOU-VILLAGES. Wines made from Gamay are sold as Anjou Gamay. Best producers: M Angeli★, Fesles, J Pithon★, RICHOU★, Yves Soulez, Touche Noire. Best years: (2000) 99 **98** 97 96 95.

**ANJOU-VILLAGES AC** *Loire Valley, France* As the Anjou AC is such a blanket term, used to describe red, white, rosé and fizz of inconsistent quality, the better Anjou red producers asked for a separate AC. Since 1985, 46 villages have been entitled to the AC Anjou-Villages, only for red wine from Cabernet Franc and Cabernet Sauvignon. Some extremely attractive dry, fruity reds are emerging in the region, with better aging potential than ANJOU ROUGE. Anjou-Villages Brissac is a superior subappellation. Best producers: Bablut★, Closel★, P Delesvaux★, Haute-Perche★, Laffourcade, J-Y Lebreton★★, V Lebreton★, Ogereau★, Pierre-Bise★, Putille★, RICHOU (Vieilles Vignes★★), Pierre Soulez★, Tigné★, la Varière★. Best years: (2000) 99 **98 97 96 95 90**.

**ANSELMI** *Soave DOC, Veneto, Italy* Roberto Anselmi, with PIEROPAN, has shown that much-maligned SOAVE can have personality when carefully made. Using ultra-modern methods he has honed the fruit flavours of his San Vincenzo★ and Capitel Foscarino★★ and introduced small-barrel-aging for single-vineyard Capitel Croce★★ and luscious, Sauternes-like I Capitelli★★ (sometimes ★★★). All sold under the regional IGT. Best years: (I Capitelli) 1998 **97 96 95 93 92 90 88**.

**ANTINORI** *Tuscany, Italy* World-famous Florentine family firm that has been involved in wine since 1385, but it is Piero Antinori, the current head, who has made the Antinori name synonymous with quality and innovation. The quality of its CHIANTI CLASSICO wines like Badia a Passignano★ (Riserva★★), Pèppoli★, Villa Antinori★ and Tenute Marchese Riserva★★ is consistently good, but it was its development of the SUPER-TUSCAN concept of superior wines outside the DOC that launched a quality revolution during the 1970s. Introducing small-barrel-aging to Tuscany, TIGNANELLO★★ (Sangiovese-Cabernet) and SOLAIA★★★ (Cabernet-based) can be great wines. Other interests include VINO NOBILE, La Braccesca★★ and BOLGHERI's Tenuta Belvedere Guado al Tasso★★ (Cabernet-Merlot). Ownership further afield includes PRUNOTTO in Piedmont, Pian delle Vigne in BRUNELLO DI MONTALCINO, the Tormaresca wines from PUGLIA, and ATLAS PEAK in California. Best years: (reds) 1999 98 **97 96 95 94 93 90 88**. See also Castello della Sala.

**ANTONOPOULOS** *Patras AO, Peloponnese, Greece* Boutique winery that nobly eschews the use of weedkiller in the vineyard. Burgundian barrel-fermented Chardonnay★★ and Cabernet New Oak★ are international in style. Collection★ red is a promising Agiorgitiko-Cabernet blend.

**ARAGÓN** *Spain*  Most of Aragón, stretching from the Pyrenees south to Spain's central plateau, used to be responsible for much of the country's cheap red wine. There have been improvements, especially in the cooler, hilly, northern SOMONTANO DO. Further south, winemaking is improving in Campo de Borja DO, Calatayud DO and, particularly, CARIÑENA DO; these 3 areas have the potential to be a major budget-price force in a world mad for beefy reds.

**ARAUJO** *Napa Valley AVA, California, USA*  Boutique winery founded in 1990 when a San Francisco businessman, Bart Araujo, bought the Eisele Vineyard, one of California's most outstanding individual vineyard sites. A small winery has been built on the property. The Cabernet Sauvignon★★★ is the flagship wine and there is also a Sauvignon Blanc★★★, blended with Viognier, and a limited-production Syrah★★★ was first released in 1993. These outstanding wines are made in small quantities and are difficult to obtain outside NAPA VALLEY, where they can be found only in the finest restaurants.

**ARBOIS AC** *Jura, France*  The largest of the specific ACs in the Jura region. The whites are made from Chardonnay or the local Savagnin, which can give the wines a sherry-like flavour that is most concentrated in *vin jaune*. There is also a rare, sweet *vin de paille*. Good sparkling CRÉMANT DE JURA is made mainly from Chardonnay. Best reds and sparklers are from the commune of Pupillin. Best producers: Ch. d'Arlay★, Aviet★, Bourdy★, Désiré★, Dugois★, J Foret★, F Lornet★, H Maire★, P Overnoy★, la Pinte★, J Puffeney★, Pupillin co-op★, Rijckaert★, Rolet★, A & M Tissot, J Tissot★, Tournelle★.

**ARGIANO** *Brunello di Montalcino DOCG, Tuscany, Italy*  The mini-renaissance continues: renewed investment and the hand of Giacomo Tachis can be seen in radically refashioned BRUNELLO★★ (Riserva★★★) that is both rich and accessible, and scintillating Solengo★★★ (a blend of Cabernet, Merlot, Sangiovese and Syrah). Good ROSSO DI MONTALCINO★, too. Best years: (Brunello) (1996) 95 **94 93 91 90**.

**ARGIOLAS** *Sardinia, Italy*  This new Italian star makes adept versions of the Sardinian DOC wines Cannonau★, Monica and Vermentino★ di Sardegna, but the best wines are the vino da tavola blends. Turriga★★ is a powerful, spicy red; Angialis★★ a golden, sweet white. New red blend Kore looks promising. All the wines are good value.

**ARNEIS** Italian grape grown in the ROERO hills in PIEDMONT. Arneis is DOC in Roero, producing dry white wines which, at best, have an attractive nutty, herbal perfume. They can be expensive. Best producers: Almondo★, Araldica/Alasia★, Brovia★, Carretta★, CERETTO★, Cascina Chicco★, Correggia★, Deltetto★, GIACOSA★, Malabaila★, Malvirà★, Angelo Negro★, Castello di Neive★, PRUNOTTO★, Vietti★, Gianni Voerzio★.

**CH. L'ARROSÉE★★** *St-Émilion Grand Cru AC, Grand Cru Classé, Bordeaux, France*  This small property, just south-west of the small historic town of St-Émilion, makes really exciting wine: rich, chewy and wonderfully luscious, with a comparatively high proportion (40%) of Cabernet Sauvignon. Drink after 5 years, but may be cellared for 10 or more. Best years: (2000) (99) 98 97 96 95 **94 90 89 88 86 85 83 82**.

**ARROWOOD VINEYARDS WINERY** *Sonoma Valley AVA, California, USA*
Dick Arrowood was the winemaker at CHATEAU ST JEAN during its glory
years of Chardonnay. In 1988 he started his own winery, which was
purchased in 2000 by MONDAVI. The wines have mostly been tip-top –
beautifully balanced Cabernet★★, superb Merlot★★, lovely, velvety
Chardonnay★★ and a crisp, fragrant Viognier★★. Whites should be
drunk young, reds with a little age. Best years: (reds) 1998 97 **96 95 94
93 92 91 90**; (whites) 1999 98 **97 96 95**.

**ISMAEL ARROYO** *Ribera del Duero DO, Castilla y León, Spain* This family
bodega is one of the best RIBERA DEL DUERO producers, making long-lived,
tannic wines, headed by Val Sotillo Reserva★★, Gran Reserva★★ and
Crianza★. Best years: (Val Sotillo Reserva) **1996 95 94 91 90**.

**ARVINE** Swiss variety from the VALAIS in the communes of Vétroz and
Martigny. The best grapes come from Fully and the Mont d'Or of Sion.
Arvine has a bouquet of peach and apricot, and develops a spicy,
honeyed character with age. Of Switzerland's indigenous grapes,
Arvine gives the wines with the best aging potential. Best producers:
Chappaz★, Caves Imesch★, Dom. du Mont d'Or★.

**ASCHERI** *Piedmont, Italy* Winemaker in PIEDMONT for at least 5 centuries,
Ascheri's style is forward and appealingly drinkable, whether it be
BAROLO (Vigna dei Pola★, Sorano★★), Dolcetto d'Alba (Vigna Nirane★)
or NEBBIOLO D'ALBA. New are Syrah and Viognier sold as Montelupa
Rosso and Bianco. The Cristina Ascheri MOSCATO D'ASTI is delightful.

**ASTI DOCG** *Piedmont, Italy* Asti Spumante, the world's best-selling
sweet sparkling wine, was long derided as light and cheap, though
promotion to DOCG signalled an upturn in quality. Made in the
province of Asti south-east of Turin, under the new appellation (which
includes the rarer MOSCATO D'ASTI) the wine is now called simply Asti.
Its light sweetness and refreshing sparkle make it ideal with fruit, rich
cakes and a wide range of sweet dishes. Drink young. Best producers:
Araldica, Bera★, Cinzano★, Contero, Giuseppe Contratto★★, Cascina
Fonda★, FONTANAFREDDA, Gancia★, Martini & Rossi★, Cascina Pian d'Oro.

**ATA RANGI** *Martinborough, North Island, New Zealand* Small, high-quality
winery run by 2 families. Stylish, concentrated wines include big, rich
Chardonnay★★, seductively perfumed cherry/plum Pinot Noir★★★
and an impressive Cabernet Sauvignon-Merlot-Syrah blend called
Célèbre★★. Young Vines Pinot Noir falls well short of the standard set
by its big brother. Best years: (Pinot Noir) (2001) (00) 99 **98 97 96 94**.

**ATLAS PEAK** *Atlas Peak AVA, Napa, California, USA* These hillside
vineyards, now owned by ANTINORI of Italy, are demonstrating a new sense
of direction after several years adrift. The 100% Sangiovese has been
improving throughout the 1990s, as has Consenso★, a tasty Cabernet-
Sangiovese blend. Both can age for 5–10 years. Chardonnay and
Cabernet are recent additions. Best years: (reds) 1998 97 **96 95**.

**AU BON CLIMAT** *Santa Maria Valley AVA, California, USA* Pace-
setting winery in this cool region, run by the talented Jim Clendenen,
who spends much time in BURGUNDY and PIEDMONT. The result is lush
Chardonnay★★, intense Pinot Noir★★ (Isabelle bottling can be ★★★)
and BORDEAUX styles under the Vita Nova label. Watch out for Italian

varietals under the Il Podere dell' Olivos label and Cold Heaven Viogniers. QUPE operates from the same winery. Best years: (reds) (1998) 97 **96 95 94 91 90 89 87 86**; (whites) (1999) 98 **97 95 92 90**.

**AUCKLAND** *North Island, New Zealand* Vineyards in the region of Auckland are centred around the small districts of Henderson, KUMEU/HUAPAI and Waimauku. Many of the better wines are made in the recently established districts of WAIHEKE ISLAND and Matakana. Clevedon, south of Auckland, is another fledgling area that shows promise. Best producers: COLLARD★, Heron's Flight.

**CH. AUSONE★★★** *St-Émilion Grand Cru AC, 1er Grand Cru Classé, Bordeaux, France* This elegant property, situated on what are perhaps the best slopes in ST-EMILION, made a much-vaunted return to form in the 1980s, and is maintaining high standards. Owner Alain Vauthier's richly textured wines gain added complexity from the high proportion (50%) of Cabernet Franc. Best years: (2000) 99 98 97 96 95 94 **93 90 89 88 86 85 83 82**.

**AUXEY-DURESSES AC** *Côte de Beaune, Burgundy, France* Auxey-Duresses is a backwater village up in the hills behind MEURSAULT. The reds should be light and fresh but can often lack ripeness. At its best, and at 3–5 years, the white is dry, soft, nutty and hinting at the creaminess of a good Meursault, but at much lower prices. Of the Premiers Crus, Les Duresses is the most consistent. Best producers: (reds) Comte Armand★★, J-P Diconne★, Jessiaume Père et Fils, Maison LEROY, Duc de Magenta★, M Prunier★, P Prunier★; (whites) R Ampeau★, d'Auvenay (Dom. LEROY)★★, J-P Diconne★, DROUHIN★★, J-P Fichet★, Olivier LEFLAIVE★, Maison LEROY★, Duc de Magenta★, M Prunier★. Best years: (reds) 1999 98 **96 95 93 90**; (whites) (2000) 99 **97 96 95**.

**AVIGNONESI** *Vino Nobile di Montepulciano DOCG, Tuscany, Italy* The Falvo brothers of Avignonesi led Montepulciano's revival as one of TUSCANY's best zones. Although VINO NOBILE★★ is often the best of the dry wines, the many international wines, Il Marzocco★ (Chardonnay), Il Vignola★ and Toro Desiderio★★ (previously Merlot, now Merlot-Cabernet), have received more attention. The VIN SANTO★★★ is the most sought after in Tuscany, and a rare red version from Sangiovese, Occhio di Pernice★★★, is just something else. Best years: (Vino Nobile) (1998) 97 96 **95 94 93 91 90 88**.

**AYL** *Saar, Germany* A top Saar village. The best-known vineyard in Ayl is Kupp, which produces classy, slaty off-dry and sweet Rieslings on its steep slopes. Best producers: Bischöflicher Konvikt, Peter Lauer★, Dr Heinz Wagner★. Best years: 1999 **97 95 94 93 90**.

**BABICH** *Henderson, North Island, New Zealand* Family-run winery with some prime vineyard land in MARLBOROUGH and HAWKE'S BAY. Irongate Chardonnay★ is an intense, steely wine that needs plenty of cellaring, while intense, full-flavoured varietal reds under the Winemakers Reserve label (which replaces Mara) show even greater potential for development. Flagship label Patriarch features Chardonnay★★ and Cabernet Sauvignon★★, both from Hawke's Bay. Marlborough wines include a stylish Sauvignon Blanc★, a tangy Riesling and a light, fruity Pinot Gris. Best years: (Hawke's Bay) (2000) 99 **98 96 94**.

**BACKSBERG ESTATE** *Paarl WO, South Africa*  Well-established Cape estate with a sound range spanning most classic white and red varieties. Michael and Jill Back's joint venture with well-known Californian winemaker Zelma Long and her viticulturist husband Phil Freese has produced a new vineyard project and a Sauvignon Blanc called Simunye (Zulu for 'we are one'). Freese, who also consults here, has re-energized the red grape vineyards. Klein Babylonstoren★, Cabernet Sauvignon★ and Merlot all show denser fruit and more supple tannins. Chardonnay★, from old vines, is the top white. A worker-empowerment/Back project has created the Freedom Road label. Best years: (Chardonnay) **1999 98 97 96 95**.

**BAD DÜRKHEIM** *Pfalz, Germany*  This spa town has some good vineyards and is the headquarters of the dependable Vier Jahreszeiten Kloster Limburg co-op. Best producers: Kurt DARTING★, Fitz-Ritter, Pflüger, Karl Schaefer★. Best years: (whites) 1999 98 **97 96 93 92**.

**BAD KREUZNACH** *Nahe, Germany*  Spa town with 22 individual vineyard sites, the best wines coming from the steepest sites such as Brückes, Kahlenberg and Krötenpfuhl. Not to be confused with the NAHE district Bereich Kreuznach. Best producers: Paul Anheuser, Anton Finkenauer, Carl Finkenauer, Reichsgraf von Plettenberg. Best years: (whites) 1999 98 **97 93 90**.

**BADEN** *Germany*  Very large wine region stretching from FRANKEN to the Bodensee. Recently took the lead in making dry whites and reds which show off the fuller, softer flavours Germany can produce in the warmer climate of its southerly regions. Many of the best non-Riesling German wines of the future will come from here, as well as many of the best barrel-fermented and barrel-aged wines. Good co-operative cellars at Achkarren, Sasbach, Durbach, Bickensohl, Bötzingen and Königsschaffhausen.

**BAGA**  Important red grape in BAIRRADA, which is one of the few regions in Portugal to rely mainly on one variety. Also planted in much smaller quantities in DAO and the RIBATEJO. It can give deep, blackberryish wine, but aggressive tannin is a continual problem.

**BAILEYS** *North-East Victoria, Australia*  Old, traditional winery at Glenrowan, where Australia's most famous bush bandit, Ned Kelly, made his last stand. Now owned by Fosters and, after a shaky start, showing real improvement from the 1998 vintage (1920s Block Shiraz★). Also some of Australia's most luscious fortified Muscat and Tokay (Winemakers Selection★★) – still heavenly and irresistible stickies, but I can't help thinking they were better a few years ago.

**BAIRRADA DOC** *Beira Litoral, Portugal*  Bairrada was for long the source of many of Portugal's best red table wines, if now overtaken by the DOURO and ALENTEJO. These can brim over with intense raspberry and blackberry fruit, though the tannin levels are severe and may take quite a few years to soften. The whites are coming on fast with modern vinification methods. Best producers: (reds) Caves ALIANCA, Quinta das Bágeiras★, Quinta do Carvalhinho★, Gonçalves Faria★★, Caves Messias (Garrafeira★), Luis PATO★★, Caves Primavera (Garrafeira★), Quinta da Rigodeira★, Casa de Saima★, Caves SAO

JOAO★★, SOGRAPE, Sidónio de Sousa★; (whites) Quinta da Rigodeira★, Casa de Saima★, SOGRAPE (Reserva★, Quinta de Pedralvites★), Quinta do Valdoeiro★. Best years: (reds) (2000) 97 **96 95 94 92 91 90**.

**BALATONBOGLÁR WINERY** *Transdanubia, Hungary* The dominant winery in the Lake Balaton region benefited from heavy investment, and the expertise of viticulturist Richard Smart and flying winemaker Kym Milne has resulted in a range of tasty, inexpensive, slightly sweet wines sold under the Chapel Hill label in the UK. Now owned by Henkell and Söhnlein, a large German sparkling wine producer.

**BALEARIC ISLANDS** *Spain* Medium-bodied reds and soft rosés were the mainstays of Mallorca's two vineyard areas, the Binissalem DO and Pla i Llevant DO, until the fledgling Anima Negra winery began turning out its stunning, deep reds from the native Callet grape, taking everyone by surprise. Best producers: Anima Negra★★, Franja Roja (J L Ferrer), Jaume Mesquida, Miguel Oliver, Herederos de Ribas.

**BANDOL AC** *Provence, France* A lovely fishing port with vineyards high above the Mediterranean, producing some of the best reds and rosés in Provence. The Mourvèdre grape gives Bandol its character – gentle raisin and honey softness with a herby fragrance. The reds happily age for 10 years, sometimes more, but can be very good at 3–4. The rosés, delicious and spicy but often too pricy, should be drunk young. There is a small amount of neutral, overpriced white. Best producers: (reds) Bastide Blanche★★, Bunan★, Cagueloup, Frégate★, le Gallantin★, J P Gaussen★★, l'Hermitage★, Lafran-Veyrolles★, Mas Redorne★, la Noblesse★, PIBARNON★, Pradeaux★★, Ray-Jane★★, Romassan★, Ste-Anne★, des Salettes★, la Suffrène★★, TEMPIER★★, Terrebrune★★, la Tour de Bon★, Vannières★. Best years: (2000) 99 98 97 **96 95 93 90 89 88**.

**BANFI** *Brunello di Montalcino DOCG, Tuscany, Italy* High-tech American-owned firm which is now a force in Italy. Noted winemaker Ezio Rivella (here from 1977 to 1999) did much to establish Banfi's reputation. BRUNELLO★★, Chardonnay (Fontanelle★★), Cabernet (Tavernelle★★) and Merlot (Mandrielle★★) are very successful, but even better are Brunello Riserva Poggio all'Oro★★★ and SUPER-TUSCANS Summus★★★ (a blend of Sangiovese, Cabernet and Syrah) and Excelsus★★★ (Cabernet-Merlot). Also has cellars (Vigne Regali) in PIEDMONT for GAVI and fizz. Best years: (top reds) 1997 **96 95 94 93 90**.

**BANNOCKBURN** *Geelong, Victoria, Australia* The experience gleaned from vintage stints at Burgundy's Domaine DUJAC is reflected in Gary Farr's powerful, gamy Pinot Noir★ and MEURSAULT-like Chardonnay★★, which are among Australia's best or most notorious wines – depending on your view. I prefer the much-improved Shiraz★★, influenced by Rhône's Alain GRAILLOT. (Note that there was no estate-grown wine in 1998 due to a freak hailstorm.) Best years: (Chardonnay) (1999) **97 96 95 94 92 89 88**.

**BANYULS AC** *Roussillon, France* One of the best *vin doux naturels*, made mainly from Grenache, with a strong plum and raisin flavour. Rimage – vintaged early bottlings – and tawny styles are the best. Generally served as an apéritif in France and deserves a wider audience. Try sampling it mid-afternoon with some macaroons or plain cake. Best producers: Casa Blanca, Cellier des Templiers★, Clos des Paulilles★, l'Étoile★, Mas Blanc★★, la RECTORIE★★, la Tour Vieille★, Vial Magnères★.

**BARBADILLO** *Jerez y Manzanilla DO, Andalucía, Spain* The largest sherry company in the coastal town of Sanlúcar de Barrameda makes a wide range of good to excellent wines, in particular salty, dry manzanilla styles (Solear★★ and Principe★★) and intense, nutty, but dry amontillados and olorosos, led by Oloroso del Tío Río★★. Neutral-flavoured dry white Castillo de San Diego is a best seller in Spain.

**BARBARESCO DOCG** *Piedmont, Italy* This prestigious red wine, grown near Alba in the LANGHE hills south-east of Turin, is often twinned with its neighbour BAROLO to demonstrate the nobility of the Nebbiolo grape. Barbaresco can be a shade softer and less powerful. The wine usually takes less time to mature and is often considered the most approachable of the two, as exemplified by the international style of GAJA. But, as in Barolo, traditionalists also excel, led by Bruno GIACOSA. Even though the area is relatively compact (509ha/1257 acres), wine styles can differ significantly between vineyards and producers. Best vineyards: Asili, Bricco di Neive, Costa Russi, Crichet Pajè, Gallina, Marcorino, Martinenga, Messoirano, Moccagatta, Montestefano, Ovello, Pora, Rabajà, Rio Sordo, San Lorenzo, Santo Stefano, Serraboella, Sorì Paitin, Sorì Tildin. Best producers: Abrigo★, Barbaresco co-op★, Piero Busso★★, CERETTO★★, Cigliuti★★, Stefano Farina★★, Fontanabianca★★, GAJA★★★, GIACOSA★★★, Marchesi di Gresy★★, Moccagatta★★, Fiorenzo Nada★★, Castello di Neive★★, Paitin★★, Oddero★, Pelissero★★, Pio Cesare★, Prunotto★★, La Spinetta★★, Albino Rocca★★, Bruno Rocca★★, Sottimano★★, Vietti★★. Best years: (2000) (99) 98 97 96 **95 93 90 89 88 86 85 82**.

---

**BARBERA** A native of north-west Italy, Barbera vies with Sangiovese as the most widely planted red grape in the country. When grown for high yields its natural acidity shows through, producing vibrant quaffers. Low yields from the top PIEDMONT estates create intensely rich and complex wines. Oaked versions can be stunning.

---

**BARBERA D'ALBA DOC** *Piedmont, Italy* Some of the most outstanding Barbera comes from this appellation. The most modern examples are supple and generous and can be drunk almost at once. More intense, dark-fruited versions require a minimum 3 years' age, but might improve for as much as 8. Best producers: G Alessandria★, ALTARE★, Azelia★★, Boglietti★, Brovia★, Cascina Chicco★, CERETTO★, Cigliuti★, CLERICO★, Elvio Cogno★, Aldo CONTERNO★, Giacomo CONTERNO★, Conterno-Fantino★, Corino★, Correggia★★, Fontanabianca★, A Ghisolfi★, Elio Grasso★, Silvio Grasso★, Giuseppe MASCARELLO★, Moccagatta★, M Molino★★, Monfalletto-Cordero di Montezemolo★★, Oberto★★, Parusso★★, Pelissero★, Pio Cesare, F Principiano★★, PRUNOTTO★★, Renato RATTI★, Albino Rocca★★, Bruno Rocca★★, SANDRONE★★, P Scavino★★, Aldo e Riccardo Seghesio★, La Spinetta★★, Vajra★★, Mauro Veglio★★, Giovanni Viberti★, Vietti★★, Gianni Voerzio★★, Roberto VOERZIO★★★. Best years: 1998 **97 96 95 93 91 90 89**.

**BARBERA D'ASTI DOC** *Piedmont, Italy* While Dolcetto d'Asti is usually light and simple, wines made from Barbera show a greater range of quality. Unoaked and barrique-aged examples can compete with the best BARBERA D'ALBA and rival some of the better Nebbiolo-based reds. Best examples can be kept for 5–6 years, occasionally longer. Best producers: G Accornero★, Araldica/Alasia★, La Barbatella★★, Pietro Barbero★★, Bava★, Bertelli★★, Braida★★, Bricco Mondalino★, Cascina Castlèt★, Giuseppe Contratto★, Coppo★★, Il Mongetto★★, Martinetti★★, PRUNOTTO★★, Cantine Sant'Agata★, Scarpa★, F & M Scrimaglio★, La Spinetta★, Vietti★★. Best years: (1999) 98 **97 96 95 93 91 90 89**.

**BARDOLINO DOC** *Veneto, Italy* Substantial zone centred on Lake Garda, giving, at best, light, scented red and rosé (chiaretto) wines to be drunk young, from the same grape mix as neighbouring VALPOLICELLA. Best producers: Cavalchina★, Colle dei Cipressi, Corte Gardoni★, Girasole, Gorgo, Guerrieri-Rizzardi★, MASI, Le Vigne di San Pietro★, Fratelli Zeni.

**BAROLO DOCG** *Piedmont, Italy* Renowned red wine, named after a village south-west of Alba, from the Nebbiolo grape grown in 1284ha (3272 acres) of vineyards in the steep LANGHE hills. Its status as 'king of wines and wine of kings' for a time proved to be more of a burden than a benefit among Italians, who considered its austere power too much for modern palates, with tough, chewy tannins which took years of cask-aging to soften. But for over a decade, many winemakers have applied new methods to make Barolo that is fresher, cleaner, better balanced and ready sooner, with richer colour, richer fruit and softer tannins yet without sacrificing Barolo's noble character. Distinct styles of wine are made in the zone's villages. Barolo and La Morra make the most perfumed wines; Monforte and Serralunga the most structured; Castiglione Falletto strikes a balance between the two. Barolo is nowadays frequently labelled by vineyards, though the producer's reputation often carries more weight. Best vineyards: Bricco Boschis, Bricco delle Viole, Brunate, Bussia Soprana, Cannubi, Cerequio, Fiasco, Ginestra, Marcenasco, Monfalleto, Monprivato, Pianpolvere Soprano, Rocche di Castiglione, Rocche di La Morra, Santo Stefano di Perno, La Serra, Vigna Rionda, Villero. Best producers: C Alario★★, ALTARE★★, Azelia★★, Boglietti★★, Bongiovanni★★, Brovia★★, CERETTO★★, CHIARLO★, CLERICO★★, Aldo CONTERNO★★★, Giacomo CONTERNO★★★, Conterno-Fantino★★, Corino★★, Luigi Einaudi★★, GAJA★★★, GIACOSA★★★, Elio Grasso★★, M Marengo★★, B MASCARELLO★★★, G MASCARELLO★★★, Monfalletto-Cordero di Montezemolo★★, Oberto★★, Oddero★★, Parusso★★, Pio Cesare★★, E Pira & Figli★★, Pira★★, F Principiano★★, PRUNOTTO★★, Renato RATTI★★, Revello★★, Rocche dei Manzoni★★, SANDRONE★★★, P Scavino★★, M Sebaste★★, Vajra★★, Mauro Veglio★★, Vietti★★, Vigna Rionda★★, Gianni Voerzio★★, Roberto VOERZIO★★. Best years: (1998) (97) 96 95 **93 90 89 88 86 85**.

**BAROSSA VALLEY** See pages 56–7.

**JIM BARRY** *Clare Valley, South Australia* Initially very much a white wine outfit, with the famous Florita vineyard as the source of perfumed, classy Rieslings★. Now creating bigger waves with reds such as McCrae Wood Cabernet-Malbec★ and Shiraz★★, and the heady, palate-busting Armagh Shiraz★★★. Best years: (Armagh Shiraz) (1999) (98) 96 95 **93 92 90**.

# BAROSSA

*South Australia*

The Barossa Valley, an hour or so's drive north of Adelaide in South Australia, is the centre of the Australian wine industry, producing or processing up to 60% of the nation's wine. Penfolds, Orlando, Yalumba and other giants have their headquarters here. However, this percentage is based mostly on grapes trucked in from other regions, because the Barossa's vineyards themselves grow less than 10% of Australia's grapes. Yet these Barossa-grown grapes, once rejected for their low yields, are now increasingly prized.

Why? Well, it's highly likely that the world's oldest vines are in the Barossa. The valley was settled in the 1840s by Prussian immigrants who brought with them vines from Europe, most importantly, as it turned out, cuttings from the Syrah (or Shiraz) variety of France's Rhône Valley. And because Barossa has never been affected by the phylloxera louse, which destroyed much of the world's vineyards in the late 19th century, today you can still see gnarled, twisted old vines sporting just a few tiny bunches of priceless fruit that were planted by refugees from Europe all of a century-and-a-half ago and are still tended by their descendants. A new wave of winemakers has taken up the cause of the Barossa vines with much zeal and no small amount of national pride, and they have begun to produce from them some of the deepest, most fascinating wines, not just in Australia, but in the world.

## GRAPE VARIETIES

Shiraz is prized above all other Barossa grapes, able to conjure headswirling, palate-dousing flavours. Barossa is the main source of Shiraz grapes for Penfolds Grange, the wine that began the revolution in Australian red wine in the 1950s. Cabernet Sauvignon is also excellent and similarly potent, as are the deliciously earthy Rhône varieties of Grenache and Mourvèdre. All these varieties are largely grown on the valley floor, but just to the east lie the Barossa Ranges, and in these higher, cooler vineyards, especially in those of the neighbouring Eden Valley, some of Australia's best and most fashionable Rieslings are grown, along with excellent Semillon and Chardonnay. But even here you can't get away from Shiraz, and some thrilling examples come from the hills.

## CLASSIFICATIONS

Barossa is a recently created zone within the Australian system of Geographical Indications and includes the regions of Barossa Valley and Eden Valley, which themselves have numerous tiny sub-regions.

See also GRANGE, SOUTH AUSTRALIA; and individual producers.

(Barossa Valley Shiraz) (2001) 00 98 97 **96 95 94 91 90 88 87**; (Eden Valley Riesling) 1999 **98 97 96 95 94 92 91 90 88 87**

## BEST PRODUCERS

**Shiraz-based reds**
Barossa Valley Estates (E & E Shiraz), BASEDOW, Bethany, Grant BURGE (Meshach), Charles Cimicky, Elderton (Command Shiraz), Glaetzer, Greenock (Creek Block Shiraz, Seven Acres Shiraz), HENSCHKE (Mount Edelstone, HILL OF GRACE), Hewitson, Jenke, Trevor Jones, Langmeil, Peter LEHMANN (Stonewell), Mamre Brook, Charles MELTON, Miranda (Show Reserve Old Vine Shiraz), MOUNTADAM (Patriarch), ORLANDO, PENFOLDS (Bin 28 Kalimna, GRANGE), ROCKFORD (Basket Press), ST HALLETT (Faith, Blackwell, Old Block), Saltram (No. 1 Shiraz), Three Rivers, Torbreck (Run Rig), Turkey Flat, Veritas (Hanisch), YALUMBA.

**Riesling**
Bethany, Grant BURGE, Leo Buring (Leonay), Heggies (Botrytis Riesling), HENSCHKE (Julius), Hewitson, Peter LEHMANN, MOUNTADAM (David Wynn), ORLANDO (St Helga, Steingarten), Pewsey Vale, Richmond Grove, ROCKFORD, Ross Estate, ST HALLETT, YALUMBA.

**BARSAC AC** *Bordeaux, France* Barsac, largest of the 5 communes in the SAUTERNES AC and producing fine sweet wines to similar high standards, also has its own AC, which is used by most, but by no means all, of the top properties. In general, the wines are a little less luscious than other Sauternes, but from good estates they can be marvellous. Best producers: (Classed Growths) CLIMENS★★★, COUTET★★, DOISY-DAENE★★, Doisy-Dubroca★, DOISY-VEDRINES★★, Myrat★, NAIRAC★★, Suau★; (others) Cru Barréjats★, Piada. Best years: 1999 98 97 **96 95 90 89 88 86 83 76 75**.

**BASEDOW** *Barossa Valley, South Australia* Basedow has changed hands twice in recent years but now looks set for stability. The popular wood-aged Semillon★ is partnered by a soft, rich Shiraz★ and Cabernet★, a heavyweight Chardonnay and a new super-premium Johannes Shiraz★★.

**BASSERMANN-JORDAN** *Deidesheim, Pfalz, Germany* Since the arrival of winemaker Ulrich Mell with the 1996 vintage, this famous estate has resumed making the rich yet elegant Rieslings of ★ and ★★ quality which long made its name synonymous with great Deidesheim and FORST wines. Best years: (2000) **99** 98 **97** 96 90 89 88 86 81 79 76 71.

**CH. BASTOR-LAMONTAGNE★** *Sauternes AC, Cru Bourgeois, Bordeaux, France* Year after year this estate produces luscious, honeyed sweet wine at a price which allows us to enjoy high-class SAUTERNES without taking out a second mortgage. Best years: 1999 98 97 **96 95 94 90 89 88 86 85 83**.

**CH. BATAILLEY★** *Pauillac AC, 5ème Cru Classé, Haut-Médoc, Bordeaux, France* A byword for value for money and reliability among the Pauillac Classed Growth estates. Marked by a full, obvious blackcurrant fruit, not too much tannin and a luscious overlay of creamy vanilla. Lovely to drink at only 5 years old, the wine continues to age well for up to 15 years. Best years: (2000) 99 96 95 **94 90 89 88 86 85 83 82**.

**BÂTARD-MONTRACHET AC** *Grand Cru, Côte de Beaune, Burgundy, France* This Grand Cru produces some of the world's greatest whites – they are full, rich and balanced, with a powerful mineral intensity of fruit and fresh acidity. There are 2 associated Grands Crus: Bienvenues-Bâtard-Montrachet and the minuscule Criots-Bâtard-Montrachet. All can age for a decade. Best producers: Blain-Gagnard★★★, CARILLON★★★, DROUHIN★★★, J-N GAGNARD★★★, GAGNARD-DELAGRANGE★★★, JADOT★★★, LATOUR★★, Dom. LEFLAIVE★★★, Olivier LEFLAIVE★★★, Marc Morey★★★, Pierre Morey★★★, Michel Niellon★★★, RAMONET★★★, SAUZET★★★, VERGET★★★. Best years: (2000) 99 98 97 96 95 **92 90 89**.

**DOM. DE LA BAUME** *Vin de Pays d'Oc, Languedoc, France* The French outpost of BRL HARDY, chiefly making varietal wines. The operation was set up in 1989, when the estate's winemaking equipment was completely renewed. The winery now makes 7 wines of which the whites★ regularly outperform the reds. Chardonnay, Sauvignon Blanc, Merlot, Cabernet Sauvignon and Shiraz are sold under the La Baume label, and include contract fruit; there are also 2 premium wines, a Merlot and a Chardonnay-Viognier blend, under the Domaine de la Baume label. For the latter wines, the grapes come exclusively from the surrounding 40-ha (100-acre) estate.

**LES BAUX-DE-PROVENCE AC** *Provence, France* This AC has proved that organic farming can produce spectacular results mainly due to the warm dry climate. Good fruit and inspirational winemaking produce some of the best reds in the south of France. Since 1994, TREVALLON has been VdP des BOUCHES-DU-RHONE. Best producers: Mas de la Dame★, Mas de Gourgonnier★, Mas Ste-Berthe★, Terres Blanches★, TREVALLON★★★. Best years: (2000) 99 98 **97 96 95 94 93 91 90 89**.

**BÉARN AC** *South-West France* While the rest of South-West France has been busy producing some unusual and original flavours in recent years, Béarn hasn't managed to cash in. The wines (90% red and rosé) just aren't special enough, despite some decent grape varieties. Best producers: Bellocq co-op, Cauhapé, Clos Lapeyre, Nigri.

**CH. DE BEAUCASTEL** *Châteauneuf-du-Pape AC, Rhône Valley, France* François Perrin makes some of the richest, most tannic reds★★★ in CHATEAUNEUF-DU-PAPE, with an unusually high percentage of Mourvèdre and Syrah, which can take at least a decade to show at their best. The white Vieilles Vignes★★★, made almost entirely from Roussanne, is exquisite, too. Perrin also produces a range of southern reds under the Domaine Perrin label. Best years: (reds) (1999) 98 97 96 95 **94 93 90 89 88 86 85 83 82 81**; (whites) (1999) 98 97 96 95 **94 93 92 90 89 88**.

**BEAUJOLAIS AC** *Beaujolais, Burgundy, France* Famous red wine from a large area of rolling hills and valleys in southern Burgundy. Much Beaujolais nowadays appears as BEAUJOLAIS NOUVEAU or Beaujolais Primeur, but Beaujolais AC is the basic appellation. In the north, toward Mâcon, most of the reds qualify either as BEAUJOLAIS-VILLAGES or as a single Cru (10 villages which produce better but more expensive wine: BROUILLY, CHENAS, CHIROUBLES, COTE DE BROUILLY, FLEURIE, JULIENAS, MORGON, MOULIN-A-VENT, REGNIE, ST-AMOUR). In the south, toward Lyon, most of the wine is simple AC Beaujolais, a light red to be drunk very young, which should be lovely and fresh but is now too often dilute. Beaujolais Supérieur means wine with a minimum strength of 1% more alcohol than simple Beaujolais. A little white is made from Chardonnay. The Éventail de Vignerons Producteurs is a high-profile marketing group. Best producers: (reds) P M Chermette★, DUBOEUF, DROUHIN, H Fessy★, JADOT, de la Madone★, Terres Dorées (J-P Brun).

**BEAUJOLAIS NOUVEAU** *Beaujolais AC, Burgundy, France* This is the first release of bouncy, fruity Beaujolais on the third Thursday of November after the harvest. Once a simple celebration of the new vintage, then a much-hyped beano, now increasingly *passé*. Quality is generally reasonably good. The wine usually improves by Christmas and the New Year, and the best ones are perfect for summer picnics.

**BEAUJOLAIS-VILLAGES AC** *Beaujolais, Burgundy, France* Beaujolais-Villages can come from any one of 38 villages in the north of the region. Carefully made, it can represent all the excitement of the Gamay grape at its best. Best villages: Beaujeu, Lancié, Lantignié, Leynes, Quincié, St-Étienne-des-Ouillières, St-Jean-d'Ardières. Best producers: Daumas★, G Descombes★, DUBOEUF, Janin★, Lacondemine★, Miolane★, Dom. Perrier★, Pivot★, M Tête★, Ch. Thivin★. Best years: **2000 99 98**.

**BEAULIEU VINEYARD** *Napa Valley AVA, California, USA* The late André Tchelistcheff had a major role in creating this icon for Napa Cabernet Sauvignon as winemaker from the late 1930s to the 50s. After he left,

59

Beaulieu missed a few beats and lived on its reputation for too long, even though Tchelistcheff continued to consult. However, recent bottlings of the Private Reserve Cabernet Sauvignon★★ signal a return to form. A meritage red called Tapestry★★ is also top-notch. Recent bottlings of Chardonnay★ from CARNEROS have been a pleasant surprise. Best years: (Private Reserve) (1998) 97 96 95 94 92 91 **90 87 86 85 84**.

**BEAUMES-DE-VENISE** *Rhône Valley, France* Area famous for its sweet wine: MUSCAT DE BEAUMES-DE-VENISE, France's best-known *vin doux naturel*. The local red wine is also very good, one of the meatier COTES DU RHONE-VILLAGES, with a ripe, plummy fruit in warm years. Best producers: (reds) Bernardins, les Goubert★, local co-op.

**BEAUNE AC** *Côte de Beaune, Burgundy, France* Beaune gives its name to the southern section of the COTE D'OR, the COTE DE BEAUNE. Most of the wines are red, with delicious, soft red-fruits ripeness. There are no Grands Crus but some excellent Premiers Crus (Boucherottes, Bressandes, Clos des Mouches, Fèves, Grèves, Marconnets, Teurons, Vignes Franches). There's an increasing production of white – DROUHIN makes an outstandingly good, creamy, nutty Clos des Mouches★★★. Best producers: (growers) GERMAIN★★, LAFARGE★★, Albert Morot★★, TOLLOT-BEAUT★★; (merchants) BOUCHARD PERE ET FILS★★(since 1996), Champy★★, Chanson★, DROUHIN★★, Camille Giroud★★, JADOT★★, JAFFELIN, LABOURE-ROI, THOMAS-MOILLARD★. Best years: (reds) 1999 98 **97** 96 **95 93** 90; (whites) (2000) 99 **97** 96 **95**.

**CH. BEAU-SÉJOUR BÉCOT★★** *St-Émilion Grand Cru AC, 1er Grand Cru Classé, Bordeaux, France* Demoted from Premier Grand Cru Classé in 1986 and promoted again in 1996, this estate is now back on top form. Brothers Gérard and Dominique Bécot produce firm, ripe, richly textured wines that need at least 8–10 years to develop. Best years: (2000) 99 98 97 96 95 **94 90 89 88 86 85**.

**BEAUX FRÈRES** *Willamette Valley AVA, Oregon, USA* A venture that has generated much interest due to the participation of wine critic Robert Parker; co-owner and winemaker Mike Etzel is his brother-in-law (hence the name). The aim has been to make ripe, unfiltered Pinot Noir★★ that expresses the essence of the grape and vineyard. Its immediate success has attracted a cult following. Second label Belles Soeurs★ is also good. Best years: 1999 98 97 96 **94 93**.

**GRAHAM BECK WINES** *Robertson WO, South Africa* This is now a two-cellar operation. One is in Robertson, where cellarmaster Pieter Ferreira concentrates on Cap Classique sparkling, including an elegantly rich NV Brut from Pinot Noir and Chardonnay, and a toastily fragrant and creamy barrel-fermented blanc de blancs★. Shiraz★ has become his second passion. Cabernet and Merlot are promising. The flavourful, balanced Chardonnay★ carries the flag for still white wine. Charles Hopkins runs the other cellar in Franschhoek. His Graham Beck Coastal range is making waves with Shiraz★ and The Old Road Pinotage★.

**BEDELL CELLARS** *Long Island, New York State, USA* Winemaker Kip Bedell earned a reputation in the 1980s for high-quality, BORDEAUX-styled Merlot★, Cabernet Sauvignon★ and a red blend called Cupola★★. In the 90s, other wineries began imitating Bedell's vineyard management techniques, contributing to a quality increase throughout the region. Bedell sold the winery in 2000, but remains as winemaker. Best years: 1998 97 **95 94 91**.

**BEIRAS** *Portugal* This large central Portuguese province includes the leading DOCs of DAO and BAIRRADA, as well as new DOCs Távora/Varosa and Beira Interior. A number of important wines are made at the Vinho Regional level, using Portuguese red and white grape varieties along with international grapes such as Cabernet Sauvignon and Chardonnay. Best producers: Caves ALIANCA (Galeria), Quinta de Foz de Arouce★★, D F J VINHOS, Luis PATO (João Pato★, Vinha Formal★★), Caves SAO JOAO (Quinta do Poco do Lobo).

*Luis Pato*

Vinha Formal
1999

VINHO REGIONAL BEIRAS

*Criado e engarrafado por*
*Luis Pato, Anadia, Portugal*
PRODUCE OF PORTUGAL

**CH. BELAIR★** *St-Émilion Grand Cru AC, 1er Grand Cru Classé, Bordeaux, France* Belair is located on the limestone plateau next to AUSONE. Under the direction of winemaker Pascal Delbeck the estate has been run biodynamically since 1994, and the effects are beginning to be felt with the soft, stylish wines on good form. Best years: (2000) 99 98 96 95 **94 90 89 88 86 85 83 82**.

**BELLAVISTA** *Franciacorta DOCG, Lombardy, Italy* Winemaker Mattia Vezzola specializes in FRANCIACORTA sparkling wines with a very good Cuvée Brut★★ and 4 distinctive Gran Cuvées★★ (including an excellent rosé). Riserva Vittorio Moretti Extra Brut★★ is made in exceptional years. Also produces lovely still wines, including white blend Convento dell'Annunciata★★★, Chardonnay Uccellanda★★ and red Casotte★ (Pinot Nero) and Solesine★★ (Cabernet-Merlot).

**BELLET AC** *Provence, France* A tiny AC of usually overpriced wine because of the local tourist market, mostly white, in the hills behind Nice. Ch. de Crémat★ and Ch. de Bellet★ are the most important producers but my favourite is Delmasso★.

**BENDIGO** *Victoria, Australia* Warm, dry, former gold-mining region, which produced some decent wines in the 19th century, then faded away completely until it was triumphantly resurrected by Balgownie in 1969, and other wineries followed (including Chateau Leamon, Water Wheel, Heathcote, Jasper Hill, Passing Clouds, Blackjack and YELLOWGLEN). The best wines are rich, ripe Shiraz and Cabernet.

**BENZIGER** *Sonoma Valley AVA, California, USA* Since the sale of the Glen Ellen brand in 1993, the Benzigers have focused on varietals from their SONOMA VALLEY estate vineyard and from other SONOMA COUNTY areas. Merlot★ and Zinfandel★ are consistently good, and quality is on the rise with CARNEROS Chardonnay★ and Tribute★ meritage blends. Imagery Series wines are often of high quality. Best years: (reds) (1999) 98 97 96 95 **94 92 91**.

**BERBERANA** *Rioja DOC, Rioja, Spain* A dynamic new boss has transformed one of RIOJA's largest companies. Berberana has bought Lagunilla and formed a partnership with MARQUES DE GRINON, and is making a pleasant, lightly oaked Crianza and respectable Reservas and Gran Reservas. Best years: (Reserva) **1996 95 94 91**.

**BERCHER** *Burkheim, Baden, Germany* The Bercher brothers run one of the top estates of the KAISERSTUHL. The high points are the powerful new oak-aged Spätburgunder (Pinot Noir) reds★★ and Weissburgunder★ (Pinot Blanc) and Grauburgunder★★ (Pinot Gris) dry whites, which marry richness with perfect balance. Drink young or cellar for 3–5 years or more. Best years: (whites) **1999 98 97 96 94 93**; (reds) (1999) **97 96 93**.

**BERGERAC AC** *South-West France* Bergerac is the main town of the Dordogne and the overall AC for this underrated area on the eastern edge of Bordeaux. The grape varieties are mostly the same as those used in the BORDEAUX ACS. The red is generally like a light, fresh claret, a bit grassy but with a good, raw blackcurrant fruit and hint of earth. In general drink young although a few estate reds can age for at least 3–5 years. The whites are generally lean and dry for quick drinking. Best producers: l'Ancienne Cure, Belingard, la Colline, Court-les-Mûts, Eyssards, Gouyat, la Jaubertie★, Moulin Caresse, Panisseau, TOUR DES GENDRES★, Tour des Verdots, Tourmentine. Best years: (reds) (2000) **98 96 95 93 90 89 88**.

**BERGKELDER** *Stellenbosch, South Africa* Now part of DISTELL (the new company formed by the merger of Stellenbosch Farmers' Winery and Distillers Corporation), the Bergkelder buys in wine and grapes from contracted growers in various regions. The flagship range is Stellenryck, reserved for classic varieties such as Cabernet Sauvignon★ and moving towards a vineyard-based focus. Fleur du Cap is a good-value budget label: the standard range concentrates on accessibility with good varietal fruit; a new, unfiltered range aims at greater individuality. Best years: (Stellenryck, Fleur du Cap reds) **1997 96 95 94 93 92 91 90**.

**BERINGER VINEYARDS** *Napa Valley AVA, California, USA* Beringer produces a full range of wine, but, in particular, offers a spectacular range of top-class Cabernet Sauvignons. The Private Reserve Cabernet can be ★★★ and is one of NAPA VALLEY's finest yet most approachable; the Chabot Vineyards★★, when released under its own label, can be equally impressive. Beringer makes red★★ and white★ Alluvium (meritage wines) from Knight's Valley and the red earns high marks. The Reserve Chardonnay★★ is a powerful wine that should age well. HOWELL MOUNTAIN Merlot★★ from Bancroft Vineyard is also very good. Now owned by Aussie brewing giant Fosters; what changes, if any, will that cause? Best years: (Cabernet Sauvignon) (1999) 98 97 96 95 94 93 **92 91 90 87 86 85 84 81**.

**BERNKASTEL** *Mosel, Germany* Both a town in the Middle Mosel and a large Bereich. Top wines, however, will come only from vineyard sites within the town – the most famous of these is the overpriced DOCTOR vineyard. Many wines from the Graben and Lay sites are as good or better and cost a fraction of the price. Best producers: Hansen-Lauer★, Dr LOOSEN★★, J J PRÜM★★, Dr H Thanisch★, J WEGELER ERBEN★★.

**BEST'S** *Grampians, Victoria, Australia* Small winery run by Viv Thomson, who makes attractive wines from estate vineyards first planted in 1868. Tasty, clear-fruited Great Western Bin No. 0 Shiraz★ and Great Western Cabernet★ are good, and the Riesling★ shows flashes of brilliance. Tropical-fruity, finely balanced Chardonnay★ is variable, delicious at best; Thomson Family Reserve★★ is a super-Shiraz label. Best years: (reds) 1998 **96 95 94 92 91 90 88 87 84 80 76**.

**BETHEL HEIGHTS** *Willamette Valley AVA, Oregon, USA* Oregon winery with a reputation for stylish Pinot Noirs★★ which are delicious young but can also age a little. Subtle Chardonnay Reserve★ is gathering acclaim, too. Best years: (reds) (1999) 98 **97** 96.

**CH. BEYCHEVELLE★** *St-Julien AC, 4ème Cru Classé, Haut-Médoc, Bordeaux, France* Although ranked as a 4th Growth, this beautiful château at best makes wine of 2nd Growth quality. The wine has a charming softness even when young, but takes at least a decade to mature into the cedarwood and blackcurrant flavour for which ST-JULIEN is famous. In the best years it is worth its high price and, after a period of inconsistency, quality has become more regular in the late 1990s. Second wine: Réserve de l'Amiral. Best years: (2000) 99 98 97 96 95 **90 89 86 85 83 82**.

**BEYERSKLOOF** *Stellenbosch WO, South Africa* Red wine maestro Beyers Truter concentrates on only 2 varieties at this property he owns in partnership with the Krige brothers of KANONKOP. The striking, supple Cabernet★★ is a multiple award winner. Truter's favourite Pinotage★ has bountiful ripe juiciness; quaffable when young, recent vintages show more aging ability. Grapes are mainly bought in, but 1998 saw the first crop from this small winery's own vineyards. Best years: (Cabernet Sauvignon) **1998 97 96 95 94 93**.

**BIANCO DI CUSTOZA DOC** *Veneto, Italy* Dry white wine similar to neighbouring SOAVE, but the addition of up to 30% Tocai Friulano can give extra richness. Drink young. Best producers: Cavalchina★, Corte Gardoni, Gorgo★, Lamberti/GIV, Montresor★, Le Vigne di San Pietro★.

**BIENVENUES-BÂTARD-MONTRACHET AC** See Bâtard-Montrachet.

**BIERZO DO** *Castilla y León, Spain* Sandwiched between the rainy mountains of GALICIA and the arid plains of CASTILLA Y LEON, Bierzo makes mostly commonplace reds. But the best ones, fruity and grassy green, are a revelation and quite unlike any in Spain save for their Galician neighbours. Ideally the wines are made entirely from the Mencía grape. Best producers: Pérez Caramés, Prada a Tope.

**JOSEF BIFFAR** *Deidesheim, Pfalz, Germany* Gerhard Biffar runs this reliable estate, making dry and sweet Rieslings from top sites in Deidesheim, Ruppertsberg and WACHENHEIM. Consistent ★ quality from recent vintages. Drink young or cellar for 5 years plus. Best years: 1999 98 **97 96 94 93 92 90**.

**BILLECART-SALMON** *Champagne AC, Champagne, France* Top-notch CHAMPAGNE house and one of the few still under family control. The wines are extremely elegant, fresh and delicate, becoming simply irresistible with age. The non-vintage Brut★★, non-vintage Brut Rosé★★, Blanc de Blancs★★★, vintage Cuvée N-F Billecart★★★ and Cuvée Elisabeth Salmon Rosé★★ are all excellent. Best years: (1995) **91 90 89 88 86 85 82**.

**BINGEN** *Rheinhessen, Germany* This is a small town and also a Bereich, the vineyards of which fall in both the NAHE and RHEINHESSEN. The best vineyard in the town is the Scharlachberg, which produces some exciting wines, stinging with racy acidity and the whiff of coal smoke. Best producer: Villa Sachsen. Best years: (whites) 1999 98 **97 96 90**.

**BIONDI-SANTI** *Brunello di Montalcino DOCG, Tuscany, Italy* Estate that in less than a century created both a legend and an international standing for BRUNELLO DI MONTALCINO. The modern dynamism of the zone owes more to other producers, however, since quality has slipped over the last 2 decades. Yet the very expensive Riserva★★, with formidable levels of extract, tannin and acidity, deserves a minimum 10 years' further aging after release before serious judgement is passed on it. Jacopo Biondi-Santi, while preparing to take over the running of the estate from his father Franco, has created his own range of wines, including Sassoallora★★, a barrique-aged Sangiovese, and Cabernet-based blend Schidione★★. Best years: (Riserva) 1990 88 85 83 82 **75 71 64 55 45 25.**

**BLAGNY AC** *Côte de Beaune, Burgundy, France* The red wine from this tiny hamlet above MEURSAULT and PULIGNY-MONTRACHET can be fair value, if you like a rustic Burgundy. The white is sold as Puligny-Montrachet, Meursault Premier Cru or Meursault-Blagny. Best producers: R Ampeau★★, Lamy-Pillot★★, Dom. Matrot★★. Best years: (red) 1999 98 **97** 96 **95 93 90.**

**DOMAINE PAUL BLANCK** *Alsace AC, Alsace, France* Philippe Blanck and his winemaker cousin Frédéric had a run of good vintages in the 1990s and the Blanck wines are improving all the time. From a huge range, Vieilles Vignes Riesling★★★ and Gewurztraminer★★★ from the Furstentum Grand Cru stand out. Riesling Schlossberg★★★ and Pinot Gris Altenberg★★ also offer depth and finesse. Best years: (Grand Cru Riesling) 1999 98 97 96 **95 94 93 92 90 89 88.**

**BLANQUETTE DE LIMOUX AC** *Languedoc-Roussillon, France* Many southern white wines are singularly flat and dull, but this fizz is sharp and refreshing. The secret lies in the Mauzac grape, which makes up over 80% of the wine and gives it its striking 'green apple skin' flavour. The Champagne method is used to create the sparkle. The more rustic *méthode rurale*, finishing off the original fermentation inside the bottle, is used under a separate appellation – Blanquette Méthode Ancestrale. Best producers: Collin, Fourn★, Guinot, Martinolles, SIEUR D'ARQUES co-op, les Terres Blanches. See also Crémant de Limoux AC and pages 260–1.

**WOLF BLASS** *Barossa Valley, South Australia* Wolf Blass stands as one of the most important men in the modern Australian wine world for mastering reds and whites of high quality and consistency which were nonetheless *easy* to enjoy. Blass reds, blended from many regions and aged mostly in American oak barrels, have a delicious mint and blackcurrant, easy-going charm. The Rieslings are soft and sweetish, and other whites also possess juicy fruit and sweet oak. Gold Label Riesling★★ from CLARE and Eden Valleys is impressively intense. Black Label★★, the top label for reds released at 4 years old, is expensive but good. New single-vineyard varietals look promising. Now owned by Beringer Blass, the burgeoning wine division of Fosters. Best years: (Black Label) 1998 **96** 95 94 92 91 90 88 86 82.

**BLAUBURGUNDER** See Pinot Noir.

**BLAUER LEMBERGER** See Blaufränkisch.

**BLAUFRÄNKISCH** Good, ripe Blaufränkisch has a taste similar to raspberries and white pepper or even beetroot. It does well in Austria, where it is the principal red wine grape of BURGENLAND. The Hungarian vineyards (where it is called Kékfrankos) are mostly just across the border on the other side of the Neusiedlersee. Called Lemberger in Germany, where almost all of it is grown in WÜRTTEMBERG. Also successful in WASHINGTON STATE.

**BODEGAS Y BEBIDAS** *Spain* The largest wine-producing company in Spain, with wineries including CAMPO VIEJO, AGE and Marqués del Puerto in RIOJA, Vinícola de Navarra, Casa de la Viña in VALDEPEÑAS, Bodegas Alanís in Ribeiro, and others in La MANCHA and JUMILLA. The new Tarsus★ winery in Ribera del Duero highlights the company's up-market ambitions.

**JEAN-CLAUDE BOISSET** *Burgundy, France* From humble origins, Boisset has become a power in the land, with new acquisitions each year; 1997 saw the addition of Moreau in CHABLIS and 1998 brought RHONE négociant Michel Bernard into the fold. He has expanded into BEAUJOLAIS by taking control of Cellier des Samsons and Mommessin-Thorin. Others controlled by Boisset include JAFFELIN, Bouchard Aîné, Ropiteau and companies in the Rhône and SAVOIE. The Boisset group markets a vast quantity of Burgundy, but for the most part it is merely adequate. However, from 1999, various Boisset-owned vineyards have been brought together under the name Domaine de la Vougeraie★★.

**BOLGHERI DOC** *Tuscany, Italy* In 1994, this zone near the coast south of Livorno extended its DOC beyond simple white and rosé to cover red wines based on Cabernet, Merlot and Sangiovese in various combinations, while creating a special category for SASSICAIA. The DOC Rosso Superiore now covers wines from the prestigious estates of Grattamacco★★, Le Macchiole★★, ORNELLAIA★★★, Michele Satta★★ and ANTINORI's Guado al Tasso★★. Best years (since 1994): (reds) (1999) 98 97 **96 95 94**.

**BOLLINGER** *Champagne AC, Champagne, France* One of the great CHAMPAGNE houses, with good non-vintage (Special Cuvée★★) and vintage wines (Grande Année★★★), made in a full, rich, rather old-fashioned style. (Bollinger is one of the few houses to ferment its base wine in barrels.) It also produces a range of rarer vintage Champagnes, including a Vintage RD★★★ and Vieilles Vignes Françaises Blanc de Noirs★★ from ancient, ungrafted Pinot Noir vines. Best years: **1992 90 89 88 85 82 79**.

**BONNES-MARES AC** *Grand Cru, Côte de Nuits, Burgundy, France* A large Grand Cru straddling the communes of CHAMBOLLE-MUSIGNY and MOREY-ST-DENIS. Less famous than many Grands Crus, but commendably consistent over the last few decades. Bonnes-Mares generally has a deep, ripe, smoky plum fruit, which starts red and chewy and matures over 10–20 years. Best producers: d'Auvenay (Dom. LEROY)★★★, BOUCHARD PERE ET FILS★★, Champy★★, DROUHIN★★, DUJAC★★★, Robert Groffier★★★, JADOT★★★, D Laurent★★★, J-F Mugnier★★, ROUMIER★★★, VOGUE★★★. Best years: (2000) 99 98 97 96 95 93 **90 89 88 85 78**.

**BONNEZEAUX AC** *Loire Valley, France* One of France's great sweet wines, Bonnezeaux is a zone within the larger COTEAUX DU LAYON AC. Like SAUTERNES the wine is influenced by noble rot, but the flavours are different, as only Chenin Blanc is used. Extensive recent plantings have made quality less reliable. It can age very well in good vintages. Best producers: M Angeli★★★, Fesles★★★, des Grandes Vignes★★, Laffourcade, Petits Quarts★★, Petit Val★★, René Renou★★, Terrebrune★★, la Varière★★. Best years: (2000) 99 **97** 96 95 94 **93 90 89 88 85 83 79 78 76 71 64 59 47**.

**BONNY DOON** *Santa Cruz Mountains AVA, California, USA* Iconoclastic operation under Randall Grahm, who revels in the unexpected. He has a particular love for RHONE, Italian and Spanish varietals and for fanciful brand names: Le Cigare Volant★★ is a blend of Grenache and Syrah and is Grahm's homage to CHATEAUNEUF-DU-PAPE. Old Telegram★★ is 100% Mourvèdre; Roussanne★★ is an impressive Rhône-style white. Particularly delightful are his Ca' del Solo Italianate wines, especially a bone-dry Malvasia Bianca★ and a white blend, Il Pescatore, his answer to VERDICCHIO. He also makes a lovely Syrah from Santa Maria★★, Cardinal Zin★ Zinfandel, a pure Riesling from WASHINGTON and eaux de vie. Grahm

has now spread his net even wider and has 3 new wines from European vineyards: a MADIRAN★, a Vin de Pays d'Oc Syrah and a Grenache from NAVARRA. Best years: (Rhônes) (1998) 97 **96 95 94 92**.

**CH. LE BON PASTEUR★★** *Pomerol AC, Bordeaux, France* Small château which has established an excellent reputation under the ownership of Michel Rolland, one of Bordeaux's leading winemakers. Wines from le Bon Pasteur have been expensive in recent years, but they are always deliciously soft and full of lush fruit. Best years: (2000) 99 98 97 96 95 94 **93 90 89 88 85 83 82**.

**BORBA DOC** *Alto Alentejo, Portugal* Promising DOC in the Alto ALENTEJO, specializing in rich, raspberry-fruited reds, but should be improving faster than it is. Best wines are still from the local co-op. Best years: (2000) **99 97 96 95 94**.

**BORDEAUX AC** *Bordeaux, France* One of the most important ACs in France. It can be applied to straightforward reds and rosés as well as to the dry, medium and sweet white wines of the entire Gironde region. Most of the best wines are allowed more specific district or commune ACs (such as MARGAUX or SAUTERNES) but a vast amount of Bordeaux's wine – delicious, atrocious and everything in between – is sold as Bordeaux AC. At its best, straight red Bordeaux is marked by bone-dry grassy fruit and an attractive earthy edge, but far more frequently the wines are tannic and raw – and often overpriced. Good examples usually benefit from a year or so of aging. Bordeaux Blanc, once a byword for flabby, fruitless and oversulphured brews, is, on the other hand, joining the modern world with an increasing number of refreshing, pleasant, clean wines. These may be labelled varietally, as Bordeaux Sauvignon. Drink as young as possible. Best producers: (reds) Bonnet, Dourthe (Numéro Un), Ducla, Sirius, Thieuley★, Tour de Mirambeau, le Trébuchet; (whites) l'Abbaye de Ste-Ferme★, CARSIN★, DOISY-DAENE★, Dourthe (Numéro Un), d:vin★, LYNCH-BAGES★, MARGAUX (Pavillon Blanc★★), Reynon★, Roquefort★, Sours, Thieuley★, Tour de Mirambeau★. See also pages 68–71.

**BORDEAUX CLAIRET AC** *Bordeaux, France* Pale red wine, virtually rosé, making a limited comeback in Bordeaux. The name 'claret', now applied to *any* red wine from the Bordeaux region, derives from *clairet*. Best producers: Bertinerie, Grand-Mouëys, Penin, Thieuley.

**BORDEAUX-CÔTES DE FRANCS AC** *Bordeaux, France* For an appellation which started with such a bang, I'm a little disappointed that this tiny area east of ST-EMILION hasn't made more progress. The Thienpont family (Puygueraud) continues to be the driving force here. Best producers: les Charmes-Godard★, Laclaverie★, Francs★, Marsau, Moulin la Pitié, la Prade, Puygueraud★★. Best years: (2000) 98 97 96 **95 94 90 89 88 86 85 83.**

**BORDEAUX SUPÉRIEUR AC** *Bordeaux, France* This AC covers the same area as the basic BORDEAUX AC but the wines must have an extra 0.5% of alcohol, a lower yield and a longer period of maturation. Many of the petits châteaux are labelled Bordeaux Supérieur. Best producers (reds): l'Abbaye de Ste-Ferme, les Arromans, Barreyre, de Bouillerot, Laville, Parenchère★, Penin★, Reignac★, de Seguin.

**BOSCARELLI** *Vino Nobile di Montepulciano DOCG, Tuscany, Italy* Arguably Montepulciano's best producer, Paola de Ferrari and her sons Luca and Niccolò, with guidance from star enologist Maurizio Castelli, craft rich and stylish reds. VINO NOBILE★★, Riserva del Nocio★★ and the barrique-aged Sangiovese Boscarelli★★ are all brilliant. Best years: (1998) 97 **96 95 94 93 91 90 88 85.**

**BOSCHENDAL** *Paarl WO, South Africa* The multi-million-rand re-vamp at this huge Anglo-American-owned property has already delivered improvements in the wines. Shiraz★, Merlot and a Grand Reserve Merlot-Cabernet Franc blend display elegant concentration. Full, flavoursome Chardonnay★ and Sauvignon Blanc lead the whites, followed by a pack of more commercial wines. Le Grand Pavillon NV and rich vintage Boschendal Brut remain sound Cap Classique bubblies.

**BOUCHARD FINLAYSON** *Walker Bay, Overberg WO, South Africa* Paul Bouchard's Burgundian know-how and financial support underline this first Franco-South African joint venture. Winemaker Peter Finlayson is committed to Pinot Noir and his 'domaine' Galpin Peak★ can elevate Cape Pinots to an international level. Chardonnay★ (several labels, variously sourced grapes, including home-grown Missionvale) and a flinty, fresh Sauvignon Blanc lack nothing in quality. Best years: (Pinot Noir) **1999 98 97 96 95.**

**BOUCHARD PÈRE ET FILS** *Beaune, Burgundy, France* Important merchant and vineyard owner, with vines in some of Burgundy's most spectacular sites, including CORTON, CORTON-CHARLEMAGNE, Chevalier-Montrachet and le MONTRACHET. The firm is owned by Champagne whiz-kid Joseph Henriot, who is starting to realize the full potential here. Wines from the company's own vineyards are sold under the Domaines du Château de Beaune label. Don't touch anything pre-1996.

**BOUCHES-DU-RHÔNE, VIN DE PAYS DES** *Provence, France* Wines from 3 areas: the coast, a zone around Aix-en-Provence and the Camargue. Mainly full-bodied, spicy reds, but rosé can be good. Best producers: Château Bas, de Boujeu, l'Île St-Pierre, Mas de Rey, TREVALLON★★★, Valdition.

# BORDEAUX RED WINES

*Bordeaux, France*

 This large area of South-West France, centred on the historic city of Bordeaux, produces a larger volume of fine red wine than any other French region. Wonderful Bordeaux-style wines are produced in California, Australia, South Africa and South America, but the home team's top performers are still unbeatable. Around 580 million bottles of red wine a year are produced here. The best wines, known as the Classed Growths, account for a tiny percentage of this figure, but some of their lustre rubs off on the lesser names, making this one of the most popular wine styles.

## GRAPE VARIETIES

Bordeaux's reds are commonly divided into 'right' and 'left' bank wines. On the left bank of the Gironde estuary, the red wines are dominated by the Cabernet Sauvignon grape, with varying proportions of Cabernet Franc, Merlot and Petit Verdot. At best they are austere but perfumed with blackcurrant and cedarwood. The most important left bank areas are the Haut-Médoc (especially the communes of Margaux, St-Julien, Pauillac and St-Estèphe) and, south of the city of Bordeaux, the ACs of Pessac-Léognan and Graves. On the right bank, Merlot is the predominant grape, which generally makes the resulting wines more supple and fleshy than those of the left bank. The key areas for Merlot-based wines are St-Émilion and Pomerol.

## CLASSIFICATIONS

Red Bordeaux is made all over the region, from the northern tip of the Gironde estuary to the southern end of the Entre-Deux-Mers. At its most basic, the wine is simply labelled Bordeaux or Bordeaux Supérieur. Above this are the more specific ACs covering sub-areas (such as the Haut-Médoc) and individual communes (such as Pomerol, St-Émilion or Margaux). Single-estate Crus Bourgeois are the next rung up on the quality ladder, followed by the Classed Growths of the Médoc, Graves and St-Émilion. Many of these châteaux also make 'second wines', which are cheaper versions of their Grands Vins. Curiously Pomerol, home of Château Pétrus, arguably the most famous red wine in the world, has no official pecking order.

---

See also BORDEAUX, BORDEAUX CLAIRET, BORDEAUX-COTES DE FRANCS, BORDEAUX SUPERIEUR, CANON-FRONSAC, COTES DE BOURG, COTES DE CASTILLON, FRONSAC, GRAVES, HAUT-MEDOC, LALANDE-DE-POMEROL, LISTRAC-MEDOC, LUSSAC-ST-EMILION, MARGAUX, MEDOC, MONTAGNE-ST-EMILION, MOULIS, PAUILLAC, PESSAC-LEOGNAN, POMEROL, PREMIERES COTES DE BLAYE, PREMIERES COTES DE BORDEAUX, PUISSEGUIN-ST-EMILION, ST-EMILION, ST-ESTEPHE, ST-GEORGES-ST-EMILION, ST-JULIEN; and individual châteaux.

---

(2000) 98 96 95 **90 89 88 86 85 83 82 78 70 66 62 61**

## BEST PRODUCERS

**Graves, Pessac-Léognan** Dom. de CHEVALIER, FIEUZAL, HAUT-BAILLY, HAUT-BRION, la LOUVIERE, la MISSION-HAUT-BRION, PAPE-CLEMENT, SMITH-HAUT-LAFITTE, la Tour-Haut-Brion.

**Margaux** FERRIERE, MALESCOT ST-EXUPERY, Ch. MARGAUX, PALMER, RAUZAN-SEGLA.

**Pauillac** GRAND-PUY-LACOSTE, LAFITE-ROTHSCHILD, LATOUR, LYNCH-BAGES, MOUTON-ROTHSCHILD, PICHON-LONGUEVILLE, PICHON-LONGUEVILLE-LALANDE, PONTET-CANET.

**Pomerol** le BON PASTEUR, Certan-de-May, Clinet, la CONSEILLANTE, l'EGLISE-CLINET, l'EVANGILE, la FLEUR-PETRUS, GAZIN, LAFLEUR, LATOUR-A-POMEROL, PETIT-VILLAGE, PETRUS, le PIN, TROTANOY, VIEUX-CHATEAU-CERTAN.

**St-Émilion** ANGELUS, l'ARROSEE, AUSONE, BEAU-SEJOUR BECOT, Beauséjour, CANON, CANON-LA-GAFFELIERE, CHEVAL BLANC, la Dominique, FIGEAC, Grand Mayne, MAGDELAINE, la Mondotte, Moulin St-Georges, PAVIE, Pavie-Macquin, TERTRE-ROTEBOEUF, TROPLONG-MONDOT, VALANDRAUD.

**St-Estèphe** CALON-SEGUR, COS D'ESTOURNEL, HAUT-MARBUZET, MONTROSE.

**St-Julien** BEYCHEVELLE, BRANAIRE, DUCRU-BEAUCAILLOU, GRUAUD-LAROSE, LAGRANGE, LANGOA-BARTON, LEOVILLE-BARTON, LEOVILLE-LAS-CASES, LEOVILLE-POYFERRE, ST-PIERRE, TALBOT.

# BORDEAUX WHITE WINES

*Bordeaux, France*

 This is France's largest fine wine region but, except for the sweet wines of Sauternes and Barsac, Bordeaux's international reputation is based solely on its reds. From 52% of the vineyard area in 1970 white wines now represent only 15% of the present 115,200ha (284,500 acres) of vines. Given the size of the region, the diversity of Bordeaux's white wines should come as no surprise. There are dry, medium and sweet styles, ranging from dreary to some of the most sublime white wines of all. Bordeaux's temperate southern climate – moderated by the influence of the Atlantic and of 2 rivers, the Dordogne and the Garonne, is ideal for white wine production, particularly south of the city along the banks of the Garonne.

## GRAPE VARIETIES

Sauvignon Blanc and Sémillon, the most important white grapes, are both varieties of considerable character and are usually blended together. They are backed up by smaller quantities of Muscadelle, Ugni Blanc and Colombard.

## DRY WINES

With the introduction of new technology and new ideas, many of them influenced by the New World, Bordeaux has become one of France's most exciting white wine areas. The wines, not only of Pessac-Léognan, an AC created for the best areas of the northern Graves in 1987, but also of basic Bordeaux Blanc and Entre-Deux-Mers, the 2 largest white wine ACs in Bordeaux, have improved beyond recognition over the last decade. At their best, dry Bordeaux whites have fresh fruit flavours of apples, peaches and apricots, balanced by a light grassiness.

## SWEET WINES

Bordeaux's most famous whites are its sweet wines made from grapes affected by noble rot, particularly those from Sauternes and Barsac. The noble rot concentrates the flavours, producing rich, honeyed wines replete with pineapple and peach flavours, and which develop a nut-oiliness and greater honeyed richness with age. On the other side of the Garonne river, Cadillac, Loupiac and Ste-Croix-du-Mont also make sweet wines; these rarely attain the richness or complexity of a top Sauternes, but they are considerably less expensive.

See also BARSAC, BORDEAUX, BORDEAUX-COTES DE FRANCS, BORDEAUX SUPERIEUR, CADILLAC, CERONS, COTES DE BLAYE, COTES DE BOURG, ENTRE-DEUX-MERS, GRAVES, GRAVES SUPERIEURES, LOUPIAC, PESSAC-LEOGNAN, PREMIERES COTES DE BLAYE, PREMIERES COTES DE BORDEAUX, STE-CROIX-DU-MONT, SAUTERNES; and individual châteaux.

## BEST YEARS

(dry) (2000) 98 96 **95 94 90 89 88 86 85 83**; (sweet) 1999 98 97 96 95 **90 89 88 86 83**

## BEST PRODUCERS

**Dry wines**

*(Pessac-Léognan)* Dom. de CHEVALIER, Couhins-Lurton, FIEUZAL, HAUT-BRION, LATOUR-MARTILLAC, LAVILLE-HAUT-BRION, la LOUVIERE, MALARTIC-LAGRAVIERE, SMITH-HAUT-LAFITTE; *(Graves)* Ardennes, Brondelle, Chantegrive, Clos Floridène, Dom. la Grave, Magneau, Rahoul, Respide-Médeville, Seuil, Vieux-Ch.-Gaubert, Villa Bel Air; *(Entre-Deux-Mers)* Bonnet, Fontenille, Nardique-la-Gravière, Ste-Marie, Toutigeac, Turcaud; *(Bordeaux AC)* l'Abbaye de Ste-Ferme, CARSIN, DOISY-DAENE (Sec), LYNCH-BAGES, Ch. MARGAUX (Pavillon Blanc), Reynon, Roquefort, Thieuley, Tour de Mirambeau; *(Premières Côtes de Blaye)* Bel-Air la Royère, Haut-Bertinerie, Jonqueyres, Mondésir-Gazin, Segonzac.

**Sweet wines**

*(Sauternes and Barsac)* CLIMENS, Clos Haut-Peyraguey, COUTET, DOISY-DAENE, DOISY-VEDRINES, FARGUES, GILETTE, GUIRAUD, LAFAURIE-PEYRAGUEY, NAIRAC, Raymond-Lafon, RIEUSSEC, Sigalas-Rabaud, SUDUIRAUT, la TOUR BLANCHE, YQUEM; *(Cadillac)* Cayla, Manos, Mémoires; *(Cérons)* Ch. de Cérons, Grand Enclos du Ch. de Cérons; *(Loupiac)* Clos Jean, Cros, Mémoires; *(Ste-Croix-du-Mont)* Loubens, la Rame.

**BOURGOGNE AC** *Burgundy, France*　Bourgogne is the French name anglicized as 'Burgundy'. This generic AC mops up all the Burgundian wine with no AC of its own, resulting in massive differences in style and quality. The best wines (red and white) will usually come from a single grower's vineyards just outside the main village ACs of the CÔTE D'OR. In today's world of high prices such wines may be the only way we can afford the joys of fine Burgundy. If the wine is from a grower, the flavours should follow a regional style. However, if the address on the label is that of a négociant, the wine could be from anywhere in Burgundy. Pinot Noir is the main red grape, with Gamay in the Mâconnais and BEAUJOLAIS. Red Bourgogne is usually light, overtly fruity in an upfront strawberry and cherry way, and should be drunk young (within 2–3 years). The rosé (from Pinot Noir) can be very pleasant but little is produced. Bourgogne Blanc is a bone-dry Chardonnay wine and most should be drunk within 2 years. Bourgogne Grand Ordinaire is the most basic appellation of all – rarely more than a quaffing wine, drunk in local bars. Best producers: (reds/growers) COCHE-DURY★, Dugat-Py★★, GERMAIN, LAFARGE★, MEO-CAMUZET★★, Pierre Morey★, Patrice Rion★★, ROUMIER★; (reds/merchants) DROUHIN★, GIRARDIN, JADOT★, LABOURE-ROI, Maison LEROY★★; (reds/co-ops) BUXY★, les Caves des Hautes-Côtes★; (whites/growers) M Bouzereau★, Boyer-Martenot★, COCHE-DURY★★, Henri Gouges★★, P Javillier★★, F Jobard★, Ch. de Meursault, Guy Roulot, SAUZET★, TOLLOT-BEAUT★; (whites/merchants) DROUHIN★, FAIVELEY, JADOT★, JAFFELIN, Olivier LEFLAIVE, RODET★; (whites/co-ops) BUXY, les Caves des Hautes-Côtes. Best years: (reds) (2000) 99 **98** 97 **96**; (whites) (2000) 99 **97 96**. See also pages 76–9.

**BOURGOGNE ALIGOTÉ AC**　See Aligoté.

**BOURGOGNE-CÔTE CHALONNAISE AC** *Côte Chalonnaise, Burgundy, France*　These vineyards have gained in importance recently, mainly because of spiralling prices on the CÔTE D'OR to the north. This AC covers vineyards in the Saône-et-Loire *département* around the villages of Bouzeron, RULLY, MERCUREY, GIVRY and MONTAGNY. Best producers: X Besson, BUXY co-op★, Villaine★. Best years: (2000) **99 98**.

**BOURGOGNE-HAUTES-CÔTES DE BEAUNE AC** *Burgundy, France*　As the supply of affordable Burgundy dwindled in the 1970s, this backwater in the hills behind the great CÔTE DE BEAUNE came into the spotlight. The red wines are lean but drinkable, as is the slightly sharp Chardonnay. Best producers: D & F Clair★, les Caves des Hautes-Côtes★, J-Y Devevey★, L Jacob★, J-L Joillot★, Ch. de Mercey (RODET)★, Naudin-Ferrand★, M Serveau★. Best years: (reds) (2000) 99 98 **97 96**; (whites) (2000) 99 **98 97 96**.

**BOURGOGNE-HAUTES-CÔTES DE NUITS AC** *Burgundy, France*　Attractive, lightweight wines from the hills behind the CÔTE DE NUITS. Best wines are the reds, with an attractive cherry and plum flavour. The whites tend to be rather dry and flinty. Best producers: (reds) FAIVELEY★, A-F Gros★, M Gros★, A Guyon★, les Caves des Hautes-Côtes★, B Hudelot★, JAYER-GILLES★★, THOMAS-MOILLARD★; (whites) les Caves des Hautes-Côtes★, Y Chaley, Champy★, J-Y Devevey★, B Hudelot★, JAYER-GILLES★★, Thévenot-le-Brun★, THOMAS-MOILLARD★, A Verdet★. Best years: (reds) (2000) 99 **98 97 96**; (whites) (2000) **99** 98 97.

**BOURGOGNE-IRANCY AC**　See Irancy AC.

**BOURGOGNE PASSE-TOUT-GRAINS AC** *Burgundy, France* Gamay with a minimum of 33% Pinot Noir; fruity, fresh, and best drunk young. Best producers: BUXY co-op, Y Chaley, C Cornu, Maison LEROY, Taupenot-Merme, G Thomas.

**BOURGUEIL AC** *Loire Valley, France* Fine red wine from between Tours and Angers. Made with Cabernet Franc, topped up with a little Cabernet Sauvignon; in hot years results can be superb. Given 5–10 years of age, the wines can develop a wonderful berry fragrance. Best producers: (reds) l'Abbaye★, Amirault★, Audebert (estate wines★), T Boucard★, P Breton★, la Butte★, Caslot★, Caslot-Galbrun★, Max Cognard★, J-F Demont★, DRUET★★, Forges★, Dom. La Lande★, Lamé-Delille-Boucard★, Nau Frères★, Raguenières. Best years: (2000) 99 **97 96 95** 90 89 88 86 85. See also St-Nicolas-de-Bourgueil.

**BOUVET-LADUBAY** *Saumur AC, Loire Valley, France* Fizz producer owned by the Champagne house TAITTINGER. The basic range (Bouvet Brut, Bouvet Rosé) is good. Cuvée Saphir, the top-selling wine, is oversweet, but Trésor (Blanc★ and Rosé★), fermented in oak casks, is very good. Weird and wonderful Rubis★ sparkling red is worth trying. Also sells non-sparkling wine from VOUVRAY and SAUMUR.

**BOUVIER** Austrian and Slovenian grape short on acidity and so mainly used for sweet to ultra-sweet wines, where it achieves richness but rarely manages to offer any other complexity. Best producers: Weinkellerei Burgenland, KRACHER★, OPITZ★.

**BOUZY** *Coteaux Champenois AC, Champagne, France* A leading CHAMPAGNE village growing good Pinot Noir, which is used mainly for *white* Champagne. However, in outstanding years a little still red wine is made. It is light and high in acidity. Best producers: Bara★, E Barnaut★, A Clouet★. Best years: 1998 96 **95 90 89**.

**BOWEN ESTATE** *Coonawarra, South Australia* Doug Bowen makes some of COONAWARRA's best reds from estate grapes: peppery yet profound Shiraz★★ and Cabernet★★ with powerful flavours, easily taking the high alcohol levels from the sugar-ripe fruit in their stride. Chardonnay★ is improved and now among the best in Coonawarra. Best years: (reds) (1999) 98 97 **96 94 91** 90 88 86 84 80 79.

**BRACHETTO** Piedmontese grape revived in dry versions and in sweet, frothy types with a Muscat-like perfume, as exemplified by Brachetto d'Acqui DOCG. Best producers: (dry) Correggia★, Scarpa★; (Brachetto d'Acqui) BANFI★, Braida★, Piero Gatti, G Marenco★.

**CH. BRANAIRE★★** *St-Julien AC, 4ème Cru Classé, Haut-Médoc, Bordeaux, France* After a long period of mediocrity Branaire chose the difficult 93 and 94 vintages to signal its renewed ambition. Subsequent vintages have confirmed a welcome return to full, soft, chocolaty form. Best years: (2000) 98 97 96 95 **94 93**.

**BRAND'S** *Coonawarra, South Australia* Low-profile COONAWARRA firm, owned by MCWILLIAMS, with 100ha (250 acres) of new vineyards as well as some ancient vines now over 100 years old. An unsubtle, peachy Chardonnay is good, and ripe Cabernet★ and Cabernet-

Merlot★ are increasingly attractive. New life is being breathed into Shiraz★, and Patron's Blend★★ shows how good Coonawarra Shiraz can be. Best years: (reds) 1998 **97 96 94 92 90**.

**CH. BRANE-CANTENAC** *Margaux AC, 2ème Cru Classé, Haut-Médoc, Bordeaux, France*  Early signs from the late 90s suggest Brane-Cantenac is back on form after a prolonged downturn. I hope so, because MARGAUX AC needs more reliable quality producers. I look forward to tasting again those gentle plummy, chocolaty flavours – not fragrant but lovely – that once made this one of my favourite châteaux. Best years: (2000) 99 98 97 96 95 **90 89 88 86**.

**BRAUNEBERG** *Mosel, Germany*  Small village in the Middle Mosel. Its most famous vineyard sites are Juffer and Juffer Sonnenuhr, whose wines have a honeyed richness and creamy gentleness rare in the Mosel. Best producers: Bastgen★, Fritz HAAG★★, Willi Haag★, Paulinshof★, M F RICHTER★★. Best years: 1999 98 **97** 95 **93 90**.

**BREAKY BOTTOM** *Sussex, England*  Small vineyard tucked in the South Downs near Lewes; it was badly flooded during 2000. Peter Hall is a wonderfully quirky, passionate grower, making dry, nutty Seyval Blanc★ that becomes creamy and Burgundy-like after 3–4 years. His crisp Müller-Thurgau★ is full of hedgerow pungency. Sparkling Seyval Blanc is a new venture.

**BREGANZE DOC** *Veneto, Italy*  Small DOC in the hills east of Verona and north of Vicenza. A red primarily from Merlot and a dry white based on Tocai Friulano are supplemented by a range of varietals, including Cabernet and Vespaiolo. Best producers: Bartolomeo da Breganze co-op, MACULAN★★, Vigneto Due Santi.

**BODEGAS BRETÓN** *Rioja DOC, Rioja, Spain*  Pedro Bretón has set this winery apart from the bevy of commercially minded bodegas launched in the mid-1980s. Single-vineyard Dominio de Conté★ is the best expression of their aim to return to RIOJA traditions. Alba★★ is a high-quality varietal Tempranillo. Best years: (reds) **1996 95 94 91 90 89**.

**GEORG BREUER** *Rüdesheim, Rheingau, Germany*  Medium-sized estate run by Bernhard Breuer, producing quality dry Riesling from vines on the Rüdesheimer Berg Schlossberg★★ and Rauenthaler Nonnenberg★★. Wines like the Rivaner (Müller-Thurgau, fermented dry) and Grauer Burgunder see a little oak. Best years: 1999 98 **97** 96 **94 93 90**.

**BRIGHT BROTHERS** *Ribatejo, Portugal*  The Fiúza-Bright winemaking operation is located in the town of Almeirim in the RIBATEJO but wines are also made from ESTREMADURA, BAIRRADA, DOURO (TFN★) and TERRAS DO SADO (Palmela Reserva★). Australian Peter Bright combines his enthusiasm for native grapes such as the Baga and Sercial-Arinto with familiar names like Chardonnay, Sauvignon Blanc, Cabernet and Merlot. Bright also makes a range of wines for PENAFLOR in Argentina.

**JEAN-MARC BROCARD** *Chablis AC, Burgundy, France*  Dynamic winemaker who has built up his modern 80ha (200-acre) domaine almost from scratch. Except for his Premiers Crus (including Montée de la Tonnerre★★, Montmains★★) and slow-evolving Grands Crus (les Clos★★ stands out), all the fruit is machine-picked and vinified in steel tanks. Vieilles Vignes★ is usually the best of the regular CHABLIS. Brocard also produces a range of Bourgogne Blancs★ from different soil types. Best years: (top crus) (1999) 98 **97 96 95 94 93 90 89**.

**BROKENWOOD** *Hunter Valley, New South Wales, Australia* High-profile winery with delicious, unfashionable Semillon★★ and fashionable Chardonnay★. Best wine is classic HUNTER Graveyard Vineyard Shiraz★★★; the Rayner Vineyard MCLAREN VALE Shiraz★★ is also a stunner. Cricket Pitch★ blended reds and whites are cheerful, fruity ready-drinkers. Best years: (Graveyard Vineyard Shiraz) 1997 96 94 **91 88 87 86**.

**BROUILLY AC** *Beaujolais, Burgundy, France* Largest of the 10 Crus; at its best, the wine is soft, fruity and gluggable. Can also make ideal BEAUJOLAIS NOUVEAU. Best producers: la Chaize★, H & J-P Dubost, DUBOEUF (Combillaty, Ch. de Nervers★), Fouilloux, Hospices de Beaujeu★, A Michaud★, Pierreux, Ruet, Ch. des Tours★. Best years: 1999 **98 97 96**.

**BROWN BROTHERS** *North-East Victoria, Australia* Highly successful family winery that has outgrown its small producer tag. There is a huge range of varietal table wines – and vintage fizz is consistently good. Focusing on cool King Valley and mountain-top Whitlands for its premium grapes.

**BRÜNDLMAYER** *Kamptal, Niederösterreich, Austria* Willi Bründlmayer makes wine in a variety of Austrian and international styles, but his dry Riesling★★ from the great Heiligenstein vineyard and Grüner Veltliner (Ried Lamm★★★) are the best. Good Sekt. Best years: (whites) (2000) 99 98 **97 95 94 93 92 91 86 83 79**.

**BRUNELLO DI MONTALCINO DOCG** *Tuscany, Italy* Powerful red wine produced from Sangiovese (known locally as Brunello). Traditionally needed over 10 years to soften, but modern practices result in more fruit-rich wines, yet still tannic enough to age spectacularly. Best producers: Altesino★ (Montosoli★★), ARGIANO★★, BANFI★★, Barbi★, Baricci★, BIONDI-SANTI★★, La Campana★★, Caparzo★★ (La Casa★★), Casanova di Neri★★, CASTELGIOCONDO★★, Centolani (Friggiali★, Pietranera★★), La Cerbaiola★★, Cerbaiona★★, Ciacci Piccolomini d'Aragona★★, Donatella Cinelli Colombini★★, Col d'Orcia★★, COSTANTI★★★, Due Portine-Gorelli★★, Fuligni★★, La Gerla★, Maurizio Lambardi★★, Lisini★★, Mastrojanni★★, Siro Pacenti★★, Pian delle Vigne★★/ANTINORI, Agostina Pieri★★, Pieve Santa Restituta★★, La Poderina★★, Poggio Antico★★, Poggio di Sotto★, Il Poggiolo★★, Il Poggione★★, Livio Sasseti-Pertimali★★, Scopetone★, Soldera (Case Basse★★), Talenti★★, Valdicava★★, Val di Suga★. Best years: (1999) (98) (97) 96 95 94 **93 91 90 88 85 83 82**.

**BUCELAS DOC** *Estremadura, Portugal* A tiny but historic DOC. The wines are whites based on the Arinto grape (noted for its high acidity). For attractive, modern examples try Quinta da Murta or Quinta da Romeira (Morgado de Santa Catherina).

**BUENA VISTA** *Carneros AVA, California, USA* Clear, lucid, appealing wines, especially a delicious Pinot Noir and a fairly simple but tasty unoaked Sauvignon. Reserve★ Chardonnay, Cabernet and Merlot are capable of aging. Best years: (Cabernet) (1999) 98 97 **95 94 91 90**.

**BUGEY VDQS, VIN DU** *Savoie, France* An area of scattered vineyards halfway between Lyon and SAVOIE. The best wines are the whites, from Chardonnay, Pinot Gris, Mondeuse Blanche, Altesse and Jacquère. Roussette du Bugey is usually a blend of Altesse and Chardonnay. Best producers: Bel-Air, Crussy, Monin, Peillot.

# BURGUNDY RED WINES

*Burgundy, France*

Rich in history and gastronomic tradition, the region of Burgundy (Bourgogne in French) covers a vast tract of eastern France, running from Auxerre, south-east of Paris, to the city of Lyon. As with its white wines, Burgundy's red wines are extremely diverse, sometimes frustratingly so. The explanation for this lies partly in the fickle nature of Pinot Noir, the area's principal red grape, and partly in the historical imbalance of supply and demand between growers – who grow the grapes and make and bottle much of the best wine – and merchants, whose efforts have established the reputation of the wines internationally.

## GRAPE VARIETIES

Pinot Noir is one of the world's most ancient varieties, prone to mutation – there are several dozen variations in Burgundy alone – and the range of flavours you get from the grape vividly demonstrates this. A red Épineuil from near Auxerre in the north of the region will be light, chalky, strawberry-flavoured; a Pinot from the Mâconnais toward Lyon will be rustic and earthy; and in between in the Côte d'Or – the heartland of red Burgundy – the flavours sweep through strawberry, raspberry, damson and cherry to a wild, magnificent maturity of Oriental spices, chocolate, mushrooms and truffles. Gamay, the grape of Beaujolais to the south, is best at producing juicy fruit flavours of strawberry and plum, demanding in most cases neither aging nor undue respect.

## WINE REGIONS

The top red Burgundies come from the Côte d'Or, home to world-famous Grand Cru vineyards such as Clos de Vougeot, Chambertin, Musigny, Richebourg and la Tâche. Givry and Mercurey in the Côte Chalonnaise are up-and-coming, as are the Hautes-Côtes hills behind the Côte d'Or, and light but pleasant reds as well as good pink sparkling Crémant can be found near Chablis in the north. Mâconnais' reds are generally earthy and dull. Beaujolais really is best at producing bright, breezy wines full of fruit, for quaffing at a mere one year old.

See also ALOXE-CORTON, AUXEY-DURESSES, BEAUJOLAIS, BEAUNE, BLAGNY, BONNES-MARES, BOURGOGNE, BOURGOGNE-COTE CHALONNAISE, BOURGOGNE-HAUTES-COTES DE BEAUNE, CHAMBERTIN, CHAMBOLLE-MUSIGNY, CHASSAGNE-MONTRACHET, CHOREY-LES-BEAUNE, CLOS DE LA ROCHE, CLOS ST-DENIS, CLOS DE TART, CLOS DE VOUGEOT, CORTON, COTE DE BEAUNE, COTE DE NUITS, COTE D'OR, CREMANT DE BOURGOGNE, ECHEZEAUX, FIXIN, GEVREY-CHAMBERTIN, GIVRY, LADOIX, MACON, MARSANNAY, MERCUREY, MEURSAULT, MONTHELIE, MOREY-ST-DENIS, MOULIN-A-VENT, MUSIGNY, NUITS-ST-GEORGES, PERNAND-VERGELESSES, PULIGNY-MONTRACHET, RICHEBOURG, La ROMANEE-CONTI, ROMANEE-ST-VIVANT, RULLY, ST-AUBIN, ST-ROMAIN, SAVIGNY-LES-BEAUNE, La TACHE, VOLNAY, VOSNE-ROMANEE, VOUGEOT; and individual producers.

(1999) 98 97 96 95 **93 90 89 88**

### BEST PRODUCERS

**Côte de Nuits** B Ambroise, Dom. l'Arlot, Robert Arnoux, Denis Bachelet, G Barthod, Burguet, Charlopin-Parizot, R Chevillon, CLAIR, J-J Confuron, Confuron-Cotétidot, B Dugat-Py, DUJAC, Engel, Michel Esmonin, Féry-Meunier, Geantet-Pansiot, Gouges, GRIVOT, Anne Gros, Hudelot-Noëllat, JAYER-GILLES, Dom. LEROY, H Lignier, MEO-CAMUZET, Mongeard-Mugneret, Denis Mortet, Mugneret-Gibourg, Mugnier, Perrot-Minot, Ponsot, RION, Dom. de la ROMANEE-CONTI, Roty, Rouget, ROUMIER, ROUSSEAU, Dom. THOMAS-MOILLARD, VOGUE.

**Côte de Beaune** Ampeau, ANGERVILLE, Comte Armand, J-M Boillot, CHANDON DE BRIAILLES, COCHE-DURY, Courcel, GERMAIN, V GIRARDIN, Michel LAFARGE, LAFON, Dom. Matrot, Montille, Albert Morot, Pousse d'Or, RAMONET, TOLLOT-BEAUT.

**Côte Chalonnaise** Brintet, H & P Jacqueson, Joblot, M Juillot, Thénard, Villaine.

**Beaujolais** F & J Calot, Chignard, Lapierre, Ch. du MOULIN-A-VENT, M Tête, Thivin.

**Merchants** BOUCHARD PERE ET FILS (since 1996), Champy, DROUHIN, DUBOEUF, FAIVELEY, Camille Giroud, JADOT, LABOURE-ROI, D Laurent, Olivier LEFLAIVE, Maison LEROY, Nicolas Potel, Remoissenet, RODET.

**Co-ops** BUXY, les Caves des Hautes-Côtes, Fleurie.

# BURGUNDY WHITE WINES

*Burgundy, France*

 White Burgundy has for generations been thought of as the world's leading dry white wine. The top wines have a remarkable succulent richness of honey and hazelnut, melted butter and sprinkled spice, yet are totally dry. Such wines are all from the Chardonnay grape and the finest are generally grown in the communes of Aloxe-Corton, Meursault, Puligny-Montrachet and Chassagne-Montrachet, where limestone soils and the aspect of the vineyard provide perfect conditions for even ripening of grapes.

*WINE STYLES*

However, Burgundy encompasses many more wine styles than this, even if no single one quite attains the peaks of quality of those 4 villages on the Côte de Beaune.

Chablis in the north traditionally produces very good steely wines, aggressive and lean when young, but nutty and rounded – though still very dry – after a few years. Modern Chablis is generally a softer, milder wine, easy to drink young, and sometimes enriched with aging in new oak barrels.

There is no doubt that Meursault and the other Côte d'Or villages can produce stupendous wine, but it is in such demand that unscrupulous producers are often tempted to maximize yields and cut corners on quality. Consequently white Burgundy from these famous villages must be approached with caution. Lesser-known villages such as Pernand-Vergelesses and St-Aubin often provide good wine at lower prices.

The Côte Chalonnaise is becoming more interesting for quality white wine now that oak barrels are being used more often for aging. Rully and Montagny are the most important villages, though Givry and Mercurey can produce nice white, too.

The minor Aligoté grape makes some reasonable acidic wine, especially in Bouzeron. Further south, the Mâconnais is a large region, two-thirds planted with Chardonnay. The wine used to be dull and flat and not all that cheap, but there is some fair sparkling Crémant de Bourgogne, and some very good vineyard sites, in particular in St-Véran and in Pouilly-Fuissé. Increasingly stunning wines can now be found.

---

See also ALOXE-CORTON, AUXEY-DURESSES, BATARD-MONTRACHET, BEAUJOLAIS, BEAUNE, BOURGOGNE, BOURGOGNE-COTE CHALONNAISE, CHABLIS, CHASSAGNE-MONTRACHET, CORTON, CORTON-CHARLEMAGNE, COTE DE BEAUNE, COTE DE NUITS, COTE D'OR, CREMANT DE BOURGOGNE, FIXIN, GIVRY, LADOIX, MACON, MARSANNAY, MERCUREY, MEURSAULT, MONTAGNY, MONTHELIE, MONTRACHET, MOREY-ST-DENIS, MUSIGNY, NUITS-ST-GEORGES, PERNAND-VERGELESSES, PETIT CHABLIS, POUILLY-FUISSE, POUILLY-LOCHE, PULIGNY-MONTRACHET, RULLY, ST-AUBIN, ST-ROMAIN, ST-VERAN, SAVIGNY-LES-BEAUNE, VOUGEOT; and individual producers.

MEURSAULT-CHARMES
APPELLATION MEURSAULT 1er CRU CONTROLÉE
1997
Domaine des Comtes LAFON
Mis en bouteilles à la propriété    Clos de la Barre
21190 Meursault
FRANCE
75 cl                PRODUIT DE FRANCE

## BEST YEARS

(2000) 99 **97** 96 **95 92 90 89**

## BEST PRODUCERS

**Chablis** J-C Bessin, Billaud-Simon, J-M BROCARD, D Dampt, DAUVISSAT, D & E Defaix, DROIN, DURUP, W Fèvre, J-P Grossot, Laroche, Louis MICHEL, G Picq, RAVENEAU, G Robin, Simonnet-Febvre, Vocoret.

**Côte d'Or** G Amiot, R Ampeau, d'Auvenay (LEROY), Blain-Gagnard, Jean Boillot, J-M Boillot, Bonneau du Martray, M Bouzereau, Y Boyer-Martenot, CARILLON, CHANDON DE BRIAILLES, COCHE-DURY, Marc Colin, Colin-Deléger, Arnaud Ente, J-P Fichet, Fontaine-Gagnard, J-N GAGNARD, GAGNARD-DELAGRANGE, Guffens-Heynen (VERGET), P Javillier, F Jobard, R Jobard, LAFON, R Lamy-Pillot, Dom. LEFLAIVE, Dom. Matrot, F Mikulski, Bernard Morey, Marc Morey, Pierre Morey, M Niellon, P Pernot, J & J-M Pillot, RAMONET, G Roulot, SAUZET.

**Côte Chalonnaise** S Aladame, H & P Jacqueson.

**Mâconnais** D & M Barraud, Bonhomme, Corsin, Deux Roches, Ferret, Forest, Ch. FUISSE, la Greffière, Guffens-Heynen, J-J Litaud, Luquet, Merlin, Robert-Denogent, R Saumaize, Thévenet, Valette.

**Merchants** BOUCHARD PERE ET FILS, Champy, DROUHIN, FAIVELEY, V GIRARDIN, JADOT, LABOURE-ROI, Louis LATOUR, Olivier LEFLAIVE, Maison LEROY, Rijckaert, RODET, VERGET.

**Co-ops** BUXY, la CHABLISIENNE.

**VON BUHL** *Deidesheim, Pfalz, Germany* Large estate, leased to the Japanese Sanyo group. The wines are rarely subtle, but have full fruit and a confident Riesling character. Best years: **1999 98 97 96 94 90**.

**BUITENVERWACHTING** *Constantia WO, South Africa* This beautifully restored property is part of the Cape's original CONSTANTIA wine farm. Its history is reflected in the traditional, Old World-style wines; a graceful, intricate Chardonnay★, penetrating, zesty Sauvignon Blanc★★ and light, racily dry Riesling. Aristocratic BORDEAUX blend Christine★★ is regularly one of the most complex and elegant. Best years: (whites) **2000 99 98 97**; (reds) **1996 95 94 93 92 91**.

**BULL'S BLOOD** *Eger, Hungary* Kékfrankos (Blaufränkisch) grapes often replace robust Kadarka in the blend but the blood has somewhat thinned, partly due to producers making lighter, more export-friendly styles, and partly due to inferior raw materials resulting from grape shortages. Winemakers Tibor Gal (of Egervin) and Vilmos Thummerer are stepping up quality on the back of stringent new regulations.

**GRANT BURGE** *Barossa Valley, South Australia* A leading producer in the BAROSSA, making chocolaty Filsell Shiraz★ and Cameron Vale Cabernet★, opulent Summers Chardonnay★, minerally Thorn Riesling★ and oaky Zerk Semillon. Top label is rich but somewhat oak-dominated Meshach Shiraz★★. Shadrach Cabernet★★ and RHONE-style blend, Holy Trinity★, are recent additions. Best years: (Meshach) **1998 96 95 94 91 90**.

**BURGENLAND** *Austria* 4 regions: Neusiedlersee, including Seewinkel for sweet Prädikat wines; Neusiedlersee-Hügelland, famous for sweet wines, now also big reds and fruity dry whites; Mittelburgenland, for robust Blaufränkisch reds; and Südburgenland, for good reds and dry whites. Best producers: FEILER-ARTINGER★★★, Gernot Heinrich★, Hans Igler★, Juris★, Kollwentz★, KRACHER★★★, Krutzler★★, M & A Nittnaus★★, OPITZ★, Peter Schandl★, Ernst Triebaumer★★, Umathum★★, VELICH★★, Robert Wenzel★.

**BURGUNDY** See Bourgogne AC and pages 76–9.

**BÜRKLIN-WOLF** *Wachenheim, Pfalz, Germany* With nearly 100ha (250 acres) of vineyards, this is one of Germany's largest privately owned estates. Under director Christian von Guradze, a champion of vineyard classification, it has shot back up to the first rank of the region's producers since the 1994 vintage. The powerful, spicy dry Rieslings are now ★ to ★★, with the magnificent dessert wines ★★★. Best years: **1999 98 97 96 95 94 93 90 89 86**.

**BURMESTER** *Port DOC, Douro, Portugal* Shipper established since 1730 and recently on the up. Vintage port★★ is much improved, as is the Vintage released under the Quinta Nova de Nossa Senhora do Carmo★ label. This highly regarded quinta was purchased by Burmester in 1991. As well as refined 10- and 20-year-old tawnies, there are some outstanding old colheitas★★ which extend back over 100 years. Also good recent Late Bottled Vintage★ and oak-aged DOURO red, Casa Burmester★. Best years: (Vintage) **1997 95 94**.

**BURRWEILER** *Pfalz, Germany* An exception in the PFALZ, Burrweiler is the region's only wine village with a slate soil like the MOSEL, most notably in the excellent Schäwer site. Elegant dry Rieslings and some fine dessert wines. Best producer: Herbert Messmer★. Best years: **1999 98 97 94 93**.

**BUXY, CAVE DES VIGNERONS DE** *Côte Chalonnaise, Burgundy, France*
Based in the Côte Chalonnaise, this ranks among Burgundy's top co-operatives, producing affordable, well-made Chardonnay and Pinot Noir. The light, oak-aged BOURGOGNE Pinot Noir★ and the red and white Clos de Chenôves★, as well as the nutty, white MONTAGNY★, are all good, reasonably priced, and delicious with 2–3 years' age.

**BUZET AC** *South-West France* Good Bordeaux-style red wines from the same mix of grapes and at a lower price. There is very little rosé and the whites are rarely exciting. Best producers: les Vignerons de Buzet (especially Baron d'Ardeuil★, Ch. de Gueyze★ and Cuvée 44★), Tissot.

**BYRON VINEYARD** *Santa Maria Valley AVA, California, USA* After new owner MONDAVI built a new winery and acquired reputable vineyards, founder Ken 'Byron' Brown has been making better than ever Pinot Noir and Chardonnay. His Reserve Pinot★★ is full of spicy cherry fruit, and the Reserve Chardonnay★★ with mineral notes and fine balance can age for several years. Regular Chardonnay is often good value and new Rhône blends look promising. Best years: (Chardonnay) (1999) **98 97 96 95 94 92**.

**CA' DEL BOSCO** *Franciacorta DOCG, Lombardy, Italy* Model estate, headed by Maurizio Zanella, making some of Italy's finest and most expensive wines: outstanding sparklers in FRANCIACORTA Brut★★, Dosage Zero★, Satén★★ and the prestige Cuvée Annamaria Clementi★★; good Terre di Franciacorta Rosso★, remarkably good Chardonnay★★★, Pinero★★ (Pinot Nero) and a BORDEAUX blend, Maurizio Zanella★★★.

**CABARDÈS AC** *Languedoc, France* Next door to MINERVOIS but, as well as the usual Mediterranean grape varieties, Cabernet Sauvignon and Merlot are allowed. At best, full-bodied, chewy and rustically attractive. Best producers: Cabrol, Jouclary, Pennautier, Salitis, Ventenac.

**CABERNET D'ANJOU AC** *Loire Valley, France* Can be made from both Cabernets and generally demi-sec. Now made to drink young, but there are still a few remarkable old vintages from the 1940s and 50s around. Best producers: Bablut, Ogereau, Passavant, Putille, Tigné.

**CABERNET FRANC** Often unfairly dismissed as an inferior Cabernet Sauvignon, Cabernet Franc comes into its own in cool zones or areas where the soil is damp and heavy. It can have a leafy freshness linked to raw but tasty blackcurrant-raspberry fruit. In France it thrives in the LOIRE VALLEY and BORDEAUX, especially ST-EMILION and POMEROL where it accounts for 19% of the planting. Italy has used the variety with considerable success for generations in the north-east, particularly in FRIULI and ALTO ADIGE. Experiments with Cabernet Franc on CALIFORNIA'S North Coast and in WASHINGTON STATE show promise. There are also some good South African, Chilean and Australian examples.

**CABERNET SAUVIGNON** See pages 82–3.

**CADILLAC AC** *Bordeaux, France* Sweet wine from the southern half of the PREMIERES COTES DE BORDEAUX. Styles vary from fresh, semi-sweet to richly botrytized. The wines have greatly improved in recent vintages. Drink young. Best producers: CARSIN, Cayla★, Ch. du Juge (Dupleich), Manos★, Mémoires★, Reynon, Ste-Catherine.

# CABERNET SAUVIGNON

 Wine made from Cabernet Sauvignon in places like Australia, California, Chile, Bulgaria, even in parts of southern France, has become so popular now that many people may not realize where it all started – and how Cabernet has managed to become the great, all-purpose, omnipresent red wine grape of the world.

*WINE STYLES*

**Bordeaux Cabernet** It all began in Bordeaux. With the exception of a clutch of Merlot-based beauties in St-Émilion and Pomerol, all the greatest red Bordeaux wines are based on Cabernet Sauvignon, with varying amounts of Merlot, Cabernet Franc, and possibly Petit Verdot also blended in. The blending is necessary because by itself Cabernet makes such a strong, powerful, aggressive and assertive wine. Dark and tannic when young, the great Bordeaux wines need 10–20 years for the aggression to fade, the fruit becoming sweet and perfumed as fresh blackcurrants, with a fragrance of cedarwood, of cigar boxes mingling magically among the fruit. It is this character which has made red Bordeaux famous for at least 2 centuries.

**Cabernet worldwide** When winemakers in other parts of the world sought role models to try to improve their wines, most of them automatically chose Cabernet Sauvignon. It was lucky that they did, because not only is this variety easy to grow in almost all conditions – cool or warm, dry or damp – but that unstoppable personality always powers through. The cheaper wines are generally made to accentuate the blackcurrant fruit and the slightly earthy tannins. They are drinkable young, but able to age surprisingly well. The more ambitious wines are aged in oak barrels, often new ones, to enhance the tannin yet also to add spice and richness capable of developing over a decade or more. Sometimes the Cabernet is blended – usually with Merlot, but occasionally, as in Australia, with Shiraz.

**European Cabernets** Many vineyards in southern France now produce good, affordable Cabernet. Some of the best wines from Spain have been Cabernet, and Portugal has also had success. Italy's red wine quality revolution was sparked off by the success of Cabernet in Tuscany, and all the leading regions now grow it; Austria is beginning to make progress and even southern Germany is having a go. Eastern Europe, in particular Bulgaria, provides us with some of the most affordable, decent quality reds in the world.

**New World Cabernets** California's reputation was created by its strong, weighty Cabernets, though in recent vintages winemakers are working with a lighter hand. Both Australia and New Zealand place more emphasis on upfront fruit in their Cabernets. Chile has made the juicy, blackcurranty style very much her own, and Argentina and South Africa are showing they want to join in too.

## BEST PRODUCERS

### France

*Bordeaux* Dom. de CHEVALIER, COS D'ESTOURNEL, GRUAUD-LAROSE, LAFITE-ROTHSCHILD, LATOUR, LEOVILLE-LAS-CASES, LYNCH-BAGES, Ch. MARGAUX, MOUTON-ROTHSCHILD, PICHON-LONGUEVILLE, RAUZAN-SEGLA; *Midi* MAS DE DAUMAS GASSAC, TREVALLON.

### Other European Cabernets

*Italy* ANTINORI (SOLAIA), BANFI, Col d'Orcia (Olmaia), CA' DEL BOSCO, GAJA, LAGEDER, MACULAN, Montevetrano, ORNELLAIA, QUERCIABELLA (Camartina), RAMPOLLA, REGALEALI, San Leonardo, SASSICAIA, TERRICCIO.

*Spain* MARQUES DE GRINON, TORRES.

### New World Cabernets

*Australia* CAPE MENTELLE, CULLEN, Giaconda, HOWARD PARK, MOSS WOOD, MOUNT MARY, PENFOLDS (Bin 707), PETALUMA, WYNNS, YARRA YERING.

*New Zealand* Esk Valley, GOLDWATER, MATUA VALLEY, STONYRIDGE, TE MATA, VILLA MARIA.

*USA* (California) ARAUJO, Bryant Family, BERINGER, CAYMUS, DALLA VALLE, DIAMOND CREEK, DOMINUS, DUNN, Grace Family, Harlan, La Jota, LAUREL GLEN, Peter MICHAEL, Miner, MONDAVI, NEWTON, PHELPS, Plumpjack, RIDGE, Screaming Eagle, SHAFER, SILVER OAK, SPOTTSWOODE, STAG'S LEAP; (Washington) ANDREW WILL, LEONETTI, QUILCEDA CREEK.

*Chile* ALMAVIVA, CARMEN (Gold Reserve), MONTES (Alpha), SANTA RITA (Casa Real), SENA, VINA CASABLANCA (Santa Isabel).

*Argentina* CATENA.

*South Africa* BEYERSKLOOF, BUITENVERWACHTING, Neil ELLIS, KANONKOP, MEERLUST, RUSTENBERG, SAXENBURG, THELEMA.

**CAHORS AC** *South-West France* Important South-West red wine region.
This dark, often tannic wine is made from at least 70% Auxerrois
(Bordeaux's Malbec) and has an unforgettable, rich plummy flavour
when ripe and well made. Ages well. Best producers: la Caminade,
Cayrou★, Cèdre★★, Clos la Coutale★, Clos de Gamot★, Clos
Triguedina★, Côtes d'Olt co-op, Gaudou, Gautoul★, Haute-Serre★,
Lagrezette★★, Lamartine★. Best years: (2000) 98 **96 95 94 90 89 88 86 85.**

**CAIN CELLARS** *Napa Valley AVA, California, USA* This Spring Mountain
estate appears to be solidly on track. Cain Five★★ is a particularly
pleasing, slow-maturing red BORDEAUX blend. Cain Concept is a red
Bordeaux blend made from hillside vineyards. Also attractive are
lower-priced drink-me-now red Cain Cuvée★ and strongly flavoured
white Sauvignon Musqué★. Best years: (Cain Five) (1999) 97 96 95 94
**93 92 91 90 87 86 85.**

**CALABRIA** *Italy* One of Italy's poorest regions. CIRO, Donnici, Savuto and
Scavigna reds from the native Gaglioppo grape, and whites from Greco, are
much improved thanks to greater winemaking expertise.

**CALERA** *San Benito, California, USA* A pace-setter for California Pinot
Noir with 4 different estate wines: Reed Vineyard★★, Selleck
Vineyard★★★, Jensen Vineyard★★★ and Mills★★. They are complex,
fascinating wines with power and originality and capable of aging. Mt
Harlan Chardonnay★★ is excitingly original too. Small amounts of
Viognier★★ are succulent with sensuous fruit. Best years: (reds) 1998 **97
96 95 94 92 91 90 88 87 86 85**; (whites) 1999 **98 97 96 95**.

**CALIFORNIA** *USA* California's importance is not simply in being the
leading wine producer in the USA. Most of the great revolutions in
technology and style that have transformed the expectations and
achievements of winemakers in every country of the world – including
France – were born in the ambitions of a band of Californian winemakers
during the 1960s and 70s. They challenged the old order with its
regulated, self-serving elitism, democratizing the world of fine wine, to the
benefit of every wine drinker. This revolutionary fervour is less evident
now. And there are times when Californians seem too intent on
establishing their own particular New World old order. A few figures: there
are 160,000ha (400,000 acres) of wine grapes, producing over 500
million gallons of wine annually, about 90% of all wine made in the USA. A
large proportion comes from the hot, inland CENTRAL VALLEY. See also
Central Coast, Mendocino County, Monterey County, Napa Valley, San
Luis Obispo County, Santa Barbara County, Sonoma County.

**CALITERRA** *Curicó, Chile* A joint venture between MONDAVI and
Chadwick (as is SENA), with an impressive portfolio: sprightly citrus-
edged Chardonnay★ from CASABLANCA, silky CURICO Merlot and intense,
grassy Sauvignon Blanc. Whites have impressed more than reds, but
new, oaky Arboleda reds, including a fine Carmenère, are promising.

**CH. CALON-SÉGUR★** *St-Estèphe AC, 3ème Cru Classé, Haut-Médoc,
Bordeaux, France* Long considered one of ST-ESTEPHE's leading
châteaux but in the mid-1980s the wines were not as good as they

should have been. Recent vintages have been more impressive, with better fruit and a suppler texture. Second wine: Marquis de Ségur. Best years: (2000) 99 98 96 95 **90 89 86 82**.

**CAMBRIA WINERY** *Santa Maria Valley AVA, California, USA* The biggest winery in SANTA BARBARA COUNTY. Most of the production, and generally the best bet, is Chardonnay (Katherine's Vineyard★★ and Reserve★★), with the remainder devoted to Pinot Noir, Syrah and Sangiovese. Look for fine Julia's Vineyard Pinot Noir★. Best years: (Chardonnay) (1999) **98 97 96 95**.

**CAMPANIA** *Italy* Until recently Italy's south was a desert for the wine lover, but now 3 regions lead the revolution there. While many have been clamouring for the new wines of PUGLIA and SICILY, in Campania moves toward quality have been underpinned by the likes of enologist Riccardo Cotarella. Other producers besides the venerable MASTROBERARDINO have finally begun to realize the potential of its soil, climate and grapes, especially the red Aglianico. DOCs of note are FALERNO DEL MASSICO, Fiano di Avellino, Greco di Tufo, Ischia, TAURASI and VESUVIO. The leading new wine is Montevetrano★★★, made from Cabernet, Merlot and Aglianico at the Montevetrano estate near Salerno, but also look for top Aglianico reds from Galardi and Orazio Rillo that fall outside the main DOCs.

**CAMPILLO** *Rioja DOC, País Vasco, Spain* An up-market subsidiary of FAUSTINO MARTINEZ, producing some exciting new red RIOJAS★. The wines are often Tempranillo-Cabernet Sauvignon blends, with masses of ripe, velvety fruit. Best years: (Reserva) 1996 **95 94 89 87**.

**CAMPO VIEJO** *Rioja DOC, Rioja, Spain* The largest producer of RIOJA. The Reservas★ and Gran Reservas★ are reliably good, as are the elegant, all-Tempranillo Reserva Viña Alcorta★ and the barrel-fermented white Viña Alcorta★. Albor Tempranillo is a good modern young Rioja, packed with fresh, pastilley fruit. Best years: (Reserva) **1996 95 94 91 89**.

**CANARY ISLANDS** *Spain* Tacoronte-Acentejo, Lanzarote, La Palma, Hierro, Abona, Valle de Güimar, Valle de la Orotava and Ycoden-Daute-Isora: a total of 8 DOs for the Canaries – there's local politics for you! The sweet Malvasia from Lanzarote or La Palma is worth a try, otherwise stick with the young reds, made mostly from Listán Negro. Best producers: El Grifo, Bodegas Monje, Viña Norte.

**CANBERRA DISTRICT** *New South Wales, Australia* Cool, high altitude (800m/2600ft) may sound good but excessive cold and frost (especially in spring 1998) can be problematic. Lark Hill and Helm make exciting Riesling, Lark Hill and Brindabella Hills some smart Cabernet blends and Clonakilla increasingly sublime Shiraz (with a dollop of Viognier). BRL HARDY is pouring money in here. Best producers: Brindabella Hills★, Clonakilla (Shiraz★★), Doonkuna★, Helm, Lark Hill★.

**CANNONAU** Sardinian grape variety essentially the same as Spain's Garnacha and France's Grenache Noir. In SARDINIA it produces deep, tannic reds but lighter, modern, dry red wines are gaining in popularity, although traditional sweet and fortified styles can still be found. Best producers: (modern reds) ARGIOLAS, SELLA & MOSCA; Dolianova, Dorgali, Jerzu, Ogliastra, Oliena, Santa Maria La Palma and Trexenta co-ops.

**CANOE RIDGE VINEYARD** *Columbia Valley AVA, Washington, USA* Successful Washington outpost of California's CHALONE group, with reliable and tasty Chardonnay★, Merlot★ and Cabernet★. The reds can age pretty well. Best years: (1999) 98 97 **96 95**.

**CH. CANON★** *St-Émilion Grand Cru AC, 1er Grand Cru Classé, Bordeaux, France* Canon can make some of the richest, most concentrated ST-EMILIONS, but it went into steep decline before being purchased in 1996 by Chanel. Expect a return to great things. The 3.5-ha (8.65-acre) vineyard of Grand Cru Classé Ch. Curé-Bon has recently been added to the estate. In good vintages the wine is tannic at first but is worth aging 10–15 years. Second wine: Clos J Kanon. Best years: (2000) 99 98 96 95 **90 89 88 86 85 83 82**.

**CANON-FRONSAC AC** *Bordeaux, France* This AC is the heart of the FRONSAC region. The wines are quite sturdy when young but can age for 10 years or more. Best producers: Barrabaque★, Canon★, Canon-de-Brem★, Canon-Moueix★, Cassagne-Haut-Canon★, la Fleur-Cailleau, Grand-Renouil★, Moulin-Pey-Labrie★, Pavillon, Vrai-Canon-Bouché. Best years: (2000) 98 97 96 95 **94 90 89 88**.

**CH. CANON-LA-GAFFELIÈRE★★** *St-Émilion Grand Cru AC, Grand Cru Classé, Bordeaux, France* Owner Stéphan de Neipperg has placed this property, located at the foot of the town of ST-EMILION, at the top of the list of Grands Crus Classés. The wines are firm, rich and concentrated. Also under the same ownership are Clos l'Oratoire★ and the remarkable *micro-cuvée* La Mondotte★★. Best years: (2000) 99 98 97 96 95 94 **93 90 89 88 85**.

**CH. CANTEMERLE★** *Haut-Médoc AC, 5ème Cru Classé, Bordeaux, France* With la LAGUNE, the most southerly of the Crus Classés. The wines are delicate in style and excellent in ripe vintages. Second wine: Villeneuve de Cantemerle. Best years: (2000) 99 98 97 96 95 **90 89 83 82**.

**CANTERBURY** *South Island, New Zealand* The long, cool ripening season of the arid central coast of South Island favours white varieties, particularly Chardonnay, Pinot Gris, Sauvignon Blanc and Riesling, as well as Pinot Noir. The northerly Waipara district produces Canterbury's most exciting wines, especially from Riesling and Pinot Noir. Best producers: GIESEN★, Mountford★, PEGASUS BAY★★, Daniel Schuster★, Waipara West★.

**CAPEL VALE** *Geographe, Western Australia* Radiologist Peter Pratten's winery makes fine Riesling★, Gewürztraminer, Chardonnay★ and Semillon-Sauvignon Blanc★, often blending Capel fruit with Mount Barker. Reserve whites and reds are increasingly classy. CV is a second label. Best years: (whites) **1999 98 97 96 95 93 92**.

**CAPE MENTELLE** *Margaret River, Western Australia* Leading MARGARET RIVER winery, owned by French luxury giant LVMH. Cape Mentelle's visionary founder, David Hohnen, produces full-throttle Cabernet★★ and Shiraz★★, impressive Chardonnay★★, tangy Semillon-Sauvignon Blanc★★ and wonderfully chewy Zinfandel★★ which effectively expresses Hohnen's CALIFORNIA training. All wines benefit from cellaring – whites up to 5 years, reds 8–10. Best years: (reds) (1998) 96 95 **92 91** 90 **88** 86 83 82 78.

**CH. CARBONNIEUX** *Pessac-Léognan AC, Cru Classé de Graves, Bordeaux, France* Carbonnieux is the largest of the GRAVES Classed Growth properties, now part of the PESSAC-LEOGNAN AC. The white★ is a pleasant, mildly oaked wine. The red is generally balanced and enjoyable but rarely memorable. Second wine: la Tour-Léognan. Best years: (whites) 1999 98 **96 95 94** 90 89 88 85; (reds) (2000) 98 96 95 **90 89 88** 86.

**CAREMA DOC** *Piedmont, Italy* Lighter than most other Nebbiolos, these wines can have great elegance and perfume. Production is confined to the local co-op (Carema Carema★) and Luigi Ferrando (White Label★, Black Label★★). Best years: (1999) (98) 97 96 **95 93** 90 88 85.

---

**CARIGNAN** The dominant red grape in the south of France is responsible for much boring, cheap, harsh wine. But when made by carbonic maceration, the wine can have delicious spicy fruit. Old vines are capable of thick, rich, impressive reds, with which it is now making a name for itself in CALIFORNIA and Chile. There is also some interest in South Africa. Although initially a Spanish grape (as Cariñena or Mazuelo), it is not that widespread there, but is useful for adding colour and acidity in RIOJA and CATALUÑA, and has gained unexpected respect in PRIORAT.

---

**CARIGNANO DEL SULCIS DOC** *Sardinia, Italy* Carignano is now starting to produce wines of quite startling quality. Rocca Rubia★★, a barrique-aged Riserva from the co-op at Santadi, with rich, fleshy and chocolaty fruit, is one of SARDINIA's best reds. In a similar vein, but more structured and concentrated, is Terre Brune★★. Best producer: Santadi co-op. Best years: (reds) (2000) 99 98 **97 96** 95.

**LOUIS CARILLON & FILS** *Puligny-Montrachet AC, Côte de Beaune, Burgundy, France* Excellent family-owned estate in PULIGNY-MONTRACHET. The emphasis here is on traditional, finely balanced whites of great concentration, rather than new oak. Look out for the Premiers Crus les Referts★★, Champs Canet★★ and les Perrières★★, and the tiny but exquisite production of Bienvenues-BATARD-MONTRACHET★★★. Reds from CHASSAGNE-MONTRACHET★, ST-AUBIN★ and MERCUREY★ are good, too. Best years: (whites) (2000) 99 97 96 **95 92** 90.

**CARIÑENA DO** *Aragón, Spain* The largest DO of ARAGON, baking under the mercilessly hot sun in inland eastern Spain, Cariñena has traditionally been a land of cheap, deep red, alcoholic wines from the Garnacha grape. However, a switch to Tempranillo grapes has begun, and some growers now pick earlier. International grape varieties like Cabernet Sauvignon are being planted widely. Best producers: Bodegas San Valero (Monte Ducay, Don Mendo), Señorío de Urbezo.

**CARMEN** *Maipo, Chile* Sister winery to SANTA RITA. Innovative young winemaker Alvaro Espinoza has left after an 8-year stint, but the winemaking remains in good hands. Best wines include complex, well-structured Gold Reserve Cabernet Sauvignon★★, plummy Reserve Merlot★ and Grande Vidure-Cabernet★. Whites are less successful but Reserve Chardonnay★ is much improved. New Nativa Chardonnay★ and Cabernet★★ show promise.

**CARMENET VINEYARD** *Sonoma Valley AVA, California, USA* Carmenet sets out to make BORDEAUX-style reds and whites and is probably one of California's most successful exponents of both, producing deep, complex reds★★ and long-lived, barrel-fermented whites★★. Best years: (reds) (1999) 98 97 96 95 94 **92 91 90 88 87 86**.

**CARMIGNANO DOCG** *Tuscany, Italy* Red wine from the west of Florence, renowned since the 16th century and revived in the 1960s by Capezzana. The blend (85% Sangiovese, 15% Cabernet) is one of Tuscany's more refined wines and can be very long-lived. Although Carmignano is DOCG for its red wine, notable as Riserva, DOC applies to a lighter red Barco Reale, a rosé called Vin Ruspo and fine VIN SANTO. Best producers: Ambra★ (Vigne Alte★★), Artimino★, Capezzana★ (Riserva★★), Le Farnete/E Pierazzuoli★ (Riserva★★), Il Poggiolo★, Villa di Trefiano★. Best years: (1999) 98 **97 96 95 94 93 90 88 85**.

**CARMO, QUINTA DO** *Alentejo, Portugal* Well-established estate, part-owned by Domaines Rothschild. Estate red★ and second label Dom Martinho have been complex and ageworthy, but quality is increasingly variable. And that's not really acceptable when you can supposedly call upon top Bordeaux expertise and finance. Best years: 1997 **95 94 93 92 90 89 87**.

**CARNEROS AVA** *California, USA* Hugging the northern edge of San Francisco Bay, Carneros includes parts of both NAPA and SONOMA Counties. Windswept and chilly with morning fog off the Bay, it is a top cool-climate area, suitable for Chardonnay and Pinot Noir as both table wine and a base for sparkling wine. Merlot is also coming on well. Best producers: ACACIA★★, BUENA VISTA, Carneros Creek★, DOMAINE CARNEROS★★, MUMM NAPA (Winery Lake)★, David Ramey★★, RASMUSSEN★★, SAINTSBURY★★.

**CARNUNTUM** *Niederösterreich, Austria* Wine region south of the Danube and east of Vienna, with a strong red wine tradition. Best producers: Walter Glatzer, Markowitsch, Pitnauer★.

**CH. CARSIN** *Premières Côtes de Bordeaux AC, Bordeaux, France* With an Australian winemaker – Mandy Jones – and a winery designed and built by an Australian engineering company, what could you expect other than aromatic and fruity New World-style wines? Carsin delivers the goods with well-oaked, drink-young white Cuvée Prestige★ and red Cuvée Noire★. Also peach and citrus vin de table Etiquette Gris★ and a sweet Cadillac. Best years: 1999 **98 97 96 95 94**.

**CASABLANCA, VALLE DE** *Aconcagua, Chile* Coastal valley with a cool climate personality that is Chile's strongest proof of regional style. Whites dominate, with best results from Chardonnay, Sauvignon Blanc and Gewürztraminer. Even so, the rare reds are very good. Best producers: (whites) CONCHA Y TORO★, CASA LAPOSTOLLE★, ERRAZURIZ★, Veramonte, VILLARD ESTATE, VINA CASABLANCA★★. Best years: (whites) 2000 **99 98 97**.

**CASA LAPOSTOLLE** *Rapel, Chile* Joint venture between Marnier-Lapostolle and Chile's Rabat family, with Michel Rolland at the winemaking helm. Cuvée Alexandre Merlot★★ and Chardonnay★ both have the intensity for several years' aging. Clos Apalta★★ is a top-class Merlot and Carmenère-based blend. Best years: (reds) 1999 98 **97 96 95**.

**CASSIS AC** *Provence, France* A picturesque fishing port near Marseille. Because of its situation, its white wine is the most overpriced on the French Riviera. Based on Ugni Blanc and Clairette, the wine can be good if fresh. The red wine is dull but the rosé can be pleasant (especially from a single estate). Best producers: Bagnol★, Clos Ste-Magdelaine★, Ferme Blanche★, Fontblanche, Mas de Boudard, Mas Fontcreuse.

**CASTEL DEL MONTE DOC** *Puglia, Italy* An arid, hilly zone, and an ideal habitat for the Uva di Troia grape, producing long-lived red wine of astonishing character. There is also varietal Aglianico, some good rosé, and the whites produced from international varieties are improving. Best producers: ANTINORI (Tormaresca), RIVERA★, Santa Lucia, Torrevento★. Best years: (1999) 98 97 **96 95 94 93 91 90 88**.

**CASTELGIOCONDO** *Brunello di Montalcino DOCG, Tuscany, Italy* FRESCOBALDI's estate is the source of fine BRUNELLO★, Brunello Riserva★★ and excellent Merlot Lamaione★★. The vineyards are also providing grapes for the much-trumpeted joint venture with MONDAVI, Luce, a Sangiovese-Merlot blend; so far, I'm unconvinced, but the addition of a second wine, Lucente, may help.

**CASTELLARE** *Chianti Classico DOCG, Tuscany, Italy* Publisher Paolo Panerai's fine estate in the west of the Classico zone produces excellent Chianti Classico★ and deeper, richer Riserva★★. Canonico di Castellare★ (Chardonnay), Coniale di Castellare★★ (Cabernet Sauvignon), and Spartito di Castellare★ (Sauvignon Blanc) are all ripe and fruity. Top wine I Sodi di San Niccolò★★ is an unusual Sangiovese-Malvasia blend, intense but finely perfumed.

**CASTELLBLANCH** *Cava DO, Cataluña, Spain* One of the world's largest quality sparkling wine companies, owned by another giant CAVA company, FREIXENET. Brut Zero and Cristal Seco are fresh, simple fizzes.

**CASTILLA-LA MANCHA** *Spain* Biggest wine region in Spain at over 600,000ha (1.5 million acres); hot, dry country with poor clay-chalk soil. The DOs of the central plateau, La MANCHA and VALDEPEÑAS, make white wines from the Airén grape, and some good reds from the Cencibel (Tempranillo). Méntrida DO, the new Manchuela DO and Almansa DO make rustic reds. Most ambitious wines made here fall outside the DOs: those from MARQUÉS DE GRIÑÓN's Dominio de Valdepusa★★ estate and the Dehesa de Carrizal★ estate, both in the Toledo mountains, and Manuel Manzaneque's Sierra de Alcaraz★★ vineyards in Albacete province are of the highest standard.

**CASTILLA Y LEÓN** *Spain* This is Spain's harsh, high plateau, with long cold winters and hot summers (but always cool nights). A few rivers, notably the Duero, temper this climate and afford fine conditions for viticulture. After many decades of winemaking ignorance, with a few exceptions like VEGA SICILIA, the situation has changed radically for the better in 2 of the region's DOs, RIBERA DEL DUERO and RUEDA, and is fast improving in the other 3, BIERZO, Cigales and TORO.

**CATALUÑA** *Spain* Standards vary among the region's 9 DOs. PENEDES, between Barcelona and Tarragona, has the greatest number of technically equipped wineries in Spain, but doesn't make a commensurate number of superior wines. Alella, up the coast, makes attractive whites, and inland COSTERS DEL SEGRE makes potentially excellent reds and whites. In the south, mountainous, isolated PRIORAT has become a new icon for its heady, raging reds, and other promising wines are coming from the hills of Tarragona and Terra Alta. Ampurdán-Costa Brava, by the French border, is showing signs of life. Cataluña also makes most of Spain's CAVA sparkling wines. A new Catalunya DO allowing inexpensive blends from anywhere around the region was approved in 2000. See also Conca de Barberá.

**NICOLAS CATENA** *Mendoza, Argentina* One of Argentina's most progressive export-orientated wine producers. The Esmeralda winery produces good international-style Chardonnay, oak-aged Cabernet Sauvignon and powerful Agrelo vineyard Malbec, with second label Alamos Ridge providing a rather leaner interpretation. Catena's takeover of La Rural has delivered a reasonable new Malbec and

soft, jammy Merlot under the Rutini label. Smartly packaged Argento Malbec is soft but undistinguished. Most impressive is the Alta range of Chardonnay★★, Cabernet★★ and Malbec★★ from Luján de Cuyo.

**DOMAINE CAUHAPÉ** *Jurançon AC, South-West France* Henri Ramonteu has been a major influence in JURANCON, proving that the area can make complex dry whites as well as more traditional sweet wines. Dry, unoaked Jurançon Sec is labelled Chant de Vignes★. Top wines are sweet Noblesse du Temps★★ and barrel-fermented Quintessence★★★.

**CAVA DO** *Spain* Cava, the Catalan and hence Spanish name for CHAMPAGNE-method fizz, is made in 159 towns and villages in northern Spain, but more than 95% are in CATALUNA. Grapes used are the local trio of Parellada, Macabeo and Xarel-lo. The best-value, fruitiest Cavas are generally the youngest, with no more than the minimum 9 months' aging. Some good Catalan Cavas are made with Chardonnay and maybe Pinot Noir. A number of top-quality wines are now produced but are seldom seen abroad, since their prices are too close to those of Champagne to attract international customers. Best producers: Can Feixes, Can Ràfols dels Caus, CASTELLBLANCH, Castell de Vilarnau, CODORNIU★, FREIXENET, JUVE Y CAMPS★, MARQUES DE MONISTROL★, Parxet, RAIMAT, Raventós i Blanc, Rovellats, Agustí Torelló, Jané Ventura.

**CAYMUS VINEYARDS** *Napa Valley AVA, California, USA* Caymus Cabernet Sauvignon is a ripe, intense and generally tannic style that is good in its regular bottling★ and can be outstanding as a Special Selection★★★. Conundrum is an exotic, full-flavoured blended white. Mer Soleil★, a new label for MONTEREY Chardonnay, was an instant success. Best years: (Special Selection) (1999) (98) (97) 96 95 94 92 91 90 **87 86 85 84 80**.

**DOMAINE CAZES** *Rivesaltes, Roussillon, France* The Cazes brothers make outstanding MUSCAT DE RIVESALTES★★, RIVESALTES Vieux★★ and the superb Aimé Cazes★★, but also produce a wide range of red and white table wines, mainly as COTES DU ROUSSILLON and Vin de Pays des Côtes Catalanes. Look out for the soft, fruity red le Canon du Maréchal★, the Cabernet-based vin de pays le Credo★ and the small production of barrel-fermented Chardonnay. Best years: (reds) **1998 96 95 94**.

**CELLIER LE BRUN** *Marlborough, New Zealand* Champagne-method specialist, with vintage blanc de blancs★★, and tasty blended vintage and non-vintage bubblies. Founder Daniel Le Brun has now sold up and established a new MARLBOROUGH winery, Le Brun Family Cellars.

90

**CENCIBEL** See Tempranillo.
**CENTRAL COAST AVA** *California, USA* Huge AVA covering virtually every vineyard between San Francisco and Los Angeles, with a number of sub-AVAs, such as Santa Cruz, Santa Ynez, SANTA MARIA and MONTEREY, which include some excellent cooler areas for Pinot Noir and Chardonnay. See also Monterey County, San Luis Obispo County, Santa Barbara County.

**CENTRAL OTAGO** *South Island, New Zealand* The only wine region in New Zealand with a continental rather than maritime climate. Technically the ripening season is long and cool, suiting Pinot Noir, Gewürztraminer and Chardonnay, but there are usually periods of considerable heat during the summer to intensify flavour. Long autumns have also produced some excellent Rieslings. There are already 31 wineries and an explosion of plantings, some in good areas like Bannockburn and Gibbston Valley, others in areas that could prove decidedly marginal. An area to watch. Best producers: Chard Farm★, FELTON ROAD★★, Gibbston Valley★, Mount Difficulty★, Mount Edwards★, Quartz Reef★, Rippon Vineyards★.

**VALLE CENTRAL** *Chile* The heart of Chile's wine industry, encompassing the valleys of MAIPO, RAPEL, CURICO and MAULE. Most major producers are located here, and the key factor determining mesoclimate differences is the distance relative to the coastal and Andean Cordilleras.
**CENTRAL VALLEY** *California, USA* This vast area grows over 50% of California's wine grapes, used mostly for cheaper styles of wine, along with brandies and grape concentrate. Viewed overall, the quality has improved over the past few years, but it is a hot area, where irrigated vineyards tend to produce excess tonnage of grapes. It has often been said that it is virtually impossible to produce exciting wine in the Central Valley, but in fact the climatic conditions in the northern half are not that unlike those in many parts of Spain and southern France. During the 1990s, growers in the Lodi AVA expanded vineyards to 22,000ha (55,000 acres), making Lodi the volume leader for Chardonnay, Merlot, Zinfandel and Cabernet. Lodi Zinfandel shows some potential. Other sub-regions with claims to quality are the Sacramento Valley and the Delta area. Best producers: MONDAVI Woodbridge, Sutter Home.
**CERETTO** *Piedmont, Italy* This merchant house, run by brothers Bruno and Marcello Ceretto, has gained a reputation as one of the chief modern producers in BAROLO. With the help of enologist Donato Lanati, Barolo (from Bricco Rocche★★ and more recently Brunate★★ and Prapò★★), BARBARESCO (Bricco Asili★★), BARBERA D'ALBA Piana★ and white Arneis Blangè have recently been living up to their reputation. At the La Bernardina estate, Ceretto also produces Chardonnay★, Viognier (La Bernardina Bianco★), Cabernet★, Pinot Nero, Syrah (La Bernardina Monsordo★★) and sparkling Brut.
**CÉRONS AC** *Bordeaux, France* An AC for sweet wine in the GRAVES region of Bordeaux. The soft, mildly honeyed wine is not quite as sweet as SAUTERNES and not so well known, nor so highly priced. Most producers now mainly make dry wine under the Graves label. Best producers: Ch. de Cérons★, Chantegrive, Grand Enclos du Château de Cérons★, Seuil. Best years: 1999 98 **97 96 95 90 89**.

**L A CETTO** *Baja California, Mexico*  Mexico's most successful winery relies on mists and cooling Pacific breezes to temper the heat of the Valle de Guadalupe. Italian Carmelo Magoni makes ripe, fleshy Petite Sirah, oak-aged Cabernet Sauvignon, Zinfandel and Nebbiolo. Chardonnay lacks acidity but, paradoxically, Cetto makes a decent stab at fizz.

**CHABLAIS** *Vaud, Switzerland*  A sub-region of the VAUD, south-east of Lake Geneva. Most of the vineyards lie on the alluvial plains but 2 villages, Yvorne and AIGLE, benefit from much steeper slopes and produce tangy whites and good reds. Most of the thirst-quenchingly dry whites are made from Chasselas, or Dorin as it is called locally. The reds are made from Pinot Noir, as is a rosé speciality, Oeil de Perdrix, an enjoyable summer wine. Drink whites and rosés young. Best producers: Henri Badoux, Delarze, Grognuz, J & P Testuz.

**CHABLIS AC** *Burgundy, France*  Chablis, halfway between Paris and Dijon, is Burgundy's northernmost outpost. Chardonnay ripens here with difficulty and there is a dreadful record of frost, which makes pricing volatile. Chablis is always white and dry, but with a steely mineral fruit which can make for delicious drinking. An increasing number of producers are experimenting with oak barrel-aging, resulting in some full, toasty, positively rich dry whites. In general straight Chablis AC should be drunk young, but the better ones can improve for 3–5 years. Best producers: J-C Bessin★, Billaud-Simon★, Pascal Bouchard★, Boudin★, J-M BROCARD★, la CHABLISIENNE★, Dampt★, D & E Defaix★, DROIN★, DROUHIN★, DURUP★, J-P Grossot★, LABOURE-ROI★, Laroche★, Long-Depaquit★, Malandes★, Marroniers★, MICHEL★, Mosnier★, L Pinson★, Vocoret★. Best years: (2000) 99 **98 97 96 95 92** 90.

**CHABLIS GRAND CRU AC** *Burgundy, France*  The 7 Grands Crus (Bougros, les Preuses, Vaudésir, Grenouilles, Valmur, les Clos and les Blanchots) facing south-west across the town of Chablis are the heart of the AC. Oak barrel-aging takes the edge off taut flavours, adding a rich warmth to these fine wines. DROIN and Fèvre are the most enthusiastic users of new oak, but use it less than they used to. Never drink young: 5–10 years is needed before you can see why you spent your money. Best producers: J-C Bessin★★, Billaud-Simon★★, la CHABLISIENNE★★, J Dauvissat★★★, R & V DAUVISSAT★★★, D & E Defaix★★, DROIN★★, W Fèvre★★, Laroche★★, Long-Depaquit★★, MICHEL★★, Pinson★★, RAVENEAU★★, Servin★, Vocoret★. Best years: (2000) 99 98 97 96 **95 94 92 90 89 88 85**.

**CHABLIS PREMIER CRU AC** *Burgundy, France*  Just over a quarter of CHABLIS' vineyards are designated Premier Cru. Some are on splendid slopes (the best are Montée de Tonnerre, Vaillons, Mont de Milieu and Fourchaumes), but many newer ones are on slopes of questionable quality. The good ones are excellent value. The wines should taste bigger and more intensely mineral than basic Chablis and may take 5 years to show full potential. Best producers: J-C Bessin★★, Billaud-Simon★★, J-M BROCARD★★, la CHABLISIENNE★★, Collet★, D Dampt★★, R & V DAUVISSAT★, D & E Defaix★★, DROIN★★, DURUP★, W Fèvre★★, Laroche★, MICHEL★★, Picq★★, RAVENEAU★★, Vocoret★★. Best years: (2000) 99 98 97 **96 95 93 92 90 89 88**.

**LA CHABLISIENNE** *Chablis, Burgundy, France*  Substantial co-op producing nearly a third of all CHABLIS. The wines are reliable and can aspire to greatness. The best are the oaky Grands Crus – especially les Preuses★★ and Grenouilles (sold as Ch. Grenouille★★) – but the basic unoaked Chablis★, the Cuvée Vieilles Vignes★★ and the numerous Premiers Crus★ are good, as is the red BOURGOGNE Épineuil from Pinot Noir. Best years: (whites) (2000) 99 **98 97 96 95 90**; (reds) (2000) **99 98**.

**CHALONE** *Monterey County, California, USA* Producers of full-blown but slow-developing Chardonnay★★ and concentrated Pinot Noir★★ from vineyards on the arid eastern slope of the Coastal Range in mid-MONTEREY COUNTY. Also makes very good Pinot Blanc★ and Chenin Blanc★, as well as Reserve bottlings of Pinot Noir★★ and Chardonnay★★★. These are strongly individualistic wines. Echelon is a second label. Best years: (Chardonnay) 1998 97 **96 95 94 93 92 91 90 89 85**; (Pinot Noir) 1998 **97 96 95 94 92 91 90 88 86 83**.

**CHAMBERS** *Rutherglen, Victoria, Australia* Family winery making sheer nectar in the form of Muscat and Tokay. The secret is Bill Chambers' ability to draw on ancient stocks put down in wood by earlier generations. His 'Special'★★ and 'Rare'★★★ blends are national treasures. The Cabernet and Shiraz are good, the whites pedestrian.

**CHAMBERTIN AC** *Grand Cru, Côte de Nuits, Burgundy, France* The village of GEVREY-CHAMBERTIN, the largest CÔTE DE NUITS commune, has no fewer than 8 Grands Crus (Chambertin, Chambertin-Clos-de-Bèze, Chapelle-Chambertin, Charmes-Chambertin, Griotte-Chambertin, Latricières-Chambertin, Mazis-Chambertin and Ruchottes-Chambertin), which can produce some of Burgundy's greatest and most intense red wine. Its rough-hewn fruit, seeming to war with fragrant perfumes for its first few years, creates remarkable flavours as the wine ages. Chambertin and Chambertin-Clos-de-Bèze are the greatest sites, but overproduction is a recurrent problem with some producers. Best producers: Denis Bachelet★★, CLAIR★★★, P Damoy★, DROUHIN★★, Dugat-Py★★★, FAIVELEY★★, R Groffier★★★, JADOT★★, D Laurent★★, Dom. LEROY★★★, Denis Mortet★★, H Perrot-Minot★★, Ponsot★★, Dom. Remy★, Rossignol-Trapet★, J Roty★, ROUMIER★★, ROUSSEAU★★★. Best years: (2000) 99 98 97 96 95 93 **91** 90 **89 88 85**.

**CHAMBERTIN-CLOS-DE-BÈZE AC** See Chambertin AC.

**CHAMBOLLE-MUSIGNY AC** *Côte de Nuits, Burgundy, France* AC with the potential to produce the most fragrant, perfumed red Burgundy, when not over-cropped. Encouragingly, more young producers are now bottling their own wines. Best producers: G Barthod★★, DROUHIN★★, DUJAC★★, R Groffier★★, JADOT★★, Dom. LEROY★★, Marchand-Grillot★★, D Mortet★★, T Mortet★★, J-F Mugnier★★, RION★★, ROUMIER★★★, VOGUE★★. Best years: (2000) 99 98 **97** 96 **95** 93 90 89.

**CHAMPAGNE** See pages 94–5.

**CHAMPAGNE ROSÉ** *Champagne, France* Good pink CHAMPAGNE has a delicious fragrance of cherries and raspberries. The top wines can age well, but most should be drunk on release. Best producers: (vintage) BILLECART-SALMON (Cuvée Elisabeth Salmon Brut★★), BOLLINGER★★, Charbaut★, Gosset★★, Charles HEIDSIECK★★, Jacquesson★★, MOET & CHANDON★★, POL ROGER★★, Louis ROEDERER★, VEUVE CLICQUOT★★; (non-vintage) Paul Bara★, E Barnaut★★, Beaumont des Crayères★, BILLECART-SALMON★★, Egly-Ouriet★★, Jacquart★, KRUG★★★, LANSON★, LAURENT-PERRIER★★, MOET & CHANDON★, PERRIER-JOUET (Blason de France★), RUINART★, TAITTINGER★, Vilmart★. Best years: (1998) (96) (95) **91** 90 89 88 86 85 82. See also pages 94–5.

# CHAMPAGNE AC

*Champagne, France*

 The Champagne region produces the most celebrated sparkling wines in the world. East of Paris, it is the most northerly AC in France – a place where grapes struggle to ripen fully. Champagne is divided into 5 distinct areas – the best are the Montagne de Reims, where the Pinot Noir grape performs brilliantly, and the Chardonnay-dominated Côte des Blancs south of Épernay. If you buy a bottle of Coteaux Champenois, a still wine from the area, you can see why they decided to make bubbly instead; it tastes mean and tart, but is transformed by the Champagne method into some of the most complex wines of all.

That's the theory anyway, and for 150 years or so the Champenois have suavely persuaded us that their product is second to none. It can be, too, except when it is released too young or sweetened to make up for a lack of richness. A combination of high prices and competition from other sparkling wines has produced a glut of Champagne. But as Champagne expertise begins to turn out exciting sparklers in California, Australia and New Zealand, the Champagne producers must re-focus on quality or lose much of their market for good.

The Champagne trade is dominated by large companies or houses, called négociants-manipulants, recognized by the letters NM on the label. The récoltants-manipulants (recognized by the letters RM) are growers who make their own wine.

## STYLES OF CHAMPAGNE

**Non-vintage** Most Champagne is a blend of 2 or more vintages. Quality varies enormously, depending on who has made the wine and how long it has been aged. Most Champagne is sold as Brut, which is a dry, but not bone-dry style. Strangely, Extra Dry denotes a style less dry than Brut.

**Vintage** Denotes Champagne made with grapes from a single vintage. As a rule, it is made only in the best years.

**Blanc de Blancs** A lighter, and at best highly elegant, style of Champagne made solely from the Chardonnay grape.

**Blanc de Noirs** A white Champagne, but made entirely from black grapes, either Pinot Noir, Pinot Meunier, or a combination of the two. Generally rather solid.

**Rosé** Pink Champagne, made either from black grapes or (more usually) by mixing a little still red wine into white Champagne.

**De luxe cuvée** In theory the finest Champagne and certainly always the most expensive, residing in the fanciest bottles.

See also CHAMPAGNE ROSE; and individual producers.

(1998) (96) 95 **90 89 88 85 83 82**

## BEST PRODUCERS

**Houses** BILLECART-SALMON, BOLLINGER, Cattier, Charbaut, Delamotte, Delbeck, DEUTZ, Drappier, Duval-Leroy, Gosset, Alfred GRATIEN, Charles HEIDSIECK, Henriot, Jacquesson, KRUG, LANSON, LAURENT-PERRIER, Bruno Paillard, Joseph PERRIER, PERRIER-JOUET, Philipponnat, POL ROGER, POMMERY, Louis ROEDERER, RUINART, Salon, TAITTINGER, VEUVE CLICQUOT.

**Growers** Bara, Barnaut, Beaufort, Beerens, Callot, Charpentier, Chartogne-Taillet, Diebolt Vallois, Daniel Dumont, Egly-Ouriet, René Geoffroy, Gimonnet, A Jaquart, Lamiable, Larmandier, Larmandier-Bernier, Launois, Margaine, Mathieu, G Michel, Moncuit, Alain Robert, Secondé, Selosse, de Sousa, Tarlant, Vilmart.

**Co-ops** Beaumont les Crayères, Nicolas FEUILLATTE, Jacquart, Mailly co-op.

**De luxe cuvées** Belle Époque (PERRIER-JOUET), N-F Billecart (BILLECART-SALMON), Blanc de Millénaires (Charles HEIDSIECK), Clos de Mesnil (KRUG), Comtes de Champagne (TAITTINGER), Cristal (Louis ROEDERER), Cuvée Josephine (Joseph PERRIER), Cuvée Sir Winston Churchill (POL ROGER), Cuvée William Deutz (DEUTZ), Dom Pérignon (MOET & CHANDON), Dom Ruinart (RUINART), Grand Siècle (LAURENT-PERRIER), Grande Dame (VEUVE CLICQUOT), Noble Cuvée (LANSON), Vintage RD (BOLLINGER).

**CHANDON DE BRIAILLES** *Savigny-lès-Beaune AC, Côte de Beaune,*
*Burgundy, France* The de Nicolays, mother and daughter, combine
modern sophistication with traditional values to produce rich but
refined reds from SAVIGNY-LES-BEAUNE★★, PERNAND-VERGELESSES★★,
ALOXE-CORTON★★ and CORTON★★★, and an equally good range of
whites from Pernand-Vergelesses★★, Corton★★★ and CORTON-
CHARLEMAGNE★★★. Best years: (reds) 1999 98 **97** 96 **95 93 90**.

**CHAPEL DOWN** *Kent, England* David Cowderoy is winemaker at this high-
tech winery, producing 1 million bottles a year from grapes grown in
the vineyards at Tenterden as well as bought-in grapes. Epoch Brut
Non-Vintage and Vintage are among England's better sparkling
wines. The curious but flavoursome wood-aged red Epoch I is worth a
punt. Bacchus, Schönburger and oaked Ortega are very good whites.

**CHAPEL HILL** *McLaren Vale, South Australia* Chapel Hill has some great
mature MCLAREN VALE vineyards and the winemaking expertise of Pam
Dunsford (ex-WYNNS and SEAVIEW). She blends McLaren Vale and
COONAWARRA in her Cabernet Sauvignon★★, while Shiraz★★ is all
McLaren Vale. Good unwooded Chardonnay★ (Reserve★★), and
fascinating, bone-dry, honey-scented Verdelho★★. In 2000 the winery
was bought by the Swiss Thomas Schmidheiny group, which also owns
CUVAISON in California. Best years: (Shiraz) (1998) 97 **96 95 94** 93 91.

**CHAPELLE-CHAMBERTIN AC** See Chambertin AC.

**LA CHAPELLE LENCLOS** *Madiran AC, South-West France* Patrick
Ducournau has tamed the savage Tannat grape with controlled
oxygenation during barrel aging. The Chapelle Lenclos★★ and
Domaine Mauréou★ reds are ripe and concentrated, though they still
need at least 5 years to mature. Best years: 1999 98 96 **95 94 93 90**.

**M CHAPOUTIER** *Rhône Valley, France* These days, Chapoutier is very
much in the vanguard of progress, both in viticulture and in
winemaking, and is producing a full range of serious and exciting
wines. The HERMITAGE la Sizeranne★★ and le Pavillon★★★, white
Hermitage Cuvée de l'Orée★★★, CROZES-HERMITAGE★★, ST-JOSEPH★★
and CHATEAUNEUF-DU-PAPE★★ are all good. Jointly owns Domaine des
Béates (Cuvée Terra d'Or★★) in PROVENCE.

**CHARDONNAY** See pages 98–9.

**CHARMES-CHAMBERTIN AC** See Chambertin AC.

**CHASSAGNE-MONTRACHET AC** *Côte de Beaune, Burgundy, France*
Some of Burgundy's greatest white wine vineyards (part of le
MONTRACHET and BATARD-MONTRACHET, all of Criots-Bâtard-Montrachet)
are within the village boundary. The white Chassagne Premiers Crus
are not as well known, but can offer nutty, toasty wines, especially if
aged for 4–8 years. Ordinary white Chassagne-Montrachet is usually
enjoyable; the red is a little earthy, peppery and plummy and can be an
acquired taste. Look out for reds from the following Premiers Crus: Clos
de la Boudriotte, Clos St-Jean and Clos de la Chapelle. Best producers:
(whites) F d'Allaines★, G Amiot★★, Blain-Gagnard★★, M Colin★★, Colin-
Deléger★★, Fontaine-Gagnard★★, J-N GAGNARD★★, GAGNARD-
DELAGRANGE★★, V GIRARDIN★★, Jouard★★, H Lamy★, Duc de Magenta★★,
B Morey★★, M Morey★★, M Niellon★★★, RAMONET★★; (reds) G Amiot★,
CARILLON★, R Clerget★, V GIRARDIN★★, B Morey★, RAMONET★★. Best years:
(whites) (2000) 99 98 **97** 96 **95** 92 90 89; (reds) 1999 98 **97** 96 **95 93 90**.

**CHASSELAS** Chasselas is considered a table grape worldwide. Only in BADEN (where it is called Gutedel) and Switzerland (called Dorin, Perlan or Fendant) is it thought to make decent light, dry wines with a slight prickle for everyday drinking. A few Swiss examples rise above this.

**CH.CHASSE-SPLEEN★** *Moulis AC, Cru Bourgeois, Haut-Médoc, Bordeaux, France* Chasse-Spleen is not a Classed Growth – but during the 1980s it built a tremendous reputation for ripe, concentrated and powerful wines under the late proprietor, Bernadette Villars. The château is now run by Villars' daughter Claire and is finding it difficult to return to the sublime form of the old days. Second wine: l'Ermitage de Chasse-Spleen. Best years: (2000) 99 96 95 **94 90 89 88 86 83 82**.

**CHÂTEAU-CHALON AC** *Jura, France* The most prized – and pricy – *vin jaune*, Jura's great speciality. It is difficult to find, even in the Jura. Best producers: Baud★★★, Berthet-Bondet★★, Bourdy★★, Chalandard★★★, Credoz★★, Durand-Perron★★, J Maclé★★★, H Maire★★.

**CHÂTEAU-GRILLET AC★★** *Rhône Valley, France* This rare and *very* expensive RHONE white, made from Viognier, has a magic reek of orchard fruit and harvest bloom when young and it can age well. The late 1980s and early 90s were poor, but this single-property AC has much improved since 1993. Best years: (2000) **99 98 97 96 95 93**.

**CHATEAU LAZARIDIS** *Thrace, Greece* A pioneering family operation, with a spectacular post-modernist winery and a long-term plan to repatriate vines planted by ancient Greeks in southern Italy. Production is currently based mainly on noble French varieties with relatively long cask- and bottle-aging. The Lazaridis red★ is very dense and concentrated but still fresh and young, and both white and red Maghiko Vouno★ show great potential. Best years: (reds) (2000) 99 97 **96 95 94 93 91**.

**CHATEAU MONTELENA** *Napa Valley AVA, California, USA* Napa winery producing well-balanced Chardonnay★★ and a Cabernet★★ that is impressive, if slow to develop. There is also a fascinating, soft Zinfandel-Sangiovese blend, St Vincent★★. Best years: (Cabernet) (1998) 97 96 95 94 **93 92 91 90 87 86 85 84 82**; (Chardonnay) (1999) 98 97 **96 95 94 93 92**.

**CHATEAU MUSAR** *Ghazir, Lebanon* Founded by Gaston Hochar in the 1930s and now run by his Bordeaux-trained son Serge, Musar is famous for having made wine every year bar two (1976 and 84) throughout Lebanon's civil war. From an unlikely blend of Cabernet Sauvignon, Cinsaut and Syrah comes a wine of real, if wildly exotic, character – full, with lush, sweet, spicy fruit and deceptively good aging potential. Hochar himself says that red Musar★ 'should be drunk at 15 years'. There is also a rosé, and a white from local grape varieties Obaideh (90%) and Merwah (10%) – Chardonnay and Sémillon lookalikes respectively. Best years: (reds) (1995) (94) (93) **92 91** 90 89 **87 85 83 81** 77 72 70 69 64; (whites) **1994**.

**CHATEAU ST JEAN** *Sonoma Valley AVA, California, USA* Once known almost entirely for its range of Chardonnays (Belle Terre★★ and Robert Young★★), St Jean has emerged as a producer of delicious Cabernet Sauvignon★★ and a meritage-style red called Cinq Cépages★★. A Reserve Merlot★★, released for the first time in 1995, is also worth seeking out. Best years: (whites) (1999) 98 97 **96 95 94 92 91 90**; (reds) (1998) 97 96 95 **94 93 92 91 90 89**.

# CHARDONNAY

I'm always getting asked, 'When will the world tire of Chardonnay?' And I reply 'Not in my lifetime.' The wine critics may pine for something else to write about, and the wine experts may decide that they want to explore the flavours available from other grape varieties, but for the vast majority of wine drinkers the Chardonnay revolution has only just begun, and to many people good dry white wine simply equals Chardonnay. And that's that. The amount of Chardonnay grown has increased dramatically over the last 10 years or so: it is now claimed to be the fourth most-planted white grape variety in the world.

*WINE STYLES*

**France** Although a relatively neutral variety if left alone (this is what makes it so suitable as a base wine for top-quality Champagne-method sparkling wine), the grape can ripen in a surprising range of conditions, developing a subtle gradation of flavours going from the sharp apple core greenness of Chardonnay grown in Champagne or the Loire, through the exciting, bone-dry yet succulent flavours of white Burgundy, to a round, perfumed flavour in Languedoc-Roussillon.

**Other regions** Italy produces Chardonnay that is bone dry and lean as well as fat, spicy and lush. Spain does much the same. A few South African examples are beginning to show what the variety is really capable of there, but California and Australia have virtually created their reputations on great viscous, almost syrupy, tropical fruits and spice-flavoured Chardonnays. They've both toned down the flavours now, though New Zealand is currently producing some wonderfully exotic wine, and Chile and Argentina have found it easy to grow and are rapidly learning how to make fine wine from it too. Add Germany, Austria, Canada, New York State, Greece, Slovenia, Moldova, Romania, even China, and you'll see it can perform almost anywhere.

**Using oak** The reason for all these different flavours lies in Chardonnay's wonderful susceptibility to the winemaker's aspirations and skills. The most important manipulation is the use of the oak barrel for fermenting and aging the wine. Chardonnay is the grape of the great white Burgundies and these are fermented and matured in oak (not necessarily new oak); the effect is to give a marvellous round, nutty richness to a wine that is yet savoury and dry. This is enriched still further by aging the wine on its lees.

The New World winemakers sought to emulate the great Burgundies, thus planting Chardonnay and employing thousands of oak barrels (mostly new) and their success – and the enthusiasm with which wine drinkers embraced the wine – has caused winemakers everywhere else to see Chardonnay as the perfect variety – easy to grow, easy to turn into wine and easy to sell to an adoring public.

## BEST PRODUCERS

**France** *Chablis* J-C Bessin, DAUVISSAT, DROIN, Laroche, MICHEL, RAVENEAU; *Côte d'Or* G Amiot, R Ampeau, J-M Boillot, Bonneau du Martray, BOUCHARD, M Bouzereau, CARILLON, COCHE-DURY, Marc COLIN, DROUHIN, A Ente, J-N GAGNARD, GAGNARD-DELAGRANGE, V GIRARDIN, JADOT, F Jobard, R Jobard, LAFON, Lamy-Pillot, LATOUR, Dom. LEFLAIVE, Dom. Matrot, B Morey, M Niellon, RAMONET, Roulot, SAUZET, VERGET; *Mâconnais* D & M Barraud, Ferret, Ch. FUISSE, Guffens-Heynen, Merlin, Rijckaert, Thévenet, Valette.

**Other European Chardonnays**
*Austria* VELICH.

*Germany* JOHNER, REBHOLZ.

*Italy* BELLAVISTA, CA' DEL BOSCO, GAJA, LAGEDER, Vie di Romans, Castello della SALA.

*Spain* ENATE, Manzaneque, TORRES, Señorío de Otazu.

**New World Chardonnays**
*Australia* Giaconda, HOWARD PARK, LEEUWIN, LENSWOOD, MOUNTADAM, PENFOLDS, PETALUMA, PIERRO, ROSEMOUNT, TYRRELL'S.

*New Zealand* CLOUDY BAY, ISABEL, KUMEU RIVER, NEUDORF, PEGASUS BAY, TE MATA.

*USA* ARROWOOD, AU BON CLIMAT, BERINGER, CALERA, CHALONE, FERRARI-CARANO, FLOWERS, KISTLER, MARCASSIN, MATANZAS CREEK, MERRYVALE, Peter MICHAEL, NEWTON, Pahlmeyer, David Ramey, ROCHIOLI, SAINTSBURY, SHAFER, STEELE, R Talbott.

*South Africa* GLEN CARLOU, HAMILTON RUSSELL, MEERLUST, MULDERBOSCH, THELEMA, VERGELEGEN.

*South America* CATENA, VILLARD, VINA CASABLANCA.

**CHATEAU STE MICHELLE** *Washington State, USA* A pioneering winery with an enormous range of wines, including several attractive vineyard-designated Chardonnays★, Cabernet Sauvignons★ and Merlots★, especially the Cold Creek Vineyard★★ wines. Makes good Riesling, both dry and sweet, and increasingly interesting red Meritage★ and white Sauvignon. COLUMBIA CREST began as a budget second label for good-value wines and has blossomed into a stand-alone winery. Partnership with Italy's ANTINORI and Germany's Ernst LOOSEN have produced dark, powerful red Col Solare★ and a good dry Riesling Eroica★. Best years: (reds) (1999) 98 97 96 **95 94**.

**CHÂTEAUNEUF-DU-PAPE AC** *Rhône Valley, France* A large vineyard area between Orange and Avignon that used to be one of the most abused of all wine names. Now, much Châteauneuf comes from single estates and deservedly ranks as one of France's top reds. Always get an estate wine, distinguished by the papal coat of arms embossed on the neck of the bottle. Only 5% of Châteauneuf is white. Made mainly from Grenache Blanc, Bourboulenc and Clairette, these wines can be surprisingly good. The top reds, particularly the increasing number of old-vine cuvées, will age for 8 years or more, while the whites are best young. Best producers: (reds) Auteuil★★, L Barrot★★, BEAUCASTEL★★★, Beaurenard★★, H Bonneau★★, Bosquet des Papes★★, Dom. du Caillou★★, les Cailloux★★, Chante-Perdrix★★, CHAPOUTIER★★, la Charbonnière★★, G Charvin★★, les Clefs d'Or★★, Clos du Mont Olivet★★, CLOS DES PAPES★★★, Crouzet-Feravel★★, Font du Loup★★, FONT DE MICHELLE★★, Fortia★★, la Gardine★★, Grand Tinel★★, la Janasse★★, Marcoux★★, Montpertuis★★, la Nerthe★★, Pégaü★★, RAYAS★★★, Roger Sabon★★, Tardieu-Laurent★★, Pierre Usseglio★★, Vieux Donjon★★, VIEUX TELEGRAPHE★★, Villeneuve★★; (whites) BEAUCASTEL★★★, CLOS DES PAPES★★, FONT DE MICHELLE★★, Grand Veneur★★, Marcoux★★, RAYAS★★, St-Cosme★★, VIEUX TELEGRAPHE★. Best years (reds): (1999) 98 97 **96 95 94 93 91 90 89 88**.

**CHAVE** *Rhône Valley, France* Jean-Louis Chave, son of founder Gérard, has deservedly achieved superstar status in recent years. His red HERMITAGE★★★ is one of the world's great wines, surpassed only by the Cuvée Cathelin★★★, produced only in exceptional years. His wonderful white Hermitage★★★ sometimes even outlasts the reds, as it quietly moves toward its honeyed, nutty zenith. Also produces a small amount of excellent red ST-JOSEPH★★. Expensive, but worth the money. Best years: (reds) (1999) 98 97 96 95 94 **92** 91 90 89 **88 86 85 83 82 81 79 78**; (whites) (1999) 98 97 96 95 94 **93 92 91 90 89 88 83**.

**CHÉNAS AC** *Beaujolais, Burgundy, France* The smallest of the BEAUJOLAIS Crus, Chénas wines, usually quite tough when young, benefit from 2 or more years' aging when they take on chocolaty tones. Best producers: G Braillon★, L Champagnon★, DUBOEUF (Manoir des Journets)★, G Granger★, H Lapierre★★, Daniel Robin★, B Santé★. Best years: (2000) **99 98 97 96 95**.

**CHENIN BLANC** One of the most underrated white wine grapes in the world. In the LOIRE VALLEY, where it is also called Pineau de la Loire, it is responsible for the great sweet wines of QUARTS DE CHAUME and BONNEZEAUX, as well as being the variety for VOUVRAY, sweet or dry, and much other Anjou white. It is also the main grape for the Loire sparkling wines. In South Africa, Chenin (also known as Steen) accounts for 24% of the vineyard area and is used for everything from easy-drinking, dryish whites through botrytized desserts to modern barrel-fermented versions, and also for brandy. CALIFORNIA, with a few exceptions like Chappellet, only employs it as a useful blender. New Zealand and Australia have produced good varietal examples.

**CH. CHEVAL BLANC★★★** *St-Émilion Grand Cru AC, 1er Grand Cru Classé, Bordeaux, France* The leading ST-EMILION estate and likely to remain so for the foreseeable future. Right on the border with POMEROL, it seems to share some of its sturdy richness, but with an extra spice and fruit that is impressively, recognizably unique. An unusually high percentage (60%) of Cabernet Franc is used in the blend. Best years: (2000) 99 98 97 96 95 94 90 89 88 **86 85 83 82**.

**CHEVALIER-MONTRACHET AC** See Montrachet AC.

**DOM. DE CHEVALIER** *Pessac-Léognan AC, Cru Classé de Graves, Bordeaux, France* This estate, mainly devoted to red, can produce some of Bordeaux's finest wines. The red★★ always starts out dry and tannic but over 10–20 years gains heavenly cedar, tobacco and black-currant flavour. The brilliant white★★★ is both fermented and aged in oak barrels; in the best vintages it will still be improving at 15–20 years. Best years: (reds) (2000) 99 98 97 96 95 **90 89 88 85 83 78**; (whites) (2000) 99 98 97 96 95 **94 90 89 88 85 83 82**.

**CHEVERNY AC** *Loire Valley, France* A little-known area south of Blois. The local speciality is the white Romorantin grape, used to make a bone-dry wine with the AC Cour Cheverny, but the best whites are from Chardonnay. Also pleasant Sauvignon, Pinot Noir and Gamay and a bracing Champagne-method fizz. Best producers: Cazin, Cheverny co-op, Courtioux, Gendrier★, Gueritte, Salvard, Sauger, Tessier, Tué Boeuf★.

**CHIANTI DOCG** *Tuscany, Italy* The most famous of all Italian wines, but there are many styles, depending on what grapes are used, where they are grown, and by which producer. It can be a light, fresh, easy-drinking red wine, but with a characteristic hint of bitterness, like a slightly aggressive Beaujolais, or it can be an intense, structured yet sleek wine in the same league as the best Bordeaux. The vineyards are scattered over central Tuscany. There are 8 sub-zones: Classico (with its own DOCG), Colli Aretini, Colli Fiorentini, Colli Senesi, Colline Pisane, Montalbano, Rufina and most recently Montespertoli. Sangiovese is the main grape; traditionally it was blended with the red Canaiolo and the white Malvasia and Trebbiano. Modern winemakers often ignored the others, especially the white, and made Chianti from Sangiovese alone or blended with 10–15% of Cabernet, Merlot or Syrah. The DOCG for Chianti Classico sanctions this, and other zones are expected to follow suit. See also Chianti Classico, Chianti Colli Fiorentini, Chianti Colli Senesi, Chianti Rufina, Super-Tuscans.

**CHIANTI CLASSICO DOCG** *Tuscany, Italy* The original (if slightly enlarged) CHIANTI zone in the hills between Florence and Siena. Classico has led the trend in making richer, more structured and better-balanced wines. Nonetheless, many producers use their best grapes for high-profile SUPER-TUSCANS. Since the 95 vintage, Classico can be made from 100% Sangiovese; the Riserva may now be aged in barrel for 2 instead of 3 years but must only use red grapes. The finest Riserva wines can improve for a decade or more. Many of the estates also offer regular bottlings of red wine, round and fruity, for drinking about 2–5 years after the harvest. Best producers: (Riservas) Castello di AMA★★, ANTINORI★★, Badia a Coltibuono★★, Brancaia★, Cacchiano★, Capaccia★★, Casaloste★, CASTELLARE★, Castell'in Villa★, Cecchi (Villa Cerna★), Cennatoio★, Collelungo★★, Colombaio di Cencio★, Dievole★, Casa Emma★★, FELSINA★★, Le Filigare★, FONTERUTOLI★★★, FONTODI★★, ISOLE E OLENA★★, La Massa★★, Melini★, Monsanto★★, Monte Bernardi★, Il Palazzino★, Paneretta★, Panzanello★,

Poggerino★, Poggiopiano★, Poggio al Sole (Casasilia★★★), Querceto★, QUERCIABELLA★★, Castello di RAMPOLLA★★, RICASOLI (Castello di Brolio★★), RIECINE★★, Rocca di Castagnoli★★, Rocca di Montegrossi★★, RUFFINO★★, San Felice★★, San Giusto a Rentennano★★, San Polo in Rosso★, Terrabianca★, Valtellina★★, Vecchie Terre di Montefili★★, Verrazzano★, Vicchiomaggio★★, Vignamaggio★, Villa Cafaggio★★, VOLPAIA★★. Best years: (2000) (99) **98 97 96 95 93 90 88**. See also Super-Tuscans.

**CHIANTI COLLI FIORENTINI** *Chianti DOCG, Tuscany, Italy*   Colli Fiorentini covers the hills around Florence. The wines traditionally are made to drink young, though some estates make Riservas of real interest. Best producers: Baggiolino★, Le Calvane, Il Corno, Corzano e Paterno★, Dell'Ugo, Lanciola II★, Pasolini dall'Onda★, Petreto, Petriolo, Poppiano★, La Querce, Sammontana, San Vito in Fior di Selva.

**CHIANTI COLLI SENESI** *Chianti DOCG, Tuscany, Italy*   This CHIANTI subzone consists of a vast area of Siena province (including the towns of Montalcino, Montepulciano and San Gimignano). Wines range from everyday quaffers to fairly elegant Riservas. Best producers: Carpineta Fontalpino★, Casale-Falchini★, Farnetella★, Ficomontanino★, Grattavecchi★, Montemorli, Pacina★, Paradiso★, Pietraserena★, Il Poggiolo★, Signano, Villa Sant'Anna.

**CHIANTI RUFINA** *Chianti DOCG, Tuscany, Italy*   Smallest of the CHIANTI subzones, situated in an enclave of the Apennine mountains to the east of Florence, where wines were noted for exceptional strength, structure and longevity long before they joined the ranks of Chianti. Today the wines, particularly the long-lived Riserva from SELVAPIANA and Montesodi from the ancient FRESCOBALDI estate of Castello di Nipozzano, match the best of CHIANTI CLASSICO. Best producers: (Riservas) Basciano★★, Tenuta di Bossi★, Il Cavaliere, Colognole, FRESCOBALDI★★, SELVAPIANA★★, Travignoli, Villa di Vetrice. Best years: (2000) 99 98 **97 96 95 94 93 90 88 86 85**.

**MICHELE CHIARLO** *Piedmont, Italy*   From his winery base south of Asti, Michele Chiarlo produces stylish wines from several PIEDMONT zones. Single-vineyard BAROLOS★★ and BARBARESCOS★ top the list, but BARBERA D'ASTI★★ and GAVI★ are reliable, too. Piedmont's new Monferrato DOC embraces Countacc!★, a Nebbiolo-Barbera-Cabernet Sauvignon blend, and barrique-aged white blend Plenilunio.

**CHIMNEY ROCK** *Stags Leap AVA, California, USA* After a shaky start, winemaker Doug Fletcher stepped in to put Chimney Rock on the right track, with powerful yet elegantly shaped Cabernet Sauvignon★★ and a Reserve-style meritage blend called Elevage★★. The wines are superb, with deep elements of fruit, opening into a long, layered finish. Best years: (1999) 98 97 96 95 **94 92 91 90** 87.

**CHINON AC** *Loire Valley, France* Best red wine of the LOIRE VALLEY, made mainly from Cabernet Franc. Full of raspberry fruit and fresh summer earth when young, can improve for 20 years; always worth buying a single-estate wine. Best producers: Philippe Alliet★★, B Baudry★★, J & C Baudry★, P Breton★, Coulaine★, COULY-DUTHEIL★, Delaunay★, DRUET★★, la Grille★, Joguet★, Lenoir★, Moulin à Tan★, Noblaie★, J-M Raffault★, Olga Raffault★. Best years: (2000) **99 97 96 95** 90 89 85 83 82 78 76.

**CHIROUBLES AC** *Beaujolais, Burgundy, France* Lightest, most delicately fragrant of the BEAUJOLAIS Crus; expensive for only a slightly superior BEAUJOLAIS-VILLAGES. Best producers: Cheysson★, de la Grosse Pierre★, G Passot★, J Passot★. Best years: (2000) **99** 98.

**CHIVITE** *Navarra DO, Navarra, Spain* The longtime leader in wine exports from NAVARRA, owned and run by the Chivite family. The wine is reliable to good but the reds, in particular, could be a bit more lively. The top range is called Colección 125 and includes a red Reserva★, white Blanco★ made from Chardonnay, and a characterful sweet Vendimia Tardía★★ from Moscatel (Muscat Blanc à Petits Grains). Best years: (reds) **1996 95 94** 92; (whites) **1999 98 97** 96.

**CHOREY-LÈS-BEAUNE AC** *Côte de Beaune, Burgundy, France* One of those tiny, forgotten villages that make good, if not great, Burgundy at prices most of us can still afford, with some committed producers too. Can age for 5–8 years. Best producers: Arnoux Père et Fils★, DROUHIN★, GERMAIN★, Maillard Père et Fils★, TOLLOT-BEAUT★★. Best years: 1999 98 **97 96 95** 93 90.

**CHURCHILL** *Port DOC, Douro, Portugal* Established in 1981, when it was the first new port shipper for 50 years. The wines are very good, notably Vintage★★, LBV★, Crusted★★, single quinta Agua Alta★★ and well-aged quirky dry white ports. Best years: (Vintage) 1997 94 **91** 85; (Agua Alta) (1998) 96 **95 92** 87.

**CHURCH ROAD** *Hawke's Bay, New Zealand* Church Road (formerly known as The McDonald Winery) is a premium-wine project owned by MONTANA, New Zealand's largest producer. There's a dry but balanced Cabernet-Merlot★ blend and a plummy Reserve Merlot★. Super-premium blend Tom★, first released in 1999, has Bordeaux-style austerity but good depth. Stylish Reserve Chardonnay★ is rich and smooth with flavours of peach, grapefruit and hazelnut. Best years: (reds) (1999) 98 **96 95** 94.

**CINSAUT** Found mainly in France's southern RHONE, PROVENCE and the MIDI, giving a light wine with fresh, but rather fleeting, neutral fruit. Popular as a blender in South Africa and Lebanon's CHATEAU MUSAR.

**CIRÒ DOC** *Calabria, Italy* The fact that this was the wine offered to champions in the ancient Olympics seemed a more potent reason to buy it than for quality. Yet Cirò Rosso, a full-bodied red from the

Gaglioppo grape, has improved remarkably of late. New wines, such as Librandi's Gravello★★ (an oak-aged blend with Cabernet), are even better. The DOC also covers a dry white from Greco and a rare dry rosé. Best producers: Caparra & Siciliani★, Librandi★, San Francesco★. Best years: (reds) (2000) 99 98 **97 96 95 93 90 88**.

**BRUNO CLAIR** *Marsannay, Côte de Nuits, Burgundy, France* Based in MARSANNAY, Bruno Clair produces a large range of excellent wines from a broad span of vineyards there, as well as in GEVREY-CHAMBERTIN, GIVRY, SAVIGNY and VOSNE-ROMANÉE. Most of his wine is red, but there is a small amount of white (CORTON-CHARLEMAGNE★★) and a delicious Marsannay rosé★. Top wines are CHAMBERTIN Clos de Bèze★★★, Gevrey-Chambertin Clos St-Jacques★★★ and vineyard-designated Marsannay reds★★. Best years: (top reds) (2000) 99 98 97 96 **95 93 90**.

**CLAIRETTE DE DIE AC** *Rhône Valley, France* One of the undeservedly forgotten sparkling wines of France, made from a minimum of 75% Muscat, off-dry with a creamy bubble and an orchard-fresh fragrance. The *méthode Dioise* is used, which preserves the Muscat scent. Drink young. Best producers: Achard-Vincent★, A Andrieux, Clairette de Die co-op★, Jacques Faure, Georges Raspail★.

**A CLAPE** *Cornas, Rhône Valley, France* The leading estate in CORNAS. Clape's wines★★ are consistently among the best in the RHÔNE – dense, tannic and full of rich, roasted fruit. Clape also makes fine CÔTES DU RHÔNE, both red★ and white★, and decent ST-PÉRAY★. Best years: (Cornas) (1999) 98 97 96 95 **94 92 91 90 89 88 86 85**.

**LA CLAPE** *Coteaux du Languedoc AC, Languedoc, France* The mountain of La Clape rears unexpectedly from the flat coastal fields south-east of Narbonne. The vineyards here are a Cru within the COTEAUX DU LANGUEDOC AC and produce some of the best Hérault wines. There are excellent whites from Bourboulenc and Clairette, plus some good reds and rosés, mainly from Carignan. The whites and reds can age. Best producers: Mire l'Étang, Pech-Céleyran★, Pech-Redon (Blanc), Vires. Best years: (reds) (2000) 99 98 **96 95 93 90 91**.

**CLARENDON HILLS** *McLaren Vale, South Australia* Controversial MCLAREN VALE winery making a name for high-priced, highly extracted, unfined and unfiltered reds. Single-vineyard Astralis★★★ – a hugely concentrated Shiraz from old vines aged in 100% French new oak – fetches similar prices to GRANGE. Other Shiraz★★ labels offer rather better value, while Merlot★★ and Cabernet Sauvignon★★ aim to rub shoulders with great red BORDEAUX. Several cuvées of Old Vines Grenache (all ★★) are marked by saturated black cherry fruit and high alcohol. Questions have been raised over the long-term potential of the wines, but all should mature well (for as much as 25 years in the case of Astralis). Best years: 1998 97 96 95 **94**.

**CLARE VALLEY** *South Australia* Historic upland valley north of Adelaide with a deceptively moderate climate, able to grow fine, aromatic Riesling, marvellously textured Semillon, rich, robust Shiraz and Cabernet blends and earthy but voluptuous Grenache. Best producers: (whites) Tim ADAMS★★, Jim BARRY★, Wolf BLASS (Gold Label★★), Leo Buring (Leonay★★), GROSSET★★★, KNAPPSTEIN★★, LEASINGHAM★, MITCHELL★★, Mount Horrocks★★, PETALUMA★★, Pike; (reds) Tim ADAMS★★, Jim BARRY★★, LEASINGHAM★, MITCHELL★★, Pike★★, WENDOUREE★★★.

**CH. CLARKE** *Listrac-Médoc AC, Bordeaux, France* This property had millions spent on it by the late Baron Edmond de Rothschild during the late 1970s, and the wines have reaped the benefit. And from the 98 vintage, leading Bordeaux winemaker Michel Rolland has been consultant enologist. The wines have an attractive blackcurrant fruit, though they never quite escape the typical Listrac earthiness. But with a name like Clarke, how could they possibly fail to be seductive? There is also a small production of dry white wine, le Merle Blanc. Best years: (2000) 99 98 96 **95 90 89 88**.

**DOMENICO CLERICO** *Barolo DOCG, Piedmont, Italy* Domenico Clerico has been one of the top BAROLO producers for more than a decade. He produces consistently impressive Barolos (Ciabot Mentin Ginestra★★★, Pajana★★★, Percristina★★★) and one of the best Barberas★ (Trevigne★★), all wonderfully balanced. His range also includes LANGHE Arte★★, a barrique-aged blend of Nebbiolo and Barbera. Best years: (Barolos) (1998) (97) 96 95 **94 93 92 91 90 89 88**.

**CH. CLIMENS★★★** *Barsac AC, 1er Cru Classé, Bordeaux, France* The leading estate in BARSAC, with a deserved reputation for fabulous, sensuous wines, rich and succulent yet streaked with lively lemon acidity. Easy to drink at 5 years, but a good vintage will be richer and more satisfying after 10–15 years. Second wine: les Cyprès (also delicious). Best years: 1999 98 97 96 95 **90 89 88 86 83 76 75**.

**CLOS BAGATELLE** *St-Chinian AC, Languedoc-Roussillon, France* For long a reference for quality wines in ST-CHINIAN. Now run by siblings Luc and Christine Simon, who produce 4 red cuvées and a MUSCAT DE ST-JEAN-DE-MINERVOIS. Top wine La Gloire de Mon Père★ is aged in 100% new oak barrels; Sélection in only 25%. Unoaked Marie et Mathieu★ is fruit-driven, and Cuvée Camillie has spicy, herbal aromas.

**CLOS DU BOIS** *Alexander Valley AVA, California, USA* Winery showcasing gentle, fruit-dominated flavours of SONOMA Chardonnay, Merlot and Cabernet. Top vineyard selections can be exciting, especially the Calcaire Chardonnay★★, as well as the rich, strong Briarcrest Cabernet Sauvignon★★ and Marlstone★★, a red BORDEAUX blend. Best years: (reds) 1998 **97 96 95 94 91 90 88 87 86**.

**CLOS CENTEILLES** *Minervois AC, Languedoc, France* Although labels still feature the name Domergue, this estate has been retitled. From vineyards close to Caunes-Minervois, Daniel Domergue and his wife Patricia Boyer are producing both excellent MINERVOIS La Livinière and innovative vins de pays. The impressive Clos de Centeilles★★ is their top wine; Capitelle de Centeilles★ and Carignanissime★ are 100% Cinsaut and Carignan respectively. Best years: 1999 98 97 **96 95 94 93**.

**CLOS DE LA COULÉE-DE-SERRANT** *Savennières AC, Loire Valley, France* Outstanding estate of only 7ha (17 acres) which merits its own AC within the boundaries of SAVENNIÈRES. The Joly family runs the property biodynamically and the estate wine★★ is a concentrated, long-lived Chenin Blanc with a fascinating honeyed, floral bouquet. Also produces better value Savennières Roche aux Moines★★ and Becherelle★. Best years: (2000) 99 **97** 96 95 **93 90 88 85 83 82**.

**CLOS MOGADOR** *Priorat DO, Cataluña, Spain* René Barbier Ferrer was one of the pioneers who relaunched the reputation of PRIORAT in the 80s. The wine★★ is a ripe, intense, brooding monster built to age. He also acts as

105

consultant at nearby Clos Erasmus★★★, where the wine receives extended oak aging. Best years: 1999 98 97 96 **95 94 93 92 91 90**.

**CLOS DES PAPES** *Châteauneuf-du-Pape AC, Rhône Valley, France* Paul Avril is one of the outstanding CHATEAUNEUF-DU-PAPE producers. His reds★★★ have an unusually high proportion of Mourvèdre, which explains their longevity, but enough Grenache to be approachable in their youth and provide the initial blast of fruit. The whites★★ take on the nutty character of aged Burgundy after a decade. Best years: (reds) (1999) 98 97 96 95 **94 93 92 90 89 88 83 81 79**.

**CLOS RENÉ**★ *Pomerol AC, Bordeaux, France* This is wonderfully plummy, juicy, fleshy wine. You can drink Clos René young, but it also ages well for at least 10 years. Sometimes sold under the label Moulinet-Lasserre. Best years: (2000) 98 96 **95 94 90 89 88 85 83 82**.

**CLOS DE LA ROCHE AC** *Grand Cru, Côte de Nuits, Burgundy, France* The best and biggest of the 5 MOREY-ST-DENIS Grands Crus. It has a lovely, bright, red-fruits flavour when young, and should become richly chocolaty or gamy with age. Best producers: DROUHIN★★★, DUJAC★★★, Léchenaut★★★, Dom. LEROY★★★, H Lignier★★★, Henri Perrot-Minot★★, Ponsot★★★, ROUSSEAU★★★. Best years: (2000) 99 98 97 96 95 93 **90 89 88**.

**CLOS ST-DENIS AC** *Grand Cru, Côte de Nuits, Burgundy, France* This small (6.5ha/16 acre) Grand Cru, which gave its name to the village of MOREY-ST-DENIS, produces wines which are sometimes light, but should be wonderfully silky, with the texture that only great Burgundy, so far, can give. Best after 10 years or more. Best producers: Charlopin★★, DUJAC★★, Georges Lignier★★, Ponsot★★★. Best years: (2000) 99 98 97 96 95 **93 90 89**.

**CLOS DE TART AC**★★ *Grand Cru, Côte de Nuits, Burgundy, France* Grand Cru in the village of MOREY-ST-DENIS, and entirely owned by the Mommessin family. The wine, light and elegant at first, can develop a delicious savoury richness as it ages. Best years: (2000) 99 98 97 96 95 **93 90 85**.

**CLOS UROULAT** *Jurançon AC, South-West France* Charles Hours makes stunningly good Jurançon, but in tiny quantities. Dry Cuvée Marie★★ balances ripe fruit with a deliciously refreshing finish. The richly textured sweet Jurançon★★ pulls together lemon, lime, honey and apricot: enjoyable young, but magnificent when aged. Best years: 1999 **98 96 95 93 90 89 88 87 83**.

**CLOS DU VAL** *Napa Valley AVA, California, USA* A sometimes overlooked producer of elegant Cabernet Sauvignon★, Chardonnay★, Merlot★, Pinot Noir and Zinfandel★. The Reserve Cabernet★ can age with the best. Ariadne★★, a Semillon-Viognier blend, is a lovely aromatic white. Best years: (Cabernet) (1999) 98 97 96 95 **94 92 91 90 87 86 85 84**.

**CLOS DE VOUGEOT AC** *Grand Cru, Côte de Nuits, Burgundy, France* Enclosed by Cistercian monks in the 14th century, and today a considerable tourist attraction, this large (50ha/125 acre) vineyard is now divided among 82 owners. As a result of this division, Clos de Vougeot has become one of the most unreliable Grand Cru Burgundies, but the better wine tends to come from the upper and middle parts. When it is good it is wonderfully fleshy, turning dark and exotic with 10 years' age or more. Best producers: B Ambroise★★★, Amiot-Servelle★★, Chopin-Groffier★★★, J-J Confuron★★★,

R Engel★★★, FAIVELEY★★, GRIVOT★★★, Anne Gros★★★, Haegelen-Jayer★, JADOT★★★, Dom. LEROY★★★, MEO-CAMUZET★★★, D Mortet★★★, Mugneret★★★. Best years: (2000) 99 98 97 96 95 93 **91 90 88**.

**CLOUDY BAY** *Marlborough, South Island, New Zealand* New Zealand's most successful winery. Cloudy Bay achieved cult status with the first release of its zesty, herbaceous Sauvignon Blanc★★ in 1985. New and very different Sauvignon Blanc Te Koko★★ is a rich, creamy, oak-matured, bottle-aged wine. Cloudy Bay also makes Chardonnay★★, a late-harvest Riesling★★, Pinot Noir★ and Pelorus★★, a high-quality old-style Champagne-method fizz. New non-vintage Pelorus★ is also good. Best years: (Sauvignon Blanc) (2001) **00 99 96**.

**J-F COCHE-DURY** *Meursault, Côte de Beaune, Burgundy, France* Jean-François Coche-Dury is a modest superstar, quietly turning out some of the finest wines on the COTE DE BEAUNE. His best wines are his CORTON-CHARLEMAGNE★★★ and MEURSAULT Perrières★★★, but everything he makes is excellent, even his BOURGOGNE Blanc★★. His red wines, from VOLNAY★★ and MONTHELIE★, tend to be significantly cheaper than the whites and should be drunk younger, too. Best years: (whites) (2000) 99 97 96 95 **92 90 89**.

**COCKBURN** *Port DOC, Douro, Portugal* Best known for its Special Reserve ruby, Cockburns has much more than that to offer. Cockburns Vintage★★ is stylishly cedary and Quinta dos Canais★★ is a fine single quinta, while the aged tawnies★★ are famously refined and nutty. Best years: (Vintage) 1997 94 **91 83 70 67 63 60 55**; (dos Canais) 1995 **92**.

**CODORNÍU** *Cava DO, Cataluña, Spain* The biggest Champagne-method sparkling wine company in the world. Anna de Codorníu★ and Jaume Codorníu★ are especially good but all the sparklers are better than the CAVA average. Drink young for freshness.

Codorníu also owns the RAIMAT estate in COSTERS DEL SEGRE and the still wine companies of Masía Bach in the PENEDES and Bodegas Bilbaínas in RIOJA, in addition to the quality-conscious California winery Artesa.

**COLCHAGUA, VALLE DE** *Valle del Rapel, Chile* RAPEL sub-region and home to many exciting estates including CALITERRA's Arboleda winery and the acclaimed Clos Apalta vineyard of CASA LAPOSTOLLE. Merlot and Carmenère both do very well here. San Fernando and Chimbarongo are the best-known sub-zones. Best producers: Bisquertt★★, CALITERRA★, CASA LAPOSTOLLE★★, Casa Silva★★, CONO SUR★★, MONTES★, MONT GRAS★.

**COLDSTREAM HILLS** *Yarra Valley, Victoria, Australia* Although South-corp purchased this formerly public company in 1996, James Halliday still holds the reins. Only YARRA VALLEY grapes are used, with the exception of the James Halliday export label. Pinot Noir★ is consistently good rather than great: sappy and smoky with cherry fruit and clever use of all-French oak. Chardonnay★ (Reserve Chardonnay★★) has subtlety and delicacy but real depth as well. Reserve Cabernet★ is good, though not always ripe. Best years: (Pinot Noir) **1998 97 96 94 92 91 88**.

**COLLARD** *Henderson, Auckland, New Zealand* White wine is the greatest strength of this small family winery, including Rothesay Chardonnay★ and Sauvignon Blanc★, HAWKE'S BAY Chardonnay★★, and MARLBOROUGH Chardonnay★, Sauvignon★ and Riesling★. The dry Chenin Blanc is one of New Zealand's better examples. Red wines are less interesting, with the exception of light, fruity Marlborough Queen Charlotte Pinot Noir. Best years: (Chardonnay) 2000 99 **98 96 94**.

**COLLI BOLOGNESI DOC** *Emilia, Italy* Wines from this zone in the Apennine foothills near Bologna were traditionally slightly sweet and frothy in style. Today some winemaking concessions have begun to be made to international taste, resulting in fine Cabernets★★ from Bonzara and Terre Rosse. Other good red wines are produced from Merlot, and increasing amounts of dry white wine are made from Sauvignon, Pignoletto and Pinot Bianco. Best producers: Bonzara (Cabernet★★, Merlot★), Gaggioli-Vigneto Bagazzana, San Vito, Terre Rosse★★, Vallona★. Best years: (reds) (2000) 99 98 **97 96 95 94 93**.

**COLLI EUGANEI DOC** *Veneto, Italy* The sheer hills south of Padova produce an array of DOC wines, still and sparkling, that are mainly taken lightly. One serious exception is the Vignalta estate, for Merlot-Cabernet blend Gemola★★. Best producers: Ca' Lustra★, Vignalta★★, Villa Sceriman. Best years: (reds) (2000) 99 98 **97 95 94 93 90**.

**COLLI ORIENTALI DEL FRIULI DOC** *Friuli-Venezia Giulia, Italy* North-east Italian DOC, covering 20 different types of wine. Best known for its sweet whites from Verduzzo in the Ramandolo sub-zone and the delicate Picolit, but it is the reds, from the indigenous Refosco and Schioppettino, as well as imports like Cabernet and dry whites, from Tocai, Ribolla, Pinot Bianco and Malvasia Istriana, that show how exciting the wines can be. Prices are high. Best producers: Bosco Romagno★, Ca' Ronesca★, Dario Coos★, Dorigo★, Dri★, Le Due Terre★★, L FELLUGA★★, Adriano Gigante★, Livon★, Meroi★, Miani★★, Rocca Bernarda★, Rodaro★, Ronchi di Cialla★, Ronchi di Manzano★★, Ronco delle Betulle★, Ronco del Gnemiz★★, Ronco dei Roseti★, Scubla★, Specogna★, Torre Rosazza★, La Viarte★, Le Vigne di Zamò★. Best years: (whites) (2000) 99 **98 97 96 95**.

**COLLI PIACENTINI DOC** *Emilia-Romagna, Italy* Home to some of Emilia-Romagna's best wines, this DOC covers 11 different types, the best of which are Cabernet Sauvignon and the red Gutturnio (an appealing blend of Barbera and Bonarda) as well as the medium-sweet white and bubbly Malvasia. Best producers: Barattieri (Vin Santo★), Campominosi, Fugazza★, Montesissa (Gutturnio Riserva Bosca del Sole★), Mossi★, Il Poggiarello (Sauvignon★), Romagnoli, La Stoppa★ (Cabernet★★), La Tosa (Cabernet Sauvignon★). Best years: (reds) (2000) 99 98 **97 96 95 94**.

**COLLINES RHODANIENNES, VIN DE PAYS DES** *Rhône Valley, France* Region between Vienne and Valence. The best wines are varietal Gamay and Syrah, although there are some good juicy Merlots, too. Best producers: COLOMBO★, P Gaillard★, Pochon★, ST-DESIRAT co-op, Tain-l'Hermitage co-op, Vernay★. Best years: (reds) (2000) **99 98 97**.

**COLLIO DOC** *Friuli-Venezia Giulia, Italy* These hills are the home of some of the country's best and most expensive dry white wines. The zone produces 19 types of wine, including 17 varietals, which range from the local Tocai and Malvasia Istriana to the more international. The best white and red wines are ageworthy. Best producers: Borgo

Conventi★, Borgo del Tiglio★★, La Castellada★, Fiegl★, L FELLUGA★★, Mario Felluga★, GRAVNER★★★, JERMANN★★, Edi Keber★, Renato Keber★★, Livon★, Matijaz Tercic★, Primosic★, Princic★, Puiatti★, Stanislao Radikon★, Russiz Superiore★, SCHIOPETTO★★, Castello di Spessa★, Subido di Monte★, Vazzoler★, Venica & Venica★, Villanova★, Villa Russiz★★. Best years: (whites) (2000) 99 98 **97 96 95 93 90**.

**COLLIOURE AC** *Roussillon, France*  This tiny fishing port tucked away in the Pyrenean foothills only a few miles from the Spanish border is also an AC, and makes a throat-warming red wine that is capable of aging for a decade but is marvellously aggressive when young. Best producers: (reds) Dom. de Baillaury★, Casa Blanca, Cellier des Templiers★, Clos des Paulilles★, Mas Blanc★★, la RECTORIE★★, la Tour Vieille★. Best years: (2000) 99 **98 96 95 94 93 91 90**.

**COLOMBARD**  In France, Colombard traditionally has been distilled to make Armagnac and Cognac, but is now emerging as a table wine grape in its own right, notably as a Vin de Pays des COTES DE GASCOGNE. At its best, it has a lovely, crisp acidity and fresh, aromatic fruit. The largest plantings of the grape are in CALIFORNIA, where it generally produces rather less distinguished wines. Australia has some fair examples, and South Africa can also produce attractive basic wines.

**JEAN-LUC COLOMBO** *Cornas AC, Rhône Valley, France*  Colombo is a modernist who has caused controversy with his criticism of traditional methods. His powerful, rich CORNAS has far less tannic grip than some. Top cuvées are les Ruchets★★ and the lush late-harvest la Louvée★★, made in tiny quantities. Among négociant wines now produced, CHATEAUNEUF-DU-PAPE Les Bartavelles★★ stands out. Also produces good COTES DU RHONE★ and vins de pays from the RHONE and elsewhere. Best years: (Cornas) (1999) 98 97 **95 94 91 90 88**.

**COLUMBIA CREST** *Washington State, USA*  Columbia Crest started life as a second label for CHATEAU STE MICHELLE but has evolved into a full-scale producer of good-value, good-quality wines. Grand Estates Merlot★ and Grand Estates Chardonnay★ are strong suits. For fruit intensity, drink both with 2–3 years' age. There is also a promising, intense Syrah★. Best years: (reds) (2000) (99) 98.

**COLUMBIA WINERY** *Columbia Valley AVA, Washington State, USA*  Under the guidance of David Lake MW, Columbia manages to produce an assortment of serviceable wines along with several standouts from Red Willow Vineyard. The best include deeply fruited, built-to-last Cabernet Sauvignon★ and a fruity, smoky-styled Syrah★★. Merlot★ has improved in recent vintages. Best years: (reds) (1999) 98 97 **95**.

**COMMANDARIA** *Cyprus*  Dark brown, treacly wine made from red Mavro and white Xynisteri grapes, sun-dried for 2 weeks before vinification and solera aging. Pretty decent stuff but only potentially one of the world's great rich wines. A lighter, drier style is also produced.

**COMTÉS RHODANIENS, VIN DE PAYS DES** *Rhône Valley and Savoie, France*  Most of the wines are red, from Syrah, Gamay, Cinsaut and Grenache, but the whites, particularly those from Viognier, Sauvignon Blanc and Chardonnay, are good too. Best producers: Rouoms co-op, ST-DESIRAT co-op★, Tain-l'Hermitage co-op, les Vignerons Ardèchois.

**CONCA DE BARBERÁ DO** *Cataluña, Spain* Quality wine area, but most of its production is sold to CAVA producers. Cool climate here is ideal and TORRES grows excellent Chardonnay, Cabernet Sauvignon, Pinot Noir, Merlot and Tempranillo. Best producers: Sanstravé (Gasset Chardonnay★), TORRES (Milmanda★★, Grans Muralles★★).

**CONCHA Y TORO** *Maipo, Chile* Chile's biggest winery has 3200ha (7900 acres) of vineyard resources and has recently secured the services of the brilliant Ignacio Recabarren (ex-VINA CASABLANCA), so look for fireworks from now on. Top whites include Amelia Chardonnay★, Casillero del Diablo Sauvignon Blanc★ and Trio Chardonnay★. Chardonnay is also the pick of the new Terrunyo range. Don Melchor Cabernet Sauvignon★★ leads the reds, along with vibrant Casillero del Diablo and Trio Merlots★. See also Almaviva.

**CONDRIEU AC** *Rhône Valley, France* Because of the demand for this wonderfully fragrant wine made entirely from Viognier, Condrieu is decidedly expensive. Unfortunately, quality is alarmingly variable. Condrieu is a sensation everyone should try at least once, but make sure you choose a good producer. Best drunk young. Best producers: G Barge★★, P & C Bonneford★★, L Chèze★★, COLOMBO★★, CUILLERON★★★, DELAS★★, P Dumazet★★, C Facchin★, GUIGAL★★★, Monteillet★★★, Niéro★★, A Paret★★, A Perret★★, C Pichon★★, R Rostaing★★, St-Cosme★★, G Vernay★★, F Villard★★★. Best years: 2000 99 **98 97 96 95**.

**CONO SUR** *Rapel, Chile* Dynamic sister winery to CONCHA Y TORO, whose Chimbarongo Pinot Noir★ put both grape and region on the Chilean map. The new, partly CASABLANCA-sourced 20 Barrels Pinot★ is more austere than the sweet, fleshy RAPEL versions. 20 Barrels Merlot★★ and Cabernet Sauvignon★★ are also very promising. Isla Negra offers easy-drinking blended wines.

**CH. LA CONSEILLANTE★★** *Pomerol AC, Bordeaux, France* Elegant, exotic, velvety wine that blossoms beautifully after 5 to 6 years but can age much longer. Best years: (2000) 99 98 96 95 **94 90 89 88 86 85**.

**CONSTANTIA WO** *South Africa* The historical heart of South African wine is now flying the flag of New World quality. The land originally granted to Simon van der Stel in 1685 was divided into 3 on his death: 2 estates, Groot Constantia and KLEIN CONSTANTIA, still exist, while BUITENVERWACHTING is partly carved from the third portion. Further along the same slopes STEENBERG and Uitsig are extending the valley's reputation for quality. A sixth, tiny winery, High Constantia, has recently started up. While the 2 original 'Constantia' estates continue tradition with some wines based on the famed 18th-century sweet Constantias, white varieties, especially Sauvignon, are thrusting this cool-climate area into the limelight. Best producers: BUITENVERWACHTING★★, KLEIN CONSTANTIA★★, STEENBERG★★.

**ALDO CONTERNO** *Barolo DOCG, Piedmont, Italy* Arguably BAROLO's finest producer. Good Dolcetto d'Alba★, excellent Barbera d'Alba Conca Tre Pile★★, a barrique-aged LANGHE Nebbiolo Il Favot★★, blended red Quartetto★★ and 2 Langhe Chardonnays, unoaked Printaniè and Bussia d'Or★, fermented and aged in new wood. Pride of the range, though, are his Barolos from the hill of Bussia. In top vintages produces Barolos Vigna Colonello★★★, Vigna Cicala★★★ and excellent Granbussia★★★, as well as a blended regular Barolo called Bussia

Soprana★★. All these Barolos, though accessible when young, need several years to show their true majesty, but retain a remarkable freshness. Best years: (Barolos) (1998) (97) 96 95 **93 90 89 88 86 85 82**.

**GIACOMO CONTERNO** *Barolo DOCG, Piedmont, Italy* Aldo's elder brother Giovanni has always taken a more traditional approach to winemaking. His flagship wine is BAROLO Monfortino★★★, but Barolo Cascina Francia★★★ is also superb. Powerful, earthy Dolcetto★ and Barbera★ are also made. Best years: (Monfortino) 1990 89 88 **87 86 85 82 79 78 74 71**.

**CONTINO** *Rioja DOC, Rioja, Spain* An estate on some of the finest RIOJA land, half-owned by CVNE. The wine, including a Reserva★, a single-vineyard Viña del Olivo★★ and an innovative Graciano★ varietal, is made by CVNE. Skipped the 92 and 93 vintages to solve cellar problems. Best years: **1996 95 94 86 85 82**.

**COONAWARRA** *South Australia* On a limestone belt thinly veneered with terra rossa soil, this flat patch of land can produce sublime Cabernet with blackcurrant leafy flavours and spicy Shiraz that age for many years. Chardonnay and Riesling can be good. An export-led boom has seen hundreds of new vineyards planted. Many are in darker, clay-based soils rather than the legendary terra rossa, and, in view of some disappointing light reds, I wonder if Coonawarra's great reputation is not at risk. Best producers: BOWEN★, HOLLICK★ (Ravenswood★★), KATNOOK★★, LECONFIELD★★, LINDEMANS★★, Majella★★, MILDARA★, ORLANDO★, PARKER★, PENFOLDS★★, PENLEY★★, PETALUMA★★★, ROSEMOUNT★★, Rouge Homme★, WYNNS★★.

**COOPERS CREEK** *Auckland, New Zealand* A specialist in wines from HAWKE'S BAY and MARLBOROUGH grapes, and successful producer of Chardonnay★, especially Swamp Road Chardonnay★, and tangy Marlborough Sauvignon Blanc★. Dry Riesling★ and Late Harvest Riesling★ styles are also good. A smart range of Reserve reds from Hawke's Bay includes complex Merlot★ and elegant Cabernet Sauvignon★. Best years: (Chardonnay) (2000) 99 **98 96**.

**CORBANS** *Auckland, Gisborne and Marlborough, New Zealand* New Zealand's second-largest wine company was bought by the largest, MONTANA, in 2000. Brand names include Cooks, Stoneleigh, Longridge, Huntaway and Robard & Butler. Stoneleigh Sauvignon Blanc★ and Rhine Riesling★★, both made with MARLBOROUGH fruit, capture the best of each variety and display their regional styles well. Private Bin Chardonnay★, Noble Rhine Riesling★★ and Merlot are good, small-production wines. There's a consistently good Champagne-method sparkler called Amadeus★. Flagship wines from top varieties and all major wine regions are now produced under the Cottage Block label. Best years: (Hawke's Bay reds) 2000 99 **98 96 95**.

**CORBIÈRES AC** *Languedoc, France* This AC now produces some of the best reds in the LANGUEDOC, with juicy fruit and more than a hint of wild hillside herbs. Excellent young, they age for years when from the best estates. White Corbières is adequate – drink as young as possible. Best producers: (reds) Baillat★, Bel Eveque★, Caraguilhes★, Ch.

Cascadais★, Étang des Colombes★, Fontsainte★, Grand Crès★, Grand Moulin★, Haut-Gléon★, Hélène★, l'Ille★, LASTOURS★, Mansenoble★, MONT TAUCH co-op★, les Palais★, St-Auriol★, Vaugelas★, VOULTE-GASPARETS★. Best years: (reds) (2000) 99 **98 96 95 93 91 90 89.**

**CORNAS AC** *Rhône Valley, France* Northern Rhône's up-and-coming star, whose wines are especially attractive since those of neighbouring HERMITAGE and COTE-ROTIE have spiralled upward in price in recent years. When young, the wine is a thick, impenetrable red, almost black in the ripest years. Most need 10 years' aging. Best producers: T Allemand★★, R Balthazar★★, CLAPE★★, COLOMBO★★, Courbis★★, DELAS★★, E & J Durand★★, JABOULET★★, J Lemencier★★, LIONNET★★, Tain l'Hermitage co-op★, Tardieu-Laurent★★, Dom. du Tunnel★★, VERSET★★, A Voge★★. Best years: (2000) 99 98 97 96 95 **94 91 90 89 88 85 83 80 78.**

**CORSE AC, VIN DE** *Corsica, France* Overall AC for Corsica with 5 superior sub-regions: Calvi, Cap Corse, Figari, Porto Vecchio and Sartène. PATRIMONIO and AJACCIO are entitled to their own ACs. Things are improving on this lovely island, but slowly. The most distinctive wines, mainly red, come from local grapes (Nielluccio and Sciacarello for reds, Vermentino for whites). There are some rich sweet Muscats – especially from MUSCAT DE CAP CORSE. Best producers: Clos Culombu★, Clos Landry★, Leccia★, Maestracci★, Péraldi★, Renucci★, Torraccia, UVAL.

**CORSICA** *France* This Mediterranean island has made some pretty dull and undistinguished wines in the past. The last decade has seen a welcome trend toward quality, with co-ops and local growers investing in better equipment and planting noble grape varieties – such as Syrah, Merlot, Cabernet Sauvignon and Mourvèdre for reds, and Chardonnay and Sauvignon Blanc for whites – to complement the local Nielluccio, Sciacarello and Vermentino. Whites and rosés are pleasant for drinking young; reds are more exciting and can age for 3–4 years. See also Ajaccio, Corse, l'Île de Beauté, Muscat de Cap Corse, Patrimonio.

**CORTESE** White grape variety planted primarily in south-eastern PIEDMONT in Italy; it can produce good, fairly acidic, dry whites. Sometimes labelled simply as Cortese del Piemonte, it is also used for GAVI.

**CORTON AC** *Grand Cru, Côte de Beaune, Burgundy, France* This is the only red Grand Cru in the COTE DE BEAUNE and ideally the wines should have the burliness and savoury power of the top COTE DE NUITS wines, combined with the more seductively perfumed fruit of Côte de Beaune. Red Corton should take 10 years to mature, but too many modern examples never make it. Very little white Corton is made. Best producers: Bonneau du Martray★★, CHANDON DE BRIAILLES★★★, Dubreuil-Fontaine★★, Guyon★★, JADOT★★★, Dom. LEROY★★★, MEO-CAMUZET★★, Rapet★★, Senard★, TOLLOT-BEAUT★★★. Best years: (reds) (2000) 99 98 97 96 95 **93 91 90 89 88.**

**CORTON-CHARLEMAGNE AC** *Grand Cru, Côte de Beaune, Burgundy, France* Corton-Charlemagne, at the top of the famous Corton hill, is the largest of Burgundy's white Grands Crus. It can produce some of the most impressive white Burgundies – rich, buttery and nutty with a fine mineral quality. The best show their real worth only at 10 years or more. Best producers: Bonneau du Martray★★★, BOUCHARD PERE ET FILS★★★, CHANDON DE BRIAILLES★★★, COCHE-DURY★★★, DROUHIN★★, FAIVELEY★★, V GIRARDIN★★★, JADOT★★, LATOUR★★★, Rapet★★, Rollin★★, ROUMIER★★, TOLLOT-BEAUT★★★, VERGET★★. Best years: (2000) 99 98 97 96 95 **92 90 89 88**.

**CH. COS D'ESTOURNEL★★★** *St-Estèphe AC, 2ème Cru Classé, Haut-Médoc, Bordeaux, France* Top name in ST-ESTEPHE, and one of the leading châteaux in all Bordeaux. Despite a high proportion of Merlot (just under 40%), the wine is classically made for aging and usually needs 10 years to show really well. Recent vintages have been dark, brooding and packed with long-term potential. Second wine: les Pagodes de Cos. Best years: (2000) 99 98 97 96 95 **94 93 90 89 88 86 85 83 82**.

**COSTANTI** *Brunello di Montalcino DOCG, Tuscany, Italy* One of the original, highly respected Montalcino estates, run by Andrea Costanti, making first-rate BRUNELLO★★ and Rosso★★, as well as a tasty partially barrique-aged Sangiovese called Vermiglio★. The archetypal Brunello of this zone is austere, elegant and long-lived, epitomized by the Costanti Riserva★★★. New Calbello wines from the hill of Montosoli include excellent Rosso★★ and promising Merlot-Cabernet blend Ardingo★★. Best years: (Brunello) 1995 94 93 **91** 90 **88 86 85 82**.

**COSTERS DEL SEGRE DO** *Cataluña, Spain* Originally created to cope with the huge RAIMAT estate near Lérida in western CATALUNA. A great array of grape varieties is grown, with the accent on French varieties. Quality is generally good and prices moderate. Best producers: Celler de Cantonella★★, Castell del Remei★★, RAIMAT (Mas Castell Cabernet Sauvignon★). Best years: (reds) (1999) 98 **96 95 94**.

**COSTIÈRES DE NÎMES AC** *Languedoc, France* A large improving AC between Nîmes and Arles in the Gard. The reds are generally bright and perfumed, while the rosés are good young gluggers. Only a little white is produced, usually tasty modern versions of Marsanne and Roussanne. Best producers: l'Amarine★, Belle-Coste, Grande-Cassagne★, Mas des Bressades★, Mas Carlot (Paul Blanc★), Mourgues du Grès★, Nages★, la Tuilerie★. Best years: (2000) 99 **98 96 95 94 93 91 90**.

**CÔTE DE BEAUNE** *Côte d'Or, Burgundy, France* Southern part of the COTE D'OR; beginning at the hill of Corton, north of the town of BEAUNE, the Côte de Beaune progresses south as far as les Maranges, with white wines gradually taking over from red. The Côte de Beaune AC refers only to rare reds and whites from the vineyards on the hill to the west of the town of Beaune.

**CÔTE DE BEAUNE-VILLAGES AC** *Côte de Beaune, Burgundy, France* Red-wine AC covering 16 villages, such as AUXEY-DURESSES, LADOIX, MARANGES. Most producers use their own village name, but if the wine is a blend from several villages it is sold as Côte de Beaune-Villages. It can also cover the red-wine production of mainly white-wine villages such as MEURSAULT. Best producers: DROUHIN★, J-P Fichet★, JADOT★. Best years: 1999 **98 97 96 95**.

**CÔTE DE BROUILLY AC** *Beaujolais, Burgundy, France* A steep hill in the middle of the BROUILLY AC, producing extra-ripe grapes. The wine is good young but can age well for several years. Best producers: Conroy★, H Fessy★, Geoffray★★, Lacondemine★, Pivot★, O Ravier★, Ch. Thivin★★, Viornery★, la Vôute des Crozes. Best years: (2000) **99 98**.

113

**CÔTE CHALONNAISE** See Bourgogne-Côte Chalonnaise.

**CÔTE DE NUITS** *Côte d'Or, Burgundy, France* This is the northern part of the great CÔTE D'OR and is *not* an AC. Almost entirely red wine country, the vineyards start in the southern suburbs of Dijon and continue south in a narrow swathe to below the town of NUITS-ST-GEORGES. The villages are some of the greatest wine names in the world – GEVREY-CHAMBERTIN, VOUGEOT and VOSNE-ROMANÉE etc.

**CÔTE DE NUITS-VILLAGES AC** *Côte de Nuits, Burgundy, France* This appellation is specific to the villages of Corgoloin, Comblanchien and Prémeaux in the south of the Côte de Nuits and Brochon and FIXIN in the north. Although not much seen, the wines (mostly red) are often good, not very deep in colour but with a nice cherry fruit. Best producers: (reds) D Bachelet★★, Chopin-Groffier★★, JAYER-GILLES★, Gérard Julien★, RION★★, P Rossignol★. Best years: (reds) (2000) 99 98 **97 96 95**.

**CÔTE D'OR** *Burgundy, France* Europe's most northern great red wine area and also the home of some of the world's best dry white wines. The name, meaning 'golden slope', refers to a 48-km (30-mile) stretch between Dijon and Chagny which divides into the CÔTE DE NUITS in the north and the CÔTE DE BEAUNE in the south.

**CÔTE ROANNAISE AC** *Loire Valley, France* In the upper Loire; the nearest large town is Lyon, the capital of BEAUJOLAIS, and so it is logical that the chief grape variety here is Gamay. Most of the wine produced is red and should generally be drunk young. Best producers: J-C Chaucesse, Demon★, Lapandéry, M Lutz, Montroussier, J Plasse, R Serol, P & M Vial.

**CÔTE-RÔTIE AC** *Rhône Valley, France* The Côte-Rôtie, or 'roasted slope', produces one of France's greatest red wines. The Syrah grape bakes to super-ripeness on these steep slopes, and the small amount of white Viognier sometimes included in the blend gives an unexpected exotic fragrance in a red wine. Lovely young, it is better aged for 10 years. Best producers: Gilles Barge★★, Bonnefond★★, Dom. de Bonserine★★, B Burgaud★★, Clusel-Roch★★, Y CUILLERON★★, DELAS★★, Duclaux★★, Y Gangloff★★, V Gasse★★, J-M Gérin★★, GUIGAL★★, JAMET★★★, JASMIN★★, R Rostaing★★, M Ogier★★, Tardieu-Laurent★★★, F Villard★★. Best years: (2000) 99 98 97 96 95 **94 91 90 89** 87 85 83 78.

**COTEAUX D'AIX-EN-PROVENCE AC** *Provence, France* This AC was the first in the south to acknowledge that Cabernet Sauvignon can enormously enhance the traditional, local grape varieties such as Grenache, Cinsaut, Mourvèdre, Syrah and Carignan. The red wines produced here can age. Some quite good fresh rosé is made, while the white wines, mostly still traditionally made, are pleasant but hardly riveting. Best producers: (reds) Ch. Bas★, les Bastides★, Dom des Béates★★, Calissanne★, Fonscolombe★, Mas Ste-Berthe, Revelette★, Salen, Ch. du Seuil, la Vallongue, Vignelaure★; (whites) Beaupré, Calissanne★, Fonscolombe, Revelette, Ch. du Seuil. Best years: (2000) 99 **98 97 96 95 94 93 91 90**.

**COTEAUX DE L'ARDÈCHE, VIN DE PAYS DES** *Rhône Valley, France* Wines from the southern part of the Ardèche. Look out for the increasingly good varietal red wines made from Cabernet Sauvignon, Syrah, Merlot or Gamay and dry, fresh white wines from Chardonnay, Viognier or Sauvignon Blanc. Best producers: Colombier, Louis LATOUR, Pradel, ST-DESIRAT CO-Op, les Vignerons Ardèchois.

**COTEAUX DE L'AUBANCE AC** *Loire Valley, France* Smallish AC parallel to the COTEAUX DU LAYON AC. It is now enjoying a renaissance for its sweet or semi-sweet white wines made from Chenin Blanc. Sweet styles can improve for 10–25 years. Best producers: Bablut★★, Charbotières★, Haute-Perche★, Montgilet★★, RICHOU★★, Rochelles, la Varière★. Best years: (2000) 99 **97 96 95 93 90**.

**COTEAUX CHAMPENOIS AC** *Champagne, France* The AC for still wines from Champagne. Fairly acid with a few exceptions, notably from BOUZY and Ay. The best age for 5 years or more. Best producers: Bara★, BOLLINGER★, Egly-Ouriet★, LAURENT-PERRIER, Joseph PERRIER, Ch. de Saran★ (MOET & CHANDON). Best years: (1998) 96 **95 90 89**.

**COTEAUX DU LANGUEDOC AC** *Languedoc, France* A large and increasingly successful AC situated between Montpellier and Narbonne in the LANGUEDOC, producing over 40 million bottles of beefy red and tasty rosé wines. Eleven of the best villages (crus) can now add their own names to the AC name, including Cabrières, la CLAPE, Montpeyroux, PIC ST-LOUP, St-Drézery and St-Georges-d'Orques. Best producers: Abbaye de Valmagne, l'Aiguelière★★, Auphilhac★, Calage★, Cazeneuve★, Clavel★, la Coste★, l'HORTUS★, Jougla★, Lascaux★, MAS BRUGUIERE★, Mas des Chimères★,

MAS JULLIEN★, Mas de Lavabre★★, Mas de Mortiès★, PEYRE ROSE★★, Prieuré de St-Jean de Bébian★★, Puech-Haut★, St-Martin de la Garrigue★, Terre Megère. Best years: (2000) 99 98 **96 95 93 91**.

**COTEAUX DU LAYON AC** *Loire Valley, France* Sweet wine from the Layon Valley south of Angers. The wine is made from Chenin Blanc grapes that, ideally, are attacked by noble rot. In great years like 1990 and 89, and from a talented grower, this can be one of the world's exceptional sweet wines. Seven villages are entitled to use the Coteaux du Layon-Villages AC (one of the best is Chaume) and put their own name on the label, and these wines are definitely underpriced for the quality. Two sub-areas, BONNEZEAUX and QUARTS DE CHAUME, have their own ACs. Best producers: P Baudouin★★★, Baumard★★, Bidet★, Breuil★, Cady★★, P Delesvaux★★★, Forges★★, Guimonière★★, Ogereau★, Pierre-Bise★, J Pithon★, Plaisance★, J Renou★★, Roulerie★★, Sablonettes★★, Sauveroy★, Soucherie★★, Yves Soulez★★, Touche Noire★. Best years: (2000) 99 **97** 96 **95 90 89 88 85 83 76**.

**COTEAUX DU LYONNAIS AC** *Burgundy, France* Good, light, BEAUJOLAIS-style reds and a few whites and rosés from scattered vineyards between Villefranche and Lyon. Drink young.

**COTEAUX DU TRICASTIN AC** *Rhône Valley, France* From the southern Drôme these are light, fresh reds and rosés with attractive juicy fruit. Only a little of the nutty white is made but is worth looking out for. Drink it young. Best producers: Grangeneuve★, Lônes, St-Luc, la Tour d'Elyssas, Vieux Micocoulier. Best years: (2000) 99 **98 97 96 95**.

**COTEAUX VAROIS AC** *Provence, France* An area to watch with new plantings of classic grapes. Best producers: Alysses★, Bremond, Calisse★, Deffends★, Garbelle, Routas★, Ch. St-Estève, St-Jean-le-Vieux★, St-Jean-de-Villecroze★, Triennes★. Best years: (2000) 99 **98 97 96 95 94 93 91 90**.

**CÔTES DE BERGERAC AC** *South-West France* The AC covers good-quality reds made from the same grapes as BERGERAC AC but with a higher minimum alcohol level. Côtes de Bergerac Moelleux AC is the name for sweet wines. Best producers: Bélingard, les Marnières, TOUR DES GENDRES★, Tour des Verdots★. Best years: (2000) 98 **96 95 94 90**.

**CÔTES DE BLAYE AC** *Bordeaux, France* The main AC for white wines from the right bank of the Gironde estuary. Almost all the best whites are now dry. Drink young. Best producer: Cave de Marcillac.

**CÔTES DE BOURG AC** *Bordeaux, France* Mainly a red wine area to the south of the COTES DE BLAYE, where the best producers and the local co-op at Tauriac make great efforts. The reds are earthy but blackcurrant and can age for 6–10 years. Very little white is made, most of which is dry and dull. Best producers: Barbe, Brulesécaille★, Bujan, FALFAS★, Fougas★, Guerry, Haut-Guiraud, Haut-Macô★, Macay, Mercier, Nodoz★, ROC DE CAMBES★★, Rousset, Tauriac co-op, Tayac★. Best years: (2000) 99 98 **96 95 94 90 89 88**.

**CÔTES DE CASTILLON AC** *Bordeaux, France* Red wine area just to the east of ST-EMILION. As the price of decent red Bordeaux climbs ever upward, Côtes de Castillon wines have remained a good, reasonably priced alternative – a little earthy but full and round. Depending on the vintage the wine is enjoyable between 3 and 10 years after the vintage. Best producers: Domaine de l'A★, Aiguilhe★, Belcier★, Cantegrive, Cap-de-Faugères★, Clos de l'Eglise★, Côte-Montpezat★, Lapeyronie★, Pitray, Poupille★, Robin★, Vieux-Ch.-Champs-de-Mars. Best years: (2000) 99 98 **96 95 94 90 89 88 86 85**.

**CÔTES DE DURAS AC** *South-West France* AC between ENTRE-DEUX-MERS and BERGERAC in the Lot-et-Garonne, with 2 very active co-ops which offer extremely good, fresh, grassy reds and whites from traditional BORDEAUX grapes. Drink the wines young. Best producers: Amblard, Cours, Clos du Cadaret, Duras co-op, Grand-Mayne, Landerrouat co-op, Lafon, Laulan. Best years: (reds) (2000) **98 96 95 94**.

**CÔTES DE FRANCS** See Bordeaux-Côtes de Francs.

**CÔTES DU FRONTONNAIS AC** *South-West France* From north of Toulouse, some of the most distinctive reds – often superb and positively silky in texture – of South-West France. Négrette is the chief grape, but too many producers are now coarsening it with Cabernet, which rather defeats the object. Best producers: Baudare, Bellevue-la-Forêt★, la Colombière, Ferran, Flotis, Laurou, Montauriol, la Palme, Plaisance, le Roc★, St-Louis. Best years: (2000) 99 **98 97 96 95 94**.

**CÔTES DE GASCOGNE, VIN DE PAYS DES** *South-West France* Mainly white wines from the Gers *département*. This is Armagnac country, but the tangy-fresh, fruity table wines are tremendously good – especially when you consider that they were condemned as unfit for anything but distillation a decade ago. Best producers: Aurin, Brumont, GRASSA★, Union des Producteurs PLAIMONT★, Hugh Ryman, Dom. de Joy, Dom. St-Lannes.

**CÔTES DU JURA AC** *Jura, France* The regional AC for Jura covers a wide variety of wines, including local specialities *vin jaune* and *vin de paille*. The Savagnin makes strong-tasting whites and Chardonnay is used for some good dry whites and Champagne-method fizz. The reds and rosés can be good when made from Pinot Noir, but with the local Poulsard and Trousseau the wines can be a bit weird. Drink young.

Best producers: Ch. d'Arlay★★, Berthet-Bondet★★, Bourdy★★, Chalandard★, Clavelin★, Durand-Perron★★, Ch. de l'Étoile★, Joly★, A Labet★★, Maclé★★, Reverchon★, Rijckaert★, Rolet★★, A & M Tissot★. Best years: (whites) (2000) 99 98 **97 96 95 94 92 90** 89 88 86 85.

**CÔTES DU LUBÉRON AC** *Rhône Valley, France* Wine production is dominated by the co-ops east of Avignon. The light, easy wines are refreshing and for drinking young. Best producers: Ch. la Canorgue, Ch. de l'Isolette★, Val Joanis, Ch. de Mille, la Sable, la Tour-d'Aigues co-op, Vendran. Best years: (2000) **99 98 97 96 95**.

**CÔTES DU MARMANDAIS AC** *South-West France* Marmandais producers aim to make Bordeaux lookalikes, and the red wines achieve a fair amount of success. Syrah is also permitted. Best producers: Beaulieu, Cave de Beaupuy, Chantecoucou, Cocumont co-op.

**CÔTES DE MONTRAVEL AC** See Montravel AC.

**CÔTES DE PROVENCE AC** *Provence, France* Large AC mainly for fruity reds and rosés to drink young, showing signs of improvement in recent years. Whites are mostly forgettable. Best producers: Barbeyrolles, la Bernarde★, Commanderie de Bargemore★, Commanderie de Peyrassol★, la Courtade★★, Coussin Ste-Victoire★, Dragon★, Esclans★, l'Estandon, Féraud★, Gavoty★, Hauts de St-Jean, Maravenne★, Mentone, Minuty★, Ott★, Pampelonne, Rabiega★, Réal Martin★, RICHEAUME★, Rimauresq★, les Maîtres Vignerons de St-Tropez, Sorin★, Vannières★. Best years: (reds) (2000) 99 **98 97 96 95 94 93 91 90**.

**CÔTES DU RHÔNE AC** *Rhône Valley, France* The general appellation for the whole RHONE VALLEY. Over 90% is red and rosé mainly from Grenache with some Cinsaut, Syrah, Carignan and Mourvèdre to add lots of warm, spicy southern personality. Modern winemaking has revolutionized the style, and today's wines are generally juicy, spicy and easy to drink, ideally within 2 years. Most wine is made by the co-ops and there are now many examples with depth and structure. Best producers: (reds) Beaurenard, A Brunel★, CLAPE★, COLOMBO★, Coudoulet de Beaucastel★, Cros de la Mure★, Fonsalette★, FONT DE MICHELLE★, Gramenon★★, GRAND MOULAS★, Grand Prebois★, GUIGAL★, JABOULET, la Janasse★, Lionnet★, J-M Lombard★, Mont-Redon, la Mordoreé★, l'ORATOIRE ST-MARTIN★, REMEJEANNE★, M Richaud★, Ste-Anne★, Santa Duc★, Tardieu-Laurent★, Tours★; (whites) CLAPE★, P Gaillard★, Pélaquié, REMEJEANNE★, Ste-Anne★. Best years: (reds) (2000) **99 98 97 95 94 93 90**.

**CÔTES DU RHÔNE-VILLAGES AC** *Rhône Valley, France* AC for wines with a higher minimum alcohol content than straightforward COTES DU RHONE, covering 16 villages in the southern Rhône that have traditionally made superior wine (especially Cairanne, Séguret, Valréas, Sablet, Visan, Chusclan, Laudun). Almost all the best are spicy reds that can age well. Best producers: Achiary★, Alary★, l'Ameillaud★, Amouriers★, Beaurenard★, Bressy-Masson★, Daniel Brusset★, Charbonnière★, Combe★, Cros de la Mure★, les Goubert, Gourt de Mautens★★, Gramenon★, GRAND MOULAS★, les Hautes Cances★, JABOULET★, la Janasse★, l'ORATOIRE ST-MARTIN★, Pélaquié★, Piaugier★, Rabasse-Charavin★, M Richaud★, ST-GAYAN★, Ste-Anne★, la Soumade★, Tours★, Trapadis★, Trignon★, Verquière★. Best years: (2000) 99 **98 97 95 94 93 90**.

**CÔTES DU ROUSSILLON AC** *Roussillon, France* Large AC covering much of ROUSSILLON. Mainly red wine; most of the white is unmemorable. Production is dominated by the co-ops, some enlightened, but estates are making their presence felt. Best producers: (reds) Vignerons Catalans, Casenove★, CAZES, Chênes★, J-L COLOMBO★, Ferrer-Ribière★, Forca Réal, GAUBY★★, Jau, Joliette, Laporte, Mas Crémat★, Piquemal, Rivesaltes co-op, Salvat, Sarda-Malet★. Best years: (reds) (2000) 99 **98 96 95**.

**CÔTES DU ROUSSILLON-VILLAGES AC** *Roussillon, France* AC for red wines from the best sites in the northern part of CÔTES DU ROUSSILLON. Villages Caramany, Latour-de-France, Lesquerde and Tautavel may add their own name, but wines from Caramany and Latour have been poor lately. Best producers: Agly co-op, Vignerons Catalans, CAZES★, Chênes★, Clos des Fées, Fontanel, Forca Réal, Gardiès★, GAUBY★★, Jau, Joliette, Mas Crémat★, Schistes. Best years: (reds) (2000) 99 98 **96 95**.

**CÔTES DE ST-MONT VDQS** *South-West France* A good VDQS for firm but fruity reds and some fair rosés and dry whites. Best producer: Union des Producteurs PLAIMONT.

**CÔTES DU TARN, VIN DE PAYS DES** *South-West France* Wines from around Albi. Sharp but fruity whites, and young reds are enjoyable too. Best producers: Chaumet-Lagrange, Gayrel, Labastide-de-Levis co-op.

**CÔTES DE THAU, VIN DE PAYS DES** *Languedoc, France* Wines from the shores of Lake Thau to the west of the Mediterranean town of Sète. Whites are often surprisingly good for the MIDI. Best producers: Gaujal, Genson, UCA Vignerons Garrigues, Pinet co-op, Pomérols co-op.

**CÔTES DE THONGUE, VIN DE PAYS DES** *Languedoc, France* Mainly red wines, from north-east of Béziers. Most are dull quaffers made from Carignan, but recent plantings of classic grapes by dynamic estates can produce excellent results. Best producers: l'Arjolle★, Bellevue, les Chemins de Bassac, Condamine l'Evêque, Croix Belle.

**CÔTES DU VENTOUX AC** *Rhône Valley, France* Increasingly successful AC, with vineyards on the slopes of Mt Ventoux in the RHÔNE VALLEY near Carpentras. When the wine is well made from a single estate or blended by a serious merchant, the reds can have a lovely juicy fruit, or in the case of JABOULET and Pesquié, some real stuffing. There is only a little white. Best producers: Anges★, Brusset, Champ-Long, JABOULET, Pesquié★, Union des Caves du Ventoux, la Vieille Ferme.

**CÔTES DU VIVARAIS VDQS** *Rhône Valley, France* In the Ardèche and northern Gard, typical southern Rhône grapes (Grenache, Cinsaut, Carignan) produce light, fresh reds and rosés for drinking young, but plantings of classic varieties (Cabernet Sauvignon and Syrah) are producing deep-flavoured wines of surprising quality and irresistible price. Best producers: Chais du Vivarais, Vigier, les Vignerons Ardèchois.

**COTNARI** *Romania* A hilly region close to the border with Moldova, whose warm mesoclimate is well suited to the development of noble rot. Romania's finest sweet wines are made here using a blend of Grasa, Tamîîoasă, Francusa and Fetească Albă grapes.

**CÔTTO, QUINTA DO** *Douro DOC and Port DOC, Douro, Portugal* Table wine expert in Lower DOURO. Basic red and white Quinta do Côtto are reasonable, and Grande Escolha★★ is one of Portugal's best reds, oaky and powerful when young, rich and cedary when mature. Best years: (Grande Escolha) (1997) 95 **94 90 87 85 82**.

**COULY-DUTHEIL** *Chinon, Loire Valley, France* Large merchant house responsible for 10% of the CHINON AC. Uses its own vineyards for the best wines, particularly Clos de l'Écho★ and Clos de l'Olive★. Top négociant blend is la Baronnie Madeleine★, which combines delicious raspberry fruit with a considerable capacity to age. Also sells a range of other Touraine wines. Best years: (2000) 99 97 **96 95 90 89 86 85.**

**PIERRE COURSODON** *St-Joseph AC, Rhône Valley, France* Family-owned domaine producing rich ST-JOSEPH from very old vines. The red wines★ need up to 5 years to show all the magnificent cassis and truffle and violety richness of the best Rhône reds, especially the top wine, called la Sensonne★★. Whites are good too. Best years: (reds) (1999) 98 97 **96 95 94 90 89 88 86 85 83.**

**CH. COUTET★★** *Barsac AC, 1er Cru Classé, Bordeaux, France* BARSAC'S largest Classed Growth property has languished behind its neighbour CLIMENS for a generation, but has shown great improvement in recent years. Extraordinarily intense Cuvée Madame★★★ is made in exceptional years. Best years: 1999 98 97 96 95 **90 89 88.**

**COWRA** *New South Wales, Australia* Very promising district with a reliable warm climate and good water supplies for irrigation. It produces soft, peachy Chardonnay and spicy, cool-tasting Shiraz. Best producers: Arrowfield★, Cowra Estate, Richmond Grove, ROTHBURY★, Charles Sturt University★, Windowrie Estate.

**CRAGGY RANGE** *Hawke's Bay, North Island, New Zealand* Exciting new venture funded by a wealthy American family and managed by brilliant viticulturist Steve Smith. Extensive vineyards in HAWKE'S BAY and MARLBOROUGH are being established. So far contract grapes have been used to make some impressive wines: ripe, pungent Sauvignon Blanc★, tangy Raupara Road Riesling★ and vibrant Strugglers Flat Pinot Noir★ all come from Marlborough grapes. Elegant Apley Road Vineyard Chardonnay★ is from grapes grown in Hawke's Bay.

**CRASTO, QUINTA DO** *Douro DOC and Port DOC, Douro, Portugal* Well-situated property belonging to the Roquette family. Very good traditional LBV★★ and Vintage★★ port and thoroughly enjoyable red DOURO★, especially Reserva★★ and varietal Touriga Nacional★★. Best years: (port) 1997 **95 94**; (red) 1997 **96 95 94.**

**CRÉMANT D'ALSACE AC** *Alsace, France* Good Champagne-method sparkling wine from Alsace, usually made from Pinot Blanc. Reasonable quality, if not great value for money. Best producers: BLANCK★, Dopff au Moulin★, Dopff & Irion, J Gross★, KUENTZ-BAS, Muré★, Ostertag★, P Sparr★, A Stoffel★, TURCKHEIM co-op★.

**CRÉMANT DE BOURGOGNE AC** *Burgundy, France* Most Burgundian Crémant is white and is made either from Chardonnay alone or blended with Pinot Noir. The result, especially in ripe years, can be full, soft, almost honey-flavoured – if you give the wine the 2–3 years' aging needed for mellowness to develop. The best rosé comes from Chablis and Auxerre in northern Burgundy. Best producers: A Delorme, Lucius-Grégoire, Parigot-Richard, Simonnet-Febvre; and the co-ops at Bailly★ (the best for rosé), Lugny★, St-Gengoux-de-Scissé and Viré.

**CRÉMANT DE DIE AC** *Rhône Valley, France* AC for traditional-method fizz made entirely from the Clairette Blanche grape. Less aromatic than CLAIRETTE DE DIE.

**CRÉMANT DE JURA AC** *Jura, France* AC created in 1995 for fizz from Jura. Annual production is around 2 million bottles, largely Chardonnay-based, with Poulsard for the pinks.

**CRÉMANT DE LIMOUX AC** *Languedoc-Roussillon, France* Sparkling wine made from a blend of Chardonnay, Chenin Blanc and Mauzac; the wines generally have more complexity than straight BLANQUETTE DE LIMOUX. Drink young. Best producers: l'Aigle★, Antech, Fourn★, Guinot, Laurens★, Martinolles★, SIEUR D'ARQUES★, Valent.

**CRÉMANT DE LOIRE AC** *Loire Valley, France* The AC for Champagne-method sparkling wine in Anjou and Touraine, with more fruit and yeast character than those of VOUVRAY and SAUMUR. The wine is good to drink as soon as it is released and can be excellent value. Best producers: des Baumard★, Berger Frères★, Brizé★, la Gabillière, Girault, GRATIEN & MEYER★, Lambert★, Langlois-Château★, Dom. Michaud★, Oisly-et-Thésée co-op★, Passavant★.

**CRIOTS-BÂTARD-MONTRACHET AC** See Bâtard-Montrachet AC.

**LUCIEN CROCHET** *Sancerre AC, Loire Valley, France* Textbook SANCERRE, both red and white. Best are the domaine-bottled wines, including ripe, perfumed red la Croix du Roy★ and zesty, gooseberryish white le Chêne★. Premium Cuvée Prestige white and red (both ★★), made from late-harvested old vines, have the depth and structure to age. Best years: (Cuvée Prestige) 2000 **99 97 96 95**.

**CROFT** *Port DOC, Douro, Portugal* Vintage ports★★ can be deceptively light in their youth, but they develop into subtle, elegant wines. Single-quinta Quinta da Roêda★★ is fine in the most recent vintages. Best years: (Vintage) 1994 91 **77 70 66 63 60 45 35 27**; (Roêda) 1997 95.

**CROZES-HERMITAGE AC** *Rhône Valley, France* The largest of the northern Rhône ACs. Ideally, the reds should have a full colour and a strong, meaty but rich flavour. You can drink them young but in ripe years the wine improves greatly for 2–5 years from a hillside site. The best whites are fresh, clean and racy. In general drink white Crozes young before the floral perfume disappears. Best producers: (reds) Albert Belle★, CHAPOUTIER★ (Varonnières★), B Chave★, Colombier★, Laurent Combier★ (Clos des Grives★), DELAS★, O Dumaine★, Fayolle★, GRAILLOT★★, JABOULET★ (Thalabert★★), Pavillon★, Pochon★, Remizières★, G Robin★, M Sorrel★, Tardieu-Laurent★★; (whites) B Chave★, Colombier★, Laurent Combier★, DELAS★, O Dumaine★, Ferraton★, GRAILLOT★★, JABOULET★, Pochon★, Pradelle★, M Sorrel★. Best years: (reds) (2000) 99 **98 97 96 95 94 91 90 89 88**; (whites) (2000) **99 98 97 96 95 94**.

**HANS CRUSIUS** *Traisen, Nahe, Germany* Dr Peter Crusius produces Rieslings from the Traiser Bastei★ and Schlossböckelheimer Felsenberg★ vineyards which manage to be rich, clean and flinty all at the same time. Best years: (1999) 98 96 **95 94 93 98 83**.

**YVES CUILLERON** *Condrieu AC, Rhône Valley, France* With wines like Cuilleron's you can understand CONDRIEU's fame and perhaps even forgive it its high price. Les Chaillets Vieilles Vignes★★★ is everything wine made from Viognier should be: opulent and rich, with perfumed honey and apricot aromas. La Petite Côte★★ is also exceptional, and the late-harvest les Ayguets★★★ is an extraordinary sweet whirl of dried apricots, honey and barley sugar. Condrieu's young star also turns a hand to ST-JOSEPH reds★★ and whites★★ and tiny quantities of ripe, dark, spicy COTE-ROTIE★★. Best years: (Condrieu) **1999 98 97 96 95**.

**CULLEN** *Margaret River, Western Australia* One of the original and best MARGARET RIVER vineyards, run by the Cullen women: winemaker Vanya and her mother Diana. The Chardonnay★★ is one of the region's richest and most complex; the Sauvignon-Semillon blend★★, also complex, has a long-lasting, nutty aftertaste. The Cabernet-Merlot★★★ is gloriously soft, deep and scented; prospects for this wine have risen even higher now the Reserve bottling has been discontinued. Best years: (reds) 1998 97 **96 95 94 92 91 90 86 84 82**.

**CURICÓ, VALLE DE** *Valle Central, Chile* Most of the big producers here have planted Cabernet Sauvignon, Merlot, Chardonnay and Sauvignon Blanc. The long growing season provides good fruit concentration. Best producers: Canepa★, Echeverría★, MONTES★, SAN PEDRO★, Miguel TORRES★, VALDIVIESO★, Veramonte★.

**CUVAISON** *Napa Valley AVA, California, USA* Cuvaison built a reputation for brooding red wines in the 1970s. Now, in a more modern style, it produces tasty, focused Merlot★, sound Cabernet Sauvignon★ and good but less thrilling Chardonnay. Most should be drunk young. Best years: (Merlot) (1999) 98 97 **96 95 94 92 91 90 88**.

**CVNE** *Rioja DOC, Rioja, Spain* Compañía Vinícola del Norte de España is the full name of this firm, but it's usually known as 'coonay'. Viña Real★ is one of RIOJA's only remaining well-oaked whites; the Viña Real Reserva★ and Gran Reserva★ reds can be rich and meaty, and easily surpass the rather commercial Crianzas; the top Imperial Gran Reserva★★ is long-lived and impressive. Best years: (reds) **1996 95 94 92 91 90 89 88 87 86 85 81**.

**DIDIER DAGUENEAU** *Pouilly-Fumé AC, Loire Valley, France* Didier Dagueneau is known as the wild man of POUILLY-FUME. In fact he is a much-needed innovator and quality fanatic in a complacent region. His wines generally benefit from 4 or 5 years' aging and, although at times unpredictable, are generally intense and complex. Probably best known for the barrel-fermented Sauvignon Blanc called Silex★★ and another entitled Pur Sang★★. Best years: 2000 99 98 **97 96 95 94 93 90**.

**DALLA VALLE** *Napa Valley AVA, California, USA* Stunning hillside winery founded in 1986 by the late Gustav Dalla Valle, now producing some of NAPA's most esteemed Cabernets. Foremost among them is Maya★★★, a magnificent blend of Cabernet Sauvignon and Cabernet Franc. The straight Cabernet Sauvignon★★★ is almost as rich. New Pietre Rosse★★ is richly cherryish 100% Sangiovese. Cabernet-based reds drink well at 10 years, but will keep for 20 or more. Best years: (1999) 98 97 96 95 94 **93 92 91 90**.

**ROMANO DAL FORNO** *Valpolicella DOC, Veneto, Italy* On his small estate at Illasi, outside the VALPOLICELLA classico area, Romano Dal Forno makes one of the most impressive wines of the appellation. His Valpolicella Superiore★★ from the Monte Lodoletta vineyard is a model of power and grace, though his RECIOTO DELLA VALPOLICELLA★★★ and AMARONE★★★, from the same source, are even more voluptuous. Best years: (Amarone) 1995 94 93 **91 90 89 88 86 85**.

121

**DÃO DOC** *Beira Alta, Portugal* Dão has steep slopes ideal for vineyards, and a great climate for growing local grape varieties; yet only in the last decade have white wines been freshened up, and reds begun to realize their long-promised potential – but many still have a long way to go. Best producers: (reds) Caves ALIANÇA, Boas Quintas (Fonte do Ouro★), Quinta de Cabriz★, Quinta das Maias★, Quinta da Pellada (Tinta Roriz, Touriga Nacional★), Quinta dos ROQUES (Tinta Roriz★, Touriga Nacional★★, Reserva★★), Quinta de Sães★, Casa de Santar★, Caves SAO JOAO★★, SOGRAPE★; (whites) Quinta de Cabriz, Quinta das Maias★, Quinta dos ROQUES★, Quinta de Sães★, Casa de Santar★, SOGRAPE★. Best years: (reds) (2000) 99 **97 96 95 94 92**.

**D'ARENBERG** *McLaren Vale, South Australia* Chester Osborn makes blockbuster Dead Arm Shiraz★★, Footbolt Old Vine Shiraz★, Custodian Grenache★ and numerous blends from very low-yielding old vines. These are big, brash, character-filled wines, but seem to have lost a little heft recently. Best years: (top reds) 1998 97 96 **95 92 91 90**.

**KURT DARTING** *Bad Dürkheim, Pfalz, Germany* Darting makes full, four-square wines in BAD DÜRKHEIM (Spielberg), Ungstein (Ungsteiner Herrenberg Riesling Spätlese★★) and WACHENHEIM (Mandelgarten), including rich, peachy Kabinett★ from Dürkheim. Best years: 1999 98 **97 96 93 92**.

**RENÉ & VINCENT DAUVISSAT** *Chablis AC, Burgundy, France* One of the top domaines in CHABLIS, specializing in concentrated wines from 2 Grand Cru and 3 Premier Cru sites. This is Chablis at its most complex – refreshing, seductive and beautifully structured, with the fruit balancing the subtle influence of mostly older oak. Look out in particular for the Forêt★★, the more aromatic Vaillons★★★ and the powerful les Clos★★★. Best years: 1999 98 97 96 95 **92 90 89**.

**MARCO DE BARTOLI** *Sicily, Italy* Marco De Bartoli is most noted for a dry but unfortified MARSALA-style wine called Vecchio Samperi; his version of what he believes Marsala was before the first English merchant, John Woodhouse, fortified it for export. Released as 10★-, 20★★- and 30-year-old★★ wines, these are dry, intense and redolent of candied citrus peel, dates and old, old raisins. Also excellent is the MOSCATO PASSITO DI PANTELLERIA Bukkuram★★.

**DE BORTOLI** *Riverina, New South Wales, Australia* Large family-owned winery producing a truly sublime botrytized Noble One Semillon★★★ that is head and shoulders above the rest of a vast range of inexpensive RIVERINA quaffers. In the YARRA VALLEY De Bortoli is also crafting some better Chardonnay★, Shiraz★, Cabernet★ and Pinot Noir★★. Good-value second labels are Windy Peak and Gulf Station. Best years: (Botrytis Semillon) 1997 96 95 **94 93 90 87 82**.

**DEHLINGER** *Russian River AVA, California, USA* Outstanding Pinot Noir★★★ from estate vineyards in the cool Russian River region a few miles from the Pacific, best at 5–10 years old. Also makes solid Chardonnay★★ and bold, peppery Syrah★★, and recent vintages of Cabernet★★★ and Bordeaux Blend★★ (Cabernet-Merlot) reflect a surge in quality. Best years: (reds) (1999) 98 97 96 95 **94 93 92 91 90 87**.

**MARCEL DEISS** *Alsace AC, Alsace, France* Founded in 1949 and now run by Jean-Michel Deiss. For many years Deiss has been fanatical about distinctions of terroir, so it was not surprising when in 1998 the estate became biodynamic. The finest wines are the Rieslings★★★ from the Grands Crus Altenberg and Schoenenbourg, which in top years also yield stunning Sélection de Grains Nobles★★★. Although Deiss claims to be less interested in Pinot Gris★★, his wines from this variety, as well as his Gewurztraminers★★★, Pinot Noirs★★ and blended Grand Vin d'Altenberg de Bergheim★, are vibrant and delicious. Best years: (Grand Cru Riesling) 1998 97 96 **95 94 93 92 90 89 88 85**.

**DELAS FRÈRES** *Rhône Valley, France* An underrated and rapidly improving merchant based near Tournon, now part of DEUTZ, selling wines from the entire Rhône Valley. Wines from its own northern Rhône vineyards have improved greatly in recent years. Look out for the aromatic CONDRIEU★★, best drunk young, as well as its single-vineyard, dense, powerful HERMITAGE★★ (les Bessards★★★), which needs as much as a decade to reach its peak, and the perfumed single-vineyard COTE-ROTIE la Landonne★★★. The CROZES-HERMITAGE★★ is an increasingly good buy. Best years: (premium reds) (1999) 98 97 96 95 **94 91 90 89 88 86 85 83 78**; (whites) (1999) 98 **97 96 95 94 93**.

**DELATITE** *Mansfield, Victoria, Australia* The Ritchies' high-altitude vineyard, in sight of VICTORIA's snowfields, grows delicate, aromatic Riesling★★ and Gewurztraminer★★; there is also subtle Chardonnay★ and extravagantly fruity reds. The Pinot Noir★ is perfumed, and Devil's River★★ is a very smart, minty Bordeaux blend. Best years: (Riesling) 1999 **98 96 94 93 92 90 87 86 82**.

**DELEGAT'S** *Henderson, Auckland, North Island, New Zealand* Family winery specializing in Chardonnay, Cabernet-Merlot and Sauvignon Blanc from the HAWKE'S BAY and MARLBOROUGH (under Oyster Bay★ label) regions. Prices are keen and quality is improving, which is reflected in Reserve Chardonnay★ and Reserve Merlot. Best years: (Hawke's Bay reds) 2000 99 **98 96**.

**DENBIES** *Surrey, England* A giant among English vineyards, with 107ha (265 acres) planted on the chalky soils outside Dorking and a well-equipped winery producing 400,000 bottles a year. The wines, from 18 different vine varieties, range from the inadequate to the exciting. The Dornfelder red is memorable for an English effort, the Pinot Noir, sparklers★ and botrytized whites★ are good, and the dry whites at here are perfumed and refreshing. John Worontschak is consultant winemaker and should make a big difference.

**DEUTZ** *Champagne AC, Champagne, France* Probably better known for its CALIFORNIA and New Zealand fizz than for its Champagne. Unfairly so, perhaps, because this small company, now owned by ROEDERER, produces excellent, medium-priced Champagne. The non-vintage★ is always reliable, but the top wines are the Blanc de Blancs★★ and the weightier Cuvée William Deutz★★. Best years: (1995) **93 90 89 88 85**.

**DÉZALEY** *Vaud, Switzerland* The top wine commune in the VAUD, making surprisingly powerful, minerally wines from the Chasselas grape. Best producers: L Bovard★, Conne, Dubois Fils★, Les Frères Dubois, J D Fonjallaz (l'Arbalète)★, Pinget★, J & P Testuz.

**D F J VINHOS** *Portugal* In the early 1990s, UK wine shippers D & F began working with one of Portugal's finest winemakers, José Neiva; in 1999 this relationship evolved into D F J Vinhos, with a range that is now available both locally and internationally. The Bela Fonte brand includes varietal reds Baga, Jaen and Touriga Franca and a white Bical, all from BEIRAS. Other labels include Rocha do Monte from TERRAS DO SADO, Senda do Vale★ from RIBATEJO, and even a red from the ALGARVE, Cataplana★. At the top end are the Grand'Arte reds, including an intensely fruity, peppery Trincadeira★★.

**DIAMOND CREEK VINEYARDS** *Napa Valley AVA, California, USA* Small estate specializing in Cabernet: Volcanic Hill★★★, Red Rock Terrace★★ and Gravelly Meadow★★. Traditionally huge, tannic wines that, when tasted young, I swear won't ever come round. Yet there's usually a sweet inner core of fruit that envelops the tannin over 10–15 years, and recent releases show wonderful perfume and balance in their youth. Best years: (1999) 98 97 96 95 94 92 91 90 **87 86 85 84 80 75.**

**DIEL, SCHLOSSGUT** *Burg Layen, Nahe, Germany* Armin Diel made his name with dry wines, and some of Germany's finest new oak-aged whites during the 1980s. However, since 1990 it has been classic-style Rieslings which have been attracting headlines. Spätlese and Auslese from Dorsheim's top sites are regularly ★★, Eiswein ★★★. Best years: 1999 98 **97** 96 **95** 93 90 89 88.

**DISTELL** *Stellenbosch, South Africa* The company formed by the merger, at the end of 2000, between Distillers Corporation and South Africa's largest merchant-producer, Stellenbosch Farmers' Winery (founded in 1925). Many brands introduced in SFW's early days are still best-sellers. Top-of-the-range Zonnebloem has agreeable, if simple, reds and whites. J C le Roux makes well-crafted Cap Classique sparkling wines, including ripe, yeasty Pongrácz NV★. Two wineries in PAARL, Nederburg and Plaisir de Merle★, also fall under the Distell umbrella, but are run separately. Nederburg's standard range is sound if unexciting. Its best-known botrytized dessert, Edelkeur★, is sold only through an annual auction. Plaisir de Merle is the company's showpiece: winemaker Niel Bester worked at Ch. MARGAUX for Paul Pontallier. The Cabernet Sauvignon★ has ripe tannin and supple fruit and seems to be back on form after a few lacklustre vintages. Both it and the minty Merlot are best with up to 5 years' aging. Other Distell partners include Le Bonheur, MEERLUST, Neethlingshof, STELLENZICHT and a handful of others.

**CH. DOISY-DAËNE★★** *Sauternes AC, 2ème Cru Classé, Bordeaux, France* A consistently good property in BARSAC (although it uses the SAUTERNES AC for its wines) and unusual in that the sweet wine is made exclusively from Sémillon. It ages well for 10 years or more. The extra-rich Extravagant★★★ is produced in exceptional years. Doisy-Daëne Sec★ is a good, perfumed, dry white. Drink young. Best years: (sweet) 1999 98 97 96 95 **90 89 88** 86 83 82 79; (dry) 1999 98 **96 95 94** 90.

**CH. DOISY-VÉDRINES★★** *Sauternes AC, 2ème Cru Classé, Bordeaux, France* Next door to DOISY-DAENE, Doisy-Védrines is a richly botrytized wine, fatter and more syrupy than most BARSAC wines. Like its neighbour, it also sells its wines under the SAUTERNES AC. Best years: (sweet) 1999 98 97 96 95 **90 89 88** 86 85 83.

**DOLCETTO** One of Italy's most charming native grapes, producing purple wines bursting at the seams with fruit. Virtually exclusive to PIEDMONT, it is DOC in 7 zones, with styles ranging from intense and rich in Alba, Ovada and Dogliani, to lighter, more perfumed versions in Acqui and ASTI. Usually best drunk within 1–2 years, top wines can age up to 4 years. Best producers: (Alba) Alario★★, ALTARE★★, Boglietti★, Bongiovanni★★, Bricco Maiolica★, Brovia★★, Elvio Cogno★★, G CONTERNO★, Conterno-Fantino★★, B Marcarini★, B MASCARELLO★, G MASCARELLO★★, Paitin★, Pelissero★★, PRUNOTTO★, Albino Rocca★★, SANDRONE★★, Vajra★★, Vietti★, Gianni Voerzio★, Roberto VOERZIO★★; (Dogliani) Abbona★, Chionetti★★, Einaudi★★, Gillardi★, San Fereolo★★, San Romano★.

**DÔLE** *Valais, Switzerland* Red wine from the Swiss VALAIS that must be made from at least 51% Pinot Noir, the rest being Gamay. Dôle is generally a light wine – the deeper, richer (100% Pinot Noir) styles have the right to call themselves Pinot Noir. Best producers: M Clavien, J Germanier, Caves Imesch, Mathier, Caves Orsat.

**DOMAINE BOYAR** *Bulgaria* From its beginnings as a marketing company for a number of Bulgarian wineries, Domaine Boyar has become the largest producer in the country. With its brand-new Australian-built Blueridge Estate winery at Sliven, in addition to the Iambol and Shumen wineries, plus a recent merger with the Seaboard Corporation of America (owners of Vinprom's ROUSSE and Korton wineries), Boyar is setting out to establish a higher-quality image for its wines.

**DOMAINE CARNEROS** *Carneros AVA, California, USA* From its founding in 1987, this TAITTINGER-owned sparkling wine house has shown great promise. Both the vintage Brut★ and the Blanc de Blancs★★ now match Taittinger's fizz from Champagne. De luxe Le Rêve★★ blanc de blancs is made in the best years, and there's a tasty still Pinot Noir★.

**DOMAINE CHANDON** *Napa Valley AVA, California, USA* The first French-owned (MOET & CHANDON) sparkling wine producer in California has shown remarkable consistency and good quality with reasonably priced non-vintage bubblies. The Reserve★ bottlings, rich and creamy, are especially good. Blanc de Blancs★, made entirely from CARNEROS Chardonnay, is a welcome addition. Étoile★★ is an aged de luxe wine, and there are delicious rosés★★, too. Shadow Creek is the budget line.

**DOMAINE DROUHIN OREGON** *Willamette Valley AVA, Oregon, USA* Burgundy wine merchant Robert DROUHIN bought 40ha (100 acres) in OREGON in 1987, with plans to make fine Pinot Noir, and this has certainly been achieved. The regular Pinot Noir★ is silky smooth, and the de luxe Pinot Noir Laurène★★ is supple, voluptuous, and one of Oregon's finest. Chardonnay★ has established itself well since its first release in 1996. Best years: (Pinot Noir) (1999) 98 97 96 **94 93**.

**DOMAINE VISTALBA** *Argentina* All the reds from this French-owned company have dark, concentrated fruit, increasing in complexity through the Fabre Montmayou range. The almost black, chocolate-and-damsons Grand Vin★★ is a splendidly topsy-turvy Bordeaux blend: Malbec plus Merlot and Cabernet Sauvignon. The reds from a second MENDOZA winery, Altos de Temporada, are also potentially excellent. Dual variety reds from Río Negro, under the Infinitus label, are erratic; whites are good but trail behind.

**DOMECQ** *Jerez y Manzanilla DO, Andalucía and Rioja DOC, País Vasco, Spain*
The largest of the sherry companies, best known for its reliable fino, La Ina★. At the top of the range, dry Amontillado 51-1A★★★, Sibarita Palo Cortado★★★ and Venerable Pedro Ximénez★★ are spectacular. Domecq also makes light, elegant Marqués de Arienzo RIOJA★.

**DOMINUS** *Napa Valley AVA, California, USA* Red wine only from this property owned by Christian MOUEIX, director of Bordeaux superstar PETRUS. Wines are based on Cabernet with leavenings of Merlot and Cabernet Franc. The dense, rich 1990 and 94 (both ★★) are the finest yet. Early vintages were mercilessly tannic, but recent ones show improvement. Best years: (1999) 97 96 95 94 91 **90**.

**DONAULAND** *Niederösterreich, Austria* Amorphous wine region on both banks of the Danube stretching from just north of Vienna west to St Polten. Best are the dry Grüner Veltliners from the Wagram area. Best producers: Karl Fritsch, Wimmer-Czerny.

**H DÖNNHOFF** *Oberhausen, Nahe, Germany* Helmut Dönnhoff is the quiet winemaking genius of the NAHE, conjuring from a string of top sites some of the most minerally dry and naturally sweet Rieslings in the world. The very best are the subtle, long-lived wines from the Niederhäuser Hermannshöhle★★★ vineyard. Eiswein★★★ is equally exciting. Best years: (2000) 99 98 **97** 96 95 **94 93** 91 90 89 88 86 83 76 **71**.

**DORDOGNE, VIN DE PAYS DE LA** *South-West France* Rare but good-value wines from an attractive area of France; Sémillon-based whites best drunk young, some Chardonnay (Ch. la Jaubertie), and various fruity BERGERAC-style reds that can age for 1–2 years.

**DOURO DOC** *Douro, Portugal* As well as a flood of port and basic table wine, some of Portugal's top, soft-textured red wines come from here. Also good whites, made from the more aromatic white port grape varieties. White wines are best young, but red wines may improve for 10 years or even more. Best producers: (reds) Maria Doroteia Serôdio Borges (Fojo★★), BRIGHT BROTHERS (TFN★), Quinta do COTTO (Grande Escolha★★), Quinta do CRASTO★★, FERREIRA (Barca Velha★), Quinta da Leda★★), Quinta da Gaivosa★★, NIEPOORT (Passadouro★★, Redoma★★), Quinta do NOVAL★, Quinta do Portal (Grande Reserva★), RAMOS PINTO (Duas Quintas★), Quinta de la ROSA★, SOGRAPE (Reserva★), Quinta do Vale Dona Maria★★, Quinta do Vale da Raposa (single varietals★), Vallado★. Best years: (reds) (2000) 99 97 **96 95 94 92** 91 **90**.

**DOW** *Port DOC, Douro, Portugal* The grapes for Dow's Vintage ports★★★ come mostly from the Quinta do Bomfim, which is also the name of the excellent single quinta★★★. Dow ports are all relatively dry compared with those of GRAHAM and WARRE (the 2 other major brands belonging to the Symington family), and there are some excellent aged tawnies★★. Best years: (Vintage) 1997 94 91 **85 83 80 77 70** 66 63 60 55 45; (Bomfim) 1995 92 90 **87 86 84**.

**JEAN-PAUL DROIN** *Chablis AC, Burgundy, France* Jean-Paul Droin sells some of his production to NUITS-ST-GEORGES merchant LABOURE-ROI, but bottles 14 different wines under his own label. Apart from CHABLIS★ and PETIT CHABLIS, all of Droin's are fermented and/or aged in oak barrels. The best wines are the big, buttery Chablis Premiers Crus – Montmains★★ and Vosgros★★ – and Grands Crus – Vaudésir★ and Grenouilles★★. Best years: (top crus) 1999 98 97 **96 95 90**.

**DROMANA ESTATE** *Mornington Peninsula, Victoria, Australia* Garry Crittenden went against the trend when he chose low-fertility soils in a wind-protected site for his first Dromana plantings in 1982. The pay-off can be tasted in fragrant, restrained Pinot Noir★ and Chardonnay★★ and elegant if rather leafy Cabernet-Merlot★. Italian varietals under the Garry Crittenden 'i' label, mostly from King Valley grapes, are of special interest. Schinus is a popular second label. Best years: (Chardonnay) 1999 **98 97 96 94 91**.

**JOSEPH DROUHIN** *Beaune, Burgundy, France* One of the best Burgundian merchants, now Japanese-owned, with substantial vineyard holdings in CHABLIS and the COTE D'OR, and DOMAINE DROUHIN OREGON, USA. Drouhin makes a consistently good, if expensive, range of wines from all over Burgundy. Look for BONNES-MARES★★, ROMANEE-ST-VIVANT★★★, BEAUNE Clos des Mouches (red★★ and white★★★), le Musigny★★★ and le MONTRACHET★★★ from the Domaine du Marquis de Laguiche. Drouhin offers better value in Chablis★ and less glamorous Burgundian ACs, such as RULLY★ and ST-AUBIN★. The BEAUJOLAIS is always good, but overall Drouhin's whites are (just) better than the reds. Quality reds and whites should be aged for at least 5 years, often better nearer 10. Best years: (reds) (2000) 99 98 97 96 95 **93 90 89 88 85**; (whites) (2000) 99 98 **97** 96 95 **92 90**.

**PIERRE-JACQUES DRUET** *Bourgueil, Loire Valley, France* A passionate producer of BOURGUEIL and small quantities of CHINON. Druet makes 5 Bourgueils – les Cent Boisselées★, Cuvée Beauvais★, Cuvée Grand Mont★★, Cuvée Reservée★ and Vaumoreau★★ – each a complex expression of the Cabernet Franc grape, but lacking obvious, upfront fruit. Best aged for 3–5 years. Best years: (2000) **99 97 96 95 90 89 88 85**.

**DRY CREEK VALLEY AVA** *Sonoma, California, USA* Best known for Sauvignon Blanc, Zinfandel and Cabernet Sauvignon, this valley runs west of ALEXANDER VALLEY AVA, and similarly becomes hotter moving northwards. Best producers: DRY CREEK VINEYARDS★, Duxoup★, FERRARI-CARANO★★, GALLO (Chardonnay★), Michel-Schlumberger★, NALLE★★, Pezzi King★, Preston★, QUIVIRA★★, Rafanelli (Zinfandel★★★).

**DRY CREEK VINEYARD** *Dry Creek Valley AVA, California, USA* An early advocate of Fumé Blanc, Dave Stare remains faithful to the brisk racy style of Fumé★ and also makes a serious Reserve Fumé Blanc★★ which improves with aging. A drink-young Chardonnay (Reserve★) is attractive, but the stars here are red Meritage, Merlot★ and Old Vine Zinfandel★★. Best years: (reds) (1999) 98 97 **95 94 92 91**.

**DRY RIVER WINES** *Martinborough, North Island, New Zealand* Low yields, careful selection and an uncompromising attitude to quality at this tiny winery, owned by the meticulous Dr Neil McCallum, have helped create some of the country's top Gewürztraminer★★★ and Pinot Gris★★, together with an intense and seductively smooth Pinot Noir★★★, a sleek Chardonnay★★★ and powerful, long-lived Riesling★★★. Best years: (2001) 00 99 98 **96 94**.

**GEORGES DUBOEUF** *Beaujolais, Burgundy, France* Known, with some justification, as the King of Beaujolais, Duboeuf is responsible for more than 10% of the wine produced in the region. Given the size of his operation, the quality of the wines is high. Duboeuf also makes and blends wine from the Mâconnais and the RHONE VALLEY. His BEAUJOLAIS

NOUVEAU is usually reliable, but his top wines are those he bottles for small growers, particularly Jean Descombes★★ in MORGON, Domaine des Quatre Vents★, la Madone★ in FLEURIE and Domaine de la Tour du Bief★ in MOULIN-A-VENT. His ST-VÉRAN★ can be very good.

**DUCKHORN** *Napa Valley AVA, California, USA* This Californian winery has earned a well-deserved reputation for its Merlot★ (Estate Merlot★★), if you like a chunky, tannic style, but the Cabernet Sauvignon★ and Sauvignon Blanc★ provide easier drinking. Paraduxx, a Zinfandel-Cabernet blend, is new to the range; Decoy is the budget line. Best years: (Merlot) (1999) 98 97 96 95 94 93 **92 91 90**; (Cabernet Sauvignon) (1999) 97 96 95 94 **93 92 91 90 87 86.**

**CH. DUCRU-BEAUCAILLOU★★★** *St-Julien AC, 2ème Cru Classé, Haut-Médoc, Bordeaux, France* Traditionally the epitome of ST-JULIEN, mixing charm and austerity, fruit and firm tannins. Vintages in the mid-80s and early 90s were flawed, but recent vintages show vast improvement. Welcome back to the premier league. Second wine: la Croix de Beaucaillou. Best years: (2000) 99 98 97 96 95 **94 85 83 82.**

**DUJAC** *Morey-St-Denis AC, Côte de Nuits, Burgundy, France* Owner Jacques Seysses is one of Burgundy's most influential winemakers. His estate is based in MOREY-ST-DENIS, and there are also some choice vineyards in CHAMBOLLE-MUSIGNY, ECHEZEAUX and GEVREY-CHAMBERTIN. The wines are all perfumed and elegant, including a small quantity of Morey-St-Denis★ white wine, but the outstanding Dujac bottlings are the 3 Grands Crus – CLOS DE LA ROCHE★★★, BONNES-MARES★★★ and CLOS ST-DENIS★★ – all of which age for a decade or more. Best years: (top reds) (2000) 99 98 96 95 **93 91 90 89 85.**

**DUNN VINEYARDS** *Howell Mountain AVA, California, USA* Massive, concentrated, hauntingly perfumed, long-lived Cabernet Sauvignon★★★ is the trademark of Randy Dunn's wines from HOWELL MOUNTAIN. His NAPA VALLEY Cabernets★★ are less powerful. Best years: (1999) 97 96 95 94 93 92 91 90 **88 87 86 85 84 82.**

**DURBACH** *Baden, Germany* Unusually for BADEN, Riesling (here called Klingelberger) is something of a speciality in Durbach. Another speciality is Traminer, here called Klevner (normally a synonym for Pinot Blanc!). Best producers: Durbach co-op, Andreas Laible★★, Heinrich Männle, von Neveu, Wolff-Metternich. Best years: (dry whites) 1999 **98 97 96 94.**

**DURIF** See Petite Sirah.

**JEAN DURUP** *Chablis, Burgundy, France* The largest vineyard owner in CHABLIS, Jean Durup is a great believer in unoaked Chablis, which tends to be clean without any great complexity. Best are the Premiers Crus Fourchaume★ and Montée de Tonnerre★★. Wines appear under a variety of labels, including l'Églantière, Ch. de Maligny and Valéry.

**ÉCHÉZEAUX AC** *Grand Cru, Côte de Nuits, Burgundy, France* The village of Flagey-Échézeaux, down in the plain away from the vineyards, is best known for its 2 Grands Crus, Échézeaux and the smaller and more prestigious Grands-Échézeaux, which are sandwiched between the world-famous CLOS DE VOUGEOT and VOSNE-ROMANÉE. Few of the 80 growers here have really made a name for themselves, but there are some fine wines with a smoky, plum richness and a soft texture that age well over 10–15 years to a gamy, chocolaty depth. Best producers:

R Arnoux★★, BOUCHARD Père et Fils★★, Cacheux-Sirugue★★★, DROUHIN★★, DUJAC★★★, R Engel★★★, GRIVOT★★★, JAYER-GILLES★★★, Mongeard-Mugneret★★, Mugneret-Gibourg★★★, Dom. de la ROMANEE-CONTI★★★, E Rouget★★★. Best years: (2000) 99 98 97 96 95 **93 90 89**.

**EDEN VALLEY** See Barossa, pages 56–7.

**CH. L'ÉGLISE-CLINET**★★★ *Pomerol AC, Bordeaux, France* A tiny 5.5-ha (13-acre) domaine in the heart of the POMEROL plateau, l'Église-Clinet has a very old vineyard – one of the reasons for the depth and elegance of the wines. The other is the winemaking ability of owner Denis Durantou. The wine is expensive and in limited supply, but worth seeking out. It can be enjoyed young, though the best examples should be cellared for 10 years or more. Best years: (2000) 99 98 97 96 95 **94 93 90 89 86 85**.

**EIKENDAL VINEYARDS** *Stellenbosch WO, South Africa* Winemaker Josef Krammer's wines are unflamboyant, though individual and complex. The deep, well-drained slopes of Helderberg produce an elegant, balanced Chardonnay★ with an aging ability unusual in South Africa, and a light-textured but flavoursome Merlot★. Best years: (Chardonnay) **2000 99 98 97 96**.

**NEIL ELLIS** *Stellenbosch WO, South Africa* A leading winemaker/négociant, renowned for full, vigorous Sauvignon Blancs★ from cooler areas and striking Stellenbosch reds (blackcurranty Cabernet Sauvignon★★ and supple Cabernet-Merlot★), Ellis has turned his attention to Shiraz★. Ageworthy single-vineyard Shiraz★, Pinotage★ and Cabernet★★, and a silky Pinot Noir★ from cool Elgin confirm his versatility. Best years: (whites) **2000 99 98 97**; (reds) **1999 98 97 96**.

**ELTVILLE** *Rheingau, Germany* This large wine town makes some of the RHEINGAU's most racy Riesling wines. Best producers: J B Becker★, J Fischer, Langwerth von Simmern★. Best years: 1999 **98 97 96 90 89**.

**EMILIA-ROMAGNA** *Italy* Central-eastern region in Italy, divided into the provinces of Emilia (in the west) and ROMAGNA (in the east). It is chiefly infamous for LAMBRUSCO in Emilia. See also Colli Bolognesi, Colli Piacentini.

**ENATE** *Somontano DO, Aragón, Spain* Enate and VINAS DEL VERO seem to be slugging it out for supremacy in the SOMONTANO DO. Barrel-fermented Chardonnay★ is rich, buttery and toasty, Gewürztraminer★ is exotic and convincing. Imported grape varieties also feature in the red Crianza, Reserva (100% Cabernet Sauvignon) and Reserva Especial★★ (Cabernet-Merlot). Best years: (reds) **1998 96 95 94**.

**ENTRE-DEUX-MERS AC** *Bordeaux, France* This AC increasingly represents some of the freshest, snappiest dry white wine in France. In general, drink the latest vintage, though better wines will last a year or two. Sweet wines are sold as PREMIERES COTES DE BORDEAUX, St-Macaire, LOUPIAC and STE-CROIX-DU-MONT. Best producers: Bel Air, Bonnet★, Castelneau, Fontenille★, Launay, Moulin-de-Launay, Nardique-la-Gravière★, Ste-Marie★, Tour-de-Mirambeau, Toutigeac★, Turcaud★.

**ERBACH** *Rheingau, Germany* Erbach's famous Marcobrunn vineyard is one of the top spots for Riesling on the Rhine. The village wines are elegant, off-dry; those from Marcobrunn more powerful and imposing. Best producers: Jakob Jung★, von Knyphausen★, SCHLOSS REINHARTS-HAUSEN★, Schloss Schönborn★. Best years: 1999 98 **97 96 94 93 92**.

**ERBALUCE DI CALUSO DOC** *Piedmont, Italy* Usually a dry or sparkling
♀ white from the Erbaluce grape, but Caluso Passito, where the grapes
are semi-dried before fermenting, can be a great sweet wine. Best
producers: (Caluso Passito) Cieck★, Ferrando★, Orsolani★, M Pachié.
**ERDEN** *Mosel, Germany* Village in the Middle MOSEL, whose most famous
♀ vineyards are Prälat and Treppchen. The wines are rich and succulent
with a strong mineral character. Best producers: J J Christoffel★★, Dr
LOOSEN★★★, Mönchhof★. Best years: 1999 98 **97** 96 **95 94** 93 90.

**ERMITAGE** Swiss name for the Marsanne grape of the northern RHONE
⚇ VALLEY. Mostly found in the central VALAIS, where it produces a range
of wines from slightly sweet to lovely honeyed dessert wines. Best
producers: Chappaz★, Dom. du Mont d'Or★, Orsat (Marsanne Blanche★).

**ERRÁZURIZ** *Aconcagua, Chile* American winemaker Ed Flaherty has
🍷 brought a welcome consistency to this producer's wines. Using red
grapes from relatively low-yielding
Aconcagua slopes north of Santiago,
as well as traditional supplies from
south of Santiago, there is a uniquely
crunchy Merlot★★, impressively
concentrated Cabernet Sauvignon★★
from the Don Maximiano vineyards
(also source of SENA) and Syrah
Reserva★★. Slick-textured, citrussy Chardonnay Reserva★ from
CASABLANCA heads the whites. Best years: (reds) (1999) 98 **97** 96 95.

**ESPORÃO** *Reguengos DOC, Alentejo, Portugal* Huge estate in the heart of
🍷 the ALENTEJO, with Australian David Baverstock producing a broad
range of wines. The principal labels are Esporão (red★★ and white★
reservas), Monte Velho and Alandra, and there are some excellent
varietals: Trincadeira★, Aragonês★, Cabernet Sauvignon★ and
Touriga Nacional★. Best years: (reds) 1999 98 **97 96 95** 94 92.

**EST! EST!! EST!!! DI MONTEFIASCONE DOC** *Lazio, Italy* Modest white
♀ accorded its undeserved reputation because of an apocryphal story of
a bishop's servant who thought he'd made a major discovery in this
wine. The most credible exception is Falesco's Poggio dei Gelsi★. Far
better is the same producer's barrique-aged Merlot Montiano★★★.
Best producers: Bigi (Graffiti), Falesco★, Mazziotti (Canuleio★).

**CH. DES ESTANILLES** *Faugères AC, Languedoc, France* The Louisons
🍷🍷 know that quality begins in the vineyard. Their best site is the Clos de
Fou, with its very steep schistous slope planted with Syrah; the grape
'dominates' the top red cuvée★★ (i.e. 100% – but the AC regulations do
not allow them to say so). Also a wood-fermented and aged rosé, plus
fine COTEAUX DU LANGUEDOC white★. Best years: (reds) 1999 98 **97 96 95** 94.

**ESTREMADURA** *Portugal* Portugal's most productive region, occupying the
western coastal strip and with an increasing number of clean, characterful
wines. The leading area is ALENQUER, recently promoted to DOC status along
with Arruda, Óbidos and Torres Vedras, and there are also the IPRs of
Alcobaça and Encostas d'Aire. However, much of the wine, including some
of the region's best, is simply labelled as Vinho Regional Estremadura. Spicy,

130

perfumed reds are often based on Periquita, but Cabernet Sauvignon and Touriga Nacional contribute to top examples, which can benefit from 4 or 5 years' age. Top producers also make fresh, aromatic whites. Best producers: Quinta da Abrigada★, Caves ALIANCA, Arruda co-op, D F J VINHOS (Grand'Arte Touriga Nacional★, Manta Preta★), Quinta de Pancas★, Casa SANTOS LIMA. See also Bucelas. Best years: (reds) (2000) **99 98 97 96 95**.

**L'ÉTOILE AC** *Jura, France* A tiny area within the COTES DU JURA which has its own AC for whites, mainly Chardonnay and Savagnin, and for *vin jaune*. There is good Champagne-method fizz too. Best producers: Ch. de l'Étoile★, Dom. Joly★, Dom. de Montbourgeau★★, Quintigny★.

**CH. L'ÉVANGILE★★** *Pomerol AC, Bordeaux, France* A neighbour to PETRUS and CHEVAL BLANC, this estate is now wholly owned and managed by the Rothschilds of LAFITE-ROTHSCHILD. The wine is quintessential POMEROL – rich, fat and exotic. Recent vintages have been very good, but expect further improvement as the Rothschild team gets to work. Best years: (2000) 99 98 97 96 95 94 **93 90 89 88 85 83 82**.

**EVANS FAMILY** *Hunter Valley, New South Wales, Australia* Len Evans' tiny HUNTER vineyard grows majestic Chardonnay★★, highly regarded sparkling wine (PETALUMA-made), as well as Gamay and Pinot Noir. Nearly all the wine is sold privately or ex-winery. The 1996 sale of ROTHBURY allowed Evans to focus on the Evans Wine Company and Tower Estate. Best years: (Chardonnay) 1998 **96 95 93 88**.

**EVANS & TATE** *Margaret River, Western Australia* Important Western Australian winery originally in SWAN DISTRICT. Producer of nutty, creamy Two-Vineyards Chardonnay★, crisp Sauvignon-Semillon★, blackcurranty Cabernet-Merlot★ and a concentrated yet irresistible Shiraz★★. Best years: (Cabernet) 1998 97 **96 94 93 92 91**.

**EYRIE VINEYARDS** *Willamette Valley AVA, Oregon, USA* One of the leading Pinot Noir producers in Oregon, especially the Reserve★, but in poor years the wines can be withdrawn and thin. Chardonnay★ shows nice varietal fruit, while the popular Pinot Gris★ flies off the shelves. Best years: (Pinot Noir Reserve) (1999) 98 **97 96**.

**FAIRVIEW** *Paarl WO, South Africa* Owner Charles Back ensures that wine remains fun as well as a serious business. The latest consumer hit is Goats do Roam, a spoof on Côtes du Rhône; the first, a red with Pinotage added to the blend of Rhône grape varieties, has now been joined by a spicy, partly barrel-fermented rosé. Zinfandel-Cinsaut★ is another delightful idiosyncrasy. In three vintages, the richly textured and delicious Viognier★★ hasn't disappointed and confirms the variety's suitability to these warm PAARL vineyards. Shiraz★★, Pinotage★, Cabernet Sauvignon★, Merlot★★, Chardonnay★ and Semillon★ also perform with consistency. Charles Back also owns the progressive SPICE ROUTE WINE COMPANY and acts as guiding light to the Fair Valley workers' empowerment project. Best years: **2000 99 98 97 96 95 94**.

**JOSEPH FAIVELEY** *Nuits-St-Georges, Côtes de Nuits, Burgundy, France* This Burgundian merchant makes excellent long-lived red wines (especially CHAMBERTIN-Clos-de-Bèze★★ and Mazis-Chambertin★★), principally from its own substantial vineyard holdings. Indeed, Faiveley is more like an outsize grower than a négociant. The much cheaper MERCUREY reds★ are also attractive if on the lean side. The

Côte Chalonnaise whites from RULLY★ and Mercurey★, and the oak-aged BOURGOGNE Blanc represent good value. Best years: (top reds) (2000) 99 98 97 96 **95 93 90 89 88**; (whites) (2000) 99 98 **97 96 95 92 90**.

**FALERNO DEL MASSICO DOC** *Campania, Italy* Falernian, from north of Naples, was one of the ancient Romans' superstar wines. The revived DOC, with a white Falanghina and reds from Aglianico and Piedirosso, or Primitivo (California's Zinfandel), looks promising. Best producers: Michele Moio, Villa Matilde★. Best years: (reds) (1999) 98 97 **96 95 93**.

**CH. FALFAS★** *Côtes de Bourg AC, Bordeaux, France* Biodynamic estate making concentrated, structured wine that needs 4–5 years to soften. Le Chevalier is an old-vines cuvée. Best years: 1999 98 **96 95 94 90 89**.

**CH. DE FARGUES★★** *Sauternes AC, Cru Bourgeois, Bordeaux, France* Property run by the Lur-Saluces family, who until recently also owned Ch. d'YQUEM. The quality of this fine, rich wine is more a tribute to their commitment than to the inherent quality of the vineyard. Best years: 1997 96 95 90 89 **88 86 83**.

**FAUGÈRES AC** *Languedoc, France* Faugères, with its vineyards in the hills north of Béziers in the Hérault, was the first of the LANGUEDOC communes to make a reputation of its own. Its ripe, soft, rather plummy flavour marks it out from other Languedoc reds. Best producers: Alquier★, Léon Barral, ESTANILLES★, Faugères co-op, Fraisse, Grézan, Haut-Fabrègues, la Liquière, Ollier-Taillefer (Cuvée Castel Fossibus★), St-Antonin. Best years: (2000) 99 98 **96 95 94 93 90**.

**FAUSTINO MARTÍNEZ** *Rioja DOC, País Vasco and Rioja, and Cava DO, Spain* Family-owned and technically very well equipped, this RIOJA company makes good Reserva★ and Gran Reserva★ red Riojas in distinctive dark, frosted bottles, as well as a fruity, Beaujolais-style Vino Joven or Viña Faustina, and pleasant whites and rosés. In 1999 it introduced a fruit-driven Crianza. Best years: (reds) **1996 95 94 92 91 90 89 87 85 82 81**.

**FEILER-ARTINGER** *Rust, Neusiedlersee, Burgenland, Austria* Father and son team Hans and Kurt Feiler make Ausbruch-style dessert wines★★★ of great elegance at this medium-sized estate housed in a fine Baroque building. Their dry whites★ and reds★★ from a range of traditional Austrian and French grapes are also worthy of attention. Best years: (dessert wines) (2000) 99 98 97 **96** 95 **94 93 91**; (dry whites, reds) (2000) 99 **97 94 93 92**.

**LIVIO FELLUGA** *Colli Orientali del Friuli DOC, Friuli-Venezia Giulia, Italy* A younger generation has continued the great work of Livio Felluga, delivering both quality and quantity from this large Friuli estate. Pinot Grigio★, Picolit Riserva★★, Tocai★, Merlot-Cabernet blend Vertigo★ and raspberryish straight Merlot Riserva Sosso★★ are all class acts. Chardonnay Esperto★ is one of Friuli's best, but there's more to stimulate the palate in Terre Alte★★, an aromatic blend of Tocai, Pinot Bianco and Sauvignon. Best years: (whites): (2000) **99 98 97 96**.

**FELSINA, FATTORIA DI** *Chianti Classico DOCG, Tuscany, Italy* Full, chunky CHIANTI CLASSICO★★ wines which improve with several years' bottle age. Quality is generally outstanding; most notable are the single-vineyard Riserva Rancia★★★ and Sangiovese Fontalloro★★★. Also good VIN SANTO★★, Chardonnay Isistri★★ and Cabernet Maestro Raro★★. Best years: (Fontalloro) 1997 **95 94 93 90 88 86 85**.

**FELTON ROAD** *Central Otago, New Zealand* Runaway success with vineyards in the old goldfields of Bannockburn. Intensely fruity, seductive Pinot Noir★★ is surpassed by very limited quantities of concentrated, complex Block 3 Pinot Noir★★★. Three classy Rieslings (all ★★) cover the range from dry to sweet. Minerally, citrussy unoaked Chardonnay★★ is one of New Zealand's best; barrel-fermented Chardonnay★★ also impresses. Best years: (2000) 99 **98** 97.

**FENDANT** *Valais, Switzerland* Chasselas wine from the steep slopes of the Swiss VALAIS. Good Fendant should be ever so slightly *spritzig* with a spicy character. However, the average Fendant is thin and virtually characterless. It is best drunk *very* young, but a good example can age for years. Best producers: Chappaz, J Germanier, Gilliard, Caves Imesch, Maye & Fils, Caves Orsat.

**FERRARI** *Trento DOC, Trentino, Italy* Founded in 1902, the firm is a leader for sparkling wine. Consistent, classy wines include Ferrari Brut★, Maximum Brut★, Perlé★, Rosé★ and vintage Giulio Ferrari Riserva del Fondatore★★, aged 8 years on its lees and an Italian classic.

**FERRARI-CARANO VINEYARDS** *Dry Creek Valley AVA, California, USA* Delightful Chardonnay, with balanced, elegant fruit made in a regular and a Reserve style. The Reserve★★ is deeply flavoured with more than a touch of oak, while the regular bottling★★ has delicious apple-spice fruit. A new red wine, Siena★★ (a blend of Cabernet Sauvignon and Sangiovese), shows great promise and could outshine the Chardonnay. Merlot★ and Fumé Blanc★ are also good. Reds can improve for 5–10 years. Best years: (reds) (1999) 98 97 96 **95 94 92 91**.

**FERREIRA** *Port DOC, Douro DOC, Douro, Portugal* Old port house owned by SOGRAPE, who have taken a major role in modernizing Portugal's wine production. Ferreira is best known for excellent tawny ports: creamy, nutty Quinta do Porto 10-year-old★ or the Duque de Braganza 20-year-old★★. The Vintage Port★★ is increasingly good. Ferreira's table wine operation, known as Casa Ferreirinha, produces Portugal's most sought-after red, Barca Velha★★; made from DOURO grape varieties (mainly Tinta Roriz), it is produced only in the finest years – just 12 vintages since 1953. Marginally less good years are now sold as Casa Ferreirinha Reserva★ (previously Reserva Especial). New Quinta da Leda reds★★ are also good. Best years: (Vintage) 1997 95 94 91 **85 78 77 70 66 63**; (Barca Velha) **1991 85 83 82 81 78**; (Casa Ferreirinha Reserva/Reserva Especial) 1990 **86 80**.

**CH. FERRIÈRE**★★ *Margaux AC, 3ème Cru Classé, Haut-Médoc, Bordeaux, France* The smallest classified growth in MARGAUX, Ferrière was leased to its larger neighbour Ch. LASCOMBES until 1992, when it was purchased by the Merlaut family, owners of Ch. CHASSE-SPLEEN. It is now managed by Claire Villars, and the ripe, rich and perfumed wines are among the best in Margaux AC. Best years: (2000) 99 98 96 95 **94**.

**FETZER VINEYARDS** *Mendocino County, California, USA* Important winery balancing quality and quantity. Basic wines are good, with a tasty Syrah★; Barrel Select bottles are usually ★. Also a leader in organic viticulture with the Bonterra range: Chardonnay, Merlot, Roussanne and Zinfandel are all ★, and there's also Cabernet, Viognier★ and Sangiovese. Best years: (Barrel Select reds) (1999) 98 **97 96 95 94**.

**NICOLAS FEUILLATTE** *Champagne AC, Champagne, France* House label of the huge, high-tech Chouilly co-op, with lively, good-value non-vintage and burly, fruit-packed vintage★. Grande Cuvée Palmes d'Or★ is a powerful heavyweight. Best years: (1995) 93 **92 90 89 88 85 82**.

**FIANO** Distinctive, low-yielding southern Italian white grape variety. Best producers: (Molise) Di Majo Norante; (Fiano di Avellino DOC in Campania) Colli di Lapio★, Feudi di San Gregorio★, Marianna, MASTROBERARDINO★, Nicola Romano★, Struzziero★, Terre Dora di Paolo★ (formerly Vignadora), Vadiaperti★, Vega-D'Antiche Terre.

**CH. DE FIEUZAL** *Pessac-Léognan AC, Cru Classé de Graves, Bordeaux, France* One of the most up-to-date properties in the region and the delicious, oaky wine sells at a high price. The red★ is drinkable almost immediately, but has been disappointingly short of its fabled perfume in recent years. Less than 10% of the wine is white★★ but this has held on to the gorgeous, perfumed Fieuzal style. Second wine (red and white): l'Abeille de Fieuzal. Best years: (reds) (2000) 98 96 95 **94 90 89 88 87 86 85 83 82**; (whites) 1999 98 96 **95 94 93 90 89 88 85**.

**CH. FIGEAC★★** *St-Émilion Grand Cru AC, 1er Grand Cru Classé, Bordeaux, France* Leading property whose wine traditionally has a delightful fragrance and gentleness of texture. There is an unusually high percentage of Cabernets Franc and Sauvignon (70%) in the wine. Generally one of my favourite properties, but I haven't been happy with several recent releases. Second wine: la Grangeneuve de Figeac. Best years: (2000) 99 98 95 **90 89 88 86 85 83 82**.

**FILLIATREAU** *Saumur-Champigny, Loire Valley, France* One of the leading growers in SAUMUR-CHAMPIGNY, producing 3 richly flavoured, ageworthy Cabernet Francs – Jeunes Vignes★, Saumur-Champigny★ and Vieilles Vignes★★ – as well as SAUMUR Rouge, called Château Fouquet★. Best years: (2000) **99 97 96 95 90 89 85**.

**FINGER LAKES AVA** *New York State, USA* Cool region in central NEW YORK STATE. Riesling, Chardonnay and sparkling wines are the trump cards here, but Pinot Noir and Cabernet Franc are increasingly successful. Best producers: Dr Konstantin Frank, FOX RUN, LAMOREAUX LANDING, Silver Thread, Hermann J Wiemer.

**FITOU AC** *Languedoc-Roussillon, France* One of the success stories of the 1980s. Quality subsequently slumped, but with the innovative MONT TAUCH co-op taking the lead, Fitou is once again an excellent place to seek out dark, herb-scented reds. Best producers: Bertrand-Berge, les Fenals, Lerys, MONT TAUCH co-op★, Mille Vignes, Nouvelles★, Rochelière, Dom. de Rolland, Roudène★. Best years: (2000) 99 **98 96 95 94 93**.

**FIXIN AC** *Côte de Nuits, Burgundy, France* Despite being next door to GEVREY-CHAMBERTIN, Fixin rarely produces anything really magical. The wines are often sold as COTE DE NUITS-VILLAGES. Recent vintages, though, have shown improvements, with best wines able to age for 5 years. Best producers: Champy★★, Pierre Gelin★, Alain Guyard★, D Laurent★★, Naddef★. Best years: (reds) (2000) 99 98 **97 96 95 93 90**.

**FLEURIE AC** *Beaujolais, Burgundy, France* The third-largest, but best-known BEAUJOLAIS Cru. Good Fleurie reveals the happy, carefree flavours of the Gamay grape at its best, plus heady perfumes and a delightful juicy sweetness. But demand has meant that many wines are overpriced and ordinary. Best producers: J-M Aujoux★, Berrod★, Michel Chignard★★, Clos de la Roilette★, Daumas★★, Depardon★, Deprés★★, DUBOEUF (named vineyards★), H Fessy★, Fleurie co-op★, Metrat★★, Vissoux★★. Best years: (2000) 99 **98 97 96 95**.

**CH. LA FLEUR-PÉTRUS★★** *Pomerol AC, Bordeaux, France* Like the better-known PETRUS and TROTANOY, this is owned by the dynamic MOUEIX family. Unlike its stablemates, it is situated entirely on gravel soil and tends to produce tighter wines with less immediate fruit but considerable elegance and cellar potential. Among POMEROL's top dozen properties. Best years: (2000) 99 98 97 96 95 94 **93 90 89 88 85 82**.

**FLORA SPRINGS** *Napa Valley AVA, California, USA* This winery started life as a white wine specialist, but after replanting is now best known for Cabernet Reserve★★, a BORDEAUX blend called Trilogy★★ and Merlot★★. Chardonnay Reserve★★ tops the whites. Best years: (Chardonnay) (1999) 98 **97 96 95 94 92 91**; (Trilogy) (1999) 97 96 95 94 **93 92 91**.

**FLOWERS** *Sonoma Coast AVA, California, USA* Small producer whose estate vineyard, Camp Meeting Ridge, a few miles from the Pacific Ocean, yields wines of great intensity. The Camp Meeting Ridge Pinot Noir★★★ and Chardonnay★★★ are usually made with native yeasts and offer exotic aromas and flavours. Wines from purchased fruit with a Sonoma Coast designation are ★★ in quality. Best years: (Chardonnay) 1999 **98 97 96**; (Pinot Noir) (1999) 98 97 96.

**FONSECA** *Port DOC, Douro, Portugal* Owned by the same group as TAYLOR FLADGATE & YEATMAN, Fonseca makes ports in a rich, densely plummy style. Fonseca Vintage★★★ is magnificent, the aged tawnies★★ uniformly superb. Fonseca Guimaraens★★ is the name of the 'off-vintage' wine, but off vintages here are equal to all but the best offerings of other houses. Bin No. 27★ is one of the top premium rubies. Best years: (Vintage) 1997 94 92 **85 83 77 75 70 66 63 55**.

**JOSÉ MARIA DA FONSECA** *Terras do Sado, Portugal* One of Portugal's most go-ahead wineries. Its most exciting red wines come from the ALENTEJO, in particular the fleshy, oaky d'Avillez★ from Portalegre and the more profound José de Sousa Mayor★. From Setúbal, south of Lisbon, it produces the fruity though rustic red Periquita, as well as good red and dry white Quinta de Camarate★, equally good Primum white★ and red★, premium Garrafeiras RA★★ and CO★ and the famous sweet fortified Moscatel de SETUBAL, ★★ in its 20-year-old and vintage-dated 'superior' versions.

**FONTANAFREDDA** *Barolo DOCG, Piedmont, Italy* One of the largest PIEDMONT estates, based in the old BAROLO hunting lodge of the King of Italy. As well as Barolo Serralunga d'Alba★, it also produces a range of Piedmont varietals, several single-vineyard Barolos★ (La Delizia★★), 4 million bottles of ASTI and a good dry sparkler, Contessa Rosa. Best years: (Barolo) (1998) (97) 96 **90 89 88 85**.

**DOM. FONT DE MICHELLE** *Châteauneuf-du-Pape AC, Rhône Valley, France* This much-improved estate is currently among the top performers in CHATEAUNEUF-DU-PAPE. The reds★★, in particular Cuvée

Etienne Gonnet★★, and whites★ are stylish but still heady, with richness and southern herb fragrance – and not too expensive. Best years: (Etienne Gonnet red) (1999) 98 97 **96 95 90 89**.

**FONTERUTOLI, CASTELLO DI** *Chianti Classico DOCG, Tuscany, Italy* This eminent estate has belonged to the Mazzei family since the 15th century. Now, in a dramatic gesture, it has focused production on CHIANTI CLASSICO Riserva★★★. The new wine replaces the fine SUPER-TUSCAN Concerto★★ (Sangiovese with 20% Cabernet) and previously outstanding Riserva Ser Lapo★★. The excellent Sangiovese-Merlot Siepi★★★ is being retained. Belguardo MORELLINO DI SCANSANO★ is a new venture in the southern Maremma.

**FONTODI** *Chianti Classico DOCG, Tuscany, Italy* The Manetti family has built this superbly sited estate into one of the most admired in the CHIANTI CLASSICO area, with excellent *normale*★★, richer Riserva★★ and fine Riserva Vigna del Sorbo★. SUPER-TUSCAN Flaccianello della Pieve★★★, produced from a single vineyard of old vines, has served as a shining example to other producers of how excellent Sangiovese can be without the addition of other varieties. Two varietals are made under the new Case Via label; of these, the Syrah★★ is most promising. Best years: (Flaccianello) (1999) 98 97 96 95 **94 93 91 90 88 86 85**.

**FORADORI** *Teroldego Rotaliano DOC, Trentino, Italy* Producer of dark, spicy, berry-fruited wines, including a regular TEROLDEGO ROTALIANO★ and barrique-aged Granato★★. Foradori's interest in Syrah is producing excellent results, both in the varietal Ailanpa★ and the smoky, black-cherry lushness of Cabernet-Syrah blend Karanar★. Best years: (Granato) (1999) **97 96 95 93 91**.

**FORST** *Pfalz, Germany* Village with 6 individual vineyard sites, including the Ungeheuer or 'Monster'; wines from the Monster can indeed be quite savage, with a marvellous mineral intensity and richness in the best years. Equally good are the Kirchenstück, Jesuitengarten, Freundstück and Pechstein. Best producers: BASSERMANN-JORDAN★★, von BUHL★, BÜRKLIN-WOLF★★, MOSBACHER★, J WEGELER ERBEN★, Werlé★, WOLF★★. Best years: (whites) 1999 98 **97 96 95 94 93 90**.

**FOX RUN VINEYARDS** *Finger Lakes AVA, New York State, USA* A solid producer of quality wines from several grapes, including a complex Alsace-style Gewürztraminer★★, an elegant Reserve Chardonnay★ and a delightfully quaffable semi-dry Riesling. There are also spicy, attractive reds from Pinot Noir and Cabernet Franc★ and, since 1996, a complex, fruit-forward red Meritage★. Best years: 2000 **99 98 97**.

**FRANCIACORTA DOCG** *Lombardy, Italy* A Champagne-method sparkler made from Pinot and Chardonnay grapes that has held DOCG status since the mid-90s. Still whites from Pinot Bianco and Chardonnay and reds from Cabernet, Barbera, Nebbiolo and Merlot are all DOC with the appellation Terre di Franciacorta. Best producers: BELLAVISTA★★, CA' DEL BOSCO★★, Fratelli Berlucchi★, Guido Berlucchi★, Castellino★, Cavalleri★, La Ferghettina★, Enrico Gatti★, Monte Rossa★, Ricci Curbastro★, San Cristoforo★, Uberti★, Villa★.

**FRANCISCAN** *Napa Valley AVA, California, USA* Consistently good wines at fair prices, from the heart of the NAPA VALLEY. The Cuvée Sauvage Chardonnay★★ is a blockbusting, courageous mouthful, and the Cabernet Sauvignon-based meritage Magnificat★ is developing a very attractive style. Estancia is a second label, with remarkably good-value Chardonnay★ from CENTRAL COAST and Cabernet Sauvignon★ from ALEXANDER VALLEY, as well as its own Meritage★. Franciscan also owns Mount Veeder Winery, where lean but intense Cabernet Sauvignon★★ of great mineral depth and complexity is made. Best years: (Chardonnay) 1998 97 96 **95 94 91**; (Cabernet Sauvignon) (1999) 97 96 95 94 **93 91**.

**FRANKEN** *Germany* Wine region incorporated into the kingdom of Bavaria at the beginning of the 19th century and specializing in dry wines. Easily recognizable by their squat, green Bocksbeutel bottles (now more familiar because of the Portuguese wine Mateus Rosé). Silvaner is the traditional grape variety, although Müller-Thurgau now predominates. The most famous vineyards are on the hillsides around WURZBURG and IPHOFEN.

**FRANSCHHOEK WO** *South Africa* A picturesque valley encircled by breathtaking mountain peaks. The Huguenot refugees settled here in the 17th century and many of the wineries still bear French names. Semillon is a local speciality (a few vines are close to 100 years old) and the valley is best known for its white wines. However, a diverse range of reds are now showing promise, including Cabrière's Pinot Noir★, La Motte's Shiraz★ and Optima Cabernet-Merlot from L'Ormarins. Best producers: Boekenhoutskloof★, Cabrière Estate★, Jean Daneel Wines, La Motte★, L'Ormarins, La Petite Ferme.

**FRASCATI DOC** *Lazio, Italy* One of Italy's most famous whites, frequently referred to as Rome's quaffing wine. The wine is a blend of Trebbiano and Malvasia; the better examples have a higher proportion of Malvasia. Good Frascati is worth seeking out, most notably Vigna Adriana★★, from the revelationary Castel de Paolis. A number of producers are also reviving the sweet late-harvest style called Cannellino. Other light, dry Frascati-like wines come from neighbouring DOCs in the hills of the Castelli Romani and Colli Albani, including Marino, Montecompatri, Velletri and Zagarolo. Best producers: Casale Marchese★, Castel de Paolis★★, Colli di Catone★, Piero Costantini/Villa Simone★, Fontana Candida★, Zandotti★.

**FREISA** Italian PIEDMONT grape making sweet, foaming, 'happy juice' reds, now sadly rather out of fashion. Some producers are now making a dry style which is very tasty after 3 or 4 years. Best producers: Cantina del Pino, Poderi Colla, Piero Gatti, G MASCARELLO, Scarpa★, Aldo Vajra★★, Rino Varaldo, Gianni Voerzio.

**FREIXENET** *Cava DO, Cataluña, Spain* The second-biggest Spanish sparkling wine company (after CODORNIU) makes the famous Cordon Negro Brut CAVA in a vast network of cellars in San Sadurní de Noya. Despite its size and success, most of Freixenet's Cavas are unexciting.

**FRESCOBALDI** *Tuscany, Italy* Florentine company selling large quantities of inexpensive blended CHIANTIS, but from its own vineyards (some 800 ha/1980 acres in total) it produces good to very good wines at Nipozzano (especially CHIANTI RUFINA Castello di Nipozzano Riserva★★ and Montesodi★★★), Tenuta di POMINO★ and CASTELGIOCONDO★ in

BRUNELLO DI MONTALCINO. Castelgiocondo is also the early source for the much-ballyhooed new wine, Luce – a joint venture with MONDAVI. Best years: (premium reds) (1998) 97 96 **95 94 93 91 90 88 85**.

**FRIEDRICH-WILHELM-GYMNASIUM** *Trier, Ruwer, Germany* New director
♀ Helmut Kranich has brought this estate back on song after a serious lapse in performance in the early 1990s. The naturally sweet Rieslings all have an appealing delicacy and lightness, and most Spätlese and Auslese rate ★. Best years: 1999 **98 97 95 90**.

**FRIULI GRAVE DOC** *Friuli-Venezia Giulia, Italy* DOC in western Friuli
♟ covering 19 wine types. Good affordable Merlot, Refosco, Chardonnay, Pinot Grigio, Traminer and Tocai. Best producers: Borgo Magredo★, La Delizia co-op, Le Fredis★, Di Lenardo★, Orgnani★, Pighin★, Pittaro★, Plozner★, Pradio★, Russolo★, Vigneti Le Monde★, Villa Chiopris★, Vistorta★. Best years: (whites) (2000) **98 97**.

**FRIULI ISONZO DOC** *Friuli-Venezia Giulia, Italy* Classy southern neighbour
♟ of COLLIO with wines of outstanding value. The DOC covers 20 styles, including Merlot, Chardonnay, Pinot Grigio and Sauvignon. The best from neighbouring Carso are also good. Best producers: (Isonzo) Borgo San Daniele★, Colmello di Grotta★, Sergio & Mauro Drius★★, Masùt da Rive★ (Silvano Gallo), Lis Neris-Pecorari★★, Pierpaolo Pecorari★★, Giovanni Puiatti★, Ronco del Gelso★★, Tenuta Villanova★, Vie di Romans★★; (Carso) Castelvecchio, Edi Kante★★. Best years: (whites) (2000) **99 98 97 96 95**.

**FRIULI-VENEZIA GIULIA** *Italy* North-east Italian region bordering Austria and Slovenia. The hilly DOC zones of COLLIO and COLLI ORIENTALI produce some of Italy's finest whites from Chardonnay, Pinot Bianco, Pinot Grigio, Sauvignon and Tocai, and excellent reds mainly from Cabernet, Merlot and Refosco. The DOCs of Friuli Aquileia, FRIULI ISONZO, Friuli Latisana and FRIULI GRAVE, in the rolling hills and plains, produce good-value wines.

**FRONSAC AC** *Bordeaux, France* Small area west of POMEROL making very
♟ good-value Merlot-based wines. The top producers have made a considerable effort to improve in recent years. The wines are firmly structured, occasionally perfumed, and are better with at least 5 years' age. Best producers: Dalem★, la Dauphine★, Fontenil★, la Grave★, Haut-Carles★, Mayne-Vieil, Moulin-Haut-Laroque★, Puy Guilhem, la Rivière★, la Rousselle★, les Trois Croix, la Vieille Cure★, Villars★. Best years: (2000) 98 97 96 **95 94 90 89 88 86 85 83 82**.

**CH. FUISSÉ** *Pouilly-Fuissé, Mâconnais, Burgundy, France* Owner Jean-
♟ Jacques Vincent produces rich, ripe, concentrated Chardonnays. Top wines are the 3 Pouilly-Fuissés – Cuvée Première★★, the oak-fermented Ch. Fuissé★★ and the memorable, richly textured Ch. Fuissé Vieilles Vignes★★★. He also makes a fine ST-VERAN★, BEAUJOLAIS and has a négociant business specializing in wines of the Mâconnais.

**FUMÉ BLANC** See Sauvignon Blanc.

**RUDOLF FÜRST** *Bürgstadt, Franken, Germany* Paul Fürst's dry
♟ Rieslings★★ are unusually elegant for a region renowned for its earthy white wines, and his ageworthy Spätburgunder reds★★ are some of the best in Germany. Sensual, intellectual wines with excellent aging potential. Best years: (whites) 1999 98 **97 94 93 92 90 89 88**; (reds) (1999) **97 94 90**.

**JEAN-NOËL GAGNARD** *Chassagne-Montrachet AC, Côte de Beaune, Burgundy, France* Caroline Lestimé has recently taken up the reins from her father, Jean-Noël Gagnard. They consistently make some of the best wines of CHASSAGNE-MONTRACHET. Top wine is rich, toasty BATARD-MONTRACHET★★★, but other whites are first rate, too, particularly Premiers Crus Caillerets★★★ and Morgeot★★. Gagnard's reds★ are not quite as good, but are still among the most enjoyable in Chassagne. All whites are capable of extended cellaring. Best years: (whites) (2000) 99 98 **97** 96 **95 92 90**.

**GAGNARD-DELAGRANGE** *Chassagne-Montrachet AC, Côte de Beaune, Burgundy, France* Jacques Gagnard-Delagrange heads a distinguished family of interrelated winemakers – Jacques' brother is Jean-Noël GAGNARD, and the source of many of his vineyards was Jacques' father-in-law, Edmond Delagrange-Bachelet. Jacques makes excellent BATARD-MONTRACHET★★★ and CHASSAGNE-MONTRACHET Premiers Crus La Boudriotte★★ and Morgeot★★. His 2 daughters and their husbands are responsible for Domaines Blain-Gagnard (look out for Criots-Bâtard-Montrachet★★) and Fontaine-Gagnard (also Criots-Bâtard-Montrachet★★★ and several Chassagne-Montrachet Premiers Crus★★). Best years: (whites) (2000) 99 98 **97** 96 **95 92 90 89**.

**GAILLAC AC** *South-West France* The whites, mainly from Mauzac with its sharp but attractive green apple bite, are rather stern but, from a decent grower or the revitalized co-ops, can be extremely refreshing. Some more serious reds are now being made, which require some aging. The star of Gaillac at the moment is the outstanding fizz, ideally not quite dry and packed with fruit. Drink as young as possible. Best producers: Albert, Bosc-Long, Causses-Marines★, Ch. Clément Termes, J Cros, Escausses, Labarthe, Labastide-de-Lévis co-op, Mas Pignou, Plageoles★, Rotier, Técou co-op★.

**GAJA** *Barbaresco DOCG, Piedmont, Italy* Angelo Gaja brought about the transformation of PIEDMONT from an old-fashioned region that Italians swore made the finest red wine in the world yet the rest of the world disdained, to an area buzzing with excitement. He introduced international standards and charged staggeringly high prices, thus giving

other Piedmont growers the chance at last to get a decent return for their labours. Into this fiercely conservative area, full of fascinating grape varieties but proudest of the native Nebbiolo, he also introduced French grapes like Cabernet Sauvignon (Darmagi★★), Sauvignon Blanc (Alteni di Brassica★) and Chardonnay (Gaia & Rey★★). His latest coup has been to renounce the Barbaresco and Barolo DOCGs for his best wines! Gaja's traditional strength has been in single-vineyard wines from the BARBARESCO region: his Sorì San Lorenzo★★★, Sorì Tildìn★★★ and Costa Russi★★★, now sold under the LANGHE DOC, are often cited as Barbaresco's best. One single premium bottling of Barbaresco★★★ is now made. Sperss★★★ and new Conteisa★★★ – from Barolo, but sold as Langhe DOC wines – are also outstanding. Barbera Sito Rey★ and Nebbiolo-based Langhe Sito Moresco★ are less exciting. Gaja has also invested in BRUNELLO DI MONTALCINO (Pieve Santa Restituta) and BOLGHERI. Best years: (Barbaresco) (1998) 97 96 95 **94 93 90 89 88 85 82 79 78 71 61**.

**GALICIA** *Spain* Up in Spain's hilly, verdant north-west, Galicia is renowned for its Albariño whites. There are 5 DOs: RIAS BAIXAS can make excellent, fragrant Albariño, with modern equipment and serious winemaking; Ribeiro has also invested heavily in new equipment, and better local white grapes are now being used, as is the case in the mountainous Valdeorras DO. Some young reds from the Mencia grape are also made there and in the new Ribeira Sacra DO. Monterrei DO, also new, is technically backward but shows some potential with its native white grape variety, Doña Blanca. Most wines are best consumed young.

**E & J GALLO** *Central Valley, California, USA* With the release of its upscale Sonoma Estate Chardonnay and Cabernet Sauvignon in the mid-1990s, Gallo, the world's biggest winery – known for cheap wines – is at last convincing doubters it can make fine wine. Both limited production wines came from Gallo's 800ha (2000 acres) of premium vineyards in key SONOMA COUNTY AVAs. Their success led to the establishment of Gallo of Sonoma, a new label for varietals such as Zinfandel and Merlot from DRY CREEK VALLEY, Cabernet from ALEXANDER VALLEY and Chardonnay from several vineyards. New vineyards in RUSSIAN RIVER VALLEY have been planted to Pinot Noir. Yet despite this giant step up in quality, Gallo continues to produce oceans of low-priced wine that is at best ordinary. New labels such as Turning Leaf, Gossamer Bay and Garnet Point were launched in the 90s, plus small-volume brands Anapamu (Central Coast Chardonnay), Zabaco (Sonoma County wines), Marcelina (Napa wines), and Indigo Hills (Mendocino wines).

**GAMAY** The only grape allowed for red BEAUJOLAIS. In general Gamay wine is rather rough-edged and quite high in raspy acidity, but in Beaujolais, so long as the yield is not too high, it can achieve a wonderful, juicy-fruit gluggability, almost unmatched in the world of wine. Elsewhere in France, it is successful in the Ardèche and the Loire and less so in the Mâconnais. IN CALIFORNIA, the grape sold under the name of Gamay has now been identified as Valdiguié and in future the name Gamay won't be used. South Africa's very limited production has yielded mixed results.

**GARD, VIN DE PAYS DU** *Languedoc, France* Mainly reds and rosés from the western side of the RHONE delta. Most Gard red is light and spicy and increasingly attractive. Rosés can be fresh when young. With modern winemaking the whites can be good. Best producers: des Aveylans★, Baruel★, Cantarelles★, Christin, Coste Plane, Grande-Cassagne★, Guiot★, Mas des Bressades★, St-Gilles co-op.

**GARGANEGA** Italian white grape from the VENETO in north-east Italy; main component of SOAVE. Grown on hillsides, it can have class, but its reputation is tainted by excessive yields from the Veronese plain.

**GARNACHA BLANCA**  See Grenache Blanc.

**GARNACHA TINTA**  See Grenache Noir.

**GATTINARA DOCG** *Piedmont, Italy*  One of the most capricious of Italy's top red wine areas, capable of both great things and dross. Situated in northern PIEDMONT and recently elevated to DOCG, the Nebbiolo wines should be softer and lighter than BAROLO, with a delicious, black plums, tar and roses flavour if you're lucky. Vintages follow those for Barolo, but the wines should be drunk within 10 years. Best producers: Antoniolo★, G Bianchi★, Nervi★, Travaglini★.

**DOMAINE GAUBY** *Côtes du Roussillon-Villages AC, Roussillon, France*  Gérard Gauby used to make burly wines in which the fruit was hidden by very hard tannins. Recent vintages have been softer while still retaining concentration, and Gauby is now a hot property in ROUSSILLON. Highlights include powerful COTES DU ROUSSILLON-VILLAGES Vieilles Vignes★★ and Syrah-dominated la Muntada★★ as well as a vin de pays Viognier★★. Best years: 1999 98 **97 96 95 94** 93.

**GAVI DOCG** *Piedmont, Italy*  Fashionable and often overpriced, this Cortese-based, steely, lemony white can age up to 5 years, providing it starts life with sufficient fruit. La Scolca's Spumante Brut Soldati★ is an admirable sparkling wine. Best producers: Battistina★, Bergaglio★, Broglia★, La Chiara★, CHIARLO★, FONTANAFREDDA★, La Giustiniana★★, Pio Cesare, San Pietro★, La Scolca★, Tassarolo★, Villa Sparina★.

**CH. GAZIN★★** *Pomerol AC, Bordeaux, France*  One of the largest châteaux in POMEROL, next to the legendary PETRUS. The wine, traditionally a succulent, sweet-textured Pomerol, seemed to lose its way in the 1980s but is now showing real richness and a very individualistic character under the management of owner Nicolas de Baillencourt. Best years: (2000) 99 98 97 96 95 94 **90 89 88** 82.

**GEELONG** *Victoria, Australia*  Region revived in the 1960s after destruction by phylloxera in the 19th century, but expansion has been erratic so far. Potentially a match for the YARRA VALLEY. Impressive Pinot Noir, Chardonnay, Riesling, Sauvignon Blanc and Shiraz. Best producers: Austin's Barrabool, BANNOCKBURN★★, Idyll, Scotchmans Hill★★.

**GEISENHEIM** *Rheingau, Germany*  Village famous for its wine school, founded in 1872. It was here that the Müller-Thurgau grape, now one of Germany's most widely planted grapes, was bred in 1882. Geisenheim's most famous vineyard is the Rothenberg, which produces strong, earthy wines. Best producers: Johannishof, J WEGELER ERBEN, von Zwierlein. Best years: 1999 98 97 96 **93 90**.

**GERMAIN PÈRE ET FILS** *Chorey-lès-Beaune, Côte de Beaune, Burgundy, France*  The sleepy village of CHOREY-LES-BEAUNE is the source of some of the COTE D'OR's best-value reds and, along with TOLLOT-BEAUT, François Germain is the AC's best-known producer. Makes elegant red Ch. de Chorey★★, a series of richer BEAUNE Premiers Crus (Teurons★★ and Vignes Franches★★ are both delicious) and reasonably priced PERNAND-VERGELESSES Blanc. The reds are best drunk after 2–6 years in bottle. Best years: 1999 98 **97 96 95 93 90**.

**GEVREY-CHAMBERTIN AC** *Côte de Nuits, Burgundy, France*  There have been periods when the wines of Gevrey-Chambertin too often proved disappointing, but a new generation of growers has restored the reputation of Gevrey as a source of well-coloured, firmly structured,

141

powerful, perfumed wines that become rich and gamy with age. Village wines should be kept for at least 5 years, Premiers Crus and the 8 Grands Crus for 10 years or more, especially CHAMBERTIN and Clos-de-Bèze. Look for the Premier Cru Clos St-Jacques, a wine worthy of promotion to Grand Cru. Best producers: Denis Bachelet★★, L Boillot★, A Burguet★★, CLAIR★★★, P Damoy★★, DROUHIN★, C Dugat★★, B Dugat-Py★★, DUJAC★★, M Esmonin★★, FAIVELEY★★, Fourrier★★, JADOT★★, Philippe Leclerc★, Denis Mortet★★★, Rossignol★, J Roty★★, ROUSSEAU★★★, J & J-L Trapet★. Best years: (2000) 99 98 **97** 96 **95 93 90**.

---

**GEWÜRZTRAMINER** Best in France's ALSACE and also impressive in the Styria region of Austria. Quality is mixed in Australia, New Zealand, OREGON, CALIFORNIA, the Czech Republic, Germany, South Africa, Italy's ALTO ADIGE (where it is called Traminer Aromatico), Romania and Switzerland (under the name Heida). *Gewürz* means spice, and the wine certainly can be spicy and exotically perfumed, as well as being typically low in acidity. Styles vary enormously, from the fresh, light, florally perfumed wines produced in Italy to the rich, luscious, late-harvest ALSACE VENDANGE TARDIVE.

---

**GEYSER PEAK** *Alexander Valley AVA, California, USA* Australian winemaker Daryl Groom's wines tend to be accessible, fruity and fun. Best is the light, fruity Cabernet★. The Reserve Alexandre★★, a blend of Cabernet Sauvignon, Merlot, Cabernet Franc and Malbec, is made for aging, and the Shiraz Reserve★★ has a cult following. Black Collection is a label for vineyard-specific Chardonnay, Cabernet and Viognier. Best years: (reds) (1999) 98 97 **95 94 92 91**.

**GHEMME DOCG** *Piedmont, Italy* Red, Nebbiolo-based wine, from vines on the opposite bank of the Sésia to GATTINARA. The top examples are Cantalupo's Collis Carellae and Signore di Bayard. Best producers: Antichi Vigneti di Cantalupo★, G Bianchi★. Best years: (1999) (98) 97 96 95 **93 90 89 88 85**.

**BRUNO GIACOSA** *Barbaresco DOCG, Piedmont, Italy* One of the great winemakers of the LANGHE hills, and an unashamed traditionalist, leaving his BARBARESCOS and BAROLOS in cask for up to 6 years. Superb Barbarescos Asili★★★, Santo Stefano★★★ and Rabaja★★★, and Barolos including Collina Rionda★★ and Falletto★★. Also excellent Dolcetto d'Alba★, Roero Arneis★, Moscato d'Asti★★ and sparkling Extra Brut★★.

**GIESEN** *Canterbury, South Island, New Zealand* CANTERBURY's largest winery makes outstanding botrytized Riesling★★, as well as fine dry Riesling★, complex, oaky Chardonnay★, and an attractive Sauvignon Blanc★. Best years: (Riesling and Chardonnay) (2001) **99 98 97 96**.

**GIGONDAS AC** *Rhône Valley, France* Gigondas wines, mostly red and made mainly from Grenache, have fistfuls of chunky personality. Most drink well with 5 years' age, some a little more. Best producers: la Boussière★★, Brusset★★, Cassan★★, Cayron★★, Clos des Cazaux★, Cros de la Mure★★, DELAS★★, Font-Sane★★, les Goubert★, Gour de Chaule★, Grapillon d'Or★★, GUIGAL★, JABOULET★★, Longue-Toque★, Moulin de la Gardette★★, les Pallières★, Piaugier★, Raspail-Ay★★, St-Cosme★★, ST-GAYAN★, Santa-Duc★★, Tardieu-Laurent★★, la Tourade★★, Trignon★★. Best years: (2000) 99 98 **97 95 93 90**.

**CH. GILETTE★★** *Sauternes AC, Bordeaux, France* These astonishing wines are stored in concrete vats as opposed to the more normal wooden barrels. This virtually precludes any oxygen contact, and it is oxygen that ages a wine. Consequently, when released at up to 30 years old, they are bursting with life and lusciousness. Best years: **1979 78 76 75 70 67 59 55 53 49**.

**GIPPSLAND** *Victoria, Australia* Diverse wineries along the southern Victoria coast, all tiny but with massive potential. Results are still erratic. Nicholson River's BURGUNDY-style wines can hit ★★, but only occasionally. McAlister★, a BORDEAUX blend, has also produced some tasty flavours. Bass Phillip Reserve★★ and Premium★★ Pinots are among the best in Australia, with a cult following – in years like 1997 they approached the silky charm of the COTE DE NUITS.

**VINCENT GIRARDIN** *Santenay AC, Côte de Beaune, Burgundy, France* The best grower in SANTENAY and now a thriving négociant as well. Bright, glossy reds from Santenay★★, MARANGES★★ and CHASSAGNE-MONTRACHET★★ are surpassed by excellent VOLNAY★★ and POMMARD Grands Epenots★★★. Chassagne-Montrachet whites (Morgeot★★ and Caillerets★★★) are well balanced with good fruit depth. CORTON-CHARLEMAGNE★★★ is exceptional. Best years: (reds) 1999 98 **97 96 95**.

**GISBORNE** *North Island, New Zealand* Gisborne, with its hot, humid climate and fertile soils, delivers both quality and quantity. Local growers have christened their region 'The Chardonnay Capital of New Zealand' and Gewürztraminer and Chenin Blanc are also a success. Good reds, however, are hard to find. Best producers: CORBANS, MILLTON★★, MONTANA, Revington.

**GIVRY AC** *Côte Chalonnaise, Burgundy, France* An important COTE CHALONNAISE village. The reds have an intensity of fruit and ability to age that are unusual in the region. In recent years the whites have improved considerably, and there are now some attractive, fairly full, nutty examples. Best producers: Bourgeon★, Chofflet-Valdenaire★, Joblot★, F Lumpp★, Parize★, Ragot★, Sarrazin★, Thénard★. Best years: (reds) (2000) 99 98 **97 96 95**; (whites) (2000) 99 **98**.

**GLEN CARLOU** *Paarl WO, South Africa* Extensive new vineyards, mainly Chardonnay, but also some Zinfandel, Tempranillo and Mourvèdre, reveal the bullish mood in this successful partnership between the Finlaysons and Donald Hess, owner of CALIFORNIA winery The HESS COLLECTION. David Finlayson is proving himself the equal of his father Walter; his elegant standard Chardonnay★ and richer toasty Reserve★★ version are widely acclaimed, as are the spicy, silky Pinot Noir★ and Grande Classique★, a BORDEAUX blend with excellent aging potential. Best years: (Chardonnay) **1999 98 97 96**.

**CH. GLORIA★** *St-Julien AC, Cru Bourgeois, Haut-Médoc, Bordeaux, France* An interesting property, created out of tiny plots of Classed Growth land scattered all round ST-JULIEN. Generally very soft and sweet-centred, the wine nonetheless ages well. Second wine: Peymartin. Best years: (2000) 98 97 96 95 **94 90 89 88 86 85 83 82**.

**GOLAN HEIGHTS WINERY** *Golan Heights, Israel* Israel's leading quality wine producer. Cool summers, well-drained, high-altitude vineyards and winemaking that combines modern techniques with kosher strictures have all resulted in good Sauvignon Blanc★ and Cabernet★, excellent, oaky Chardonnay★★ and good bottle-fermented fizz★. Yarden is the top label; Golan and Gamla are mid-range. Expansion to new vineyards in Galilee may offset the threat to the flagship winery resulting from the Middle East peace process.

---

**GOLDMUSKATELLER**   The Moscato Giallo grape is known as Goldmuskateller in Italy's ALTO ADIGE. Here and elsewhere in Italy's northeast it makes scented wines in both dry and slightly sweet styles. Best producers: Nilo Bolognani★, Isera CO-OP★, LAGEDER★, Tiefenbrunner★.

---

**GOLDWATER ESTATE** *Waiheke Island, Auckland, New Zealand*   The founding vineyard established by Kim and Jeanette Goldwater on WAIHEKE ISLAND, New Zealand's premium red wine district. Intense, long-lived Cabernet-Merlot★★ and Merlot★★, made in an elegant, cedary style with considerable depth and structure. Also attractive MARLBOROUGH Sauvignon Blanc★ and Chardonnay★ from grapes grown under contract. New Estate Chardonnay should be exciting. Best years: (Waiheke reds) (2000) 99 **98 96 94**.

**GONZÁLEZ BYASS** *Jerez y Manzanilla DO, Andalucía, Spain*   Tio Pepe★, the high-quality fino brand of this huge top sherry firm, is the world's biggest-selling sherry. The top range of old sherries is superb: the dry Amontillado del Duque★★★, and 2 rich, complex olorosos, sweet Matusalem★★ and medium Apostoles★★. One step down is the Alfonso Dry Oloroso★. The firm pioneered the rediscovery of single-vintage (non-solera) dry olorosos★★.

DEL DUQUE
*Amontillado Muy Viejo*
*Jerez · Xérès · Sherry*
**GONZÁLEZ BYASS**

**GOULBURN VALLEY** *Victoria, Australia*   The Goulburn river is a serene, beautiful thread of contentment running through VICTORIA's parched grazing lands. Surprisingly few vineyards have been established here but these do produce some very individual wines. The region's speciality is Marsanne white. Best producers: MITCHELTON★★, Osicka★★, Plunkett, Strathbogie Ranges, TAHBILK★, David Traeger.

**GRAACH** *Mosel, Germany*   Important Middle MOSEL wine village with 4 vineyard sites, the most famous being Domprobst (also the best) and Himmelreich. A third, the Josephshöfer, is wholly owned by the von KESSELSTATT estate in Trier. The wines have an attractive fullness to balance their steely acidity, and great aging potential. Best producers: von KESSELSTATT★★, Dr LOOSEN★★, J J PRÜM★★, W SCHAEFER★★★, SELBACH-OSTER★★. Best years: 1999 98 **97** 96 **95 94 93 90**.

**GRACIA** *Rapel, Chile*   Part of the Córpora group, making a well-made range of wines at a futuristic winery. Good reds include Pinot Noir Reserva Lo Mejor★. Much Merlot and Cabernet Sauvignon, including the top red RR Reserva Caminante★★, is sourced from Aconcagua.

---

**GRACIANO**   Rare, low-yielding but excellent Spanish grape, traditional in RIOJA, NAVARRA and, as Parraleta, in SOMONTANO. It makes dense, highly structured, fragrant reds, and its high acidity adds life when blended with low-acid Tempranillo. Also grown by BROWN BROTHERS in Australia.

**GRAHAM** *Port DOC, Douro, Portugal* Part of the Symington empire, making rich, florally scented Vintage Port★★★, sweeter than DOW's and WARRE's, but with the backbone to age. In non-vintage years makes a fine wine called Malvedos★★. Six Grapes is one of the best premium rubies, and 10-year-old★ and 20-year-old★ tawnies are consistently good. Best years: (Vintage) 1997 94 91 **85 83 80 77 75 70 66 63 60**; (Malvedos) 1998 95 92 **90 87 86 84**.

**ALAIN GRAILLOT** *Crozes-Hermitage AC, Rhône Valley, France* This excellent estate, established in 1985, stands out as a producer of powerfully concentrated, rich, fruity reds. The top wine is called la Guiraude★★, but the regular Crozes★★ is wonderful too, as is the Hermitage★★. Keep reds for 5 years, though the best will become even finer with longer aging.

**GRAMPIANS** *Victoria, Australia* This recently renamed area centres on Great Western, a distinguished old viticultural area in central-western Victoria, historically known for its sparkling wine. Grampians has not expanded in the 1990s like the other southern Victoria regions but still produces some of Australia's greatest Shiraz – as table wine, sparkling red and even port-style. Best producers: BEST's★, Garden Gully★, Montara★, MOUNT LANGI GHIRAN★★, SEPPELT★★.

**CH. DU GRAND MOULAS** *Côtes du Rhône, Rhône Valley, France* Marc Ryckwaert makes first-rate COTES DU RHONE★ from Grenache and a lick of Syrah that is delicious young but will age for 2–4 years. He also produces very good COTES DU RHONE-VILLAGES (red★ and white) and a rich, Syrah-based Grande Réserve red wine called Cuvée de l'Écu★.

**CH. GRAND-PUY-DUCASSE★** *Pauillac AC, 5ème Cru Classé, Haut-Médoc, Bordeaux, France* After great improvement in the 1980s, form in the 90s was less consistent. Approachable after 5 years, but the wines can improve for considerably longer. Second wine: Artigues-Arnaud. Best years: (2000) 96 95 **94 90 89 88 86 85**.

**CH. GRAND-PUY-LACOSTE★★** *Pauillac AC, 5ème Cru Classé, Haut-Médoc, Bordeaux, France* Classic PAUILLAC, with lots of blackcurrant and cigar-box perfume. As the wine develops, the flavours mingle with the sweetness of new oak into one of Pauillac's most memorable taste sensations. Second wine: Lacoste-Borie. Best years: (2000) 99 98 97 96 95 **94 93 90 89 88 86 85 83 82**.

**GRANDS-ÉCHÉZEAUX AC** See Échézeaux AC.

**GRANGE★★★** *Barossa Valley, South Australia* In 1950 Max Schubert, chief winemaker at PENFOLDS, visited Europe and the legend of Grange, the prototype for the reds that made Australia famous, began. Determined to make a wine that could match the quality and aging capacity of great BORDEAUX reds, and undeterred by the lack of Cabernet Sauvignon grapes or French oak barrels, he set to work with BAROSSA Shiraz and barrels made from the more pungent American oak. Only after years of being ignored and misunderstood did Schubert achieve recognition for his wine, a stupendously complex, thrillingly rich red that only begins to reveal its magnificence after 10 years in bottle. Produced using premium grapes primarily from the Barossa and MCLAREN VALE, it is acknowledged as Australia's greatest red. Best years: 1995 94 93 92 91 **90 88 86 84 83 80 76 71 67 66 63 62 55 53 52**.

**GRANGEHURST** *Stellenbosch WO, South Africa* Production is growing at this boutique winery, and a new 15-ha (37-acre) site has been purchased, but quality remains paramount. Nikela★, a new Cabernet-Pinotage-Merlot blend, joins the hand-crafted range as owner/winemaker Jeremy Walker's answer to the Cape blend. There is also a modern Pinotage★, savoury and ripe, and a Cabernet-Merlot★★ with powerful clarety appeal. Best years: **1998 97 96 95 94 93 92.**

**DOMAINE DE LA GRANGE DES PÈRES** *Vin de Pays de l'Hérault, Languedoc, France* It hasn't taken long for owner Laurent Vaillé to establish his tiny domaine as a LANGUEDOC legend – the first vintage was only in 1992. With only 500 cases produced each year, demand is high for the meticulously crafted unfiltered red★★. 1995 was the first vintage of a white★★ which is produced in even smaller quantities. Best years: (red) 1999 98 97 **96 95 94 93 92.**

**GRANS-FASSIAN** *Leiwen, Mittel Mosel, Germany* Leiwen owes its reputation largely to Gerhard Grans' success during the late 1980s. His naturally sweet Rieslings have gained in sophistication over the years: Spätlese★★ and Auslese★★ from Trittenheimer Apotheke are particularly impressive. Eiswein is a speciality and ★★★ in good vintages. Best years: (Spätlese) 1999 98 **97 96 95 93 90.**

**YVES GRASSA** *Vin de Pays des Côtes de Gascogne, South-West France* Innovative COTES DE GASCOGNE producer, who transformed Gascony's thin raw whites into some of the snappiest, fruitiest, almost-dry wines in France. Grassa also makes oak-aged★ and late-harvest★ styles.

**ALFRED GRATIEN** *Champagne AC, Champagne, France* This small company makes some of my favourite CHAMPAGNE. Its wines are made in wooden casks, which is very rare nowadays. The non-vintage★★ blend is usually 4 years old when sold, rather than the normal 3 years. The vintage★★★ is deliciously ripe and toasty when released but can age for another 10 years. Unusually, the prestige cuvée is a non-vintage, Cuvée Paradis★★. Best years: (1995) **90 89 88 87 85 83 82.**

**GRATIEN & MEYER** *Loire Valley, France* Owner of the quality-minded CHAMPAGNE house Alfred GRATIEN, Gratien & Meyer was recently bought by German sparkling wine company Henkell & Söhnlein. In the Loire the company's reputation rests on its Champagne-method SAUMUR MOUSSEUX, particularly its attractively rich, biscuity Cuvée Flamme★ and the Cuvée Flamme Rosé. Also a producer of still SAUMUR white wine and the red SAUMUR-CHAMPIGNY, it produces a little CREMANT DE LOIRE★ – and the sparkling red Cuvée Cardinal is unusual and fun.

**GRAVES AC** *Bordeaux, France* The Graves region covers the area south of Bordeaux to Langon, but the generally superior villages in the northern half broke away in 1987 to form the PESSAC-LEOGNAN AC. Nowadays a new wave of winemaking is sweeping through the southern Graves, and there are plenty of clean, bone-dry white wines, with lots of snappy freshness, as well as more complex soft, nutty barrel-aged whites, and some juicy, quick-drinking reds. Best producers: Archambeau, Ardennes★, le Bonnat, Brondelle★, Chantegrive★, Clos Floridène★, Dom. la Grave★, l'Hospital, Landiras, Magence, Magneau★, Rahoul★, Respide-Médeville★, St-Robert, Seuil★, Vieux-Ch.-Gaubert★, Villa Bel Air★. Best years: (reds) (2000) 98 **96 95 94 90 89 88 86 85 83 82;** (whites) (2000) **98 96 95 94 90 89 88.**

**GRAVES SUPÉRIEURES AC** *Bordeaux, France* White Graves, dry, medium or sweet, with a minimum alcohol level of 12% as opposed to 11% for Graves. The AC has never really caught on because of the confusion between dry and sweet wines, but the sweet wines can, in good years, make decent substitutes for the more expensive SAUTERNES. Best producers: (sweet) Clos St-Georges, Léhoul. Best years: (sweet) **1998 97 96 95 90 89 88 86.**

**GRAVNER** *Friuli-Venezia Giulia, Italy* Josko Gravner, Friuli's most zealous winemaker, sets styles with wood-aged wines of uncommon stature, though some remain outside the COLLIO DOC. Along with prized and high-priced Chardonnay★★, Sauvignon★★ and Ribolla Gialla★, he combines 6 white varieties in Breg★★. Reds are Rosso Gravner★ (predominantly Merlot) and Rujno★★ (Merlot-Cabernet Sauvignon).

**GRECHETTO** Italian grape centred on UMBRIA, making tasty, anise-tinged dry whites. Also used in VIN SANTO in TUSCANY. Best producers: Antonelli, Barberani-Vallesanta, Caprai, Falesco★, Palazzone, Castello della SALA.

**GRECO** See Grechetto.

**GREEN POINT VINEYARDS** *Yarra Valley, Victoria, Australia* MOET & CHANDON's Aussie offshoot makes Pinot Noir-Chardonnay Champagne-method fizz, including regular Chandon Australia and premium sparklers under the Green Point label (Vintage Brut★★, Vintage Brut Rosé★★). Now also producing still wines from Chardonnay and Pinot Noir, in a fairly oaky style. The Domaine Chandon label is used in the Australian market and is the name of the winery.

**GRENACHE BLANC** A common white grape in the south of France, but without many admirers. Except me, that is, because I love the pear-scented wine flecked with anise that a good producer can achieve. Generally best within a year of the vintage, although the odd old-vine example can age. Grown as Garnacha Blanca in Spain.

**GRENACHE NOIR** Among the world's most widely planted red grapes – the bulk of it in Spain, where it is called Garnacha Tinta. It is a hot-climate grape and in France it reaches its peak in the southern RHONE, especially in CHATEAUNEUF-DU-PAPE, where it combines great alcoholic strength with rich raspberry fruit and a perfume hot from the herb-strewn hills. It is given more tannin, acid and structure by blending with Syrah, Mourvèdre, Cinsaut or other southern French grapes. It can make wonderful rosé in TAVEL, LIRAC and COTES DE PROVENCE, as well as in NAVARRA in Spain. It forms the backbone of the impressive, newly rediscovered reds of PRIORAT, and in RIOJA it adds weight to the Tempranillo. It is also the basis for the *vins doux naturels* of BANYULS and MAURY. Also widely grown in CALIFORNIA and SOUTH AUSTRALIA, where it has become a surprisingly trendy and headily enjoyable quaffer. It has only recently been accorded much respect as imaginative winemakers realized there was a great resource of century-old vines capable of making wild and massively enjoyable reds that no one was taking any notice of. See also CANNONAU.

147

**G** **GRGICH HILLS CELLAR**

**GRGICH HILLS CELLAR** *Rutherford AVA, California, USA* Mike Grgich
was winemaker at CHATEAU MONTELENA when its Chardonnay shocked
the Paris judges by finishing ahead of French versions in the famous
1976 tasting. At his own winery he makes ripe, tannic Cabernet★ and
a huge, old-style Zinfandel★, but his reputation has been made by big,
ripe, oaky Chardonnay★★ that is one of NAPA's best-selling high-priced
wines. Best years: (Chardonnay) 1999 88 97 **96 95 94** 92 91 90.

**GRIGNOLINO** Italian red grape native to PIEDMONT that can produce pale-
coloured but intensely flavoured wines. DOC in the Monferrato Casalese
and Asti, and also made in Alba. HEITZ makes a version in CALIFORNIA.
Best producers: G Accornero★, Braida, Bricco Mondalino★, Cantine
Sant' Agata, Scarpa, La Tenaglia, Viarengo, Vinchio e Vaglio Serra co-op.

**GRIOTTE-CHAMBERTIN AC** See Chambertin AC.

**GRISTINA VINEYARDS** *Long Island, New York State, USA* A long-standing
producer acquired in 2000 by Vincent Galluccio, who immediately
embarked on expanding facilities and plantings. Stars are the elegant
Chardonnay★ and cherry-vanilla Merlot. Best years: **1998 97 95**.

**JEAN GRIVOT** *Vosne-Romanée, Côte de Nuits, Burgundy, France* Étienne
Grivot took time to settle down but has now reconciled his father's
traditional styles and former consultant Guy Accad's experimentation
into a high-quality interpretation of his own. He has made brilliant wines
since 1995, especially RICHEBOURG★★★ and NUITS-ST-GEORGES les
Boudots★★. Expensive. Best years: (2000) 99 98 97 96 95 **94** 93.

**GROS PLANT DU PAYS NANTAIS VDQS** *Loire Valley, France* From the
marshy salt-flats around Nantes, Gros Plant can be searing stuff, but
this acidic wine is well suited to the seafood guzzled in the region. Look
for a *sur lie* bottling and drink the youngest available. Best producers:
Chiron, J Guindon, J Hallereau, Herbauges, la Preuille, Sauvion.

**GROSSET** *Clare Valley, South Australia* Jeffrey Grosset is a perfectionist,
crafting tiny quantities of hand-made wines in his Auburn winery. A
Riesling specialist, he bottles Watervale★★★ separately from Polish
Hill★★★; both are supremely good and age well. Cabernet blend
Gaia★★ is smooth and seamless. Also outstanding Piccadilly (ADELAIDE
HILLS) Chardonnay★★★ and very fine Pinot Noir★★ and Semillon-
Sauvignon★★. Best years: (Riesling) 1999 **98 97 96 95 94** 92 90 87 86.

**GROVE MILL** *Marlborough, New Zealand* Mid-sized producer with a strong
quality focus. Full-bodied Sauvignon Blanc★ is a feature of their range,
together with a ripe, rich, remarkably smooth Chardonnay★ and tangy,
pungent Riesling★★.

**CH. GRUAUD-LAROSE★★** *St-Julien AC, 2ème Cru Classé, Haut-Médoc,
Bordeaux, France* One of the largest ST-JULIEN estates, now owned by
the same family as CHASSE-SPLEEN and HAUT-BAGES-LIBERAL. Until the
1970s these wines were classic, cedary St-Juliens. Since the early 80s,
the wines have been darker, richer and coated with new oak, yet have
also shown an unnerving animal quality. They're certainly impressive,
but it is hard to say whether the animal or the cedar will prevail after
20 years or so of aging in bottle. Second wine: Sarget de Gruaud-
Larose. Best years: (2000) 99 98 97 96 95 94 93 **90 89 88 86 85 83 82**.

148

**GRÜNER VELTLINER**   Grown in every Austrian wine region with the exception of Styria. The grape is at its best, however, in KAMPTAL, KREMSTAL, and the WACHAU, where the soil and cool climate bring out all the lentilly, white-peppery aromas in the fruit.

**GUELBENZU** *Navarra DO, Spain*   Family-owned bodega making good Guelbenzu Crianza★, from Tempranillo, Cabernet and Merlot, and rich concentrated Evo★, made mostly from Cabernet Sauvignon. The new Lautus★ is made from old vines and incorporates Garnacha in the blend. Best years: 1998 **97 96 95 94 93 92 90**.

**GUIGAL** *Côte-Rôtie AC, Rhône Valley, France*   Marcel Guigal is among the most famous names in the Rhône, producing wines from his company's own vineyards in COTE-ROTIE under the Château d'Ampuis label as well as the Guigal range from purchased grapes. La Mouline, la Turque and la Landonne all rate ★★★ in most critics'

opinions, but I have to add the proviso that with all these oaky wines I find the unique beauty and fragrance of Côte-Rôtie difficult to discern. I'm more of a fan of the fragrant CONDRIEU★★. HERMITAGE★★ is also good, as is the cheaper COTES DU RHONE★. GIGONDAS★ is reasonably chunky. Best years: (top reds) (1999) 98 97 95 **94 91 90 89 88 85 83 82**.

**CH. GUIRAUD**★★ *Sauternes AC, 1er Cru Classé, Bordeaux, France*   A property that was hauled up from near extinction by the Canadian Narby family, convinced that Guiraud could be one of SAUTERNES' greatest wines. Selecting only the best grapes and using 50% new oak each year, they have returned Guiraud to the top-quality fold. Keep best vintages for 10 years or more. Second wine (dry): G de Guiraud. Best years: 1999 98 97 96 95 90 **89 88 86 85 83**.

**GUNDERLOCH** *Nackenheim, Rheinhessen, Germany*   Fritz and Agnes Hasselbrach's estate has become one of the nation's best. Sensationally concentrated and luscious Beerenauslese★★★ and Trockenbeerenauslese★★★ dessert Rieslings are among the world's most expensive wines. Dry and off-dry Rieslings, at least ★, however, are good value. Late-harvest Spätlese and Auslese are ★★ year in, year out. Best years: (Spätlese) (2000) 99 98 **97** 96 95 **94 93 92 90 89**.

**GUNDLACH-BUNDSCHU** *Sonoma Valley AVA, California, USA*   This family-owned winery was founded in 1858. Since then it has had its ups and downs but for the last couple of decades it has been mostly up. The Rhinefarm Vineyard Cabernet Sauvignon★★ is outstanding, with lean herbal tones opening up to a big, juicy, fruity centre, and Rhinefarm Vineyard Merlot★★ is beautifully crafted and elegant. The Chardonnay★ is rich but not over the top and a Riesling is delightfully different. The Zinfandel★ and Cabernet merit at least short-term cellaring. Best years: (reds) (1999) 98 97 **95 94 92 91**.

**FRITZ HAAG** *Braunenberg, Mosel, Germany*   MOSEL grower with vineyards in the Braunenberger Juffer and Braunenberger Juffer Sonnenuhr. Pure, elegant Rieslings at least ★ quality, with Auslese reaching ★★ or ★★★. Best years: 1999 98 97 **96 95 94 93 92 91 90 88 85 83 79 76 75 71**.

**REINHOLD HAART** *Piesport, Mosel, Germany*  Theo Haart produces sensational Rieslings – with blackcurrant, peach and citrus aromas – from the great Piesporter Goldtropfchen★★ vineyard. Ausleses are invariably ★★★. Best years: (Spätlese) 1999 98 97 **96 95 94 93 91 90 89.**

**HAMILTON RUSSELL VINEYARDS** *Walker Bay, Overberg WO, South Africa*  Owner Anthony Hamilton-Russell and winemaker Kevin Grant are a determined duo. Classic Pinot Noir and Chardonnay are their holy grails, individuality their philosophy. From 1999, new Burgundian clones provide a fruitier profile and higher quality plateau to the regular Pinot Noir★. The regular Chardonnay★ maintains the restrained house style. Ashbourne Pinot Noir★★ and Chardonnay★★ have been discontinued; the concept will now be marketed under an Auction label. The Southern Right label focuses on Pinotage and Sauvignon Blanc from bought-in grapes. Best years: (Pinot Noir) **1999** 98 97 96 95; (Chardonnay) 2000 **99 98 97 96 95.**

**HANDLEY CELLARS** *Mendocino County, California, USA*  Outstanding producer of hand-crafted sparkling wines, including one of California's best Brut Rosés★ and a delicious Blanc de Blancs★★. The aromatic Gewurztraminer★★ is one of the state's finest. Two bottlings of Chardonnay, one from the DRY CREEK VALLEY★★ and an Anderson Valley★, are worth seeking out. Best years: (1999) **98 97 95 94**.

**HANGING ROCK** *Macedon Ranges, Victoria, Australia*  Highly individual, gutsy sparkling wine, Macedon non-vintage★★ stands out at John and Anne (née Tyrrell) Ellis's ultra-cool-climate vineyard high in the Macedon Ranges. Tangy estate-grown Sauvignon Blanc★ is mouthwatering stuff, while Heathcote Shiraz★★, from a warmer neighbouring region, is the best red.

**HARDYS** *McLaren Vale, South Australia*  Fine quality across the board comes from the flagship label of the BRL Hardy group. Varietals under the Siegersdorf and Nottage Hill labels are tasty and affordable everyday wines, among Australia's most reliably good gluggers. Top of the tree are the commemorative Eileen Hardy Shiraz★★★ and Thomas Hardy Cabernet★★★, both dense reds for hedonists. Eileen Hardy Chardonnay★★ is rich, heady, oak-perfumed and complex. Newer releases include the attractively packaged Tintara Shiraz★★ and Grenache★★, plus 'ecologically aware' Banrock Station★, the inexpensive Insignia wines and great-value sparkling wine under the Omni label. Premium sparklers are made by the much-respected Ed Carr. Best years: (Eileen Hardy Shiraz) 1998 97 96 95 **93 88 87 81 79 70**. See also Leasingham, Reynell.

**HARGRAVE VINEYARD** *Long Island, New York State, USA*  It took Hargrave's thrilling reds and whites produced from an old potato plantation to establish LONG ISLAND as a serious wine region in the 1980s and spark a grape-growing explosion on the island's North Fork. The vineyard changed hands in 1999, and the new Italian owners, Castello di Borghese, have begun planting the region's first Sangiovese. Best years: 1998 **97 95**.

**HARTENBERG ESTATE** *Stellenbosch WO, South Africa*  An old winery making a strong return to the Cape super-league under a young and enthusiastic team. The warmer Bottelary Hills area favours reds, especially Shiraz★, Merlot★ and Cabernet★. More unusual are

Zinfandel and the Cape's sole Pontac; both reflect winemaker Carl Schultz' high standards. Whites are well served by a firm, flavoursome Chardonnay and, unusually for these north-facing slopes, a vigorous, limy Riesling. Best years: (reds) **1997 96 95 94**.

**HATTENHEIM** *Rheingau, Germany* Fine RHEINGAU village with 13 vineyard sites, including a share of the famous Marcobrunn vineyard. Best producers: SCHLOSS REINHARTSHAUSEN★★, Schloss Schönborn★. Best years: (1999) 98 96 **95 94 93 92 90**.

**CH. HAUT-BAGES-LIBÉRAL★** *Pauillac AC, 5ème Cru Classé, Haut-Médoc, Bordeaux, France* Little-known PAUILLAC property that has quietly been gathering plaudits for some years now: loads of unbridled delicious fruit, a positively hedonistic style – and its lack of renown keeps the price just about reasonable. The wines will age well but are ready to drink at 5 years. Best years: (2000) 99 98 96 95 **94 90 89 86 85**.

**CH. HAUT-BAILLY★★** *Pessac-Léognan AC, Cru Classé de Graves, Bordeaux, France* The softest and most charming wines among the GRAVES Classed Growths, which showed welcome improvement in the late 1980s. Drinkable very early, but ages well. Second wine: la Parde-de-Haut-Bailly. Best years: (2000) 99 98 96 95 **93 90 89 88 86 85 83 82**.

**CH. HAUT-BATAILLEY★** *Pauillac AC, 5ème Cru Classé, Haut-Médoc, Bordeaux, France* Despite being owned by the Borie family of DUCRU-BEAUCAILLOU, this estate has produced too many wines that are light, pleasant, attractively spicy, but lacking real class and concentration. Recent vintages have shown improvement and the wine is becoming a bit more substantial. Best years: (2000) 97 96 95 **90 89 85 83 82**.

**CH. HAUT-BRION** *Pessac-Léognan AC, 1er Cru Classé, Graves, Bordeaux, France* The only Bordeaux property outside the MEDOC and SAUTERNES to be included in the great 1855 Classification, when it was accorded First Growth status. The excellent gravel-based vineyard is now part of Bordeaux's suburbs. The red wine★★★ almost always deserves its exalted status, and there is also a small amount of white★★★ which, at its best, is magically rich yet marvellously dry, blossoming out over 5–10 years. Second wine: (red) Bahans-Haut-Brion. Best years: (red) (2000) 99 98 97 96 95 94 93 **90 89 88 86 85 83 78**; (white) (2000) 99 98 97 **96 95 94 92 90 89 88**.

**CH. HAUT-MARBUZET★★** *St-Estèphe AC, Cru Bourgeois, Haut-Médoc, Bordeaux, France* Impressive ST-ESTEPHE wine with great, rich, mouthfilling blasts of flavour and lots of new oak. Best years: (2000) 99 98 97 96 95 **94 93 90 89 88 86 85 83 82**.

**HAUT-MÉDOC AC** *Bordeaux, France* The finest gravelly soil is here in the southern half of the MEDOC peninsula, and Haut-Médoc AC covers all the decent vineyard land not included in the 6 village ACs (MARGAUX, MOULIS, LISTRAC, ST-JULIEN, PAUILLAC and ST-ESTEPHE). The wines vary somewhat in quality and style. Best producers: Beaumont, Belgrave★, Camensac, CANTEMERLE★, Charmail★, Cissac★, Citran★, Coufran★, la LAGUNE★★, Lanessan★, Malescasse, Maucamps★, Ramage-la-Batisse, Sénéjac, SOCIANDO-MALLET★★, la Tour-Carnet, la Tour-du-Haut-Moulin★, Verdignan, Villegeorge. Best years: (2000) 96 **95 94 90 89 88 86 85**.

**HAUT-MONTRAVEL AC** See Montravel AC.

**HAUTES-CÔTES DE BEAUNE AC** See Bourgogne-Hautes-Côtes de Beaune AC.

**HAUTES-CÔTES DE NUITS AC** See Bourgogne-Hautes-Côtes de Nuits AC.

**HAWKE'S BAY** *North Island, New Zealand* One of New Zealand's oldest and most prestigious wine regions. The high number of sunshine hours, moderately predictable weather during ripening and a complex array of soil patterns make it ideal for a wide range of winemaking styles. Chardonnay, Cabernet Sauvignon and Merlot are the area's greatest strengths, although Syrah has good potential. Sauvignon Blanc is generally a bit flat. Best producers: CHURCH ROAD★, Clearview★, CRAGGY RANGE★, Esk Valley★★, MATUA VALLEY★★, Mission, MORTON ESTATE★, NGATARAWA★, C J Pask, Sacred Hill★, TE MATA★★, Trinity Hill, Vidal★, VILLA MARIA★★, Unison★★.

**DR HEGER** *Ihringen, Baden, Germany* Joachim Heger specializes in powerful, dry Grauburgunder, Weissburgunder and red Spätburgunder★ with Riesling a sideline. Grauburgunder from the Winklerberg★★ is serious stuff. Best years: 1999 **98 97 96 94 93 90 89 88**.

**HEIDA** Swiss name for the grape thought to be either the Savagnin of the French Jura or the Gewürztraminer. In the Swiss VALAIS it is known as Paien. Above the town of Visp at Visperterminen, Heida is grown at heights of around 1000m (3280ft), the highest-altitude vineyards in Europe, and the wine is correspondingly pungent and mountain mad. Best producers: Chanton, St Jodern.

**CHARLES HEIDSIECK** *Champagne AC, Champagne, France* Charles Heidsieck, under Rémy-Cointreau ownership, is the most consistently fine of all the major houses, with ★★★ vintage Champagne. The non-vintage★★ is regularly of vintage quality, especially those cuvées★★ marked by a bottling date (for example, Mis en Caves en 1996). Best years: (1995) **90 89 88 85 82**.

**HEITZ CELLARS** *Napa Valley AVA, California, USA* Star attraction here is the Martha's Vineyard Cabernet Sauvignon★★. Heitz also produces a Bella Oaks Vineyard Cabernet Sauvignon★, a Trailside Vineyard Cabernet★ and a straight Cabernet★ that takes time to understand but can be good. After 1992, phylloxera forced the replanting of Martha's Vineyard and bottling only resumed in 1996. Many believe that early bottlings of Martha's Vineyard are among the best wines ever produced in CALIFORNIA. Grignolino Rosé is an attractive picnic wine. Best years: (Martha's Vineyard) 1992 91 **86 85 75**; (Bella Oaks) 1997 95 **93 91 87 86**.

**HENRIQUES & HENRIQUES** *Madeira DOC, Madeira, Portugal* The wines to look for are the 10-year-old★★ and 15-year-old★★ versions of the classic varieties. Vibrant Sercial and Verdelho, and rich Malmsey and Bual are all fine examples of their styles. Henriques & Henriques also has vintage Madeiras of extraordinary quality.

**HENRY OF PELHAM** *Niagara Peninsula VQA, Ontario, Canada* Winery making concentrated wines from low-yielding vines. Best are Reserve Chardonnay★, Proprietor's Reserve Riesling★, Riesling Icewine★ and a Cabernet-Merlot blend. Best years: 1999 98 **97 95**.

**HENSCHKE** *Eden Valley, South Australia* Fifth-generation winemaker Stephen Henschke and his viticulturist wife Prue make some of Australia's grandest reds from old vines in Eden Valley. Top wine, HILL OF GRACE★★★, is stunning, and Mount Edelstone Shiraz★★★ and Cyril Henschke Cabernet★★ are also brilliant wines. The whites are full and intensely flavoured too, led by the seductive, perfumed Julius Riesling★★ and the toasty yet fruity Louis Semillon★★. Best years: (reds) (1998) 97 96 **94 92 91 90 88 86 84 82 80 78 72**.

**HÉRAULT, VIN DE PAYS DE L'** *Languedoc, France* A huge region, covering the entire Hérault *département*. Red wines predominate, based on Carignan, Grenache and Cinsaut, and most of the wine is sold in bulk. But things are changing. There are lots of hilly vineyards with great potential, and MAS DE DAUMAS GASSAC is merely the first of many exciting reds from the region. The whites are improving too. Best producers: Bosc, Capion★, la Fadèze, GRANGE DES PERES★★, Jany, Limbardié★, MAS DE DAUMAS GASSAC★★, Moulines.

**HERMITAGE AC** *Rhône Valley, France* Great Hermitage, from steep vineyards above the town of Tain l'Hermitage in the northern RHONE, is revered throughout the world as a rare, rich red wine – expensive, memorable and classic. Not all Hermitage achieves such an exciting blend of flavours, but the best growers, with mature red Syrah vines, can create superbly original wine, needing 5–10 years' aging even in a light year and a minimum of 15 years in a ripe vintage. White Hermitage, from Marsanne and Roussanne, is less famous but the best wines, made by traditionalists, can outlive the reds, sometimes lasting as long as 40 years. Some winemakers are making modern, fruity, fragrant whites that are attractive at 1–2 years old. Best producers: A Belle★★, CHAPOUTIER★★ (since 1988), CHAVE★★★, B Chave★★, Colombier★★, COLOMBO★ (white★★), DELAS★★★ (les Bessards★★★), B Faurie★★, Fayolle★★, M Ferraton★★, A GRAILLOT★★, J-L Grippat★★, GUIGAL★★, JABOULET (la Chapelle★★★), J-M Sorrel★★, M Sorrel★★, Tain l'Hermitage co-op★★, Tardieu-Laurent★★, de Vallouit★★. Best years: (reds) (2000) 99 98 97 96 95 **94 92 91 90 89 88 85 83 82 78 71 70**.

**JAMES HERRICK** *Vin de Pays d'Oc, Languedoc, France* When Herrick and his Aussie partners planted 175ha (435 acres) of Chardonnay between Narbonne and Béziers, many locals thought he was mad. His neatly trellised rows with drip-feed irrigation are a real contrast to his neighbours' traditionally straggling vines. Chardonnay is an attractive blend of tropical fruit and French elegance. A reserve bottling★ is more concentrated. Red, Cuvée Simone, has disappointed. The brand and vineyards are now owned by Australia's Southcorp group.

**THE HESS COLLECTION** *Mount Veeder AVA, California, USA* NAPA VALLEY producer earning rave reviews for its Cabernet Sauvignon★★, which shows all the intense lime and black cherry originality of its MOUNT VEEDER fruit, without coating it with impenetrable tannins. Hess Select is the budget label. Best years: (Cabernet) (1999) (98) (97) 96 95 94 **93** 91 **90**.

THE **HESS COLLECTION**
NAPA VALLEY CABERNET SAUVIGNON
1995
ESTATE GROWN ON MOUNT VEEDER
PRODUCED AND BOTTLED IN THE HESS COLLECTION WINERY
NAPA, CALIFORNIA, USA • ALCOHOL 13% BY VOLUME

**HESSISCHE BERGSTRASSE** *Germany* Small, warm wine region near Darmstadt. Much of the winemaking is by the co-op, Bergsträsser Winzer, although the Staatsweingut also makes some good wines. There has been less flirtation with new grape varieties here than elsewhere in Germany, and Riesling is still the most prized grape. Eisweins are a speciality.

**HEURIGER** *Austria* Fresh, young wine drunk in the many taverns in the Viennese hills. Once the wine is a year old it is called der Alte, or 'old chap'. No really good wine is sold as Heuriger, yet a few swift jugs of it can make for a great evening – but keep the aspirin handy.

**HEYL ZU HERRNSHEIM** *Nierstein, Rheinhessen, Germany* Historical estate whose main strength is substantial dry whites from the Riesling, Weissburgunder and Silvaner grapes. However, the Auslese and higher Prädikat wines of recent vintages have been of ★★ and – sometimes – ★★★ quality. In future only wines from the top sites (Brudersberg, Pettenthal, Hipping, Ölberg) will carry the vineyard designation. Other high-quality wines will be sold under the 'Rotschiefer' name. Best years: 1999 98 97 96 **93 90 89 88**.

**HIDALGO** *Jerez y Manzanilla DO, Andalucía, Spain* Hidalgo's Manzanilla La Gitana★★ is deservedly one of the best-selling manzanillas in Spain. Hidalgo is still family-owned, and only uses grapes from its own vineyards. Brands include Mariscal★, Fino Especial and Miraflores, Amontillado Napoleon★★, Oloroso Viejo★★ and Jerez Cortado★★.

**HILL OF GRACE★★★** *Eden Valley, South Australia* A stunning wine with dark, exotic flavours made by HENSCHKE from a single plot of Shiraz. The Hill of Grace vineyard was first planted in the 1860s, and the old vines produce a powerful, structured wine with superb ripe fruit, chocolate, coffee, earth, leather and more. Can be cellared for 20 years or longer. Best years: (1997) 96 95 94 **93 92 91** 90 88 86 85 84 82 78 72.

**HILLTOP** *Neszmély, Hungary* Based in the Neszmély wine region just south of the Danube, this dynamic company, with its showpiece winery, is lucky enough to have the right grapes in the right place. On the protected slopes between the Danube and the Transdanubian Mountains, aromatic varieties such as Irsay Oliver and Gewürztraminer thrive alongside Chardonnay and Merlot. Grapes are also bought in from other regions. Chief winemaker Akos Kamocsay is one of Hungary's most respected and has gained a solid international reputation. Hilltop's top brand is Riverview.

**HILLTOPS** *New South Wales, Australia* Promising high-altitude cherry-growing region with a small but fast-growing area of vineyards around the town of Young. Special potential for reds from Cabernet Sauvignon and Shiraz. Best producers: Demondrille, Grove Estates, MCWILLIAM'S (Barmway vineyard).

**FRANZ HIRTZBERGER** *Wachau, Niederösterreich, Austria* One of the WACHAU's top growers. Hirtzberger's finest wines are the concentrated, elegant Rieslings from Singerriedel★★★ and Hochrain★★. The best Grüner Veltliner comes from the Honivogl site★★★. Best years: (2000) 99 98 97 96 **95 94 93 92 91 90 88 86 83 79 77 71**.

**HOCHHEIM** *Rheingau, Germany* Village best known for having given the English the word 'Hock' for Rhine wine, but with good individual vineyard sites, especially Domdechaney, Hölle (or Hell!) and Kirchenstück. Best producers: Franz KÜNSTLER★★★, W H Schafer, Domdechant Werner. Best years: 1999 98 97 96 **94 93 92 90**.

**HOGUE CELLARS** *Yakima Valley AVA, Washington State, USA* Good, ripe, brambly Reserve Cabernet Sauvignon★, often blended with Merlot, and supple, elegant Merlots★. The Chardonnay is pleasant without being memorable. Best years: (reds) (1999) 98 97 **96 95 94**.

**HOLLICK** *Coonawarra, South Australia*   Run by viticulturist Ian Hollick, this winery makes a broader range of good wines than is usually found in COONAWARRA: an irresistible sparkling Merlot★ (yes, *Merlot*), subtle Chardonnay★, tobaccoey Cabernet-Merlot★ and a richer Ravenswood Cabernet Sauvignon★★. Attractive Sauvignon-Semillon and limy Riesling★ are also good. Best years: (reds) 1998 **96 94 93 91 90 88**.

**DOMAINE DE L'HORTUS** *Pic St-Loup, Coteaux du Languedoc AC, Languedoc, France*   From a first vintage in 1990, Jean and Marie-Thérèse Orliac have created one of the leading estates in this upcoming region. Cuvée Classique★, a ready-to-drink unoaked Mourvèdre-Syrah-Grenache blend, has delightful flavours of herbs, plums and cherries. Big brother Grande Cuvée★★ needs some time for the fruit and oak to come into harmony. Promising new white l'Hortus Grande Cuvée★ is a blend of Chardonnay and Viognier. Best years: (Grande Cuvée red) 1999 98 97 **96 95 94 93**.

**HOSPICES DE BEAUNE** *Côte de Beaune, Burgundy, France*   Scene of a theatrical auction on the third Sunday in November each year, the Hospices is an historical foundation which sells wine from its holdings in the COTE D'OR to finance its charitable works. The quality of the wine-making has increased immeasurably since 1994, partly thanks to the building of a new state-of-the-art winery on the outskirts of Beaune. The wines are matured and bottled by the purchaser, which can cause variations in quality, and pricing reflects charitable status rather than common sense. Best years: (top reds) 1999 98 97 96 95 **85**; (top whites) (2000) 99 97 96 **95 94**.

**HOUGHTON** *Swan District, Western Australia*   WESTERN AUSTRALIA's biggest winery, with a huge output of 'White Burgundy' (called Houghton's HWB in the EU). Good Sauvignon-Semillon★ and Chenin Blanc; also recently improved Chardonnay and attractive Riesling★. With the inclusion of more grapes from the south of the state, the reds have improved, especially Houghton and Moondah Brook Cabernets★ and Shiraz★. The super-duper Jack Mann commemorative Cabernet blend★★ was released in 1997 to a well-deserved fanfare.

**VON HÖVEL** *Konz-Oberemmel, Saar, Germany*   Eberhard von Kunow has always made unusually rich, succulent wines for a region renowned for steely Rieslings, but since 1993 quality has taken another leap; wines are now almost all ★★. Most wines age impressively for 10 years or more. Best years: (2000) 99 97 96 95 **94 93 90 89 88 85**.

**HOWARD PARK** *Great Southern, Western Australia*   Founded by the talented John Wade, who established several top COONAWARRA reds, Howard Park has been an important player in high-quality Australian Cabernet over the last 15 years. New owners have implemented winery expansion. The classic Cabernet Sauvignon-Merlot★★★, built for long cellaring, is matched by intense, floral Riesling★★★, and a classy Chardonnay★★ is not far behind. Second label Madfish is good for Shiraz★ and dry white. Best years: (Cabernet-Merlot) 1997 96 94 93 92 **90 89 88 86**; (Riesling) 2000 98 97 **96 95 94 93 91 90 88 86**.

**HOWELL MOUNTAIN AVA** *Napa Valley, California, USA*   NAPA's north-eastern corner is noted for powerhouse Cabernet Sauvignon and Zinfandel as well as exotic, full-flavoured Merlot. Best producers: BERINGER (Merlot)★★, DUCKHORN★, DUNN★★, La Jota★★, Liparita★.

**HUADONG WINERY** *Shandong Province, China* The first producer of varietal and vintage wines in China, Huadong has received massive investments from its multinational joint owners (Allied DOMECQ) as well as state support. But money can't change climates, and excessive moisture from the summer rainy season causes problems. Riesling and Chardonnay (under the Tsingtao label) were the first wines to be exported, but most of the noble varieties have been planted.

**HUET SA** *Vouvray AC, Loire Valley, France* Gaston Huet has passed this estate to his son-in-law, Noël Pinguet, but still takes a keen interest in the complex, traditional Vouvrays which can age for up to 50 years. The estate produces wines from 3 excellent sites – le Haut Lieu, Clos du Bourg and le Mont – which can be dry★★, medium-dry★★ or sweet★★★, depending on the vintage. Also very good Vouvray Mousseux★★. Best years: (2000) **99 98 97** 96 95 **93 90 89 88 85 76 64 61 59 47**.

**HUGEL ET FILS** *Alsace AC, Alsace, France* Arguably the most famous name in Alsace. As well as wines from its own vineyards, Hugel buys in grapes for basic wines. Best wines are sweet ALSACE VENDANGE TARDIVE★★ and Sélection de Grains Nobles★★★. The Tradition wines are generally rather dull, but the Jubilée wines are often of ★★ quality. Best years: (Vendange Tardive Riesling) 1998 97 96 **95 90 89 88 87 83**.

**HUNTER VALLEY** *New South Wales, Australia* NEW SOUTH WALES' oldest wine region overcomes a tricky climate to make fascinating, ageworthy Semillon and rich, buttery Chardonnay. The reds meet less universal approval. Shiraz is the mainstay, aging well but often developing a leathery overtone. Cabernet can deliver occasional success but Pinot Noir is less suited. Premium region is the Lower Hunter Valley; the Upper Hunter has few wineries but extensive vineyards. Best producers: Allandale★★, BROKENWOOD★★, De Iuliis, Kulkunbulla, LAKE'S FOLLY★, LINDEMANS★★, Lowe Family, MCWILLIAM'S★, Meerea Park★, ROSEMOUNT★★, ROTHBURY★, TYRRELL'S★★.

**HUNTER'S** *Marlborough, South Island, New Zealand* One of MARLBOROUGH's stars, with fine, if austere, Sauvignon★★, savoury, Burgundian Chardonnay★★, vibrant Riesling★ and sophisticated Pinot Noir★. Attractive fizz★ has technical input from Tony Jordan, GREEN POINT's ex-general manager. Best years: (Sauvignon Blanc) (2001) **00 99 97 96**.

**ÎLE DE BEAUTÉ, VIN DE PAYS DE L'** *Corsica, France* Some increasingly good wines are being made from Syrah, Cabernet Sauvignon, Nielluccio, Sciaccarello and Merlot (reds); Grenache and Barbarossa (rosés); Chardonnay and Vermentino (whites). Best producers: Marana co-op, Samuletto, UVAL co-op.

**INNISKILLIN** *Niagara Peninsula, Ontario, Canada* One of Canada's leading wineries, producing good Pinot Noir★, a beautifully rounded Klose Vineyard Chardonnay★ and thick, rich, Vidal icewine★★. Winemaker Karl Kaiser is also achieving good results with Cabernet Franc. Another Inniskillin winery is in the somewhat drier OKANAGAN VALLEY in British Columbia, a partnership between the winery and the Inkameep Indian Band. Best years: (icewine) (1999) **98 97 95 94 92 89**.

**IPHOFEN** *Franken, Germany* One of the 2 most important wine towns in FRANKEN (the other is WÜRZBURG) for dry Riesling and Silvaner. Both are powerful, with a pronounced earthiness. Best producers: JULIUSSPITAL★, Johann Ruck★, Wirsching★. Best years: (2000) 99 **98 97 94 93 92 90**.

**IRANCY AC** *Burgundy, France* Formerly known as Bourgogne-Irancy and labelled simply Irancy from 1996, this northern outpost of vineyards, just south-west of CHABLIS, is an unlikely champion of the clear, pure flavours of the Pinot Noir grape. But red Irancy can be delicate and lightly touched by the ripeness of plums and strawberries, and can age well. There is also a little rosé. Best producers: Bienvenu, J-M BROCARD, Cantin, A & J-P Colinot★, Delaloge, Patrice Fort★, Simonnet-Febvre. Best years: (2000) 99 **98 97 96** 95.

**IRON HORSE VINEYARDS** *Sonoma County, California, USA* Outstanding sparkling wines with Brut★★ and the Blanc de Blancs★★ delicious on release but capable of aging. A blanc de noirs★ called 'Wedding Cuvée' and a Brut Rosé★ complete the line-up. Table wines include Cabernets★, a lovely Pinot Noir★★, a barrel-fermented Chardonnay★, a zesty Sauvignon and a seductive Viognier★. Best years: (reds) (1999) 98 97 96 95 **94 92 91 90**; (Chardonnay) 1999 98 97 96 95 **92 91 90**.

**IROULÉGUY AC** *South-West France* A small AC in the Basque Pyrenees. Cabernet Sauvignon, Cabernet Franc and Tannat give robust reds that are softer than MADIRAN. Production of white from Petit Courbu and Manseng has recently restarted. Best producers: Arretxea, Brana★, Etxegaraya, Ilarria★, Irouléguy co-op (Mignaberry★). Best years: (reds) (2000) 98 **97 96 95 94**.

**ISABEL ESTATE** *Marlborough, New Zealand* Grapegrowers (for CLOUDY BAY) turned award-winning winemakers Michael and Robyn Tiller is blazing a trail with Sauvignon Blanc★★ that equals the country's best. Aromatic, plum-and-cherry Pinot Noir★★, stylish, concentrated Chardonnay★★, and promising Riesling★ and Pinot Gris★ complete the impressive line-up. An estate to follow. Best years: (Pinot Noir) (2001) 99 **98 96 94**.

**ISOLE E OLENA** *Chianti Classico DOCG, Tuscany, Italy* Long one of the pacesetters in Chianti Classico, this fine estate is run by Paolo De Marchi. His CHIANTI CLASSICO★★, characterized by a clean, elegant and spicily perfumed fruit, excels in every vintage. The powerful SUPER-TUSCAN Cepparello★★★, made from 100% Sangiovese, is the top wine. Excellent Syrah★★, Cabernet Sauvignon★★★, Chardonnay★★, and VIN SANTO★★★. Best years: (Cepparello) 1998 97 96 95 **94 93 91 90 88 86**.

**CH. D'ISSAN** *Margaux AC, 3ème Cru Classé, Haut-Médoc, Bordeaux, France* This lovely moated property has disappointed me far too often in the past but is beginning to pull its socks up. When successful, the wine can be one of the most elegant but delicate in the MARGAUX AC. Best years: (2000) 99 98 97 96 95 **90 89 85 83 82 78**.

**PAUL JABOULET AÎNÉ** *Rhône Valley, France* During the 1970s, Jaboulet led the way in raising the world's awareness of the great quality of RHÔNE wines, yet during the 80s the quality of wine faltered. But recent vintages, fuller of fruit, less manipulated and proud of their origins, make it look as though Jaboulet is back on the quality bandwagon. Best wines are top red HERMITAGE la Chapelle★★★ and white Chevalier de Stérimberg★★. Also excellent CROZES-HERMITAGE Thalabert★★ and Raymond Rouré★★, fine juicy ST-JOSEPH le Grand Pompée, concentrated CORNAS Domaine St-Pierre★★ and sweet, perfumed MUSCAT DE BEAUMES-DE-VENISE★★. Best years: (la Chapelle) (1999) 98 97 96 95 **94 91 90 89 88 78**.

# JEREZ Y MANZANILLA DO/SHERRY

*Andalucía, Spain*

The Spanish now own the name outright. From 1996 'British sherry' and 'Irish sherry' ceased to exist. At least in the EU, the only wines that can be sold as sherry come from the triangle of vineyard land between the Andalucian towns of inland Jerez de la Frontera, and Sanlúcar de Barrameda and Puerto de Santa María by the sea.

The best sherries can be spectacular. Three main factors contribute to the high quality potential of wines from this region: the chalky-spongy albariza soil where the best vines grow, the Palomino Fino grape – unexciting for table wines but potentially great once transformed by the sherry-making processes – and a natural yeast called flor. All sherry must be a minimum of 3 years old, but fine sherries age in barrel for much longer. Sherries must be blended through a solera system. About a third of the wine from the oldest barrels is bottled, and the barrels topped up with slightly younger wine from another set of barrels and so on, for a minimum of 3 sets of barrels. The idea is that the younger wine takes on the character of older wine, as well as keeping the blend refreshed.

## MAIN SHERRY STYLES

**Finos, manzanillas and amontillados** These sherries derive their extraordinary, tangy, pungent flavours from flor. Young, newly fermented wines destined for these styles of sherry are deliberately fortified very sparingly to just 15–15.5% alcohol before being put in barrels for their minimum of 3 years' maturation. The thin, soft, oatmeal-coloured mush of flor grows on the surface of the wines, protecting them from the air (and therefore keeping them pale) and giving them a characteristic sharp, pungent tang. Manzanillas are fino-style wines that have matured in the cooler seaside conditions of Sanlúcar de Barrameda, where the flor grows thickest and the fine tang is most accentuated. True amontillados are simply fino sherries that have continued to age after the flor has died (after about 5 years) and so finish their aging period in contact with air. These should all be bone dry. Medium-sweet amontillados are merely concoctions for the export market.

**Oloroso** This type of sherry is strongly fortified after fermentation to deter the growth of flor. Olorosos therefore mature in barrel in contact with the air, which gradually darkens them while they develop rich, intense, nutty and raisiny flavours.

**Other styles** Palo cortado is an unusual, deliciously nutty, dry style somewhere in between amontillado and oloroso. Sweet oloroso creams and pale creams are almost without exception enriched solely for the export market.

See also individual producers.

## BEST PRODUCERS AND WINES

Argüeso (Manzanilla San Léon, Manzanilla Fina Las Medallas).

BARBADILLO (Manzanilla Eva, Manzanilla Príncipe, Solear Manzanilla Fina Vieja, Amontillado Príncipe, Amontillado de Sanlúcar, Oloroso del Tío Río, Oloroso Seco).

Delgado Zuleta (Manzanilla La Goya).

Díez Mérito (Don Zoilo Imperial Amontillado and Fino, Victoria Regina Oloroso).

DOMECQ (Amontillado 51-1A, Sibarita Palo Cortado, Fino La Ina, Venerable Pedro Ximénez).

Garvey (Palo Cortado, Amontillado Tio Guillermo, Pedro Ximénez).

GONZALEZ BYASS (Tio Pepe Fino, Matusalem Oloroso Muy Viejo, Apostoles Oloroso Viejo, Amontillado del Duque Seco y Muy Viejo, Noé Pedro Ximénez, Oloroso Viejo de Añado).

HIDALGO (Manzanilla La Gitana, Manzanilla Pasada, Jerez Cortado).

LUSTAU (Almacenista single-producer wines, Old East India Cream, Puerto Fino).

OSBORNE (Fino Quinta, Bailén Oloroso, Solera India Pedro Ximénez).

Sánchez Romate (Pedro Ximénez Cardenal Cisneros).

VALDESPINO (Amontillado Coliseo, Amontillado Tio Diego, Cardenal Palo Cortado, Inocente Fino, Pedro Ximénez Solera Superior).

Williams & Humbert (Pando Fino, Manzanilla Alegria).

**JACKSON ESTATE** *Marlborough, South Island, New Zealand* An established grapegrower with vineyards in MARLBOROUGH's most prestigious district, Jackson Estate turned its hand to winemaking in 1991, making appley Sauvignon Blanc★ that improves with a little age, restrained but full-flavoured Chardonnay and complex traditional-method fizz★. Best years: (Sauvignon Blanc) (2001) 00 **99 97 96**.

**LOUIS JADOT** *Beaune, Burgundy, France* A leading merchant based in Beaune with a broad range matched only by DROUHIN, and with rights to some estate wines of the Duc de Magenta★★. Jadot has extensive vineyard holdings for red wines, but it is the firm's whites which have earned its reputation. Excellent in Grands Crus like BATARD-MONTRACHET★★★ and CORTON-CHARLEMAGNE★★ but Jadot also shows a more egalitarian side by producing good wines in lesser ACs like ST-AUBIN★ and RULLY★. After leading white Burgundy in quality during the 1970s, the 80s were less thrilling, but in the 90s Jadot returned to form. Best years: (top reds) 1999 98 97 96 **95 93 90 89**.

**JAFFELIN** *Beaune, Burgundy, France* Now owned by BOISSET, Jaffelin sells a large range of wine from the COTE D'OR, the COTE CHALONNAISE and BEAUJOLAIS. The lesser ACs – RULLY★, ST-ROMAIN★, BOURGOGNE Blanc and Beaujolais – are the best value, but don't overlook the BEAUNE les Avaux★★. Despite introducing a sound range of Village wines, Boisset's aim of making Jaffelin into the group's quality standard-bearer has yet to be achieved. Best years: (2000) 99 98 **97 96 95**.

**JAMET** *Côte-Rôtie AC, Rhône Valley, France* Jean-Paul and Jean-Luc Jamet are 2 of the most talented growers of COTE-ROTIE. If anything, the wines★★★ from this excellent estate have improved since they took over from their father, Joseph. The wines age well for a decade or more. Best years: (1999) 98 97 96 95 **94 91 90 89 88 87 85 83 82**.

**JARDIN DE LA FRANCE, VIN DE PAYS DU** *Loire Valley, France* This vin de pays covers most of the LOIRE VALLEY, and production often exceeds 50 million bottles – mostly of white wine, from Chenin Blanc and Sauvignon Blanc, and usually very cheap to buy. There is an increasing amount of good Chardonnay made here, too. The few reds and rosés are generally light and sharp. Best producers: Ackerman-Laurance, Bablut, Couillaud, Forges, Hauts de Sanziers, Touche Noire.

**ROBERT JASMIN** *Côte-Rôtie AC, Rhône Valley, France* Robert Jasmin was tragically killed in 1999, but his son Patrick is sure to continue to produce some of the most aromatic red wines★★ in this northern section of the RHONE VALLEY. The wines have an exuberance of gluggable young fruit and a beguiling scent. They are at their best after 4–5 years, but are capable of keeping for longer. Best years: (1999) 98 **97 96 94 92 91 90 89 88 85 83**.

**JASNIÈRES AC** *Loire Valley, France* Tiny AC north of Tours making long-lived, bone-dry whites from Chenin Blanc. Best producers: Nicolas (Bellivière)★, J Gigou★★. Best years: (2000) **99 98 97** 96 95 **93 92 90 85**.

**ROBERT JAYER-GILLES** *Côte de Nuits, Burgundy, France* Robert Jayer-Gilles produces expensive but sought-after wines, heavily dominated by new oak. Good ALIGOTE★, wonderful Hautes-Côtes de Nuits Blanc★★, as well as structured reds, including ECHEZEAUX★★★ and NUITS-ST-GEORGES les Damodes★★. Best years: (top reds) (2000) 99 98 97 96 95 **93 91 90**.

**JEREZ Y MANZANILLA DO/ SHERRY** See pages 158–9.

**JERMANN** *Friuli-Venezia Giulia, Italy* Silvio Jermann, in the COLLIO zone of north-east Italy, produces non-DOC Chardonnay★, Sauvignon Blanc★, Pinot Bianco★ and Pinot Grigio. Vintage Tunina★★ is based on Sauvignon-Chardonnay, and barrel-fermented Chardonnay★★ was called 'Where the dreams have no end' but has, incredibly, been renamed 'Were dreams, now it is just wine'. The wines are plump but pricy. Vinnae★ is based on Ribolla; Cabernet★ blends the 2 Cabernet grapes.

**JOHANNISBERG** *Rheingau, Germany* Probably the best known of all the Rhine wine villages, with 10 vineyard sites, including the famous Schloss Johannisberg. Best producers: Prinz von Hessen★, Johannishof★★, Schloss Johannisberg★. Best years: 1999 98 **97 96 94 93 90**.

**KARL-HEINZ JOHNER** *Bischoffingen, Baden, Germany* Johner specializes in new oak-aged wines from his native BADEN. The vividly fruity Pinot Noir★ and Pinot Blanc★ are excellent, the Chardonnay SJ★ is Germany's best example of this varietal, and the rich, silky Pinot Noir SJ★★ can be one of Germany's finest reds. Best years: (Pinot Noir) (1999) 98 **97 96 93 90**.

**JORDAN** *Alexander Valley AVA, Sonoma, California, USA* Ripe, fruity Cabernet Sauvignon★ with a cedar character rare in California. The Chardonnay★ is balanced and attractive. J★★ fizz is an excellent mouthful, now made independently by Judy Jordan's J Wine Co. Best years: (reds) (1999) 98 **97 96 95 94 91 87 86**.

**JORDAN VINEYARDS** *Stellenbosch WO, South Africa* Ted and Shelagh Jordan purchased this farm in the early 1980s and planted premium varieties on its many different slopes. Son and daughter-in-law, Gary and Kathy, took full advantage of this forward thinking on their return from studying and working in California. A nutty Chardonnay★ heads the strong white range; improving Cabernet★ and Merlot★ are modern but understated. Cobblers Hill★, a Bordeaux blend, best shows the impressive level the farm is capable of achieving. Best years: (Chardonnay) **1999 98 97 96**.

**TONI JOST** *Bacharach, Mittelrhein, Germany* Husband and wife team Peter and Linde have put the MITTELRHEIN on the map. From the Bacharacher Hahn site come some delicious, racy Rieslings★ including well-structured Halbtrockens★; Auslese★★ adds creaminess without losing that pine-needle scent. Best years: 1999 98 **97 96 94 93 92 90 89**.

**J P VINHOS** *Terras do Sado, Portugal* The name has changed since the João Pires Muscat brand was sold, but the winemaking is as forward-looking as ever, using Portuguese and foreign grapes with equal ease. Quinta da Bacalhôa★ is an oaky, meaty Cabernet-Merlot blend, Tinto da Ânfora★ rich and figgy, white Herdade de Santa Marta★ greengagey and mouthfilling, and Cova da Ursa★ a tasty, toasty rich Chardonnay that walks on the wild side. Portugal's finest sparkling wine, vintage-dated Loridos Extra Bruto★ is a pretty decent Champagne lookalike, made from Chardonnay. Also decent Moscatel de SETUBAL★.

**JULIÉNAS AC** *Beaujolais, Burgundy, France* One of the more northerly BEAUJOLAIS Crus, Juliénas makes delicious, 'serious' Beaujolais which can be big and tannic enough to develop in bottle. Best producers: G Descombes★, DUBOEUF★, P Granger★, Ch. de Juliénas★, J P Margerand★, R Monnet★, Pelletier★ B Santé★, M Tête★★. Best years: 2000 **99 98**.

**JULIUSSPITAL WEINGUT** *Würzburg, Franken, Germany* A 16th-century charitable foundation known for its dry wines – especially Silvaners from IPHOFEN and WURZBURG. Look out for the Würzburger Stein vineyard wines, sappy Müller-Thurgau, grapefruity Silvaners★★ and petrolly Rieslings★★. Back on form in 1999, after curiously disappointing 1998 and 97 vintages. Best years: 1999 **96 95 94 93 92 90**.

**JUMILLA DO** *Murcia and Castilla-La Mancha, Spain* Jumilla's reputation in Spain is for big alcoholic reds. Reds and fruity rosés are made from Monastrell (Mourvèdre), so the potential is there, and there are also a few boring whites. Best producers: Casa de la Ermita, Induvasa (Finca Luzón), Agapito Rico, Julia Roch (Casa Castillo).

**JURA** See Arbois, Château-Chalon, Côtes du Jura, l'Étoile.

**JURANÇON AC** *South-West France* The sweet white wine made from late-harvested and occasionally botrytized grapes can be heavenly. The rapidly improving dry wine, Jurançon Sec, can be ageworthy. Best producers: Bellegarde★, Bru-Baché★★, Castera★, CAUHAPE★★, Clos Lapeyre★, CLOS UROULAT★★, Clos Thou★, Larrédya, Souch★. Best years: (sec) (2000) **99 98 96 95 94 93**.

**JUVÉ Y CAMPS** *Cava DO and Penedès DO, Cataluña, Spain* Juvé y Camps is ultra-traditional – and expensive. Unusually among the Catalan companies, most of the grapes come from its own vineyards. Fruitiest CAVA is Reserva de la Familia Extra Brut★, but the rosé and the top brand white Cava Gran Juvé also are good.

**KAISERSTUHL** *Baden, Germany* A 4000-ha (10,000-acre) volcanic stump rising to 600m (2000ft) and overlooking the Rhine plain and south BADEN. Best producers: BERCHER★★, Bickensohl co-op, Dr HEGER★★, JOHNER★, Franz Keller★, Königsschaffhausen co-op, Salwey★. Best years: 1999 **98 97 96 93**.

**KALLSTADT** *Pfalz, Germany* A warm climate combined with the excellent Saumagen site results in the richest dry Rieslings in Germany. These, and the dry Weissburgunder and Muskateller, can stand beside the very best from ALSACE, while Pinot Noir is also showing it likes the chalk soil. Best producer: KOEHLER-RUPRECHT★★. Best years: 1999 98 **97 96 95 93 92 90 89 88 85 83**.

**KAMPTAL** *Niederösterreich, Austria* Wine region centred on the town of Langenlois, making some impressive dry whites, particularly Riesling and Grüner Veltliner. Best producers: BRUNDLMAYER★★, Ehn★, Hirsch★, Schloss Gobelsburg★. Best years: (1999) 98 **97 95 94 93**.

**KANONKOP ESTATE** *Stellenbosch WO, South Africa* Red wine supremo Beyers Truter celebrated 20 years as Kanonkop's winemaker in 2000. Some of the world's first Pinotage vines, planted in the 1950s, produce his standard Pinotage★★ and lavishly new-oaked Auction Reserve★★. The Auction Reserve together with the red BORDEAUX blend Paul Sauer★★ and Cabernet Sauvignon★ uphold an enviable red wine reputation. Sadly, the estate was severely damaged by the fires which swept the region in January 2000; 8ha (20 acres) of young Pinotage vines were destroyed and have since been replanted. The Krige brothers, owners of the estate, are partners with Truter in nearby BEYERSKLOOF and a new red wine property, Bouwland, where the first Pinotage★ has proven well up to scratch. Best years: (Paul Sauer) **1997 96 95 94 92 91**.

**KARTHÄUSERHOF** *Trier, Ruwer, Germany*    Top Ruwer estate which has
♀ gone from strength to strength since Christoph Tyrell and winemaker
Ludwig Breiling took charge in 1986. Rieslings combine aromatic
extravagance with racy brilliance. Since 93 most wines are ★★, some
Auslese and Eiswein ★★★. Best years: 1999 97 96 95 **94 93 90 89 88 86**.

**KATNOOK ESTATE** *Coonawarra, South Australia*    Chardonnay★★ has
♀🏛 consistently been the best of the fairly expensive whites, though
the Riesling★ and the Sauvignon★ are pretty good, too. Reds are led
by well-structured Cabernet Sauvignon★ and treacly Shiraz★, with new
flagship red, Odyssey★★, reaching a higher level. Best years: (red) 1998
97 96 **94 93 91 90 88**.

**KÉKFRANKOS** See Blaufränkisch.

**KENDALL-JACKSON** *Sonoma County, California, USA*    Jess Jackson
♀🏛 founded KJ in bucolic Lake County in 1982 after buying a vineyard
there. The operation has since grown from under 10,000 cases to over
2 million. Early success with Vintner's Reserve Chardonnay was
fuelled by a style of winemaking favouring sweetness, but in the
1990s Jackson redirected energies toward something a bit more
challenging. Today's Chardonnays are 100% barrel fermented and
oak aged. Most varietals, including ambitious Grand Reserves, are
blends from several AVAs. The line-up has experienced a complete
quality makeover, exemplified by Cabernet Sauvignon and Pinot Noir.

**KENWOOD VINEYARDS** *Sonoma Valley AVA, California, USA*    From
♀🏛 humble beginnings, this winery is now home to one of California's
best Sauvignon Blancs★★. Kenwood Zinfandels★ have always been
first rate (Jack London★★, Mazzoni Vineyard★ and Nuns Canyon★)
and Kenwood also makes a range of concentrated Cabernet
Sauvignons. Best years: (1999) 98 97 96 **95 94 93 91 90**.

**VON KESSELSTATT** *Trier, Mosel, Germany*    Good Riesling★ and rich,
♀ fragrant Spätlese and Auslese★★ wines from some top sites at GRAACH
(Josephshöfer) in the MOSEL, Scharzhofberg in the Saar and at Kasel in
the Ruwer. Best years: (1999) 98 97 96 95 **94 93 91 90 89**.

**KHAN KRUM** *Eastern Region, Bulgaria*    Australian flying winemakers
♀ brought new skills, which the all-Bulgarian winemaking team are
now putting into practice making some of Bulgaria's better modern
whites: oaky Reserve Chardonnays and delicate, apricoty Riesling-
Dimiat Country Wine. Research by agent Lovico International has led
to the production of fruitier wines.

**KIEDRICH** *Rheingau, Germany*    Small village whose top vineyard is the
♀ Gräfenberg, giving extremely long-lived, minerally Rieslings. Wines
from Sandgrub and Wasseros are also often good. Best producer:
WEIL★★. Best years: 1999 98 97 96 **95 94 93 92 90**.

**KING ESTATE** *Oregon, USA*    OREGON's biggest producer of Pinot Noir and
♀🏛 Pinot Gris★. Both wines are made in a user-friendly style but the Pinot
Noir is inconsistent. The Reserve Pinot Noir and Reserve Pinot Gris★
offer greater depth. Best years: (Reserve Pinot Gris) (2000) 99 **98 97**.

**KIONA** *Yakima Valley AVA, Washington State, USA*    A small operation in
♀🏛 sagebrush country, Kiona has a growing reputation for its barrel-
fermented Chardonnay★, big, rich Cabernet Sauvignon★ and
delightful sweet or dry Riesling★. Kiona also makes a Lemberger★, a
juicy red wine that has achieved cult status in the Pacific Northwest.

**KISTLER** *Sonoma Valley AVA, California, USA* One of California's hottest Chardonnay producers. Wines are made from many different vineyards (Kistler Vineyard, Durell Vineyard and Dutton Ranch can be ★★★; McCrea Vineyard and the ultra-cool climate Camp Meeting Ridge Vineyard ★★). All possess great complexity with good aging potential. Kistler also makes a number of single-vineyard Pinot Noirs★★ that go from good to very good. Best years: (Dutton) (1999) 98 **97 96 95 94 93 92 91 90**; (Durell) (1999) 98 97 96 **95 94 93 91 90**; (Kistler) (1999) 98 97 96 **95 94 91 90**; (McCrea) (1999) 98 97 96 **95 94 93 92 91 90**.

**KLEIN CONSTANTIA** *Constantia WO, South Africa* Since 1980, the Jooste family have turned this winery into a South African showpiece. Sauvignon Blanc★★, crisp and vivid, benefits from winemaker Ross Gower's experience in New Zealand. A toasty butterscotch Chardonnay★, often botrytis-brushed Riesling★ and Vin de Constance★★, a Muscat dessert wine based on the 18th-century CONSTANTIA examples, highlight the area's aptitude for white wine. Reds have not risen to the same level, although this may change as current vineyards start to bear. Recently purchased STELLENBOSCH vineyards are destined to produce an export-only label. Recently released Shiraz looks promising. Best years: (whites) **2000 99 98 97 96 95 93 92 91**.

**KNAPPSTEIN** *Clare Valley, South Australia* In 1995 Tim Knappstein quit the company, now part of PETALUMA, to focus on his own LENSWOOD VINEYARDS, high in the ADELAIDE HILLS. However, the Knappstein brand is still a market leader, with fine Riesling★★ and Gewürztraminer★, subtly-oaked Semillon-Sauvignon★, Cabernet★, Cabernet-Merlot and Chardonnay. Former Petaluma winemaker Andrew Hardy took charge in 1996, and he has pumped new enthusiasm into the wines. Best years: (Cabernet Sauvignon) (1998) 96 **94 90 86**.

**EMMERICH KNOLL** *Unterloiben, Wachau, Niederösterreich, Austria* Since the late 1970s publicity-shy Emmerich Knoll has made some of the best Austrian dry white wines. His Riesling and Grüner Veltliner are packed with fruit and are rich and complex. They rarely fail to reach ★★ quality, with Grüner Veltliner and Riesling from both the Loibenberg and Schütt sites ★★★. They repay keeping for 5 years or more. Best years: (2000) 99 98 97 **96 95 94 93 92 90 89 88 86 85**.

**KOEHLER-RUPRECHT** *Kallstadt, Pfalz, Germany* Bernd Philippi makes powerful, very concentrated dry Rieslings★★★ from the Kallstadter Saumagen site, the oak-aged botrytized Elysium★★ and, since 1991, Burgundian-style Pinot Noirs★. Philippi is also co-winemaker (with Bernhard Breuer) at Mont du Toit in South Africa, where they have been producing ground-breaking wines since 1998. Best years: (Riesling) 1999 98 97 96 95 **94 93 92 90 89 88 83 79**.

**ALOIS KRACHER** *Illmitz, Burgenland, Austria* Austria's greatest sweet winemaker. Nouvelle Vague wines are aged in barriques while Zwischen den Seen wines are spared oak. The Scheurebe Beerenauslesen and TBAs, and the Welschrieslings, Chardonnay-Welschrieslings and Grand Cuvée are all ★★★. The Bouviers★ (often labelled Kracher Beerenauslese) are also good. With the 97 vintage

Kracher has also catapulted himself into the first rank of Austrian red wine producers. Best years: (whites) (2000) 98 **96 95 94 93 91** 89 86 81.

**KREMSTAL** *Niederösterreich, Austria* Wine region on both sides of the Danube around the town of Krems, producing some of Austria's best whites, particularly dry Riesling and Grüner Veltliner. Best producers: Mantlerhof★, Sepp Moser★, Nigl★★, NIKOLAIHOF★★, Franz Proidl★, Salomon★. Best years: (2000) 99 98 **97 95 94 93**.

**KRUG** *Champagne AC, Champagne, France* Serious CHAMPAGNE house, making seriously expensive wines. The non-vintage, Grande Cuvée★★, used to knock spots off most other de luxe brands but has begun to get a bit too cumbersome for its own good. Also an impressive vintage★★, a rosé★★ and ethereal single-vineyard Clos du Mesnil★★★ blanc de blancs. Now owned by LVMH, so the style may change and – heretical as it is to say so – maybe for the better. Best years: (1990) **89 88 85 82 81** 79.

**KUENTZ-BAS** *Alsace AC, Alsace, France* A small négociant, with high-quality wines from its own vineyards (labelled Réserve Personnelle) and from purchased grapes (Cuvée Tradition). Look out for the Eichberg Grand Cru★★ and the excellent ALSACE VENDANGE TARDIVE★★ wines. Best years: (Grand Cru Riesling) (1999) 98 97 96 **95 94 93** 92 90 89.

---

**KUMEU/HUAPAI** *Auckland, North Island, New Zealand* A small but significant viticultural area north-west of Auckland. The 11 wineries profit from their proximity to New Zealand's capital. Most producers make little or no wine from their home region. Best producers: COOPERS CREEK★, Harrier Rise, KUMEU RIVER★, MATUA VALLEY★★, NOBILO.

---

**KUMEU RIVER** *Kumeu, Auckland, North Island, New Zealand* This family winery has been transformed by New Zealand's first Master of Wine, Michael Brajkovich, who has created a range of adventurous, high-quality wines: a big, complex, award-winning Chardonnay★★★, softly stylish Merlot★, complex oak-aged Pinot Gris★, Auckland's best Pinot Noir and a newly released premium Merlot-Malbec-Cabernet Franc blend called Melba★★. Best years: (Chardonnay) (1999) 98 **96 94 93**.

**KUNDE ESTATE** *Sonoma Valley, California, USA* The Kunde family have grown wine-grapes in SONOMA COUNTY for at least 100 years; in 1990 they started producing wines, with spectacular results. A powerful, buttery Reserve Chardonnay★★ gets rave reviews, as does the Century Vines Zinfandel★★, while the explosively fruity Viognier★★ is a real beauty. Best years: (Chardonnay) (1999) 98 **97 96 95 94**.

**FRANZ KÜNSTLER** *Hochheim, Rheingau, Germany* Gunter Künstler makes the best dry Rieslings in the RHEINGAU. They are powerful, minerally wines★★, with everything from the Hölle site worthy of ★★★. In 1996 he bought the run-down Aschrott estate, which more than doubled his vineyard area. The sweet wine quality has been erratic lately, but the best are fantastic. Best years: (2000) 99 98 97 96 **94 93 92 90 89 88**.

**KWV** *Paarl, South Africa* The KWV's conversion from co-op to company was celebrated with huge investment in the cellar. The standard range has been rationalized, while the grander Cathedral Cellar line-up has been enlarged with more premium varietals; both moves have advanced overall quality. This is shown to best advantage in Cathedral Cellar's bright-fruited, well-oaked Triptych★ BORDEAUX-style blend, rich bold Cabernet★ and modern-style Pinotage. Topping everything, in price if in no other way, is the single-vineyard Perold, the first a Shiraz, though varieties may change from year to year. Whites are generally less exciting, though Cathedral Cellar barrel-fermented Chardonnay shows pleasing fruit/oak balance and the standard Chenin Blanc is a consistent, fruity, off-dry crowd-pleaser. Port-style fortifieds remain superb value, particularly Vintage★★.

**LA AGRICOLA** *Mendoza, Argentina* One of Argentina's great success stories. Dynamic owner José Zuccardi saw the potential for export before his compatriots and set about creating a range of utterly enjoyable easy-drinking wines. La Agricola now exports about 70% of its wine under a number of labels, including Santa Julia and Picajuan Peak. Its greatest success is its basic reds★, often from Italian or Spanish grape varieties. Reserves are also good, if oaky, but top of the line 'Q' still needs to prove itself. Whites are good but less exciting.

**CH. LABÉGORCE-ZÉDÉ★** *Margaux AC, Bordeaux, France* One of the most improved domaines in the MARGAUX AC. Much of the credit goes to manager Luc Thienpont, whose family purchased the estate in 1979. The balance between concentration and finesse is always good. Age for 5 years or more. Second wine: Domaine Zédé. A third wine, Z de Zédé, is a simple Bordeaux AC. Best years: (2000) 99 98 97 96 **95 94 90 89 88**.

**LABOURÉ-ROI** *Nuits-St-Georges, Burgundy, France* Price-conscious and generally reliable merchant, yet no longer so consistent as before as supply struggles to keep up with demand. The CHABLIS★ and MEURSAULT★ are very correct wines, and NUITS-ST-GEORGES★, CHAMBOLLE-MUSIGNY★, GEVREY-CHAMBERTIN★, BEAUNE★ and VOLNAY★ are usually good. Best years: (reds) (2000) 99 98 **97** 96 **95 93** 90.

**LADOIX AC** *Côte de Beaune, Burgundy, France* Most northerly village in the CÔTE DE BEAUNE and one of the least known. Best wines sell under the ACs CORTON or ALOXE-CORTON, and the less good ones as Ladoix-Côte de Beaune or CÔTE DE BEAUNE-VILLAGES. There are several good growers and Ladoix wine, mainly red, quite light in colour and a little lean in style, is reasonably priced. Best producers: (reds) P André★, Cachat-Occuidant★, E Cornu★, Prince Florent de Merode★, A & J-R Nudant★; (whites) P André★, E Cornu★, R & R Jacob★, VERGET★. Best years: (reds) 1999 98 **97 96** 95.

**MICHEL LAFARGE** *Côte de Beaune, Burgundy, France* The doyen of VOLNAY, Michel Lafarge has now virtually handed over to his son, Frédéric. The MEURSAULT produced under this label is not thrilling, but all the red wines can be outstanding, notably Volnay Clos des Chênes★★★, Volnay Clos du Château des Ducs★★★ (a monopole) and less fashionable BEAUNE Grèves★★. Bourgogne Rouge★ is good value. Top wines are accessible when young but can age up to 10 years or more. Best years: (top reds) 1999 98 97 96 95 **93 91 90 89 88**.

**CH. LAFAURIE-PEYRAGUEY★★★** *Sauternes AC, 1er Cru Classé, Bordeaux, France* One of the most improved SAUTERNES properties of the 1980s and now frequently one of the best Sauternes of all. The wines can age well too. Best years: 1999 98 97 96 95 90 89 **88 86 85 83**.

**CH. LAFITE-ROTHSCHILD★★★** *Pauillac AC, 1er Cru Classé, Haut-Médoc,*
*Bordeaux, France* This PAUILLAC First Growth is frequently cited as
the epitome of elegance, indulgence and expense. The wine was
inconsistent in the 1970s and early 80s but there has been great
improvement since. If vintages of the late 80s were excellent, those of
96, 97 and 98 have been superb, with added depth and body to match
the wine's traditional finesse. Second wine: les Carruades de Lafite-
Rothschild. Best years: (2000) 99 98 97 96 95 94 90 89 88 **86 85 82**.

**CH. LAFLEUR★★★** *Pomerol AC, Bordeaux, France* Using some of
POMEROL's most traditional winemaking, this tiny estate can seriously
rival the great PETRUS for sheer power and flavour, and indeed in
certain years has nudged ahead of Pétrus for hedonistic richness and
concentration. Best years: (2000) 99 98 97 96 95 94 93 90 **89 88 86 85**.

**LAFON** *Meursault, Côte de Beaune, Burgundy, France* A leading
producer in MEURSAULT and one of Burgundy's current superstars, with a
reputation and prices to match. From biodynamic viticulture Dominique
Lafon produces rich, powerful Meursaults that spend as long as 2 years
in barrel and age superbly in bottle. As well as excellent Meursault,
especially Clos de la Barre★★★, les Charmes★★★ and les Perrières★★★,
Lafon makes a tiny amount of le MONTRACHET★★★ and some really
individual and exciting red wines from VOLNAY★★ (Santenots du
Milieu★★★) and MONTHELIE★★. Since 1999 the Lafons also own a MACON★
domaine. Best years: (whites) (2000) 99 97 96 95 **93 92 90 89**.

**CH. LAFON-ROCHET ★** *St-Estèphe AC, 4ème Cru Classé, Haut-Médoc,*
*Bordeaux, France* Good-value, affordable Classed Growth claret.
Recent vintages have seen an increase of Merlot in the blend, making
the wine less austere. Delicious and blackcurrant after 10 years. Best
years: (2000) 98 97 96 95 **94 90 89 88 86 85 83 82 79**.

**LAGEDER** *Alto Adige DOC, Trentino-Alto Adige, Italy* Leading producer in
ALTO ADIGE. Produces medium-priced varietals under the Lageder label,
and pricy estate and single-vineyard wines including Cabernet★ and
Chardonnay★★ under the Löwengang label, Sauvignon Lehenhof★★,
Cabernet Cor Römigberg★★, Pinot Bianco Haberlehof★★ and Pinot
Grigio Benefizium Porer★★. Also owns the Casòn Hirschprunn estate,
source of excellent Alto Adige varietals, including Chardonnay★, Pinot
Grigio★ and Sauvignon★, and blended red Casòn★★ (Merlot-Cabernet)
and whites Etelle★★ and Contest★★.

**LAGO DI CALDARO DOC** *Trentino-Alto Adige, Italy* At its best a lovely,
barely red, youthful glugger from the Schiava grape, tasting of straw-
berries and cream and bacon smoke. However, much overproduced
Caldaro scarcely passes muster as red wine at all. Known in German as
Kalterersee. Kalterersee Auslese (Lago di Caldaro Scelto) is not sweet,
but has 0.5% more alcohol. Best producers: Brigl, Caldaro co-op★,
Baron Dürfeld de Giovanelli★, LAGEDER★, J Niedermayr, Prima & Nuova/
Erste & Neue★, San Michele Appiano co-op, Schloss Sallegg★, Elena Walch.

**CH. LAGRANGE★★** *St-Julien AC, 3ème Cru Classé, Haut-Médoc, Bordeaux,*
*France* Since the Japanese company Suntory purchased this estate in
1983, the leap in quality has been astonishing. No longer an amiable,
shambling ST-JULIEN, this has become a single-minded wine of good
fruit, meticulous winemaking and fine quality. Second wine: les Fiefs de
Lagrange. Best years: (2000) 99 98 97 96 95 **94 93 90 89 88 86 85**.

**LAGREIN** Highly individual black grape variety, planted only in Italy's Trentino-Alto Adige region, producing deep-coloured, brambly, chocolaty reds called Lagrein Dunkel, and full-bodied yet attractively scented rosé (known as Kretzer). Best producers: Colterenzio co-op (Cornell★), Graziano Fontana★, Franz Gojer★, Gries co-op★, Hofstätter★, LAGEDER★, Laimburg★, Muri-Gries★, J Niedermayr★, I Niedriest★, Plattner-Waldgries★, Hans Rottensteiner★, Santa Maddalena co-op★, Simoncelli★, Terlano co-op★★, Thurnhof★★, Tiefenbrunner★, Zemmer★.

**CH. LAGREZETTE** *Cahors AC, South-West France* Splendid CAHORS estate owned by Alain-Dominique Perrin, boss of luxury jewellers Cartier. Since 1991, wines have been made in a modern cellar under the eye of Michel Rolland. There's supple, fruity Moulin Lagrezette, oak-aged Chevaliers and Ch. Lagrezette★. Sometimes, Cuvée Dame Honneur★★ and le Pigeonnier★★ are also produced, mainly from Auxerrois.

**CH. LA LAGUNE**★★ *Haut-Médoc AC, 3ème Cru Classé, Haut-Médoc, Bordeaux, France* Consistently excellent Classed Growth – full of the charry, chestnut warmth of good oak and a deep, cherry-blackcurrant-plum sweetness which, after 10 years or so, becomes outstanding claret. Best years: (2000) 98 96 95 **94 90 89 88 86 85 83 82**.

**LAKE'S FOLLY** *Hunter Valley, New South Wales, Australia* Erratic wines with an eager following, thanks to charismatic Dr Max Lake. In best years, austere Chardonnay★★ ages slowly to a masterly antipodean yet Burgundy-like peak. The red is generally ★, but not consistent. Best years: (red) 1999 97 **96 94 91 89 85 83 81**; (white) 1998 97 **96 94 92 91**.

**LALANDE-DE-POMEROL AC** *Bordeaux, France* To the north of its more famous neighbour POMEROL, this AC produces full, ripe wines with an unmistakable mineral edge that are very attractive to drink at 3–4 years old, but age reasonably well too. Even though they lack the concentration of top Pomerols, the wines are not particularly cheap. Best producers: Annereaux★, Belles-Graves, Bertineau-St-Vincent★, Clos de l'Église, la Croix-Cheneveille, la Croix-St-André★, la Fleur de Boüard★, Fougeailles, Garraud★, Grand Ormeau★, Haut-Chaigneau★, Haut-Surget, les Hauts Conseillants, Sergant, Siaurac, Tournefeuille, Viaud★. Best years: (2000) 98 96 **95 94 90 89 88 85 83 82**.

**LAMBRUSCO** *Emilia-Romagna, Italy* Lambrusco is actually a black grape variety, grown in 4 DOC zones on the plains of Emilia, and 1 around Mantova in LOMBARDY, but it is the screwcap bottles of red and white non-DOC Lambrusco that have made the name famous, even though some of them may contain no wine from the Lambrusco grape at all. Originally a dry or semi-sweet fizzy red wine, whose high acidity partnered the rich local food, good dry Lambrusco (especially Lambrusco di Sorbaia and Grasparossa di Castelvetro) is worth trying. Best producers: Barbieri, Barbolini, F Bellei★, Casali, Cavicchioli★, Chiarli, Vittorio Graziano★, Oreste Lini, Stefano Spezia, Venturini Baldini.

**LAMOREAUX LANDING** *Finger Lakes AVA, New York State, USA* One of the most important wineries in this top-quality Eastern region. Its Chardonnay★ is a consistent medal winner, and the Pinot Noir★ is the region's best. Merlot★ and Cabernet Franc★ are also attractive, as are Riesling★ and a limited-production blanc de blancs. Best years: (2000) **99 98**.

**CH. LANESSAN** ★ *Haut-Médoc AC, Cru Bourgeois, Haut-Médoc, Bordeaux, France* Attractive but occasionally austere Cru Bourgeois from the commune of Cussac-Fort-Médoc. Hardly ever uses new oak barrels, yet can achieve Fifth Growth standard and is rarely overpriced. Tends to be at its best in top vintages and can easily age for 8–10 years. Second wine: Dom. de Ste-Gemme. Best years: (2000) 98 96 **95 90 89 88 85 83 82**.

**LANGHE DOC** *Piedmont, Italy* Important new DOC covering wines from the Langhe hills around Alba. The range of varietals such as Chardonnay, Barbera and Nebbiolo include many *vino da tavola* blends of the highest order. Best producers: (reds) ALTARE★★, ASCHERI★, Boglietti (Buio★★), Bongiovanni (Falletto★★), CERETTO★★, CHIARLO★, Cigliuti★★, D CLERICO★★, A CONTERNO★★, Conterno-Fantino (Monprà★★), Luigi Einaudi★, GAJA★★★, A Ghisolfi★★, Marchesi di Gresy (Virtus★★), F Nada (Seifile★★), Parusso (Bricco Rovella★★), Rocche dei Manzoni (Quatr Nas★), Vajra★, G Voerzio (Serrapiu★★), R VOERZIO★★. Best years: (reds) (1999) 98 **97 96 95 93 90**.

**CH. LANGOA-BARTON** ★★ *St-Julien AC, 3ème Cru Classé, Haut-Médoc, Bordeaux, France* Owned by the Barton family since 1821, Langoa-Barton is usually lighter in style than its ST-JULIEN stablemate LEOVILLE-BARTON, but it is still extremely impressive and reasonably priced. Drink after 7 or 8 years, although it may keep for 15. Second wine: Réserve de Léoville-Barton (a blend from the young vines of both Barton properties). Best years: (2000) 99 98 96 95 **90 89 88 86 85 83 82**.

**LANGUEDOC-ROUSSILLON** *Midi, France* This vast area of southern France, running from Nîmes to the Spanish border and covering the *départements* of the GARD, HERAULT, Aude and Pyrénées-Orientales, is still a source of undistinguished cheap wine, but is also one of France's most exciting wine regions. The transformation is the result of better grape varieties, temperature-controlled vinification and ambitious producers, from the heights of MAS DE DAUMAS GASSAC to very good local co-ops. The best wines are the reds, particularly those from CORBIERES, FAUGERES, MINERVOIS and PIC ST-LOUP, and some new-wave Cabernets, Merlots and Syrahs, as well as the more traditional *vins doux naturels*, such as BANYULS, MAURY and MUSCAT DE RIVESALTES; but we are now seeing exciting whites as well, particularly as new plantings of Chardonnay, Marsanne, Roussanne, Viognier and Sauvignon Blanc mature. See also Bouches-du-Rhône, Collioure, Costières de Nîmes, Coteaux du Languedoc, Côtes du Roussillon, Côtes du Roussillon-Villages, Côtes de Thau, Côtes de Thongue, Fitou, Muscat de Frontignan, Muscat de Mireval, Oc, St-Chinian, Vallée du Paradis.

**LANSON** *Champagne AC, Champagne, France* Owners Marne & Champagne are the dominant force in own-label cheap Champagne, but fortunately seem determined to maintain Lanson as their quality flagship. Non-vintage Black Label ★ is reliable stuff and, like the rosé ★ and vintage ★★ wines, especially de luxe Noble Cuvée ★★, improves greatly with aging. Best years: (1995) **93 90 89 88 85 83 82 79**.

**LA ROSA** *Cachapoal, Rapel, Chile* Old family operation rejuvenated by a new winery, La Palmeria. Unoaked Chardonnay★ is pure apricots and figs, and the Merlot★ one of the better wines from RAPEL. Reserva and Gran Reserva wines (often ★★) are a step up in quality.

**CH. LASCOMBES** *Margaux AC, 2ème Cru Classé, Haut-Médoc, Bordeaux, France* Traditionally a hauntingly beautiful, perfumed MARGAUX but during the 1990s the wines were flat and unenjoyable. We can only hope for a return to better things. Best years: (2000) 96 95 **90 89 88 86 85**.

**CH. DE LASTOURS** *Corbières AC, Languedoc, France* A large estate in CORBIÈRES, with some exciting wines. The top white is Blanc de Blancs, but the best wines are the reds – particularly Cuvée Simon Descamps ★ and the oaky Cuvée Boisée ★. Best years: (reds) 1999 **98 96 95 94 93 90**.

**CH. LATOUR** ★★★ *Pauillac AC, 1er Cru Classé, Haut-Médoc, Bordeaux, France* Latour's great reputation is based on powerful, long-lasting classic wines. Throughout the 1950s, 60s and 70s the property stood for consistency and a refusal to compromise in the face of financial pressure. Strangely, in the early 80s there was an attempt to make lighter, more fashionable wines with mixed results. The late 80s saw a return to classic Latour, much to my relief. Its reputation for making fine wine in less

successful vintages is well deserved. After 30 years in British hands, it is now French-owned. Second wine: les Forts de Latour. Best years: (2000) 99 98 97 96 95 94 93 90 **89 88 86 82 78 75 70**.

**LOUIS LATOUR** *Beaune, Burgundy, France* Controversial merchant almost as well known for his COTEAUX DE L'ARDÈCHE Chardonnays as for his Burgundies. Latour's white Burgundies are much better than the reds, although the red CORTON-Grancey ★★ can be very good. Latour's oaky CORTON-CHARLEMAGNE ★★★, from his own vineyard, is his top wine, but there is also good CHEVALIER-MONTRACHET ★★, BÂTARD-MONTRACHET ★★ and le MONTRACHET ★★★. Even so, as these are the greatest white vineyards in Burgundy, there really should be more top performances. Best years: (top whites) (2000) 99 97 96 95 **92 90 89**.

**CH. LATOUR-MARTILLAC** *Pessac-Léognan AC, Cru Classé de Graves, Bordeaux, France* A GRAVES Classed Growth that for many years positively cultivated an old-fashioned image but which is now a property to watch. The vineyard is strictly organic, and has many ancient vines. In the past, the reds★ were deep, dark and well structured but they lacked charm. Things improved considerably in the 1980s and again in the late 90s. Since 1986 new-style vinification has also transformed the whites★★. Best years: (reds) (2000) 99 98 97 96 95 **90 88 86 85 83 82**; (whites) 1999 98 **96 95 94 93 90 89 88**.

**CH. LATOUR-À-POMEROL** ★★ *Pomerol AC, Bordeaux, France* Directed by Christian MOUEIX of PÉTRUS fame, this property makes luscious wines with loads of gorgeous fruit and enough tannin to age well. Best years: (2000) 99 98 96 95 **94 90 89 88 85 83 82**.

**LATRICIÈRES-CHAMBERTIN AC** See Chambertin AC.

**LAUREL GLEN** *Sonoma Mountain AVA, California, USA* Owner/winemaker Patrick Campbell makes only Cabernet ★★ at his mountaintop winery. This is rich wine with deep fruit flavours, aging after 6–10 years to a perfumed, complex BORDEAUX style. Counterpoint is a label for wine that does not make it into the top-level Cabernet. Terra Rosa is made from bought-in wine and bargain-label Reds has been made from wines from Chile and Argentina. Best years: (1999) 97 96 95 94 **93 92 91 90**.

**LAURENT-PERRIER** *Champagne AC, Champagne, France* Large, family-
owned CHAMPAGNE house, offering flavour and quality at reasonable
prices. Non-vintage★ is a bit lean and dry, but the vintage★★ is
delicious, and the top wine, Cuvée Grand Siècle★★★, is among the
finest Champagnes of all. Good rosé, as non-vintage★★ and vintage
Alexandra Grand Siècle★★★. Best years: (1995) **93 90 88 85 82**.

**L'AVENIR ESTATE** *Stellenbosch WO, South Africa* It took only a few years
for owner Marc Wiehe and winemaker François Naudé to gain local
and international recognition. While Pinotage★ and Chenin Blanc are
Naudé's passion, all grapes receive careful attention. The entire range
is imbued with stylish individuality; Cabernet★ and Chardonnay★
look particularly promising. Best years: **2000 99 98 97 96 95 94**.

**CH. LAVILLE-HAUT-BRION★★★** *Pessac-Léognan AC, Cru Classé de
Graves, Bordeaux, France* This is the white wine of the MISSION-HAUT-
BRION and is one of the finest white GRAVES, with a price tag to match.
Fermented in barrel, it needs 10 years or more to reach its savoury
but luscious peak. Best years: 1999 98 97 96 95 **94 93 90 89 85 83**.

---

**LAZIO** *Italy* Region best known for FRASCATI, Rome's white glugger. There
are also various bland whites from Trebbiano and Malvasia, such as EST!
EST!! EST!!! DI MONTEFIASCONE. The region's best are red table wines based on
Cabernet and Merlot from the likes of Castel de Paolis (Quattro Morio★★)
and Paolo di Mauro (Vigna del Vassallo★★).

**LEASINGHAM** *Clare Valley, South Australia* Another wing of the BRL HARDY
group, Leasingham is CLARE VALLEY's biggest winery, and well respected.
Once prostituted on 4-litre casks, the Stanley Leasingham name now
stands for rich, chocolaty reds laced with coconutty American oak. Bin
56 Cabernet-Malbec★ and Bin 61 Shiraz★, once great bargains, are
rising in price, while recently minted Classic Clare Shiraz★★ and
Cabernet★ are high-alcohol, heavily oaked, overpriced blockbusters.
Riesling★★ can be among the area's best; respectable Chardonnay★ and
Semillon-Sauvignon as well. Sparkling Shiraz is excellent.

**L'ECOLE NO 41** *Washington State, USA* The velvety and deeply
flavoured Seven Hills Merlot★ from this fine winery can be
marvellous, as can the Cabernet★. However, the reds don't always
shine. A rich, intense Semillon★★ is very good and the Chardonnay★
could well reach a similar level. Best years: (reds) (1999) 98 97 **96**.

**LECONFIELD** *Coonawarra, South Australia* Leconfield's popular appeal
continues under winemaker Phillippa Treadwell. Cabernet★ is finely
crafted, Merlot★ is a stunner and peppery Shiraz★★ is set to hit the
heights in years to come. Best years: (reds) 1998 **96 95 94 93 91**.

**LEEUWIN ESTATE** *Margaret River, Western Australia* MARGARET RIVER's high
flier, with pricy Chardonnay (at best ★★★) that gets Burgundy lovers
drooling into their bibs. The Cabernets have been patchy, but at best
are ★★, blackcurranty yet with a cool, lean edge. Best years: (white)
**1998 96 95 93 92 91 87 86 85 82 80**.

**DOM. LEFLAIVE** *Puligny-Montrachet, Côte de Beaune, Burgundy, France*
Famous white Burgundy producer, with extensive holdings in some of
the world's greatest vineyards (BATARD-MONTRACHET, CHEVALIER-
MONTRACHET and, since 1990, le MONTRACHET). The price of the wines is

correspondingly high, although 1986–92 produced many disappointing wines. A new winemaking team, led by Anne-Claude Leflaive and including the talented Pierre Morey, and the adoption of biodynamic growing soon turned things around. The top wines here – les Pucelles★★★, Chevalier-Montrachet★★★, Bâtard-Montrachet★★★ and Bienvenues-Bâtard-Montrachet★★★ – are consistently delicious and can age for up to 20 years. Best years: (2000) 99 98 97 96 95 **94 93**.

**OLIVIER LEFLAIVE FRÈRES** *Puligny-Montrachet, Côte de Beaune, Burgundy, France* Former co-manager of Dom. LEFLAIVE, négociant Olivier Leflaive specializes in crisp, modern white wines from the COTE D'OR and the COTE CHALONNAISE, but standards are not as consistent as they should be. The best-value wines are those from lesser ACs – ST-ROMAIN , MONTAGNY★, ST-AUBIN★ and RULLY★ – but the rich, oaky BATARD-MONTRACHET★★★ is the star turn of talented winemaker Franck Grux. Best years: (2000) 99 98 **97** 96 **95 92**.

**PETER LEHMANN** *Barossa Valley, South Australia* Lehmann buys grapes from many BAROSSA smallholders and owns the superb Stonewell plot, source of his best Shiraz★★★. Splendidly juicy old-fashioned, fruit-packed reds (Grenache★, Mentor★★ and Eight Songs Shiraz★★). Also lemony Semillon★★ and dry, long-lived Riesling★★ from Eden Valley. Best years: (Stonewell Shiraz) (1998) 96 95 94 **93 91 90** 89.

**JOSEF LEITZ** *Rüdesheim, Rheingau, Germany* The Leitz family makes the best dry and off-dry Rieslings in RUDESHEIM, especially from the Berg Rottland★★ and Berg Schlossberg★★ sites. Many wines offer excellent value for money. Best years: 1999 98 **97** 96 **94 93 92** 90 89.

**LENSWOOD VINEYARDS** *Adelaide Hills, South Australia* Tim and Annie KNAPPSTEIN traded their CLARE VALLEY holdings for a new venture in the cool-climate ADELAIDE HILLS. They quickly established a fine reputation for Chardonnay★★ and Pinot Noir★★, and Sauvignon Blanc★★, Semillon★ and Cabernets★ are well on the way. Recent vintages of the Pinot Noir in particular should be causing YARRA VALLEY producers sleepless nights. Best years: (Pinot Noir) 1998 **97** 96 95 94 93.

**LENZ WINERY** *Long Island AVA, New York State, USA* Leading LONG ISLAND winery going from strength to strength. The Merlot★ is elegant and powerful with soft, balanced tannins; dry Gewürztraminer★ is spicy and tasty. In good vintages the Pinot Noir★ has deep, ripe fruit. Chardonnay★ is mostly oaked and Cabernet Franc is appealing. Brut-style sparkling wine★ is hard to find, but worth the search. Best years: 1999 98 97 **96** 95.

**LEONETTI CELLAR** *Washington State, USA* The Cabernet★★★ and Merlot★★ produced here are immense, with concentrated fruit and enough tannin to chew on but not be blasted by. The tiny production is usually sold out within hours. Sangiovese★ is also pretty interesting. Best years: (1999) 98 97 **96 95 94 93** 92.

**CH. LÉOVILLE-BARTON★★★** *St-Julien AC, 2ème Cru Classé, Haut-Médoc, Bordeaux, France* Made by Anthony Barton, whose family has run this ST-JULIEN property since 1826, this fine claret is a traditionalist's delight. Dark, dry and tannic, the wines are difficult to taste young, therefore often underestimated, but over 10–15 years they achieve a lean yet sensitively proportioned beauty rarely equalled in Bordeaux. Moreover, they are extremely fairly priced. Second wine: Réserve de Léoville-Barton. Best years: (2000) 99 98 97 96 95 **94 93** 90 89 88 86.

**CH. LÉOVILLE-LAS-CASES★★★** *St-Julien AC, 2ème Cru Classé, Haut-Médoc, Bordeaux, France*  The largest of the 3 Léoville properties, with the highest profile of all the ST-JULIENS, making wines of startlingly deep, dark concentration. I now find them so dense and thick in texture that it is difficult to identify them as St-Julien. Second wine: Clos du Marquis. The death of Michel Delon, the genius behind the property, in 2000, may have an effect on the wine style. We shall see. Best years: (2000) 99 98 97 96 95 94 **93 90 89 88 86 85 83 82**.

**CH. LÉOVILLE-POYFERRÉ★★** *St-Julien AC, 2ème Cru Classé, Haut-Médoc, Bordeaux, France*  Since the 1986 vintage Didier Cuvelier has gradually increased the richness of the wine without wavering from its austere style. A string of excellent wines in the 90s frequently show more classic ST-JULIEN style than those of illustrious neighbour LEOVILLE-LAS-CASES. Second wine: Moulin-Riche. Best years: (2000) 99 98 97 96 95 **94 90 89 86 85 83 82**.

**DOMAINE LEROY** *Vosne-Romanée, Côte de Nuits, Burgundy, France*  In 1988 Lalou Bize-Leroy bought the former Domaine Noëllat in VOSNE-ROMANEE, renaming it Domaine Leroy which should not be confused with her négociant house, Maison LEROY, or the Dom. d'Auvenay, her personal estate. Here she produces fiendishly expensive, though fabulously concentrated, wines with biodynamic methods and almost ludicrously low yields from top vineyards such as CHAMBERTIN★★★, CLOS DE VOUGEOT★★★, MUSIGNY★★★, RICHEBOURG★★★ and ROMANEE-ST-VIVANT★★★. Best years: (top reds) (2000) 99 98 97 96 95 93 90 **89**.

**MAISON LEROY** *Auxey-Duresses, Côte de Beaune, Burgundy, France*  Négociant tucked away in the back streets of AUXEY-DURESSES, Leroy co-owns Domaine de la ROMANEE-CONTI, though is no longer involved in its management. However, its own cellar contains an extraordinary range of gems, often terrifyingly expensive, dating back to the beginning of the century. Best years: (reds) **1980 71 59 49 47 45**.

**LIEBFRAUMILCH** *Pfalz, Rheinhessen, Nahe and Rheingau, Germany*  Sweetish and low in acidity, Liebfraumilch eased millions of beginners into wine drinking in the 1980s, but it now has a downmarket image and sales are plummeting. It can come from the PFALZ, RHEINHESSEN, NAHE or the RHEINGAU and must be made of 70% Riesling, Silvaner, Müller-Thurgau or Kerner grapes.

**LIGURIA** *Italy*  Thin coastal strip of north-west Italy, running from the French border at Ventimiglia to the Tuscan border. Best-known wines are the Riviera Ligure di Ponente, Cinqueterre Colli di Luna and Rossese di Dolceacqua DOCs.

**LIMOUX AC** *Languedoc, France*  The first AC in the LANGUEDOC to allow producers to use Chardonnay and Chenin Blanc, which must be vinified in oak. Production is dominated by the SIEUR D'ARQUES co-op, whose best wines, Toques et Clochers★, fetch high prices at the annual charity auction. Dom. de l'Aigle★ and Dom. Bégude★ are also good.

**LINDEMANS** *Murray River, Victoria, Australia*  Large, historic company now part of Southcorp. Wines come from various regions. Best include HUNTER VALLEY Shiraz★★ (and Reserve Steven Vineyard Shiraz★★); Hunter River Semillon★★; elegant COONAWARRA St George Cabernet★;

173

spicy Limestone Ridge Shiraz-Cabernet★★; and flagship Pyrus★★ – a BORDEAUX blend. Also an impressive, if oaky, PADTHAWAY Chardonnay★ and the mass-market Bin 65 Chardonnay★ – several million cases a year and growing, and it still tastes good! Best years: (Hunter Shiraz) 1998 96 **95 94 91** 87 86 83 82 80 79 73 70 65; (Hunter Semillon) (1999) 98 96 95 92 91 **90 89 87 86** 80 79 78 75 72 68; (Coonawarra reds) 1998 96 **94 93 91 90 88 86 85 82**.

**JEAN LIONNET** *Cornas, Rhône Valley, France* Jean Lionnet produces dense, tannic CORNAS★★ in a fairly modern style. The emphasis here is on new oak aging. Because the wines can seem closed when young, it's worth waiting for 6–7 years, especially for his Cuvée Rochepertuis★★. Lionnet also produces impressive COTES DU RHONE★ from his younger Cornas vines, and a little white ST-PERAY★. Best years: (Cuvée Rochepertuis) (1999) 98 97 96 95 **94 92 91** 90 89 88 85 83.

**LIRAC AC** *Rhône Valley, France* An excellent but underrated AC between TAVEL and CHATEAUNEUF-DU-PAPE. The reds have the dusty, spicy fruit of Châteauneuf without quite achieving the intensity of the best examples. They age well but are delicious young. The rosé is refreshing, with a lovely strawberry fruit, and the white can be good – drink them both young before the perfume goes. Best producers: Aquéria★, Bouchassy★, la Genestière, Lafond-Roc-Epine★, Maby, Mont-Redon★, la Mordorée★★, Pélaquié★, Roger Sabon★★, St-Roch★, Ségriès★, Tavel co-op★. Best years: (2000) **98 97 96 95 94** 93 91 90.

**LISTRAC-MÉDOC AC** *Haut-Médoc, Bordeaux, France* Set back from the Gironde and away from the best gravel ridges, Listrac is 1 of the 6 specific ACs within the HAUT-MEDOC. The wines can be good without ever being thrilling, and are marked by solid fruit, a slightly coarse tannin and an earthy flavour. More Merlot is now being used to soften the style. Best producers: CLARKE, Ducluzeau, Fonréaud, Fourcas-Dupré★, Fourcas-Hosten, Fourcas-Loubaney, Grand Listrac co-op, Mayne-Lalande★, Saransot-Dupré. Best years: (2000) 96 **95 90 89 88 86** 85.

**LOCOROTONDO DOC** *Puglia, Italy* Nutty, crisp, dry white from the south. Drink young. Neighbouring Martina Franca DOC is essentially the same. Best producers: Borgo Canale, Cardone, Leone de Castris, Locorotondo co-op, Torrevento.

**LOIRE VALLEY** *France* The Loire river cuts right through the heart of France. The middle reaches are the home of world-famous SANCERRE and POUILLY-FUME. The region of TOURAINE makes good Sauvignon Blanc and Gamay, while at VOUVRAY and MONTLOUIS the Chenin Blanc makes some pretty good fizz and still whites, ranging from sweet to very dry. The Loire's best reds are made in SAUMUR-CHAMPIGNY, CHINON and BOURGUEIL, mainly from Cabernet Franc, with ANJOU-VILLAGES improving fast. Anjou is famous for ROSE D'ANJOU but the best wines are white, either sweet from the Layon Valley or very dry Chenin from SAVENNIERES. Near the mouth of the river around Nantes is MUSCADET. See also Anjou Blanc, Anjou Rouge, Bonnezeaux, Cabernet d'Anjou, Cheverny, Côte Roannaise, Coteaux de l'Aubance, Coteaux du Layon, Crémant de Loire, Gros Plant du Pays Nantais, Jardin de la France, Jasnières, Menetou-Salon, Muscadet, Pouilly-sur-Loire, Quarts de Chaume, Quincy, Reuilly, Rosé de Loire, St-Nicolas-de-Bourgueil, Saumur, Saumur Mousseux, Touraine Mousseux.

**LOMBARDY** *Italy* Lombardy, richest and most populous of Italian regions, is a larger consumer than producer. Many of the best grapes go to provide base wine for Italy's thriving *spumante* industry. However, there are some interesting wines in OLTREPO PAVESE, VALTELLINA, LUGANA and high-quality sparkling and still wines in FRANCIACORTA.

**LONG ISLAND** *New York State, USA* Long Island has 2 AVAs: North Fork, which has more maritime exposure, and the Hamptons, of jetset fame. This cool region has a long growing season and concentration of fruit in the wines can be wonderful in a good year. However, hurricanes have ruined some vintages. The industry embarked on a growth spurt in the late 1990s. Best grapes are Chardonnay, Merlot and Cabernet Franc. Best producers: BEDELL★★, GRISTINA, HARGRAVE, LENZ★, Palmer★, Pellegrini★, Pindar, Schneider★.

**DR LOOSEN** *Bernkastel, Mosel, Germany* Loosen's estate has portions of some of the MOSEL's most famous vineyards: Treppchen and Prälat in ERDEN, Würzgarten in URZIG, Sonnenuhr in WEHLEN, Himmelreich in GRAACH and Lay in BERNKASTEL. Most of Ernst Loosen's wines achieve ★★, and Spätlese and Auslese from Wehlen, Ürzig and Erden frequently ★★★. One of Germany's foremost protagonists of organic methods, his simple Riesling is great, year in year out. A joint venture with CHATEAU STE MICHELLE in WASHINGTON is proving exciting. Best years: (2000) 99 98 97 96 95 **94 93 92 90 89 88 85 76**. See also J L Wolf.

**LÓPEZ DE HEREDIA** *Rioja DOC, Rioja, Spain* Family-owned RIOJA company, still aging wines in old oak casks. Younger red wines are called Viña Cubillo★, and mature wines Viña Tondonia★ and Viña Bosconia★. Good, oaky whites, especially Viña Gravonia★. Best years: (Viña Tondonia) **93 91 87 86 85 78 76**.

**LOUPIAC AC** *Bordeaux, France* A sweet wine area across the Garonne river from BARSAC. The wines are attractively sweet without being gooey. Drink young in general, though they can age. Best producers: Clos Jean★, Cros★, Loupiac-Gaudiet, Mémoires★, Dom. du Noble, Ricaud, les Roques. Best years: 1999 98 **97 96 95 90 89 88 86**.

**CH. LA LOUVIÈRE** *Pessac-Léognan AC, Bordeaux, France* The star of PESSAC-LEOGNAN's non-classified estates, its reputation almost entirely due to André Lurton. Well-structured reds★★ and fresh, Sauvignon-based whites★★ are excellent value. Best years: (reds) (2000) 99 98 96 95 **94 93 90 89 88 86 85**; (whites) 1999 98 97 96 95 **94 93 90 89 88**.

**LUGANA DOC** *Lombardy, Italy* Medium-bodied white (occasionally sparkling) from the Trebbiano di Lugana grape. Well-structured wines from the better producers can develop excitingly over a few years. Best producers: Ca' dei Frati★★, Ottella★, Roveglia★, Visconti★, Zenato★.

**LUNA** *Napa Valley, California, USA* Led by winemaker John Kongsgaard (ex-NEWTON), Luna has been attracting attention recently with its ambitious SUPER-TUSCAN-style Sangiovese★, stylish Pinot Grigio and attractive Merlot. Best years: (reds) 1998 **97 96**.

**PIERRE LUNEAU-PAPIN** *Muscadet de Sèvre-et-Maine AC and Muscadet des Coteaux de la Loire AC, Loire Valley, France* Meticulous producer who specializes in unoaked Muscadets for the long haul: his top wine, le 'L' d'Or★, ages brilliantly. Oak-fermented wines, although interesting, are variable. Best years: ('L' d'Or) 2000 **99 98 97 96 95 90**.

**LUNGAROTTI** *Torgiano DOC, Umbria, Italy*  Leading producer of TORGIANO. Also makes fine red San Giorgio★★ (Cabernet-Sangiovese), white Torgiano and Chardonnay Palazzi★. His Torgiano Riserva★★ (Vigna Monticchio) is now DOCG.

**LUSSAC-ST-ÉMILION AC** *Bordeaux, France*  Much of the wine from this AC, which tastes like a lighter ST-ÉMILION, is made by the first-rate local co-op and should be drunk within 4 years of the vintage; certain properties are worth seeking out. Best producers: Barbe-Blanche★, Bel-Air, Bellevue, Courlat, Croix-de-Rambeau, la Grenière, Haut-Milon, Lyonnat★, Vieux-Ch.-Chambeau. Best years: (2000) 98 **96 95 90 89 88**.

**EMILIO LUSTAU** *Jerez y Manzanilla DO, Andalucía, Spain*  Specializes in supplying 'own-label' wines to supermarkets. Quality is generally good, and there are some real stars at the top, especially the Almacenista range★★: very individual sherries from small, private producers.

**CH. LYNCH-BAGES** *Pauillac AC, 5ème Cru Classé, Haut-Médoc, Bordeaux, France*  I am a great fan of Lynch-Bages red★★★ – with its almost succulent richness, its gentle texture and its starburst of flavours, all butter, blackcurrants and mint, and it is now one of PAUILLAC's most popular wines. Because of its Fifth Growth status, it was inclined to be underpriced; I couldn't say that now, but it's still worth the money. It is impressive at 5 years, beautiful at 10 and irresistible at 20. Second wine: Haut-Bages-Avérous. White wine: Blanc de Lynch-Bages★. Best years: (reds) (2000) 99 98 97 96 95 **94 90 89 88 86 85 83 82**.

**MÂCON AC** *Mâconnais, Burgundy, France*  The basic Mâconnais AC, but most whites in the region are labelled under the superior MÂCON-VILLAGES AC. The wines are rarely exciting. Chardonnay-based Mâcon Blanc, especially, is a rather expensive basic quaffer. Drink young. Mâcon Supérieur has a slightly higher minimum alcohol level. Best producers: Bertillonnes, Bruyère, DUBOEUF. Best years: 2000 **99 98**.

**MÂCON-VILLAGES AC** *Mâconnais, Burgundy, France*  Mâcon-Villages should be an enjoyable, fruity, fresh wine for everyday drinking at a fair price, but because it is made from Chardonnay, the wines are often overpriced. Forty-three villages in the region can call their wine Mâcon-Villages or add their own name, as in Mâcon-Lugny. Co-ops dominate production. Best villages: Chaintré, Chardonnay, Charnay, Clessé, Davayé, Igé, Lugny, Prissé, la Roche Vineuse, St-Gengoux-de-Scissé, Uchizy, Viré. Best producers: D & M Barraud★★, A Bonhomme★★, Deux Roches★, E Gillet★, Greffière★★, J-J Litaud★, Jean Manciat★, O Merlin★★, Robert-Denogent★★, Rijckaert★, Roally★, Saumaize-Michelin★, de la Soufrandise★, J Thévenet★★, Valette★★, VERGET★★, J-J Vincent★. Best years: (2000) 99 **98 97 96 95 94 93**.

**MACULAN** *Breganze DOC, Veneto, Italy*  Fausto Maculan makes an impressive range of BREGANZE DOC led by Cabernet-Merlot blend Fratta★★ and Cabernet Palazzotto★, along with excellent reds★★ and whites★★ from the Ferrata vineyards, but his most impressive wines are sweet Torcolato★★ and outstanding Acininobili★★★ made mainly from botrytized Vespaiolo grapes.

**MADEIRA DOC** *Madeira, Portugal*  The subtropical holiday island of Madeira seems an unlikely place to find a serious wine. However, Madeiras are very serious indeed and the best can survive to a great age. Internationally famous by the 17th century, modern Madeira was shaped by the phylloxera epidemic 100 years ago, which wiped out the vineyards. Replantation was with hybrid vines inferior to the 'noble' and traditional Malvasia (or Malmsey), Boal (or Bual), Verdelho and Sercial varieties. There are incentives to replant with noble grapes, but progress is slow (having now crept up to 15% of total plantings). The typically burnt, tangy taste of inexpensive Madeira comes from the process of heating in huge vats. The better wines are aged naturally in the subtropical warmth. All the wines are fortified early on and may be sweetened with fortified grape juice before bottling. Basic 3-year-old Madeira is made mainly from Tinta Negra Mole, whereas higher-quality 5-year-old (Reserva), 10-year-old (Reserva Velha), 15-year-old (Extra Reserva) and vintage wines (from a single year, aged in cask for at least 20 years) tend to be made from 1 of the 4 'noble' grapes. Best producers: Barbeito, Barros e Souza, H M Borges, HENRIQUES & HENRIQUES, Vinhos Justino Henriques, MADEIRA WINE COMPANY, Pereira d'Oliveira.

**MADEIRA WINE COMPANY** *Madeira DOC, Madeira, Portugal* This company ships more than half of all Madeira exported in bottle. Among the brand names are Blandy's, Cossart Gordon, Leacock and Rutherford & Miles. Now controlled by the Symington family from the mainland. Big improvements are taking place in 5-, 10- and 15-year-old wines.

**MADIRAN AC** *South-West France* In the gentle hills of Vic-Bilh, north of Pau, there has been a steady revival of the Madiran AC as viticulturists have gradually discovered ways to propagate the difficult Tannat vine successfully. Several of the best producers are now using new oak, and this certainly helps to soften the rather aggressive wine. Best producers: Aydie★★, Barréjat★, Berthoumieu★, Bouscassé★★, Capmartin★, la CHAPELLE LENCLOS★★, Caves de Crouseilles, Laffitte-Teston★, MONTUS★★, Mouréou★, Union des Producteurs PLAIMONT. Best years: (2000) 98 **97 96 95 94 90 89 88 85.**

**CH. MAGDELAINE★★** *St-Émilion Grand Cru AC, 1er Grand Cru Classé, Bordeaux, France* Owned by the quality-conscious company of MOUEIX, these are dark, rich, aggressive wines, yet with a load of luscious fruit and oaky spice. In lighter years the wine has a gushing, easy, tender fruit and can be enjoyed at 5–10 years. Best years: (2000) 99 98 97 96 95 **90 89 88 85 82 75.**

**MAIPO, VALLE DEL** *Valle Central, Chile* Birthplace of the Chilean wine industry and increasingly encroached upon by Chile's capital, Santiago. Cabernet is king and many of Chile's premium-priced reds come from here. Good Chardonnay is produced from vineyards close to the Andes. Best producers: CARMEN★, CONCHA Y TORO★, SANTA CAROLINA, SANTA RITA★, TARAPACA.

**MÁLAGA DO** *Andalucía, Spain* Málaga is a curious blend of sweet wine, alcohol and juices (some boiled up and concentrated, some fortified, some made from dried grapes) and production is dwindling. The label generally states colour and sweetness. The best are intensely nutty, raisiny and caramelly. The much-admired Scholtz Hermanos ceased operations in 1996. Best producer: López Hermanos★★.

177

**CH. MALARTIC-LAGRAVIÈRE**★ *Pessac-Léognan AC, Cru Classé de Graves, Bordeaux, France* A change of ownership in 1997 and massive investment in the vineyard and cellars should lead to improvements at this underperforming GRAVES Classed Growth. The tiny amount of white★ is made from 100% Sauvignon Blanc and usually softens after 3–4 years into a lovely nutty wine. Best years: (reds) (2000) 99 98 97 96 **90 89**; (whites) 1999 98 97 96 95 **94**.

**MALBEC** A red grape, rich in tannin and flavour, from South-West France. A major ingredient in CAHORS wines, it is also known as Cot or Auxerrois. At its best in Argentina and Chile where it produces lush-textured, ripe, damsony reds. In CALIFORNIA, it sometimes appears in BORDEAUX-style blends; it has a similar role in South Africa. Also grown in Australia.

**CH. MALESCOT ST-EXUPÉRY**★★ *Margaux AC, 3ème Cru Classé, Haut-Médoc, Bordeaux, France* Once one of the most scented, exotic reds in BORDEAUX, a model of perfumed MARGAUX. In the 1980s Malescot lost its reputation as the wine became pale, dilute and uninspired, but it is beginning to rediscover that cassis and violet perfume and return to its former glory. Best years: (2000) 99 98 97 96 95 94 **93 90**.

**MALVASIA** This grape is widely planted in Italy and is found there in many guises, both white and red. In Friuli, it is known as the Malvasia Istriana and produces light, fragrant wines of great charm, while in TUSCANY, UMBRIA and the rest of central Italy it is used to improve the blend for wines like ORVIETO and FRASCATI. On the islands, Malvasia is used in the production of rich, dry or sweet wines in Bosa and Cagliari (in SARDINIA) and in Lipari off the coast of SICILY to make really tasty, apricotty sweet wines. As a black grape, Malvasia Nera is blended with Negroamaro in southern PUGLIA, while in PIEDMONT a paler-skinned relation produces frothing light reds in Castelnuovo Don Bosco, just outside Turin. Variants of Malvasia also grow in Spain and mainland Portugal. On the island of MADEIRA it produces sweet, varietal fortified wine, usually known by its English name: Malmsey.

**LA MANCHA DO** *Castilla-La Mancha, Spain* Spain's vast central plateau is Europe's biggest delimited wine area. Whites are never exciting but nowadays are often fresh and attractive. Reds can be light and fruity, or richer. New DO regulations in 1995 allowed for much-needed irrigation and the planting of new grape varieties, including Viura, Chardonnay, Cabernet Sauvignon, Merlot, Petit Verdot and Syrah. There is still some rough, old-style wine, but progress is fast. Best producers: Fermin Ayuso Roig (Viña Q Estola), Vinícola de Castilla (Castillo de Alhambra, Señorío de Guadianeja★), la Magdalena co-op, Nuestra Señora de la Cabeza co-op (Casa Gualda), Parra Jiménez, Rodriguez y Berger (Viña Santa Elena★), Julian Santos Aguado (Don Fadrique), Torres Filoso (Arboles de Castillejo★), Casa de la Viña.

**DOMAINE ALBERT MANN** *Alsace AC, Alsace, France* Powerful, flavoursome and ageworthy wines from a range of Grand Cru vineyards, including intense, minerally Rieslings from Furstentum★★ and Rosenberg★★ and rich Furstentum Gewurztraminer★★. An impressive range of Pinot Gris culminates in astonishingly concentrated Sélection de Grains Nobles from Furstentum★★★. Best years: (Sélection de Grains Nobles Gewurztraminer) 1998 97 94 **89**.

**MARANGES AC** *Côte de Beaune, Burgundy, France*  AC in the southern COTE DE BEAUNE. Generally attractive light red wines, though many growers sell them as COTE DE BEAUNE-VILLAGES. Less than 5% of production is white. Best producers: B Bachelet★, M Charleux★, Contat-Grangé★, DROUHIN, GIRARDIN★★, Rijckaert★. Best years: (reds) 1999 98 **97 96 95**.

**MARCASSIN** *Sonoma County, California, USA*  Helen Turley has always had a reputation for full-power, flavour-packed wines, but at her own winery she is focusing on cool-climate Chardonnay and Pinot Noir. Incredible depth and restrained power are the hallmarks here. Tiny quantities of single-vineyard Chardonnays from Gauer Ranch's Upper Barn, Lorenzo Vineyard, Hudson Vineyard and the 4-ha (10-acre) Marcassin Vineyard often rank ★★★. Best years: (1999) 98 97 **96 95**.

**MARCHE** *Italy*  Adriatic region producing increasingly good white VERDICCHIO and reds from Montepulciano and Sangiovese led by ROSSO CONERO and ROSSO PICENO. Good wines from international varieties such as Cabernet, Chardonnay and Sauvignon Blanc are becoming more common.

**MARCILLAC AC** *South-West France*  Strong, dry red wines (there is a little rosé), largely made from the local grape Fer. The reds are rustic but full of fruit and should be drunk between 2 and 5 years. Best producers: Marcillac-Vallon co-op, Philippe Teulier.

**MARGARET RIVER** *Western Australia*  First Australian region planted on the advice of scientists in the late 1960s. Quickly established its name as a leading area for Cabernet, with marvellously deep, BORDEAUX-like structured reds. Now Chardonnay, concentrated and opulent, vies with Cabernet for top spot, but there is also fine grassy Semillon, tropical Sauvignon and spicy, fruity Verdelho. Best producers: Brookland Valley★, CAPE MENTELLE★★★, CULLEN★★★, Devil's Lair★, EVANS & TATE★, LEEUWIN ESTATE★★, MOSS WOOD★★, PIERRO★★, VASSE FELIX★, Xanadu★.

**MARGAUX AC** *Haut-Médoc, Bordeaux, France*  AC centred on the village of Margaux but including Soussans and Cantenac, Labarde and Arsac. Gravel banks dotted through the vineyards mean that the wines are rarely heavy and should have a divine perfume when mature at 7–12 years. Best producers: (Classed Growths) BRANE-CANTENAC★, Dauzac★, FERRIERE★★, Giscours★, ISSAN★, Kirwan★, LASCOMBES★, MALESCOT ST-EXUPERY★★, MARGAUX★★★, PALMER★★, PRIEURE-LICHINE★, RAUZAN-SEGLA★★, Tertre★; (others) ANGLUDET★, Bel-Air Marquis d'Aligre★, la Gurgue★, LABEGORCE-ZEDE★, Monbrison★, SIRAN★. Best years: (2000) 99 96 95 **90 89**.

**CH. MARGAUX★★★** *Margaux AC, 1er Cru Classé, Haut-Médoc, Bordeaux, France*  The greatest wine in the MEDOC. Has produced almost flawless wines since 1978, as great as any MARGAUX ever made. Inspired winemaker Paul Pontallier continues to produce the best from this great terroir. There is also some delicious white, Pavillon Blanc★★, made from Sauvignon Blanc, but it must be the most expensive BORDEAUX AC wine by a mile. Second wine: (red) Pavillon Rouge★★. Best years: (reds) (2000) 99 98 97 96 95 94 93 90 89 88 86 **85 83 82 81 79 78**; (whites) 1999 98 97 96 **95 94 90 89 88**.

**MARLBOROUGH** *South Island, New Zealand* Marlborough has enjoyed such spectacular success as a quality wine region that it is difficult to imagine that the first vines were planted as recently as 1973. Long, cool and relatively dry ripening and free-draining stony soils are the major assets. Its snappy, aromatic Sauvignon Blanc first brought the region fame worldwide. Fine-flavoured Chardonnay, steely Riesling, elegant Champagne-method fizz and luscious botrytized wines are the other successes. Pinot Noir is a work in progress. **Best years:** CELLIER LE BRUN, Clifford Bay★★, CLOUDY BAY★★, DELEGAT'S (Oyster Bay)★, Forrest Estate★★, GROVE MILL★★, HUNTER'S★★, ISABEL★★, JACKSON ESTATE★, Lawson's Dry Hills★, MONTANA, Nautilus★, SERESIN★★, VAVASOUR★★, Wither Hills★.

**MARNE ET CHAMPAGNE** *Champagne AC, Champagne, France* Family firm, the second-largest producer in CHAMPAGNE, selling over 20 million bottles, mainly for supermarkets, under dozens of different labels. The best known is Alfred Rothschild, which is the second-biggest-selling Champagne in France. The company controls two well-known brands under Besserat de Bellefon and LANSON.

**MARQUÉS DE CÁCERES** *Rioja DOC, Rioja, Spain* Go-ahead RIOJA winery making crisp, aromatic, modern whites★ and rosés★, and fleshy, fruity reds (Reservas★) with the emphasis on aging in bottle, not barrel. There is a new luxury red, Gaudium★. **Best years:** (reds) 1996 95 94 92 91 90 89 87 85 82 78.

**MARQUÉS DE GRIÑÓN** *Rioja DOC, Rioja and Rueda DO, Castilla y León, Spain* From his home, non-DO estate at Malpica, near Toledo and Madrid, Carlos Falcó (the eponymous Marqués de Griñón) has expanded into the Duero and now into RIOJA, after selling a stake in his company to BERBERANA. Minty Cabernet de Valdepusa★★ and Durius red (blended from TORO and RIBERA DEL DUERO) have been joined by barrel-fermented Chardonnay, Petit Verdot★★, Syrah★★ and the top blend, Eméritus★★, from his own estate, 2 Marqués de Griñón red Riojas (a lightly oaked young wine★ and a Reserva★), and white non-DO Durius★. **Best years:** (reds) 1998 97 95 94 92 91 90 89.

**MARQUÉS DE MONISTROL** *Cava DO and Penedès DO, Cataluña, Spain* Now owned by the Arco group (led by BERBERANA). Brut Selección★ is a fresh, fruity CAVA. The still whites, a Blanc de Blancs and Blanc en Noirs, are good; the reds, long unexceptional, have gained from the introduction of a young Merlot. Drink the youngest available.

**MARQUÉS DE MURRIETA** *Rioja DOC, Rioja, Spain* The RIOJA bodega that most faithfully preserves the traditional style of long aging. Ultra-conservative, yet sporting glistening new fermentation tanks and a Californian bottling line. The latest move has been to release more wines under their splendidly ornate Castillo de Ygay★★ label. No longer do these wait 20 years for release. A new, more modern-styled, up-market cuvée, Dalmau★★, was introduced in 1999. Whites are dauntingly oaky, reds packed with savoury mulberry fruit. **Best years:** (reds) 1995 94 92 91 89 87 85 68 64; (whites) 1992 91 86 85 78.

**MARQUÉS DE RISCAL** *Rioja DOC, País Vasco, and Rueda DO, Castilla y León, Spain* A producer which has restored its reputation for classic pungent RIOJA reds (Reserva★). The expensive, Cabernet-based Barón de Chirel★★ cuvée is made only in selected years. Increasingly aromatic Rueda whites★. Cellar problems during the 1990s are now supposed to have been corrected; let's hope so. Best years: (Barón de Chirel) 1996 95 **94** 91.

**MARSALA DOC** *Sicily, Italy* Fortified wines, once as esteemed as sherry or Madeira. A taste of an old Vergine (unsweetened) Marsala, fine and complex, will show why. Today most is sweetened. Purists say this mars its delicate nuances, but DOC regulations allow for sweetening Fine and Superiore versions. Best producers: DE BARTOLI★, Florio (Baglio Florio★, Terre Arse★), Pellegrino (Soleras★, Vintage★).

**MARSANNAY AC** *Côte de Nuits, Burgundy, France* Village almost in Dijon, best known for its rosé, pleasant but quite austere and dry. The red is rapidly proving itself as one of Burgundy's most fragrant wines. There is little white. Best producers: R Bouvier★, P Charlopin★★, CLAIR★★, Collotte★, Fougeray de Beauclair★, Geantet-Pansiot★★, JADOT, D Mortet★★, J & J-L Trapet★. Best years: (reds) (2000) 99 **98 97 96** 95.

**MARSANNE** Undervalued grape yielding rich, nutty wines in the northern Rhône (HERMITAGE, CROZES-HERMITAGE, ST-JOSEPH and ST-PERAY), often with the more lively Roussanne. Also planted in Switzerland (as Ermitage), and performs well in Australia at MITCHELTON★★ and TAHBILK★★.

**MARTINBOROUGH** *North Island, New Zealand* A cool, dry climate, free-draining soil and a passion for quality are this region's greatest assets. Mild autumn weather promotes intense flavours balanced by good acidity in all varieties: top Pinot and complex Chardonnay, intense Cabernet, full Sauvignon Blanc and honeyed Riesling. Best producers: ATA RANGI★★, DRY RIVER★★★, MARTINBOROUGH VINEYARD★★, Nga Waka★, PALLISER ESTATE★★.

**MARTINBOROUGH VINEYARD** *Martinborough, North Island, New Zealand* Famous for Pinot Noir★★ but also makes impressive Chardonnay★★, spicy Riesling★, and luscious botrytized styles★★ when vintage conditions allow. A new winemaker has replaced the talented Larry McKenna – watch this space. Best years: (Pinot Noir) (2001) 99 **98 96** 94.

**MARTÍNEZ BUJANDA** *Rioja DOC, País Vasco, Spain* Family-owned firm that makes some of the best modern RIOJAS. Whites and rosés are young and crisp, reds★ are full of fruit *and* age well. The single-vineyard Finca Valpiedra★★ is a major newcomer. Best years: (reds) 1996 **95 94 92** 91 90 87 86 85.

**LOUIS M MARTINI** *Napa Valley, California, USA* During the 1980s the wines from this NAPA winery changed from being deep and rich to relatively light. Recently it has returned to a more concentrated style based on single vineyards and a range of Reserve wines, so far with mixed results. The Monte Rosso Zinfandel★ and Cabernet Sauvignon★ can be very good, Chardonnays are mostly pretty good and the Merlot shows most improvement. Best years: (reds) (1999) 98 97 **96 95 94** 91.

**MARZEMINO** This red grape of northern Italy's TRENTINO province makes deep-coloured, plummy and zesty reds that are best drunk within 3–5 years. Best producers: Battistotti★, Bossi Fedrigotti, Casata Monfort, La Cadalora★, Cavit★, Concilio Vini★, Isera co-op★, Letrari★, Mezzacorona, Simoncelli★, Spagnolli★, De Tarczal★, Vallarom★, Vallis Agri★.

**MAS BRUGUIÈRE** *Pic St-Loup, Coteaux du Languedoc AC, Languedoc,*
*France* One of the top domaines in this quality-oriented region. The
basic red★ has rich, spicy Syrah character, while top-of-the-range Fûts
de Chêne★★, now renamed La Grenadière, develops buckets of black
fruit and spice after 3 years. Calcadiz is an easy-drinking red from
young vines. The Roussanne white★ is aromatic, fruity and
refreshingly crisp.

**MAS DE DAUMAS GASSAC** *Vin de Pays de l'Hérault, Languedoc, France*
Aimé Guibert is the longest established quality producer in the
Languedoc, proving that the HERAULT, normally associated with cheap
table wine, is capable of producing great
red wines that can age in bottle. The
Daumas Gassac rosé is dull; however, the
tannic yet rich Cabernet Sauvignon-based
red★★ and the fabulously scented white★★
(Viognier, Muscat, Chardonnay and Petit
Manseng) are impressive, if expensive.
Sweet Vin de Laurance★★★ is a new
triumph. Best years: (reds) 1999 98 97 96
95 94 **93 90**.

**MAS JULLIEN** *Coteaux du Languedoc AC, Languedoc, France* Olivier
Jullien makes fine wines from traditional MIDI varieties, with such
success that bottles have to be rationed. Red can frequently rate ★★★,
white★ is also good stuff. Also late-harvest Clairette Beudelle. Best
years: (reds) 1998 97 **96 95 94 93 91**.

**BARTOLO MASCARELLO** *Barolo DOCG, Piedmont, Italy* One of the great
old-fashioned producers of BAROLO★★★, yet the wines have an
exquisite perfume and balance. The Dolcetto★ and Barbera★ can need
a little time to soften. Best years: (Barolo) (1998) (97) 96 95 93 **90 89 88
86 85 82 78**.

**GIUSEPPE MASCARELLO** *Barolo DOCG, Piedmont, Italy* The old house
of Giuseppe Mascarello (now run by grandson Mauro) is renowned
for dense, vibrant Dolcetto d'Alba (Bricco★★) and intense Barbera
(Codana★★), but the pride of the house is BAROLO from the
Monprivato★★★ vineyard. Best years: (Monprivato) (1998) 97 95 **93 91
90 89 88 85 82 78**.

**MASI** *Veneto, Italy* Family firm, one of the driving forces in VALPOLICELLA.
Brolo di Campofiorin★ (effectively if not legally a *ripasso* Valpolicella),
is worth looking out for, as is AMARONE (Mazzano★★ and Campolongo
di Torbe★★). Toar★ is a blend of Corvina and other native varieties;
Osar★ a blend of the obscure Oseleta with Corvina. The wines of
Serègo Alighieri★★ are also produced by Masi. Best years: (Amarone):
**1995 93 90 88 86 85**.

**MASTROBERARDINO** *Campania, Italy* This family firm has long flown the
flag for CAMPANIA in southern Italy, though it has now been joined by
others. Best known for red TAURASI★ and white Greco di Tufo★ and
Fiano di Avellino★. Best years: (Taurasi Radici) 1996 95 **94 93 90 89 88 86
85 83 82 81 79**.

**MATANZAS CREEK** *Sonoma Valley AVA, California, USA* Sauvignon
Blanc★ is taken very seriously here, and the results show in a
complex, zesty wine; Chardonnay★★ is rich and toasty but not

overblown. Merlot★★ has established a high reputation, with a silky, mouthfilling richness. Limited-edition Journey Chardonnay★★ and Merlot★★ are opulent but pricy. Best years: (Chardonnay) 1998 **97 96 95 94 93** 91 90; (Merlot) 1997 96 **95 94 93 92 91** 90.

**MATUA VALLEY** *Waimauku, Auckland, North Island, New Zealand* Family company producing a wide range of often adventurous and always full-flavoured wines from 4 regions. Best are the sensuous, scented Ararimu Chardonnay★★, lush and strongly varietal Gewürz-traminer★, a creamy oak-aged Sauvignon Blanc★, tangy MARLBOROUGH Sauvignon Blanc★ (Shingle Peak), fine Merlot★ and Ararimu Cabernet Sauvignon★★. Best years: (Ararimu Cabernet) 1998 **96 94 92 91**

**CH. MAUCAILLOU★** *Moulis AC, Cru Bourgeois, Haut-Médoc, Bordeaux, France* Maucaillou shows that you don't have to be a Classed Growth to make high-quality claret. Expertly made by the Dourthe family, it is soft but classically flavoured. It matures quickly but ages well for 10–12 years. Best years: (2000) 99 98 96 **95 90 89 88 86 85 83** 82.

**MAULE, VALLE DEL** *Valle Central, Chile* The most southerly of Valle CENTRAL's sub-regions, characterized by wet winters and a large day/night temperature difference. White varieties (mostly Chardonnay and Sauvignon Blanc) outnumber red by nearly 2 to 1, but Merlot's success on clay soils looks set to shift the balance. Best producers: (whites) J Bouchon, CARMEN★, SANTA RITA★, Terra Noble.

**MAURY AC** *Roussillon, France* A *vin doux naturel* made mainly from Grenache Noir. This strong, sweetish wine can be made in either a young, fresh style or the locally revered old *rancio* style. Best producers: Mas Amiel★★, la Coume du Roy★, Maury co-op★, Maurydoré★, la Pleiade★.

**MAXIMIN GRÜNHAUS** *Grünhaus, Ruwer, Germany* The best estate in the Ruwer valley and one of Germany's greatest. Dr Carl von Schubert vinifies separately the wines of his 3 vineyards (Abtsberg, Bruderberg and Herrenberg), making chiefly dry and medium-dry wines of great subtlety. In good vintages the wines are easily ★★★ and the Auslese will age for decades; even QbA and Kabinett wines can age for many years. Best years: 1999 97 96 95 **94 93 92** 90 **89 88 85** 83 79 76 75 71.

**MAZIS-CHAMBERTIN AC** See Chambertin AC.

**MAZOYÈRES-CHAMBERTIN AC** See Chambertin AC.

**McLAREN VALE** *South Australia* Sunny maritime region just south of Adelaide, with about 50 small wineries, plus big boys HARDYS, SEAVIEW and now ROSEMOUNT and BLASS. Once a 'port' area, nowadays it produces full-bodied wines from Chardonnay, Sauvignon Blanc, Shiraz, Grenache and Cabernet. Best producers: CHAPEL HILL★★, CLARENDON HILLS★★, Coriole★, D'ARENBERG★★, Fox Creek★★, Andrew Garrett, HARDYS★★, Ingoldby, Kangarilla Road★, Maxwell★, Geoff MERRILL★, REYNELL★, ROSEMOUNT★★, Tatachilla★, WIRRA WIRRA★★.

**McWILLIAM'S** *Riverina, New South Wales, Australia* Large family winery whose best wines are the Mount Pleasant range from the Lower HUNTER VALLEY: classic bottle-aged Semillons, including Elizabeth★★ and Lovedale★★, buttery Chardonnays★ and special-vineyard Shirazes★ – Old Paddock, Old Hill and Rose Hill. Classy liqueur Muscat★★ from RIVERINA, and excellent table wines from Barwang★ vineyard near HILLTOPS. Best years: (Hunter Semillon) 1998 96 95 93 **91 90 86 84 82** 80 79.

**MÉDOC AC** *Bordeaux, France* The Médoc peninsula north of Bordeaux
on the left bank of the Gironde river produces a good fistful of the
world's most famous reds. These are all situated in the HAUT-MÉDOC, the
southern, more gravelly half of the area. The Médoc AC, for reds only,
covers the northern part. Here, in these flat clay vineyards, the
Merlot grape dominates. The wines can be attractive in warm years:
dry but juicy. Best at 3–5 years old. Best producers: la Cardonne,
Escurac, les Grands Chênes★, Greysac, Lacombe-Noaillac, Lafon★,
Loudenne, les Ormes-Sorbet★, Patache d'Aux, POTENSAC★★, Ramafort,
Rollan-de-By★, la Tour-de-By★, la Tour-Haut-Caussan★, la Tour-St-
Bonnet, Vieux-Robin. Best years: (2000) 96 95 94 **90 89 88 86 85 82**.

**MEERLUST** *Stellenbosch WO, South Africa* Owner Hannes Myburgh
maintains his late father's faith in the Bordeaux varieties: his complex
Rubicon★ was one of the Cape's first Bordeaux blends. Italian
cellarmaster Giorgio Dalla Cia's passion is Merlot★; refined with good
aging potential. Impressive Chardonnay★★ is full and toasty. Best
years: (Rubicon) **1997** 96 95 94 92 91; (Chardonnay) **1998** 97 96 95.

**ALPHONSE MELLOT** *Sancerre AC, Loire Valley, France* Long-established
grower and négociant. The négociant business includes decent wines
from POUILLY-FUMÉ and MENETOU-SALON, but the most interesting come
from the family's own vineyards in SANCERRE. Domaine la Moussière★
is unoaked with fresh and intense citrus flavours; the oaked Cuvée
Edmond★★ can seem overly wooded at first and needs a few years to
mature to a fascinating, fully integrated flavour. Much improved reds.
Best years: (Cuvée Edmond) 2000 99 **98 97 96 95 90 89**.

**CHARLES MELTON** *Barossa Valley, South Australia* One of the leading
lights in the renaissance of hand-crafted Shiraz, Grenache and
Mourvèdre in the BAROSSA. Fruity Grenache rosé Rose of Virginia★,
RHONE blend Nine Popes★★, varietal Grenache★★ and smoky Shiraz★★
have all attained cult status. Cabernet Sauvignon is variable, but ★★ at
best. Best years: (Nine Popes) 1998 97 **96 95 94 93 92 91**.

**MENDOCINO COUNTY** *California, USA* The northernmost county of the
North Coast AVA. It includes Anderson Valley AVA, a cool east–west
valley opening up to the Pacific Ocean and an excellent area for
sparkling wines and the occasional Pinot Noir; and Redwood Valley
AVA, a warmer area with good Zinfandel and Cabernet. Best producers:
FETZER, Goldeneye, HANDLEY CELLARS★★, Husch, Lazy Creek★, McDowell
Valley★, Navarro★★, PACIFIC ECHO★, Parducci, ROEDERER★★.

**MENDOZA** *Argentina* The most important wine region in Argentina,
accounting for about 90% of fine wine production. Situated in the
eastern foothills of the Andes on a similar latitude to Chile's Santiago,
the region's bone-dry climate produces powerful, high-alcohol red
wines. High-altitude sub-regions like Tupungato now produce better
whites, particularly Chardonnay. Further from the mountains, Maipú
and Luján de Cuyo are ideal for Malbec, Syrah and Cabernet. Best
producers: Luigi Bosca, CATENA★, DOMAINE VISTALBA★, Finca El Retiro★, LA
AGRICOLA★, NORTON★, Nieto Senetiner (Cadus★★).

**MENETOU-SALON AC** *Loire Valley, France* Extremely attractive, chalky-
clean Sauvignon whites and cherry-fresh Pinot Noir reds and rosés from
west of SANCERRE. Best producers: Chatenoy★, Chavet★, J-P Gilbert★,
H Pellé★, J-M Roger★, J Teiller★. Best years: 2000 99 98 97 96.

**MÉO-CAMUZET** *Vosne-Romanée, Côte de Nuits, Burgundy, France* Super-quality estate, thanks in no small measure to the advice of Henri Jayer, a third of whose property it gained in 1988. New oak barrels and luscious, rich fruit combine in superb wines, which also age well. CLOS DE VOUGEOT★★★, RICHEBOURG★★★ and CORTON★★ are the grandest wines, along with the VOSNE-ROMANEE Premiers Crus, aux Brulées★★, Cros Parantoux★★★ and les Chaumes★★. Also fine NUITS-ST-GEORGES Boulot★★. Best years: (2000) 99 98 97 96 95 93 **92 90 89**.

**MERCUREY AC** *Côte Chalonnaise, Burgundy, France* Most important of the 4 main COTE CHALONNAISE villages. The red is usually pleasant and strawberry-flavoured, sometimes rustic, and can take some aging. There is not much white but I like its buttery, even spicy, taste. Best at 3–4 years old. Best producers: (reds) FAIVELEY★★, E Juillot★, M Juillot★★, Lorenzon★, F Raquillet★, RODET (Chamirey★), de Suremain★★, Villaine★★; (whites) FAIVELEY (Clos Rochette★), Genot-Boulanger★, M Juillot★, O LEFLAIVE★, RODET (Chamirey★). Best years: (reds) (2000) 99 98 **97 96 95**.

**MERLOT** See pages 186–7.

**GEOFF MERRILL** *McLaren Vale, South Australia* High-profile winemaker with an instinctive feel for wine. Under the Geoff Merrill brand he fields nicely bottle-aged Reserve Cabernet, a light, early-picked, slightly eccentric style, Reserve Shiraz★ and a Chardonnay★ (Reserve is ★★). The cheaper Mount Hurtle brand has a moreish Grenache rosé.

**MERRYVALE** *Napa Valley AVA, California, USA* A Chardonnay powerhouse (Reserve★★★, Silhouette★★★, Starmont★★), but reds are not far behind, with BORDEAUX-blend Profile★★ and juicy Reserve Merlot★. Best years: (Chardonnay) 1999 98 **97 96 95**.

**LOUIS MÉTAIREAU** *Muscadet de Sèvre-et-Maine AC, Loire Valley, France* Classic Muscadets with considerable intensity, thanks to low yields and careful winemaking. Styles range from lighter Petit Mouton to concentrated Cuvée LM★ and Cuvée One★.

**MEURSAULT AC** *Côte de Beaune, Burgundy, France* The biggest and most popular white wine village in the COTE D'OR. There are no Grands Crus, but a whole cluster of Premiers Crus. The general standard is better than in neighbouring Puligny. The golden wine is lovely to drink young but better aged for 5–8 years. Virtually no Meursault red is now made. Best producers: R Ampeau★★, Michel Bouzereau★★, Boyer-Martenot★★, COCHE-DURY★★, DROUHIN★★, A Ente★★, J-P Fichet★★, V GIRARDIN★★, Grivault★★, JADOT★★, P Javillier★★, Rémi Jobard★★★, François Jobard★★★, LAFON★★★, Dom. Matrot★★, Dom. Michelot★★, Michelot-Buisson★, Pierre Morey★★, Potinet-Ampeau★, J Prieur★★, G Roulot★★. Best years: (2000) 99 **97 96 95 92 89**.

**CH. MEYNEY★** *St-Estèphe AC, Cru Bourgeois, Haut-Médoc, Bordeaux, France* One of the most reliable ST-ESTEPHES, producing broad-flavoured wine with dark, plummy fruit. Second wine: Prieur de Meyney. Best years: (2000) 99 96 95 **94 90 89 88 86 83 82 75**.

**PETER MICHAEL WINERY** *Sonoma County, California, USA* British-born Sir Peter Michael caught the wine bug and turned a country retreat into an impressive winery known for its small-batch wines. Les Pavots is the estate red BORDEAUX blend, and Mon Plaisir★ and Cuvée Indigne★ are his top Chardonnays, both noted for their deep, layered flavours. Best years: (Chardonnay) (1999) 98 97 **95 94 92**.

# MERLOT

Red wine without tears. That's the reason Merlot has vaulted from being merely Bordeaux's red wine support act, well behind Cabernet Sauvignon in terms of class, to being the red wine drinker's darling, planted like fury all over the world. It is able to claim some seriousness and pedigree, but – crucially – can make wine of a fat, juicy character mercifully low in tannic bitterness, which can be glugged with gay abandon almost as soon as the juice has squirted from the press. Yet this doesn't mean that Merlot is the jelly baby of red wine grapes. Far from it.

## WINE STYLES

**Bordeaux Merlot** The great wines of Pomerol and St-Émilion are largely based on Merlot and the best of these can mature for 20–30 years. In fact there is more Merlot than Cabernet Sauvignon planted in Bordeaux, and I doubt if there is a single red wine property that does not have some growing, because the variety ripens early, can cope with cool conditions and is able to bear a heavy crop of fruit. In a cool, damp area like Bordeaux, Cabernet Sauvignon cannot always ripen, so the soft, mellow character of Merlot is a fundamental component of the blend even in the best Médoc estates.

**Other European Merlots** The south of France has briskly adopted the variety, but in the hot Languedoc the grape often ripens too fast to express its full personality and can seem a little simple and even raw-edged. Italy has long used very high-crop Merlot to produce a simple, light quaffer in the north, particularly in the Veneto, though Friuli and Alto Adige make fuller styles and there are some very impressive Tuscan examples. The Italian-speaking Swiss canton of Ticino is often unjustly overlooked for intensely fruity, oak-aged versions. Eastern Europe should provide fertile pastures for Merlot and so far the most convincing, albeit simple, styles have come from Hungary and Bulgaria, although the younger examples are almost invariably better than the old. Spain has developed good Merlot credentials since the mid-1990s.

**New World Merlots** Youth is also important in the New World, nowhere more so than in Chile. Chilean Merlot has leapt to the front of the pack of New World examples with gorgeous garnet-red wines of unbelievable crunchy fruit richness that cry out to be drunk virtually in their infancy. California Merlots often have more serious pretensions, but the nature of the grape is such that its soft, juicy quality still shines through. The cooler conditions in Washington State have produced some impressive wines, and the east coast of the US has produced good examples from places such as Long Island. With some French input, South Africa is starting to get Merlot right, and in New Zealand, despite the cool, damp conditions, some gorgeous rich examples have been made. Only Australia seems to find Merlot problematic – but there's so much other ripe fruit in Australian reds that maybe Merlot isn't a necessity there.

## BEST PRODUCERS

### France
*Bordeaux* (St-Émilion) ANGELUS, AUSONE, BEAU-SEJOUR BECOT, BELAIR, MAGDELAINE, le TERTRE-ROTEBOEUF, TROPLONG-MONDOT; (Pomerol) le BON PASTEUR, l'EGLISE-CLINET, l'EVANGILE, la FLEUR-PETRUS, LAFLEUR, PETRUS, le PIN, TROTANOY, VIEUX-CHATEAU-CERTAN.

### Other European Merlots
*Italy* (Veneto) MACULAN; (Friuli) Livio FELLUGA; (Tuscany) AMA, AVIGNONESI, CASTELGIOCONDO, Ghizzano, Le Macchiole, ORNELLAIA, Petrolo, Tua Rita, Valtellina; (Lazio) Falesco.

*Spain* (Penedès) Can Ràfols dels Caus.

*Switzerland* Christian Zundel.

### New World Merlots
*USA* (California) ARROWOOD, BERINGER, CHATEAU ST JEAN, DUCKHORN, FERRARI-CARANO, MATANZAS CREEK, NEWTON, Pahlmeyer, Paloma, SHAFER, Swanson; (Washington) ANDREW WILL, LEONETTI; (New York) BEDELL, LENZ.

*Australia* Brookland Valley, CLARENDON HILLS, James Irvine, KATNOOK ESTATE, Maxwell, Pepper Tree, PETALUMA, Tatachilla, YARRA YERING.

*New Zealand* Esk Valley, GOLDWATER, C J Pask, VILLA MARIA.

*South Africa* Morgenhof, SAXENBURG (Private Collection), SPICE ROUTE, STEENBERG, THELEMA, VEENWOUDEN, VERGELEGEN.

*Chile* CARMEN, CASA LAPOSTOLLE (Cuvée Alexandre, Clos Apalta), Casa Silva, ERRAZURIZ, LA ROSA (La Palmeria), VALDIVIESO, VINA CASABLANCA.

**LOUIS MICHEL** *Chablis AC, Burgundy, France*  The prime exponent of unoaked CHABLIS. The top Crus – Montmains★★★, Montée de Tonnerre★★★ and les Clos★★★ – are wonderfully fresh, mineraly and long-lived. Best years: (top crus) 1999 98 97 96 **95 92 90 88**.

**MIDI** *France*  A loose geographical term, virtually synonymous with LANGUEDOC-ROUSSILLON, covering the vast, sunbaked area of southern France between the Pyrenees and the RHONE VALLEY.

**MILDARA** *Murray River, Victoria, Australia*  Based on the Murray River, but the best wines are from COONAWARRA vineyards, including the popular Jamieson's Run (blended red and a Chardonnay), Robertson's Well Cabernet Sauvignon★ and Saltram in the BAROSSA. Owns BAILEYS, Wolf BLASS, Andrew Garrett, Ingoldby, ROTHBURY, Mount Ida, Yarra Ridge, YELLOWGLEN, and was itself bought in 1996 by Fosters, the lager lads.

**MILLTON** *Gisborne, North Island, New Zealand*  Organic vineyard using biodynamic methods, whose top wines include the sophisticated Clos St Anne Chardonnay★★, botrytized Opou Vineyard Riesling★★ and complex barrel-fermented Chenin Blanc★. Recent vertical tastings of Chardonnays and Rieslings spanning over a decade indicated just how well both wines age. Best years: (whites) 1999 **98 96 94**.

**MINERVOIS AC** *Languedoc, France*  Attractive, mostly red wines from north-east of Carcassonne. Big companies like Nicolas have worked with local co-ops to produce good, juicy, quaffing wine at reasonable prices. The best wines are made by the estates: full of ripe, red fruit and pine-dust perfume, for drinking young. It can age, especially if a little new oak has been used. Since 1997, a village denomination, La Livinière, which is delimited to 4 communes, can be appended to the Minervois label. Best producers: (reds) Aires Hautes★, CLOS CENTEILLES★★, Coupe-Roses★, Pierre Cros★, Fabas★, Gourgazaud★, la Grave, Maris★, Oupia★, Piccinini★, Pujol, Ste-Eulalie★, la TOUR BOISÉE★, Vassière, Villerambert-Julien★, Violet★. Best years: (2000) **99 98 96 95**.

**CH. LA MISSION-HAUT-BRION★★★** *Pessac-Léognan AC, Cru Classé de Graves, Bordeaux, France*  Traditionally I have found la Mission's wines long on power but short on grace, but in the difficult years of the 1990s they showed consistency allied to intensity and fragrance. Best years: (2000) 99 98 97 96 95 94 **93 90 89 88 85 82 81 79 78 75**.

**MISSION HILL** *British Columbia, Canada*  Spring 2001 saw the expansion of Mission Hill's winery, allowing it to process grapes from its extensive vineyard holdings in the OKANAGAN VALLEY. Kiwi (ex-MONTANA) winemaker John Simes has strengthened the winery's red wines of late: excellent Chardonnay★★ and Pinot Gris are joined by Merlot★, Cabernet Sauvignon, Shiraz★, and a red meritage blend, Oculus★.

**MITCHELL** *Clare Valley, South Australia*  Jane and Andrew Mitchell turn out some of CLARE VALLEY's fruitiest cellarable Riesling★ and a classy barrel-fermented Growers Semillon★ which both deserve a wider audience. Growers Grenache★ is a huge unwooded and spirity lump of fruit, but if you're in the mood... Peppertree Shiraz★★ and Cabernet Sauvignon★ are plump, chocolaty and typical of the region.

**MITCHELTON** *Goulburn Valley, Victoria, Australia*  Victoria's most consistently fine Riesling★★. Oaked Marsanne★★, released at 4 years old, is a speciality. GOULBURN VALLEY Shiraz★ was introduced in 1996 and followed by Marsanne★★ and Viognier★ – all three classic examples.

Print label Shiraz★★ and Reserve Cabernet★ are increasingly deep and structured. Best years: (Print label) 1998 96 **95 94 92 90**.

**MITTELRHEIN** *Germany*   Small, northerly wine region. About 75% of the wine here is Riesling but, unlike other German regions, the Mittelrhein has been in decline over the last few decades. The vineyard sites are steep and difficult to work – although breathtaking. The best growers (like Toni JOST★★) cluster around Bacharach in the south and Boppard in the north, and produce wines of a striking mineral tang and dry, fruity intensity.

**MOËT & CHANDON** *Champagne AC, Champagne, France*   Moët & Chandon's enormous production of more than 25 million bottles a year dominates the CHAMPAGNE market. Good non-vintage★ can be delightful – soft, creamy and a little spicy, and consistency is pretty good. The vintage★★ usually has considerable style, while the rosé★ shows a Pinot Noir floral fragrance depressingly rare in modern Champagne. Dom Pérignon★★★ is the de luxe cuvée. It can be one of the greatest Champagnes of all, but you've got to age it for a number of years or you're wasting your money. Best years: (1995) **93 92 90 88 86 85 82**.

**MONBAZILLAC AC** *South-West France*   BERGERAC's leading sweet wine. Most is light and forgettable, from the efficient co-op. This style won't age, but a truly rich, late-harvested Monbazillac can last 10 years. Best producers: l'Ancienne Cure★, Bélingard (Blanche de Bosredon★), la Borderie★, Grande Maison★, Haut-Bernasse, Hébras, Theulet★, Tirecul-la-Gravière★★, Treuil-de-Nailhac★. Best years: 1999 98 **97 96 95**.

**ROBERT MONDAVI** *Napa Valley, California, USA*   Robert Mondavi is a Californian institution, based in NAPA. Best known for the regular Cabernet Sauvignon★, open and fruity with the emphasis on early drinkability, and the Reserve Cabernet★★★, possessing enormous depth and power. A regular★ and a Reserve★ Pinot Noir are velvety smooth and supple wines with style, perfume and balance. For many years the Mondavi trademark wine was Fumé (Sauvignon Blanc), but in recent years Chardonnay★ (Reserve★★) has become the winery leader, although the quality is inconsistent. Mondavi also owns ARROWOOD in SONOMA, BYRON in SANTA BARBARA COUNTY, OPUS ONE in Napa in partnership with the Rothschilds, as well as the Mondavi Woodbridge winery, where inexpensive varietal wines are produced. The La Famiglia range, made in Napa, is based chiefly on Italian varietals. Mondavi is involved in SENA in Chile, and in Italy has an association with FRESCOBALDI (CASTELGIOCONDO), producing a SUPER-TUSCAN named Luce. In France's LANGUEDOC Mondavi makes wines under the Vichon Mediterranean label, but plans for a new premium red from vineyards next to MAS DE DAUMAS GASSAC have been thwarted. Best years: (Cabernet Sauvignon Reserve) (1999) 98 97 96 95 94 **93 92 91 88 87 86 85 84 82**; (Chardonnay Reserve) 1999 98 97 96 **95 94 92 91 90**.

**MONTAGNE-ST-ÉMILION AC** *Bordeaux, France*   A ST-EMILION satellite which can produce rather good red wines. The wines are normally ready to drink in 4 years but age quite well in their slightly earthy way. Best producers: Bonneau, Calon, Corbin, Faizeau, Laurets, Moines, Montaiguillon, Négrit, Roc-de-Calon, Rocher Corbin, Roudier, Vieux-Ch.-St-André. Best years: (2000) 98 **96 95 94 90 89 88 85 82**.

**MONTAGNY AC** *Côte Chalonnaise, Burgundy, France* Wines from this
Côte Chalonnaise village can be rather lean, but are greatly improved
now that some producers are aging their wines for a few months in new
oak. Generally best with 2–5 years' bottle age. Best producers: S
Aladame★★, BOUCHARD PERE ET FILS★, BUXY CO-OP★, Davenay★, FAIVELEY,
LATOUR★, O LEFLAIVE★, A Roy★, J Vachet★. Best years: (2000) **99 98 96**.

**MONTALCINO** See Brunello di Montalcino DOCG.

**MONTANA** *Auckland, Gisborne, Hawke's Bay and Marlborough, New
Zealand* Easily the country's largest winemaker, especially since its
purchase of CORBANS in 2000, Montana has consistently made some of
New Zealand's best-value wines. The MARLBOROUGH Sauvignon Blanc★
and GISBORNE Chardonnay★ are in a considerable way to thank for
putting New Zealand on the international map. To show that big can
also be best, the company has established CHURCH ROAD★, a small (by
Montana standards) winery in HAWKE'S BAY. Estate bottlings,
particularly Ormond Estate Chardonnay★★, also bode well. Makes
consistent Lindauer fizz and, with the help of the CHAMPAGNE house
DEUTZ, austere yet full-bodied Deutz Marlborough Cuvée NV Brut★★.

**MONTECARLO DOC** *Tuscany, Italy* Both reds (Sangiovese with Syrah)
and whites (Trebbiano with Sémillon and Pinot Grigio) are distinctive.
Non-DOC wines can include Cabernet, Merlot, Pinot Bianco, Roussanne
and Vermentino. Best producers: Buonamico★, Carmignani★,
Montechiari★, Wandanna★. Best years: (reds) (2000) **99 98 97 96 95 93**.

**MONTECILLO** *Rioja DOC, Rioja, Spain* Owned by sherry firm OSBORNE,
making high-quality RIOJAS in young and mature styles. Red and white
Crianza★ is young and fruity. Rich, fruity red Gran Reservas★ are
aged in French oak barrels and combine delicacy with flavour. The
Viña Cumbrero and Viña Monty brands were abandoned in 2000.
Best years: (reds) 1996 **95 94 91 88 87 86 82 81**.

**MONTEFALCO DOC** *Umbria, Italy* Sangiovese-based Montefalco Rosso,
often good, is outclassed by dry Sagrantino di Montefalco (now DOCG) and
Sagrantino Passito, a glorious sweet red made from dried grapes. Best
producers: (Sagrantino) Adanti★, Antonelli★, Caprai★ (25 Anni★★★),
Colpetrone★★. Best years: (Sagrantino) (1999) (98) 97 96 95 **94 93 91 90 88**.

**MONTEPULCIANO** Grape, grown mostly in eastern Italy (unconnected
with TUSCANY's Sangiovese-based wine VINO NOBILE DI MONTEPULCIANO).
Can produce deep-coloured, fleshy, spicy wines with moderate tannin
and acidity. Besides MONTEPULCIANO D'ABRUZZO, it is used in ROSSO CONERO
and ROSSO PICENO in the MARCHE and also in UMBRIA, Molise and PUGLIA.

**MONTEPULCIANO D'ABRUZZO DOC** *Abruzzo, Italy* The Montepulciano
grape's most important manifestation. Quality varies from the insipid
or rustic to the concentrated and characterful. Best producers: Cataldi
Madonna★, Cornacchia★, Filomusi Guelfi, Illuminati★, Marramiero★,
Masciarelli★★, Elio Monti★, Montori★, Nicodemi★, Cantina Tollo★,
Umani Ronchi★, Roxan★, La Valentina★, Valentini★★★, Ciccio
Zaccagnini★. Best years: (2000) 99 **98 97 95 94 93 90 88 85**.

**MONTEREY COUNTY** *California, USA* Large CENTRAL COAST county south
of San Francisco Bay in the Salinas Valley. The most important AVAs
are Arroyo Seco, CHALONE, Carmel Valley and Santa Lucia Highlands.

Best grapes are Chardonnay, Riesling and Pinot Blanc, with some good Cabernet Sauvignon, Merlot in Carmel Valley and Pinot Noir in the cool north of the county. Best producers: Barnett Vineyard★, Bernardus★★, CHALONE★★, Estancia★, Mer Soleil★★, Morgan★, Talbott★★, Testarossa★★.

**MONTES** *Curicó, Chile* This has to be one of Chile's most frustratingly erratic producers, but Reserve Malbec★ and Alpha Syrah★★ show what winemaker Aurelio Montes can do at his best. The Sauvignon Blanc★ has improved dramatically recently, and Montes Alpha Cabernet Sauvignon★ and Merlot★ are slowly revealing a satisfying mixture of fruit ripeness and structure. Ultra-premium Montes Alpha M★ is at last beginning to live up to its price and pretensions.

**MONTEVERTINE** *Tuscany, Italy* Based in the heart of CHIANTI CLASSICO, Montevertine is famous for its non-DOC wines, particularly Le Pergole Torte★★★. This was the first of the SUPER-TUSCANS made solely with the Sangiovese grape, and it remains one of the best. A little Canaiolo is included in the excellent Il Sodaccio★★ and Montevertine Riserva★★. Best years: (Le Pergole Torte) 1997 96 95 **93 92 90** 88 86 85.

**MONT GRAS** *Rapel, Chile* Reds are, so far, well ahead of the whites at this superbly equipped new winery in COLCHAGUA. Reserva Merlot★ and Cabernet★ are oaky but with good plum and berry fruit. New plantings on Ninquén hill, including Syrah, with much lower yields, will provide the real excitement in upcoming vintages.

**MONTHELIE AC** *Côte de Beaune, Burgundy, France* Attractive, mainly red wine village lying halfway along the COTE DE BEAUNE behind MEURSAULT and VOLNAY. The wines generally have a lovely, cherry fruit and make pleasant drinking at a good price. Best producers: COCHE-DURY★, P Garaudet★★, R Jobard★, LAFON★★, Olivier LEFLAIVE★, Monthelie-Douhairet★, Potinet-Ampeau★, G Roulot★★, de Suremain★. Best years: (reds) 1999 98 **97 96 95**; (whites) (2000) 99 **97 96**.

**MONTILLA-MORILES DO** *Andalucía, Spain* Sherry-style wines that are sold almost entirely as lower-priced sherry substitutes. However, the wines *can* be superb, particularly the top dry amontillado, oloroso and rich Pedro Ximénez styles. Best producers: Alvear (top labels★★), Aragón, Gracia Hermanos, Pérez Barquero★, Toro Albalá★.

**MONTLOUIS AC** *Loire Valley, France* Situated on the opposite bank of the Loire to the VOUVRAY AC, Montlouis wines are made from the same Chenin grape and in similar styles (dry, medium and sweet and Champagne-method fizz) but tend to be a touch more rustic. Two-thirds of the production is Mousseux, a green, appley fizz which is best drunk young. The still wines need aging for 5–10 years, particularly the sweet or Moelleux version. Best producers: Chidaine★, Deletang★★, Levasseur, Dom des Liards/Berger★, Moyer★, Taille aux Loups★★. Best years: (2000) 99 **98 97 96 95** 90 89 88 86 85.

**MONTRACHET AC** *Côte de Beaune, Burgundy, France* This world-famous Grand Cru straddles the boundary between the villages of CHASSAGNE-MONTRACHET and PULIGNY-MONTRACHET. Produces wines with a unique combination of concentration, finesse and perfume; white Burgundy at its most sublime. Another Grand Cru, Chevalier-Montrachet, immediately above it on the slope yields a slightly leaner wine that is less explosive in its youth, but good examples will become ever more fascinating over 20 years or more. Best producers: G Amiot★★★, Colin★★★, DROUHIN (Laguiche)★★★, LAFON★★★, LATOUR★★★, Dom. LEFLAIVE★★★, RAMONET★★★, Dom. de la ROMANEE-CONTI★★★, Thénard★★★. Best years: (2000) 99 98 97 96 95 **93 92 90 89 86 85**.

**MONTRAVEL AC** *South-West France*  Dry, medium-dry and sweet white wines from the western end of the BERGERAC region. Sweetish ones from Côtes de Montravel AC and fully sweet from Haut-Montravel AC. Production is declining. Best producers: le Bondieu, Gourgueil, Moulin Caresse, Perreau, Pique-Sègue, Puy-Servain, le Raz.

**CH. MONTROSE**★★ *St-Estèphe AC, 2ème Cru Classé, Haut-Médoc, Bordeaux, France*  A leading ST-ESTEPHE property, once famous for its dark, brooding wine that would take around 30 years to reach its prime. In the late 1970s and early 80s the wines became lighter, but Montrose has now returned to a powerful style, though softer than before. Recent vintages have been extremely good. Second wine: la Dame de Montrose. Best years: (2000) 99 98 97 96 95 94 93 90 **89 86**.

**MONT TAUCH, LES PRODUCTEURS DU** *Fitou, Languedoc-Roussillon, France*  A big, quality-conscious co-op producing a large range of MIDI wines, from good gutsy FITOU★ and CORBIERES to rich MUSCAT DE RIVESALTES★ and light but gluggable Vin de Pays du Torgan. Top wine: Terroir de Tuchan★. Best years: (reds) 1999 98 **97 96 95 94**.

**CH. MONTUS** *Madiran AC, South-West France*  Alain Brumont has led MADIRAN's revival, using 100% Tannat and deft public relations. The top wine is aged in new oak. He has 3 properties: Montus★★★, Bouscassé★★ and Meinjarre. Montus and Bouscassé also make enjoyable dry PACHERENC DU VIC-BILH★, while Bouscassé has fine Moelleux★★. Best years: (reds) 1998 97 96 95 **94 93 91 90 89 88 85**.

**MORELLINO DI SCANSANO DOC** *Tuscany, Italy*  Morellino is the local name for the Sangiovese grape in this small town in south-west TUSCANY. The wines can be broad and robust, but more and more well-mannered and delightfully perfumed examples are appearing. Best producers: E Banti★, Carletti/Poliziano (Lohsa★), Cecchi★, Il Macereto★, Mantellassi★, Mazzei/FONTERUTOLI★, Morellino di Scansano co-op★, Moris Farms★, Le Pupille★★. Best years: (2000) 99 **98 97 96 95 93 90**.

**MOREY-ST-DENIS AC** *Côte de Nuits, Burgundy, France*  Morey has 5 Grands Crus (Clos des Lambrays, CLOS DE LA ROCHE, CLOS ST-DENIS, CLOS DE TART and a share of BONNES-MARES) as well as some very good Premiers Crus. Basic village wine tends to be dilute and dull, but from a quality grower the wine has good fruit and acquires an attractive depth as it ages. A tiny amount of startling nutty white wine is also made. Best producers: Pierre Amiot★, Arlaud★★, Castagnier-Vadey★, CLAIR★★, DUJAC★★★, Dom. des Lambrays★★, G Lignier★★, H Lignier★★★, H Perrot-Minot★★, Ponsot★★, Rossignol-Trapet★, ROUMIER★★, ROUSSEAU★★, Serafin★★. Best years: (2000) 99 98 **97 96 95 93 90 89 88**.

**MORGON AC** *Beaujolais, Burgundy, France*  Most of the wine produced in this BEAUJOLAIS Cru has a soft, cherry fruit for very easy drinking, but from a good grower and from the slopes of the Mont du Py the wine can be thick and dark, acquiring a perfume of cherries as it ages. Best producers: Georges Brun★, Calot★★, la Chanaise (Piron★), G Charvet★, Collonge★, L-C Desvignes★, DUBOEUF (J Descombes★★), J Foillard★, M Lapierre★, Plateau de Bel-Air★, P Savoye★. Best years: (2000) 99 98 **97 96 95**.

**MORNINGTON PENINSULA** *Victoria, Australia* Exciting cool-climate maritime region dotted with small vineyards, often owned by monied Melbourne hobbyists. Chardonnay here runs the gamut from honeyed to harsh; Pinot Noir can be very stylish indeed in warmer years. Best producers: DROMANA★, King's Creek, Main Ridge★, Massoni★, Moorooduc Estate★, Paringa, Port Phillip Estate★, STONIER'S★★, T'Gallant★.

**MORRIS** *Rutherglen, Victoria, Australia* Historic winery, ORLANDO-owned, making traditional favourites like liqueur Muscat★★ and Tokay★★ (Old Premium is ★★★), 'ports', 'sherries' and robust table wines from Shiraz★, Cabernet★, Durif★ and Blue Imperial (Cinsaut).

**MORTON ESTATE** *Katikati, North Island, New Zealand* The winery in the tiny town of Katikati; the vineyards are in HAWKE'S BAY. Best wines are the robust, complex Black Label Chardonnay★★, a rich and gamy Black Label Merlot★, the best Hawke's Bay Pinot Noir★ yet, berries and cedar Black Label Merlot-Cabernet Sauvignon★★ and a successful fizz★. Best years: (Black Label Merlot-Cabernet) (1998) **96 95 94 91**.

**GEORG MOSBACHER** *Deidesheim, Pfalz, Germany* This small estate makes dry white and dessert wines in the wine village of FORST. Best of all are the dry Rieslings★★ from the Forster Ungeheuer site, which are among the lushest in Germany. Delicious young, but worth cellaring for more than 3 years. Best years: 1999 98 **97 96 94 93 90 89**.

**MOSCATO D'ASTI DOCG** *Piedmont, Italy* Utterly beguiling, delicately scented, gently bubbling wine, made from Moscato Bianco grapes grown in the hills between Asti and Alba in north-west Italy. The DOCG is the same as for ASTI Spumante, but only select grapes go into this wine, which is frizzante (semi-sparkling) rather than fully sparkling. The best are thrillingly grapy and low in alcohol. Drink while they're bubbling with youthful fragrance. Best producers: Araldica/Alasia★, ASCHERI★, Bava★, Bera★, Braida★, Caudrina★★, Cascina Castlèt★, Giuseppe Contratto★, Coppo★, Cascina Fonda★, Forteto della Luja★, Icardi★, Marenco★, Beppe Marino★, La Morandina★, Marco Negri★, Perrone★, Cascina Pian d'Or★, Saracco★★, Scagliola★, La Spinetta★★, I Vignaioli di Santo Stefano★.

**MOSCATO PASSITO DI PANTELLERIA DOC** *Sicily, Italy* The Muscat of Alexandria grape is used to make this powerful dessert wine. Pantelleria is a small island south-west of SICILY, closer to Africa than it is to Italy. The grapes are picked in mid-August and laid out in the hot sun to dry and shrivel for a couple of weeks. They are then crushed and fermented to give an amber-coloured, intensely flavoured sweet Muscat. The wines are best drunk within 5–7 years of the vintage. Best producers: Benanti★, D'Ancona★, DE BARTOLI (Bukkuram★★), Donnafugata (Ben Ryé★), MID (Tanit), Murana (Martingana★★, Khamma★, Mueggen★), Nuova Agricoltura co-op★, Pellegrino.

**MOSEL-SAAR-RUWER** *Germany* Not a coherent wine region, but a collection of vineyard areas on the Mosel and its tributaries, the Saar and the Ruwer. The Mosel river rises in the French Vosges before forming the border between Germany and Luxembourg. In its first German incarnation in the Upper Mosel the fairly dire Elbling grape holds sway, but with the Middle Mosel begins a series of villages responsible for some of the world's very best Riesling wines: PIESPORT, BRAUNEBERG, BERNKASTEL, GRAACH, WEHLEN, URZIG and ERDEN. The wines are not big or powerful, but in good years they have tremendous slatiness and an ability to blend the greenness of citrus leaves and fruits with the golden warmth of honey. Great wines are rarer in the lower part of the valley as the Mosel swings round into Koblenz, although Winningen is an island of excellence. The Saar can produce wonderful, piercing wines in villages such as Serrig, AYL, OCKFEN and Wiltingen. The Ruwer produces slightly softer wines; the estates of MAXIMIN GRUNHAUS and KARTHAUSERHOF are on every list of the best in Germany.

**LENZ MOSER** *Rohrendorf-bei-Krems, Kremstal, Austria* Important merchant buying growers' wines and bottling them as 'Selection'. Also fine Burgenland wines from the Klosterkeller Siegendorf and Weinviertel wines (including Cabernet Sauvignon!) from Malteser Ritterorden.

**MOSS WOOD** *Margaret River, Western Australia* Pioneer winery with silky smooth, rich but structured Cabernet★★. Chardonnay★★ can be rich and peachy; Pinot Noir★ can be erratic but is magical at best. Semillon★★, both oaked and unoaked, is consistently fascinating. Best years: (reds) 1996 95 **94** 93 91 90 87 86 85 83 80 77 75.

**J P MOUEIX** *Bordeaux, France* As well as owning PETRUS, la FLEUR-PETRUS, MAGDELAINE, TROTANOY and other properties, the Moueix family runs a thriving merchant business specializing in the wines of the right bank, particularly POMEROL and FRONSAC. Quality is generally high.

**MOULIN-À-VENT AC** *Beaujolais, Burgundy, France* BEAUJOLAIS Cru that can resemble a full, chocolaty Burgundy, tasting more of Pinot Noir than Gamay, after 6–10 years' bottle age. Best producers: Bertola★, Cellier des Samsons★, L Champagnon★, G Charvet★, Chauvet★, P M Chermette★, Desperrier★, Diochon★, DUBOEUF (single domaines★), Gay-Coperet★, P Granger★, Ch. des Jacques★★, Janin★★, Janodet★, Margerand★, Ch. du Moulin-à-Vent★★, B Santé★, la Tour du Bief★★, R Trichard★, Vissoux★. Best years: (2000) 99 **98 97 96 95**.

**MOULIS AC** *Haut-Médoc, Bordeaux, France* Small AC within the HAUT-MEDOC. Much of the wine is excellent – delicious at 5–6 years old, though good examples can age 10–20 years – and not overpriced. Best producers: Anthonic, Biston-Brillette, Brillette, CHASSE-SPLEEN★, Duplessis, Dutruch-Grand-Poujeau, Gressier-Grand-Poujeaux, MAUCAILLOU★, Ch. Moulin-à-Vent, POUJEAUX★★. Best years: (2000) 96 95 **94** 90 89 88 86 85 83 82.

**MOUNTADAM** *Eden Valley, South Australia* The late David Wynn and his Bordeaux-educated son Adam planted this property high in the Eden Valley from scratch. It is now a subsidiary of CAPE MENTELLE. Rich, buttery Chardonnay★★ has a worldwide reputation. There is also sumptuous Pinot★, bold Cabernet-Merlot blend The Red★, and fruity David Wynn and Eden Ridge organic labels. Patriarch★★★ is a rich, fruit-laden premium Shiraz. Best years: (reds) 1998 96 **94** 93 91 90 87 84; (Chardonnay) **1998** 97 96 94 92 91 90.

**MOUNT LANGI GHIRAN** *Grampians, Victoria, Australia* World-famous winery which made its reputation with remarkable dark plum, chocolate and pepper Shiraz★★. Later releases are still good, though can be erratic. Delightful Riesling★, honeyed Pinot Gris★ and melony unwooded Chardonnay★. Joanna★★ Cabernet is dark and intriguing. Best years: (reds) 1998 97 96 95 **94 93 92 90 89 86**.

**MOUNT MARY** *Yarra Valley, Victoria, Australia* Classic property using only estate-grown grapes along Bordeaux lines, with dry white 'Triolet'★★ blended from Sauvignon Blanc, Semillon and Muscadelle, and Cabernets Quintet★★★ from all 5 Bordeaux red grapes that ages beautifully. The Pinot Noir★★ is almost as good. Best years: (Cabernets Quintet) (1997) 96 95 94 **92 91 90 88 84 80**.

**MOUNT VEEDER AVA** *Napa Valley, California, USA* Cabernet Sauvignon and Zinfandel wines, made in a typical rough-hewn style, come from this small mountain AVA in NAPA's south-west corner. Best producers: Chateau Potelle★, Robert Craig★★, HESS COLLECTION★★, Lokoya, Mayacamas★, Mount Veeder Vineyards★.

**MOURVÈDRE** The variety originates from south-eastern Spain, where it is called Monastrell. It needs lots of sunshine to ripen, which is why it performs well on the Mediterranean coast at BANDOL. It is increasingly important as a source of colour, body and tarry, pine-needle flavour in the wines of CHATEAUNEUF-DU-PAPE and parts of the MIDI. It is beginning to make a reputation in Australia and CALIFORNIA, where it is frequently known as Mataro. It is also appearing in many parts of South Africa.

**MOUTON-CADET** *Bordeaux AC, Bordeaux, France* The most widely sold red BORDEAUX in the world was created by Baron Philippe de Rothschild in the 1930s. Blended from the entire Bordeaux region, the wine is correct but uninspiring – and never cheap. Also a white and rosé.

**CH. MOUTON-ROTHSCHILD★★★** *Pauillac AC, 1er Cru Classé, Haut-Médoc, Bordeaux, France* Baron Philippe de Rothschild died in 1988, having raised Mouton from a run-down Second Growth to its promotion to First Growth in 1973, and a reputation as one of the greatest wines in the world. It can still be the most magnificently opulent of the great MEDOC reds, although there were signs of inconsistency in the early 90s. Recent vintages have been back on top form. When young, this wine is rich and indulgent on the palate, aging after 15–20 years to a complex bouquet of blackcurrant and cigar box. There is also a white wine, Aile d'Argent. Second wine: Petit-Mouton. Best years: (red) (2000) 99 98 97 96 95 94 **89 88 86 85 83 82 70**.

**MUDGEE** *New South Wales, Australia* Small, long-overlooked region neighbouring HUNTER VALLEY, with a higher altitude and marginally cooler temperatures. Major new plantings are giving it a fresh lease of life; ROSEMOUNT is leading the charge with impressive, if expensive Mountain Blue Shiraz-Cabernet★★ and the Hill of Gold★★ range of varietals. Other producers aren't yet making best use of their very good fruit. Best producers: Andrew Harris★, Huntington Estate★, Miramar★, Montrose★, ROSEMOUNT★★, Thistle Hill.

**MUGA** *Rioja DOC, Rioja, Spain* A traditional family winery making high-quality, rich red RIOJA★, especially the Gran Reserva, Prado Enea★. It is the only bodega in Rioja where every step of red winemaking is still carried out in oak containers. In recent years, the whites and rosés have been good too. The modern Torre Muga Reserva★ marks a major stylistic change. Best years: (Torre Muga Reserva) 1996 **95 94 91**.

195

**MULDERBOSCH** *Stellenbosch WO, South Africa* Any fears that new ownership of this small property might lead to a drop in standards are unfounded. Winemaker Mike Dobrovic's sleek, gooseberry-infused Sauvignon Blanc★★ is a model of consistency and a deserved cult wine; drink young and fresh. Purity with intensity are also the hallmarks of Chardonnay★★ and Steen-op-Hout★ (Chenin Blanc brushed with oak). Faithful Hound, a Cabernet-Merlot blend and the sole red, is claret-like, though easy-drinking. Best years: (Chardonnay) **1998 97 96 95**.

**EGON MÜLLER** *Scharzhofberg, Saar, Germany* Not only some of the greatest German wines but also the most expensive. The ultimate sweet versions are the estate's Auslese, Beerenauslese, Trockenbeerenauslese and Eiswein, all ★★★. Regular Kabinett and Spätlese wines are pricy but classic. Best years: 1999 97 96 95 **94 93 91** 90 **89 88 83 76 75 71**.

**MÜLLER-CATOIR** *Neustadt-Haardt, Pfalz, Germany* An eye-opener for those who are sceptical about Germany's ability to make wines in an international idiom. Produces wine of a piercing fruit flavour and powerful structure unsurpassed in Germany, including ★★★ Riesling, Scheurebe and Rieslaner; ★★ Gewürztraminer, Muskateller and Pinot Noir; Weissburgunder★. Best years: 1999 98 **97 96 94 93 92 90 89 88**.

**MÜLLER-THURGAU** The workhorse grape of Germany, largely responsible for LIEBFRAUMILCH. When yields are low it produces pleasant floral wines; but this is rare since modern clones are all super-productive. It is occasionally better in England – though the odd good examples, with a slightly green edge to the grapy flavour, come from Austria, Switzerland, Luxembourg and Italy's ALTO ADIGE. New Zealand used to pride itself on making the world's best Müller-Thurgau, although acreage is in rapid decline.

**G H MUMM** *Champagne AC, Champagne, France* Mumm's top-selling non-vintage brand, Cordon Rouge, is usually disappointing and frequently out-performed by its Californian counterpart, MUMM NAPA. A new winemaker has set about improving quality, but since it's now the Formula One Grand Prix Champagne, most of it will get sprayed over the drivers, whatever the quality. Best years: 1995 **90 89 88 85 82**.

**MUMM NAPA** *Napa Valley AVA, California, USA* The French CHAMPAGNE house MUMM and Seagram Classic Wines of California started Mumm Napa in 1983. Some reports have it that the French owners are sorry they did because the bubbly coming out of California has been simply too good. The style has now become leaner and drier, which is a pity, but both Cuvée Napa Brut Prestige and Vintage Reserve★ are good. A blanc de noirs★ is far better than most pink Champagnes. Tête de Cuvée DVX★★ has become the star turn.

**MURFATLAR** *Romania* Region to the west of the Black Sea, producing excellent late-harvest wines (including botrytized versions) from Pinot Gris★, Chardonnay and Muscat Ottonel. Sparkling wines are now being made, too. The maritime influence tends to mean warm nights, with resultant low acidity levels, often a fault in the Cabernet Sauvignon and Merlot. When they work it out, Murfatlar should be a good source of ripe, soft reds. Best producer: Murfatlar Winery.

**MUSCADET AC** *Loire Valley, France*   In 1994, Muscadet became the general AC for the region around Nantes in north-west France, with 3 high-quality zones: MUSCADET DES COTEAUX DE LA LOIRE, MUSCADET COTES DE GRAND LIEU and MUSCADET DE SEVRE-ET-MAINE. Producers who make basic Muscadet AC are allowed higher yields but cannot use the term *sur lie* on the labels. Inexpensive and best drunk young and fresh, a perfect match for the local seafood. Best producer: la Preuille.

**MUSCADET DES COTEAUX DE LA LOIRE AC** *Loire Valley, France*   The smallest of the 3 high-quality zones of MUSCADET AC. Yields are lower than for the basic AC. Best producers: Jacques Guindon, LUNEAU-PAPIN.

**MUSCADET CÔTES DE GRAND LIEU AC** *Loire Valley, France*   The AC for the best vineyards around Lac de Grand Lieu, south-west of Nantes. The vines have to be 7 years old before they merit the AC. Best producers: Serge Bâtard★, Bel-Air, Herbauges★.

**MUSCADET DE SÈVRE-ET-MAINE AC** *Loire Valley, France*   The Maine and Sèvre rivers converge south of Nantes and give their name to this AC. Look out for the term *sur lie* on a label – the wine is bottled directly off its sediment or lees, retaining a creamy, yeasty flavour and a slight prickle of carbon dioxide. Most is drunk young but the best can age several years. Best producers: G Bossard★, Chasseloir★, Chéreau-Carré★, Dorices★, Marquis de Goulaine, l'Hyvernière★, LUNEAU-PAPIN★, METAIREAU★, Quatre Routes★, la Ragotière★, Sauvion★, la Touché★.

**MUSCAT** See pages 198–9.

**MUSCAT OF ALEXANDRIA**   Muscat of Alexandria rarely shines in its own right but performs a useful job worldwide, adding perfume and fruit to what would otherwise be dull, neutral white wines. It is common for sweet and fortified wines throughout the Mediterranean basin and in South Africa (where it is also known as Hanepoot), as well as being a fruity, perfumed bulk producer there and in Australia.

**MUSCAT DE BEAUMES-DE-VENISE AC** *Rhône Valley, France*   Some of the best Muscat *vin doux naturel* in France comes from the attractive village of BEAUMES-DE-VENISE in the southern Rhône. It is certainly sweet but with a fruity acidity and a bright fresh feel to it. Best drunk young to get all that lovely grapy perfume at its peak. Best producers: Baumalric★, Beaumes-de-Venise co-op, Bernardins★, CHAPOUTIER★, Coyeux, Durban★★, Fenouillet★, JABOULET★, Vidal-Fleury★.

**MUSCAT BLANC À PETITS GRAINS** See Muscat.

**MUSCAT DE CAP CORSE AC** *Corsica, France*   New AC for fortified wine made from Muscat à Petits Grains, covering 17 communes on CORSICA. Best producers: Arena★, Catarelli★, Clos Nicrosi★, Gentile★, Leccia★, Orenga de Gaffory★.

**MUSCAT DE FRONTIGNAN AC** *Languedoc, France*   Well-known Muscat *vin doux naturel* on the Mediterranean coast. With colours ranging from bright gold to deep orange, it is quite impressive but can seem rather cloying. Muscat de Mireval AC, a little further inland, can have a touch more acid freshness, and quite an alcoholic kick. Best producers: (Frontignan) Cave du Muscat de Frontignan, la Peyrade★, Robiscau; (Mireval) la Capelle, Mas des Pigeonniers, Moulinas.

**MUSCAT DE MIREVAL AC** See Muscat de Frontignan AC.

# MUSCAT

It's strange, but there's hardly a wine grape in the world which makes wine that actually tastes of the grape itself. Yet there's one variety which is so joyously, exultantly grapy that it more than makes up for all the others – the Muscat, generally thought to be the original wine vine. In fact there seem to be about 200 different branches of the Muscat family, but the one that always makes the most exciting wine is called Muscat Blanc à Petits Grains. These berries can be crunchily green, golden yellow, pink or even brown, and the wines they make may be pale and dry, rich and golden, subtly aromatic or as dark and sweet as treacle.

*WINE STYLES*

**France** Muscat is grown from the far north-east right down to the Spanish border, yet is rarely accorded great respect in France. This is a pity because the dry, light, hauntingly grapy Muscats of Alsace are some of France's most delicately beautiful wines. It pops up sporadically in the Rhône Valley, especially in the sparkling wine enclave of Die. Mixed with Clairette, the Clairette de Die Tradition is a fragrant grapy fizz that should be better known. Muscat de Beaumes-de-Venise could do with being less well known because quality has suffered in recent years. But its success has encouraged the traditional fortified winemakers of Languedoc-Roussillon, especially in Frontignan and Rivesaltes, to make fresher, more perfumed wines rather than the usual flat and syrupy ones.

**Italy** Muscat is grown in Italy for fragrantly sweet or (rarely) dry table wines in the north and for *passito*-style wines (though the less fine Muscat of Alexandria makes most of the rich southern Moscato). Yet the greatest Muscats in Italy are those of Asti, where it is called Moscato Bianco. As either Asti Spumante or Moscato d'Asti, this brilliantly fresh fizz can be a blissful drink. Italy also has red varieties: the Moscato Nero for rare sweet wines in Lazio, Lombardy and Piedmont; and Moscato Rosa and Moscato Giallo for delicately sweet wines in Trentino-Alto Adige and Friuli-Venezia Giulia.

**Other regions** Muscat is a component of some Tokajis in Hungary, Crimea has shown how good it can be in the Massandra fortified wines, and the Muscats of Samos and Patras are among Greece's finest wines. As Muskateller in Austria and Germany it makes both sweet and dry subtly aromatic wines. In Spain, Moscatel de Valencia is sweet, light and sensational value. Moscatel de Grano Menudo is on the resurgence in Navarra and has been introduced in Mallorca. Portugal's Moscatel de Setúbal is also wonderfully rich and complex. California grows Muscat, often calling it Muscat Canelli, but South Africa and Australia make better use of it. With darker berries, and called Brown Muscat in Australia and Muscadel in South Africa, it makes some of the world's most sweet and luscious fortified wines, especially in north-east Victoria in Australia.

## BEST PRODUCERS

### Sparkling Muscat
*France* (Clairette de Die) Achard-Vincent, Clairette de Die co-op.

*Italy* (Asti) G Contratto, Gancia; (Moscato d'Asti) Fratelli Bera, Braida, Caudrina, Saracco, La Spinetta.

### Dry Muscat
*Austria* (Muskateller) Lackner-Tinnacher, F X PICHLER, E & M TEMENT.

*France* (Alsace) J Becker, A Boxler, Dirler, Kientzler, KUENTZ-BAS, Rolly Gassmann, Schléret, SCHOFFIT, WEINBACH, ZIND-HUMBRECHT.

*Germany* (Muskateller) BERCHER, Dr HEGER, MULLER-CATOIR, REBHOLZ.

*Spain* (Alicante) Bocopa co-op; (Penedès) TORRES (Viña Esmeralda).

*Italy* (Goldmuskateller) LAGEDER, Tiefenbrunner.

### Sweet Muscat
*Australia* (Liqueur Muscat) ALL SAINTS, BAILEYS, Buller, Campbells, CHAMBERS, MCWILLIAM'S, MORRIS, SEPPELT, Stanton & Killeen.

*France* (Alsace) E Burn, René Muré, SCHOFFIT; (Beaumes-de-Venise) Bernardins, Durban, Paul JABOULET, Vidal-Fleury; (Frontignan) Peyrade; (Rivesaltes) CAZES, Jau, Laporte.

*Greece* SAMOS CO-OP.

*Italy* (Goldmuskateller) Viticoltori Caldaro, Thurnhof; (Pantelleria) DE BARTOLI, Murana.

*Portugal* (Moscatel de Setúbal) J M da FONSECA, J P VINHOS.

*South Africa* KLEIN CONSTANTIA.

*Spain* (Navarra) Camilo Castilla, CHIVITE, OCHOA; (Alicante) Gutiérrez de la Vega, Enrique Mendoza.

199

**MUSCAT DE RIVESALTES AC** *Roussillon, France* Made from Muscat Blanc
à Petits Grains and Muscat of Alexandria, the wine can be very good
indeed, especially since several go-ahead producers are now allowing
the skins to stay in the juice for longer periods, thereby gaining
perfume and fruit. Best producers: Cave de Baixas (Ch. les Pins★),
Casenove★, CAZES★★, Chênes★, Destavel, Fontanel★, Forca Réal★,
Jau★, Laporte★, Mas Rous, Piquemal★, Sarda-Malet★.

**MUSCAT DE ST-JEAN-DE-MINERVOIS AC** *Languedoc, France* Up in
the remote and wild Minervois hills, a small appellation for fortified
Muscat made from Muscat à Petits Grains. Less cloying than some
Muscats from the plains of LANGUEDOC-ROUSSILLON, more tangerine and
floral. Best producers: Barroubio, Vignerons de Septimanie.

**MUSIGNY AC** *Grand Cru, Côte de Nuits, Burgundy, France* One of a
handful of truly great Grands Crus, combining power with an
exceptional depth of fruit and lacy elegance – an iron fist in a velvet
glove. Understandably expensive. A tiny amount of white Musigny is
produced by de VOGUE. Best producers: DROUHIN★★★, JADOT★★★, D
Laurent★★★, Dom. LEROY★★★, J-F Mugnier★★★, J Prieur★★, ROUMIER★★★,
VOGUE★★★. Best years: (2000) 99 98 97 96 95 93 **90 89 88 85 78**.

**NAHE** *Germany* Wine region named after the River Nahe which rises
below Birkenfeld and joins the Rhine by BINGEN, just opposite RUDESHEIM in
the RHEINGAU. Riesling, Müller-Thurgau and Silvaner are the main grapes,
but the Rieslings from this geologically complex region are considered
some of Germany's best. The finest vineyards are those of Niederhausen
and SCHLOSSBOCKELHEIM, situated in the dramatic, rocky Upper Nahe Valley,
and at Dorheim and Münster in the lower Nahe.

**CH. NAIRAC★★** *Barsac AC, 2ème Cru Classé, Bordeaux, France* This
Second Growth estate is an established star in BARSAC which, by dint
of enormous effort and considerable investment, produces a wine
sometimes on a par with the First Growths. The influence of aging in
new oak casks, adding spice and even a little tannin, makes this sweet
wine a good candidate for aging 10–15 years. Best years: 1999 98 97
96 95 90 89 88 **86 83**.

**NALLE WINERY** *Dry Creek Valley AVA, California, USA* Owner and
winemaker Doug Nalle is one of the leading producers of Zinfandel in
California. He is one of that rare breed that would rather not talk to
the press. 'All I'm doing is making the best Zinfandel I can make', he
once explained. Which seems pretty fair. So that's what he does, and
his Zinfandel★★ is consistently excellent, though also consistently
more expensive of late. Best years: (1999) 98 97 96 **95 94 93 92 91 90**.

**NAPA VALLEY** See pages 202–3.

**NAPA VALLEY AVA** *California, USA* An AVA designed to be so inclusive
that it is almost completely irrelevant. It includes vineyards that are
outside the Napa River drainage system – such as Pope Valley and
Chiles Valley. Because of this a number of sub-AVAs have been and are
in the process of being created, but few have any real claim to being
discernibly different from their neighbours, and many fear that these
sub-AVAs will simply dilute the magic of Napa's name. Best producers:
BEAULIEU★, BERINGER★★, CAIN★, CAYMUS★★, CHATEAU MONTELENA★, CHIMNEY

ROCK★, Clos Pegase★, CLOS DU VAL★, CUVAISON, DALLA VALLE★★, DIAMOND CREEK★★, DOMAINE CHANDON★, DUCKHORN★, DUNN★★, FLORA SPRINGS★★, FRANCISCAN★, Harlan Estate★★★, HEITZ CELLARS★, HESS COLLECTION★★, Miner★★, MONDAVI★★, MUMM NAPA★, NEWTON★★, OPUS ONE★★, PHELPS★, PINE RIDGE★, SCHRAMSBERG★★, SHAFER★★, SILVERADO★, SPOTTSWOODE★★, STAG'S LEAP★★, STERLING★, TURLEY★★, ZD Wines★. See also Carneros, Howell Mountain, Mount Veeder, Napa Valley, Oakville, Rutherford.

**NAVARRA DO** *Navarra, Spain* This buzzing region has increasing numbers of vineyards planted to Cabernet Sauvignon, Merlot and Chardonnay in addition to Tempranillo, Garnacha and Moscatel de Grano Menudo (Muscat à Petits Grains). This translates into a wealth of juicy reds, barrel-fermented whites and modern sweet Muscats, but quality is still more haphazard than it should be. Best producers: Camilo Castilla (Capricho de Goya Muscat★★), CHIVITE★, GUELBENZU★, Magaña★, Vicente Malumbres, Alvaro Marino★, Castillo de Monjardin★, Vinícola Navarra, Nekeas co-op (Merlot★★), OCHOA★, Palacio de la Vega★, Piedemonte Olite co-op★, Príncipe de Viana★, Senorio de Otazu★. Best years: (reds) 1996 **95 94 93 89**.

**NEBBIOLO** The grape variety responsible for the majestic wines of BAROLO and BARBARESCO, found almost nowhere outside north-west Italy. Its name derives from the Italian for fog, *nebbia*, because it ripens late when the hills are shrouded in autumn mists. It needs a thick skin to withstand this fog, so often gives wines with a very tannic character that needs years to soften. When grown in the limestone soils of the Langhe hills around Alba, Nebbiolo produces wines that are only moderately deep in colour but have a wonderful array of perfumes and an ability to develop great complexity with age – rivalled only by Pinot Noir and Syrah. Barolo is usually considered the best and longest-lived of the Nebbiolo wines; the myth that it needs a decade or more to be drinkable has been dispelled by new-style Barolo, yet the best of the traditional styles are more than worth the wait. Barbaresco, Barolo's neighbour, is somewhat more approachable though styles vary between the traditional and the new. NEBBIOLO D'ALBA and ROERO produce lighter styles. The variety is also used for special barrique-aged Nebbiolos in the Alba area, such as ALTARE's Vigna Arborina and Aldo CONTERNO's Il Favot, now in the LANGHE DOC. Nebbiolo is also the principal grape for reds of northern PIEDMONT – CAREMA, GATTINARA and GHEMME. In LOMBARDY it is known as Chiavennasca and is the main variety of the Valtellina DOC and VALTELLINA SUPERIORE DOCG wines. Outside Italy, Australia shows the greatest potential. Trials in CALIFORNIA have not been encouraging.

**NEBBIOLO D'ALBA DOC** *Piedmont, Italy* Red wine from Nebbiolo grown around Alba, but excluding the BAROLO and BARBARESCO zones. Vineyards in the LANGHE and ROERO hills, by the Tanaro river, are noted for sandy soils that produce a fragrant, fruity style for early drinking, though some growers make wines that improve for 5 years or more. Best producers: Alario★, ALTARE★, ASCHERI★, Cascina Chicco★, CERETTO, Correggia★★, FONTANAFREDDA, GIACOSA★, G MASCARELLO★, PRUNOTTO★, RATTI★, SANDRONE★, Scarpa★, Vietti★. Best years: (2000) (99) **98 97 96 95**.

# NAPA VALLEY

*California, USA*

 From the earliest days of California wine, and through all its up and downs, the Napa Valley has been the standard-bearer for the whole industry and the driving force behind quality and progress. The magical Napa name – derived from an Indian word for plenty – applies to the fertile valley itself, the county in which it is found and the AVA for the overall area, but this appellation is so wide-ranging as to be virtually meaningless. The most significant vine-growing area is the valley floor running from Calistoga in the north down to Carneros, below which the Napa River flows out into San Pablo Bay. Some of the best vineyards are tucked into the mountain slopes at the valley sides or in selected spots at higher altitudes.

The valley was first settled by immigrants in the 1830s, and by the late 19th century Napa, and in particular the area around the communities of Rutherford and Oakville, had gained a reputation for exciting Cabernet Sauvignon. Despite the long, dark years of Prohibition, this reputation survived and when the US interest in wine revived during the 1970s, Napa was ready to lead the charge.

## GRAPE VARIETIES

Most of the classic French grapes are grown and recent replantings have done much to match varieties to the most suitable locations. Cabernet Sauvignon is planted in profusion and Napa's strongest reputation is for varietal Cabernet and Bordeaux-style (or Meritage) blends, mostly Cabernet-Merlot. Pinot Noir and Chardonnay, for both still and sparkling wines, do best in the south, from Yountville down to Carneros. Zinfandel is grown mostly at the north end of the valley. Syrah and Sangiovese are relatively new here.

## SUB-REGIONS

There is as much as a 10° temperature difference between torrid Calistoga and Carneros at the mouth of the valley, cooled by Pacific fog and a benchmark for US Pinot Noir and cool-climate Chardonnay. About 20 major sub-areas have been identified along the valley floor and in the mountains, although there is much debate over how many have a real claim to individuality. Rutherford, Oakville and Yountville in the mid-valley produce Cabernet redolent of dust, dried sage and ultra-ripe blackcurrants. Softer flavours come from Stags Leap further south and Spring Mountain to the west. Deep Cabernets hail from Diamond Mountain and Mount Veeder along the Mayacamas mountain range to the west, while Howell Mountain in the north-east has stunning Zinfandel.

See also CARNEROS AVA, HOWELL MOUNTAIN AVA, MOUNT VEEDER AVA, NAPA VALLEY AVA, OAKVILLE AVA, RUTHERFORD AVA; and individual producers.

ESTATE 1998 BOTTLED

EISELE VINEYARD
NAPA VALLEY

Cabernet Sauvignon

ARAUJO
ESTATE WINES

## BEST YEARS

(2000) 99 98 97 **95 94 92 91 90 87 86**

## BEST PRODUCERS

**Cabernet Sauvignon and Meritage blends**
Abreu, Altamura, Anderson's Conn Valley, S Anderson, ARAUJO, Barnett (Rattlesnake Hill), BEAULIEU, BERINGER, Bryant Family, Buehler (Reserve), Burgess Cellars, Cafaro, CAIN CELLARS, Cakebread, CAYMUS, Chateau Montelena, Chateau Potelle (VGS), CHIMNEY ROCK, CLOS DU VAL, Clos Pegase, Colgin, Conn Creek (Anthology), Corison, Cosentino, Robert Craig, DALLA VALLE, Del Dotto, DIAMOND CREEK, DOMINUS, DUCKHORN, DUNN, Elyse, Etude, Far Niente, Fisher, FLORA SPRINGS, Folie à Deux, Forman, FRANCISCAN, Freemark Abbey (Bosché Vineyard), Frog's Leap, Grace Family, Groth, Harlan Estate, HEITZ, HESS, Jarvis, Lewis Cellars, Livingston, Lokoya, Long Vineyards, Markham, MERRYVALE, Miner, MONDAVI, Monticello, NEWTON, NIEBAUM-COPPOLA, Oakford, Oakville Ranch, OPUS ONE, Pahlmeyer, Paradigm, Robert Pecota, Peju Province (HB Vineyard), PHELPS, Plumpjack, Pride Mountain, Quintessa, Raymond, Rombauer (Meilleur du Chai), Rudd Estate, Saddleback, St Clement, Screaming Eagle, Seavey, SHAFER, SILVER OAK, SILVERADO, SPOTTSWOODE, Staglin Family, STAG'S LEAP WINE CELLARS, STERLING, Von Strasser, Swanson, The Terraces, Philip Togni, Viader, Villa Mt Eden (Signature Series), Vine Cliff, Vineyard 29, Whitehall Lane, ZD.

203

**NELSON** *South Island, New Zealand*   A range of mountains separates Nelson from MARLBOROUGH at the northern end of South Island. Nelson is made up of a series of small hills and valleys with a wide range of mesoclimates, supporting most of the grape varieties grown in NZ: Chardonnay, Riesling and Sauvignon Blanc do well. Best producers: Greenhough, NEUDORF★★, SEIFRIED★/Redwood Valley.

**NEUCHÂTEL** *Switzerland*   Swiss canton with high-altitude vineyards, mainly Chasselas whites and Pinot Noir reds. Three small areas (Schloss Vaumarcus, Hôpital Poutalès, Dom. de Champrevèyres) have a special AC. Best producers: Ch. d'Auvernier, Thierry Grosjean, Montmillon, Porret.

**NEUDORF** *Nelson, South Island, New Zealand*   Owners Tim and Judy Finn make stylish and often innovative wines and have resisted the temptation to expand production, preferring instead to fine-tune the quality of their wines by careful vineyard and winery management. Best are gorgeous, honeyed Chardonnay★★, Sauvignon Blanc★★, rich but scented Pinot Noir★★ and Riesling★. Best years: (Chardonnay) (2001) 99 **98 96 94**.

**NEW SOUTH WALES** *Australia*   Australia's most populous state. The RIVERINA, a hot, irrigated area of 9000ha (22,000 acres) grows 14% of Australia's grapes and is definitely showing signs of improvement. The HUNTER VALLEY, MUDGEE, COWRA and HILLTOPS are smaller, premium-quality regions hugging the coastal highlands. Orange is a high-altitude inland district. Fashionable CANBERRA is an area of tiny vineyards at chilly altitudes, as is Tumbarumba at the base of the Snowy Mountains.

**NEWTON VINEYARDS** *Napa Valley AVA, California, USA*   Spectacular winery and vineyards above St Helena. Estate Cabernet Sauvignon★★, Merlot★★ and Claret★ are some of California's most balanced and ageworthy examples. Newton pioneered the unfiltered Chardonnay★★★ style and this lush mouthful remains one of California's best. Newtonian★ is the excellent second label, sold chiefly in export markets. French luxury giant LVMH took a controlling interest in 2000. Age the Chardonnays for up to 5 years, reds for 10–15. Best years: (Cabernet Sauvignon) (1999) 98 97 96 **95 94 92 91 90**; (Merlot) (1999) 98 97 96 95 93 92 91 **90**; (Chardonnay) 1999 98 97 96 **95 94 93 91**.

**NEW YORK STATE** *USA*   Wine grapes were first planted on Manhattan Island in the mid-17th century but it wasn't until the early 1950s that a serious wine industry began to develop in the state as vinifera grapes were planted to replace natives such as *Vitis labrusca*. The most important region is the FINGER LAKES in the north of the state, with the Hudson River also showing some form, but LONG ISLAND is the most exciting area. Consistency and quality have increased markedly in recent years, as improved vineyard practices help growers cope with the sometimes erratic weather. Best producers: BEDELL★★, FOX RUN★, HARGRAVE/Castello di Borghese, LAMOREAUX LANDING★, LENZ★, Millbrook★, Palmer, Schneider★, Silver Thread★, Hermann J Wiemer.

**NGATARAWA** *Hawke's Bay, North Island, New Zealand*  One of HAWKE'S BAY's better producers. Viticulture is organic, with Chardonnay, botrytized Riesling and a Cabernet-Merlot blend produced under the premium Alwyn Reserve label. The Glazebrook range includes attractive Chardonnay★ and Cabernet-Merlot★, both of which are best drunk within 5 years. Best years: (reds) (2000) **98 96**.

**NIAGARA PENINSULA** *Ontario, Canada*  Sandwiched between lakes Erie and Ontario, the Niagara Peninsula benefits from regular through-breezes created by the Niagara escarpment, the cool climate bringing out distinctive characteristics in the wine. Chardonnay leads the way in dry whites, with Riesling and Vidal making good icewine. Pinot Noir is proving the most successful red grape, but Merlot and Cabernet Sauvignon are improving. Best producers: Cave Spring★, Chateau des Charmes★, HENRY OF PELHAM★, INNISKILLIN★, Konzelmann★, Marynissen, Reif Estate★, Stoney Ridge, THIRTY BENCH WINERY.

**NIEBAUM-COPPOLA ESTATE** *Rutherford AVA, California, USA*  Movie director Coppola has turned the historical Inglenook Niebaum winery into an elaborate tourist destination. Rubicon★, a BORDEAUX blend, lacked grace in the early vintages but with Coppola's greater involvement in the 1990s the wine has taken on a more attractive personality. It still needs 5–6 years of aging. Coppola offers Zinfandel under the Edizione Pennino★ label and Cabernet Franc★ under Coppola Family Wines. Best years: (Rubicon) (1999) 97 96 95 **94 93 91 87 86**.

**NIEPOORT** *Port DOC, Douro, Portugal*  Remarkable small port shipper of Dutch origin, run by the widely respected Dirk Niepoort. Outstanding Vintage ports★★★, old tawnies★★★ and Colheitas★★★ and a single-quinta wine: Quinta do Passadouro★★. Unfiltered LBVs★★ are among the best in their class – intense and complex. He also produces fine red★★ and white★★ DOURO Redoma and red Passadouro★★. Best years: (Vintage) 1997 94 92 91 87 85 83 **82 80 77 70 66 63 58 55 45 42 27**; (Passadouro) 1997 95 94 92.

**NIERSTEIN** *Rheinhessen, Germany*  Both a small town and a large Bereich which includes the infamous Grosslage Gutes Domtal. The town boasts 23 vineyard sites and the top ones (such as Ölberg, Orbel, Hipping and Pettenthal) are some of the best in the whole Rhine Valley. Best producers: Heinrich Braun★, GUNDERLOCH★, HEYL ZU HERRNSHEIM★★, ST ANTONY★★. Best years: 1999 98 **97 96 94 93**.

**NIKOLAIHOF** *Wachau, Niederösterreich, Austria*  The Saahs family of Mautern makes some of the best wines in the WACHAU as well as in nearby Krems-Stein in KREMSTAL, including steely, intense Rieslings from their small plot in the famous Steiner Hund vineyard, always ★★. Best years: 1999 98 **97 95 94 92 91 90 86 79 77**.

**NOBILO** *Kumeu/Huapai, Auckland, North Island, New Zealand*  New Zealand's third-largest winery – now owned by Australian giant BRL HARDY – produces a wide range of wines, from popular medium-dry White Cloud to single-vineyard varietals. Dixon Vineyard Chardonnay★, a lush, intensely flavoured wine, is Nobilo's 'prestige' label. Sleek Sauvignon Blanc★ and Chardonnay★ from Nobilo's newly developed MARLBOROUGH vineyard are rapidly moving toward centre-stage. In 1998 Nobilo bought SELAKS, a mid-sized company with wineries in AUCKLAND and MARLBOROUGH.

**NORTON** *Luján de Cuyo, Mendoza, Argentina* Austrian-owned winery using superb-quality fruit, but the winemaking has lacked a bit of spark. The arrival of super-consultant Michel Rolland from France should inject some life into the wines. Reserva level (terracotta label) reds★ can pack plenty of fruit. Top-of-the-range Privada★★ is a powerful, ripe wine suitable for cellaring. Best years: (reds) (2000) **99 97 96**.

**NOVAL, QUINTA DO** *Port DOC, Douro, Portugal* Owned by French insurance giant AXA's subsidiary AXA-Millésimes, this immaculate property is the source of extraordinary Quinta do Noval Nacional★★★, made from ungrafted vines – probably the best vintage port made, but virtually unobtainable except at auction. Other Noval ports (including Noval Vintage★★ and single-quinta Silval★★) are now excellent too. Also fine colheitas★★ and some stunning 40-year-old tawnies★★★. Best years: (Nacional) 1997 94 87 85 **70 66 63 62 60 31**; (Vintage) 1997 95 94 91 **87 85 70 66 63 60**.

**NUITS-ST-GEORGES AC** *Côte de Nuits, Burgundy, France* This large AC is one of the few relatively reliable 'village' names in Burgundy. Although it has no Grands Crus, many of its Premiers Crus (it has 38!) are extremely good. The red can be rather slow to open out, often needing at least 5 years. Minuscule amounts of white are made by Gouges★, l'Arlot, Chevillon and RION. Best producers: l'Arlot★★, R Arnoux★★, J Chauvenet★★, R Chevillon★★★, J-J Confuron★★, FAIVELEY★★, Gouges★★, GRIVOT★★, JAYER-GILLES★★, D Laurent★★★, MEO-CAMUZET★★, A Michelot★★, Mugneret★★★, RION★★, THOMAS-MOILLARD★★. Best years: (reds) (2000) 99 98 97 96 95 **93 91 90 88**.

**NYETIMBER** *West Sussex, England* Brainchild of two expatriate Chicagoans, making top-quality, trophy-winning, traditional-method sparkling wines, clearly showing England's potential in this field. First production Première Cuvée 1992★★ was all Chardonnay. The 1993 Classic Cuvée★★ has 30% Pinot Noir and some Meunier in the blend.

**OAKVILLE AVA** *Napa Valley, California, USA* This region is similar in many respects to RUTHERFORD, which lies immediately to the north. Planted primarily to Cabernet Sauvignon, the area contains some of the best vineyards (MONDAVI, OPUS ONE, Screaming Eagle), producing wines that display lush, ripe black fruits and firm tannins.

**OC, VIN DE PAYS D'** *Languedoc-Roussillon, France* Vin de Pays wanted to concentrate on good quality from international varieties, but problems of overproduction and consequently underripeness have dogged attempts to smarten up its reputation. Occasional fine red or white wine shows what can be done. Best producers: l'Aigle★, Dom. de la BAUME (whites★), Clovallon★, HERRICK, J Lurton, Mas Cremat★, Ormesson★, Pech-Céleyran (Viognier★), Quatre Sous★, St-Saturnin★, SKALLI-FORTANT, VAL D'ORBIEU (top reds★), Virginie.

**OCHOA** *Navarra DO, Navarra, Spain* Javier Ochoa has completely modernized the family bodega and his 68ha (168 acres) of vineyards. The wines are fresh, clean and fruity, with particularly good Merlot, Cabernet Sauvignon★, Tempranillo★ and sweet Muscat★. Best years: (reds) 1996 **95 94 93 92 91 90**.

**OCKFEN** *Saar, Germany* Village with one famous individual vineyard site, the Bockstein. The wines can be superb in a sunny year, never losing their cold steely streak but packing in delightful full-flavoured

fruit as well. Best producers: Dr Fischer, Heinz Wagner★★, ZILLIKEN★★.
Best years: 1999 **97 95 93 90**.

**OKANAGAN VALLEY** *British Columbia, Canada*  The oldest and most important wine-producing region of British Columbia and first home of Canada's rich, honeyed icewine. The Okanagan Lake helps temper the bitterly cold nights but October frosts can be a problem. Chardonnay, Pinot Blanc and Pinot Noir are the top performing grapes. South of the lake, Cabernet and Merlot are now being grown successfully. Best producers: Blue Mountain★, Burrowing Owl★, Gehringer★, INNISKILLIN, MISSION HILL★, Quail's Gate, SUMAC RIDGE★, Tinhorn Creek.

**OLTREPÒ PAVESE DOC** *Lombardy, Italy*  Oltrepò Pavese is Italy's main source of Pinot Nero, used mainly for sparkling wines that may be called Classese when made by the Champagne method here, though base wines supply *spumante* industries elsewhere. The region supplies Milan's everyday wines, often fizzy, though still reds from Barbera, Bonarda and Pinot Nero and whites from the Pinots, Riesling and, lately, Chardonnay can be impressive. Best producers: Anteo, Il Bosco/Zonin, Cà di Frara★, Le Fracce★, Frecciarossa★, Fugazza, Mazzolino★, Monsupello★, Montelio★, Piccolo Bacco dei Quaroni, Santa Maria della Versa co-op★, Vercesi del Castellazzo★, Bruno Verdi★. Best years: (reds) 2000 99 **98 97 96 95 93 90**.

**OMAR KHAYYAM** *Maharashtra, India*  Champagne-method sparkling wine produced from a blend of Chardonnay, Ugni Blanc, Pinot Noir, Pinot Meunier – and Thompson Seedless. The Thompson is now being used less and less as plantings of the other varieties come on stream. Technology, thanks to CHAMPAGNE consultants PIPER-HEIDSIECK, together with high-sited, irrigated vineyards, generally produce a firm, fresh, chunky sparkler – and quality is becoming more consistent. A demi-sec style, Marquise de Pompadour, is also made and an excellent pink fizz. Attention is now turning to table wines.

**WILLI OPITZ** *Neusiedlersee, Austria*  The eccentric and publicity-conscious Willi Opitz produces a remarkable, unusual range of dessert wines from his tiny 2-ha (5-acre) vineyard, including red Eiswein. The best are ★★, but dry wines are simpler and less consistent.

**OPPENHEIM** *Rheinhessen, Germany*  Village whose reputation has suffered from the sale of much inferior wine under the Oppenheimer Krötenbrunnen label. In its steepest sites, such as Sackträger, it can be one of the better villages in RHEINHESSEN, where the deep soils give relatively earthy, weighty wines. Best producers: Guntrum, Koch, Kühling-Gillot. Best years: 1999 98 **97 96 93**.

**OPUS ONE★★** *Oakville AVA, California, USA*  Joint venture between Robert MONDAVI and the late Baron Philippe de Rothschild of MOUTON-ROTHSCHILD. The first vintage (1979) was released in 1983. At that time, the $50 price was the most expensive for any California wine, though others have reached way beyond it now. The various Opus bottlings since 1979 have been in the ★★ range and have only recently touched the standard of the Mondavi Reserve Cabernet. Best years: (1999) 98 97 96 95 94 93 92 91 **90 88 87 86 85 84**.

**DOMAINE DE L'ORATOIRE ST-MARTIN** *Côtes du Rhône AC, Rhône Valley, France*  Careful fruit selection in the vineyard is the secret of Frédéric and François Alary's concentrated COTES DU RHONE-VILLAGES reds and whites. The Haut-Coustias white★ is ripe with aromas of peach and exotic fruits, while its red namesake★★ is a concentrated concoction of raspberries, herbs and spice. Top red Cuvée Prestige★★ is deep and intense with darkly spicy fruit.

**OREGON** *USA* Oregon shot to international stardom in the early 1980s following some perhaps overly generous praise of its Pinot Noir, but the state has failed to consolidate this position. Not that Oregon Pinot Noir can't be attractive, but it rarely offers more than a black cherry fruit, generally without much complexity. Chardonnay can be quite good in an austere, understated style. The rising star is Pinot Gris which, in Oregon's cool climate, can be delicious with surprising complexity. Pinot Blanc is also gaining momentum. The Willamette Valley is considered the best growing region, with Dundee hills the best sub-region, although the more Bordeaux-like climate of the Umpqua and Rogue Valleys can produce good Cabernet Sauvignon and Merlot. Best producers: ADELSHEIM★, AMITY★, Archery Summit★, Argyle★, BEAUX FRERES★★, BETHEL HEIGHTS★, Cameron★, Cristom, DOMAINE DROUHIN OREGON★, Elk Cove★, Eola Hills, Erath, EYRIE★, Henry Estate, KING ESTATE, PANTHER CREEK★, PONZI★, Rex Hill★★, SOKOL BLOSSER★, Torii Mor, WillaKenzie, Ken Wright, Yamhill Valley★.

**ORLANDO** *Barossa Valley, South Australia* Australia's second-biggest wine company is owned by Pernod-Ricard and encompasses MORRIS, Wickham Hill, Gramps, Richmond Grove and Wyndham Estate, and MUDGEE wineries Craigmoor and Montrose. Top wines under the Orlando name are COONAWARRA reds St Hugo★ and Jacaranda Ridge★, and individualistic Eden Valley Rieslings St Helga★ and Steingarten★★, but Orlando has lacked strength at the premium end. Rich Centenary Hill Barossa Shiraz★★ might change that, as might renewed efforts in Mudgee. Jacob's Creek basics are deservedly Australia's most successful brand abroad. Best years: (St Hugo Cabernet) **1996** 94 92 90 86 82.

**ORNELLAIA, TENUTA DELL'** *Bolgheri, Tuscany, Italy* This beautiful property was developed by Lodovico Antinori, brother of Piero, after he left the family firm, ANTINORI, to strike out on his own. The red Ornellaia★★★, a Cabernet-Merlot blend, bears comparison with neighbouring SASSICAIA. The white Poggio alle Gazze★★ is made solely with Sauvignon. An outstanding Merlot, Masseto★★★, is produced in small quantities. Best years: (Ornellaia) (1998) 97 96 95 **94 93 92 90** 88.

**ORVIETO DOC** *Umbria, Italy* Traditionally a lightly sweet *abboccato* white wine, Orvieto is now usually dry and characterless. In the superior Classico zone, however, the potential for richer, more biscuity wines exists. Not generally a wine for aging. There are also some very good botrytis-affected examples. Best producers: (dry) Barberani-Vallesanta★, La Carraia★, Decugnano dei Barbi★, Palazzone★, Castello della SALA★, Salviano★, Conte Vaselli★, Le Velette★; (sweet) Barberani-Vallesanta★, Decugnano dei Barbi★, Palazzone★, Castello della SALA★★.

**OSBORNE** *Jerez y Manzanilla DO, Andalucía, Spain* The biggest drinks company in Spain, Osborne does most of its business in brandy and other spirits. Its sherry arm in Puerto de Santa María specializes in the light Fino Quinta★. Amontillado Coquinero★, rich, intense Bailén Oloroso★★ and Solera India★★ are very good indeed.

**OVERBERG WO** *South Africa*   One of South Africa's most southerly wine regions, prized for cool-climate viticulture, embracing the upland area of Elgin as well as the coastal ward of Walker Bay. In Elgin, Sauvignon, Chardonnay, Riesling and Pinot Noir vindicate the decision to replace valuable apple orchards. Walker Bay was opened up (at the time illegally) by HAMILTON RUSSELL in the mid-1970s, who remained the only producer until BOUCHARD FINLAYSON started in the early 90s. They have since been joined by others. Pinot Noir is the holy grail of the majority, although Pinotage is also doing well. **Best producers:** (Elgin) Paul Cluver, Neil ELLIS; (Walker Bay) BOUCHARD FINLAYSON★★, HAMILTON RUSSELL VINEYARDS★★, WhaleHaven, Wildekrans.

**PAARL WO** *South Africa*   Paarl is South Africa's second most densely planted region after Worcester, accounting for 16.5% of all vineyards. There is great diversity of soil and climate here, favouring everything from Cap Classique sparkling wines to sherry styles. Currently, Rhône varieties Viognier and Shiraz are setting the quality pace. Wellington and FRANSCHHOEK are smaller designated areas within the Paarl region. **Best producers:** (Paarl) BACKSBERG★, BOSCHENDAL, FAIRVIEW★★, GLEN CARLOU★★, DISTELL (Plaisir de Merle★, Nederburg), VEENWOUDEN★★, VILLIERA★★, Welgemeend★; (Wellington) Claridge.

**PACHERENC DU VIC-BILH AC** *South-West France*   Individual whites from an area overlapping the MADIRAN AC in north-east Béarn. The wines are mainly dry but there are some medium-sweet/sweet late-harvest wines. Most Pacherenc is best drunk young. **Best producers:** Aydie, Berthoumieu★, Brumont★, Crampilh★, Damiens, Laffitte-Teston★, Union des Producteurs PLAIMONT★. **Best years:** (2000) **97 96 95**.

**PACIFIC ECHO** *Anderson Valley AVA, California, USA*   Known until 1998 as Scharffenberger Cellars, this winery was somewhat erratic, but money from POMMERY has upgraded the facility, and recent vintages have been greatly improved. The Brut★★, with lovely toasty depth, and the exuberant Rosé★★ are excellent. The blanc de blancs Prestige Cuvée★★ is one of California's finest sparklers.

**PADTHAWAY** *South Australia*   This wine region has always been the alter-ego of nearby COONAWARRA, growing whites to complement Coonawarra's reds. But today some excellent reds are made, and even GRANGE now has some Padthaway grapes. ORLANDO's premium Shiraz, Lawson's★, is 100% Padthaway, HARDYS' Eileen Hardy Shiraz★★★ is half Padthaway and LINDEMANS' Padthaway Chardonnay★ is a serious white. Padthaway Sauvignon Blanc is also some of Australia's tastiest. **Best producers:** Browns of Padthaway, HARDYS★★, Henry's Drive★★, LINDEMANS★, ORLANDO★, Padthaway Estate, SEPPELT.

**BODEGAS PALACIO** *Rioja DOC, País Vasco, Spain*   Founded in 1894 by Don Cosme Palacio, then the owner of VEGA SICILIA. Relaunched in the late 1980s by then owner Jean Gervais and POMEROL winemaker Michel Rolland, whose Cosme Palacio y Hermanos★★ has become a cult wine in Spain. Sold in 1998 to the owners of Viña Mayor, a RIBERA DEL DUERO winery. **Best years:** (reds) **1996 95 94 92 91**.

209

**ALVARO PALACIOS** *Priorat DO, Cataluña, Spain* Although he was only in his 20s, Alvaro Palacios was already a veteran with Bordeaux and Napa experience when he launched his boutique winery in the rough hills of southern CATALUNA in the late 1980s. He is now one of the driving forces of the area's sensational rebirth. His expensive, highly concentrated reds★★★ from old Garnacha vines and a dollop of Cabernet Sauvignon, Merlot and Syrah have won a cult following. Best years: 1998 **97** 96 **95 94 93 92 90.**

**PALETTE AC** *Provence, France* Tiny AC just east of Aix-en-Provence. Even though the local market pays high prices, I find the reds and rosés rather tough and charmless. However, Ch. Simone, the only producer of white Palette, manages to achieve a wine of some flavour from basic southern grapes. Best producers: Crémade, Ch. Simone★.

**PALLISER ESTATE** *Martinborough, North Island, New Zealand* State-of-the-art winery producing some of New Zealand's best Sauvignon Blanc★★ (certainly the best outside MARLBOROUGH) and Riesling★, with some impressive, rich-textured Pinot Noir★★. Exciting botrytized dessert wines appear in favourable vintages. Méthode★ fizz is also impressive. Best years: (Pinot Noir) (2001) 99 **98 96 94.**

**CH. PALMER★★** *Margaux AC, 3ème Cru Classé, Haut-Médoc, Bordeaux, France* This estate was named after a British major-general who fought in the Napoleonic Wars. Palmer was the leading property in MARGAUX AC during the 1960s and 70s until the Mentzelopolous family took over at Ch. MARGAUX in 1977. The wine is wonderfully perfumed, with irresistible plump fruit, but sometimes would benefit from rather more body and intensity. The very best vintages can age for 30 years or more. Second wine: Alter Ego (previously Réserve-du-Général). Best years: (2000) 99 98 96 95 **90 89 88 86 85 83 82 79.**

**PANTHER CREEK** *Willamette Valley AVA, Oregon, USA* Ron and Linda Kaplan have picked up where former owner Ken Wright left off, producing rich, cherryish Pinot Noirs with good aging potential. Single-vineyard bottlings such as Shea★★, Bednarik★★ and Freedom Hill★★ have extra opulence and complexity. Best years (1999) 98 **97** 96.

**CH. PAPE-CLÉMENT** *Pessac-Léognan AC, Cru Classé de Graves, Bordeaux, France* The expensive red wine★★ from this GRAVES property has not always been as consistent as it should be – but things have looked up considerably since the exciting 1986 vintage. In style it is mid-way between the refinement of HAUT-BRION and the firmness of la MISSION-HAUT-BRION. Also a small production of a much-improved white wine★★. Second wine: (red) Clémentin. Best years: (reds) (2000) 99 98 97 96 95 94 **90 89 88 86**; (white) (2000) 99 98 **97** 96.

---

**PARELLADA** This Catalan exclusivity is the lightest of the trio of simple white grapes that go to make CAVA wines in north-eastern Spain. It also makes still wines, light, fresh and gently floral, with good acidity. Drink it as young as possible, while it still has the benefit of freshness.

---

**PARKER COONAWARRA ESTATE** *Coonawarra, South Australia* Red wine specialist whose top label, cheekily named Parker Estate First Growth★★ in imitation of illustrious BORDEAUX reds, has enjoyed much critical acclaim and auction success. It is released only in better years and is built to age well. Second label Parker Estate Terra Rossa★ is lighter and leafier.

**LUIS PATO** *Bairrada, Beira Litoral, Portugal* Leading 'modernist' in BAIRRADA, passionately convinced of the Baga grape's ability to make great reds on clay soil. Wines such as the Vinhas Velhas★★, Vinha Barrosa★★, Vinha Pan★★ and the flagship Quinta do Ribeirinho Pé Franco★★ (from ungrafted vines) now rank among Portugal's finest new reds. Exciting new white, Vinha Formal★★, is 100% Bical. Best years: (reds) 1997 **96 95** 92.

**PATRIMONIO AC** *Corsica, France* Good, underrated wines from northern CORSICA. Reds and rosés are based on the local Nielluccio grape, whites are increasingly made from Malvasia. Best producers: Arena★, Gentile, Leccia★, Orenga de Gaffory★. Best years: (reds) (2000) **99 98 97 96 95**.

**PAUILLAC AC** *Haut-Médoc, Bordeaux, France* The deep gravel banks around the town of Pauillac in the HAUT-MÉDOC are the heartland of Cabernet Sauvignon. For many wine lovers, the king of red wine grapes finds its ultimate expression in the 3 Pauillac First Growths (LATOUR, LAFITE-ROTHSCHILD and MOUTON-ROTHSCHILD). The large AC also contains 15 other Classed Growths, including PICHON-LONGUEVILLE-LALANDE, PICHON-LONGUEVILLE and LYNCH-BAGES. The uniting characteristic of Pauillac wines is their intense blackcurrant fruit flavour and heady cedar and pencil-shavings perfume. These are the longest-lived of Bordeaux's great red wines. Best producers: Armailhac★, BATAILLEY★, Clerc-Milon★, Duhart-Milon★, Fonbadet, GRAND-PUY-DUCASSE★, GRAND-PUY-LACOSTE★★, HAUT-BAGES-LIBÉRAL★, HAUT-BATAILLEY★, LAFITE-ROTHSCHILD★★★, LATOUR★★★, LYNCH-BAGES★★★, MOUTON-ROTHSCHILD★★★, Pibran★, PICHON-LONGUEVILLE★★★, PICHON-LONGUEVILLE-LALANDE★★★, PONTET-CANET★★. Best years: (2000) **96 95 90 94 90 89 88 86 85 83 82**.

**CH. PAVIE★** *St-Émilion Grand Cru AC, 1er Grand Cru Classé, Bordeaux, France* Pavie produces supple, aromatic wines which will happily evolve for a decade yet never lose the soft, unctuous charm of the fruit and the sweet oak. Recent vintages have lacked guts but a change of ownership in 1998 should signal a rapid improvement. Best years: (2000) 99 98 96 95 **90 89 88 86 85 83 82**.

**PÉCHARMANT AC** *South-West France* Lovely red wines from this small AC north-east of BERGERAC. The wines are quite light in body but have a delicious, full, piercing flavour of blackcurrants and attractive grassy acidity. Good vintages will easily last 10 years and end up indistinguishable from a good HAUT-MÉDOC. Best producers: Bertranoux, Champarel, Clos Peyrelevade, Costes, Haut-Pécharmant, la Métairie, Tiregand★. Best years: (2000) **99 96 95 90 89 88 86**.

**PEDROSA** *Ribera del Duero DO, Castilla y León, Spain* Delicious, elegant reds★ (Pérez Pascuas Gran Reserva★★), both young and oak-aged, from a family winery in the little hill village of Pedrosa del Duero. The wines are not cheap, but far less pricy than some stars of this fashionable region. Best years: (reds) (1999) 96 **95 94 92 91 90 89 86**.

**PEGASUS BAY** *Waipara, Canterbury, New Zealand* Matthew Donaldson and Lynette Hudson fashion lush, mouthfilling Chardonnay★★, an almost chewy Pinot Noir★, a powerful Sauvignon Blanc-Semillon★★ and a very stylish Riesling★★ – an impressive portfolio from this upcoming region. All will age well. Best years: (2001) 00 99 **98 97 96**.

**PEMBERTON** *Western Australia* Exciting new region, deep in the karri forests of the south-west, full of promise for cool-climate Pinot Noir, Chardonnay, Merlot and Sauvignon Blanc. Leading wineries include Salitage, run by Denis (LEEUWIN ESTATE) Horgan's brother John; Picardy, founded by Bill Pannell of MOSS WOOD fame; Chestnut Grove, part-owned by the Langes from Alkoomi; Smithbrook, part-owned by PETALUMA; and Bronzewing Estate, owned by John Kosovich of SWAN winery Westfield. Some large outfits such as HOUGHTON have moved in.

**PEÑAFLOR** *Mendoza, Argentina* The biggest wine producer in Argentina. Investment in its fine wine arm, Trapiche, along with the expertise of Bordeaux enologist Michel Rolland, is beginning to deliver results. Punchy Sauvignon★ from high-altitude vineyards, grassy Chenin Blanc★ and rich, melony Chardonnay. Iscay★ is the new flagship red.

**PENEDÈS DO** *Cataluña, Spain* The wealthy CAVA industry is based in Penedès, and the majority of the still wines are white, made from the Cava trio of Parellada, Macabeo and Xarel-lo, clean and fresh when young, but never exciting. Better whites are made from Chardonnay. The reds are variable, the best made from Cabernet Sauvignon and/or Tempranillo and Merlot. Best producers: Albet i Noya★, Can Feixes★, Can Ràfols dels Caus★ (Caus Lubis Merlot★★), Cavas Hill, JUVE Y CAMPS★, Jean León★, MARQUES DE MONISTROL★, Masía Bach★, Albert Milá i Mallofré, Puig y Roca★, TORRES★★, Vallformosa, Jané Ventura.

**PENFOLDS** *Barossa Valley, South Australia* Part of Australia's Southcorp Wines group, Penfolds proves that quality *can* go in hand with quantity and is regarded as the dominant force in Australian wine. Makes the country's greatest red wine, GRANGE★★★, and a welter of superbly rich, structured reds from Magill Estate★★ through St Henri★, Bin 707 Cabernet★★★, Bin 389 Cabernet-Shiraz★★, Bin 28 Kalimna★★ and Bin 128 Coonawarra Shiraz★ to Koonunga Hill and Rawson's Retreat cheapies (Riesling★). Still very much a red wine name, although making a spirited bid for white-wine fame with new Chardonnay and Semillon from ADELAIDE HILLS, led by overpriced Yattarna★★, dubbed, with tongue in cheek, the 'white Grange'. Also makes tasty wooded Semillon★★ and lemony Semillon-Chardonnay★★. Best years: (Grange) (1995) 94 93 92 91 **90 88 86 84 83 80 76 71 67 66 65 63 62 55 53 52**; (other reds) 1998 96 **94 93 92 91 90 88 86 84 83 82 80 78 76 71**.

**PENLEY ESTATE** *Coonawarra, South Australia* Kym Tolley, a member of the PENFOLD family, combined the names when he left Southcorp and launched Penley Estate in 1991. From 1997 Cabernet Sauvignon★★ has been outstanding and matches its lavish packaging. Chardonnay and Hyland Shiraz can reach ★★; fizz★ is also worth a try, as is the recently released Merlot★. Best years: (Cabernet) 1998 **96 94 93 92 91**.

**PERNAND-VERGELESSES AC** *Côte de Beaune, Burgundy, France* The little-known village of Pernand-Vergelesses contains a decent chunk of the great Corton hill, including much of the best white CORTON-CHARLEMAGNE Grand Cru vineyard. The red wines sold under the village name are very attractive when young with a nice raspberry pastille fruit and a slight earthiness, and will age for 6–10 years. As no one ever links poor old Pernand with the heady heights of Corton-Charlemagne, the whites sold under the village name can be a bargain. The wines can be a bit lean and dry to start with but fatten up beautifully after 2–4 years in bottle. Best producers: (reds) Besancenot-Mathouillet★, Champy, CHANDON DE BRIAILLES★★, C Cornu★, Denis Père et Fils★, Dubreuil-Fontaine★, Laleure-Piot★, Rapet★, Rollin★; (whites) CHANDON DE BRIAILLES★★, Chanson, Dubreuil-Fontaine★, GERMAIN, A Guyon, JADOT, Laleure-Piot★, J-M Pavelot★, Rapet★, Rollin★★. Best years: (reds) 1999 98 **97 96 95** 93; (whites) (2000) 99 **97 96 95**.

**JOSEPH PERRIER** *Champagne AC, Champagne, France*   This is the sole CHAMPAGNE house left in Châlons-en-Champagne (previously called Châlons-sur-Marne). In 1998 Alain Thiénot took a controlling interest in the house. The NV Cuvée★ is biscuity and creamy. Prestige Cuvée Josephine★★ has length and complexity, but the much cheaper Cuvée Royale Vintage★★ is the best deal. Best years: (1995) **90 89 88** 85.

**PERRIER-JOUËT** *Champagne AC, Champagne, France*   Perrier-Jouët used to be the one classy performer in the clutch of CHAMPAGNE houses formerly owned by media and spirits giant Seagram. But sadly, latest sightings of Perrier-Jouët show that it, along with its stablemates, has begun to lose the plot. Vintage can be OK, and de luxe cuvée Belle Époque★★, white and rosé, is still classy, but Perrier-Jouët is no longer a label to seek out. Best years: (1995) **92 90 89 88 85** 82.

**PERVINI** *Primitivo di Manduria DOC, Puglia, Italy*   Premium venture from the Perrucci family, long-established bulk shippers of basic Puglian wines. There's real quality and a modern outlook across the range of Primitivo-based reds (PRIMITIVO DI MANDURIA★★). Whites and rosés are decent, simple wines to drink young. Best years: (reds) (2000) 99 98 **97 96**.

**PESQUERA** *Ribera del Duero DO, Castilla y León, Spain*   Viña Pesquera reds, richly coloured, firm, fragrant and plummy-tobaccoey, are among Spain's best. Made by the small firm of Alejandro Fernández, they are 100% Tempranillo and sold as Crianzas★★, with expensive Reservas★★ and Pesquera Janus★★★ in the best years. Condado de Haza (Alenza★★) is a separate estate. Best years: (1999) 96 **95 94 93 92 91 90 89 86** 85.

**PESSAC-LÉOGNAN AC** *Bordeaux, France*   AC created in 1987 for the northern (and best) part of the GRAVES region and including all the Graves Classed Growths. The supremely gravelly soil tends to favour red wines over the rest of the Graves. Now, thanks to cool fermentation and the use of new oak barrels, this is also one of the most exciting areas of France for top-class white wines. Best producers: (reds) Brown, CARBONNIEUX★, les Carmes Haut-Brion★, Dom. de CHEVALIER★★, FIEUZAL★★, HAUT-BAILLY★★, HAUT-BRION★★★, Larrivet Haut-Brion★, LATOUR-MARTILLAC★, la LOUVIERE★★, MALARTIC-LAGRAVIERE★, la MISSION-HAUT-BRION★★★, PAPE-CLEMENT★★, SMITH-HAUT-LAFITTE★, la Tour-Haut-Brion★★; (whites) CARBONNIEUX★, Dom. de CHEVALIER★★★, Couhins-Lurton★★, FIEUZAL★★, HAUT-BRION★★★, LATOUR-MARTILLAC★★, LAVILLE-HAUT-BRION★★★, la LOUVIERE★★, MALARTIC-LAGRAVIERE★★, Rochemorin★, SMITH-HAUT-LAFITTE★★. Best years: (reds) (2000) 99 98 96 95 94 **90 89 88** 82; (whites) (2000) 99 98 **96 95 94 93** 90 89 88 86 85.

**PETALUMA** *Adelaide Hills, South Australia* This publicly listed company, which includes KNAPPSTEIN and MITCHELTON and has major interests in WESTERN AUSTRALIA and MORNINGTON PENINSULA wineries, is run by Brian Croser, probably Australia's most influential winemaker. Champagne-method Croser★ is stylish but lean. The Chardonnay★★ and COONAWARRA Cabernet-Merlot★★★ are consistently outstanding and CLARE Riesling★★ is at the fuller end of the spectrum and matures superbly. Vineyard Selection Tiers Chardonnay★★★ is ridiculously expensive. Best years: (reds) 1998 97 **96 94 93 92 91 90 88**.

**PETIT CHABLIS AC** *Chablis, Burgundy, France* Once this denoted the outlying parts of the CHABLIS region. Then the vineyards were upgraded to full Chablis. Now more land has been planted even further away. The wine is often thin but can be appealing when drunk young. Too close to regular Chablis in price, though.

**PETITE SIRAH** Long used as a blending grape in California but used also for varietal wines, Petite Sirah is supposed to be the Durif of southern France, although there is now some doubt about that. At its best in California and Mexico, the wine has great depth and strength; at worst it can be monstrously huge and unfriendly. Best producers: L A CETTO (Mexico), Fife, FETZER, Foppiano, Ravenswood★★, RIDGE★★, Stags Leap Winery★★, TURLEY★★.

**PETIT VERDOT** A rich, tannic red variety, grown mainly in Bordeaux's HAUT-MEDOC to add depth, colour and violet fragrance to top wines. Late-ripening and erratic yield limit its popularity, but warmer-climate plantings in Australia, California, Argentina and Spain are giving exciting results.

**CH. PETIT-VILLAGE★★** *Pomerol AC, Bordeaux, France* This top POMEROL wine, sterner in style than its neighbours, is owned by AXA-Millésimes, who also own PICHON-LONGUEVILLE. In general it is worth aging the wine for 8–10 years at least. Best years: (2000) 99 98 96 95 94 90 **89 88 85 82**.

**CH. PÉTRUS★★★** *Pomerol AC, Bordeaux, France* Now one of the most expensive red wines in the world (alongside other fine wines from POMEROL, such as le PIN), but only 40 years ago Pétrus was virtually unknown. The powerful, concentrated wine produced here is the result of the caring genius of Pétrus' co-owners since 1962, the MOUEIX family, who have maximized the potential of the vineyard of almost solid clay, although the impressive average age of the vines has been much reduced by recent replantings. Drinkable for its astonishingly rich, dizzying blend of fruit and spice flavours after a decade, but top years will age for much longer, developing exotic scents of tobacco and chocolate and truffles as they mature. Best years: (2000) 99 98 97 96 95 94 93 90 89 **88 85 82 79 75 71**.

**DOMAINE PEYRE ROSE** *Coteaux du Languedoc AC, Languedoc, France* Organic viticulture, ultra-low yields and total absence of oak are all marks of the individuality of Marlène Soria's wines. Syrah is the dominant grape in both the raisin and plum-scented Clos des Cistes★★ and the dense, velvety Syrah Léone★★. An attractive white★ is a recent addition to the range. Best years: (reds) 1999 98 **97 96 95 94 93**.

**CH. DE PEZ**★ *St-Estèphe AC, Cru Bourgeois, Haut-Médoc, Bordeaux, France* One of ST-ESTEPHE's leading non-Classed Growths, de Pez makes mouthfilling, satisfying claret with sturdy fruit. Slow to evolve, good vintages often need 10 years or more to mature. Now owned by CHAMPAGNE house ROEDERER. Best years: (2000) 98 97 96 95 94 **90 89 88**.

**PFALZ** *Germany* Germany's most productive wine region makes a lot of mediocre wine, but the quality estates are capable of matching the best that Germany has to offer. The Mittelhaardt has a reputation for Riesling, especially round the villages of WACHENHEIM, FORST and Deidesheim, though Freinsheim, Ungstein, KALLSTADT, Gimmeldingen and Haardt also produce fine Riesling as well as Scheurebe, Rieslaner and Pinot Gris. In the Südliche Weinstrasse the warm climate makes the area an ideal testing ground for Spät-, Weiss- and Grauburgunder (Pinot Noir, Pinot Blanc and Pinot Gris), as well as Gewürztraminer, Scheurebe, Muscat and red Dornfelder, the latter often dark and tannic, if not elegant, sometimes with oak barrique influence. See also Bad Dürkheim, Burrweiler.

**JOSEPH PHELPS** *Napa Valley AVA, California, USA* Joseph Phelps' Insignia★★ red (Cabernet, Merlot and Cabernet Franc) is consistently one of California's top reds, strongly fruit-driven with a lively spicy background. Phelps' pure Cabernets include Napa Valley★, a medium-weight wine, and Backus Vineyard★★, beautifully balanced with solid ripe fruit. Best years: (Insignia) 1999 98 97 96 95 94 93 92 **91 89 87 85**.

**CH. DE PIBARNON** *Bandol AC, Provence, France* Blessed with excellently located vineyards, Pibarnon has risen to fulfil its potential since Comte Henri St-Victor took over in 1977. The red★★ develops a truffly, wild herb character with age. Average white and a ripe, strawberryish rosé complete the range. Best years: (red) (1999) 98 97 **96 95 94 93 91 90 89 88 85 82**.

**FRANZ X PICHLER** *Wachau, Niederösterreich, Austria* Austria's most famous producer of dry wines has a reputation as the country's 'bad boy'. Demand for his ★★★ Rieslings and Grüner Veltliners far outstrips supply. Premium wines 'M' (for monumental) and Unendlich, an alcoholically potent but perfectly balanced dry Riesling, are amazing. It is seldom that a wine leaves Pichler's cellar that is not of ★★ quality. Best years: (2000) 99 98 **97 95 94 93 92 90 86**.

**CH. PICHON-LONGUEVILLE**★★★ *Pauillac AC, 2ème Cru Classé, Haut-Médoc, Bordeaux, France* Despite its superb vineyards with the potential for making great PAUILLAC, Pichon-Longueville (called Pichon-Baron until 1988) wines were 'also-rans' for a long time. In 1987 the management was taken over by Jean-Michel Cazes of LYNCH-BAGES and, since then, there has been a remarkable change in fortune. Recent vintages have been of First Growth standard, with firm tannic structure and rich dark fruit. Cellar for at least 10 years, although it is likely to keep for 30. Second wine: les Tourelles de Pichon. Best years: (2000) 99 98 97 96 95 94 **90 89 88 86 82**.

**CH. PICHON-LONGUEVILLE-LALANDE**★★★ *Pauillac AC, 2ème Cru Classé, Haut-Médoc, Bordeaux, France* Pichon-Longueville-Lalande has been run since 1978 by the inspirational figure of Madame de Lencquesaing, who has led the property ever upwards through her

215

superlative vineyard management and winemaking sensitivity. Divinely scented and lush at 6–7 years, the wines usually last for 20 at least. Things dipped at the end of the 1980s, but recent efforts have been excellent. Second wine: Réserve de la Comtesse. Best years: (2000) 99 98 97 96 95 94 **93 90 89 88 86 85 83 82 81**.

**PIC ST-LOUP** *Coteaux du Languedoc AC, Languedoc, France* The vineyards of this Cru, arranged around a steep outcrop of limestone north of Montpellier, produce some of the best reds in the Languedoc. This is one of the coolest growing zones in the MIDI. Syrah does particularly well and, along with Grenache and Mourvèdre, it is the dominant variety. Whites from Marsanne, Roussanne, Rolle and Viognier are beginning to show promise. Best producers: Cazeneuve★, l'Euzière, l'HORTUS★, Lascaux★, MAS BRUGUIERE★, Mas de Lavabre★★, Mas de Mortiès★. Best years: (reds) (2000) 99 **98 96 95 93 90**.

**PIEDMONT** *Italy* This is the most important Italian region for the tradition of quality wines. In the north, there is CAREMA, GHEMME and GATTINARA. To the south, in the LANGHE hills, there's BAROLO and BARBARESCO, both masterful examples of the Nebbiolo grape, and other wines from Dolcetto and Barbera grapes. In the Monferrato hills, in the provinces of Asti and Alessandria, the Barbera, Moscato and Cortese grapes hold sway. Recent changes in the system have created the broad new DOCs of Colline Novaresi in the north, Langhe and Monferrato in the south and the regionwide Piemonte appellation designed to classify all wines of quality from a great range of grape varieties. See also Asti, Erbaluce di Caluso, Gavi, Moscato d'Asti, Nebbiolo d'Alba, Roero.

**PIEROPAN** *Veneto, Italy* Leonildo and Teresita Pieropan produce excellent SOAVE Classico★ and, from 2 single vineyards, Calvarino★★ and La Rocca★★, the definitive wines of this zone. There is an excellent Recioto di Soave Le Colombare★★, and an opulent Passito della Rocca★★, a barrique-aged blend of Sauvignon, Riesling Italico and Trebbiano di Soave. Single-vineyard Soaves can improve for 5 years or more, as can the Recioto and other sweet styles.

**PIERRO** *Margaret River, Western Australia* Yet another of MARGARET RIVER's winemaking doctors, Mike Peterkin, makes Pierro Chardonnay★★★ by the hatful, yet still it is a masterpiece of power and complexity. The Semillon-Sauvignon-Chardonnay blend★ is full with just a hint of leafiness, while Pinot Noir continues to improve as the vines age. A dark, dense Cabernet★★ is the serious, BORDEAUX-like member of the family. Fire Gully is the second label, using bought-in grapes. Best years: (Chardonnay) **1998 97** 96 95 94 93 92 91 90 87 86.

**PIESPORT** *Mosel, Germany* The generic Piesporter Michelsberg wines, soft, sweet and easy-drinking, have nothing to do with the excellent Rieslings from the top Goldtröpfchen site. With their intense peach and blackcurrant aromas they are unique among MOSEL wines. Best producers: GRANS-FASSIAN★, R HAART★★, Kurt Hain★, von KESSELSTATT★, Weller-Lehnert. Best years: 1999 98 **97 96 95 93 92 90 89 88 83**.

**CH. LE PIN★★★** *Pomerol AC, Bordeaux, France* Now one of the most expensive wines in the world, with prices at auction overtaking those for PETRUS. The 1979 was the first vintage and the wines, which are concentrated but elegant, are produced from 100% Merlot. The tiny 2-ha (5-acre) vineyard lies close to those of TROTANOY and VIEUX-CH.-CERTAN. Best years: (2000) 99 98 97 96 95 94 **90 89 88 86 85 83 82 81**.

**PINE RIDGE WINERY** *Stags Leap District AVA, California, USA* Within an ever-changing roster, Pine Ridge offers wines from several NAPA AVAs, but its flagship Cabernet remains the supple, plummy Stags Leap District★. Andrus Reserve Cabernet★★ has more richness and power. CARNEROS District Merlot★ is spicy and cherry fruited, and Carneros Chardonnay★ looks good. OREGON's Archery Summit is a sister label. Best years: (reds) 1998 97 96 **95 94 92 91**.

**PINGUS, DOMINIO DE** *Ribera del Duero DO, Castilla y León, Spain* Peter Sisseck's tiny vineyard and winery have attracted worldwide attention since 1995 due to the extraordinary depth and character of the cult wine they produce, Pingus★★★. Second wine Fleur de Pingus★★ is also delicious. Best years: (1999) 98 **97 96 95**.

**PINOT BIANCO** See Pinot Blanc.

**PINOT BLANC** Wine made from the Pinot Blanc grape has a clear, yeasty, appley taste, and good examples can age to a delicious honeyed fullness. In France its chief power-base is in ALSACE, where it is taking over the 'workhorse' role from Sylvaner and Chasselas. Most CREMANT D'ALSACE now uses it as the principal variety. Important in northern Italy as Pinot Bianco, in southern Germany and Austria as Weissburgunder and successful in Hungary, Slovakia, Slovenia and the Czech Republic. Promising new plantings in CALIFORNIA, OREGON and Canada.

**PINOT GRIGIO** See Pinot Gris.

**PINOT GRIS** At its finest in France's ALSACE, where it is often called Tokay-Pinot Gris; with reasonable acidity and a deep colour the grape produces fat, rich wines that mature wonderfully. It is very occasionally used in BURGUNDY to add fatness to a wine. As Pinot Grigio it is grown in northern Italy, where it produces some of the country's most popular yet boring dry whites, but also some of the most exciting. Also successful in Austria and Germany as Ruländer or Grauer Burgunder, and as Malvoisie in the Swiss VALAIS. There are some good Romanian and Czech examples, as well as spirited ones in Hungary (as Szürkebarát). In a crisp style, it is very successful in OREGON and showing some promise in CALIFORNIA and Canada's OKANAGAN VALLEY. Becoming fashionable in New Zealand and beginning to appear in Australia.

**PINOT MEUNIER** The most widely planted grape in the CHAMPAGNE region. A vital ingredient in Champagne, along with Pinot Noir and Chardonnay – though it is the least well known of the 3.

**PINOT NERO** See Pinot Noir.
**PINOT NOIR** See pages 218–19.

# PINOT NOIR

There's this myth about Pinot Noir that I think I'd better lay to rest. It goes something like this. Pinot Noir is an incredibly tricky grape to grow; in fact Pinot Noir is such a difficult customer that the only place that regularly achieves magical results is the thin stretch of land known as the Côte d'Or, between Dijon and Chagny in France, where mesoclimate, soil conditions and 2000 years of experience weave an inimitable web of pleasure.

This just isn't so. The thin-skinned, early-ripening Pinot Noir is undoubtedly more difficult to grow than other great varieties like Cabernet or Chardonnay, but that doesn't mean that it's impossible to grow elsewhere – you just have to work at it with more sensitivity and seek out the right growing conditions. And although great red Burgundy is a hauntingly beautiful wine, many Burgundians completely fail to deliver the magic, and the glorious thing about places like New Zealand, California, Oregon, Australia and Germany is that we are seeing an ever increasing number of wines that are thrillingly different from anything produced in Burgundy, yet with flavours that are unique to Pinot Noir.

## WINE STYLES

**France** All France's great Pinot Noir wines do come from Burgundy's Côte d'Or. Rarely deep in colour, they should nonetheless possess a wonderful fruit quality when young – raspberry, strawberry, cherry or plum – that becomes more scented and exotic with age, the plums turning to figs and pine, and the richness of chocolate mingling perilously with truffles and well-hung game. Strange, challenging, hedonistic. France's other Pinots – in north and south Burgundy, the Loire, Jura, Savoie, Alsace and now occasionally in the south of France – are lighter and milder, and in Champagne its pale, thin wine is used to make sparkling wine.

**Other European regions** During the 1990s, helped by good vintages, German winemakers made considerable efforts to produce serious Pinot Noir (generally called Spätburgunder). Italy, where it is called Pinot Nero, and Switzerland (as Blauburgunder) both have fair success with the variety. Austria and Spain have produced a couple of good examples, and Romania, the Czech Republic and Hungary produce significant amounts of generally low quality.

**New World** Light, fragrant wines have bestowed upon Oregon the reputation for being 'another Burgundy'; but I get more excited about the marvellously fruity, erotically scented wines of California's Carneros and Russian River Valley regions, and the original offerings from outposts such as Santa Maria Valley, south of San Francisco. New Zealand is the most important southern hemisphere producer with wines of thrilling fruit and individuality. Australia is beginning to find its way and new Burgundian clones bode well for South African Pinot Noir. Even Chile has a few fine producers.

## BEST PRODUCERS

**France** *Burgundy* (growers) B Ambroise, ANGERVILLE, Comte Armand, Denis Bachelet, G Barthod, J-M Boillot, CHANDON DE BRIAILLES, R Chevillon, J-J Confuron, Dugat-Py, DUJAC, Engel, Anne Gros, GRIVOT, Hudelot-Noëllat, LAFARGE, LAFON, Dom. LEROY, H Lignier, MEO-CAMUZET, Montille, Denis Mortet, J-F Mugnier, Ponsot, RION, Dom. de la ROMANEE-CONTI, E Rouget, ROUMIER, ROUSSEAU, TOLLOT-BEAUT, VOGUE; (merchants) DROUHIN, FAIVELEY, JADOT, V GIRARDIN, LABOURE-ROI, D Laurent, RODET.

**Germany** FURST, JOHNER, Meyer-Näkel, MULLER-CATOIR, REBHOLZ.

**Italy** CA' DEL BOSCO, Hoffstätter, Marchesi Pancrazi, Castello della SALA.

**New World Pinot Noirs**
*USA* (California) ACACIA, AU BON CLIMAT, CALERA, CHALONE, DEHLINGER, Etude, Gary Farrell, FLOWERS, Hurtford Court, KISTLER, Landmark, Lane Tanner, Littorai, J ROCHIOLI VINEYARDS, SAINTSBURY, SANFORD, Talley, WILLIAMS SELYEM; (Oregon) Archery Summit, BEAUX FRERES, Bethel Heights, Cristom, DOMAINE DROUHIN, PANTHER CREEK, Rex Hill, Torii Mor, WillaKenzie, Ken Wright.

*Australia* BANNOCKBURN, Bass Phillip, COLDSTREAM HILLS, Diamond Valley, Freycinet, Giaconda, LENSWOOD VINEYARDS, Paringa Estate, YARRA YERING.

*New Zealand* ATA RANGI, DRY RIVER, FELTON ROAD, ISABEL, MARTINBOROUGH VINEYARD, NEUDORF, Rippon, Wither Hills.

*South Africa* BOUCHARD FINLAYSON, HAMILTON RUSSELL.

*Chile* CARMEN, CONO SUR, GRACIA, VALDIVIESO, VILLARD ESTATE.

219

**PINOTAGE** A Pinot Noir x Cinsaut cross, conceived in South Africa in 1925 but not widely planted until the 1950s. Currently enjoying international popularity, the variety's champion is Beyers Truter of KANONKOP. New-style Pinotage, wooded or unwooded, has plum, banana and marshmallow flavours. There are several examples from New Zealand, a few from CALIFORNIA and Canada, and a little is grown in Brazil and Zimbabwe. Best South African producers: BACKSBERG, Bellingham (Premium★), BEYERSKLOOF★, Clos Malverne, FAIRVIEW★, GRANGEHURST★, Kaapzicht★, KANONKOP★★, L'AVENIR★, Simonsig★, Uiterwyk★, WARWICK★, Wildekrans.

**PIPER-HEIDSIECK** *Champagne AC, Champagne, France* Traditionally one of CHAMPAGNE's least distinguished brands, though the owners, Remy, have made great improvements. The non-vintage★ is gentler and more biscuity than it used to be, and can develop complexity. The de luxe cuvée, Champagne Rare★★, is best. Best years: (1995) **90 89 85 82**.

**PIPERS BROOK VINEYARDS** *Northern Tasmania, Australia* Keenly sought wines combining classy design, highish prices, clever marketing and skilled winemaking by Andrew Pirie. Steely Riesling★★, classically reserved Chardonnay★★, fragrant Gewürztraminer★★ and refreshing Pinot Gris★ are highlights. Purchased the Heemskerk-Rochecombe group in 1998 and in the same year made probably its best wines yet, led by the release of a traditional-method sparkling wine, Pirie★★, that may achieve ★★★ with a little extra age. Best years: (Riesling) **1999 98 97 95 94 92 91 90 84 82**.

**PLAIMONT, L'UNION DES PRODUCTEURS** *Madiran AC, Côtes de St-Mont VDQS and Vin de Pays des Côtes de Gascogne, South-West France* This grouping of 3 Gascon co-ops is the largest, most reliable and most go-ahead producer of COTES DE GASCOGNE and COTES DE ST-MONT. The whites, full of crisp fruit, are reasonably priced and are best drunk young. The reds, especially Ch. St-Go★ and de Sabazan★, are very good too. Also good MADIRAN and PACHERENC DU VIC-BILH.

**PLANETA** *Sicily, Italy* Rapidly expanding, young and dynamic estate. Chardonnay★★ is already one of the best in southern Italy; Cabernet Sauvignon★ and Merlot★ are improving every year. Rich, peppery Santa Cecilia★★ (Nero d'Avola-Syrah) is aiming for international stardom. Basic La Segreta red★ and white★ are marvellously fruity.

**PLANTAGENET** *Great Southern, Western Australia* Influential winery in the region, contract-making wine for smaller outfits and producing its own flavourful range, notably spicy Shiraz★★, limy Riesling★★, melony/nutty Chardonnay★★, plump Pinot Noir★★ and classy Cabernet Sauvignon★★. Best years: 1998 97 **96 95 94 93** 91 **90** 88 86 85.

**POLIZIANO** *Vino Nobile di Montepulciano, Tuscany, Italy* A leading light in Montepulciano. VINO NOBILE★★ is far better than average, especially the Riserva Vigna Asinone★★, while the SUPER-TUSCANS Elegia★★ (Sangiovese but no longer made) and Le Stanze★★★ (now Cabernet Sauvignon-Merlot) are packed with fruit and sweet oak. VIN SANTO★★ is unctuous. Best years: (Vino Nobile) (1999) (98) 97 **96 95 93 90**.

**POL ROGER** *Champagne AC, Champagne, France* Makers of Winston Churchill's favourite CHAMPAGNE and for many years a great favourite of the British market. The non-vintage White Foil★ has sadly lost some personality over the last few years. Pol Roger also produces a vintage★★, a vintage rosé★★, a vintage Grand Cru Chardonnay★★ and a vintage Réserve Spécial★★. Its top Champagne, called Cuvée Sir Winston Churchill★★, is a deliciously refined drink. All vintage wines will improve with another 5 years' keeping or more. **Best years:** (1995) **93 90 89 88 86 85 82**.

**POMEROL AC** *Bordeaux, France* One of the most famous and expensive of the BORDEAUX ACS, Pomerol includes some of the world's most sought-after red wines. The AC's unique quality lies in its deep clay in which the Merlot grape flourishes. The result is seductively rich, almost creamy wine with wonderful mouthfilling fruit flavours. **Best producers:** Beauregard★, Bonalgue, le BON-PASTEUR★★, Certan-de-May★★, Clinet★★, Clos l'Eglise★, CLOS RENE★, la CONSEILLANTE★★, l'EGLISE-CLINET★★★, l'EVANGILE★★, la FLEUR-PETRUS★★, GAZIN★★, LAFLEUR★★★, LATOUR-A-POMEROL★★, Mazeyres, Montviel, PETIT-VILLAGE★★, PETRUS★★★, le PIN★★★, Sales★, TROTANOY★★, VIEUX-CHATEAU-CERTAN★★. **Best years:** (2000) 98 96 95 94 **90 89 88 86 85 83 82**.

**POMINO DOC** *Tuscany, Italy* Small zone, east of Florence in the hills above CHIANTI RUFINA, noted for its historical use of French varieties in both red (Merlot and Cabernet blended with Sangiovese) and white (where, unusually, Trebbiano plays a supporting role to Pinot Bianco and Chardonnay). FRESCOBALDI's Pomino Il Benefizio★ (a barrique-fermented Chardonnay) was a trendsetting Tuscan white. **Best producers:** FRESCOBALDI★, SELVAPIANA (Petrognano★). **Best years:** (reds) (1999) 98 97 96 **95 93 90 88**.

**POMMARD AC** *Côte de Beaune, Burgundy, France* The first village south of Beaune. At their best, the wines should have full, round, beefy flavours. Can age well, often for 10 years or more. There are no Grands Crus but les Rugiens Bas, les Épenots and les Arvelets (all Premiers Crus) occupy the best sites. **Best producers:** Comte Armand★★★, J-M Boillot★★, Courcel★★★, Dancer★, P Garaudet★, M Gaunoux★, V GIRARDIN★★★, LAFARGE★★, D Laurent★★, Lejeune★, Montille★★, A Mussy★, J & A Parent★, Ch. de Pommard★, Pothier-Rieusset★, Pousse d'Or★. **Best years:** 1999 98 97 96 95 **93 92 90 89 88**.

**POMMERY** *Champagne AC, Champagne, France* Warmly regarded house owned by LVMH and performing well under the innovative leadership of winemaker Prince Alain de Polignac, a descendant of the celebrated Madame Pommery. Restrained non-vintage Brut Royal★ is often surpassed by another non-vintage, Apanage★, but 'Summertime' blanc de blancs and 'Wintertime' blanc de noirs seem superfluous additions to the range. Austere vintage Brut★★ is delicious, and the prestige Cuvée Louise, both white★★ and rosé★★, is the epitome of discreet elegance. **Best years:** (1995) **92 91 90 89 88 85 82 81 80 76 75**.

**CH. PONTET-CANET★★** *Pauillac AC, 5ème Cru Classé, Haut-Médoc, Bordeaux, France* The vineyards of this property are located close to those of MOUTON-ROTHSCHILD. The wines used to be rather lean and uninteresting but since 1979, when the Tesserons of LAFON-ROCHET bought the property, there has been a gradual return to form – big, chewy, intense claret which develops a beautiful blackcurrant fruit. Now one of the best-value of the Classed Growths. **Best years:** (2000) 99 98 97 96 95 **94 90 89 86 85 83 82**.

**PONZI** *Willamette Valley AVA, Oregon, USA* OREGON pioneer that has recently taken on a new lease of life. The latest Chardonnay is good and Pinot Noir★ original and attractive. Decent Pinot Gris and delicious sweet Vino Gelato★★. Best years: (reds) (1999) 98 **97 94**.

**PORT** See pages 224–5.

**CH. POTENSAC★★** *Médoc AC, Cru Bourgeois, Bordeaux, France* Potensac's fabulous success is based on quality, consistency and value for money. Owned and run by the Delon family, of LEOVILLE-LAS-CASES, the wine can be drunk at 4–5 years, but fine vintages will improve for at least 10 years. Best years: (2000) 99 98 97 96 95 **94 93 90 89 88 86 85**.

**POUILLY-FUISSÉ AC** *Mâconnais, Burgundy, France* Chardonnay from 5 villages, including Pouilly and Fuissé. For several years high prices and low quality meant this was a wine to avoid, but now it is beginning to find a sensible price level and there are some committed growers producing buttery, creamy wines that can be delicious at 2 years but will often develop beautifully for up to 10. Best producers: Corsin★★, C & T Drouin★, J-A Ferret★★★, M Forest★★, Ch. FUISSE★★★, Guffens-Heynen (VERGET)★★★, R Lassarat★★, Léger-Plumet★, R Luquet★, Robert-Denogent★★, Saumaize-Michelin★★, de la Soufrandise★, Valette★. Best years: (2000) 99 98 **97 96 95 94 93 90**.

**POUILLY-FUMÉ AC** *Loire Valley, France* Fumé means 'smoked' in French and a good Pouilly-Fumé has a pungent smell often likened to gunflint. The only grape allowed is the Sauvignon Blanc, and the extra smokiness comes from a flinty soil called silex. Despite the efforts of a few producers, this is a seriously underperforming and overpriced AC. The word 'fumé' was annexed by Californian producers such as MONDAVI★ to attach to their Sauvignon Blanc wines. Best producers: Berthiers★, Henri Bourgeois★, A Cailbourdin★, J-C Chatelain★, Didier DAGUENEAU★★★, Serge Dagueneau★, M Deschamps★, Ladoucette★, Landrat-Guyollot★, Masson-Blondelet★, R Pabiot, M Redde, G Saget, Tinel-Blondelet★, Ch. de Tracy★. Best years: 2000 99 98 **97 96 95 90**.

**POUILLY-LOCHÉ AC** *Mâconnais, Burgundy, France* Loché is a village to the east of Fuissé which has added the name of Pouilly to its own. The wines are no better than many MACON-VILLAGES – not a patch on POUILLY-FUISSE. Best producer: Cordier★. Best years: (2000) **99 98 97**.

**POUILLY-SUR-LOIRE AC** *Loire Valley, France* Light appley wines from the Chasselas grape from vineyards around Pouilly-sur-Loire, the town which gave its name to POUILLY-FUME. Drink as young as possible.

**POUILLY-VINZELLES AC** *Mâconnais, Burgundy, France* Like POUILLY-LOCHE, the village of Vinzelles adds the name of Pouilly to its own. Best producer: Valette★. Best years: (2000) **99 98 97**.

**CH. POUJEAUX★★** *Moulis AC, Cru Bourgeois, Haut-Médoc, Bordeaux, France* Poujeaux is one reason why MOULIS AC is attracting attention: the wines have a delicious chunky fruit and new-oak sweetness. Attractive at 6–7 years old, good vintages can easily last for 20–30 years. Best years: (2000) 99 98 97 96 95 **94 93 90 89 88 86 85 83 82**.

**PRAGER** *Wachau, Niederösterreich, Austria* One of the pioneers of the region, who produced the first Riesling Trockenbeerenauslese★★★ in the WACHAU in 1993. Also top dry Rieslings from the Achleiten and Klaus vineyards★★★ and excellent Grüner Veltliners from the Achleiten vineyard★★. Best years: (2000) 99 98 97 **96 95 93 92 90 86**.

**PREMIÈRES CÔTES DE BLAYE AC** *Bordeaux, France*   An improving AC on the right bank of the Gironde. The fresh, Merlot-based reds are ready at 2–3 years but will age for more. The whites are usually sold under the COTES DE BLAYE AC. Best producers: Bel-Air la Royère★, Haut-Bertinerie★, Haut-Grelot, Haut-Sociando, Jonqueyres★, Loumède, Mondésir-Gazin★, Rolande-la-Garde, Segonzac★, Sociondo, Tourtes. Best years: (2000) 98 **96 95 94 90 89 88**.

**PREMIÈRES CÔTES DE BORDEAUX AC** *Bordeaux, France*   Hilly region overlooking GRAVES and SAUTERNES across the Garonne. For a long time the AC was best known for its Sauternes-style sweet wines, particularly from the communes of CADILLAC, LOUPIAC and STE-CROIX-DU-MONT, but the juicy reds and rosés have now forged ahead. These are usually delicious at 2–3 years old but should last for 5–6 years. Dry whites are designated BORDEAUX AC. Best producers: (reds) Brethous★, CARSIN★, Chelivette, Clos Ste-Anne, Grand-Mouëys★, Haux★, Jonchet, Juge (Dupleich), Lamothe-de-Haux★, Langoiran, Melin, Puy-Bardens★, Reynon★, le Sens, Suau, Tanesse. Best years: (reds) (2000) **98 96 95 94 90**.

**CH. PRIEURÉ-LICHINE★** *Margaux AC, 4ème Cru Classé, Haut-Médoc, Bordeaux, France*   Once owned by Alexis Lichine, possibly the greatest promoter of high-quality French wines this century, but sold by his son Sacha in 1999. The wine has a gentle, perfumed style, though it does not lack tannin and keeps well for 10–15 years. Best years: (2000) 99 98 96 95 **94 90 89 88 86 85 83 82**.

**PRIMITIVO DI MANDURIA DOC** *Puglia, Italy*   The most important appellation for PUGLIA's Primitivo grape, which has been enjoying a renaissance of interest since it was found to be identical to California's Zinfandel. The best wines combine outstanding ripeness and concentration with a knockout alcohol level. Best producers: Felline★★, PERVINI★★, Giovanni Soloperto. Best years: (2000) 99 98 **97 96**.

**PRIMO ESTATE** *Adelaide Plains, South Australia*   Innovative Joe Grilli stuck his winery in one of Australia's hottest climates but works miracles with his own grapes and those from outlying areas. The premium label is Joseph: Grilli adapts the Italian *amarone* method for Moda Amarone Cabernet-Merlot★★ (★★★ with 10 years age!), makes a fantastic, dense but eye-popping Joseph fizz★★ and uses a novel pruning technique to achieve 'cooler' flavours in Double Pruned Cabernet★. He also does a sensuous Botrytis Riesling★★, fabulous honeyed fortified Fronti★★★, surprising dry white Colombard★ – and superb olive oil★★★. Best years: (Cabernet-Merlot Joseph) 1998 97 **96 95 93 92 90**.

**PRIORAT DO** *Cataluña, Spain*   A hilly, isolated district with very low-yielding vineyards planted on precipitous slopes of deep slate soil. Old-style fortified *rancio* wines used to attract little attention. Then in the 1980s a group of young winemakers revolutionized the area, bringing in state-of-the-art winemaking methods and grape varieties such as Cabernet Sauvignon and Merlot to back up the native Garnacha and Cariñena. Their rare, expensive wines have taken the world by storm. Ready at 5 years old; the best will last much longer. Best producers: Cims de Porrera★★, CLOS MOGADOR★★★, Clos i Terrasses★★★ (Clos Erasmus), Costers del Siurana★★, Josep Maria Fuentes★★, Mas Martinet★★, Alvaro PALACIOS★★★, Pasanau Germans (Finca la Planeta★★), Rotllan Torra★★, Scala Dei★, Vall-Llach★★. Best years: (reds) (1998) **96 95 94 93 92 90**.

# PORT DOC

*Douro, Portugal*

The Douro region in northern Portugal, where the grapes for port are grown, is wild and beautiful. Steep hills covered in vineyard terraces plunge dramatically down to the Douro river. Grapes are one of the only crops that will grow in the inhospitable climate, which gets progressively drier the further inland you travel. But not all the Douro's grapes qualify to be made into increasingly good port. A quota is established every year, and the rest are made into table wines.

Port grapes (including Touriga Francesa, Tinta Roriz, Touriga Nacional, Tinta Barroca, Tinta Cão and Tinta Amarela) are partially fermented, and then *aguardente* (grape spirit) is added – fortifying the wine, stopping the fermentation and leaving sweet, unfermented grape sugar in the finished port.

## PORT STYLES

**Vintage** Finest of the ports matured in bottle, made from grapes from the best vineyards. Vintage port is not 'declared' every year, but during the second year in cask, if the shipper thinks the standard is high enough. It is bottled after 2 years, and may be consumed not long afterwards, not uncommon in the USA; at this stage it packs quite a punch. The British custom of aging for 20 years or more can yield exceptional mellowness.

**Single quinta** A true single-quinta wine comes from an individual estate; however, many shippers sell their vintage port under a quinta name in years which are not declared as a vintage. It is quite possible for these 'off vintage' ports to equal or even surpass the vintage wines from the same house.

**Tawny** Matured in cask for 10, 20 or 30 years before bottling and sale, older tawnies have delicious nut and fig flavours. Cheap tawny is a blend of ruby and white port and is both dilute and raw.

**Colheita** Tawny from a single vintage, matured in cask for at least 7 years – potentially the finest of the aged tawnies.

**Late Bottled Vintage (LBV)/Late Bottled** Port matured for 4–6 years in cask then usually filtered to avoid sediment forming in the bottle. Traditional unfiltered examples have much more flavour and, if released young, can often be aged for another 5 years or more.

**Crusted** Rarely seen today, this is a blend of good ports from 2–3 vintages, bottled without filtration after 3–4 years in cask. A deposit (crust) forms in the bottle and the wine should be decanted.

**Ruby** The youngest red port. Ruby port should be bursting with young, almost peppery fruit but rarely achieves this level of quality.

**Vintage Character** or Premium Ruby has an average of 3–5 years' age. A handful represent good value.

**White** Only the best taste dry and nutty from wood-aging; most are coarse and alcoholic, best drunk chilled with tonic water.

### BEST YEARS

1997 94 92 91 **85 83 80 77 70 66 63 60 55 48 47 45 35 34 27 12 08 04 1900**

### BEST PRODUCERS

**Vintage** BURMESTER, Cálem, CHURCHILL, COCKBURN, CRASTO, CROFT, Delaforce, DOW, FERREIRA, FONSECA, Gould Campbell, GRAHAM, Quarles Harris, Infantado, Martinez, NIEPOORT, NOVAL (including Nacional), Offley, Osborne, RAMOS PINTO, ROSA, SMITH WOODHOUSE, TAYLOR, Vale Dona Maria, VESUVIO, WARRE.

**Single quinta** BURMESTER (Quinta Nova de Nossa Senhora do Carmo), CHURCHILL (Agua Alta), COCKBURN (Quinta dos Canais), CROFT (Quinta da Roêda), Delaforce (Quinta da Corte), DOW (Quinta do Bomfim, Senhora da Ribeira), FONSECA (Guimaraens, Quinta do Panascal), GRAHAM (Malvedos), Martinez (Quinta da Eira Velha), NIEPOORT (Quinta do Passadouro), NOVAL (Silval), SMITH WOODHOUSE (Madalena), TAYLOR (Quinta de Vargellas), WARRE (Quinta da Cavadinha).

**Aged tawny** Barros, BURMESTER, Cálem, COCKBURN, DOW, FERREIRA, FONSECA, GRAHAM, Krohn, NIEPOORT, NOVAL, RAMOS PINTO, ROSA, SANDEMAN, TAYLOR, WARRE.

**Colheita** Barros, Feist, Krohn, NIEPOORT, NOVAL.

**Traditional Late Bottled Vintage** CHURCHILL, CRASTO, NIEPOORT, NOVAL, RAMOS PINTO, ROSA, SMITH WOODHOUSE, Vale da Mina, WARRE.

**White** CHURCHILL, NIEPOORT.

225

**PROSECCO DI CONEGLIANO-VALDOBBIADENE DOC** *Veneto, Italy* The Prosecco grape gives soft, scented wine made sparkling by a second fermentation in tank, though Prosecco can also be still, or *tranquillo*. Generally, however, it is a *spumante* or *frizzante* for drinking young. Cartizze, from a vineyard area of that name, is the most refined. Best producers: Adami★, Bernardi★, Bisol★, Carpenè Malvolti★, Le Colture, Col Vetoraz★, Nino Franco★, Ruggeri & C★, Tanorè★, Zardetto★.

**PROVENCE** *France* Provence is home to France's oldest vineyards but the region is better known for its nudist beaches and arts festivals than for its wines. However, it seems even Provence is caught up in the revolution sweeping through the vineyards of southern France. The area has 5 small, high-quality ACs (BANDOL, les BAUX-DE-PROVENCE, BELLET, CASSIS and PALETTE), but most of the wine comes from the much larger areas of the COTES DE PROVENCE, COTEAUX VAROIS, Coteaux de Pierrevert and COTEAUX D'AIX-EN-PROVENCE. Provençal reds and rosés are generally better than whites.

**J J PRÜM** *Bernkastel, Mosel, Germany* Estate making some of Germany's best Riesling in sites like the Sonnenuhr★★★ in WEHLEN, Himmelreich★★ in GRAACH and Lay★★ and Badstube★★ in BERNKASTEL. All have great aging potential. Best years: (1999) 98 97 96 95 **94 93 91 90 89** 88 86 85 83 79 76 75 71.

**S A PRÜM** *Wehlen, Mosel, Germany* There are a confusing number of Prüms in the MOSEL – the best known is J J PRÜM, but Raimund Prüm of S A Prüm comes a decent second. The estate's most interesting wines are Riesling from Wehlener Sonnenuhr, especially Auslese★★, but it also makes good wine from sites in BERNKASTEL★, GRAACH★ and Zeltingen★. Best years: 1999 **97 95 93 90 88 86 85**.

**PRUNOTTO** *Barolo DOCG, Piedmont, Italy* One of the great BAROLO producers, whose winemaker Giuseppe Colla pioneered the concept of single-vineyard wines in the region; bought by ANTINORI in 1989. Highlights include BARBERA D'ALBA Pian Romualdo★★, BARBERA D'ASTI Costamiòle★★, NEBBIOLO D'ALBA Occhetti★, Barolo Bussia★★★ and Cannubi★★ and new BARBARESCO Briz Turot★★. Also produces good MOSCATO D'ASTI★, BARBERA D'ASTI Fiulot★ and ROERO Arneis★. Best years: (Barolo) (1998) (97) 96 95 **94 93 90 89 88 86 85 82**.

**PUGLIA** *Italy* This southern region is a prolific source of blending wines, but exciting progress has been made with native varieties: Uva di Troia in CASTEL DEL MONTE; Negroamaro in SALICE SALENTINO and other reds and rosés of the Salento peninsula; white Greco for characterful Gravina, revived by Botromagno; and Verdeca and Bianco d'Alessano for LOCOROTONDO and Martina Franca. But it is the red Primitivo (CALIFORNIA's Zinfandel), led by examples from the likes of PERVINI and Felline, that is set to make the biggest impact, whether under the PRIMITIVO DI MANDURIA DOC or more general IGTs.

**PUISSEGUIN-ST-ÉMILION AC** *Bordeaux, France* Small ST-EMILION satellite AC. The wines are usually fairly solid but with an attractive chunky fruit and usually make good drinking at 3–5 years. Best producers: Bel-Air, Branda, Durand-Laplagne★, Fongaban, Guibeau, Laurets, Producteurs Réunis, Soleil. Best years: (2000) **98 96 95 94 90 89 88**.

**PULIGNY-MONTRACHET AC** *Côte de Beaune, Burgundy, France*  Puligny is one of the finest white wine villages in the world and adds the name of its greatest Grand Cru, le MONTRACHET, to its own. There are 3 other Grands Crus (BATARD-MONTRACHET, Bienvenues-BATARD-MONTRACHET and Chevalier-MONTRACHET) and 11 Premiers Crus. The flatter vineyards use the Puligny-Montrachet AC. Good vintages really need 5 years' aging, while Premiers Crus and Grands Crus may need 10 years and can last for 20 or more. Only about 3% of the AC is red wine. Best producers: J-M Boillot★★, CARILLON★★★, J Chartron★, G Chavy★★, DROUHIN★★, A Ente★★, JADOT★★, LABOURE-ROI★, Larue★★, LATOUR★, Dom. LEFLAIVE★★★, O LEFLAIVE★, P Pernot★★, Ch. de Puligny-Montrachet★, RAMONET★★, RODET★, SAUZET★★, G Thomas★. Best years: (2000) 99 **97** 96 **95 92**.

**PYRENEES** *Victoria, Australia*  Robust, often eucalyptus-scented reds from Shiraz and Cabernet Sauvignon are the trademark of this hilly central VICTORIA district, but ripe Sauvignon Blanc and Chardonnay can also impress. Champagne-method fizz from TALTARNI and French-owned Blue Pyrenees offer good quality. Best producers: Blue Pyrenees, Dalwhinnie★★, Redbank★, Summerfield★, TALTARNI★, Warrenmang.

**QUARTS DE CHAUME AC** *Grand Cru, Loire Valley, France*  The Chenin grape finds one of its most rewarding mesoclimates here. Quarts de Chaume is a 40-ha (100-acre) Cru within the larger COTEAUX DU LAYON AC and, as autumn mists begin to curl off the river Layon, noble rot attacks the grapes. The result is intense, sweet wines which can last for longer than almost any in the world – although many can be drunk after 5 years. Best producers: des Baumard★★★, Bellerive★★, Laffourcade★, Pierre-Bise★★, J Pithon★★★, Poirel★★, Joseph Renou★★. Best years: (2000) 99 **97 96 95 94 93 90** 89 88 85 83 81 78 76 70 69 64 59 47.

**QUEENSLAND** *Australia*  Queensland has the smallest production of all Australia's wine-producing states. About 30 wineries perch on rocky hills in the main region, the Granite Belt, near the NEW SOUTH WALES border. New region Burnett, north-west of Brisbane, is showing some promise. Best producers: Bald Mountain, Kominos, Robinson's, Stone Ridge.

**QUERCIABELLA** *Chianti Classico DOCG, Tuscany, Italy*  This model of a modern CHIANTI producer serves up a gorgeously scented, rich-fruited Chianti Classico★★. But it has made an even greater splash with its two SUPER-TUSCANS: BURGUNDY-like white Batàr★★ from Pinot Bianco and Chardonnay, and tobaccoey, spicy Sangiovese-Cabernet blend Camartina★★★. Best years: (Camartina) 1997 96 95 **94 93 91 90 88**.

**QUILCEDA CREEK VINTNERS** *Washington State, USA*  This tiny winery has built a cult following in Washington because of a big, rich Cabernet Sauvignon★★★. The wine can be a bit overpowering, but it does open up to stunning effect after a while in the glass and it has good aging potential. Since 1997 a less expensive Columbia Valley Red★★ has been produced from a blend of Cabernets Sauvignon and Franc and Merlot. Best years: (Cabernet) (1999) 98 97 96 95 **94 92**.

**QUINCY AC** *Loire Valley, France*  Intensely flavoured, dry white wine from Sauvignon Blanc vineyards west of Bourges. Can age for a year or two but always keeps a rather aggressive gooseberry flavour. Best producers: D Jaumier, Mardon★, J Rouzé. Best years: 2000 **99 97 96**.

**QUINTARELLI** *Valpolicella DOC, Veneto, Italy* Giuseppe Quintarelli is the great traditional winemaker of VALPOLICELLA. His philosophy is one of vinifying only the very best grapes and leaving nature to do the rest. His Classico Superiore★★ is left in cask for about 4 years and his famed AMARONE★★★ and RECIOTO★★ for 7 years or more before release. There is also Alzero★★, a spectacular Amarone-style wine from both Cabernets. Best years: (Amarone) **1993** 91 **90** 88 86 85 83.

**QUIVIRA** *Dry Creek Valley AVA, California, USA* Among the best of the new-wave Zinfandel★★ producers; established the trend for bright, fruity early-drinking wine under former winemaker Doug NALLE. The wines are immediately delicious and have the balance to age well. The Dry Creek Cuvée★ (Grenache, Mourvèdre, Syrah and Zinfandel) is dangerously delightful. Lively Sauvignon Blanc★ is another crowd-pleaser. Best years: (Zinfandel) (1999) 98 97 96 **95 94 91** 90.

**QUPÉ** *Santa Maria Valley AVA, California, USA* Owner/winemaker Bob Lindquist makes a gorgeously tasty Bien Nacido Reserve Syrah★★★. His Reserve Chardonnay★★ and Bien Nacido Cuvée★★ (two-thirds Chardonnay, one-third Viognier) have sublime appley fruit and perfume. A leading exponent of RHONE-style wines, he also makes Viognier, Mourvèdre, Roussanne and Marsanne. Best years: (Reserve Syrah) 1998 97 **96 95 94 92 91 90**.

**RAÏMAT** *Costers del Segre DO, Cataluña, Spain* Owned by CODORNIU, this large, irrigated estate can make good fruity wines such as Tempranillo★, Cabernet Sauvignon★ (Mas Castell vineyard★★) and Chardonnay. Best years: (reds) 1998 **97 96 95 94 92 91** 90.

**RAMONET** *Chassagne-Montrachet, Côte de Beaune, Burgundy, France* The Ramonets (father and sons) produce some of the most complex of all white Burgundies from 3 Grands Crus (BATARD-MONTRACHET★★★, Bienvenues-BATARD-MONTRACHET★★★ and le MONTRACHET★★★) and Premiers Crus including Ruchottes★★★, Caillerets★★★, Boudriotte★★, Vergers★★, Morgeot★★ and Chaumées★★★. If you want to spare your wallet try the ST-AUBIN★★ or the CHASSAGNE-MONTRACHET white★★ or red★★. Best years: (whites) (2000) 99 98 97 96 95 **93 92 90** 89 86 85.

**JOÃO PORTUGAL RAMOS** *Alentejo, Portugal* João Portugal Ramos has the potential to become Portugal's foremost winemaker. At least a dozen producers draw on his expertise as a consultant, but he is now making his mark with his own winery and vineyards. Smoky, peppery Trincadeira★★, spicy Aragonês★★ and intensely dark-fruited Vila Santa★★ (a blend of the previous two wines topped up with Cabernet Sauvignon and Alicante Bouschet) are all superb. Marquês de Borba★ is the label for everyday red and white wines though a small amount of a brilliant red Reserva★★★ is also made. João Ramos has also taken charge of the potentially outstanding Pegos Claros★★ from the neighbouring TERRAS DO SADO region. Best years: 1999 **97**.

**RAMOS PINTO** *Douro DOC and Port DOC, Douro, Portugal* Innovative port company now controlled by ROEDERER, making complex, full-bodied Late Bottled Vintage★ and aged tawny (Quinta do Bom Retiro★). The 1994 Vintage★★ and Quinta da Ervamoira★★ are of a different order to older vintage efforts. Table wines Duas Quintas (Reserva★) and Bon Ares★ (Reserva★★) are improving rapidly. Best years: (Vintage) 1997 95 94 **83**; (table wines) (1999) 97 **95 94 92 91**.

**RAMPOLLA, CASTELLO DEI** *Chianti Classico DOCG, Tuscany, Italy* One of the outstanding CHIANTI CLASSICO★★ estates. Sammarco, sometimes ★★★, is mostly Cabernet with some Sangiovese, while the new Vigna d'Alceo★★★ adds Petit Verdot to Cabernet Sauvignon. Best years: (Sammarco) (1998) 97 96 95 **94 90 88 86 85**.

**RANDERSACKER** *Franken, Germany* Important wine village in FRANKEN, producing excellent medium-bodied dry Rieslings, dry Silvaners, spicy Traminer and piercingly intense Rieslaner. Best producers: JULIUSSPITAL★, Robert Schmitt★, Schmitt's Kinder★. Best years: (1999) 98 **97 94 93 92 90**.

**RAPEL, VALLE DEL** *Valle Central, Chile* Proving to be Chile's most exciting red wine region, Rapel is split between Valle de COLCHAGUA to the south, where Merlot, Carmenère and Cabernet Sauvignon are best suited, and Valle del Cachapoal, mostly planted to earlier-ripening Pinot Noir and Chardonnay. Best producers: CONCHA Y TORO, LA ROSA★, Porta.

**KENT RASMUSSEN** *Carneros AVA, California, USA* Tightly structured Burgundy-style Chardonnay★★ capable of considerable aging and a fascinating juicy Pinot Noir★★ are made by ultra-traditional methods. Also occasional delightful oddities like Pinotage, Alicante and Dolcetto under the Ramsay label. Best years: (1999) 98 97 95 **94 92 91 90 88**.

**RASTEAU AC** *Rhône Valley, France* Rasteau is one of the original 16 villages entitled to the COTES DU RHONE-VILLAGES AC. The AC is for a fortified red or white and a *rancio* version which is left in barrel for 2 or more years. Best producers: Beaurenard★, Cave des Vignerons, Rabasse-Charavin, la Soumade★, du Trapadis★.

**RENATO RATTI** *Barolo DOCG, Piedmont, Italy* The late Renato Ratti led the revolution in winemaking in the Alba area with BAROLO and BARBARESCO of better balance, colour and richness and softer in tannins than the traditional models. Today his son Pietro and nephew Massimo Martinelli produce exemplary modern Barolo★★ from the Marcenasco vineyards at La Morra, as well as fine BARBERA D'ALBA★, Dolcetto d'Alba★ and NEBBIOLO D'ALBA★, from choice vineyards in the zone. Villa Pattono★ is a blend of Barbera and Freisa from Monferrato.

**RAUENTHAL** *Rheingau, Germany* Sadly, only a few producers live up to the reputation earned by this RHEINGAU wine village's great Baiken and Gehrn sites, for intense, spicy Rieslings. Best producers: J B Becker★, Georg BREUER★★, August Eser. Best years: 1999 98 **97 96 94 93 90**.

**CH. RAUZAN-SÉGLA★★** *Margaux AC, 2ème Cru Classé, Haut-Médoc, Bordeaux, France* A dynamic change of winemaking regime in 1982 brought about a startling change for the better. This has been further improved from 1994 by current owners Chanel. Now the wines have a rich blackcurrant fruit, almost tarry, thick tannins and weight, excellent woody spice and superb concentration. Second wine: Ségla. Best years: (2000) 99 98 97 96 95 **94 90 89 88 86 85 83**.

**JEAN-MARIE RAVENEAU** *Chablis AC, Burgundy, France* One of the outstanding growers in CHABLIS, producing beautifully nuanced wines from 3 Grands Crus (Blanchot★★★, les Clos★★★ and Valmur★★★)

229

and 4 Premiers Crus (Montée de Tonnerre★★★, Vaillons★★, Butteaux★★★ and Chapelot★★), using a combination of oak and stainless-steel fermentation. The wines can easily age for a decade or more. Best years: (top crus) (1999) 98 97 96 **95 92 90** 89.

**RAVENSWOOD** *Sonoma Valley AVA, California, USA* Joel Peterson, one of California's leading Zin masters, established Ravenswood in 1976. During the lean years, when most Zinfandel was pink and sweet, he added an intense Chardonnay, a sometimes very good Cabernet Sauvignon★ and a tasty Merlot. But Zinfandel remains the trump card. Peterson makes several, varying the menu from year to year: the Dickerson Vineyard★★, Old Hill★★ and Old Vines★★★ are super Zins, with ripe, concentrated fruit – bold and beautiful wines. Most should be drunk at 5–15 years. Best years: (1999) 98 97 96 **95 94 92 91 90**.

**CH. RAYAS** *Châteauneuf-du-Pape, Rhône Valley, France* The most famous estate in CHATEAUNEUF-DU-PAPE. Pierre Reynaud, nephew of the eccentric Jacques Reynaud, is running this estate in his uncle's inimitable rule-breaking style, producing big, alcoholic, exotically rich reds★★★ and whites★★ which also age well. However, prices are not cheap and the wines are not consistent, but at its best Rayas is worth the money. The red is made entirely from low-yielding Grenache vines – the only such wine in the AC – while the white is a blend of Clairette, Grenache Blanc and (so rumour has it) Chardonnay. Second label Pignan is also impressive. COTES DU RHONE Ch. de Fonsalette★★ is wonderful. Best years: (Châteauneuf-du-Pape) (1999) 98 96 95 94 **93 91** 90 **89 88 86**; (whites) (1998) 97 96 95 94 **93 91 90 89 86**.

**REBHOLZ** *Siebeldingen, Pfalz, Germany* This estate in the southern PFALZ produces good Riesling★, Weissburgunder★ and Grauburgunder★, all crystalline in their clarity with vibrant fruit aromas. Top of the range are intensely mineraly dry Riesling★★ from the Kastanienbusch vineyard, powerful dry Gewürztraminer★★ and extravagantly aromatic, crisp, dry Muskateller★★. Also produces Germany's finest barrel-fermented Chardonnay★★ and most serious Spätburgunder★★ (Pinot Noir) reds. Best years: (whites) 1999 98 **97 96** 95 94 93 92 90 89; (reds) (1999) 98 97 96 **94** 93.

**RECIOTO DELLA VALPOLICELLA DOC** *Veneto, Italy* The great sweet wine of VALPOLICELLA, made from grapes picked earlier than usual and left to dry on straw mats until the end of January. The wines are deep in colour, with a rich, bitter-sweet cherryish fruit. They age well for 5–8 years, but most are best drunk young. As with Valpolicella, the Classico tag is all important. Best producers: Accordini★, ALLEGRINI★★, Bolla (Spumante)★★, Tommaso Bussola★★, Corteforte★, DAL FORNO★★, Degani★, Aleardo Ferrari★, MASI★, Giacomo Montresor★, QUINTARELLI★★, Le Ragose★, Le Salette★, Serègo Alighieri★★, Speri★, Tedeschi★, Tommasi★, Villa Bellini★, Villa Monteleone★★, Villa Spinosa★, Viviani★, Fratelli Zeni★. Best years: (1999) 98 **97 95 93 90 88 85**.

**RECIOTO DI SOAVE DOCG** *Veneto, Italy* Sweet white wine made in the SOAVE zone from dried grapes, like RECIOTO DELLA VALPOLICELLA. Garganega grapes give wonderfully delicate yet intense wines that age well for up to a decade. Two outstanding examples are ANSELMI's Recioto I Capitelli★★★ and PIEROPAN's Le Colombare★★. Best producers: ANSELMI★★★, La Cappuccina★★, Cantina del Castello, Cà

Rugate★, Coffele★, Gini★, PIEROPAN★★, Bruno Sartori★, Soave co-op, Suavia, Tamellini★★. Best years: (2000) (99) **98 97 95 93 90 88**.

**DOM. DE LA RECTORIE** *Banyuls AC and Collioure AC, Roussillon, France* Marc and Thierry Parcé are distant relations of Dr A Parcé of Mas Blanc, a famous name in BANYULS. Their COLLIOURE★★ is made for keeping, while the Banyuls Cuvée Léon Parcé★★ can be enjoyed for its youthful fruit or kept for future pleasure. The vin de pays Grenache Gris, Cuvée l'Argile★, is one of the best whites in ROUSSILLON. Best years: (reds) 1999 98 97 **96 95 94 93**.

**REGALEALI** *Sicily, Italy* The estate of the Conte Tasca d'Almerita in the highlands of central SICILY makes some of Italy's most admired wines. From native grape varieties come excellent Rosso del Conte★★ (based on Nero d'Avola) and white Nozze d'Oro★ (based on Inzolia), but the range extends to Chardonnay★★ and Cabernet Sauvignon★★ of extraordinary intensity and elegance. Almerita Brut★ (Chardonnay) may well be the finest Italian Champagne-method sparkler south of the Alps. Relatively simple Branco and Rosato are good value.

**RÉGNIÉ AC** *Beaujolais, Burgundy, France* The wines of this BEAUJOLAIS Cru are generally light and attractive but in poor years not up to scratch. Best producers: P Cinquin, Crêt des Bruyères, DUBOEUF★, H & J-P Dubost★, J-M Laforest, Pivon, Rochette★, J Trichard. Best years: (2000) **99 98**.

**REGUENGOS DOC** *Alentejo, Portugal* Promising ALENTEJO DOC with flavoursome reds epitomizing the excitingly juicy flavours of southern Portugal. Best producers: ESPORAO★★, José Maria da FONSECA★, Reguengos de Monsaraz co-op★. Best years: (2000) **99 97 95 94**.

**DOM. LA RÉMÉJEANNE** *Côtes du Rhône AC, Rhône Valley, France* First-class property making a range of strikingly individual wines. CÔTES DU RHÔNE-VILLAGES les Genèvriers★★ has the weight and texture of good CHATEAUNEUF-DU-PAPE, while CÔTES DU RHÔNE Syrah les Eglantiers★★ is superb. Both need at least 3–5 years' aging. Also good Côtes du Rhône les Chèvrefeuilles★ and les Arbousiers (red and white).

**REMELLURI** *Rioja DOC, País Vasco, Spain* Organic RIOJA estate producing wines with far more fruit than usual and good concentration for aging. Best are ★★. Best years: 1996 **95 94 91 89**.

**RETSINA** *Greece* Resinated white (and some rosé) wine common all over Greece – although both production and sales are falling steadily. The best are deliciously oily and piny, while the resin provides a mild cooling effect on the tongue. For this reason, Retsina need not be overchilled. A small amount of modern-style Retsina (Eiai) is emerging. Drink young. Best producers: Achaia-Clauss, Cambas, Kourtakis.

**REUILLY AC** *Loire Valley, France* Extremely dry but attractive Sauvignon from west of SANCERRE. Also some pale Pinot Noir red and Pinot Gris rosé. Best producers: H Beurdin★, G Cordier, C Lafond★, G Malbête, D Martin, J-M Sorbe. Best years: 2000 **99 98 97 96 95**.

**REYNELL** *McLaren Vale, South Australia* Pioneer John Reynell established Chateau Reynella in 1838. Now part of the BRL HARDY empire, wines have been labelled Reynell in Australia since 1997 although the Chateau Reynella name was until recently used for export. Prices have shot up lately, but they're not unreasonable given the quality. Basket Pressed Cabernet★★, Merlot★★ and Shiraz★★ are concentrated, tannic, ageworthy reds from low-yielding vines, some of which were planted in the 1930s. Chardonnay is rich, emphatic and oaky. Best years: (reds) **1998 96 94 92 91 90**.

**RHEINGAU** *Germany* Wine region on a south-facing stretch of the Rhine flanking the city of Wiesbaden. Traditionally considered Germany's most aristocratic wine region, both in terms of the racy, slow-maturing wines and because of the number of noble estate owners. But famous names here are no longer a guarantee of top quality, as a new generation now produces the best wines. See also Eltville, Erbach, Geisenheim, Hochheim, Johannisberg, Kiedrich, Rauenthal, Rüdesheim, Winkel.

**RHEINHESSEN** *Germany* Large wine region to the south and west of Mainz. On the Rheinterrasse between Mainz and Worms are a number of very famous top-quality estates, especially at Nackenheim, NIERSTEIN, OPPENHEIM and Bodenheim. BINGEN, to the north-west, also has a fine vineyard area along the left bank of the Rhine.

**RHÔNE VALLEY** *France* The Rhône starts out as a river in Switzerland, ambling through Lake Geneva before hurtling southwards into France. In the area south of Lyon, between Vienne and Avignon, the valley becomes one of France's great wine regions. In the northern part, where vertigo-inducing slopes overhang the river, there is not much wine produced but the little that is made is of remarkable individuality. The Syrah grape reigns here in COTE-ROTIE and on the great hill of HERMITAGE. ST-JOSEPH, CROZES-HERMITAGE and CORNAS also make excellent reds, while the white Viognier grape yields perfumed, delicate wine at CONDRIEU and at the tiny AC CHATEAU-GRILLET. In the southern part the steep slopes give way to wide plains, where the vines swelter in the hot sun, with hills both in the west and east. Most of these vineyards are either COTES DU RHONE or COTES DU RHONE-VILLAGES, reds, whites and rosés, but there are also specific ACs. The most well known of these are CHATEAUNEUF-DU-PAPE and the luscious, golden dessert wine, MUSCAT DE BEAUMES-DE-VENISE. See also Clairette de Die, Coteaux de l'Ardèche, Coteaux du Tricastin, Côtes du Lubéron, Côtes du Vivarais, Gigondas, Lirac, Rasteau, St-Péray, Tavel, Vacqueyras.

**RÍAS BAIXAS DO** *Galicia, Spain* The best of GALICIA's 5 DOs, Rías Baixas is making increasing quantities of Spain's best whites (apart from a few Chardonnays in the north-east). The magic ingredient is the characterful Albariño grape, making dry, fruity whites with a glorious fragrance and citrus tang. Drink young or with short aging. Best producers: Adegas Galegas★, Agro de Bazán★★, Quinta de Couselo★★, Granxa Fillaboa★, Lagar de Fornelos★ (La RIOJA ALTA), Lusco do Miño★★, Martin Códax★★, Gerardo Méndez Lázaro (Do Ferreiro Cepas Vellas★★), Pazo de Barrantes★ (MARQUES DE MURRIETA), Pazo de Señorans★, Bodegas Salnesur (Condes de Albarei★), Santiago Ruiz★★ (Lan), Terras Gauda★★.

**RIBATEJO** *Portugal* Portugal's second-largest wine region, now with its own DOC, straddles the river Tagus (Tejo). Hotter and drier than ESTREMADURA to the west, prolific vineyards on the fertile soils alongside the river are producing volumes of improving everyday reds and whites. There are several sub-regional DOCs. Best producers: (reds) Almeirim CO-OP, BRIGHT

BROTHERS, Casa Cadaval, Quinta do Casal Branco (Falcoaria★), D F J VINHOS, Falua, Quinta Grande, Horta da Nazaré★, Quinta da Lagoalva★.

**RIBERA DEL DUERO DO** *Castilla y León, Spain* The dark elegant reds in this DO, from Tinto Fino (Tempranillo), sometimes with Cabernet Sauvignon and Merlot, are nowadays generally more exciting than those of RIOJA. But excessive expansion of vineyards and increase in yields may threaten its supremacy. Also a few light rosés. Best producers: Alión★★, ARROYO★★, Arzuaga★, Balbás★, Hijos de Antonio Barceló★, Briego★★, Felix Callejo★, Hermanos Cuadrado García★★, Dehesa de los Canónigos★, Del Campo★, Fuentespina★, Hacienda Monasterio★, Emilio Moro★, Pago de Carraovejas★, PEDROSA★, PESQUERA★★★, PINGUS★★★, Protos★, Teófilo Reyes★★, Rodero★, Telmo Rodriguez★★, Hermanos Sastre★★★, Tarsus★★, Valderiz★★, Valduero★, Valtravieso★, VEGA SICILIA★★★, Viñedos y Bodegas★, Winner Wines★. Best years: 1999 96 **95 94 91 90 89 86 85 82**.

**BARONE RICASOLI** *Chianti Classico DOCG, Tuscany, Italy* The estate where modern CHIANTI was perfected by Baron Bettino Ricasoli in the mid-19th century has recovered its lost form. 1993 saw the start of the renaissance under the guidance of Francesco Ricasoli. The flagship wine is now Castello di Brolio Chianti Classico★★; that labelled simply Brolio is effectively a second selection. Chianti Classico Riserva Guicciarda★ is good value. Casalferro★★, a Sangiovese-Merlot red, looks certain to join the SUPER-TUSCAN élite. Best years: (Casalferro) (1998) 97 **96 95 94 93**.

**DOMAINE RICHEAUME** *Côtes de Provence AC, Provence, France* German-owned property, run on organic principles and producing impressively deep-coloured wines★ (Colomelle★★) full of smoky spice and power. Best years: (Colomelle) (1999) 98 97 **95**.

**RICHEBOURG AC** *Grand Cru, Côte de Nuits, Burgundy, France* Rich, fleshy wine from the northern end of VOSNE-ROMANEE. Most domaine-bottlings are exceptional. Best producers: GRIVOT★★★, Anne Gros★★★, A-F Gros★★★, Dom. LEROY★★★, MEO-CAMUZET★★★, Mongeard-Mugneret★★★, Dom. de la ROMANEE-CONTI★★★. Best years: (2000) 99 98 97 96 95 93 **91** 90 **89 88 85**.

**RICHOU** *Loire Valley, France* One of the leading domaines in the LOIRE, producing consistently good wines. Best are the ANJOU-VILLAGES Vieilles Vignes★★ and sweet COTEAUX DE L'AUBANCE les Trois Demoiselles★★.

**MAX FERD RICHTER** *Mülheim, Mosel-Saar-Ruwer, Germany* Racy Rieslings from some of the best sites in the MOSEL, including Wehlener Sonnenuhr★★, Brauneberger Juffer★★ and Graacher Domprobst★★. Richter's Mülheimer Helenenkloster vineyard produces a magical Eiswein★★★ virtually every year – although not in 1999. Best years: 1999 98 **97** 96 95 **94 93 90 89 88 83**.

**RIDGE VINEYARDS** *Santa Cruz Mountains AVA, California, USA* Once a Zinfandel-only winery, winemaker Paul Draper moved into Cabernet Sauvignon★★ and Petite Sirah★★ in the late 60s. The Zinfandels★★★, made with grapes from various sources, have great intensity and long life, and the other reds, led by Monte Bello Cabernet★★★, show impressive originality. Good Chardonnay★, too. Best years: (Monte Bello) 1998 97 **95 94 93 92 91 90 89 87 85 84**.

# RIESLING

I'm sad to have to make this bald statement at the start, but I feel I must. If you have tasted wines with names like Laski Riesling, Olasz Riesling, Welschriesling, Gray Riesling, Riesling Italico and the like and found them unappetizing – do not blame the Riesling grape. These wines have filched Riesling's name, but have nothing whatsoever to do with the great grape itself.

Riesling is Germany's finest contribution to the world of wine – and herein lies the second problem. German wines have fallen to such a low level of general esteem through the proliferation of wines like Liebfraumilch that Riesling, even true German Riesling, has been dragged down with it.

So what *is* true Riesling? It is a very ancient German grape, probably the descendant of wild vines growing in the Rhine Valley. It certainly performs best in the cool vineyard regions of Germany's Rhine and Mosel Valleys, but also does well in New Zealand and cool parts of Australia; yet it is widely planted in California, South Africa and Italy, and the warmer parts of Australia also grow it to good effect.

## WINE STYLES

**Germany** These wines are based on a marvellous perfume and an ability to hold on to a piercing acidity, even at high ripeness levels, so long as the ripening period has been warm and gradual rather than broiling and rushed. German Rieslings can be bone dry, through to medium and even lusciously sweet, but if they are dry, they must be made from fully ripe grapes, otherwise the acidity is excessive and the wine's body insufficient.

Young Rieslings often show a delightful floral perfume, sometimes blended with the crispness of green apples, often lime, sometimes even peach, raisin or honey, depending upon the ripeness of the grapes. As the wines age, the lime often intensifies, and a flavour perhaps of slate, perhaps of petrol/kerosene intrudes.
**Other regions** Cooler areas of Australia produce lean, limy flavours, while California generally produces a grapy style which is usually best when sweet. In the valleys of the Danube in Austria, Riesling gives stunning dry wines that combine richness with elegance. The mountain vineyards of northern Italy, and the cool vineyards of the Czech Republic, Slovakia and Switzerland can show a floral sharp style, but the most fragrant wines come from Germany, from France's Alsace, and from New Zealand, with some success from America's Pacific Northwest and New York State, and, increasingly, from the odd cool spot in Australia. South Africa's cooler regions produce delicate drier styles; there are also good late harvest and botrytized Rieslings.

In general Rieslings may be drunk young, but top dry wines can improve for many years, and the truly sweet German styles can age for generations.

## BEST PRODUCERS

### Dry Rieslings
*Austria* BRUNDLMAYER, HIRTZBERGER, J Högl, KNOLL, Nigl, NIKOLAIHOF, F-X PICHLER, Rudi Pichler, PRAGER, Freie Weingärtner WACHAU.

*France* (Alsace) P BLANCK, A Boxler, DEISS, Dirler, HUGEL, Kientzler, Kreydenweiss, KUENTZ-BAS, A Mann, Muré, Ostertag, SCHOFFIT, TRIMBACH, WEINBACH, ZIND-HUMBRECHT.

*Germany* BASSERMANN-JORDAN, Georg BREUER, BURKLIN-WOLF, GUNDERLOCH, Heymann-Löwenstein, KOEHLER-RUPRECHT, Franz KUNSTLER, J LEITZ, MULLER-CATOIR, ST ANTONY, J L WOLF.

### Non-dry Rieslings
*Germany* DIEL, DONNHOFF, GUNDERLOCH, HAAG, HAART, Heymann-Löwenstein, JOST, KARTHAUSERHOF, C Loewen, von KESSELSTATT, KUNSTLER, Dr LOOSEN, MAXIMIN GRUNHAUS, MULLER-CATOIR, Egon MULLER, J J PRUM, RICHTER, Willi SCHAEFER, WEIL.

*France* (Alsace) Léon Beyer, DEISS, HUGEL, Ostertag, TRIMBACH, WEINBACH, ZIND-HUMBRECHT.

### New World Rieslings
*Australia* Tim ADAMS, Alkoomi, Wolf BLASS, Leo Buring, DELATITE, GROSSET, HENSCHKE, HOWARD PARK, LEEUWIN, MITCHELL, MITCHELTON, ORLANDO, PETALUMA, PIPERS BROOK, PLANTAGENET, Geoff WEAVER, Wilson Vineyard, YALUMBA.

*New Zealand* CLOUDY BAY, DRY RIVER, FELTON ROAD, GIESEN, MILLTON, NEUDORF, PEGASUS BAY, Rippon, VILLA MARIA, Waipara West.

*South Africa* Neethlingshof.

*USA* (Washington) CHATEAU STE MICHELLE (Eroica), KIONA.

**RIDGEVIEW ESTATE** *West Sussex, England* Escapees from the computer industry, Christine and Michael Roberts are proving that England is naturally suited to growing grapes for sparkling wine. They are emulating CHAMPAGNE every step of the way at their South Downs vineyard. Various blends of Chardonnay, Pinot Noir and Pinot Meunier are produced under the Cuvée Merret label, each named after a swanky area of London, such as Bloomsbury★ and Belgravia. Also uses the South Ridge name.

**RIECINE** *Chianti DOCG, Tuscany, Italy* Small estate in Gaiole, made famous by the late John Dunkley, making some of the most exquisite CHIANTI. Yields are low, so there is a great intensity of fruit and a superb definition of spiced cherry flavours. New American owners have retained Irish winemaker Sean O'Callaghan, who continues to fashion still better CHIANTI CLASSICO★★, Riserva★★★ and barrique-aged La Gioia★★★. Best years: (La Gioia) 1997 96 **95 94 93 91 90 88 86 85**.

**RIESLING** See pages 234–5.

**RIESLING ITALICO** Known as Welschriesling in the rest of Europe, and not in any way related to the great Riesling of the Rhine, this grape is widely planted in northern Italy, where it produces decent dry whites. In Austria it makes some of the very best sweet wines, but tends to be rather dull and thin as a dry wine. In Hungary, where is it called Olasz Rizling, it is highly esteemed.

**CH. RIEUSSEC★★★** *Sauternes AC, 1er Cru Classé, Bordeaux, France* Apart from the peerless Ch. d'YQUEM, Rieussec is often the richest, most succulent wine of SAUTERNES. Other estates can now rival it in quality but rarely make such extravagantly rich wines. Vintages in the late 1990s have been excellent. Cellar for at least 10 years. Dry white 'R' is inexplicably dull. Second wine: Clos Labère. Owned since 1984 by LAFITE-ROTHSCHILD. Best years: 1999 98 97 96 95 90 89 **88 86 85 83**.

**RIO GRANDE DO SUL** *Brazil* High rainfall and humidity in this southernmost region of Brazil mean that fungal diseases and ripening can be a problem for winemakers here. The main grape-growing area is the Serra Gaucha, a hilly zone at an altitude of over 700m (over 2200ft). Flying winemaker John Worontschak has made progress with Cabernet Sauvignon and Merlot at Vinicola Aurora, but Chardonnay is still his most drinkable wine.

**RIOJA DOC** *Rioja, Navarra, País Vasco and Castilla y León, Spain* Rioja, in northern Spain, is not all oaky, creamy white wines and elegant, barrel-aged reds, combining oak flavours with wild strawberry and prune fruit. Over half Rioja's red wine is sold young, never having seen the inside of a barrel, and most of the white is fairly anonymous. Wine quality, as could be expected from such a large region with more than 300 producers, is inconsistent. There is far too much mediocre Rioja on the market as large producers and co-ops try to milk Rioja's reputation, and prices for grapes – and wine – have shot up in recent years, despite large harvests in 1995, 96 and 97. Luckily, perhaps, conditions were more difficult in 98, 99 and 2000. A bevy of new producers with great ambitions is changing the regional hierarchy and they, at least, are taking quality seriously. Best producers: (reds)

Allende★★, Altos de Lanzaga★★, Amézola de la Mora, Artadi★★, BARON DE LEY★, BERBERANA★, Beronia, Bodegas Bilbaínas, BRETON★★, CAMPILLO★★, CAMPO VIEJO★, Luis Cañas, CONTINO★, El Coto★, CVNE, DOMECQ★, FAUSTINO MARTINEZ★, Lan (Culmen★), LOPEZ DE HEREDIA★, MARQUES DE CACERES★, MARQUES DE GRINON★, MARQUES DE MURRIETA★, MARQUES DE RISCAL★★, Marqués de Vargas★★, MARTINEZ BUJANDA★★, MONTECILLO★, MUGA★, Navajas, PALACIO★★, REMELLURI★★, Fernando Remírez de Ganuza★★, La RIOJA ALTA★★, RIOJANAS★, Roda★★, Señorío de San Vicente★★, Viña Ijalba; (whites) Artadi★★, Beronia, BRETON★★, CAMPO VIEJO★, CVNE★, LOPEZ DE HEREDIA★, MARQUES DE CACERES★, MARQUES DE MURRIETA★, MARTINEZ BUJANDA★★, MONTECILLO★, La RIOJA ALTA★, RIOJANAS★. Best years: 1996 95 94 **91 89 87 86 85 83 82 81 78**.

**LA RIOJA ALTA** *Rioja DOC, Rioja, Spain* One of the best of the older RIOJA producers, making mainly Reservas and Gran Reservas. Its only Crianza, Viña Alberdi, fulfils the minimum age requirements for a Reserva anyway. There is a little good, lemony-oaky Viña Ardanza Reserva★ white. Red Reservas, Viña Arana★ and Viña Ardanza★★, age splendidly, and Gran Reservas, Reserva 904★★ and Reserva 890★★★ (made only in exceptional years), are among the very best of Rioja wines. Best years: (Gran Reserva 890) **1985 82 81 78**.

**RIOJANAS** *Rioja DOC, Rioja, Spain* Quality winery producing Reservas and Gran Reservas in 2 styles – elegant Viña Albina★ and richer Monte Real★ – plus the new, refined Gran Albina★★. White Monte Real Blanco Crianza★ is one of RIOJA's best. The whites and Reservas can be kept for 5 years after release, Gran Reservas for 10 or more. Best years: (Monte Real Gran Reserva) **1989 87 85 83 82 81**.

**DANIEL RION** *Nuits-St-Georges, Côte de Nuits, Burgundy, France* One of Burgundy's most consistent performers, producing concentrated but slightly austere reds from Pinot Noir. Also white NUITS-ST-GEORGES les Terres Blanches and a small amount of crisp white ALIGOTÉ★. The best wines are the VOSNE-ROMANEE les Beaux Monts★★ and les Chaumes★★, Nuits-St-Georges Clos des Argillières★★ and the village-level VOSNE-ROMANEE★★. Best years: (reds) (2000) 99 98 97 96 **95 93 90 88**.

**RIVERA** *Puglia, Italy* One of southern Italy's most dynamic producers. In the traditional mould, the CASTEL DEL MONTE Riserva Il Falcone★★ is an excellent, full-blooded southern red. There is also a series of varietals sold under the Terre al Monte label, best of which are Aglianico★, Pinot Bianco and Sauvignon Blanc.

**RIVERINA** *New South Wales, Australia* Along with RIVERLAND, this extensive irrigated region, fed by the Murrumbidgee River, provides the bulk of Australia's basic table wines. Many of Australia's best-known brands, from companies like HARDYS, MCWILLIAM'S, ORLANDO and PENFOLDS, though not mentioning either Riverina or Riverland on the label, are based on wines from these areas. There are also some remarkable sweet wines such as the Botrytis Semillon★★★ from DE BORTOLI. Other leading producers are Ballingah Estate, Cranswick Estate, Gramps, Lillypilly, Miranda★, Painter's Cove and Wilton Estate★.

**RIVERLAND** *Australia* A vast irrigated region along the Murray River, straddling 3 states (NEW SOUTH WALES, SOUTH AUSTRALIA and VICTORIA), and producing 27% of the national grape crush. Mainly given over to casks and cheaper bottles of table and fortified wine, though an

237

increasing number of producers are bringing out high-quality special selections. Best producers: Angove's, Deakin Estate, HARDYS (Banrock Station), Kingston Estate, Trentham Estate, YALUMBA (Oxford Landing).

**RIVESALTES AC** *Languedoc-Roussillon, France* *Vin doux naturel* from a large area around the town of Rivesaltes. These fortified wines are some of southern France's best and can be made from an assortment of grapes, mainly white Muscat (when it is called MUSCAT DE RIVESALTES) and Grenache Noir, Gris and Blanc. A *rancio* style ages well. Best producers: Vignerons Catalans, Casenove, CAZES★★, Chênes★, Ch. de Corneilla, Forca Réal★, GAUBY★, Ch. de Jau★, Laporte, Rivesaltes co-op, Sarda-Malet★, Terrats co-op, Trouillas co-op.

**ROBERTSON WO** *South Africa* Hot, dry inland area with lime-rich soils, uncommon in the Cape, that are ideal for wines. Chenin Blanc and Colombard are the major white wine varieties, and Chardonnay performs very well (for both still and sparkling styles). The traditional Muscadel (Muscat Blanc à Petits Grains) yields a benchmark fortified wine. A red revolution is currently under way; Shiraz, Merlot and Cabernet have made an excellent start, producing juicy, gluggable reds. Best producers: Bon Courage, Graham BECK★, De Wetshof, Robertson Winery, Springfield Estate★, Van Loveren, Zandvliet.

**CH. ROC DE CAMBES★★** *Côtes de Bourg AC, Bordeaux, France* François Mitjavile of TERTRE-ROTEBOEUF has applied enthusiasm and diligence to this property since he acquired it in 1988. Full and concentrated, with ripe dark fruit, this wine takes the COTES DE BOURG appellation to new heights. Best years: (2000) 99 98 97 96 **95 94 93 91 90 89**.

**J ROCHIOLI VINEYARDS** *Russian River Valley AVA, California, USA* Meticulous growers still selling grapes, the Rochioli family are equally good at winemaking, offering silky, black cherry Pinot Noir★★ and a richer, dramatic West Block Reserve Pinot★★★. All wines stand out, including a fine Sauvignon Blanc★★ and a range of cult Chardonnays★★. Best years: (Pinot Noir) (1999) 98 **97 95 94 92**.

**ROCKFORD** *Barossa Valley, South Australia* Wonderfully nostalgic wines from the stone winery of Robert 'Rocky' O'Callaghan, a great respecter for the old vines so plentiful in the BAROSSA, who delights in using antique machinery. Masterful Basket Press Shiraz★★, EDEN VALLEY Riesling★, Moppa Springs★ Grenache, Shiraz and Mourvèdre blend and cult sparkling red, Black Shiraz★★★. Best years: (reds) (1998) 97 96 **94 92 91 90 88 87 85**.

**ANTONIN RODET** *Mercurey, Côte Chalonnaise, Burgundy, France* Merchant based in the village of MERCUREY, specializing in COTE CHALONNAISE, but with an excellent range from throughout Burgundy. Rodet owns or co-owns 5 domaines – Ch. de Rully★, Ch. de Chamirey★, Ch. de Mercey★, Dom. de Perdrix★ and Jacques Prieur★★ – which are the source of the best wines. Don't miss the BOURGOGNE Vieilles Vignes★, one of the best inexpensive Chardonnays available. Best years: (reds) 1999 98 **97** 96 95 **93 90**; (whites) (2000) 99 97 96 **95**.

**LOUIS ROEDERER** *Champagne AC, Champagne, France* Renowned firm making some of the best, full-flavoured CHAMPAGNES around. As well as the excellent non-vintage★★ and pale vintage rosé★★ it also makes a big, exciting vintage★★, delicious vintage Blanc de Blancs★★ and the famous Roederer Cristal★★★, a de luxe cuvée which is pretty nearly always magnificent. Both the vintage wines and Cristal can usually be aged for 10 years or more; the non-vintage benefits from a bit of aging, too. Best years: (1995) **93 90 89 88 86 85**.

**ROEDERER ESTATE** *Anderson Valley AVA, California, USA* Californian offshoot of Louis ROEDERER. The Brut★★ (sold in the UK as Quartet) is somewhat austere, a step back from the upfront fruit of many California sparklers, but it will age beautifully if you can wait. The top bottling, or tête de cuvée, L'Ermitage★★★, is a stunning addition to the range of California fizz. Best years: (L'Ermitage) (1996) **94 92 91**.

**ROERO DOC** *Piedmont, Italy* The Roero hills lie across the Tanaro river from the LANGHE hills, home of BAROLO and BARBARESCO. Long noted as a source of Nebbiolo in supple, fruity red wines to drink in 2–5 years, Roero has recently made its mark with the white Arneis grape. The red wine is called simply Roero and the white Roero Arneis. Best producers: (reds) Almondo★, Carretta★, Cascina Ca' Rossa★, Cascina Chicco★, Cornarea, Correggia★, Deltetto★, Funtanin★, Malabaila, Malvirà★, Monchiero Carbone★, Angelo Negro★, Porello★. Best years: (reds) (2000) 99 **98 97 96 95**. See also Arneis.

**ROMAGNA** *Emilia-Romagna, Italy* Romagna's wine production is centred on 4 DOCs and 1 DOCG. The whites are from Trebbiano (ineffably dull), Pagadebit (showing promise as both a dry and sweet wine) and Albana (ALBANA DI ROMAGNA was upgraded to DOCG in 1987 and can be made in either dry or sweet versions). The reds are dominated by the Sangiovese grape, which ranges from young and fresh through to wines that can rival a good CHIANTI. Best producers: (Sangiovese) La Berta★, Le Calbane★, Casetto dei Mandorli★, Castelluccio★★, Celli★, Conti★, Ferrucci★, La Palazza★, Pandolfa★, Paradiso★, San Patrignano co-op–Terre del Cedro (Riserva★), Tre Monti★, Trerè★, Uccellina (Riserva★), Zerbina★★.

**LA ROMANÉE-CONTI AC** *Grand Cru, Côte de Nuits, Burgundy, France* For many extremely wealthy wine lovers this is the pinnacle of red Burgundy★★★. It is an incredibly complex wine with great structure and pure, clearly defined fruit flavour, but you've got to age it 15 years to see what all the fuss is about. The vineyard covers only 1.8ha (4½ acres), which is one reason for the high prices. Wholly owned by Dom. de la ROMANÉE-CONTI. Best years: (2000) 99 98 97 96 95 93 **91** 90 **89 88 85 78 72**.

**DOM. DE LA ROMANÉE-CONTI** *Vosne-Romanée, Côte de Nuits, Burgundy, France* This famous red wine domaine owns a string of Grands Crus in VOSNE-ROMANÉE (la TACHE★★★, RICHEBOURG★★★, ROMANÉE-CONTI★★★, ROMANÉE-ST-VIVANT★★★, ECHEZEAUX★★★ and Grands-Échézeaux★★★) as well as a small parcel of le MONTRACHET★★★. The wines are all ludicrously expensive but can be quite sublime – full of fruit when young, but capable of aging for 15 years or more to an astonishing marriage made in the heaven and hell of richness and decay. Recent vintages show a necessary return to consistency. At these prices they'd better! Best years: (2000) 99 98 97 96 95 93 90 **89 88 85 78**.

**ROMANÉE-ST-VIVANT AC** *Grand Cru, Côte de Nuits, Burgundy, France* By far the largest of VOSNE-ROMANÉE's 6 Grands Crus. At 10–15 years old the wines should reveal the keenly balanced brilliance of which the vineyard is capable, but a surly, rough edge sometimes gets in the way. Best producers: R Arnoux★★★, J-J Confuron★★★, DROUHIN★★★, Hudelot-Noëllat★★★, JADOT★★★, Dom. LEROY★★★, Dom. de la ROMANEE-CONTI★★★. Best years: (2000) 99 98 97 96 95 93 **91** 90 **89 88**.

**ROQUES, QUINTA DOS** *Dão DOC, Beira Alta, Portugal* Now the DÃO's finest producer, the wines of two estates with quite different characters are made here. Quinta dos Roques red★ is ripe and supple, while Quinta dos Maias★ is a smoky, peppery red. Both estates also have a decent dry white, but the top wines are the dos Roques Reserva★★, made from old vines and aged in 100% new oak, and Touriga Nacional★★. Best years: 1997 **96**.

**ROSA, QUINTA DE LA** *Douro DOC and Port DOC, Douro, Portugal* The Bergqvist family have transformed this spectacular property into a small but serious independent producer of both PORT and DOURO★ (Reserva★★) table wines. The Vintage Port★★ is excellent, as is unfiltered LBV★★, while Finest Reserve and 10-year-old tawny★ are also good. Best years: (Vintage) 1997 95 94 92 **91**.

**ROSÉ D'ANJOU AC** *Loire Valley, France* AC for cheap ANJOU rosé that is usually somewhere between off-dry and quite sweet. Produced predominantly from the Groslot grape, which doesn't give much colour or flavour. Most of the top producers prefer to use ROSE DE LOIRE or CABERNET D'ANJOU titles. Drink young. Best producer: Caves de la Loire.

**ROSÉ DE LOIRE AC** *Loire Valley, France* Dry rosé from ANJOU, SAUMUR and TOURAINE. It can be a lovely drink, full of red berry fruits, but drink as young as possible and chill well. Best producers: l'Echalier, Haute-Perche, Ogereau, Passavant, RICHOU, Sauveroy.

**ROSÉ DES RICEYS AC** *Champagne, France* This is a curiosity and an expensive one at that. It's a still, dark pink wine made from Pinot Noir grapes in the southern part of the CHAMPAGNE region. Best producers: Alexandre Bonnet★, Devaux★, Guy de Forez, Morel.

**ROSEMOUNT ESTATE** *Hunter Valley, New South Wales, Australia* Model winery buying and growing grapes in several regions to produce some of Australia's best, most popular wines. Top are complex, weighty Roxburgh★★ and Show Reserve★★ Chardonnays; blackcurrant COONAWARRA Cabernet★ and gutsy Balmoral Syrah★★. New Rose label Chardonnay★★ from the Orange region is very fine; MCLAREN VALE Show Reserve Shiraz★★ is too. Mountain Blue Shiraz-Cabernet★★ and Hill of Gold varietals★★ are the most exciting new wines to come out of MUDGEE for a long time, and GSM★★ (Grenache, Syrah, Mourvèdre) is a knockout. 'Split label' Semillon-Chardonnay and Shiraz-Cabernet★ are among Australia's best gluggers, but no longer such good value as they were. Recent merger with Southcorp creates a high-quality giant. Let's hope the quality stays high and the prices don't get silly. Best years: (whites) 1999 98 **97 96** 95 93 **91** 90 **89** 87.

**ROSSO CÒNERO DOC** *Marche, Italy* The best wines in this zone, on the Adriatic coast just south of Ancona, are made solely from Montepulciano, and have a wonderfully spicy richness. Winemaking has improved greatly of late. Best producers: Fazi Battaglia★, Garofoli★ (Grosso Agontano★★), Lanari★, Leopardi Dittajuti★, Marchetti (Villa Bonomi★), Mecella (Rubelliano★), Terre Cortesi Moncaro (Riserva★), Moroder★ (Dorico★★), Le Terrazze★ (Sassi Neri★★, Visions of J★★), Umani Ronchi★ (Cúmaro★★). Best years: (2000) 99 **98 97** 95 94 93 90.

**ROSSO DI MONTALCINO DOC** *Tuscany, Italy* The little brother of
BRUNELLO DI MONTALCINO spends much less time aging in wood, so
enabling the wines to retain a wonderful exuberance of flavour that
Brunello may lose through its longer cask-aging. Best producers:
Altesino★, ARGIANO★, BANFI★, Barbi★, Canalicchio di Sopra★, Caparzo★,
Casanova di Neri★★, CASTELGIOCONDO, Ciacci Piccolomini d'Aragona★★,
Col d'Orcia★, Collemattoni★, COSTANTI★, Fattoi★, La Fortuna★, Fuligni★,
La Gerla★, Due Portini-Gorelli★, Maurizio Lambardi★, Lisini★, Silvio
Nardi★, Siro Pacenti★★, Agostina Pieri★, Poggio Antico★, Il Poggiolo★,
Il Poggione★, Poggio Salvi★, Salicutti★★, San Filippo★, Talenti★,
Uccelliera★, Valdicava★. Best years: (2000) 99 **98 97 96 95 94 93 90**.

**ROSSO DI MONTEPULCIANO DOC** *Tuscany, Italy* This DOC gives
producers the option of honing the production of their grander VINO
NOBILE DI MONTEPULCIANO DOCG by diverting some of the younger, juicier
vats into bottle at an earlier stage. Some turn out a fresh, jammy,
rather innocuous style, but the best deliver delightfully plummy,
chocolaty flavours. Best producers: La Braccesca★, Buracchi,
Contucci, Dei★, Del Cerro★, Fassati★, Gracciano della Seta, Antonino
Lombardo★, Il Macchione, Nottola, Palazzo Vecchio★, POLIZIANO★, Redi,
Massimo Romeo★, Valdipiatta★. Best years: (2000) **99 98 97 96**.

**ROSSO PICENO DOC** *Marche, Italy* Though related to ROSSO CONERO, this
red is often considered a poor relative, since Sangiovese tends to be
lean and harsh in the Marche. But when the full complement (40%)
of Montepulciano is used, Rosso Piceno can be rich and seductive.
Best producers: Boccadigabbia★ (Villamagna★★), Bucci, Le Caniette★,
Cocci Grifoni★, Saladini Pilastri★ (Vigna Monte Prandone★★),
Velenosi★, Villa Pigna. Best years: (1999) **98 97 95 94 93 90**.

**ROTHBURY ESTATE** *Hunter Valley, New South Wales, Australia* Len
Evans' brainchild (now owned by Beringer Blass, a division of Fosters)
has struggled to find its way in recent years. The premium
Brokenback range of HUNTER VALLEY wines (Shiraz★, Semillon★ and
Chardonnay) has led a new quality charge. Hunter Valley Semillon★
is legendary; the Verdelho has life and zest; and there are inexpensive
varietals from MUDGEE and COWRA (Chardonnay★). Best years: (whites)
**1998 96 95 93 91 86 84 79**; (reds) 1998 **96 93 91 89 87 86 83 81 79**.

**GEORGES ROUMIER** *Chambolle-Musigny AC, Côte de Nuits, Burgundy,*
*France* Christophe Roumier has long been recognized as one of
Burgundy's top winemakers, devoting as much attention to his
vineyards as to cellar technique, believing in severe pruning, low yields
and stringent grape selection. Roumier never uses more than one-third
new oak. His best wine is often BONNES-MARES★★★, but his other Grands
Crus include MUSIGNY★★★, Ruchottes-Chambertin★★ and CORTON-
CHARLEMAGNE★★. The best value are usually the Chambolle les Cras★★
and an exclusively owned Premier Cru in MOREY-ST-DENIS, Clos de la
Bussière★★. Best years: (reds) (2000) 99 98 97 96 95 **93 90 89 88 85**.

---

**ROUSSANNE** The RHONE VALLEY's best white grape variety, frequently
blended with Marsanne. Roussanne is the more aromatic and elegant
of the two, less prone to oxidation and with better acidity, but growers
usually prefer Marsanne due to its higher yields. Now being planted in
the MIDI. Also some fascinating examples in Australia and California.

**ROUSSE** *Northern Region, Bulgaria* One of Bulgaria's largest wineries and an up-and-coming star, achieving vibrant, zesty results with Cabernet Sauvignon★ and Merlot★. The low-priced 'country' blends are good. Privatized in 1998 and now owned by the Seaboard Corporation of America, which has invested millions of dollars in new equipment, the winery is undergoing a merger with DOMAINE BOYAR.

**ARMAND ROUSSEAU** *Gevrey-Chambertin AC, Côte de Nuits, Burgundy, France* One of the most highly respected and important CHAMBERTIN estates, with vineyards in Clos-de-Bèze★★★, Mazis-Chambertin★★ and Charmes-Chambertin★★ as well as CLOS DE LA ROCHE★★★ in MOREY-ST-DENIS and GEVREY-CHAMBERTIN Clos St-Jacques★★★. The outstandingly harmonious, elegant, yet rich wines are made in a traditional style and enjoy an enviable reputation for longevity. The Chambertin★★★ is exceptionally fine. Best years: (2000) 99 98 96 95 93 **91 90** 89 88 85.

**ROUSSILLON** *France* The snow-covered peaks of the Pyrenees form a spectacular backdrop to the ancient region of Roussillon, now the Pyrénées-Orientales *département*. The vineyards produce a wide range of fairly priced wines, mainly red, ranging from the ripe, raisin-rich *vins doux naturels* to light, fruity-fresh vins de pays. After spending several years in the shadow of the LANGUEDOC renaissance, there are now some really exciting table wines, both white and red, being made in Roussillon, especially by individual estates. See also Banyuls, Collioure, Côtes du Roussillon, Côtes du Roussillon-Villages, Maury, Muscat de Rivesaltes, Rivesaltes.

**RUCHOTTES-CHAMBERTIN AC** See Chambertin AC.

**RÜDESHEIM** *Rheingau, Germany* Village producing silky, aromatic wines from some famous sites (Berg Schlossberg, Berg Rottland, Berg Roseneck and Bischofsberg). Not to be confused with the NAHE village of the same name. During the 1990s a group of young winemakers dramatically improved standards here. Best producers: Georg BREUER★★, Johannishof★, J LEITZ★★. Best years: 1999 98 **97** 96 **94** 93 90.

**RUEDA DO** *Castilla y León, Spain* The RIOJA firm of MARQUES DE RISCAL launched the reputation of this white-wine-only region in the 1970s, first by rescuing the almost extinct local grape, Verdejo, then by introducing Sauvignon Blanc. Fresh young whites have been joined by barrel-fermented wines aiming for a longer life, particularly those made by Brigitte Lurton at Belondrade y Lurton★. Best producers: Alvarez y Diez★, Antaño (Viña Mocén★), Cerrosol (Doña Beatriz), Hermanos Lurton★, MARQUES DE RISCAL★ (Sauvignon Blanc★★), Bodegas de Crianza Castilla La Vieja (Palacio de Bornos Vendimia Seleccionada★★), Javier Sanz Cantalapiedra★, Viños Sanz, Angel Rodríguez Vidal (Martinsancho★).

**RUFFINO** *Tuscany, Italy* Huge winemaking concern recently divided between two sides of the Folonari family. CHIANTI CLASSICO comes from estates at Zano★, Nozzole★ and Santedame★, though the classic is Riserva Ducale Oro★★. SUPER-TUSCANS include Chardonnay Cabreo La Pietra★★, Cabernet Cabreo Il Borgo★★, Pinot Noir Nero del Tondo★

and the unique blend of Colorino and Sangiovese in Romitorio di Santedame★★★. The original Ruffino empire also included VINO NOBILE estate Lodola Nuova and BRUNELLO Il Greppone Mazzi.

**RUINART** *Champagne AC, Champagne, France*  This is one of the oldest CHAMPAGNE houses. Ruinart has a surprisingly low profile, given the quality of its wines. The non-vintage★★ is very good, but the top wines here are the excellent, classy Dom Ruinart blanc de blancs★★★ and the Dom Ruinart Rosé★★★. Best years: (1995) **93 92 90 88 86 85 83 82.**

**RULLY AC** *Côte Chalonnaise, Burgundy, France*  One of Burgundy's most improved ACs with good-quality, reasonably priced wine. Once famous for sparkling wines, it is now best known for its still whites, often oak-aged. Reds are light, with a fleeting strawberry and cherry perfume. Best producers: (whites) Allaines★, J-C Brelière★, DROUHIN★, Dureuil-Janthial★, Duvernay, FAIVELEY★, V GIRARDIN★, JADOT★, JAFFELIN★, Olivier LEFLAIVE★, RODET★, Villaine★; (reds) A Delorme, Dureuil-Janthial★, Duvernay, la Folie, H & P Jacqueson★★. Best years: (whites) (2000) 99 **98 97 96**; (reds) (2000) 99 **98 96.**

**RUSSIAN RIVER VALLEY AVA** *Sonoma County, California, USA*  Beginning south of Healdsburg along the Russian River as it flows south-west, this wine valley cools as it meanders south-westerly towards the Pacific. It is now challenging CARNEROS as the top spot for Pinot Noir and Chardonnay. Best producers: Davis Bynum★, DEHLINGER★★★, De Loach★, Dutton-Goldfield★, Gary Farrell★★, IRON HORSE★★, ROCHIOLI★★, SONOMA-CUTRER★, Rodney Strong★, Joseph SWAN★, Marimar TORRES★★, WILLIAMS SELYEM★★.

**RUSTENBERG WINES** *Stellenbosch WO, South Africa*  A new cellar in the old dairy is part of the extensive overhaul that has brought this magnificent old farm technically up to date. Local youngster Adi Badenhorst, with experience in California and Bordeaux, heads up the cellar. The new-look, classically styled single-vineyard Five Soldiers Chardonnay★, Rustenberg★★, a BORDEAUX-style blend, and majestic Cabernet Peter Barlow★★ put this producer in the premier league. Sauvignon Blanc is ★. The Brampton varietal range remains good value. Best years: (reds) **1998 97 96**; (whites) **1999 98 97.**

**RUST EN VREDE** *Stellenbosch WO, South Africa*  Owner Jannie Engelbracht's son Jean now heads the team at this premium red wine estate. A new underground cellar, several hundred new oak wine barrels and a surge of replanting complete the transition. The wines are following suit: Merlot, Shiraz★ and Rust en Vrede★, a Cabernet-based blend designed to show off the terroir, all have fresher fruit flavours and suppler tannins. Best years: **1998 97 96 95 94 92.**

**RUTHERFORD AVA** *Napa County, California, USA*  This viticultural area in mid-NAPA VALLEY has inspired endless hours of argument over whether it has a distinct identity. The heart of the area, the Rutherford Bench, does seem to be a prime Cabernet Sauvignon zone, and many traditional old Napa Cabernets have come from Rutherford and exhibit the 'Rutherford Dust' flavour. Best producers: BEAULIEU★★, Cakebread, FLORA SPRINGS★★, Freemark Abbey, NIEBAUM-COPPOLA★.

**RUTHERGLEN** *Victoria, Australia*  This district in north-east Victoria is the home of heroic reds from Shiraz, Cabernet and Durif, and luscious, world-beating fortifieds from Muscat and Tokay (Muscadelle). Good sherry-style and vintage port-style wines. Chardonnay and Semillon are tasty but unsubtle. Best producers: (fortifieds) ALL SAINTS★★, Buller's★, Campbells★★, CHAMBERS★★, MORRIS★★, Stanton & Killeen★★.

**SAALE-UNSTRUT** *Germany* Located in the former East Germany, Saale-Unstrut's vineyards have been extensively replanted since reunification in 1989, but these vineyards must mature before first-class wines can be produced. Best producer: Lützkendorf★.

**SACHSEN** *Germany* Until recently one of Europe's forgotten wine regions on the river Elbe in former East Germany. Now beginning to produce some good wines, the best being fruity dry whites. Best producers: Schloss Proschwitz★, Schloss Wackerbarth, Klaus Zimmerling★.

**ST-AMOUR AC** *Beaujolais, Burgundy, France* The northernmost BEAUJOLAIS Cru, producing juicy, soft-fruited wine which lasts well for 2–3 years. Best producers: Billards (Loron)★, DUBOEUF★, H Fessy, J Patissier★, J-G Revillon★, M Tête★★. Best years: (2000) **99 98**.

**ST ANTONY** *Nierstein, Rheinhessen, Germany* Dr Alex Michalsky runs one of RHEINHESSEN's finest estates, making dry and off-dry Rieslings (frequently ★★) with unusual power and richness from the top sites of NIERSTEIN. Occasional sweet Auslese and higher Prädikat wines are always expansive and luscious. All wines except the regular dry Riesling★ have at least 5 years' aging potential. Best years: (1999) 98 **97** 96 **94 93 92 90 89**.

**ST-AUBIN AC** *Côte de Beaune, Burgundy, France* Some of Burgundy's best-value wines. Good reds, especially from Premiers Crus like les Frionnes and les Murgers des Dents de Chien. Also reasonably priced, oak-aged white wines. Best producers: Bernard Bachelet, D & F Clair★★, M Colin★★, DROUHIN★, JADOT★, Lamy-Pillot★, Larue★★, Olivier LEFLAIVE★, B Morey★, H Prudhon★, RAMONET★★, Roux★, G Thomas★. Best years: (reds) 1999 98 **97 96 95**; (whites) (2000) **99 97 96 95**.

**ST-CHINIAN AC** *Languedoc, France* Large AC for strong, spicy red wines with more personality and fruit than run-of-the-mill HERAULT. Best producers: Berloup co-op★, Borie la Vitarèle★, Canet-Valette★★, Cazal-Viel★, Clos Bagatelle, Combebelle, Jougla★, Mas Champart, Maurel Fonsalade★, Roquebrun co-op★, St-Chinian co-op. Best years: (2000) 99 **98 96 95 94 93 91 90**.

**ST-DÉSIRAT, CAVE DE** *St-Joseph, Rhône Valley, France* St-Désirat is the largest single producer of ST-JOSEPH wines and one of the best co-ops in the RHÔNE VALLEY. The intense, smoky red St-Joseph★ is a fantastic bargain, as are local vins de pays.

**ST-ÉMILION AC** *Bordeaux, France* The scenic Roman hill town of St-Émilion is the centre of Bordeaux's most historic wine region. The finest vineyards are on the *côtes*, or steep slopes, around the town, although an area to the west, called the *graves*, contains 2 famous properties, CHEVAL BLANC and FIGEAC. It is a region of smallholdings, with over 1000 different properties, and consequently the co-operative plays an important part. The dominant early-ripening Merlot grape gives wines with a 'come hither' softness and sweetness rare in red Bordeaux. St-Émilion AC is the basic generic AC, with 4 'satellites' (LUSSAC, MONTAGNE, PUISSEGUIN, ST-GEORGES) allowed to annex their name to it. The best producers, including the Classed Growths, are found in the more tightly controlled ST-EMILION GRAND CRU AC category. Best years: (2000) **96 95 94 90 89 88 86 85**.

**ST-ÉMILION GRAND CRU AC** *Bordeaux, France*   St-Émilion's top-quality AC, which includes the estates classified as Grand Cru Classé and Premier Grand Cru Classé. The 1996 Classification lists 55 Grands Crus Classés. Top wines in this category are better value than Premiers Grands Crus Classés and can age for 10–15 years. Best producers: (Grands Crus Classés) l'ARROSEE★★, Balestard-la-Tonnelle★, CANON-LA-GAFFELIERE★★, la Dominique★★, Grand Mayne★★, Grand Pontet★, Larmande★, Pavie-Decesse★, Pavie-Macquin★★, Soutard★, TROPLONG-MONDOT★★; (others) Faugères★, Fleur Cardinale★, Fombrauge★, la Mondotte★★, Monbousquet★, Moulin St-Georges★★, Rol Valentin★★, TERTRE-ROTEBOEUF★★★, Teyssier★, VALANDRAUD★★. Best years: (2000) 99 98 96 **95 94 90 89** 88 86 85. See also St-Émilion Premier Grand Cru Classé.

**ST-ÉMILION PREMIER GRAND CRU CLASSÉ** *Bordeaux, France*   The St-Émilion élite level, divided into 2 categories – 'A' and 'B' – with only the much more expensive CHEVAL BLANC and AUSONE in category 'A'. There are 11 'B' châteaux, with ANGELUS and BEAU-SEJOUR BECOT added in the 1996 Classification. Best producers: ANGELUS★★★, AUSONE★★★, BEAU-SEJOUR BECOT★★, Beauséjour★★, BELAIR★, CANON★, CHEVAL BLANC★★★, Clos Fourtet★, FIGEAC★★, la Gaffelière★, MAGDELAINE★★, PAVIE★★. Best years: (2000) 99 98 96 **95 94 90 89 88 86 85** 83 82.

**ST-ESTÈPHE AC** *Haut-Médoc, Bordeaux, France*   Large AC north of PAUILLAC with 5 Classed Growths. St-Estèphe wines have high tannin levels, but less weight. They are drinkable at 2–3 years, but given time (10–20 years) those sought-after flavours of blackcurrant and cedarwood do peek out. More Merlot has been planted to soften the wines. Best producers: CALON-SEGUR★★, COS D'ESTOURNEL★★★, Cos Labory★, HAUT-MARBUZET★★, LAFON-ROCHET★, Lilian-Ladouys★, Marbuzet★, MEYNEY★, MONTROSE★★, les Ormes-de-Pez★, PEZ★, Phelan Ségur★. Best years: (2000) 96 **95 94 90 89** 88 86 85 83 82.

**DOMAINE ST-GAYAN** *Gigondas AC, Rhône Valley, France*   The Meffre family have substantial holdings of vines in GIGONDAS and the COTES DU RHONE. Old vine fruit lends power to the Gigondas★ (★★ in top years), but the extensive period of barrel-aging really only suits the ripest vintages. Côtes du Rhône and Côtes du Rhône-Villages Rasteau are usually good value. Best years (Gigondas): 1998 97 96 95 **93 91 90**.

**ST-GEORGES-ST-ÉMILION AC** *Bordeaux, France*   The best satellite of ST-EMILION, with lovely, soft wines that can nevertheless age for 6–10 years. Best producers: Calon, Griffe de Cap d'Or, Macquin St-Georges★, St-André Corbin, Ch. St-Georges★, Tour-du-Pas-St-Georges★, Vieux-Montaiguillon. Best years: (2000) 99 98 **96 95 94 90 89 88 85** 83.

**ST HALLETT** *Barossa Valley, South Australia*   Bob McLean manages this revitalized winery, which makes Old Block Shiraz★★ using very old vines and open fermenters, and 2 other delightful Shirazes: Blackwell★ and Faith★. Gamekeeper's Reserve★ red and Poacher's Blend★ white can be real bargains, as can Riesling★★. Now merged with MCLAREN VALE's Tatachilla. Best years: (reds) 1998 **96 94 93 92 91 90 88 86**.

**ST-JOSEPH AC** *Rhône Valley, France* Large, mainly red AC, on the opposite bank of the Rhône to HERMITAGE. Made from Syrah, the reds have mouthfilling fruit with irresistible blackcurrant richness. Brilliant at 1–2 years, they can last for up to 8. Only a little white is made and with, up-to-date winemaking, these are usually pleasant, flowery wines to drink young, although an increasing number can age. Best producers: (reds) CHAPOUTIER★, CHAVE★★, Chêne★★, L Chèze★, COLOMBO★, Courbis★, COURSODON★, Y CUILLERON★, DELAS★, FLORENTIN★, P GAILLARD★★, GRAILLOT★★, B Gripa★★, J-L Grippat★★, JABOULET★, Monteillet★, Paret★★, A Perret★, P Pichon★, ST-DESIRAT CO-OP★, Tardieu-Laurent★★, Tunnel★, F Villard★★; (whites) Chêne★, L Chèze★, Courbis★, Y Cuilleron★, DELAS★, Ferraton★, Florentin★, P Gaillard★, B Gripa★, J-L Grippat★, JABOULET★, Monteillet★, A Perret★, Trollat★, Villard★★. Best years: (reds) (2000) 99 98 **97 96 95** 94 91; (whites) (2000) **99 98 97 96 95**.

**ST-JULIEN AC** *Haut-Médoc, Bordeaux, France* For many, St-Julien produces perfect claret, with an ideal balance between opulence and austerity and between the brashness of youth and the genius of maturity. It is the smallest of the HAUT-MEDOC ACs but almost all is first-rate vineyard land and quality is high. Best producers: BEYCHEVELLE★, BRANAIRE★★, DUCRU-BEAUCAILLOU★★★, GLORIA★, GRUAUD-LAROSE★, LAGRANGE★★, LANGOA-BARTON★★, LEOVILLE-BARTON★★★, LEOVILLE-LAS-CASES★★★, LEOVILLE-POYFERRE★★, ST-PIERRE★★, TALBOT★. Best years: (2000) 99 98 97 96 95 94 90 89 88 86 85 83 82.

**ST-NICOLAS-DE-BOURGUEIL AC** *Loire Valley, France* An enclave of just under 500ha (1250 acres) within the larger BOURGUEIL AC. Almost all the wine is red and with the same piercing red fruit flavours of Bourgueil, and much better after 7–10 years, especially in warm vintages. Best producers: P Jamet★, F Mabileau★, J-C Mabileau★, Taluau★, Vallée★. Best years: (2000) 99 **97 96 95** 90 89 85.

**ST-PÉRAY AC** *Rhône Valley, France* Rather hefty, Champagne-method fizz from Marsanne and Roussanne grapes from vineyards across the river from Valence. Still white is usually dry and solid. Best producers: Biguet★, J-F Chaboud★, CLAPE★, DELAS★, Fauterie, B Gripa★, J Lemencier★, LIONNET★, J-L Thiers★, A Voge★. Best years: (2000) 99 **98 97 96 95**.

**CH. ST-PIERRE★★** *St-Julien AC, 4ème Cru Classé, Haut-Médoc, Bordeaux, France* Small ST-JULIEN property making wines that have become a byword for ripe, lush fruit wrapped round with the spice of new oak. Drinkable early, but top vintages can improve for 20 years. Best years: (2000) 99 98 97 96 95 **94** 90 89 88 86 83 81.

**ST-ROMAIN AC** *Côte de Beaune, Burgundy, France* Out-of-the-way village producing red wines with a firm, bitter-sweet cherrystone fruit and flinty-dry whites varying between austerely acid and quirkily old-style. Usually good value by Burgundian standards, but take a few years to open out. Best producers: (reds) A Gras★, Thévenin-Monthélie★; (whites) Allaines★, Bazenet★, H & G Buisson, A Gras★★, JAFFELIN★, O LEFLAIVE★, P Taupenot, Thévenin-Monthélie★, VERGET★★. Best years: (reds) 1999 98 **97 96 95**; (whites) (2000) 99 **97 96 95**.

**ST-VÉRAN AC** *Mâconnais, Burgundy, France* Often thought of as a POUILLY-FUISSE understudy. This is gentle, fairly fruity, normally unoaked Mâconnais Chardonnay at its best, and the overall quality is good. The price is fair, too. Best to drink young. Best producers:

Barraud★, G Chagny, Corsin★★, Deux Roches★, B & J-M Drouin★, DUBOEUF★, G Guérin★, Lassarat★, Saumaize-Michelin★, J C Thévenet★★, J-L Tissier★, VERGET★, J-J Vincent★. Best years: (2000) **99 98 97 96**.

**STE-CROIX-DU-MONT AC** *Bordeaux, France* Best of the 3 sweet wine ACs that gaze jealously at SAUTERNES and BARSAC across the Garonne river (the others are CADILLAC and LOUPIAC). The wine is mildly sweet rather than splendidly rich, best drunk as an apéritif or with hors d'oeuvre. The top wines can age for at least a decade. Best producers: Crabitan-Bellevue, Loubens★, Lousteau-Vieil, Mailles, Mont, Pavillon, la Rame★. Best years: 1999 98 **97 96 95 90 89 88 86 85 83**.

**SAINTSBURY** *Carneros AVA, California, USA* New-wave, deeply committed winery using only CARNEROS fruit. Its Pinot Noirs★★ are brilliant examples of the perfume and fruit quality of Carneros; the Reserve★★★ and the exquisite Brown Ranch★★★ are deeper and oakier, while Garnet★ is a delicious, lighter style. Chardonnay★★ and Reserve Chardonnay★★ are also impressive, best after 2–3 years. Best years: (Pinot Noir Reserve) (1999) 98 **97 96 95 94 92 91**; (Pinot Noir Carneros) (1999) 98 **97 96 95 94 93**.

**SALA, CASTELLO DELLA** *Orvieto DOC, Umbria, Italy* Belongs to the ANTINORI family, making good ORVIETO★ and outstanding oak-aged Cervaro della Sala★★★ (90% Chardonnay and 10% Grechetto). Also impressive Pinot Nero★★ and sweet Muffato della Sala★★.

**SALAPARUTA, DUCA DI** *Sicily, Italy* Corvo is the brand name for Sicilian wines made by this firm. Red and white Corvo are pretty basic, but there are superior whites, Colomba Platino★ and Bianca di Valguarnera★, and 2 fine reds, Terre d'Agala★ and Duca Enrico★★.

**SALICE SALENTINO DOC** *Puglia, Italy* Probably the best of the DOCs in the Salento peninsula, turning out wines (made with Negroamaro and tempered with a dash of perfumed Malvasia Nera) that are ripe and chocolatey, acquiring hints of roast chestnuts and prunes with age. Drink after 3–4 years, although they may last as long again. The DOCs of Alezio, Brindisi, Copertino, Leverano and Squinzano have similar Rosso and Rosato. Best producers: Candido★, Leone De Castris★, Taurino★, Vallone★, Conti Zecca. Best years: (reds) 1999 98 **97 96 95 94**.

**SAMOS** *Greece* The island of Samos was granted an appellation in 1982, but its reputation for producing rich, sweet dessert wines from the Muscat grape stretches back centuries. The 2 wineries of the Samos co-op make similar Muscat-based wines. Pale green Samena dry white is made from early-picked Muscat; deep gold, honeyed Samos Nectar★★ is made from sun-dried grapes; the rarer version, Palaio, is aged for up to 20 years and very apricotty in nature; and seductively complex Samos Anthemis★ is fortified and cask-aged for up to 5 years.

**SANCERRE AC** *Loire Valley, France* Sancerre mania broke out in the 1970s, first with the white wine which can provide the perfect expression of the bright green tang of the Sauvignon grape, then with the reds and rosés, which are made from Pinot Noir. The whites, from a good grower in one of the best villages like Bué, Chavignol, Verdigny or Ménétréol in the chalky land around the hill town of Sancerre, can be deliciously refreshing; so too can the rare Pinot Noir rosé. Reds are now being taken more seriously, but still really need hot years to show best. The wines are now more consistent than those of neighbouring POUILLY. Best producers: F & J Bailly★, Bailly-Reverdy★, H Bourgeois★★, R Champault★, F Cotat★★, L CROCHET★★, A & P Dezat★, Fouassier, Gitton★, P Jolivet, A MELLOT★★, J Mellot★, P Millérioux★, Natter★, A & F Neveu★, R Neveu★, V Pinard★★, P & N Reverdy★, Reverdy-Cadet★, J-M Roger★, Vacheron★★, André Vatan★. Best years: 2000 **99 98 97 96 95 90**.

**SANDEMAN** *Port DOC, Douro, Portugal and Jerez y Manzanilla DO, Spain* No longer one of the leading port houses, but there are definite signs of improvement. Best are the aged tawnies, Imperial Aged Reserve Tawny★ and 20-year-old★★, and the single-quinta Vau (1997★★), while Signature★ is currently the best Premium Ruby style going.

**LUCIANO SANDRONE** *Barolo DOCG, Piedmont, Italy* Luciano Sandrone has become one of PIEDMONT's leading wine stylists, renowned for his BAROLO Cannubi Boschis★★★ and Le Vigne★★★, as well as BARBERA D'ALBA★★ and Dolcetto d'Alba★★, which rank with the best.

**SANFORD** *Santa Ynez Valley AVA, California, USA* Richard Sanford planted the great Benedict vineyard in the Santa Ynez Valley in 1971, thus establishing Santa Ynez and SANTA BARBARA as potentially top-quality vineyard regions. Sanford now makes sharply focused, green-edged Pinot Noir★★, Chardonnay★★ and Sauvignon Blanc★. A new series of 'Signature' Barrel Select Pinot Noir★★ is especially impressive. Best years: (Pinot Noir) (1999) 98 **97 96 95 94 92 91**.

---

**SANGIOVESE** Sangiovese rivals Trebbiano as the most widely planted grape variety in Italy, but it reaches its greatest heights in central TUSCANY. This grape has produced a wide variety of clones that make generalization difficult. Much care is being taken in the current wave of replanting, whether in CHIANTI CLASSICO, BRUNELLO DI MONTALCINO or VINO NOBILE DI MONTEPULCIANO. Styles range from pale, lively and cherryish, through the vivacious, mid-range Chiantis, to excellent top Riservas and SUPER-TUSCANS. At the latter level, Sangiovese shows itself to be one of the great grapes of the world. CALIFORNIA producers like ATLAS PEAK, SHAFER, Robert Pepi and Seghesio are now working some of their magic on this grape. Australia is taking a keen interest, with good examples from King Valley in VICTORIA (Gary Crittenden, Pizzini) and MCLAREN VALE (Coriole). Some interesting examples are also grown in Argentina and the grape is starting to appear in South African vineyards.

---

**SAN LUIS OBISPO COUNTY** *California, USA* CENTRAL COAST county best known for Chardonnay, Pinot Noir, a bit of old-vine Zinfandel and Cabernet Sauvignon. There are 5 AVAs – Edna Valley, Paso Robles, SANTA MARIA VALLEY (shared with SANTA BARBARA COUNTY), Arroyo Grande Valley and York Mountain, each of which has already grown some outstanding grapes and will surely grow a lot more. Best producers: Clairborne & Churchill★, Creston Vineyards★, Eberle★, Edna Valley★★, Justin★★, Meridian★★, Norman★, Savannah-Chanel★, Serin Peaks★★, Talley★★, Wild Horse★.

**SAN PEDRO** *Curicó, Chile* A takeover by Chile's biggest brewer, along with Jacques Lurton as consultant since 1994, turned the fortunes of San Pedro around, leading to another 1000ha (2470 acres) of planting and new facilities. Crisp, clean 35 Sur Sauvignon Blanc★, Reserva Chardonnay★, and Cabernet and Merlot★ in the Castillo de Molina range are best, though basic Gato and 35 Sur reds aren't bad, either.

**SANTA BARBARA COUNTY** *California, USA* CENTRAL COAST county, just north of Los Angeles, which is best known for Chardonnay, Riesling, Pinot Noir and Syrah. The main AVAs are Santa Ynez Valley and most of SANTA MARIA VALLEY (the remainder is in SAN LUIS OBISPO COUNTY), both leading areas for Pinot Noir. Best producers: AU BON CLIMAT★★, Babcock★, BYRON★★, CAMBRIA★, Foxen★★, Gainey★, Hitching Post★, Longona★, QUPE★★, SANFORD★★, Whitcraft★★, Zaca Mesa★.

**SANTA CAROLINA** *Maipo, Chile* Long-established winery that is at last catching up with the modern world. You'll find fresh Reserva whites★ with good fruit definition, including an excellent sweet Semillon-Sauvignon★★ from Lontué, and substantial, ripe, if oaky, Barrica Selection reds★.

**SANTA MADDALENA** *Alto Adige, Italy* Light, delicate wine from the Schiava grape grown in the hills above Bolzano. It has a perfume of black cherries, cream and bacon smoke, and can be improved with the addition of up to 10% of Lagrein. The best wines are generally from the original Classico zone. Drink young but some vintages will age. Best producers: Egger-Ramer★, Franz Gojer★, Gries co-op, LAGEDER★, Josephus Mayr★, Josef Niedermayr★, Plattner Waldgries★, Hans Rottensteiner★, Heinrich Rottensteiner★, Santa Maddalena co-op★, Thurnhof.

**SANTA MARIA VALLEY AVA** *California, USA* Cool Santa Maria Valley is coming on strong as a producer of Chardonnay, Pinot Noir and Syrah. Look for wines made from grapes grown in Bien Nacido vineyards by several small wineries. Best producers: AU BON CLIMAT★★, BYRON★★, CAMBRIA★, Camelot (KENDALL-JACKSON)★, Foxen★★, Lane Tanner (Pinot Noir★), Longona★, QUPE★★.

**SANTA RITA** *Maipo, Chile* Long-established MAIPO giant, now revitalized under winemaker Andrés Ilabaca. Plummy new red blends such as Triple C★★ (Cabernet Franc, Cabernet Sauvignon, Carmenère) and Syrah-Cabernet Sauvignon-Carmenère★ show real flair, and top-of-the-range Casa Real★★ is back on form.

**SANTENAY AC** *Côte de Beaune, Burgundy, France* Red Santenay wines often promise good ripe flavour, and are worth aging for 4–6 years in the hope that the wine will open up. The best wines, both red and white, come from les Gravières Premier Cru on the border with CHASSAGNE-MONTRACHET. Best producers: (reds) R Belland★★, D & F Clair★, M Colin★, Fleurot-Larose★, J Girardin★, V GIRARDIN★★, Monnot★, B Morey★★, L Muzard★★, Pousse d'Or★, Prieur-Brunet, Roux Père et Fils★; (whites) V GIRARDIN★★, JAFFELIN, René Lequin-Colin★. Best years: (reds) 1999 98 **97 96 95 93**; (whites) (2000) 99 **97 96 95**.

**CASA SANTOS LIMA** *Alenquer DOC, Estremadura, Portugal* A beautiful estate with an expanding range. Espiga reds and whites are light, fruity and tasty, but for more character look to the spicy red★ and creamy, perfumed white Palha-Canas, or to red and white Quinta das Setencostas★. New reds sold under the Casa Santos Lima label include

249

Touriz★ (from DOURO varieties) and varietal Touriga Nacional★, Touriga Francesa★, Trincadeira★ and Tinta Roriz★. Also a promising peachy, herby Chardonnay★. Best years: (2000) **99 98 97 96**.

**SÃO JOÃO, CAVES** *Beira Litoral, Portugal* A traditional-seeming but discreetly modernist company. It was a pioneer of cool-fermented, white BAIRRADA, and has made some very good Cabernet Sauvignons from its own vines. Rich, complex reds include outstanding Reserva★★ and Frei João★ from Bairrada and Porta dos Cavalheiros★★ from DAO – they demand at least 10 years' age to show their quality.

**SARDINIA** *Italy* Grapes of Spanish origin, like the white Vermentino and Torbato and the red Monica, CANNONAU and Carignano, dominate production on this huge, hilly Mediterranean island, but they vie with MALVASIA of Greek origin and natives like Nuragus and Vernaccia. The cooler northern part favours whites, especially VERMENTINO, while the southern and eastern parts are best suited to reds from Cannonau and Monica. The wines were powerful, alcoholic monsters, but the current trend is for a lighter, modern, more international style. Foremost among those in pursuit of quality are ARGIOLAS, SELLA & MOSCA and the Santadi co-op. See also Carignano del Sulcis, Vernaccia di Oristano.

**SASSICAIA DOC★★★** *Tuscany, Italy* This Cabernet Sauvignon-Cabernet Franc blend from the coast has done more than any other wine to gain credibility abroad for Italy. Vines were planted in 1944 to satisfy the Marchese Incisa della Rochetta's thirst for fine red Bordeaux, which was in short supply during the war. The wine remained purely for family consumption until nephew Piero Antinori (of ANTINORI) and winemaker Giacomo Tachis persuaded the Marchese to refine production practices and to release several thousand bottles from the 1968 vintage. Since then, Sassicaia's fame has increased as it consistently proved itself to be one of the world's great Cabernets, combining a blackcurrant power of blistering intensity with a heavenly scent of cigars. It is the first Italian single-owner estate wine to have its own DOC, within the BOLGHERI appellation, from the 1995 vintage. Best years: (1998) 97 96 95 **90 88 85 84 83 82 81 78 75 71 68**.

**SAUMUR AC** *Loire Valley, France* Improving dry white wines, made mainly from Chenin Blanc, but 20% Chardonnay can be added. The reds are lighter than those of SAUMUR-CHAMPIGNY. Also dry to off-dry Cabernet rosé, and sweet Coteaux de Saumur in good years. Best producers: Clos Rougeard★★, FILLIATREAU★, Hureau★, Langlois-Château★, la Renière★, Retiveau-Retif★, Roches Neuves★, St-Just★, P Vatan★★, Villeneuve★★. Best years: (whites) (2000) **99 97 96 95 90**.

**SAUMUR-CHAMPIGNY AC** *Loire Valley, France* Saumur's best red wine. Cabernet Franc is the main grape, and in hot years the wine can be superb, with a piercing scent of blackcurrants and raspberries easily overpowering the earthy finish. Delicious young, it can age for 6–10 years. Best producers: Clos Rougeard★★, Clos des Cordeliers★, Drouineau★, FILLIATREAU★★, Hureau★, Retiveau-Retif★, Roches Neuves★★, St-Just★, Val Brun★, P Vatan★, Villeneuve★★. Best years: (2000) **99 97 96 95 90**.

**SAUMUR MOUSSEUX AC** *Loire Valley, France* Reasonable Champagne-method sparkling wines made mainly from Chenin Blanc. Adding Chardonnay and Cabernet Franc makes Saumur Mousseux softer and more interesting. Usually non-vintage. Small quantities of rosé are also made. Best producers: BOUVET-LADUBAY★, GRATIEN & MEYER★, Grenelle★, la Paleine★, la Perruche★, St-Cyr-en-Bourg co-op★.

**SAUTERNES AC** *Bordeaux, France* The name Sauternes is synonymous with the best sweet wines in the world. Sauternes and BARSAC both lie on the banks of the little river Ciron and are 2 of the very few areas in France where noble rot occurs naturally. Production of these intense, sweet, luscious wines from botrytized grapes is a risk-laden and extremely expensive affair, and the wines are never going to be cheap. From good producers (most of which are Crus Classés) the wines are worth their high price – with 14% alcohol they have a richness full of flavours of pineapples, peaches, syrup and spice. Good vintages should be aged for 5–10 years, and they can often last twice as long. Best producers: BASTOR-LAMONTAGNE★, Clos Haut-Peyraguey★★, DOISY-DAENE★★, DOISY-VEDRINES★★, FARGUES★★, GILETTE★★, GUIRAUD★★, les Justices★, LAFAURIE-PEYRAGUEY★★★, Lamothe-Guignard★, Malle★, Rabaud-Promis★, Raymond-Lafon★★, Rayne-Vigneau★, RIEUSSEC★★★, St-Amand, Sigalas Rabaud★, SUDUIRAUT★★, la TOUR BLANCHE★★, YQUEM★★★. Best years: 1999 98 97 **96 95 90** 89 88 86 83.

**SAUVIGNON BLANC** See pages 252–3.

**SAUZET** *Côte de Beaune, Burgundy, France* A producer with a reputation for classic, rich, full-flavoured white Burgundies, made in an opulent, fat style, that don't always age as well as they should. Sauzet owns prime sites in PULIGNY-MONTRACHET★★ and CHASSAGNE-MONTRACHET★, as well as small parcels of BATARD-MONTRACHET★★★ and Bienvenues-BATARD-MONTRACHET★★★, and supplements grapes from its own vineyards with bought-in supplies. Best years: (2000) 99 **97** 96 **95**.

**SAVENNIÈRES AC** *Loire Valley, France* The AC for wines from Chenin Blanc, produced on steep vineyards above the Loire south of Anjou and which have always been thought of as steely and dry. They also used to appear in semi-sweet and sweet styles, and since the great 1989 and 90 vintages we've seen a revival of these. The top wines usually need at least 8 years to mature, and can age for longer. There are 2 extremely good Grand Cru vineyards with their own ACs: la Coulée-de-Serrant and la Roche-aux-Moines. Best producers: Baumard★★, Clos de Coulaine★, CLOS DE LA COULEE-DE-SERRANT★★, Closel★★, Clos des Maurières★, Épiré★★, Forges★★, Laffourcade★, Dom. aux Moines★, Pierre-Bise★★, P Soulez★, P-Y Tijou★★. Best years: (2000) 99 **97 96 95** 93 90 89 88 85 83 82 78 76 71 70 69 66.

**SAVIGNY-LÈS-BEAUNE AC** *Côte de Beaune, Burgundy, France* This large village concentrates on red wines; they are usually middle weight and best drunk 4–10 years after the vintage. The top Premiers Crus are more substantial. The white wines show a bit of dry, nutty class after 3–4 years. The wines are generally reasonably priced. Best producers: S Bize★, Camus-Bruchon★★, CHANDON DE BRIAILLES★★, Champy, B CLAIR★★, M Écard★★, J J Girard★, P Girard★, V GIRARDIN★, L Jacob★★, D Laurent★, C Maréchal★, J-M Pavelot★★, TOLLOT-BEAUT★★. Best years: (reds) 1999 98 **97 96 95** 93 90.

# SAUVIGNON BLANC

 Of all the world's grapes, the Sauvignon Blanc is leader of the 'love it or loathe it' pack. It veers from being wildly fashionable to totally out of favour depending upon where it is grown and which country's consumers are being consulted. But Sauvignon is always at its best when full rein is allowed to its very particular talents because this grape does give intense, sometimes shocking flavours, and doesn't take kindly to being put into a straitjacket.

*WINE STYLES*

**Sancerre-style Sauvignon** Although initially used largely as a blending grape in Bordeaux, where its characteristic green tang injected a bit of life into the blander, waxier Sémillon, Sauvignon first became trendy as the grape used for Sancerre, a bone-dry Loire white whose green gooseberry fruit and slightly smoky perfume inspired the winemakers of other countries to try to emulate, then often surpass the original model.

But Sauvignon is only successful where it is respected. The grape is not as easy to grow as Chardonnay, and the flavours are not so adaptable. Yet the range of styles Sauvignon produces is as wide, if less subtly nuanced, as those of Chardonnay. It is highly successful when picked not too ripe, fermented cool in stainless steel, and bottled early. New Zealand is now regarded as the top Sauvignon country, and most new producers in countries like Australia, South Africa, southern France, Hungary and Chile try to emulate this powerful mix of passionfruit, gooseberry and lime.

**Using oak** Sauvignon also lends itself to fermentation in barrel and aging in new oak, though less happily than does Chardonnay. This is the model of the Graves region of Bordeaux, although generally here Sémillon would be blended in with Sauvignon to good effect.

New Zealand again excels at this style, though there are good examples from California, Australia, northern Italy and South Africa. In Austria, a handful of producers in southern Styria (Steiermark) make powerful, aromatic versions with a touch of oak. In all these regions, the acidity that is Sauvignon's great strength should remain, with a dried apricots fruit and a spicy, biscuity softness from the oak. These oaky styles are best drunk either within about a year, or after aging for 5 years or so, and can produce remarkable, strongly individual flavours that you'll either love or loathe.

**Sweet wines** Sauvignon is also a crucial ingredient in the great sweet wines of Sauternes and Barsac from Bordeaux, though it is less susceptible than its partner Sémillon to the sweetness-enhancing 'noble rot' fungus, botrytis.

Sweet wines from the USA, South Africa, Australia and, inevitably, New Zealand range from the interesting to the outstanding – but the characteristic green tang of the Sauvignon should stay in the wine even at ultra-sweet levels.

SAUVIGNON BLANC 2000

## BEST PRODUCERS

**Top-class Sauvignons**
*France* (Pouilly-Fumé)
Chatelain, Didier DAGUENEAU,
Ladoucette, Masson-Blondelet,
Tracy; (Sancerre) H Bourgeois,
Cotat, CROCHET, A MELLOT,
Pinard, Jean-Max Roger,
Vacheron; (Pessac-Léognan)
Dom. de CHEVALIER, Couhins-
Lurton, FIEUZAL, HAUT-BRION,
SMITH-HAUT-LAFITTE.

*New Zealand* CLOUDY BAY,
Forrest Estate, GROVE MILL,
HUNTER'S, ISABEL, JACKSON ESTATE,
Lawson's Dry Hills, MONTANA,
NEUDORF, PALLISER, SELAKS,
SERESIN, VAVASOUR, VILLA MARIA,
Wither Hills.

*Italy* AVIGNONESI, GRAVNER, Edi
Kante, LAGEDER, ORNELLAIA,
SCHIOPETTO, Vie di Romans, Villa
Russiz.

**Other good Sauvignons**
*Australia* Bridgewater Mill,
Chain of Ponds, HANGING ROCK,
Karina, KATNOOK ESTATE,
LENSWOOD VINEYARDS, SHAW &
SMITH, Geoff Weaver.

*Austria* Polz, Gross, Lackner-
Tinnacher, E & M TEMENT.

*Chile* VIÑA CASABLANCA.

*New Zealand* Cairnbrae,
MONTANA, Nautilus, NOBILO, Allan
Scott, SEIFRIED.

*South Africa* BUITENVERWACHTING,
KLEIN CONSTANTIA, MULDERBOSCH,
SAXENBURG, STEENBERG,
VERGELEGEN, VILLIERA.

*Spain* (Rueda) MARQUES DE
RISCAL, Hermanos Lurton;
(Penedès) TORRES (Fransola).

*USA* (California) Abreu, ARAUJO,
Babcock, FLORA SPRINGS
(Soliloquy), KENWOOD, MATANZAS
CREEK, Robert MONDAVI (Reserve),
Murphy-Goode, Navarro,
QUIVIRA, ROCHIOLI, SPOTTSWOODE.

**SAVOIE** *France* Savoie's high Alpine vineyards, which are scattered between Lake Geneva and Grenoble and on the banks of the Rhône and Isère rivers, produce fresh, snappy white wines with loads of flavour, when made from the Altesse (or Roussette) grape. Drink them young. There are some attractive light reds and rosés, too, mainly from a group of villages south of Chambéry and, in hot years, some positively Rhône-like reds from the Mondeuse grape. Most of the better wines use the Vin de Savoie AC and should be drunk young or with 3–4 years' age. The 15 best villages, including Abymes, Apremont, Arbin, Chignin, Cruet and Montmélian, can add their own name to the AC name. Best producers: Boniface★, Bouvet★, Dupasquier★, Magnin★, C Marandon★, Monin, Neyroud, Perret★, A & M Quénard★, R Quénard★, Ripaille★, Rocailles★, C Trosset★. See also Seyssel.

**SAXENBURG** *Stellenbosch WO, South Africa* Two harvests a year are now a feature of winemaker Nico van der Merwe's life. Locally, he creates some of the Cape's most sought-after reds, led by Shiraz; the headily scented and, at times, burly Private Collection Shiraz★★ has been joined by an even richer, bigger Shiraz Select★★. Also excellent are the Cabernet★★, Merlot★ and Sauvignon Blanc★★ and Chardonnay★ under the Private Collection label. Nico is producing equally good results at Swiss businessman Adrian Bührer's other estate, Dom. Capion in the LANGUEDOC. Two Capion/Saxenburg 'Grand Vin' intercontinental blends, a red and white, unite the 2 hemispheres. Drink whites young; reds will improve for 5–8 years. Best years: (reds) 1998 **97 96 95 94 93 92 91**.

**WILLI SCHAEFER** *Graach, Mosel, Germany* It would be hard to find more classic MOSEL wines than Schaefer's naturally sweet Riesling Spätlese and Auslese from the great Domprobst vineyard of GRAACH. The balance of piercing acidity and lavish fruit is every bit as dramatic as Domprobst's precipitous slope. Made in tiny quantities and extremely long-lived, they're frequently ★★★, as is the sensational Beerenauslese Schaefer produces in good vintages. Even the QbA wines here are ★. Best years: (2000) 99 98 97 96 95 **94 93 92** 90 **89 88 85 83 79 76 71 69 59**.

**SCHEUREBE** Very popular Silvaner x Riesling crossing most widespread in Germany's RHEINHESSEN and PFALZ. Also planted in Austria, where it is sometimes sold under the name Sämling 88. At its best in Trockenbeerenauslese and Eiswein. When ripe, it has a marvellous flavour of honey, exotic fruits and the pinkest of pink grapefruit.

**SCHIOPETTO** *Friuli-Venezia Giulia, Italy* One of the legends of Italian wine, who pioneered the development of scented varietals and, above all, high-quality, intensely concentrated white wines from COLLIO. Most outstanding are Tocai★★, Pinot Bianco★★ and Sauvignon★★ which open out with age to display myriad flavours. New COLLI ORIENTALI vineyards Poderi dei Blumeri can only add further prestige.

**SCHLOSSBÖCKELHEIM** *Nahe, Germany* This NAHE village's top sites are the Felsenberg and Kupfergrübe, but good wines also come from Mühlberg and Königsfels. Best producers: CRUSIUS★, H DONNHOFF★★★, Weingutsverwaltung Niederhausen-Schlossböckelheim★. Best years: 1999 98 **96 95 94**.

**SCHLOSS LIESER** *Lieser, Mosel, Germany* Since Thomas Haag (son of Wilhelm, of the Fritz HAAG estate) took over the winemaking in 1992, this small estate has shot to the top. MOSEL Rieslings★★ that marry richness with great elegance. Best years: 1999 98 **97** 96 95 94 **93**.

**SCHLOSS REINHARTSHAUSEN** *Erbach, Rheingau, Germany* Estate formerly owned by the Hohenzollern family, which ruled Prussia, then Germany until 1918. There are several fine vineyard sites, including the great Erbacher Marcobrunn. Interesting organic Weissburgunder-Chardonnay blend from its vines in Erbacher Rheinhell, an island in the middle of the Rhine. Good Rieslings (Auslese, BA, TBA ★★★) and Sekt★. Best years: 1999 98 **97** 96 **95 94 93 92** 90 89.

**SCHLOSS SAARSTEIN** *Serrig, Saar, Germany* Fine Saar estate whose Riesling Dry can taste a little austere; better balanced are wines like the Serriger Riesling Kabinett★ or Spätlese★ and Auslese★★, which keep the startling acidity but coat it with fruit, often with the aromas of slightly unripe white peaches. Saarstein makes the occasional spectacular Eiswein★★★. Best years: 1999 **97** 95 93 92 90 89 88 86 85.

**SCHLOSS VOLLRADS** *Oestrich-Winkel, Rheingau, Germany* Following the sudden death of owner Erwein Graf Matuschka-Greiffenclau before the 1997 harvest, the running of this historic estate was taken up by its banker, Rowald Hepp, who continues to direct it. Quality seems to have got back on track with the 1999 vintage.

**DOMAINE SCHOFFIT** *Alsace AC, Alsace, France* One of the two main owners of the outstanding Rangen Grand Cru vineyard, also making a range of deliciously fruity non-cru wines. Top-of-the-tree Clos St-Théobald wines from Rangen are often ★★★ and will improve for at least 5–6 years after release, Rieslings for even longer. Best years: (Grand Cru Riesling) (1998) 97 **96 95** 94.

**SCHRAMSBERG** *Napa Valley AVA, California, USA* The first CALIFORNIA winery to make really excellent CHAMPAGNE-method sparklers from the classic grapes. Though all releases do not achieve the same heights, the best of these wines can be unequalled in California – and in most of Champagne too. The Crémant★ is an attractive sweetish sparkler, the Blanc de Noirs★★ and the Blanc de Blancs★ stand out. Top of the line is the Reserve Brut★★, which can be world class. In a bold, powerful style is J Schram★★ – rich and flavoursome and increasingly good. Vintage-dated wines can be drunk with up to 10 years' age.

**SEAVIEW** *McLaren Vale, South Australia* Best known for good, mass-market fizz★ and excellent Vintage Reserve Pinot-Chardonnay★★ and Blanc de Blancs★★ but, along with value-for-money commercial reds and whites, occasionally produces super export selection Cabernet★. Edwards & Chaffey★★ is the Reserve label for top fizz, rich Shiraz★★, Cabernet★★ and unfiltered Chardonnay★★.

**SEIFRIED ESTATE** *Nelson, South Island, New Zealand* Established in 1974 by Austrian Hermann Seifried and his New Zealand wife Agnes. The best wines include botrytized Riesling★★, Gewürztraminer★ and Sauvignon Blanc★. The Redwood Valley label is used in export markets. Best years: (2001) 00 99 **98** 96.

**SELAKS** *Kumeu/Huapai, Auckland, North Island, New Zealand* A long-established winery making fine Sauvignon Blanc-Semillon★★ and aggressive, snappy Sauvignon Blanc★★; also Chardonnay★ and

Riesling★. Selaks was purchased by NOBILO in 1998, but wine styles and quality have been maintained. Best years: (Sauvignon Blanc-Semillon) (2001) **99 97 96 94**.

**SELBACH-OSTER** *Zeltingen, Mosel, Germany* Johannes Selbach is one of the MOSEL's new generation of star winemakers, producing very pure, elegant Riesling★ from the Zeltingen Sonnenuhr site. Also good wine from WEHLEN, GRAACH and BERNKASTEL. Best years: 1999 98 97 96 95 **94 93 92 91 90 89 88 85**.

**SELLA & MOSCA** *Sardinia, Italy* Apart from the rich, port-like Anghelu Ruju★ made from semi-dried Cannonau grapes, this much-modernized old firm produces excellent dry whites, Terre Bianche★ (Torbato), La Cala★ (Vermentino) and oak-aged reds, Marchese di Villamarina★★ (Cabernet) and Tanca Farrà★★ (Cannonau-Cabernet). Best years: (Marchese di Villamarina) 96 **95 93 92 90**.

**SELVAPIANA** *Chianti DOCG, Tuscany, Italy* This estate in CHIANTI RUFINA has always produced excellent wines that are typical of the zone. But since 1990 it has vaulted into the top rank of Tuscan estates, particularly with the Riserva★★ and single-vineyard Riserva, Vigneto Bucerchiale★★★. New is another single-vineyard Riserva, Fornace★★. VIN SANTO★★ is very good. Best years: (Bucerchiale) 1998 96 95 **94 93 91 90 88 85**.

**SÉMILLON** Found mainly in South-West France, especially in the sweet wines of SAUTERNES and BARSAC where, because of its thin skin, it is prone to noble rot. Also blended with Sauvignon Blanc to make dry wine – almost all the great GRAVES Classed Growths are based on this blend. Performs well in Australia (aged Semillon from the HUNTER, BAROSSA and CLARE VALLEY can be wonderful) on its own or as a blender with Chardonnay (the accent over the é is dropped on New World labels). Sémillon is also blended with Sauvignon in Australia, New Zealand, CALIFORNIA and WASHINGTON STATE. It is enjoying a revival in the South African Cape, where it is primarily a bulk blender, but barrel-fermented varietals and blends with Sauvignon can produce outstanding results.

**SEÑA★★** *Valle del Aconcagua, Aconcagua, Chile* A MONDAVI and Chadwick family (ERRAZURIZ) partnership, currently sourced from Errázuriz's Don Maximiano vineyards, Seña is a Cabernet-Carmenère blend. By 2005, it should be composed of 5 different varieties from a single estate. It has fruit intensity and quality is high, although not enough to justify the price. Cellar for 5–10 years. Best years: 1999 **96 95**.

**SEPPELT** *Barossa Valley, South Australia, and Grampians, Victoria* Leading Australian fizz factory, from mass-produced Great Western tank-fermented, up to tasty Fleur de Lys★, and on to Drumborg★★, Harpers Range★ and Salinger★★, all made by the Champagne method from Pinot Noir and Chardonnay, all pristine and fruity with subtle yeast influence. A vintage Sauvignon fizz called Rhymney is a recent addition. Table wines are generally good, especially Great Western Shiraz★★ and Chardonnay★, Dorrien Cabernet★, Partalunga Riesling★ and wines from super-cool Drumborg. Mid-priced 'Victorian Portfolio' stars Chalambar Shiraz★ and Sunday Creek Pinot Noir★. Also makes wonderful sparkling Show Reserve Shiraz (the 85, 86, 87 and 90 are ★★★) and top-notch fortifieds (many ★★★).

**SERESIN** *Marlborough, South Island, New Zealand* London-based film producer Michael Seresin's super-premium winery is making a big impact on the MARLBOROUGH scene. Concentrated Sauvignon Blanc★★ is best within a year or two of the vintage, but creamy, mellow Chardonnay★★, succulent Pinot Gris★ and rich, oaky Pinot Noir★★ will age for up to 3 years.

**SETÚBAL DOC** *Terras do Sado, Portugal* Fortified wine from the Setúbal Peninsula south of Lisbon, which is called 'Moscatel de Setúbal' when made from at least 85% Moscatel, and 'Setúbal' when it's not. Best producers: José Maria da FONSECA★★, J P VINHOS★.

**SEYSSEL AC** *Savoie, France* Known for its feather-light, sparkling wine, Seyssel Mousseux. With the lovely sharp, peppery bite of the Molette and Altesse grapes smoothed out with a creamy yeast, it is an ideal summer gulper. The still white is light and floral, and made only from Altesse. Best producers: Mollex★, Varichon & Clerc★.

**SEYVAL BLANC** Hybrid grape (Seibel 5656 x Rayon d'Or) whose disease resistance and ability to continue ripening in a damp autumn make it a useful variety in England, Canada and NEW YORK STATE and other areas in the eastern US. Gives clean, sappy, grapefruit-edged wines that are sometimes a very passable imitation of bone-dry CHABLIS.

**SHAFER** *Stags Leap AVA, California, USA* One of the best NAPA wineries, making unusually fruity Stags Leap District Cabernet★★ and a Reserve-style Hillside Select★★★. Merlot★★ and Firebreak★★ (Sangiovese-Cabernet) are increasingly important. Chardonnay★★★, from Red Shoulder Vineyard, is classic CARNEROS style. Best years: (Cabernet Hillside Select) (1999) (98) 97 96 95 94 **93 92 91 90 85 84**.

**SHAW & SMITH** *Adelaide Hills, South Australia* Cousins Michael Hill Smith – Australia's first MW and operator of Adelaide's noted Universal wine bar – and Martin Shaw, an ex-flying winemaker, have had a runaway success with their tangy Sauvignon Blanc★ since the first vintage in 1989. Not a pair to rush in, they have gradually added an unwooded Chardonnay★ and a wooded Reserve★★ to the list, and now an impressive Merlot, Incognito. Drink the Sauvignon and unoaked Chardonnay very young, but the Reserve will keep. Best years: (Reserve Chardonnay) **1998 97 96 95 94 93 92 91**.

**SHERRY** See Jerez y Manzanilla DO, pages 158–9.

**SHIRAZ** See Syrah, pages 268–9.

**SICILY** *Italy* Sicily is emerging with a renewed spirit and attitude to wine production. The three leading estates for table wines, PLANETA, REGALEALI and Duca di SALAPARUTA, are being joined by others, including Donnafugata, the revitalized Spadafora and transformed Settesoli (headed by Diego Planeta) as well as other exciting estates such as Abbazia Santa Anastasia (whose Cabernet Sauvignon Litra★★ has been shaped by the great Giacamo Tachis). A new internal dynamism is being matched by outside investment and expertise – nowhere better illustrated than in Maurizio Miccichè's (Calatrasi) joint venture with BRL HARDY. Zonin's new 200-ha (495-acre) estate in the Caltanissetta region is set to have a major impact over the next decade. See also Alcamo, Marsala, Moscato Passito di Pantelleria.

**SIEUR D'ARQUES, LES CAVES DU** *Limoux AC and Blanquette de Limoux AC, Languedoc, France* This modern co-op makes around 90% of the still and sparkling wines of LIMOUX. The BLANQUETTE DE LIMOUX★ and CREMANT DE LIMOUX★ are both reliable, but the real excitement comes with the Toques et Clochers Chardonnays★ (occasionally ★★). The co-op also makes a range of white and red varietal vins de pays.

**SILVER OAK CELLARS** *Napa Valley, California, USA* One of California's best Cabernet Sauvignon producers, with bottlings from ALEXANDER VALLEY★★ grapes and NAPA VALLEY★★, the latter now including grapes previously earmarked for limited-release Bonny's Vineyard★★★, last produced in 1991. Forward, generous, fruity wines, impossible not to enjoy young, yet with great staying power. Best years: (Alexander Valley) (1999) (98) 97 96 95 **94 93 92 91 90 88 87** 85; (Napa Valley) (1999) (98) 97 96 95 **94 93 92 91 90 88 87 86 85 84** 82.

**SILVERADO VINEYARDS** *Stags Leap AVA, California, USA* This estate winery makes splendid Cabernet Sauvignon and Chardonnay. The regular Cabernet★ has intense fruit and is drinkable fairly young; Limited Reserve★★ has more depth and is capable of some aging. The Chardonnay★ has soft, inviting fruit and a silky finish. A fruity Merlot★ and SUPER-TUSCAN-style Sangiovese are also much in demand. Best years: (Reserve Cabernet) (1999) (98) 97 96 95 94 **93 91 90**.

**SIMI** *Alexander Valley AVA, California, USA* Historic winery recently sold to Canandaigua, although winemaker Nick Goldschmidt has stayed. The Cabernet Sauvignon★, Chardonnay★★ and Sauvignon Blanc★ (Sendal★★) attain high standards; Chardonnay Reserve occasionally reaches ★★★. Best years: (reds) (1999) 98 97 95 94 **92 91 90**.

**SION** *Valais, Switzerland* Considered one of the top wine villages in the VALAIS and best known for its pure Chasselas Fendant. Best producers: Michel Clavien★, Robert Gilliard★, Dom. du Mont d'Or★.

**CH. SIRAN★** *Margaux AC, Cru Bourgeois, Haut-Médoc, Bordeaux, France* Consistently good claret, approachable young, but with enough structure to last for as long as 20 years. Second wine: Ch. Bellegarde. Best years: (2000) 98 96 95 **90 89 86 85 83 82**.

**SKALLI-FORTANT DE FRANCE** *Languedoc-Roussillon, France* Now one of the most important producers in the South of France, Robert Skalli was an early pioneer of varietal wines in the MIDI. Modern winemaking and the planting of international grape varieties were the keys to success. The Fortant de France brand includes a range of single-variety Vins de Pays d'OC. Grenache and Chardonnay are among the best, but I am yet to be fully convinced by the top reds.

**CH. SMITH-HAUT-LAFITTE** *Pessac-Léognan AC, Cru Classé de Graves, Bordeaux, France* Large property best known for its reds★★, now one of the most improved and innovative estates in PESSAC-LEOGNAN AC since a change of ownership in 1990. There is only a little white★★ (from 100% Sauvignon) but it is a shining example of tip-top modern white Bordeaux. Best years: (reds) (2000) 99 98 97 96 95 94 **90 89**; (whites) (2000) 99 98 **96 95 94 93 92**.

**SMITH WOODHOUSE** *Port DOC, Portugal* Underrated but consistently satisfying port from this shipper in the Symington group. The Smith Woodhouse Vintage★★ is always worth looking out for, as is the single-quinta Santa Madalena in 1995, and its Late Bottled Vintage

Port★★ is the rich and characterful, figgy, unfiltered type. Best years: (Vintage) 1997 94 92 91 **85 83 80 77 70 63**.

**SOAVE DOC** *Veneto, Italy*  In the hilly Soave Classico zone near Verona, the Garganega and Trebbiano di Soave grapes can produce ripe, nutty, scented wines. However, 70% of all Soave comes from the flat fertile plains, and much of this is blended into a limp, tasteless white. Since 1992, the blend may include 30% Chardonnay, and good examples are definitely on the increase. Best producers: ANSELMI★★, Bertani★, Ca' Rugate★, La Cappuccina★, Cantina del Castello★, Coffele★, Gini★, Inama★, MASI★, Pasqua/Cecilia Beretta★, PIEROPAN★★, Portinari★, Prà★, Soave co-op, Suavia★, Tamellini★. See also Recioto di Soave DOCG.

**CH. SOCIANDO-MALLET★★** *Haut-Médoc AC, Cru Bourgeois, Haut-Médoc, Bordeaux, France*  Owner Jean Gautreau has made this one of BORDEAUX's star Crus Bourgeois. The wine has every sign of great red Bordeaux flavours to come if you can hang on for 10–15 years. Best years: (2000) 99 98 97 96 95 **94 93 90 89 88 86 85 83 82**.

**SOGRAPE** *Portugal*  Sogrape proves that it is possible to be the biggest *and* among the best, and can be credited with revolutionizing quality in some of Portugal's most reactionary wine regions. Mateus Rosé is still the company's golden egg, but Sogrape makes good to very good wines in BAIRRADA (Reserva Branco★), DOURO (Reserva Tinto★) and VINHO VERDE as well. Subsidiaries FERREIRA and Offley provide top-flight ports and Casa Ferreirinha table wines. From the high-tech Quinta dos Carvalhais winery in DAO come a premium varietal white, Encruzado★, and red, Touriga Nacional★, as well as improved Duque de Viseu★ and Grão Vasco reds and whites. Vinha do Monte is a new red from the ALENTEJO. Also owns Finca Flichman in Argentina.

**SOKOL BLOSSER WINERY** *Willamette Valley AVA, Oregon, USA*  Consistently good, buttery, toasty Chardonnay★★ (Redland) and sometimes outstanding, though not as consistent, Pinot Noir★ (Redland) with soft, rather elegant fruit. Best years: (1999) 98 **97**.

**SOLAIA★★★** *Tuscany, Italy*  One of ANTINORI's much-admired SUPER-TUSCANS, sourced from a neighbouring vineyard to TIGNANELLO, Solaia is a blend of Cabernet Sauvignon, Sangiovese and Cabernet Franc. It is intense, with rich fruit and a classic structure. It is not produced in every vintage. Best years: (1998) 97 96 95 94 93 **91 90 88 86 85**.

**SOMONTANO DO** *Aragón, Spain*  In the foothills of the Pyrenees, this region is an up-and-coming star. Reds and rosés from the local grapes (Moristel and Tempranillo) can be light, fresh and flavourful, and international varieties such as Chardonnay and Gewürztraminer are already yielding promising wines. An interesting development is the rediscovery of the soft native red grape, Moristel, and the powerful Parraleta (RIOJA's Graciano). Best producers: ENATE★, Bodega Pirineos★, VINAS DEL VERO★. Best years: (reds) (1999) 98 **97 96 95 94**.

**SONOMA COUNTY** *California, USA*  Sonoma's vine-growing area is big and sprawling, with dozens of soil types and mesoclimates, from the fairly warm SONOMA VALLEY/ALEXANDER VALLEY region to the cool Green Valley and lower RUSSIAN RIVER VALLEY. The best wines are from Chardonnay, Sauvignon Blanc, Cabernet Sauvignon, Pinot Noir and Zinfandel. Often the equal of rival NAPA in quality and originality of flavours. See also Carneros, Dry Creek Valley.

# SPARKLING WINES OF THE WORLD ___

*Made by the Traditional (Champagne) Method*

Although Champagne is still the benchmark for top-class sparkling wines all over the world, the Champagne houses themselves have taken the message to California, Australia and New Zealand via wineries they've established in these regions. However, Champagne-method fizz doesn't necessarily have to feature the original grape varieties, and this allows a host of other places to join the party. Describing a wine as Champagne method is now strictly speaking no longer allowed (only original Champagne from France is officially sanctioned to do this), but the use of a phrase like Traditional Method should not distract from the fact that these wines are still painstakingly produced using the complex system of secondary fermentation in the bottle itself.

*STYLES OF SPARKLING WINE*

**France** Non-Champagne French fizz ranges from the sublime to the near-ridiculous. The best examples have great finesse and include grapy Crémant d'Alsace, produced from Pinot Blanc and Riesling; often inexpensive yet eminently drinkable Crémant de Bourgogne, based mainly on Chardonnay; and some stylish examples from the Loire, notably in Saumur and Vouvray. Clairette de Die and Blanquette de Limoux in the south confuse the issue by following their own idiosyncratic method of production, but the result is delicious.

**Rest of Europe** Franciacorta DOCG is a success story for Italy; Asti and Lambrusco are not Champagne-method wines. In Spain, the Cava wines of Cataluña offer an affordable style for everyday drinking. German Sekt comes in two basic styles: one made from Riesling grapes, the other using Champagne varieties. England is proving naturally suited to growing grapes for sparkling wine.

**Australia and New Zealand** Australia has a wide range of styles. Blends are still being produced using fruit from many areas, but regional characters are starting to emerge. Tasmania is the rising star and makes some top fizz from its own local grapes. Red sparklers, notably those made from Shiraz, are an irresistible Australian curiosity with an alcoholic kick. Cool-climate New Zealand is coming up fast for fizz with some premium and pricy examples; as in Australia, some have Champagne connections.

**USA** Some magnificent quality examples are produced – the best ones using grapes from Carneros or the Anderson Valley. Quality has been transformed by the efforts of French Champagne houses. Oregon is also a contender in the sparkling stakes.

**South Africa** Cap Classique is the local name for the Champagne method. Many producers are jumping on the fizz bandwagon and the best are very good, but there are problems with consistency.

See also individual producers.

260

## BEST PRODUCERS

**Australia** Blue Pyrenees, BROWN BROTHERS, Cope-Williams, GREEN POINT, HANGING ROCK, PETALUMA (Croser), PIPERS BROOK (Pirie), ROCKFORD (Sparkling Shiraz), SEAVIEW, SEPPELT, TALTARNI (Clover Hill), Yarrabank, YELLOWGLEN.

**Austria** BRUNDLMAYER.

**France** (Alsace) Ostertag; (Burgundy) Caves de Bailly, Caves de Lugny; (Saumur) BOUVET-LADUBAY, GRATIEN & MEYER; (Die) Clairette de Die co-op; (Limoux) SIEUR D'ARQUES co-op; (Vouvray) Clos Naudin, HUET.

**Germany** (Franken) Rudolf FURST; (Pfalz) Bergdolt, KOEHLER-RUPRECHT; (Saar) Dr Wagner.

**Italy** (Franciacorta) BELLAVISTA, CA' DEL BOSCO; (Trento) FERRARI; (Sicily) REGALEALI.

**New Zealand** CELLIER LE BRUN, CLOUDY BAY (Pelorus), CORBANS (Amadeus), MONTANA (Deutz), MORTON ESTATE, Nautilus, PALLISER.

**Portugal** Caves ALIANCA, J P VINHOS.

**South Africa** Graham BECK, J C le ROUX (Pongrácz), Twee Jonge Zellen, VILLIERA.

**Spain** (Cava) CASTELLBLANCH, CODORNIU, FREIXENET, JUVE Y CAMPS, MARQUES DE MONISTROL, Raventós i Blanc.

**UK** CHAPEL DOWN, NYETIMBER, RIDGEVIEW, VALLEY VINEYARDS.

**USA** (California) S Anderson, DOMAINE CARNEROS, DOMAINE CHANDON, HANDLEY CELLARS, IRON HORSE, J Wine, Laetitia, MUMM NAPA, PACIFIC ECHO, ROEDERER, SCHRAMSBERG; (Oregon) Argyle.

**SONOMA-CUTRER** *Russian River Valley AVA, California, USA* Crisp,
♀ pleasant but nowadays often overrated Chardonnay from 3 vineyards.
Les Pierres is the most complex and richest of the 3, often worth ★★;
Cutrer★★ can also have a complexity worth waiting for. Russian
River Ranches★ can be rather flat and ordinary, though much
improved in recent releases. Best years: 1999 98 **97 95 94 92 91**.

**SONOMA VALLEY AVA** *Sonoma, California, USA* The oldest wine region
🍷 north of San Francisco, Sonoma Valley is situated on the western side
of the Mayacamas Mountains, which separate it from NAPA VALLEY. Best
varieties are Chardonnay and Zinfandel, with Cabernet and Merlot
from hillside sites coming on strong. Best producers: ARROWOOD★★,
CARMENET★★, CHATEAU ST JEAN★, B R Cohn, Fisher★, GUNDLACH-
BUNDSCHU★, KENWOOD★, KUNDE★, LAUREL GLEN★★, MATANZAS CREEK★★,
RAVENSWOOD★★, St Francis★, Sebastiani★.

**SOUTH AUSTRALIA** Australia's biggest grape-growing state, with more
than 50,000ha (123,000 acres) of vineyards. Covers many climates and
most wine styles from bulk wines to the very best. Old established areas are
BAROSSA, CLARE and Eden Valleys, MCLAREN VALE, Langhorne Creek,
COONAWARRA, Adelaide Plains and RIVERLAND. Newer districts creating
excitement are ADELAIDE HILLS and PADTHAWAY; the recently planted
Wrattonbully is already producing promising red wines and is, like
Coonawarra, made up of *terra rossa* soil over limestone. Mount Benson,
Robe and even Kangaroo Island also show promise.

**SOUTH-WEST FRANCE** As well as the world-famous wines of
BORDEAUX, South-West France has many lesser-known, inexpensive ACs,
VDQS and VdPs, over 10 different *départements* from the Atlantic coast to
LANGUEDOC-ROUSSILLON. Bordeaux grapes (Cabernet Sauvignon, Merlot and
Cabernet Franc for reds; Sauvignon Blanc, Sémillon and Muscadelle for
whites) are common, but there are lots of interesting local varieties as
well, such as Tannat (in MADIRAN), Petit Manseng (in JURANCON) and
Mauzac (in GAILLAC). See also Bergerac, Cahors, Côtes de Duras, Côtes du
Frontonnais, Irouléguy, Monbazillac, Montravel, Pacherenc du Vic-Bilh.

**SPÄTBURGUNDER** See Pinot Noir.
**SPICE ROUTE WINE COMPANY** *Swartland WO, South Africa* High-profile
🍷 operation established by Charles Back, owner of FAIRVIEW, international
wine marketer Jabulani Ntshangase, South Africa's leading wine
writer, John Platter, and Gyles Webb of THELEMA. Back now owns the
company but the others remain as directors. Cellarmaster Eben Sadie
produces sumptuous Chenin Blanc★ and tangy Sauvignon★, but the
real quality lies in his top reds, the big yet classically styled Flagship
trio of Pinotage★★, Merlot★★ and Syrah★★.

**SPOTTSWOODE** *Napa Valley AVA, California, USA* Replanted in the mid-
🍷 1990s, Spottswoode's beautifully situated 16-ha (40-acre) vineyard west
of St Helena has not missed a beat since the winery opened in 1982.
Deep, blackberry and cherry-fruited Cabernet Sauvignon★★★ invites
early drinking, but is best at 5–10 years. Sauvignon Blanc★★ (blended
with a little Semillon and barrel fermented) is a beautiful, sophisticated
treat. Best years: (Cabernet) (1999) 98 97 96 95 94 **93 92 91**.

**STAG'S LEAP WINE CELLARS** *Stags Leap AVA, California, USA* The winery rose to fame when its Cabernet Sauvignon came first at the Paris tasting of 1976. Cabernet Sauvignon★★ can be stunning, particularly the SLV★★★ from estate vineyards and the Fay★★; the Cask 23 Cabernet Sauvignon★ can be very good, but is overhyped. After a dip in quality, late 1990s vintages seem back on form. A lot of work has gone into the Chardonnay★★ and the style is one of NAPA's most successful. Best years: (reds) (1999) 98 97 96 95 94 93 **92 91 90 89 88 84**; (whites) 1999 98 97 96 95 **94**.

**STEELE WINES** *Lake County, California, USA* Owner and winemaker Jed Steele is a master blender. He sources grapes from all over California and shapes them into exciting wines, usually featuring vivid fruit with supple mouthfeel. But he also offers single-vineyard wines and has, in current release, 4–6 Chardonnays, most ★★. His Zinfandels★★ are often very good, as are his Pinot Noirs★★ (CARNEROS, SANTA MARIA VALLEY). The Shooting Star label provides remarkable value in a ready-to-drink style. Best years: (Zinfandels) (1999) 98 **97 95 94 93**.

**STEENBERG** *Constantia WO, South Africa* The oldest farm in the CONSTANTIA valley is seeing great results from total vineyard replanting in the early 1990s. Winemaker Nicky Versfeld's Reserve Sauvignon Blanc★★ is one of South Africa's best, smoky and flinty with underlying fruit richness. Straight Sauvignon★ is fruitier but remains subtle. Semillon★★ and Chardonnay★ are impressive. A bright-fruited, minty Merlot★★ has been joined by the blend Catharina★; both are ripe and well structured. Best years: **2000 99 98 97 96**.

**STEIERMARK** *Austria* Known as Styria in English, this wine region in south-east Austria formerly covered much of Slovenia's vineyards, too. It includes the regions of Süd-Oststeiermark, Süd-Steiermark and West-Steiermark. It is the warmest of the 4 Austrian wine zones, but the best vineyards are in cool, high-altitude sites. The best wines are Morillon (unoaked Chardonnay, though oak is catching on here as well), Sauvignon Blanc and Gelber Muskateller. Best producers: Gross★, Lackner-Tinnacher★★, Polz★, TEMENT★★.

**STELLENBOSCH WO** *South Africa* Considered the hub of the South African wine industry, this fine red wine region boasts the greatest concentration of wineries in the Cape, with vineyards straddling valley floors and stretching up the many mountain slopes. Climates and soils are as diverse as wine styles; smaller units of origin – wards – are now being demarcated to more accurately reflect this diversity. The renowned reds are matched by some excellent Sauvignon Blanc and Chardonnay, as well as modern Chenin Blanc and Semillon. The area suffered widespread fire damage in January 2000, which particularly affected Delheim, KANONKOP, Morgenhof and WARWICK. Best producers: BEYERSKLOOF★, EIKENDAL★, Neil ELLIS★★, GRANGEHURST★★, HARTENBERG★, JORDAN★, Kaapzicht, KANONKOP★★, L'AVENIR★, Le Bonheur★, Le Riche★, Lievland★, Longridge★, Louisvale, MEERLUST★, Meinert★, Morgenhof★, MULDERBOSCH★★, Neethlingshof★, Overgaauw★, RUSTEN-BERG★★, RUST-EN-VREDE★, SAXENBURG★, Simonsig★, STELLENZICHT★★, THELEMA★★, Uiterwyk★, VERGELEGEN★★, Vriesenhof★, WARWICK★.

# SUPER-TUSCANS
*Tuscany, Italy*

The term 'Super-Tuscans', first used by English and American writers, has now been adopted by Italians themselves to describe the new-style red wines of Tuscany. The 1970s and 80s were a time when enormous strides were being made in Bordeaux, Australia and California, yet these changes threatened to bypass Italy completely because of its restrictive wine laws. A group of winemakers, led by Piero Antinori, abandoned tradition to put their best efforts and best grapes into creative wines styled for modern tastes, replacing old casks with barriques, while planting Cabernet and other trendy varieties, such as Merlot, Pinot Noir and Syrah, alongside Sangiovese in vineyards that emerged with sudden grandeur as crus. Since the DOC specifically forbade such innovations, producers were forced to label their wines as plain Vino da Tavola. The 'Super-Tuscan' Vino da Tavolas, as they were quickly dubbed, were a phenomenal success: brilliant in flavour with an approachable, upfront style. Some found it hard to believe that table wines with no official credentials could outrank DOCG Chianti. A single mouthful was usually enough to convince them.

## WINE STYLES

Sangiovese and Cabernet Sauvignon are the basis for most Super-Tuscans, one usually making up the balance with the other. Both also appear varietally, with Sangiovese forming the largest group of top-quality Super-Tuscans. To some Sangiovese-based wines, a small percentage of other native varieties such as Colorino, Canaiolo or Malvasia Nera is added. Merlot has long been used as the complement to Cabernet in the Bordeaux mould but more recently has been combined with Sangiovese in exactly the same way. Syrah is of growing importance, mostly varietally, but also in innovative new blends such as Argiano's Solengo. Super-Tuscan wines also show considerable differences in vinification and aging. Top wines are invariably based on ripe, concentrated grapes from a site with special attributes.

## CLASSIFICATIONS

A law passed in 1992 has finally brought the Super-Tuscans into line with official classifications. Sassicaia now has its own DOC under Bolgheri. Chianti Classico's newly independent DOCG could cover many a Sangiovese-based Super-Tuscan, but the majority are currently sold under the region-wide IGT Toscana alongside wines made from international varieties. There are also three sub-regional IGTs, but only a few producers use these.

See also BOLGHERI, CHIANTI CLASSICO, SASSICAIA, SOLAIA, TIGNANELLO; and individual producers.

264

### BEST PRODUCERS

**Sangiovese and other Tuscan varieties** Badia a Coltibuono (Sangioveto), BOSCARELLI, CASTELLARE (I Sodi di San Niccolò), FELSINA (Fontalloro), FONTODI (Flaccianello della Pieve), ISOLE E OLENA (Cepparello), Lilliano (Anagallis), MONTEVERTINE (Le Pergole Torte, Il Sodaccio), Panera (Quattrocentenario, Terrine), Poggio Scalette (Il Carbonaione), Querceto (La Corte), RIECINE (La Gioia), RUFFINO (Romitorio di Santedame), San Giusto a Rentennano (Percarlo), VOLPAIA (Coltassala).

**Sangiovese-Cabernet and Sangiovese-Merlot blends** ANTINORI (TIGNANELLO), ARGIANO (Solengo), BANFI (Summus), Colombaio di Cencio (Il Futuro), FONTERUTOLI (Siepi), Gagliole, Montepeloso (Nardo), QUERCIABELLA (Camartina).

**Cabernet** ANTINORI (SOLAIA), Col d'Orcia (Olmaia), ISOLE E OLENA (Collezione), Nozzole (Il Pareto), RAMPOLLA (Sammarco, Vigna d'Alceo).

**Merlot** Castello di AMA (L'Apparita), AVIGNONESI, Le Macchiole (Messorio), ORNELLAIA (Masseto), Tua Rita (Redigaffi).

**Cabernet-Merlot blends** ANTINORI (Guado al Tasso), BANFI (Excelsus), Capezzana (Ghiaie della Furba), ORNELLAIA (Ornellaia), Poggio al Sole (Seraselva), POLIZIANO (Le Stanze), Le Pupille (Saffredi), TERRICCIO (Lupicaia, Tassinaia), Trinoro, Tua Rita (Giusto di Notri).

**STELLENZICHT** *Stellenbosch WO, South Africa*  Since taking over from
Andre van Rensburg, now at VERGELEGEN, winemaker Guy Webber has
aimed for more elegance, less power, an approach already evident in
the Semillon★, although his first vintage of the rich, spicy Syrah★★
has yet to be released. Sauvignon Blanc★ with gooseberry intensity
and newcomer Pinotage★ are well up to standard.

**STERLING VINEYARDS** *Napa Valley AVA, California, USA*  After a long,
disappointing period, new winemaker Rob Hunter seems to be making
his mark. Merlot is the focus here, with Three Palms★★ and
Reserve★★, both impressively packed with ripe, dense fruit, leading
the way. Reserve Cabernet★ is generally good, while the regular
bottling is at last showing signs of improvement, as is Winery Lake
Pinot Noir★. The NAPA VALLEY Chardonnay★ can be rich and intense.
Best years: (reds) 1998 97 95 94 **92 91 90 87 86 85.**

**STONIER'S** *Mornington Peninsula, Victoria, Australia*  The peninsula's
biggest winery and one of its best, partly owned by PETALUMA, is still
run by the Stonier family and winemaker Ted Dexter. Reserve
Chardonnay★★ and Reserve Pinot★★ are usually outstanding, and
there are fine standard bottlings in warm vintages. Cabernets, in the
rather herbaceous style typical of the region, continue to improve.

**STONYRIDGE** *Waiheke Island, Auckland, North Island, New Zealand*  The
leading winery on WAIHEKE ISLAND, Stonyridge specializes in reds made
from Cabernet Sauvignon, Merlot, Petit Verdot, Malbec and Cabernet
Franc. The top label, Larose★★★, is a remarkably BORDEAUX-like red of
real intensity, and one of New Zealand's most expensive wines. Best
years: (Larose) (2000) 99 98 **96 94 93 91**.

**CH. SUDUIRAUT**★★ *Sauternes AC, 1er Cru Classé, Bordeaux, France*
Together with RIEUSSEC, Suduiraut is regarded as a close runner-up to
d'YQUEM. Although the wines are delicious at only a few years old, the
richness and excitement increase enormously after a decade or so.
Very expensive and seemed to be under-performing since the mid-
1980s but now owned by AXA of PICHON-LONGUEVILLE fame and back
on song. Best years: 1999 98 97 96 95 **90 89 88 86 82 81**.

**SUHINDOL** *Northern Region, Bulgaria*  This winery is the old warhorse
among Bulgarian wineries, established in 1909, and was the first to be
privatized in 1991. It perfected the creamy, curranty, throat-soothing
style of Cabernet Sauvignon then synonymous with Bulgaria, and is
now developing some premium Cabernet and Merlot reds. The Gamza
and Gamza-Merlot blends are both worth trying. New technology and
judicious use of oak have improved quality, as in the Craftsman Creek
range. Suhindol's new planting programme will make it self-sufficient by
2008; it currently produces nearly 30 million bottles a year.

**SUMAC RIDGE** *Okanagan Valley VQA, British Columbia, Canada*
Winemaker Mark Wendenberg produces excellent Sauvignon Blanc★
and Gewürztraminer Reserve★, fine Pinot Blanc and one of Canada's
best Champagne-method fizzes, Steller's Jay Brut★. Top reds include
varietal Cabernet Sauvignon, Cabernet Franc, Merlot and Pinot Noir
and blended Meritage★. Now owned by Canadian wine giant Vincor.

**SUNTORY** *Japan*  Tomi and Noble d'Or (made from botrytized grapes) are
top brand names here for wine made exclusively from grapes grown
in Japan; this is a rarity in a country where imported wine can legally

be blended with Japanese and sold as Japanese. The grapes are classic varieties and the wines include a light but attractive Cabernet Sauvignon and a good botrytized Semillon-Sauvignon blend.

**SUPER-TUSCANS** See pages 264–5.

**SUTTER HOME** *Napa County, California, USA* Now known for White Zinfandel, Sutter Home still makes a very drinkable Amador County Zinfandel, although it doesn't achieve the intensity and richness of its Zins of the 1970s and early 80s. Reserve Cabernet is a recent hit.

**SWAN DISTRICT** *Western Australia* The original WESTERN AUSTRALIA wine region and the hottest stretch of vineyards in Australia, spread along the torrid, fertile silty flats of Perth's Swan River. It used to specialize in fortified wines, but SOUTH AUSTRALIA and north-east VICTORIA both do them better. New-wave whites and reds, especially from Moondah Brook and HOUGHTON, are fresh and generous. Best producers: Paul Conti, HOUGHTON★, Lamont, Moondah Brook★, Sandalford, Westfield.

**JOSEPH SWAN VINEYARDS** *Russian River Valley AVA, California, USA* Joseph Swan made legendary Zinfandel in the 1970s and was one of the first to age Zinfandel★★ in French oak. In the 1980s he turned to Pinot Noir★★ which is now probably the winery's best offering. After Swan's death in 1989, his son-in-law, Rod Berglund, took over and has proved a worthy successor. Best years: (1999) 98 97 **96 95 94 93 92 91**.

**SYRAH** See pages 268–9.

**LA TÂCHE AC★★★** *Grand Cru, Côte de Nuits, Burgundy, France* Along with la ROMANEE-CONTI, the greatest of the great VOSNE-ROMANEE Grands Crus, owned by Dom. de la ROMANEE-CONTI. The wine has the rare ability to provide layer on layer of flavours; keep it for 10 years or you'll only experience a fraction of the pleasure you paid big money for. Best years: (2000) 99 98 97 96 95 93 91 90 **89 88 85 78**.

**TAHBILK** *Goulburn Valley, Victoria, Australia* Wonderfully old-fashioned family company making traditionally big, gumleafy/minty reds, matured only in old wood. Regional speciality white Marsanne★★ is perfumed and attractive. Other whites tend to lack finesse, but Shiraz★ and Cabernet★ are full of character, even if they need years of cellaring. Best years: (reds) 1998 97 95 91 **90 88 86 84 81 76 71**.

**TAITTINGER** *Champagne AC, Champagne, France* The top wine, Comtes de Champagne blanc de blancs★★★, can be memorable for its creamy, foaming pleasures and the Comtes de Champagne rosé★★ is elegant and oozing class. Ordinary non-vintage★ is soft and honeyed but has been unusually inconsistent for the last few years. Another de luxe cuvée, called Vintage Collection★, is simply the vintage Brut in a fancy bottle. Best years: 1995 **93 90 89 88 86 85 82 79**.

**CH. TALBOT★** *St-Julien AC, 4ème Cru Classé, Haut-Médoc, Bordeaux, France* Chunky, soft-centred but sturdy, capable of aging well for 10–20 years. There is also an interesting white wine, Caillou Blanc de Talbot★. Second wine: Connétable Talbot. Best years: (2000) 99 98 97 96 95 **94 90 89 88 86 85 83 82**.

**TALTARNI** *Pyrenees, Victoria, Australia* Biggest winery in this region, specializing in classic, deep-flavoured, European-style Cabernet★, Shiraz★, Merlot and Malbec; also respected fizz, especially Clover Hill★ and pink Brut Tâche★ from TASMANIA. Sauvignon Blanc★★ is tangy and gooseberry-like. Best years: (reds) 1997 **96 94 93 92 91 90**.

# SYRAH/SHIRAZ

Syrah now produces world-class wines in 3 countries. In France, where Hermitage and Côte-Rôtie are 2 of the world's great reds; in Australia, where as Shiraz it produces some of the New World's most remarkable reds; and now in California, too. And wherever Syrah appears it trumpets a proud and wilful personality based on loads of flavour and unmistakable originality.

Syrah's spread round the warmer wine regions of the world has been limited, however. Syrah's heartland – Hermitage and Côte-Rôtie in the Rhône Valley – comprises a mere 270ha (670 acres) of steeply terraced vineyards, producing hardly enough wine to make more than a very rarefied reputation for themselves. For long, growers in other countries simply had no idea as to what kind of flavour the Syrah grape produced, so didn't copy it. But the situation is rapidly changing.

## WINE STYLES

**French Syrah** The flavours of Syrah are most individual, but with modern vineyard practices and modern winemaking techniques they are far less daunting than they used to be. Traditional Syrah had a savage, almost coarse, throaty roar of a flavour. And from the very low-yielding Hermitage vineyards, the small grapes often showed a bitter tannic quality. But better selections of clones in the vineyard and improved winemaking have revealed that Syrah in fact gives a wine with a majestic depth of fruit, all blackberry and damson, loganberry and plum, some quite strong tannin, and some tangy smoke, but also a warm creamy aftertaste, and a promise of chocolate and occasionally a scent of violets. It is these characteristics that have made Syrah popular throughout the south of France as an 'improving' variety for its rather rustic red wines.

**Australian Shiraz** Australia's most widely planted red variety has become, in many respects, its premium varietal. Shiraz gives spectacularly good results when taken seriously – especially in the Barossa, Clare, Eden Valley and McLaren Vale regions of South Australia. An increasingly diverse range of high-quality examples also includes those from Victoria's warmer vineyards (especially in the Grampians region), more traditional examples from New South Wales' Hunter Valley and Mudgee, and exciting elegant styles from Western Australia's Margaret River and Great Southern regions. The flavours are rich, intense, thick sweet fruit coated with chocolate, and seasoned with leather, herbs and spice. It is frequently blended with Cabernet Sauvignon to add richness to Cabernet's angular frame.

**Other regions** In California producers are turning out superb Rhône blends as well as varietal Syrahs modelled closely on Côte-Rôtie or Hermitage. In South Africa, too, some exciting wines are appearing. Both Italy and Spain in Europe, and Argentina, Chile and New Zealand in the New World are also beginning to shine.

QUPÉ

19   97

SYRAH

Santa Barbara County
Bien Nacido Reserve

PRODUCED AND BOTTLED BY ROBERT N. LINDQUIST
SANTA MARIA, CALIFORNIA · BW 6009 · ALC 14.5% BY VOL

## BEST PRODUCERS

**Top Syrah**
*France* (Rhône) Allemand, G
Barge, Burgaud, CHAPOUTIER,
CHAVE, A CLAPE, Clusel-Roch,
COLOMBO, DELAS, J-M Gerin, A
GRAILLOT, GUIGAL, JABOULET,
JAMET, Rostaing, M Sorrel,
Tardieu-Laurent, VERSET.

*USA* (California) Alban, ARAUJO,
DEHLINGER, Edmunds St John,
Havens, Jade Mountain, Lewis,
Ojai, PHELPS, QUPE, Swanson,
THACKREY, Truchard, Zaca Mesa.

**Top Shiraz**
*Australia* Tim ADAMS, Jim BARRY,
BOWEN, BROKENWOOD, Charles
Cimicky, CLARENDON HILLS,
Craiglee, Dalwhinnie, HARDYS,
Jasper Hill, HENSCHKE, Peter
LEHMANN, Charles MELTON, MOUNT
LANGI GHIRAN, PENFOLDS,
PLANTAGENET, ROCKFORD,
ROSEMOUNT, WENDOUREE, WYNNS,
YARRA YERING.

**Other good Syrah**
*France* (Languedoc) Ch. des
ESTANILLES, GAUBY, l'HORTUS;
(Rhône) Balthazar, Belle,
Combier, Courbis, COURSODON,
Durand, B Faurie, J-L Grippat,
JASMIN, Monteillet, Villard.

*Italy* Bertelli, FONTODI, ISOLE E
OLENA, Le Macchiole, Manzano,
Poggio al Sole, Villa Pillo.

*Spain* Albet i Noya, MARQUES DE
GRINON, Enrique Mendoza.

**Other good Shiraz**
*Australia* BEST'S, Grant BURGE,
CHAPEL HILL, Coriole, D'ARENBERG,
LECONFIELD, LINDEMANS, MCWILLIAM'S,
MITCHELTON, Redbank, ROSEMOUNT,
ROTHBURY, ST HALLETT, SEPPELT,
Seville Estate, TALTARNI, TYRRELL'S,
VASSE FELIX, WIRRA WIRRA, Zema.

*New Zealand* Stonecroft, TE MATA.

*South Africa* Boekenhoutskloof,
SAXENBURG, SPICE ROUTE,
STELLENZICHT.

**TARAPACÁ** *Maipo, Chile* No expense has been spared in recent vineyard and winery improvements at this long-established company, and the wine too is improving under the guidance of Sergio Correa. New premium reds include Reserva Privada Syrah★ and Last Edition★ – an unusual blend of Cabernet, Merlot, Syrah and Mourvèdre.

**TARRAWARRA** *Yarra Valley, Victoria, Australia* Clothing magnate and arts patron Marc Besen wanted to make a MONTRACHET, and hang the expense. The winemakers are on the right track: Tarrawarra Chardonnay★★ is deep and multi-faceted, but Pinot Noir★★ is just as good, with almost COTE DE NUITS flavour and concentration. Tunnel Hill is a less costly brand for both these grapes and Shiraz. Best years: **1998 97 96 95 94 92 90 89 88.**

**TASMANIA** *Australia* Tasmania is a minor state viticulturally, with only 550ha (1360 acres) of vines. The cool climate has attracted seekers of greatness in Pinot Noir and Chardonnay, but doesn't always deliver. Top Pinots are great but in a minority, Chardonnay can be superb, and there is some delicious Riesling. An important supplier of grapes for sparkling wine. Best producers: Elsewhere Vineyard★, Freycinet★★, Iron Pot Bay, Stefano Lubiana★, Moorilla★, Notley Gorge★, PIPERS BROOK★★, Spring Vale★, Stoney★★, Wellington★.

**TAURASI DOCG** *Campania, Italy* Remarkably, it was a single producer, MASTROBERARDINO, and a single vintage, 1968, that created the reputation for this red. Now the great potential of the Aglianico grape is being exploited by others, both within this DOCG and elsewhere in CAMPANIA. Drink at 5–10 years. Best producers: Caggiano★★, Feudi di San Gregorio★, MASTROBERARDINO (Radici★), Montesole, Struzziero, Terre Dora di Paolo★. Best years: 1997 96 **95 94 93 92 90 89 88 86.**

**TAVEL AC** *Rhône Valley, France* Big, alcoholic rosé from north-west of Avignon. Grenache and Cinsaut are the main grapes. Drink Tavel at one year old if you want it cheerful, heady, yet refreshing. Best producers: Aquéria★, la Forcadière★, Genestière★, GUIGAL, la Mordorée★, Vignerons de Tavel, Trinquevedel, Vieux Moulin.

**TAYLOR FLADGATE & YEATMAN** *Port DOC, Douro, Portugal* The aristocrat of the port industry, 300 years old and still going strong. Its Vintage★★★ is superb; Quinta de Vargellas★★ is an elegant, cedary, single-quinta vintage port made in the best of the 'off-vintages'. Taylor's 20-year-old★★ is a very fine aged tawny. First Estate is a successful premium ruby. The best vintage ports can be kept for at least 25 years. Best years: (Vintage) 1997 94 92 85 83 **80 77 75 70 66 63 60 55 48 45 27**; (Vargellas) 1998 96 95 91 **88 87 86 82 78 67 64 61.**

**TE MATA** *Hawke's Bay, North Island, New Zealand* HAWKE'S BAY's glamour winery and still probably its best, though now facing increasing local competition. The best-known wines are the reds, Coleraine★★★ and Awatea★★, both based on Cabernet Sauvignon with varying proportions of Merlot and Cabernet Franc. Also outstanding is Elston Chardonnay★★, a superbly crafted, toasty, spicy wine. Exceptional vintages of all 3 wines might be aged for 5–10 years. New to the range is Bullnose Syrah★, an elegant, peppery red, and an initial release of Viognier shows potential. Best years: (Coleraine) 1998 **96 95 94 91 90 89.**

**E & M TEMENT** *Ehrenhausen, Steiermark, Austria* Fanatical Manfred
Tement makes Austria's best Sauvignon Blanc★★ and Chardonnay★★
in a spectacular new hilltop winery. Both varieties are fermented and
aged in oak, giving power, depth and subtle oak character. Sauvignon
from the Zieregg site is ★★★ at best. Drink young or after brief
keeping. Best years: (2000) 99 **98 97 95** 94.

**DOM. TEMPIER** *Bandol AC, Provence, France* Leading BANDOL estate,
run by the Péyraud family and making rich, ageworthy reds from a
high percentage of Mourvèdre. The top wines are Migoua★★,
Cabassou★★ and la Tourtine★★. The rosé★ is one of Provence's best.
Best years: (1999) 98 97 96 95 **93 92 90 89 88 85 83 82**.

**TEMPRANILLO** Spain's best native red grape can make wonderful wine,
with wild strawberry and spicy, tobaccoey flavours. It is important in
RIOJA, PENEDES (as Ull de Llebre), RIBERA DEL DUERO (as Tinto Fino or Tinta
del Pais), La MANCHA and VALDEPENAS (as Cencibel), NAVARRA, SOMONTANO,
UTIEL-REQUENA and TORO (as Tinta de Toro). In Portugal it is found in the
DOURO, DAO and ESTREMADURA (as Tinta Roriz) and in ALENTEJO as
Aragonês. Wines can be deliciously fruity for drinking young, but
Tempranillo also matures well, and its flavours blend happily with oak.
It is now being taken more seriously in Argentina, and new plantings
have been made in CALIFORNIA, OREGON, Australia and South Africa.

**TEROLDEGO ROTALIANO DOC** *Trentino-Alto Adige, Italy* Teroldego is a
native TRENTINO grape variety, producing deep-coloured, grassy,
blackberry-flavoured wine on the gravel soils of the Rotaliano plain.
Best producers: Barone de Cles★, M Donati★, Dorigati★, Endrizzi★,
FORADORI★★, Conti Martini★, Mezzacorona (Riserva★), Cantina Rotaliana★,
G Sebastiani★, A & R Zeni★. Best years: (2000) 99 **97 96 95 94** 93 91 90.

**TERRAS DO SADO** *Setúbal Peninsula, Portugal* Warm, maritime-
influenced area south of Lisbon. SETUBAL produces fine sweet fortified wine,
best from José Maria da FONSECA. Many of the better reds, mostly based on
Periquita, come from the newly created Palmela DOC. A few good whites
are also made. Best producers: (reds) Caves ALIANCA (Palmela Particular★),
BRIGHT BROTHERS, José Maria da FONSECA★, J P VINHOS, Pegões co-op, João
Portugal RAMOS (Pegos Claros★★). Best years: (2000) 99 **97 96 95 94** 92 91.

**TERRICCIO, CASTELLO DEL** *Tuscany, Italy* High in the hills south of
Livorno, this producer has transformed itself from bulk red and white
wines to the status of Tuscan superstar. The top red is Lupicaia★★★
(Cabernet-Merlot), rich and concentrated with a hint of eucalyptus
and already very expensive. Tassinaia★★ is a second red from
Sangiovese, Cabernet and Merlot and is ready to drink sooner. The
barrique-fermented Chardonnay Saluccio★★ and varietal Sauvignon
Blanc Con Vento★ are the most interesting whites. Best years:
(Lupicaia) 1998 97 **96 95 94** 93.

**CH. LE TERTRE-RÔTEBOEUF**★★★ *St-Émilion Grand Cru AC, Bordeaux,*
*France* ST-EMILION's most exceptional unclassified estate. The richly
seductive, Merlot-based wines sell at the same price as the Premiers
Grands Crus Classés. Best years: (2000) 99 98 97 96 95 **94 90 89 88 86 85**.

**TEXAS** *USA* Since the planting of an experimental vineyard in 1975, Texas has risen to fifth in the ranks of US wine-producing states. The state has 5 AVAs, of which Texas High Plains is most significant. 36 wineries and some fine Chardonnay and Riesling. Thunderstorms are a menace, capable of destroying entire crops in minutes. Best producers: Cap Rock, Fall Creek, Llano Estacado, Messina Hof, Pheasant Ridge, Ste-Geneviève.

**SEAN THACKREY** *Marin County, California, USA* A small warehouse winery with a cult following for big RHONE-style red wines. Orion★★ is a powerful, dense Syrah, and the unusual Pleiades★★ is a softer non-vintage blend of Petite Sirah, Mourvèdre, Syrah and Grenache. Pleiades is ready a couple of years after release, Orion should be aged for 5 years or more. Best years: (Orion) 1997 96 95 **94 93 92 90 88 86**.

**THELEMA** *Stellenbosch WO, South Africa* Family-run winery, high in the Simonsberg mountains. Meticulous attention is paid to the vineyards, where CALIFORNIA's Phil Freese helps with innovative ideas – the latest an early warning system for mildew picked up by a computer in the cellar. Winemaker Gyles Webb is acclaimed for a range that includes a rich blackcurrant Cabernet Sauvignon★★, a ripe fleshy Merlot★, a barrel-fermented Chardonnay★★, a vibrant Sauvignon Blanc★★ and less-hyped Riesling★. Best years: (reds) 1997 96 95 94 93 92 91; (whites) **2000 99 98 97 96 95**.

**THERMENREGION** *Niederösterreich, Austria* This region, south of Vienna, takes its name from the thermal spa towns of BADEN and Bad Vöslau. Near Vienna is the village of Gumpoldskirchen with its rich and often sweet white wines. The red wine area around Baden produces large amounts of Blauer Portugieser together with a couple of good examples of Pinot Noir and Cabernet. Best producers: Biegler, Fischer, Hofer, Johanneshof★, Schellmann, Stadlmann★.

**THIRTY BENCH WINERY** *Niagara Peninsula VQA, Ontario, Canada* A collaboration of 3 winemakers, Thirty Bench is known for its low yields and intense wines. Excellent Riesling, including Late Harvest and Icewine★, has been joined by BORDEAUX-style red Reserve Blend★ and a fine barrel-fermented Chardonnay.

**DOMAINE THOMAS-MOILLARD** *Nuits-St-Georges AC, Côte de Nuits, Burgundy, France* This is the label for wines from the family-owned vineyards of négociant house Moillard-Grivot. The wines are not consistent across the range, but the best, including ROMANEE-ST-VIVANT★★★ and BONNES-MARES★★★, are very fine, in an old-fashioned, long-lived, robust style. Other good reds include NUITS-ST-GEORGES Clos de Thorey★★, BEAUNE Grèves★★ and VOSNE-ROMANEE Malconsorts★★. Red and white HAUTES-COTES DE NUITS★ stand out at the simpler end of the range. Best years: (reds) (2000) 99 98 **97** 96 95 **93 90**.

**THREE CHOIRS** *Gloucestershire, England* Martin Fowke makes an impressive range of wines at this state-of-the-art winery set in a 30-ha (73-acre) vineyard, including a zingy English Nouveau, sold at the same time as BEAUJOLAIS NOUVEAU. Premium Selection (from Seyval Blanc, Reichensteiner and Müller-Thurgau), Estate Reserve Bacchus★ and fizz★ are the main sellers.

**TICINO** *Switzerland* Italian-speaking, southerly canton of Switzerland. The most important wine of the region is Merlot del Ticino, usually soft and gluggable, but sometimes more serious with some oak barrel-aging. Best producers: Daniel Huber, Werner Stucky, Christian Zündel★.

**TIGNANELLO★★** *Tuscany, Italy* The wine that broke the mould in Tuscany. Piero ANTINORI employed the previously unheard of practice of aging in small French oak barrels and used Cabernet Sauvignon (20%) in the blend with Sangiovese. Labelled as simple vino da tavola, the quality was superb and Tignanello's success sparked off the SUPER-TUSCAN movement that has produced many of Italy's most exciting wines. Top vintages are truly great: lesser years are of decent CHIANTI CLASSICO quality. Best years: (1998) 97 96 95 **94 93 90** 88 86 85.

**TINTA RORIZ** See Tempranillo.

**TOCAI FRIULANO** Unrelated to Hungary's or Alsace's Tokay, Tocai Friulano is a north-east Italian grape producing dry, nutty, oily whites of great character in COLLIO and COLLI ORIENTALI and good wines in the Veneto's COLLI EUGANEI, as well as lots of neutral stuff in Piave. Best producers: Borgo del Tiglio★, Borgo San Daniele★, Dorigo★, Drius★, Livio FELLUGA★, Marco Felluga★, JERMANN★, Edi Keber★, Miani★★, Pierpaolo Pecorari★, Princil★, Puiatti★, Rocca Bernarda★, Ronchi di Manzano★, Paolo Rodaro★, Ronco del Gelso★★, Russiz Superiore★★, SCHIOPETTO★★, Specogna★, La Viarte★, Vie di Romans★★, Russolo, Villa Russiz★, Le Vigne di Zamò★★, Volpe Pasini★.

**TOKAJI** *Hungary and Slovakia* Strange, fascinating and unique, Tokaji wine has a sweet-sour-sweet, sherry-like tang. It comes from 28 villages on the Hungarian-Slovak border. Mists from the Bodrog river ensure that noble rot or botrytis on the Furmint, Hárslevelü and Muscotaly (Muscat Ottonel) grapes is a fairly common occurrence. Old single-vineyard Museum wines★★ from the Tokaji Kereskedöház demonstrate the area's potential, and recent international investments are exploiting it; after a long period of decline, quality is very much on the up. The current debate centres on traditional versus modern styles; oxidation or absence of it. The best wines promise ★★★ quality when they've matured a bit. Best producers: Disznókö★★, Megyer★★, Oremus★★, Pajzos★★, Royal Tokaji Wine Company★★, Istvan Szepsy★, Tokaji Kereskedöház★.

**TOLLOT-BEAUT & FILS** *Chorey-lès-Beaune, Burgundy, France* High-quality COTE DE BEAUNE reds with lots of fruit and a pronounced new oak character. The village-level CHOREY-LES-BEAUNE★★, ALOXE-CORTON★★ and SAVIGNY-LES-BEAUNE★★ wines are all excellent, as is the top BEAUNE Premier Cru Clos du Roi★★. Best years: (reds) 1999 98 97 96 **95 93 90**.

**TORGIANO DOC & DOCG** *Umbria, Italy* A zone near Perugia dominated by LUNGAROTTI. While the basic Rubesco Torgiano★ is ripely fruity, the Riserva Vigna Monticchio★★ is a fine black cherry-flavoured wine. Torgiano Riserva Rosso has been accorded DOCG.

**TORO DO** *Castilla y León, Spain* Mainly red wines, which are robust, full of colour and tannin, and pretty high in alcohol. The main grape, Tinta de Toro, is a local variant of Tempranillo, and there is some Garnacha. Whites from the Malvasía grape are generally heavy. Best producers: Viña Bajoz★, Fariña★, Frutos Villar (Muruve)★, Maurodós★★, Telmo Rodriguez★, Toresanas (Bodegas de Crianza Castilla la Vieja) ★, Vega Saúco★, Vega de Toro (Señorío de San Vicente) ★★.

**TORRES** *Penedès DO, Cataluña, Spain* Large family winery led by visionary Miguel Torres, making good wines with local grapes, Parellada and Tempranillo, but also renowned for French varieties. Viña Sol★ is a good, citrony quaffer, Viña Esmeralda★ (Muscat à Petits Grains and Gewürztraminer) is grapy and spicy, Fransola★★ (Sauvignon Blanc with some Parellada) is rich yet leafy, and Milmanda★★ is a delicate, expensive Chardonnay. Successful reds are Gran Coronas★, soft, oaky and blackcurranty (Tempranillo and Cabernet); fine, relatively rich Mas la Plana★★ (Cabernet Sauvignon); floral, perfumed Mas Borrás (Pinot Noir); and raisiny Atrium★ (Merlot). The new top-line reds, Grans Muralles★★, from a blend of Catalan grapes, and Reserva Real★★, a BORDEAUX-style blend, mark an exciting new departure for Torres. Best years: (Mas la Plana) 1995 **94 91 90 88 87 83 81 79 76**.

**MARIMAR TORRES ESTATE** *Sonoma County, California, USA* The sister of Spanish winemaker Miguel TORRES has established her own winery in the cool Green Valley region of SONOMA COUNTY, only a few miles from the Pacific Ocean. She specializes in Chardonnay and Pinot Noir. Chardonnays★★ are big, intense wines, perhaps a shade heavy on the oak, best with 2–4 years' age. The full-bodied Pinot Noirs generally achieve ★★ quality. Best years: (1999) 98 97 **95 94 92**.

**MIGUEL TORRES** *Curicó, Chile* After a long period of under-achievement from the man who re-awoke the Chilean wine industry, we are at last seeing good snappy Sauvignon Blanc★ once more, grassy, fruity Santa Digna rosé★ and a lean but blackcurranty Manso de Velasco Cabernet★. Best years: (Manso) 1997 **96 95 94**.

**TOURAINE AC** *Loire Valley, France* General AC for Touraine wines in the central LOIRE. There are 6140ha (15,170 acres) of AC vineyards, divided half and half between red or rosé and white. Most of the reds are from the Gamay and in hot years these can be juicy, rustic-fruited wines. There is a fair amount of red from Cabernets Sauvignon and Franc, too, and some good Côt (Malbec). The reds are best drunk young. Fairly decent whites come from the Chenin Blanc but the best wines are from Sauvignon Blanc. These can be a good SANCERRE substitute at half the price. Drink at one year old, though Chenin wines can last longer. Best producers: (reds and rosés) la Charmoise★, Ch. de Chenonceau★, Corbillières, J Delaunay★, Robert Denis★, Marcadet★, Oisly-et-Thésée co-op, Pavy★, Roche Blanche★; (whites) des Acacias★, Baron Briare, la Charmoise★, Ch. de Chenonceau★, X Frissant, Marcadet★, Octavie★, Oisly-et-Thésée co-op★, Pibaleau★, Pré Baron, Roche Blanche★. Best years: (2000) **99 98 97 96 95**.

**TOURAINE MOUSSEUX AC** *Loire Valley, France* A sparkling wine AC covering the entire Touraine region. The wines are rarely as good as the best VOUVRAY and CREMANT DE LOIRE. Best producers: Ch. de Chenonceau★, J Delaunay, Monmousseau.

**CH. LA TOUR BLANCHE★★** *Sauternes AC, 1er Cru Classé, Bordeaux, France* Owned by the French Ministry of Agriculture, this estate regained top form in the 1980s with the introduction of new oak barrels for fermentation, lower yields and greater selection. Full-bodied, rich and aromatic, it now ranks with the best of the Classed Growths. Second wine: Les Charmilles. Best years: 1999 98 97 96 95 **90 89 88 86**.

**DOM. DE LA TOUR-BOISÉE** *Minervois AC, Languedoc, France* Jean-Louis Poudou is one of the pioneering producers in MINERVOIS. Of most interest here is the red Cuvée Marie-Claude★, aged for 12 months in barrel, the white Cuvée Marie-Claude★, which has a hint of Muscat Blanc à Petits Grains for added aroma, and the fruity Cuvée Marielle et Frédéric★, produced from Grenache and Syrah.

**CH. TOUR DES GENDRES** *Bergerac AC, South-West France* Luc de Conti's BERGERACS are made with as much sophistication as is found in the better Crus Classés of BORDEAUX. Generously fruity Moulin des Dames★ and the more earnest la Gloire de Mon Père★ reds are mostly Cabernet Sauvignon. Full, fruity and elegant Moulin des Dames★ white is a classic Bordeaux blend of Sémillon, Sauvignon Blanc and Muscadelle. Best years: (la Gloire de Mon Père) 1999 98 **97 96 95 94 90 89 88**.

**TOURIGA NACIONAL** High-quality red Portuguese grape which is rich in aroma and fruit. Though plantings remain small, it is prized for port production as it contributes deep colour and tannin to the blend. Rapidly increasing in importance for table wines both in the DOURO and elsewhere in Portugal.

**TRÁS-OS-MONTES** *Portugal* Impoverished north-eastern province, traditionally a supplier of grapes for Mateus Rosé, with 3 IPR regions, Valpaços, Chaves and Planalto-Mirandês, but producing pretty rustic stuff. However, the Vinho Regional Trás-os-Montes/Terras Durienses covers a handful of very good DOURO-sourced reds. Best producers: RAMOS PINTO (Bons Ares★ and Reserva★★), Quinta do Sidrô (Chardonnay★), Valle Pradinhos.

**TREBBIANO** The most widely planted white Italian grape variety – far too widely, in fact, for Italy's good. As the Trebbiano Toscano, it is used as the base for Galestro and any number of other neutral, dry whites, as well as in VIN SANTO. But there are also a number of grapes masquerading under the Trebbiano name that aren't anything like as neutral. The most notable are the Trebbianos from LUGANA and ABRUZZO – both grapes capable of full-bodied, fragrant wines. Called Ugni Blanc in France, and primarily used for distilling, as it should be.

**TRENTINO** *Italy* This northern region is officially linked with ALTO ADIGE, but they are completely different. The wines rarely have the verve or perfume of Alto Adige examples, but can make up for this with riper, softer flavours, where vineyard yields have been kept in check. The Trentino DOC covers 20 different styles of wine, including whites Pinot Bianco and Grigio, Chardonnay, Moscato Giallo, Müller-Thurgau and Nosiola, and reds Schiava, Lagrein, Marzemino, Teroldego and Cabernet. Trento Classico is a special DOC for Champagne-method fizz. Best producers: N Balter★, N Bolognani★, La Cadalora★, Castel Noarna★, Cavit co-op, De Tarczal★, Dorigati, FERRARI★★, Graziano Fontana★, FORADORI★★, Isera co-op★, Letrari★, Longariva★, Conti Martini★, Maso Cantanghel★★, Maso Furli★, Maso Roveri★, Mezzacorona, Pojer & Sandri★, Pravis★, San Leonardo★, Simoncelli★, E Spagnolli★, Vallarom★, La Vis co-op. See also Teroldego Rotaliano.

**DOM. DE TRÉVALLON** *Provence, France* Iconoclastic Parisian Eloi
Dürrbach makes brilliant reds★★, mixing herbal wildness with a
sweetness of blackberry, blackcurrant and black, black plums, and a
tiny quantity of white★★★. Dürrbach's tradition-busting blend of
Cabernet Sauvignon and Syrah, no longer accepted by the appellation
les BAUX-DE-PROVENCE, is the finest wine to come out of Provence. The
wines age extremely well, but are surprisingly drinkable in their
youth. Best years: (reds) (1999) 98 97 96 **95 94 93 90 89 88 85 83 82**.

**TRIMBACH** *Alsace AC, Alsace, France* An excellent grower/merchant
whose trademark is beautifully structured, subtly perfumed elegance.
Riesling and Gewurztraminer are the specialities, but the Pinot Gris
and Pinot Blanc are first-rate too. Top wines are Gewurztraminer
Cuvée des Seigneurs de Ribeaupierre★★, Riesling Cuvée Frédéric
Émile★★ and Riesling Clos St-Hune★★★. Also very good ALSACE
VENDANGE TARDIVE★★ and Sélection de Grains Nobles★★. Best years:
(Clos St-Hune) 1997 96 95 93 **92 90 89 88 85**.

**TRITTENHEIM** *Mosel, Germany* Important MOSEL wine village with some
excellent vineyard sites, most notably the Apotheke (pharmacy) and
Leiterchen (little ladder). The wines are sleek, with crisp acidity and
plenty of fruit. Best producers: Ernst Clüsserath★, Clüsserath-Weiler★,
GRANS-FASSIAN★, Milz-Laurentiushof★. Best years: 1999 98 **97 95 93 90**.

**CH. TROPLONG-MONDOT★★** *St-Émilion Grand Cru AC, Bordeaux, France*
Consistently one of the best of ST-EMILION's Grands Crus Classés and
contentiously denied promotion to Premier Grand Cru Classé status
in 1996. The wines are beautifully structured and mouthfillingly
textured for long aging. Best years: (2000) 99 98 97 96 95 94 **93 90 89
88 86 85**.

**CH. TROTANOY★★** *Pomerol AC, Bordeaux, France* Another POMEROL
estate (along with PETRUS, la FLEUR-PETRUS, LATOUR-A-POMEROL and
others) which has benefited from the brilliant touch of the MOUEIX
family. After a dip in the mid-1980s, recent vintages are getting back
on form. Best years: (2000) 99 98 97 96 95 94 93 **90 89 88 82**.

**CAVE VINICOLE DE TURCKHEIM** *Alsace AC, Alsace, France* Very
important co-op with a reputation for good Pinot Blanc, Pinot Gris★
and Gewurztraminer★. Brand★★ and Hengst★★ bottlings of the last
two are rich and concentrated. Riesling is less reliable, but reds, rosés
and CREMANT D'ALSACE★ are consistent. Best years (Grand Cru
Gewurztraminer): 1998 97 **95 94 93 90 89 88**.

**TURLEY CELLARS** *Napa Valley AVA, California, USA* Co-founder of Frog's
Leap winery, Larry Turley has successfully launched his own winery
which specializes in powerful Zinfandel and Petite Sirah. After early
assistance from his talented winemaking sister Helen (now based at
MARCASSIN), Turley has gone on to produce ultra-ripe Zins★★ from a
number of old vineyards. They pack a wallop and are either praised
for their profound power and depth or damned for their tannic, high-
alcohol, PORT-like nature. Petite Sirah★★ is similarly built, and all the
wines can last a decade or more. Best years: (1999) 98 97 96 95 **94 93**.

**TURSAN VDQS** *South-West France* Wine of local interest only, made on
the edge of les Landes, the sandy coastal area south of Bordeaux. The
white is the most interesting: made from the Baroque grape it is clean,
crisp and refreshing. Best producers: de Bachen★, Tursan co-op.

**TUSCANY** *Italy*  Tuscany's rolling hills, clad with vines, olive trees and cypresses, have produced wine since at least Etruscan times, and today Tuscany leads the way in promoting the new image of Italian wines. Its many DOC/DOCGs are based on the red Sangiovese grape and are led by CHIANTI CLASSICO, BRUNELLO DI MONTALCINO and VINO NOBILE DI MONTEPULCIANO, as well as famous SUPER-TUSCANS like ORNELLAIA and TIGNANELLO. White wines, despite sweet VIN SANTO, and the occasional excellent Chardonnay and Sauvignon, do not figure highly. See also Bolgheri, Carmignano, Montecarlo, Morellino di Scansano, Pomino, Rosso di Montalcino, Rosso di Montepulciano, Sassicaia, Solaia, Vernaccia di San Gimignano.

**TYRRELL'S** *Hunter Valley, New South Wales, Australia*  Family-owned company with prime Lower HUNTER vineyards; the wines taste splendid on their home patch but only recently have achieved consistency on the export market. Makes superb Vat 1 Semillon★★★, generally excellent Vat 47 Chardonnay★★, and Vat 5★ and Vat 9★★ Shiraz which can be special. Vat 6 Pinot Noir★ is variable. Best years: (Semillon) (1999) 98 97 96 95 94 93 **92 90 89 87 86 79 76 74 72**; (Chardonnay) (1999) 97 **96 95 94 93 92 90 89 87 86 84** 79 76 73; (reds) (1998) 96 **95 93 92 89 87 85 84 83 81** 75 65.

**UGNI BLANC**  See Trebbiano.

**UMBRIA** *Italy*  Wine production in this Italian region is dominated by ORVIETO, accounting for almost 70% of DOC wines. However, some of the most characterful wines are reds from TORGIANO and MONTEFALCO. Latest interest centres on remarkable new reds made by the outstanding Riccardo Cotarella at estates such as Pieve del Vescovo (Lucciaio★★), la Carraia (Fobiano★★), Lamborghini (Campoleone★★) and La Palazzola (Rubino★★).

**ÜRZIG** *Mosel, Germany*  Middle MOSEL village with the famous Würzgarten (spice garden) vineyard tumbling spectacularly down to the river and producing marvellously spicy Riesling. Drink with 5 years' age or more. Best producers: J J Christoffel★★, Dr LOOSEN★★★, Mönchhof★. Best years: 1999 98 97 96 95 **94 93**.

**UTIEL-REQUENA DO** *Valencia, Spain*  Inland from Valencia, Utiel-Requena is renowned for its rosés, mostly made from the Bobal grape. Recent plantings of Tempranillo are improving the reds. Best producers: Vicente Gandía Pla, Schenk, Torre Oria, Vinival.

**VACQUEYRAS AC** *Rhône Valley, France*  The most important of the COTES DU RHONE-VILLAGES communes was promoted to its own AC in 1990. Red wines account for 95% of production; dark in colour, they have a warm, spicy bouquet and a rich deep flavour that seems infused with the herbs and pine dust of the south. Lovely to drink at 2–3 years, though good wines will age for 5 years or more. Best producers: Armouriers★, la Charbonnière★, Clos des Cazaux★, Couroulu★, DELAS★, la Fourmone (Roger Combe)★, la Garrigue★, JABOULET★, Montmirail★, Montvac★, Sang des Cailloux★, Tardieu-Laurent★, Ch. des Tours★, Vacqueyras co-op★, Verquière★. Best years: (2000) 99 98 **97 96 95 94**.

**VALAIS** *Switzerland* Swiss canton flanking the Rhône above Lake Geneva. Between Martigny and Sierre the valley turns north-east, creating an Alpine suntrap, and this short stretch of terraced vineyard land provides the majority of Switzerland's most individual wines from Fendant, Johannisberger (the local name for Silvaner), Pinot Noir and Gamay, and also including Syrah and Chardonnay, which are recent innovations. Best producers: Michel Clavien, J Germanier, R Gilliard, Caves Imesch, Mathier, Dom. du Mont d'Or★, Raymond, Zufferey.

**CH. DE VALANDRAUD**★★ *St-Émilion Grand Cru AC, Bordeaux, France* ST-EMILION's recent high-priced sensation, a big, rich, extracted wine produced from low yields from grapes mainly grown on the less favoured Dordogne plain. The first vintage was in 1991. Time will tell. Best years: (2000) 99 98 97 96 95 **94 93 92**.

**VALDEPEÑAS DO** *Castilla-La Mancha, Spain* Valdepeñas offers some of Spain's best inexpensive oak-aged reds, but these are a small drop in a sea of less exciting stuff. In fact there are more whites than reds, at least some of them modern, fresh and fruity. Best producers: Miguel Calatayud, Los Llanos★, Luís Megía, Real, Félix Solís, Casa de la Viña.

**VALDESPINO** *Jerez y Manzanilla DO, Andalucía, Spain* Old-fashioned, very high-quality family sherry business. Delicious wines include Inocente Fino★★, Tio Diego Amontillado★★, the expensive but concentrated Palo Cortado Cardenal★★★, dry amontillados Coliseo★★★ and Don Tomás★★, Don Gonzalo Old Dry Oloroso★★ and Pedro Ximénez Solera Superior★★.

**VALDIVIESO** *Curicó, Chile* Part of the Mitjan group and recipient of huge investment both in their Lontué winery and Curicó Valley vineyards. Best known for smooth Pinot Noir★ and Chardonnay, but exciting Merlot★, Cabernet Franc★ and Malbec★★ in the single-vineyard Reserves. Multi-varietal blend Caballo Loco★ is good but a long way from its goal of being Chile's answer to GRANGE. V Series Malbec★★ and Pinot Noir★★ show further elegance and complexity, but at a price. Although sparkling wines have been made here for 100 years, Champagne-method fizz is a recent introduction.

**VAL D'ORBIEU, LES VIGNERONS DU** *Languedoc-Roussillon, France* This growers' association is France's largest wine exporting company, selling in excess of 20 million cases of (mostly uninspiring) wine a year. Membership includes several of the MIDI's best co-ops (Cucugnan, Cuxac, Ribauté and Montredon) and individual producers (Dom. de Fontsainte, Ch. la Voulte-Gasparets). It also owns Cordier (BORDEAUX) and Listel, famous for dull rosés and fizzes, but with a much better range of varietal wines. Also marketed by Val d'Orbieu are Château de Jau and the excellent BANYULS and COLLIOURE estate, Clos de Paulilles. Its range of blended wines (Cuvée Chouette★, Chorus★, Pas de Deux★, Elysices★, Réserve St-Martin★ and la Cuvée Mythique★★) are a judicious mix of traditional Mediterranean varieties with Cabernet or Merlot and show welcome signs of ambition to raise quality.

**VALENCIA** *Spain* The best wines from Valencia DO in the south-east of Spain are the inexpensive, sweet, grapy Moscatels. Simple, fruity whites, reds and rosés are also good. Alicante DO to the south produces a little-known treasure, the Fondillón dry or semi-dry fortified wine, as well as a cluster of wines from native and foreign varieties made by a few quality-conscious modern wineries. Monastrell (Mourvèdre) is the main red grape variety. UTIEL-REQUENA DO specializes in rosés and light reds. Best producers: (Valencia DO) Vicente Gandía Pla, Schenk, Cherubino Valsangiacomo (Marqués de Caro); (Alicante DO) Bocopa★, Gutiérrez de la Vega (Casta Diva Muscat★★), Enrique Mendoza★★, Salvador Poveda★, Primitivo Quiles★.

**VALLE D'AOSTA** *Italy* Tiny Alpine valley sandwiched between PIEDMONT and the French Alps in northern Italy. The regional DOC covers 17 wine styles, referring either to a specific grape variety (like Gamay or Pinot Nero) or to a delimited region like Donnaz, a northern extension of Piedmont's CAREMA, producing a light red from the Nebbiolo grape. Perhaps the finest wine from these steep slopes is the sweet Chambave Moscato. Best producers: Bonin, Charrère★, Les Crêtes★, La Crotta di Vegneron★, Institut Agricole Regional★, Ezio Voyat★.

**VALLÉE DU PARADIS, VIN DE PAYS DE LA** *Languedoc, France* With a name like the valley of paradise, the wines from this area to the south-west of Narbonne ought to be heavenly. In fact, they're good, basic quaffers made principally from Carignan, Cinsaut and Grenache.

**VALLEY VINEYARDS** *Berkshire, England* Eighteen grape varieties planted over 13ha (32 acres) from which 2 Aussies, viticulturist and owner Jon Leighton and consultant winemaker John Worontschak, produce full-flavoured wines, many with antipodean-style use of oak. Fumé★ is a remarkable white Graves-lookalike and Bacchus-based Regatta is worth trying. Worontschak is also mad keen on fizz★. Overall, my feeling about this vineyard is: we ain't seen nothing yet.

**VALPOLICELLA DOC** *Veneto, Italy* This Veronese wine can range in style from a light, cherryish red to the rich, port-like RECIOTO and AMARONE Valpolicellas. Most Valpolicella from the plains is pale and insipid, and bears little comparison to Valpolicella Classico from the hills. Made from Corvina (the best grape), Rondinella and Molinara, Valpolicella Classico can be a light, cherryish red of great appeal, for drinking within 18 months of the vintage. A fuller wine of bitter-sweet complexity is made either from a particular vineyard, or by refermenting the wine on the skins and lees of the Amarone, a style called *ripasso*, which adds an exciting sweet-sour dimension to the wine. Best producers: Accordini★, ALLEGRINI★★, Bertani★, Bolla★, Brigaldara★, Brunelli, Tommaso Bussola★, Cà la Bionda★, M Castellani, Corteforte★, Corte Sant'Alda★, Degani, DAL FORNO★, Aleardo Ferrari★, Guerrieri-Rizzardi★, MASI★, Mazzi★, Pasqua/Cecilia Beretta★, QUINTARELLI★★, Le Ragose★, Le Salette★, Serègo Alighieri★, Speri★, Tedeschi★, Tommasi, Villa Bellini, Villa Monteleone★, Villa Spinosa★, Viviani, Zenato★, Fratelli Zeni★. Best years: (2000) **99 98 97 95 93 90 88**.

**VALTELLINA SUPERIORE DOCG** *Lombardy, Italy* Red wine produced on the precipitous slopes of northern LOMBARDY. There is a basic, light Valtellina DOC red, made from at least 70% Nebbiolo (here called Chiavennasca), but the best wines are made under the Valtellina Superiore DOCG as Grumello, Inferno, Sassella and Valgella. From top vintages the wines are attractively perfumed and approachable. Sfursat or Sforzato is a dense, high-alcohol red (up to 14.5%) made from semi-dried grapes. Best producers: La Castellina★, Enologica Valtellinese★, Fay★, Nino Negri★, Nera★, Rainoldi★, Conti Sertoli Salis★, Triacca★. Best years: (1998) 97 96 **95 93 90 89 88 85**.

**VASSE FELIX** *Margaret River, Western Australia* One of the originals responsible for MARGARET RIVER rocketing to fame, with decadently rich, profound Cabernet Sauvignon★★ and stylish Shiraz★★. Flagship red is the delicious Heytesbury★★. Whites are also very smart. Even so, I'm waiting for Vasse Felix to reach the next level up. Best years: (reds) 1998 97 **96 95 94 93 91 90 88 86 84 83 79**.

**VAUD** *Switzerland* With the exception of the canton of Geneva, the Vaud accounts for the vineyards bordering Lake Geneva. There are 5 regions: la Côte, Lavaux, CHABLAIS, Côtes de l'Orbe-Bonvillars and Vully. Most of the production is Dorin (Chasselas) and it can be a delightful light white. Reds are from Gamay and Pinot Noir. Best producers: Henri Badoux, Louis Bovard, Conne, Delarze, Dubois Fils, Grognuz, Massy, Obrist, Pinget, J & P Testuz.

**VAVASOUR** *Marlborough, South Island, New Zealand* First winery in the Awatere Valley near MARLBOROUGH's main wine area, enjoying spectacular success. One of New Zealand's best Chardonnays★★, a fine Pinot Noir★★ and palate-tingling Sauvignon Blanc★★.

**VEENWOUDEN** *Paarl WO, South Africa* This tiny cellar, one of the Cape's most exciting, is owned by international opera singer, Deon van der Walt, whose brother Marcel, an ex-golf pro, has become a dedicated and capable winemaker. Apart from a tiny quantity of Chardonnay, 3 reds are made, each based on BORDEAUX varieties and all noted for their consistency: sumptuous and well-oaked Merlot★★, firm and silky-fruited Veenwouden Classic★★ and Vivat Bacchus★, with a distinctive Malbec component. All are made to mature, the first 2 for up to 10 years. Best years: **1998 97 96 95 94 93**.

**VEGA SICILIA** *Ribera del Duero DO, Castilla y León, Spain* Spain's most expensive red wines, rich, fragrant, complex and very slow to mature, and by no means always easy to appreciate. This estate was the first in Spain to introduce French varieties, and over a quarter of the vines are now Cabernet Sauvignon, two-thirds are Tempranillo and the rest Malbec and Merlot. Vega Sicilia Unico★★★ – the top wine – has traditionally been given about 10 years' wood aging, but this is now being reduced and volatility evident in some vintages should now no longer occur. Second wine: Valbuena★★. A subsidiary winery producing the more modern-style Alión★★ was launched in 1995. Best years: (Unico) **1990** 86 85 83 82 81 80 79 76 75 74 70 68 64 62.

**VELICH** *Neusiedlersee, Burgenland, Austria* Former casino croupier Roland Velich makes not only Austria's most minerally and sophisticated Chardonnay★★ from old vines in the Tiglat vineyard, but since 1995 also spectacular dessert wines of ★★ and ★★★ quality. Best years: (dry white) (2000) 99 **97 95 93 92**; (sweet) (2000) (99) 98 **96 95 94 91**.

---

**VENETO** *Italy* This region takes in the wine zones of SOAVE, VALPOLICELLA, BARDOLINO and Piave in north-east Italy. It is the source of a great deal of inexpensive wine, but the Soave and Valpolicella hills are also capable of producing small quantities of high-quality wine. Other hilly areas like Colli Berici and COLLI EUGANEI produce mainly large quantities of dull staple varietal wines, but can offer the odd flash of brilliance. The great dry red of this zone is AMARONE. See also Bianco di Custoza, Breganze, Prosecco di Conegliano-Valdobbiadene, Recioto della Valpolicella, Recioto di Soave.

**VERDICCHIO DEI CASTELLI DI JESI DOC** *Marche, Italy* Verdicchio, grown in the hills near the Adriatic around Jesi and in the Apennine enclave of Matelica, has blossomed into central Italy's most promising white variety. When fresh and fruity it is the ideal wine with fish, but some Verdicchio has the size and strength to age into a white of surprising depth of flavours. A few producers, notably Garofoli with Serra Fiorese★★, age it in oak, but even without wood it can develop an almost Burgundy-like complexity. Jesi is the classical zone, but the rarer Verdicchio di Matelica can be as impressive. A little is made sparkling. Best producers: (Jesi) Brunori★, Bucci★, Colonnara★, Coroncino★★, Fazi Battaglia★, Garofoli★★, Mancinelli★, Marchetti★, Terre Cortesi Moncaro★, Monte Schiavo★, Santa Barbara★, Sartarelli★★, Tavignano★, Umani Ronchi★, Vallerosa-Bonci★, Fratelli Zaccagnini★; (Matelica) Belisario★, Bisci★, Mecella★, La Monacesca★★.

**VERGELEGEN** *Stellenbosch WO, South Africa* Since moving to this historic Anglo-American-owned farm, winemaker Andre van Rensburg has made it clear that it is destined to be one of the greats of the new century. His 2 Sauvignon Blancs are already considered benchmarks: the regular bottling★★ is assertive and racy, topped with sleek tropical fruit; the single-vineyard★★ flinty, dry and powerful. There is also a ripe-textured, stylish Chardonnay Reserve★★. The recent release of van Rensburg's first reds lived up to high expectations. Vergelegen★★, the BORDEAUX-blend flagship, shows classic mineral restraint. Mill Race Red, another Bordeaux blend, is substantial yet accessible. Merlot and Cabernet are also serious and ageworthy. Best years: (whites) 2000 99 98 97 96; (reds) 1998 97 95 94.

**VERGET** *Mâconnais, Burgundy, France* A négociant house specializing in white Burgundies, run by Jean-Marie Guffens-Heynen, an exuberant character with his own domaine. The Guffens-Heynen wines include excellent MACON-VILLAGES★ and POUILLY-FUISSE★★ but the Verget range extends to outstanding Premiers Crus and Grands Crus from the COTE D'OR, notably CHASSAGNE-MONTRACHET★★ and BATARD-MONTRACHET★★★. But beware, the wines are made in a *very* individualistic style.

**VERMENTINO** The best dry white wines of SARDINIA generally come from the Vermentino grape. Light, dry, perfumed and nutty, the best examples tend to be from the north of the island, where the Vermentino di Gallura zone is located. Occasionally it is made sweet or sparkling. Vermentino is also grown in LIGURIA and TUSCANY, though its character is quite different. Best producers: (Sardinia) ARGIOLAS★, Capichera★, Cherchi★, Gallura co-op, Piero Mancini★, Fattoria Mauritania, Santadi co-op★, SELLA & MOSCA★, Vermentino co-op.

**VERNACCIA DI ORISTANO DOC** *Sardinia, Italy* Outstanding, oxidized, almost sherry-like wines from the west of the island, which acquire complexity and colour through long aging in wood. Amber-coloured and dry, nutty and long on the finish. Best producer: Contini★.

**VERNACCIA DI SAN GIMIGNANO DOCG** *Tuscany, Italy* The dry white wines – generally light quaffers – made from the Vernaccia grape grown in the hills around San Gimignano have now been promoted to DOCG. However, whether the allowance of up to 10% Chardonnay in the blend is a forward step is debatable. There is also a San Gimignano DOC for the zone's up-and-coming reds, though the best SUPER-TUSCANS are sold as IGT wines. Best producers: Ambra delle Torri★, Le Calcinaie, Casale-Falchini★, Vincenzo Cesani★, La Lastra (Riserva★), Melini (Le Grillaie★), Montenidoli★, Panizzi★, Paradiso★, Pietrafitta★, Pietraserena★, La Rampa di Fugnano★, San Donato★, Guicciardini Strozzi, Teruzzi & Puthod (Terre di Tufi★★), Vagnoni★.

**NOËL VERSET** *Cornas AC, Rhône Valley, France* Powerful, concentrated reds★★ from some of the oldest and best-sited vines in CORNAS. Yields are tiny and it shows in the depth that Verset achieves. Worth aging for 10 years or more. Best years: (1999) 98 97 96 95 94 **91 90 89 88 85**.

**VESUVIO DOC** *Campania, Italy* Red wines based on Piedirosso and whites from Coda di Volpe and Verdeca. The evocative name Lachryma Christi del Vesuvio is now only for superior versions, which include just about anything worth drinking. Best producers: Cantine Caputo, De Angelis, Cantina Grotta del Sole, MASTROBERARDINO, Sorrentino.

**VESÚVIO, QUINTA DO★★★** *Port DOC, Douro, Portugal* A consistently top performer. Purchased by Symington in 1989, it differs from stablemates DOW, GRAHAM and WARRE in that it appears whenever the high quality can be maintained (and not just in officially declared years). A brilliant medium- to long-term port, best with at least 10 years' age. Best years: 1998 97 96 95 94 92 **91 90**.

**VEUVE CLICQUOT** *Champagne AC, Champagne, France* These Champagnes can still live up to the high standards set by the original Widow Clicquot at the beginning of the 19th century, although many are released too young. The non-vintage★ is full, toasty and satisfyingly weighty, or lean and raw, depending on your luck: the vintage★★ is fuller and the de luxe Grande Dame★★★ is hefty but impressive stuff. Grande Dame Rosé★★★ is exquisite. Best years: (1995) **93 91 90 89 88 85 82**.

**VICTORIA** *Australia* Despite its small area, Victoria has arguably more land suited to quality grape-growing than any other state in Australia, with climates ranging from hot Sunraysia and RUTHERGLEN on the Murray River to cool MORNINGTON PENINSULA and GIPPSLAND in the south. The range of flavours is similarly wide and exciting. With more than 200 wineries, Victoria leads the boutique winery boom, particularly in Mornington Peninsula. See also Bendigo, Geelong, Goulburn Valley, Grampians, Pyrenees, Yarra Valley.

**VIEUX-CHÂTEAU-CERTAN★★** *Pomerol AC, Bordeaux, France* Slow-developing, tannic red (because of the use of 45% Cabernet), which after 15–20 years finally resembles more a fragrant refined MEDOC than a hedonistic POMEROL. Best years: (2000) 99 98 96 95 94 **93 90 89 88 86 85 83 82**.

**VIEUX TÉLÉGRAPHE** *Châteauneuf-du-Pape AC, Rhône Valley, France*
One of the top names in the AC, less tannic than BEAUCASTEL perhaps, but with just as much aging potential. The vines are some of the oldest in Châteauneuf and this Grenache-based red★★ is among the best modern-style wines produced in the RHONE VALLEY. Recently purchased les Pallières in GIGONDAS and will look for similar style and quality there. There is also a small amount of white★, which is heavenly to drink at the youngest possible stage. Best years: (reds) (1999) 98 97 96 95 **93 90 89 88**.

**VILLA MARIA** *Auckland, North Island, New Zealand* Founder and co-owner George Fistonich also owns Esk Valley and Vidal. Villa Maria Reserve Cabernet★★★, Esk Valley The Terraces★★★ (a Bordeaux blend) and Vidal Merlot-Cabernet★★ are superb. Reserve Chardonnay from Vidal★★ and Villa Maria★ are power-packed wines. Also produces 2 outstanding examples of MARLBOROUGH Sauvignon Blanc: classic Wairau Valley Sauvignon Blanc★★ and even more concentrated Clifford Bay Reserve Sauvignon Blanc★★. Riesling★★ is impressive, and, at the sweeter end, so is stunning Late Harvest Riesling★★★, all from Marlborough. Best years: (Hawke's Bay reds) (2000) **98 95**.

**VILLARD ESTATE** *Casablanca, Chile* Owner Thierry Villard (formerly of ORLANDO in South Australia) has created one of Chile's most successful boutique wineries. A big, buttery Chardonnay Reserve★ and clean, crisp Sauvignon Blanc★, both from CASABLANCA, have improved further since the new winery opened in 1997. Also good MAIPO Merlot★ and Pinot Noir★.

**VILLIERA** *Paarl WO, South Africa* The down-to-earth Grier family have a knack of achieving both quality and value for money in their varied range. Their speciality is Cap Classique sparklers under the Tradition label; the vintage Monro Brut★, a Pinot Noir-Chardonnay blend with rich, biscuity flavours, has replaced Carte d'Or Brut and Première Cuvée. Winemaker Jeff Grier is known for Sauvignon Blancs (standard and Traditional Bush Vine★★); there's also a consistent Riesling★ and a delicious, partly barrel-fermented Chenin Blanc. Reds are equally good, especially the intense yet succulent BORDEAUX-style blend Cru Monro★ and newcomer Merlot-Pinotage★ – Grier's answer to a Cape blend. Best years: (whites) **2000** 99 98 97 96; (reds) **1998** 97 96 95 94.

**VIN SANTO** *Tuscany, Italy* The 'holy wine' of TUSCANY can be one of the world's great sweet wines – just occasionally, that is, for it is also one of the most wantonly abused wine terms in Italy (in particular avoid anything called *liquoroso*). Made from grapes either hung from rafters or laid on mats after harvest to dry, the resulting wines, fermented and aged in small barrels (*caratelli*) for up to 7–8 years, should be nutty, oxidized, full of the flavours of dried apricots and crystallized orange peel, concentrated and long. Also produced in UMBRIA and in TRENTINO as Vino Santo. Best producers: Altesino★★, Castello di AMA★, ANTINORI★, AVIGNONESI★★★, Badia a Coltibuono★, Fattoria Basciano★★, Cacchiano★, Capezzana★★, Carmignani★, Castell'in Villa★, FELSINA★★, FONTODI★★, ISOLE E OLENA★★★, Pieve Santa Restituta★★, POLIZIANO★★, Rocca di Montegrossi★, San Felice★★, San Giusto a Rentennano★★★, SELVAPIANA★★, Villa Pillo★, Villa Sant'Anna★★.

**VIÑA CASABLANCA** *Casablanca, Chile* This much-acclaimed estate owes its reputation to Ignacio Recabarren, recently departed to CONCHA Y TORO. We'll have to see if standards stay high, since only top wines use CASABLANCA-sourced fruit. White Label wines use vineyards in Lontué, MAIPO and San Fernando. There is rose- and lychee-filled Gewürztraminer★, excellent tangy, intense Sauvignon Blanc, quince-edged Santa Isabel Estate Chardonnay★★ and barrel-fermented Chardonnay★★ from the same estate. Reds include inky-black Cabernet Sauvignon★ and low-yield White Label Merlot★, together with the rich, juicy Merlot★★ and Cabernet★★ from the Santa Isabel Estate.

**VIÑAS DEL VERO** *Somontano DO, Aragón, Spain* SOMONTANO's largest company, specializing in New World-inspired wines. A buttery but minerally unoaked Chardonnay and its toasty barrel-fermented counterpart★ are joined by more original whites such as Clarión★, a blend of Chardonnay, Gewürztraminer and Macabeo. Flavours have unfortunately been lightening up recently, but top reds – Gran Vos★★ (Merlot-Cabernet-Pinot Noir) and the new Blecua★★ – still deliver the goods. Best years: 1998 97 96 95 94.

**VINHO VERDE DOC** *Minho and Douro Litoral, Portugal* 'Vinho Verde' can be red *or* white. 'Green' only in the sense of being young, demarcated Vinhos Verde come from north-west Portugal. The whites are the most widely seen outside Portugal and range from sulphured and acidic to aromatic, flowery and fruity. One or two that fall outside the DOC regulations are sold as Vinho Regional Minho. Best producers: Quinta de Alderiz, Quinta da Aveleda★, Quinta da Baguinha★, Encostas dos Castelos, Quinta da Franqueira★, Monção co-op (Deu la Deu Alvarinho★), Muros de Melgaço (Alvarinho★), Quintas de Melgaço, Palácio de Brejoeira★, Dom Salvador, Casa de Sezim★, Soalheiro, SOGRAPE (Gazela, Quinta de Azevedo★), Quinta de Tamariz (Loureiro★).

**VINO NOBILE DI MONTEPULCIANO DOCG** *Tuscany, Italy* The 'noble' wine' from the hills around the town of Montepulciano is made from the Sangiovese grape, known locally as the Prugnolo, with the help of a little Canaiolo and Mammolo. At its best, it combines the power and structure of BRUNELLO DI MONTALCINO with the finesse and complexity found in top CHIANTI. Unfortunately, the best was a rare beast until recently, though the rate of improvement has been impressive. The introduction of what is essentially a second wine, ROSSO DI MONTEPULCIANO, has certainly helped. Best producers: AVIGNONESI★★, Bindella★, BOSCARELLI★★, La Braccesca/ANTINORI★, Le Casalte★★, La Casella★, Contucci★★, Dei★★, Del Cerro★, Fassati★, Gracciano della Seta, Innocenti★, Il Macchione★, Nottola★, Lodola Nuova/RUFFINO, Palazzo Vecchio★, POLIZIANO★★, Redi★, Romeo★, Salcheto★, Trerose★, Valdipiatta★, Villa Sant'Anna★. Best years: (1999) 98 97 **95 93 91 90 88 85.**

---

**VIOGNIER** A poor yielder, prone to disease and difficult to vinify. The wine can be delicious: peachy, apricoty with a soft, almost waxy texture, usually a fragrance of spring flowers and sometimes a taste like crème fraîche. Traditionally grown only in the northern RHONE, it is now found in LANGUEDOC-ROUSSILLON, Ardèche and the southern Rhône as well as in CALIFORNIA, Argentina, Australia and South Africa.

**ROBERTO VOERZIO** *Barolo DOCG, Piedmont, Italy* One of the best of the new wave of BAROLO producers that came to prominence in the late 1980s. Dolcetto (Priavino★) is particularly successful, as is Vignaserra★★ – barrique-aged Nebbiolo with a little Cabernet – and the outstanding new BARBERA D'ALBA Riserva Vigneto Pozzo dell'Annunziata★★★. Barriques are also used for fashioning his Barolo, but such is the quality and concentration of fruit coming from densely planted vineyards that the oak does not overwhelm. Single-vineyard examples made in the best years are Brunate★★, Cerequio★★★, La Serra★★ and new Riserva Capalot★★★. Best years: (Barolos) (1998) 97 96 95 **93 91 90 89 88 85**.

**COMTE GEORGES DE VOGÜÉ** *Chambolle-Musigny AC, Côte de Nuits, Burgundy, France* De Vogüé owns substantial holdings in 2 Grands Crus, BONNES-MARES★★★ and MUSIGNY★★★, as well as in Chambolle's top Premier Cru, Les Amoureuses★★★. A succession of winemakers in the 1980s led to many disappointing vintages in that decade, but since 1990 the domaine has been back on magnificent form. It is the sole producer of minute quantities of Musigny Blanc★★★, but because of recent replanting the wine is now being sold as (very expensive) BOURGOGNE Blanc. Best years: (reds) (2000) 99 98 97 96 95 93 **92 91 90**.

**VOLNAY AC** *Côte de Beaune, Burgundy, France* Volnay is home to the finest red wines of the COTE DE BEAUNE in terms of elegance and class. The wines are attractive when young but the best examples can age well. The top Premiers Crus are Caillerets, Champans, Clos des Chênes, Santenots (which actually lies in MEURSAULT but is called Volnay by courtesy title) and Taillepieds. Best producers: R Ampeau★★, ANGERVILLE★★, J-M Boillot★★, J-M Bouley★★, COCHE-DURY★★, V GIRARDIN★★, LAFARGE★★, LAFON★★, Dom. Matrot★★, Montille★★★, N Potel★★, Pousse d'Or★, J Prieur★★, Roblet-Monnot★, J Voillot★★. Best years: 1999 98 97 96 **95 93 91 90 89 88**.

**VOLPAIA, CASTELLO DI** *Chianti Classico DOCG, Tuscany, Italy* Light, perfumed but refined CHIANTI CLASSICO★ (Riserva★). Two stylish SUPER-TUSCANS, Balifico★★ and Coltassala★★, are both predominantly Sangiovese. Torniello★ is Sauvignon with a dash of Sémillon.

**VOSNE-ROMANÉE AC** *Côte de Nuits, Burgundy, France* The greatest village in the COTE DE NUITS, with 6 Grands Crus and 13 Premiers Crus (notably les Malconsorts, aux Brûlées and les Suchots) which are often as good as other villages' Grands Crus. The quality of the village wine is also high. In good years the wines need at least 6 years' aging and 10–15 would be better. Best producers: Robert Arnoux★★★, Cacheux-Sirugue★★, Champy★★, B Clavelier★★, R Engel★★★, GRIVOT★★★, Anne Gros★★★, A-F Gros★★, Haegelen-Jayer★★, F Lamarche★★, Dom. LEROY★★★, MEO-CAMUZET★★★, Mongeard-Mugneret★★, Mugneret-Gibourg★★, RION★★, Dom. de la ROMANEE-CONTI★★★, THOMAS-MOILLARD★. Best years: (2000) 99 98 97 96 95 **93 91 90 89 88**.

**VOUGEOT AC** *Côte de Nuits, Burgundy, France* Outside the walls of CLOS DE VOUGEOT there are 11ha (27 acres) of Premier Cru and 5ha (12 acres) of other vines. The wine, mainly red, is not bad and a lot cheaper than any Clos de Vougeot. Best producers: Bertagna★★, Chopin-Groffier★★, C Clerget★, Dom. de la Vougeraie★★. Best years: (2000) 99 98 97 96 95 **93 91 90 89 88**.

**LA VOULTE-GASPARETS** *Corbières AC, Languedoc, France* One of the MIDI's most exciting properties, producing 3 different styles of CORBIERES from old hillside vines. Unashamedly Mediterranean in style with flavours of thyme and baked earth. The Cuvée Réservée★ and Romain Pauc★★ are the most expensive wines, but the basic Voulte-Gasparets★ is almost as good. Drink young or up to 5 years from the vintage. Best years: 1999 98 **96 95**.

**VOUVRAY AC** *Loire Valley, France* Dry, medium-dry, sweet and sparkling wines from Chenin grapes east of Tours. The dry wines acquire beautifully rounded flavours after 6–8 years. Medium-dry wines, when properly made from a single domaine, are worth aging for 20 years or more. Spectacular noble-rot-affected sweet wines were produced in 1990 and 89 with an intense peach and honey soft sweetness but an ever-present acidity. The fizz is some of the LOIRE's best. Best producers: Allias★, Aubuisières★★, Bourillon-Dorléans★★, Brédif★, Champalou★★, Clos Naudin★★, P Delaleu★, la Fontainerie★★, Ch. Gaudrelle★, HUET★★, Pichot★, F Pinon★★. Best years: (2000) 99 98 **97 96 95 93 90 89 88 85 83 78 76 75 70**.

**WACHAU** *Niederösterreich, Austria* This stunning stretch of the Danube between Krems-Stein and the monastery of Melk is Austria's top region for dry whites. Riesling is the grape here, followed by Grüner Veltliner. Best producers: F HIRTZBERGER★★★, Högl★★, Emmerich KNOLL★★★, NIKOLAIHOF★★, F X PICHLER★★★, PRAGER★★★, Freie Weingärtner WACHAU★★.

**WACHAU, FREIE WEINGÄRTNER** *Wachau, Niederösterreich, Austria* Co-op long producing fine WACHAU white wines. Since Fritz Miesbauer took over responsibility for winemaking in 1995, regular wines★ and vineyard-designated Grüner Veltliners and Rieslings★★ have reached new heights. Best years: (2000) 99 **98 97 96 95 93 92 91 90 88 86 79**.

**WACHENHEIM** *Pfalz, Germany* Wine village made famous by the BURKLIN-WOLF estate, its best vineyards are capable of producing rich, yet beautifully balanced Rieslings. Best producers: Josef BIFFAR★, BURKLIN-WOLF★★, Karl Schaefer★, WOLF★★. Best years: (1999) 98 **97 96 94 93 90**.

**WAIHEKE ISLAND** *North Island, New Zealand* GOLDWATER pioneered wine-making on this island in Auckland harbour in the early 1980s. Hot, dry ripening conditions have made high-quality Cabernet-based reds that sell for high prices. An increasing quantity of Chardonnay is appearing, together with experimental plots of Shiraz and Viognier. A tiny, highly fashionable region that will soon be home to over 30 winemakers. Best producers: Fenton★★, GOLDWATER★★, Obsidian, STONYRIDGE★★★, Te Whau★.

**WARRE** *Port DOC, Douro, Portugal* Top-quality Vintage port★★★, and a good 'off-vintage' port from Quinta da Cavadinha★★. Optima, an adequate 10-year-old tawny, is most remarkable for its unconventional clear bottle presentation. Crusted★★ and LBV★★ are very welcome traditional, full-bodied ports. Warrior★ is a reliable ruby. Age Vintage port for 15–30 years. Best years: (Vintage) 1997 94 91 85 83 80 **77 70 66 63**; (Cavadinha) 1995 92 **90 88 87 86 82 78**.

**WARWICK ESTATE** *Stellenbosch WO, South Africa* This farm has vineyards in some of the Cape's best red wine country, and owner Norma Ratcliffe has taken over once again as winemaker. Traditional BORDEAUX varieties are responsible for the most highly regarded wines: the complex Trilogy★ blend, and a refined, fragrant, varietal Cabernet Franc★. Old Bush Vine Pinotage is less consistent but, at best, is suave and velvety; quantities will be limited for a while, as around 3ha (7 acres) were destroyed in the fire of summer 2000. The new red blend, Three Cape Ladies, combines Cabernet Sauvignon, Merlot and Pinotage. Whites are represented by a full-bodied yet lightly oaked Chardonnay★. Best years: (reds) 1998 **97 96 95 94**.

**WASHINGTON STATE** *USA* Second-largest premium wine-producing state in the US. The chief growing areas are in irrigated high desert, east of the Cascade Mountains. Although the heat is not as intense as in CALIFORNIA, long summer days with extra hours of sunshine due to the northern latitude seem to increase the intensity of fruit flavours and result in both red and white wines of great depth. Cabernet, Merlot, Chardonnay, Sauvignon Blanc and Semillon produce very good wines here. Some believe that the wines of Washington State could become the best in the US. Best producers: ANDREW WILL★★, CANOE RIDGE★, CHATEAU STE MICHELLE★, COLUMBIA CREST★, COLUMBIA WINERY, Covey Run★, Durham Cellars★★, Hedges Cellars★, HOGUE CELLARS★, KIONA★, L'ECOLE NO 41★★, LEONETTI CELLAR★★★, Matthews Cellars★★, QUILCEDA CREEK★★, Salishan, WOODWARD CANYON★★.

**GEOFF WEAVER** *Adelaide Hills, South Australia* Geoff Weaver, a former chief winemaker at HARDYS, now crafts fine wines from grapes grown at his Lenswood vineyard. Quality fruit from low-yielding vines produces limy Riesling★★, crisply gooseberryish Sauvignon★★ and stylish cool-climate Chardonnay★★. Cabernet-Merlot★ is restrained but tasty.

**J WEGELER ERBEN** *Bernkastel, Mosel; Oestrich-Winkel, Rheingau; Deidesheim, Pfalz, Germany* In 1997 the Wegeler family sold their share of the huge Deinhard wine empire to concentrate on wines from their own vineyards. All 3 estates are dedicated primarily to Riesling, and today dry wines make up the bulk of production. Whether dry or naturally sweet Auslese, the best merit ★★ and will develop well with 5-plus years of aging. The MOSEL estate achieves the best standard of the 3 estates; nearly all the wines are ★. Best years: (Mosel-Saar-Ruwer) 1999 98 **97 96 95 93 90 89 88 83 76**.

**WEHLEN** *Mosel, Germany* Village whose steep Sonnenuhr vineyard produces some of the most powerful Rieslings in Germany. Best producers: Kerpen, Dr LOOSEN★★★, J J PRUM★★★, S A PRUM★★, RICHTER★★, SELBACH-OSTER★★, J WEGELER ERBEN★, Dr Weins-Prüm★.

**ROBERT WEIL** *Kiedrich, Rheingau, Germany* This estate, previously known as Dr Weil, has enjoyed huge investment input from Japanese drinks giant Suntory which, coupled with Wilhelm Weil's devotion to quality, has made it the brightest jewel in the RHEINGAU's crown. Majestic sweet Auslese, Beerenauslese and Trockenbeerenauslese Rieslings★★★ and also dry Rieslings★ are crisp and elegant in style, although the regular wines have been a little disappointing in recent vintages. Best years: 1999 98 **97** 96 **95 94 93 92 90 89**.

287

**WEINBACH** *Alsace AC, Alsace, France* This Kaysersberg estate, which produces some of the most classic wines of ALSACE, is run by Mme Colette Faller and her two daughters. The range is quite complicated. Some wines are named in honour of Mme Faller's late husband Théo★★; others are labelled Ste-Cathérine★★, and are late picked, though not technically Vendange Tardive. Also very fine are the Gewurztraminer Altenbourg Laurence★★ and the Pinot Gris Cuvée Laurence★★. The Riesling Grand Cru Schlossberg★★★ is the finest dry wine. In certain vintages the estate produces Quintessence – a super-concentrated Sélection de Grains Nobles – from Pinot Gris★★★ and Gewurztraminer★★★. All the wines are exceptionally balanced and can be aged for many years. Best years: (Grand Cru Riesling) 1999 98 97 96 **95 94 93 92 90 89 88 85 83**. See also Alsace Vendange Tardive.

**WEISSBURGUNDER** See Pinot Blanc.

**WELSCHRIESLING** See Riesling Italico.

**WENDOUREE** *Clare Valley, South Australia* Small winery using old-fashioned methods to make enormous, ageworthy reds★★★ from paltry yields off their own very old Shiraz, Cabernet, Malbec and Mataro (Mourvèdre) vines. There are tiny amounts of sweet Muscat★. Best years: 1997 96 95 94 **92 91 90 86 83 82 81 80 78 76 75**.

**WESTERN AUSTRALIA** Only the south-west corner of this vast state is suited to vines, the SWAN DISTRICT and Perth environs being the oldest and hottest area, with present attention focused on Great Southern, MARGARET RIVER, Geographe and, most recently, PEMBERTON. Quality easily rivals the best of the eastern states.

**WIEN** *Austria* Region within the city limits of Wien/Vienna. The best wines come from the south-facing sites in Grinzing, Nussdorf and Weiden; and the Bisamberg hill east of the Danube. Best producers: Bernreiter, Kierlinger, Mayer, Schilling, Wieninger★.

**WILLIAMS SELYEM** *Russian River Valley AVA, California, USA* Purchased in 1998 by John Dyson of New York, and it remains to be seen if the cult following for the Pinot Noirs★★, especially the J Rochioli Vineyard★★★, can be sustained. Traditionally the wine is big, sometimes very fruity and sometimes just a bit off the wall. Impressive Zinfandel★★, too. Best years: (Pinot Noir) (1999) 98 97 **96 95 94 92 91**.

**WINKEL** *Rheingau, Germany* RHEINGAU village whose best vineyard is the large Hasensprung Einzellage but the most famous one is Schloss Vollrads – an ancient estate that does not use the village name on its label. Best producers: August Eser, Johannishof★★, SCHLOSS VOLLRADS★ (since 1999) J WEGELER ERBEN★. Best years: 1999 98 96 **93 90**.

**WIRRA WIRRA** *McLaren Vale, South Australia* Owned by celebrated eccentric Greg Trott, who consistently makes whites with more finesse than is customary in the region. Recent years have seen rapid expansion, a spell with GREEN POINT's Tony Jordan and the arrival of HARDYS' Tim James. Well-balanced Sauvignon Blanc★, ageworthy Semillon blend★, buttery Chardonnay★★ and soft reds led by delicious The Angelus Cabernet★★, chocolaty RSW Shiraz★★ and decadent Original Blend Grenache-Shiraz★. Also a good-value 'WW' label. Best years: (reds) 1998 **96 95 94 93 92 91 90 86 82 80**.

**J L WOLF** *Wachenheim, Pfalz, Germany* Ernst Loosen, of Dr LOOSEN in the MOSEL, took over this underperforming estate in 1996. A string of concentrated dry and naturally sweet Rieslings★★ have won it a place among the region's top producers. Best years: 1999 98 **97 96**.

**WOODWARD CANYON** *Walla Walla AVA, Washington State, USA* Big barrel-fermented oaky Chardonnay★★ is the trademark wine, but there's also Charbonneau Red★ (Cabernet Sauvignon-Merlot) and Artist★★ and Dedication★★ Cabernet Sauvignons. Best years: (1999) 98 **96 95**.

**WÜRTTEMBERG** *Germany* Underperforming wine region centred on the river Neckar. More than half the wine made is red, and the best comes from Lemberger, Dornfelder or Spätburgunder (Pinot Noir) grapes. Massive yields are generally responsible for pallid wines. However, a few of the many marvellously steep sites produce perfumed reds and racy Riesling.

**WÜRZBURG** *Franken, Germany* The centre of FRANKEN wines. Müller-Thurgau is the bread-and-butter grape, some Rieslings can be great, but the real star is Silvaner. Best producers: Bürgerspital, JULIUSSPITAL★, Staatlicher Hofkeller. Best years: (2000) 99 97 **94 93 92 90**.

**WYNNS** *Coonawarra, South Australia* The name is synonymous with COONAWARRA's oldest cellars and major vineyard holdings. After a low period in the 1970s, standard Cabernet★★ and Shiraz★ have returned to form, so that they are among the best value in the land. They also age well: better vintages from the 1950s and 60s are still alive and kicking. In peak years the cream of the Cabernet is released as John Riddoch★★★ and Shiraz as Michael★★, both powerful reds, the latter incredibly oaky. There is also Chardonnay★ in an attractive, fruit-driven style plus cheap, delightful Riesling★. Best years: (premium reds) 1998 97 96 94 93 **91 90 88 86 84 82 76 66 62 55**.

**YALUMBA** *Barossa Valley, South Australia* Distinguished old firm, owned by the Hill-Smith family, making a wide range of wines including estate wines Heggies (restrained Riesling★, nice plump Merlot★, opulent Viognier★ and botrytis Riesling★★), Hill-Smith Estate (Sauvignon Blanc★) and Pewsey Vale (fine Riesling★ and Cabernet Sauvignon★). The Yalumba range is headed by 3 glorious reds: The Signature Cabernet-Shiraz★★, Octavius Shiraz★★ and The Menzies Cabernet★★ and will cellar well. Tricentenary Barossa Old Vine Grenache★★ is crunchy and satisfying. From these premium reds down to reliable quaffer Galway Shiraz, Yalumba is consistently impressive. Oxford Landing Chardonnay, Sauvignon★, Viognier★★, Merlot and Cabernet-Shiraz are highly successful quaffers. Yalumba is also the pioneer of good 2-litre casks. Angas Brut and Angas Rosé remain big-volume enjoyable fizzes for the masses (me included); Pinot-Chardonnay and Yalumba D sparklers seem to be recovering from a recent crisis of confidence, while the acquisition of TASMANIA's Jansz★ has added a class act to the flight. Fortified wines are excellent, notably Muscat★★. Best years: (The Signature red) 1996 **95 94 92 90 88**.

**YARRA VALLEY** *Victoria, Australia* With its cool climate, the fashionable Yarra is asking to be judged as Australia's best Pinot Noir region. Exciting also for Chardonnay and Cabernet-Merlot blends and as a supplier of base wine for sparklers. Best producers: Arthur's Creek★★,

COLDSTREAM HILLS★, DE BORTOLI★★, GREEN POINT VINEYARDS★, MOUNT MARY★★, Oakridge★, St Huberts★, Seville Estate★, TARRAWARRA★★, Yarra Burn★, Yarra Ridge★, YARRA YERING★★★, Yeringberg★, Yering Station★.

**YARRA YERING** *Yarra Valley, Victoria, Australia*  Bailey Carrodus creates extraordinary wines from his exceptional vineyard. The reds, labelled Dry Red No. 1★★★ (Cabernet-based) and No. 2★★★ (Shiraz-based), are profound, concentrated, ageworthy, packed with unnervingly self-confident fruit and memorable perfume. Pinot Noir★★ is expensive but gets finer and wilder by the vintage. Chardonnay★ is erratic, occasionally delicious. Best years: 1997 **95** 94 93 **92 91 90 86 82**.

**YELLOWGLEN** *Ballarat, Victoria, Australia*  Big Champagne-method fizz producer owned by Beringer Blass. Basic, high-volume lines are Pinot Chardonnay NV, Brut Crémant and Brut Rosé. Cuvée Victoria★ is the finest. 'Y' Premium and Vintage Brut are also well made. Best years: (Cuvée Victoria) **1996 95 92 90 88**.

**CH. D'YQUEM★★★** *Sauternes AC, 1er Cru Supérieur, Bordeaux, France*  Often rated the most sublime sweet wine in the world, no one can question Yquem's total commitment to quality. Despite a large vineyard (100ha/250 acres), production is tiny. Only fully noble-rotted grapes are picked, often berry by berry, and low yield means each vine produces only a glass of wine! This precious liquid is then fermented in new oak barrels and left to mature for 3½ years before bottling. It is one of the world's most expensive wines, in constant demand because of its richness and exotic flavours – loony prices or not. A dry white, Ygrec, is made in some years. LVMH has recently won a 3-year battle to take over the château's vineyard from the Lur-Saluces family, owners for 406 years. Best years: 1995 94 93 91 90 **89 88 86 83 82 81 80 79 76 75 71 67 62**.

**ZILLIKEN** *Saarburg, Saar, Germany*  Estate specializing in Rieslings★★ from the Saarburger Rausch vineyard. The Auslese and Eiswein often achieve ★★★. Best years: 1999 97 95 94 93 91 90 89 88 85 83 79 76.

**ZIND-HUMBRECHT** *Alsace AC, Alsace, France*  Olivier Humbrecht is one of France's outstanding winemakers. The family owns vines in 4 Grand Cru sites – Rangen, Goldert, Hengst and Brand – and these wines (Riesling★★, Gewurztraminer★★★, Pinot Gris★★★ and Muscat★★) are excellent, as is a range of wines from specific vineyards and *lieux dits*, such as Riesling Clos Windsbuhl★★★ and Pinot Gris Clos Jebsal★★. ALSACE VENDANGE TARDIVE wines are almost invariably of ★★★ quality. Even basic Sylvaners★ and Pinot Blancs★ are fine. Best years (Clos Windsbuhl Gewurztraminer): 1998 97 **96 95 94 93 92 90 89 88**.

**ZINFANDEL** CALIFORNIA's versatile red grape can be used to make an insipid blush wine or a big, bruising, late-harvest-style dessert wine. In-between dry styles have fruit to the fore. A few are now made in other countries, with notable examples in Australia and South Africa. Known as Primitivo in Italy. Best producers: (California) Cline Cellars★★, DRY CREEK VINEYARDS★, FETZER★, Martinelli★★★, NALLE★★★, Preston★, QUIVIRA★★, Rafanelli★★★, RAVENSWOOD★★★, RIDGE★★★, Rosenblum★★, Saddleback★★, St Francis★★, TURLEY★★★; (Australia) CAPE MENTELLE★, Kangarilla Road, LENSWOOD★.

# GLOSSARY OF WINE TERMS

**AC/AOC (APPELLATION D'ORIGINE CONTRÔLÉE)** The top category of French wines, defined by regulations covering vineyard yields, grape varieties, geographical boundaries and alcohol content. Guarantees origin and style of a wine, but not its quality.

**ACID/ACIDITY** Naturally present in grapes and essential to wine, providing balance and stability and giving the refreshing tang in white wines and the appetizing grip in reds.

**ADEGA** Portuguese for 'winery'.

**AGING** An alternative term for maturation.

**ALCOHOLIC CONTENT** The alcoholic strength of wine, expressed as a percentage of the total volume of the wine. Typically in the range of 7–15%.

**ALCOHOLIC FERMENTATION** The process whereby yeasts, natural or added, convert the grape sugars into alcohol (Ethyl alcohol, or Ethanol) and carbon dioxide.

**AMONTILLADO** Traditionally dry style of sherry. *See* Jerez y Manzanilla DO in main A–Z.

**ANBAUGEBIET** German for 'growing region'; these names will appear on labels of all QbA and QmP wines. There are 13 Anbaugebiete: Ahr, Baden, Franken, Hessische Bergstrasse, Mittelrhein, Mosel-Saar-Ruwer, Nahe, Pfalz, Rheingau, Rheinhessen, Saale-Unstrut, Sachsen and Württemberg.

**AUSBRUCH** Austrian Prädikat category used for sweet wines.

**AUSLESE** German and Austrian Prädikat category meaning that the grapes were 'selected' for their higher ripeness.

**AVA (AMERICAN VITICULTURAL AREA)** System of appellations of origin established for US wines in the 1970s.

**AZIENDA AGRICOLA** Italian for 'estate' or 'farm'. It also indicates wine made from grapes grown by the proprietor.

**BARREL AGING** Time spent maturing in wood, usually oak, during which the wines take on flavours from the wood.

**BARREL FERMENTATION** Oak barrels may be used for fermentation instead of stainless steel to give a rich, oaky flavour to the wine.

**BARRIQUE** The *barrique bordelaise* is the traditional Bordeaux oak barrel of 225 litres (50 gallons) capacity.

**BAUME** A scale measuring must weight (the amount of sugar in grape juice) to estimate potential alcohol content.

**BEERENAUSLESE** German and Austrian Prädikat category applied to wines made from 'individually selected' berries, i.e. grapes, affected by noble rot (*Edelfäule* in German). The wines are rich and sweet. Beerenauslese wines are only produced in the best years in Germany, but in Austria they are a pretty regular occurrence.

**BEREICH** German for region or district within a wine region or Anbaugebiet. Bereichs tend to be large, and the use of a Bereich name, such as Bereich Bingen, without qualification is seldom an indication of quality – in most cases, quite the reverse.

**BIODYNAMIC VITICULTURE** This approach works with

## BOTTLE SIZES

### CHAMPAGNE

| | | |
|---|---|---|
| Magnum | 1.5 litres | 2 bottles |
| Jeroboam | 3 litres | 4 bottles |
| Rehoboam | 4.5 litres | 6 bottles |
| Methuselah | 6 litres | 8 bottles |
| Salmanazar | 9 litres | 12 bottles |
| Balthazar | 12 litres | 16 bottles |
| Nebuchadnezzar | 15 litres | 20 bottles |

### BORDEAUX

| | | |
|---|---|---|
| Magnum | 1.5 litres | 2 bottles |
| Marie-Jeanne | 2.25 litres | 3 bottles |
| Double-magnum | 3 litres | 4 bottles |
| Jeroboam | 4.5 litres | 6 bottles |
| Imperial | 6 litres | 8 bottles |

the movement of the planets and cosmic forces to achieve health and balance in the soil and in the vine. Vines are treated with infusions of mineral, animal and plant materials, applied in homeopathic quantities.

**BLANC DE BLANCS** White wine made from one or more white grape varieties. Used especially for sparkling wines; in Champagne, denotes wine made entirely from the Chardonnay grape.

**BLANC DE NOIRS** White wine made from black grapes only – the juice is separated from the skins to avoid extracting any colour. Most often seen in Champagne, where it describes wine made from Pinot Noir and/or Pinot Meunier.

**BLENDING** (Assemblage) The art of mixing together wines of different origin, styles or age, often to balance out acidity, weight etc.

**BODEGA** Spanish for 'winery'.

**BOTRYTIS** See Noble Rot.

**BRUT** French term for dry sparkling wines, especially Champagne.

**CARBONIC MACERATION** Winemaking method used to produce fresh fruity reds for drinking young. Whole (uncrushed) bunches of grapes are fermented in closed containers – a process that extracts lots of fruit and colour, but little tannin.

**CAVE CO-OPÉRATIVE** French for 'co-operative cellar', where members

bring their grapes for vinification and bottling under a collective label. In terms of quantity, the French wine industry is dominated by co-ops. Often use less workaday titles, such as Caves des Vignerons, Producteurs Réunis, Union des Producteurs or Cellier des Vignerons.

**CHAMPAGNE METHOD** Traditional method used for all of the world's finest sparkling wines. A second fermentation takes place in the bottle, producing carbon dioxide which, kept in solution under pressure, gives the wine its fizz.

**CHAPTALIZATION** Legal addition of sugar during fermentation to raise a wine's alcoholic strength. More necessary in cool climates where lack of sun produces insufficient natural sugar in the grape.

**CHARTA** A German organization founded to protect the image of the best Rheingau Rieslings in 1984, recognizable by a 'double-window' motif on the bottle or label. The accent is on dry wines which are thought to go well with food. Now merged with VDP to form VDP-Rheingau, but the Charta symbol remains in use.

**CHÂTEAU** French for 'castle', used to describe a wide variety of wine estates.

**CHIARETTO** Italian for a rosé wine of medium pink colour.

**CLARET** English for red Bordeaux wines, from the French *clairet*, which was traditionally

used to describe a lighter style of red Bordeaux.

**CLARIFICATION** Term covering any winemaking process (such as filtering or fining) that involves the removal of solid matter either from the must or the wine.

**CLONE** Strain of grape species. The term is usually taken to mean laboratory-produced, virus-free clones, selected to produce higher or lower quantity, or selected for resistance to frost or disease.

**CLOS** French for a walled vineyard – as in Burgundy's Clos de Vougeot – also commonly incorporated into the names of estates (e.g. Clos des Papes), regardless of whether they are walled or not.

**COLD FERMENTATION** Long, slow fermentation at low temperature to extract maximum freshness from the grapes.

**COLHEITA** Aged tawny port from a single vintage. *See* Port in main A–Z.

**CORKED/CORKY** Wine fault derived from a cork which has become contaminated, usually with Trichloroanisole or TCA, and nothing to do with pieces of cork in the wine. The mouldy, stale smell is unmistakable.

**COMMUNE** A French village and its surrounding area or parish.

**COSECHA** Spanish for 'vintage'.

**CÔTE** French word for a slope or hillside, which is where many, but not all, of the country's best vineyards are to be found.

**CRÉMANT** French term for traditional-method sparkling wine from Alsace, Bordeaux, Burgundy, Die, Jura, Limoux, Loire and Luxembourg.

**CRIANZA** Spanish term for the youngest official category of oak-matured wine. A red Crianza wine must have had at least 2 years' aging (1 in oak, 1 in bottle) before sale; a white or rosé, 1 year.

**CRU** French for 'growth', meaning a specific plot of land or particular estate. In Burgundy, growths are divided into Grands (great) and Premiers (first) Crus, and apply solely to the actual land. In Champagne the same terms are used for whole villages. In Bordeaux there are various hierarchical levels of Cru referring to estates rather than their vineyards.

**CRU BOURGEOIS** French term for wines from the Médoc and Sauternes that are ranked immediately below the Crus Classés. Many are excellent value for money.

**CRU CLASSÉ** The Classed Growths are the aristocracy of Bordeaux, ennobled by the Classifications of 1855 (for the Médoc, Barsac and Sauternes), 1955, 1969, 1986 and 1996 (for St-Émilion) and 1947, 1953 and 1959 (for Graves). Curiously, Pomerol has never been classified. The modern classifications are more reliable than the 1855 version, which was

based solely on the price of the wines at the time of the Great Exhibition in Paris, but in terms of prestige the 1855 Classification remains the most important. With the exception of a single alteration in 1973, when Ch. Mouton-Rothschild was elevated to First Growth status, the list has not changed since 1855. It certainly needs revising.

**CUVE CLOSE** A bulk process used to produce inexpensive sparkling wines. The second fermentation, which produces the bubbles, takes place in tank rather than in the bottle.

**CUVÉE** French for the contents of a single vat or tank, but usually indicates a wine blended from either different grape varieties or the best barrels of wine.

**DÉGORGEMENT** Process in the Champagne method of removing sediment from the bottle.

**DEMI-SEC** French for medium-dry.

**DO (DENOMINACIÓN DE ORIGEN)** Spain's equivalent of the French AC quality category, regulating origin and production methods.

**DOC (DENOMINAÇÃO DE ORIGEM CONTROLADA)** The top regional classification for Portuguese wines.

**DOC (DENOMINACIÓN DE ORIGEN CALIFICADA)** Spanish quality wine category, intended to be one step up from DO. So far only Rioja qualifies.

**DOC (DENOMINAZIONE DI ORIGINE CONTROLLATA)** Italian quality wine category, regulating origin, grape varieties, yield and production methods.

**DOCG (DENOMINAZIONE DI ORIGINE CONTROLLATA E GARANTITA)** The highest tier of the Italian classification system.

**DOSAGE** A sugar and wine mixture added to sparkling wine after *dégorgement* which affects how sweet or dry it will be.

**EDELZWICKER** Blended wine from Alsace in France, usually of low quality.

**EINZELLAGE** German for an individual vineyard site which is generally farmed by several growers. The name is preceded on the label by that of the village; for example, the Wehlener Sonnenuhr is the Sonnenuhr vineyard in Wehlen. The mention of a particular site should signify a superior wine. Sadly, this is not necessarily so.

**EISWEIN** Rare, chiefly German and Austrian, late-harvested wine made by picking the grapes and pressing them while frozen. This concentrates the sweetness of the grape as most of the liquid is removed as ice. *See also* Icewine.

**FILTERING** Removal of yeasts, solids and any impurities from a wine before bottling.

**FINING** Method of clarifying wine by adding a coagulant (e.g. egg whites, isinglass or bentonite) to remove soluble particles such as proteins and excessive tannins.

**FINO** The lightest, freshest style of sherry. *See* Jerez y Manzanilla DO in main A–Z.

**FLOR** A film of yeast which forms on the top of fino sherries (and some other wines), preventing oxidation and imparting a unique tangy, dry flavour.

**FLYING WINEMAKER** Term coined in the late 1980s to describe enologists, many Australian-trained, brought in to improve the quality of wines in many underperforming wine regions.

**FORTIFIED WINE** Wine which has high-alcohol grape spirit added, usually before the initial fermentation is completed, thereby preserving sweetness.

**FRIZZANTE** Italian for semi-sparkling wine, usually made dry, but sometimes sweet.

**GARRAFEIRA** Portuguese term for wine from an outstanding vintage, with 0.5% more alcohol than the minimum required, and 2 years' aging in vat or barrel followed by 1 year in bottle for reds, and 6 months of each for whites. Also used by merchants for their best blended and aged wines. Use of the term is in decline as producers opt for the more readily recognized Reserva as an alternative on the label.

**GRAN RESERVA** Top category of Spanish wines from a top vintage, with at least 5 years' aging (2 of them in cask) for reds and 4 for whites.

**GRAND CRU** French for 'great growth'. Supposedly the best vineyard sites in Alsace, Burgundy, Champagne and parts of Bordeaux and should produce the most exciting wines.

**GRANDES MARQUES** 'Great brands' – this was once Champagne's self-appointed élite. After years of attempted reform, the Syndicat des Grandes Marques finally admitted defeat and disbanded in 1997. Quality differences between the various Champagne houses were just too great to resolve.

**GROSSLAGE** German term for a grouping of vineyards. Some are not too big, and have the advantage of allowing small amounts of higher QmP wines to be made from the grapes from several vineyards. But sometimes the use of vast Grosslage names (e.g. Niersteiner Gutes Domtal) only deceives consumers into believing they are buying something special.

**HALBTROCKEN** German for medium dry. In Germany and Austria medium-dry wine has 9–18g per litre of residual sugar, though sparkling wine is allowed up to 50g per litre. But the high acid levels in German wines can make them seem rather dry and lean.

**ICEWINE** A speciality of Canada, produced from juice squeezed from ripe grapes that have frozen on the vine. *See also* Eiswein.

**IGT (INDICAZIONE GEOGRAFICA TIPICA)** The Italian equivalent of the French vin de pays.

As in the Midi, both premium and everyday wines may share the same appellation. Many of the Super-Tuscan vini da tavola are now sold under a regional IGT.

**IPR (INDICAÇÃO DE PROVENIÊNCIA REGULAMENTADA)** The second tier in the Portuguese wine classification regulations, covering grape varieties, yields and aging requirements.

**KABINETT** Term used for the lowest level of QmP wines in Germany.

**LANDWEIN** German or Austrian country wine; the equivalent of French vin de pays. The wine must have a territorial definition and may be chaptalized to give it more alcohol.

**LATE HARVEST** *See* Vendange Tardive.

**LAYING DOWN** The storing of wine which will improve with age.

**LEES** Sediment – dead yeast cells, grape pips (seeds), pulp and tartrates – thrown by wine during fermentation and left behind after racking. Some wines are left on the fine lees for as long as possible to take on extra flavour.

**MALOLACTIC FERMENTATION** Secondary fermentation whereby harsh malic acid is converted into mild lactic acid and carbon dioxide. Normal in red wines but often prevented in whites to preserve a fresh, fruity taste.

**MANZANILLA** The tangiest style of sherry, similar to fino. *See* Jerez y Manzanilla DO in main A–Z.

**MATURATION** Positive term for the beneficial aging of wine.

**MERITAGE** American term for red or white wines made from a blend of Bordeaux grape varieties.

**MESOCLIMATE** The climate of a specific geographical area, be it a vineyard or simply a hillside or valley.

**MOELLEUX** French for soft or mellow, used to describe sweet or medium-sweet wines.

**MOUSSEUX** French for sparkling wine.

**MUST** The mixture of grape juice, skins, pips and pulp produced after crushing (but prior to completion of fermentation), which will eventually become wine.

**MUST WEIGHT** An indicator of the sugar content of juice – and therefore the ripeness of grapes.

**NÉGOCIANT** French term for a merchant who buys and sells wine. A négociant-éléveur is a merchant who buys, makes, ages and sells wine.

**NEW WORLD** When used as a geographical term, New World includes the Americas, South Africa, Australia and New Zealand. By extension, it is also a term used to describe the clean, fruity, upfront style now in evidence all over the world, but pioneered in the USA and Australia.

**NOBLE ROT** (*Botrytis cinerea*) Fungus which, when it attacks ripe white grapes, shrivels the fruit and intensifies their sugar while adding a distinctive flavour. A vital factor in creating many of the world's finest sweet wines, such as Sauternes and Trockenbeerenauslese.

**OAK** The wood used almost exclusively to make barrels for fermenting and aging fine wines.

**OECHSLE** German scale measuring must weight.

**OLOROSO** The darkest, most heavily fortified style of sherry. *See* Jerez y Manzanilla DO in main A–Z.

**OXIDATION** Overexposure of wine to air, causing loss of fruit and flavour. Slight oxidation, such as occurs through the wood of a barrel or during racking, is part of the aging process and, in wines of sufficient structure, enhances flavour and complexity.

**PASSITO** Italian term for wine made from dried grapes. The result is usually a sweet wine with a raisiny intensity of fruit. *See also* Moscato Passito di Pantelleria, Recioto di Soave, Recioto della Valpolicella and Vin Santo in main A–Z.

**PERLWEIN** German for a lightly sparkling wine.

**PÉTILLANT** French for a slightly sparkling wine.

**PHYLLOXERA** The vine aphid *Phylloxera vastatrix* attacks vine roots. It devastated European and consequently other vineyards around the world in the late 1800s soon after it arrived from America. Since then, the vulnerable *Vitis vinifera* has generally been grafted on to vinously inferior, but phylloxera-resistant, American rootstocks.

**PRÄDIKAT** Grades defining quality wines in Germany and Austria. These are (in ascending order) Kabinett (not considered as Prädikat in Austria), Spätlese, Auslese, Beerenauslese, the Austrian-only category Ausbruch, and Trockenbeerenauslese. Strohwein and Eiswein are also Prädikat wines. Some Spätleses and even a few Ausleses are now made as dry wines.

**PREMIER CRU** 'First Growth'; the top quality classification in parts of Bordeaux, but second to Grand Cru in Burgundy. Used in Champagne to designate vineyards just below Grand Cru.

**PRIMEUR** French term for a young wine, often released for sale within a few weeks of the harvest. Beaujolais Nouveau is the best-known example.

**QbA (QUALITÄTSWEIN BESTIMMTER ANBAUGEBIETE)** German for 'quality wine from designated regions'. Sugar can be added to increase the alcohol content. Usually pretty ordinary, but from top estates this category offers excellent value for money. In Austria *Qualitätswein* is equivalent to the German QbA.

**QmP (QUALITÄTSWEIN MIT PRÄDIKAT)** German for 'quality wine with distinction'. A higher category than QbA, with controlled yields and no sugar addition. QmP covers

6 levels based on the ripeness of the grapes: *see* Prädikat.

**QUINTA** Portuguese for 'farm' or 'estate'.

**RACKING** Gradual clarification of a quality wine; the wine is transferred from one barrel or container to another, leaving the lees behind.

**RANCIO** A fortified wine deliberately exposed to the effects of oxidation, found mainly in Languedoc-Roussillon, Cataluña and Spain.

**REMUAGE** Process in Champagne-making whereby the bottles, stored on their sides and at a progressively steeper angle in *pupitres*, are twisted, or riddled, each day so that the sediment moves down the sides and collects in the neck of the bottle on the cap, ready for *dégorgement*.

**RESERVA** Spanish wines that have fulfilled certain aging requirements: reds must have at least 3 years' aging before sale, of which one must be in oak barrels; whites and rosés must have at least 2 years' age, of which 6 months must be in oak.

**RÉSERVE** French for what is, in theory at least, a winemaker's finest wine. The word has no legal definition in France.

**RIPASSO** A method used in Valpolicella to make wines with extra depth. Wine is passed over the lees of Amarone della Valpolicella, adding extra alcohol and flavour, though also extra tannin and a risk of higher acidity and oxidation.

**RISERVA** An Italian term, recognized in many DOCs and DOCGs, for a special selection of superior-quality wine that has been aged longer before release. It is only a promise of a more pleasurable drink if the wine had enough fruit and structure in the first place.

**SEC** French for 'dry'. When applied to Champagne, it actually means medium-dry.

**'SECOND' WINES** A second selection from a designated vineyard, usually lighter and quicker-maturing than the main wine.

**SEDIMENT** Usually refers to residue thrown by a wine, particularly red, as it ages in bottle.

**SEKT** German for sparkling wine. The wine will be entirely German only if it is called 'Deutscher Sekt' or 'Sekt bA'. The best wines are traditional-method made from 100% Riesling.

**SÉLECTION DE GRAINS NOBLES** A super-ripe category for sweet Alsace wines, now also being used by some producers of Coteaux du Layon in the Loire. *See also* Alsace Vendange Tardive in main A–Z.

**SOLERA** Traditional Spanish system of blending fortified wines, especially sherry and Montilla-Moriles.

**SPÄTLESE** German for 'late-picked' and therefore riper grapes. Often moderately sweet, though there are now dry versions.

**SPUMANTE** Italian for 'sparkling'. Bottle-fermented wines are often referred to as *metodo classico* or *metodo tradizionale*.

**SUPÉRIEUR** French for a wine with a slightly higher alcohol content than the basic AC.

**SUPERIORE** Italian DOC wines with higher alcohol or more age potential.

**SUR LIE** French for 'on the lees', meaning wine bottled direct from the cask/fermentation vat to gain extra flavour from the lees. Common with quality Muscadet, white Burgundy, similar barrel-aged whites and, increasingly, commercial bulk whites.

**TAFELWEIN** German for table wine.

**TANNIN** Harsh, bitter, mouth-puckering element in red wine, derived from grape skins and stems, and from oak barrels. Tannins soften with age and are essential for long-term development in reds.

**TERROIR** A French term used to denote the combination of soil, climate and exposure to the sun – that is, the natural physical environment of the vine.

**TROCKEN** German for 'dry'. In most parts of Germany and Austria Trocken matches the standard EU definition of dryness – less than 9g per litre residual sugar.

**TROCKENBEEREN-AUSLESE (TBA)** German for 'dry berry selected', denoting grapes affected by noble rot (*Edelfäule* in

German) – the wines will be lusciously sweet although low in alcohol.

**VARIETAL** Wine made from, and named after, a single or dominant grape variety.

**VDP** German organization recognizable on the label by a Prussian eagle bearing grapes. The quality of estates included is usually – but not always – high. Now merged with the Charta organization.

**VDQS (VIN DÉLIMITÉ DE QUALITÉ SUPÉRIEURE)** The second-highest classification for French wines, behind AC.

**VENDANGE TARDIVE** French for late harvest. Grapes are left on the vines beyond the normal harvest time to concentrate flavours and sugars. The term is traditional in Alsace, and is now authorized in the Loire, and used especially for intensely sweet Coteaux du Layon. *See also* Alsace Vendange Tardive in main A–Z.

**VIEILLES VIGNES** French term for a wine made from vines at least 20 years old. Should have greater concentration than wine from younger vines.

**VIÑA** Spanish for 'vineyard'.

**VIN DE GARAGE** Wines made on so small a scale they could be made in one's garage. Such wines may be made from vineyards of a couple of hectares or less, and are often of extreme concentration.

**VIN DE PAILLE** Sweet wine found mainly in the Jura region of France. Traditionally, the grapes are left for 2–3 months on straw (*paille*) mats before fermentation to dehydrate, thus concentrating the sugars. The wines are sweet but slightly nutty.

**VIN DE PAYS** The term gives a regional identity to wine from the country districts of France. It is a particularly useful category for adventurous winemakers who want to use good-quality grapes not allowed under the frequently restrictive AC regulations. Many are labelled with the grape variety.

**VIN DE TABLE** French for table wine, the lowest quality level.

**VIN DOUX NATUREL (VDN)** French for a fortified wine, where fermentation has been stopped by the addition of alcohol, leaving the wine 'naturally' sweet, although you could argue that stopping fermentation with a slug of powerful spirit is distinctly unnatural.

**VIN JAUNE** A speciality of the Jura region in France, made from the Savagnin grape. In Château-Chalon it is the only permitted style. Made in a similar way to fino sherry but not fortified. Unlike fino, *vin jaune* usually ages well.

**VINIFICATION** The process of turning grapes into wine.

**VINO DA TAVOLA** The Italian term for table wine, officially Italy's lowest level of production, is a catchall that until recently applied to more than 80% of the nation's wine, with virtually no regulations controlling quality. Yet this category also provided the arena in the 1970s for the biggest revolution in quality that Italy has ever seen, with the creation of innovative, DOC-busting Super-Tuscans. *See* Super-Tuscans in main A–Z.

**VINTAGE** The year's grape harvest, also used to describe wines of a single year. 'Off-vintage' is a year not generally declared as vintage. *See* Port DOC in main A–Z.

**VITICULTURE** Vine-growing and vineyard management.

**VITIS VINIFERA** Vine species, native to Europe and Central Asia, from which almost all the world's quality wine is made.

**VQA (VINTNERS QUALITY ALLIANCE)** The Canadian equivalent of France's AC system, defining quality standards and a number of designated viticultural areas.

**WEISSHERBST** German rosé wine, a speciality of Baden.

**WO (WINE OF ORIGIN)** The South African certification system, covering grape variety, area of origin and vintage. Guarantees authenticity rather than quality and only 10% of the harvest is certified.

**YIELD** The amount of fruit, and ultimately wine, produced from a vineyard. Measured in hectolitres per hectare (hl/ha) in most of Europe and in the New World as tons/acre or tonnes/hectare.

# INDEX OF PRODUCERS

## ACKNOWLEDGEMENTS

*Editor* Maggie Ramsay; *Assistant Editor* Sarah Cooke; *DTP Consultant* Keith Bambury; *Proofreader* Hugh Morgan; *Indexer* Angie Hipkin; *Production* Kâren Connell; *Managing Editor* Anne Lawrance; *Art Director* Nigel O'Gorman; *Photography* Nigel James

# OLDER VINTAGE CHARTS *(top wines only)*

| **FRANCE** | | | | | | | | | | |
|---|---|---|---|---|---|---|---|---|---|---|
| Alsace | 90 | 89 | 88 | 85 | 83 | 81 | 76 | 71 | 69 | 61 |
| | 10◊ | 9♦ | 8♦ | 8♦ | 9◊ | 7♦ | 10♦ | 9♦ | 8◊ | 9◊ |
| Champagne (vintage) | 90 | 89 | 88 | 86 | 85 | 83 | 82 | 81 | 76 | 75 |
| | 9♦ | 8♦ | 8◊ | 7♦ | 9♦ | 8◊ | 10♦ | 8◊ | 9◊ | 9◊ |
| **Bordeaux** | 90 | 89 | 88 | 86 | 85 | 83 | 82 | 81 | 79 | 78 |
| Margaux | 10◊ | 8◊ | 7◊ | 8♦ | 8♦ | 9♦ | 8♦ | 7♦ | 6♦ | 7♦ |
| St.-Jul., Pauillac, St-Est. | 10◊ | 9◊ | 8◊ | 9◊ | 8♦ | 8◊ | 10♦ | 7♦ | 7♦ | 7♦ |
| Graves/Pessac-L. (R) | 8◊ | 8◊ | 8◊ | 6♦ | 8♦ | 8♦ | 9♦ | 7♦ | 7♦ | 8♦ |
| St-Émilion, Pomerol | 10◊ | 9◊ | 8◊ | 7♦ | 9♦ | 7◊ | 9♦ | 7♦ | 7♦ | 7♦ |
| **Bordeaux (cont.)** | 75 | 70 | 66 | 62 | 61 | 59 | 55 | 53 | 49 | 47 |
| Margaux (cont.) | 6◊ | 8♦ | 7◊ | 8◊ | 10♦ | 8◊ | 6◊ | 8◊ | 9◊ | 8◊ |
| St.-Jul. etc. (cont.) | 8♦ | 8♦ | 8♦ | 9◊ | 10♦ | 9◊ | 8◊ | 9◊ | 10◊ | 9◊ |
| Graves etc. (R) (cont.) | 6◊ | 8♦ | 8◊ | 8◊ | 10♦ | 9◊ | 8◊ | 8◊ | 10◊ | 9◊ |
| St-Émilion etc. (cont.) | 8♦ | 8♦ | 6◊ | 8◊ | 10◊ | 7◊ | 7◊ | 8◊ | 9◊ | 10◊ |
| Sauternes | 90 | 89 | 88 | 86 | 83 | 82 | 81 | 80 | 76 | 75 |
| | 10♦ | 9◊ | 9◊ | 9◊ | 9◊ | 5♦ | 6◊ | 7♦ | 8♦ | 8♦ |
| Sauternes (cont.) | 71 | 67 | 62 | 59 | 55 | 53 | 49 | 47 | 45 | 37 |
| | 8♦ | 9◊ | 8◊ | 9◊ | 8◊ | 8◊ | 10◊ | 10◊ | 9◊ | 10◊ |
| **Burgundy** | | | | | | | | | | |
| Chablis | 90 | 89 | 88 | 87 | 86 | 85 | 83 | 81 | 78 | 71 |
| | 9♦ | 8♦ | 8◊ | 6◊ | 9♦ | 9♦ | 7◊ | 8◊ | 9◊ | 9◊ |
| Côte de Beaune (W) | 90 | 89 | 88 | 86 | 85 | 83 | 79 | 78 | 71 | 69 |
| | 8♦ | 9♦ | 7◊ | 8◊ | 9♦ | 6◊ | 8◊ | 8◊ | 9◊ | 7◊ |
| Côte de Nuits (R) | 90 | 89 | 88 | 85 | 83 | 80 | 78 | 76 | 71 | 69 |
| | 10◊ | 8♦ | 8◊ | 8♦ | 6◊ | 6◊ | 9♦ | 6◊ | 9◊ | 8◊ |